Why Do You Need This New Edition?

5 good reasons why you should buy this new edition of *Readings in Social Psychology*!

1. An entirely new collection of contemporary readings (15 new articles!) help you gain exposure to new research and new approaches in the field of social psychology.

2. Updated and revised chapter introductions draw correlations among the three articles in each chapter, illustrating how they each relate to one another.

3. Hand-selected classic and newer readings are more readable than in previous editions, yet not overly simplistic nor challenging.

4. New and revised "Critical Thinking" questions at the end of each article ask readers to examine different aspects of the articles presented, as well as assess the implications of psychological research in their own lives.

5. New and revised "Chapter Integration Questions" at the end of each chapter—one of this book's most popular features—help promote critical thinking and bring together the articles in each section.

Readings in ———————————
SOCIAL PSYCHOLOGY
General, Classic, and Contemporary Selections

SEVENTH EDITION

WAYNE A. LESKO
Marymount University

PEARSON

Boston ■ New York ■ San Francisco
Mexico City ■ Montreal ■ Toronto ■ London ■ Madrid ■ Munich ■ Paris
Hong Kong ■ Singapore ■ Tokyo ■ Cape Town ■ Sydney

Acquisitions Editor: Michelle Limoges
Editorial Assistant: Christina Manfroni
Senior Marketing Manager, Psychology: Kate Stewart Mitchell
Production Editor: Karen Carter
Editorial-Production Service: Omegatype Typography, Inc.
Composition Buyer: Linda Cox
Manufacturing Buyer: JoAnne Sweeney
Electronic Composition: Omegatype Typography, Inc.
Cover Administrator: Kristina Mose-Libon

For related titles and support materials, visit our online catalog at www.ablongman.com

Between the time website information is gathered and then published, it is not unusual for some sites to have closed. Also, the transcription of URLs can result in typographical errors. The publisher would appreciate notification where these errors occur so that they may be corrected in subsequent editions.

ISBN-13: 978-0-205-59577-8
ISBN-10: 0-205-59577-4

Printed in the United States of America

10   9   8   7   6   5   4   3   2   1   RRD-VA   12   11   10   09   08

To Brennan, Marlaine, and Matt

Brief Contents

Contents

Preface

THE TYPICAL SOCIAL psychology class ranges from sophomore through graduate levels, and the members may include majors who are required to take the course as well as nonmajors who have elected to do so. Regardless of the level or the audience, many instructors—myself included—feel that a collection of readings is a valuable means of promoting an understanding of the discipline.

Most collections of readings typically fall into two categories: professional articles from journals in the field or popular articles reprinted from such magazines as *Psychology Today*. The category of professional readings may include contemporary articles, classic articles, or a combination of the two. These articles provide excellent insight into the core of social psychology by describing not only the research outcomes but also the detailed methodology for how the results were obtained. Popular articles, on the other hand, lack the scientific rigor of journal articles but often present a broad overview of a number of findings pertaining to a particular topic. Clearly, both types of readings have advantages and disadvantages associated with them, depending on the particular level at which the course is taught.

In over three decades of teaching social psychology at both the undergraduate and graduate levels, I have found that students seem to respond best to a variety of reading formats. Popular articles are easy to understand and provide a good overview, while also generating critical thinking about an issue. Research articles provide insight into the methodological issues in social psychology and help the student develop a critical attitude in evaluating research contributions and conclusions. Classic research articles familiarize the student with early research that has had a lasting impact on social psychology, while contemporary works illustrate issues currently being studied and the methods used to investigate them.

Like the first six editions, this seventh edition of *Readings in Social Psychology: General, Classic, and Contemporary Selections* is designed to provide exactly that breadth of exposure to the different sources of information available in the field. As in the previous editions, each chapter begins with an introduction to the topic, which is followed by three articles: one general (popular), one classic, and one contemporary. Each article begins with a short introduction that sets the stage, or provides a context for the article. Each article is followed by a set of Critical Thinking Questions, which ask the student to examine critically some part of the article presented, to speculate about generalizations and implications of the research, and, in some cases, to suggest new studies based on the information in the article. Each classic article is also followed by a list of Additional Related Readings for students who may wish to examine more contemporary articles on the same topic. At the end of each chapter is a section called Chapter Integration Questions. These questions are intended to link the three chapter articles, usually by identifying a theme or themes common to all of them. As with the Critical Thinking Questions, these questions can be used in their entirety or in part, as best meets the needs of the instructor.

The topical organization of *Readings in Social Psychology: General, Classic, and Contemporary Selections* (seventh edition) directly parallels that of many social psychology textbooks. As such, it can be adapted readily for use with any text or used in lieu of a text, depending on how the course is taught. Likewise, the book can be used with classes of varying levels, by structuring which articles will be emphasized and in how much detail they will be examined.

Finally, all articles are presented verbatim, in their entirety, since it is my firm belief that one valuable skill gained by students from reading research articles is the ability to abstract pertinent information from an original source. The only exception to this, necessitated by copyright ownership, is found in Table 1 of Article 14, which is an abbreviation of the Bem Sex Role Inventory.

Because the articles are presented in their original forms, some of them, especially the contemporary articles, may be difficult to understand. However, I selected these particular articles for a variety of reasons. First, the topic of each of these articles is one that not only represents the type of research being conducted on this topic today but that also usually has interest to the reader. Second, these contemporary articles were selected to give the reader a broad exposure to the different types of professional publications in the field. Most of the more difficult articles are from journals published by the American Psychological Association (APA) or the American Psychological Society (APS). In fact, if only less complex articles were included in this book, then APA and APS publications virtually would be excluded. This would be a disservice to the reader, from my view.

For even the most complex contemporary articles, I have found that users without much background in psychology (e.g., sophomores with little or no prior research exposure) can read them effectively with the proper guidance. In addition to the guidance provided by the instructor, students will benefit by reading A Note to the Reader, which follows this Preface. That section provides some useful suggestions for how to read a research article without getting lost in all of the statistics and technical detail.

At this point, perhaps some notice is in order about several of the articles. Understandably, everything is representative of the time in which it was written, both in terms of the ideas presented and the language used. Some of the classic articles in this collection were written 40 or more years ago and are out of step with current language style. Moreover, some of the descriptions made and observations offered would be considered condescending and even offensive by today's standards. Please keep this in mind, and consider the context in which each of the articles was written.

ACKNOWLEDGMENTS

At Allyn and Bacon, I would like to thank Michelle Limoges, Acquisitions Editor, and Christina Manfroni, Editorial Assistant, for their guidance and help with the format of the book. I likewise wish to extend my gratitude to Sue Freese, of Communicáto, Ltd., for her excellent copyediting of this book. In particular, I would like to thank the following individuals, who reviewed this edition: William Dragon, Cornell College; Alwyn Gilkes, Lehman College–CUNY; Tani McBeth, Portland Community College; Mark Rafter, College of the Canyons; and Benjamin Tong, California Institute of Integral Studies.

I am especially indebted to my graduate and undergraduate students in social psychology at Marymount University, whose honest feedback on the contents of the first six editions helped me create a new, improved book of readings.

I also want to thank the various friends, colleagues, and graduate assistants who helped me and provided encouragement and advice over the many editions of this collection of readings. Without their input, this work would not have been possible.

Last but not least, I thank all of the authors and publishers of the articles contained in this book for their permission to reprint these materials. Their fine work in advancing the field of social psychology is literally what made this book possible.

W. L.

A Note to the Reader

As YOU EMBARK on your study of social psychology, you will soon discover that the field is broad indeed. You will encounter many different topics, but they all are related by the common thread that defines social psychology—namely, the study of individual behavior in social situations.

As a collection of readings, this book is designed to expose you to some of the most important areas of study within social psychology. Just as the topics found in the area of social psychology are diverse, so, too, are the ways in which social psychological knowledge is disseminated. If you are new to the field, most likely you have encountered one common source of information: articles in nonprofessional sources. For example, newspaper and magazine articles may present the information from some study in social psychology. Typically nontechnical pieces directed to the general public, these articles summarize a number of studies on a given topic and are fairly easy to comprehend. Each of the 15 chapters that comprise this book begins with such an article—what I have termed a *general* reading.

A second source of information is actually the backbone of social psychology: articles that appear in professional journals of the field. These articles are the primary means by which new ideas and the results of research are shared with the professional community. While they tend to be more technical and difficult to read compared to the general works, professional articles have the advantage of providing readers with sufficient detail to draw their own conclusions, rather than be forced to rely on someone else's interpretation of the information. Some of these articles represent research that has stood the test of time and are generally regarded as *classics* in the field; the second reading found in each chapter is such an article.

Finally, the last type of article found in each chapter is labeled *contemporary*. These articles are fairly recent examples of research currently being conducted in social psychology. As noted in the Preface, these articles can be particularly challenging to read but are significant in terms of what they represent about the field of social psychology.

The format of each chapter is the same. Each opens with a brief introduction to the chapter topic; one general, one classic, and one contemporary article are then presented, in that order. Each article begins with an introduction written by me, which serves to focus your perspective before reading. Every article is then followed by Critical Thinking Questions. In some cases, these questions directly refer to information contained in the articles; in others, the questions are more speculative, asking you to go beyond the data presented. The classic articles also contain Additional Related Readings. The references included here are either recent articles that address the same issues discussed in the classic article (a way of updating the current status of research on the topic) or a topic similar to the one discussed in the original. In either case, the interested student can use these references to find more information on the topic. Finally, each chapter concludes with a section called Chapter Integration Questions. These questions relate the articles to one another, usually by having you identify a theme or themes that cut across them. Considering these questions provides another way of seeing the articles in the larger context of the topic, rather than as isolated pieces of research.

Before reading the articles in this book, it might be worthwhile to review the fundamentals of research tactics. Having such a basic understanding will help you understand even the most complex articles.

Research studies in social psychology (or indeed, in any scientifically based discipline) fall into two broad categories: correlational studies and experimental studies. A *correlation* is a finding that two variables are somehow related; that is, as one variable changes, so does the other one. For example, consider the relationship between the amount of violent content that children watch on television and their subsequent aggressive behavior. A correlation may show that the more aggressive programs a child watches, the more aggressive he or she is in playing with other children. Would such a correlation mean that watching the aggressive shows makes children more aggressive? Not necessarily. The children may be more aggressive for other reasons (e.g., maybe they eat too much candy while watching the shows), or perhaps children who are innately more aggressive are more attached to violent programs. In short, all that a correlation tells us is that two variables are related. It does *not* tell us that one variable causes the other one.

What, then, is the value of a correlation if it does not allow us to make cause-effect connections? One major value is that a correlation allows us to *predict*. That is, knowing that two variables are correlated allows us to predict the value of one when we only know the other is present. Again, using the violent programs example, if we know that there is a strong correlation between the amount of time children spend watching violent television and their subsequent aggressive behavior, then simply knowing how much violent television a child watches will allow us to predict the likelihood of his or her being aggressive.

In addition to making predictions, sometimes we want research to determine *why* something happens. In other words, we may want to determine a cause-and-effect relationship. The established way to do so is to use *experimental* research. The goal of all experimental research is to determine causation. No matter how complex a study's research design, the underlying logic of experimental research is fundamentally the same and fairly straightforward.

To understand the logic behind experimental research, along with its commonly used terms, let's look again at the example of aggressive television programming and children's behavior. Suppose we want to determine if exposure to violent television makes children more aggressive. First of all, we will need two groups of children—one watching violent television and the other watching something else—so that we can compare one group to another. But how will we form the two groups of children? We could ask the children which type of programming they prefer to watch and then group them accordingly. The problem with this approach is that we will not know if children already prone to aggression are more likely to prefer watching violent television programs.

The solution to this problem is actually quite simple: We will use *random assignment* to put the children into the groups. In other words, we will use pure chance, such as the results of a coin toss, to determine to which group each child is assigned. Why? By using chance, we are essentially creating two equal groups at the beginning of the study. For each child who is aggressive and is assigned to the one group, by chance, there will be another aggressive child assigned to the other group. In other words, individual differences cancel themselves out when we use random assignment.

Let's get back to our study design. Suppose we start out with, say, 100 children of the same age and randomly assign them to the two groups. Half of these children are assigned to a group that will watch violent television programs. This group is called the *experimental group,* since it involves the variable we are investigating—namely, exposure to violent programs. The other half of the children are assigned to a group that will watch nonviolent programs. This latter group is called the *control group,* and it will be our comparison group.

Another term you need to understand is *independent variable.* The independent variable is what the researcher is manipulating. In our example, the independent variable is whether or not the child is exposed to violent television programs. It is called *independent* because the experimenter is free to manipulate it as he or she wishes.

Let's pause for a second to look at the design of our experiment thus far. We started out with a group of children and randomly assigned them to two groups. Doing so resulted in our starting out with two equal groups. Next, we treated the two groups the same except for one thing: the independent variable. That is, half the children watched violent shows, and the other half watched nonviolent shows. Next, following exposure to the independent variable, we need some sort of way to measure the children's aggression. This outcome measure is known as the *dependent variable.* The two groups were identical to begin with (due to our random assignment), but what if we now find they are different after exposure to the independent variable? The answer is that the difference must be due to the only difference between the two groups—namely, exposure to the independent variable. Thus, a cause-and-effect relationship can be established, demonstrating that exposure to violent television programming causes children to become more aggressive.

No matter how complex a study's research design is (and you will encounter some very complex designs in the studies that follow), the logic of experimental research is the same as outlined in our experiment: Identical groups are created through random assignment, they are exposed to different conditions (the independent variable), and the outcomes are measured (the dependent variable). If a difference is observed in the dependent variable, then it must be due to the different treatments that the subjects received.

The reality of conducting research and drawing warranted conclusions obviously is a bit more complicated than our discussion would indicate. Nonetheless, if you keep in mind the basics of experimental design, you will find it easier to understand the studies that you read.

All of the articles in this collection are reprinted in their entirety. Not a word has been abridged or altered. (Again, the only exception is Article 14, which has been abbreviated due to a copyright restriction.) For the general articles, this should not be a problem for anyone. However, if this is the first time that you are reading journal articles from their primary sources, some assistance might be in order. First of all, do not allow yourself to be overwhelmed or intimidated. New students often are confused by some of the terminology that is used and are left totally dumbfounded by the detailed statistics that are usually part of such articles. Approached in the right way, these articles need not be intimidating and should be comprehensible to any reader willing to expend a little effort.

In reading a research article, I would like to make the following suggestions:

■ Most articles begin with an Abstract or end with a Summary. If these are provided, begin by carefully reading them; they will give you an overview of why the study was conducted, what was done, and what the results were.

■ Next, read the Introduction fairly carefully; this is where the authors describe previous research in the area and develop the logic for why they are conducting the experiment in the first place.

■ The Methods section describes in detail the techniques used by the researchers to conduct their study; read this section thoroughly in order to understand exactly what was done.

■ The next section, Results, is where the authors describe what was found in the study. This is often the most technically difficult part of the article; from your standpoint, you might want to skim over this part, focusing only on the sections that verbally describe what the results were. Do not worry about the detailed statistical analyses that are presented.

■ Finally, you might want to read the Discussion section in some detail; here, the authors discuss the findings and implications of the study and perhaps suggest avenues for further study.

To summarize: Each article is fairly straightforward to comprehend, provided that you do not allow yourself to get too bogged down in the details and thus frustrated. The journey may seem difficult at times, but the end result—an appreciation and understanding of the complex issues of human social behavior—will be worth it. Enjoy!

W. L.

Readings in
SOCIAL PSYCHOLOGY

Chapter One

THE FIELD OF
SOCIAL PSYCHOLOGY

AN INTRODUCTION TO a course such as social psychology often includes a section on research methods. Nonmajors confronting this topic often wonder why they need to know about research methods when in all likelihood they will never actually conduct research. Whether you are majoring in psychology or not, familiarity with research methods will benefit you, for several reasons.

First, it will help you understand the studies that make up the knowledge base of social psychology. Familiarity with methodology will allow you to make informed decisions about the conclusions drawn by various studies. Second, and perhaps more important, some knowledge of research issues will allow you to be an intelligent consumer of research information. Results of studies often are reported to the general public in newspapers and magazines. Knowing something about the methods used to produce these results will better prepare you to decide whether the conclusions drawn are warranted. Finally, it is useful to fully appreciate why the results of experimental data are needed instead of just relying on common sense. Article 1, "Folk Wisdom: Was Your Grandmother Right?" shows how folk wisdom (i.e., common sense) often is contradictory and hence not very useful as a guideline for behavior.

Research is the basic underpinning of psychological science. Given the subject matter of social psychology, it is often difficult, if not impossible, to get unbiased results if subjects know what is being observed. For that reason, psychologists, in general, and social psychologists, in particular, often have relied on deception as a means of obtaining naive subjects. But what ethical issues are involved in the use of deception? And what if deception is so widely used that subjects expect to be deceived whenever they participate in a research study? What, if any, are the alternatives to the use of deception? These are some of the questions addressed in Article 2, "Human Use of Human Subjects: The Problem of Deception in Social Psychological Experiments."

Finally, Article 3 provides some basic guidelines for making sense of the various research results we encounter on a regular basis. "How to Be a Wise Consumer of Psychological Research" gives some invaluable tools for how best to draw valid conclusions from studies. While the focus of the article is on psychological research, many of the concepts really can be applied to a variety of other science and social science disciplines as well.

ARTICLE 1 _____

At the heart of all the articles you will read in this book is *research methodology*. Given a question you want to investigate, how do you go about actually collecting data?

There are a number of different ways of conducting social psychological research. One broad distinction is between *experimental methods* and *correlational (nonexperimental) methods*. Each method has potential advantages and disadvantages. One is not necessarily better than the other; it depends on what you are investigating.

Students encountering research methods literature for the first time are often surprised at the difficulty of designing and conducting a good piece of research. It is not as easy as it might seem on the surface. Numerous artifacts that can affect the outcome of a study need to be accounted for and controlled. An examination of the introductory chapters of most social psychology texts will give you a better understanding of some of these issues.

Sometimes, a study obtains results that are quite unexpected and surprises readers. Other times, however, readers may feel that the outcome of a study was totally expected— indeed, that it was just common sense. The reaction to such an article often is to question why it is even necessary to test the obvious.

The only problem with common sense is that it is often contradictory. For example, to whom are people most attracted: people like themselves or people different from themselves? Common sense would predict that "Birds of a feather flock together"; on the other hand, "Opposites attract." So which is it? As it turns out, common sense is not such a good predictor of actual behavior. The only way to know for sure is to go out and empirically test the concept.

The following article by Robert Epstein examines a number of common-sense ideas that have been passed down to us in light of what current research tells us about their validity. The article underscores the necessity of testing ideas empirically and why even supposedly obvious notions must be exposed to scientific scrutiny.

Folk Wisdom
Was Your Grandmother Right?
■ Robert Epstein

The table next to me at Fillipi's restaurant was a noisy one. Two men and two women in their 20s and 30s were arguing about a relationship issue. One of the men—call him Male #1—would soon be leaving the country for six months. Would the passion he shared with his beloved survive? The exchange went something like this:

Female #1 (probably the girlfriend): "When you really love someone, being apart makes you care even

more. If someone is good to you, you sometimes take that for granted when the person is around every day. But when he's gone, all that good treatment is gone, too, and you realize just how much you had. You really start to yearn for him."

Male #2 (looking lustfully at Female #1, even though he seemed to be with the other woman): "That's right. The same thing happens when your parents die. You really start to miss and appreciate

Reprinted from *Psychology Today*, 1997 (November/December), *30*, 46–50, 76. Reprinted with permission from *Psychology Today* magazine. Copyright © 1997 (Sussex Publishers, Inc.).

them. You even rewrite the past, forgetting the bad things and focusing on the good times and the kindness they showed you."

Female #1 (starting to look lovingly at Male #2): "Exactly. Everyone knows that absence makes the heart grow fonder."

Then Male #1, the one probably on his way to Thailand, spoke up. "Well, but . . ." He faltered, thinking hard about going on. All eyes were on him. He took a deep breath.

And then he said, slowly and deliberately, "But don't we also say, 'Out of sight, out of mind'?"

This was not good for anyone's digestion. Female #1's face turned the color of marinara sauce. Male #2 smiled mischievously, presumably imagining himself in bed with Female #1. Female #2 looked back and forth between her date and Female #1, also apparently imagining them in bed together. And Male #1, not wanting to face the carnage, lowered his eyes and tapped out a strange rhythm on the table top with his fork. Was he thinking about the classy Thai brothels he had read about on the Internet?

TRUTH OR POPPYCOCK?

"Absence makes the heart grow fonder" and "Out of sight, out of mind" are examples of folk wisdom—folk psychology, you might say. All cultures pass along wisdom of this sort—sometimes in the form of proverbs; sometimes through songs (remember Paul Simon's "Fifty Ways to Leave Your Lover"?), rhymes (Mother Goose), or stories (Aesop's fables); sometimes through laws and public information campaigns ("Stay alive, don't drink and drive"); and always through religion ("Do unto others as you would have them do unto you").

But folk wisdom is an unreliable, inconsistent kind of wisdom. For one thing, most proverbs coexist with their exact opposites, or at least with proverbs that give somewhat different advice. Does absence truly make the heart grow fonder, or are loved ones out of mind when they're out of sight? And isn't variety the spice of life? (If Male #1 had come up with *that* one, he might have been murdered on the spot.)

Do opposites attract, or do birds of a feather flock together? Should you love the one you're with, or

would that be like changing horses in midstream? We all know that he who hesitates is lost, but doesn't haste make waste, and isn't patience a virtue, and don't fools rush in, and aren't you supposed to look before you leap?

And, sure, money is power, but aren't the best things in life supposed to be free? And since time is money, and money is power, and power corrupts, does that mean time also corrupts? Well, maybe so. After all, the Devil finds work for idle hands.

I've only covered a few well-known proverbs from the English-speaking world. Each culture passes along its own wisdom, which is not always meaningful to outsiders. In India, for example, people say, "Call on God, but row away from the docks," and Romanians advise, "Do not put your spoon into the pot that does not boil for you." In Bali they say, "Goodness shouts and evil whispers," while in Tibet the message is, "Goodness speaks in a whisper, but evil shouts."

You get the idea. Proverbs that relay wisdom about how we're supposed to live do not necessarily supply useful or reliable advice. In fact, proverbs are sometimes used merely to justify what we already do or believe, rather than as guidelines for action. What's more, we tend to *switch* proverbs to suit our current values and ideals. A young man might rationalize risky action by pointing out that "You only live once"; later in life—if he's still around—he'll probably tell you, "Better safe than sorry."

Is the situation hopeless? Can we glean any truths at all from the wisdom of the ages?

The behavioral sciences can help. Science is a set of methods for testing the validity of statements about the world—methods for getting as close to "truth" as we currently know how to get. Psychologists and other scientists have spent more than a century testing the validity of statements about human behavior, thinking, and emotions. How well does folk psychology stand up to scientific inquiry? What do we find when we test a statement like "Absence makes the heart grow fonder"? If, as I do, you sometimes rely on folk wisdom to guide your actions or teach your children, this is a question well worth considering.

Here's how five common proverbs measure up to behavioral research.

CONFESSION IS GOOD FOR THE SOUL

Psychologists don't study the soul, of course. But, says psychologist James W. Pennebaker, Ph.D., "If we define 'soul' loosely as who you are, how you feel about yourself, and how healthy you are, then confession is good for the soul." Pennebaker, a researcher at the University of Texas at Austin, is one of several behavioral scientists who have looked carefully at the results of "self-disclosure"—talking or writing about private feelings and concerns. His research suggests that for about two-thirds of us, self-disclosure has enormous emotional and physical benefits. Pennebaker's newly revised book, *Opening Up: The Healing Power of Expressing Emotion,* summarizes 15 years of compelling research on this subject.

Self-disclosure, as you might expect, can greatly reduce shame or guilt. In fact, studies of suspected criminals showed that they acted far more relaxed after confessing their crimes—despite the fact that punishment now awaited them. Self-disclosure may also provide the power behind talk therapy. "The fact that self-disclosure is beneficial," says Pennebaker, "may explain why all forms of psychotherapy seem to be helpful. Whether the therapy is behavioral or psychoanalytic, in the beginning the clients tell their stories."

Perhaps most intriguing are the physical effects of "confession." Pennebaker has found that self-disclosure may actually boost the immune system, spurring production of white blood cells that attack invading microorganisms, increasing production of antibodies, and heightening the body's response to vaccination.

But what about those other proverbs that advise us to keep our mouths shut? "Let sleeping dogs lie." "Least said is soonest mended." "Many have suffered by talking, few by silence." Can self-disclosure do harm? According to Pennebaker, self-disclosure is not likely to be beneficial when it's forced. University of Notre Dame psychologist Anita Kelly, Ph.D., has suggested, moreover, that revealing secrets may be harmful if the confidant is likely to be judgmental. And a 1989 study conducted by Maria Sauzier, M.D., of Harvard Medical School, showed that people often regret disclosures of child abuse. Sauzier found that nearly half of the parents whose children had disclosed sexual abuse (usually to the other parent or a therapist) felt that both the children and the families were harmed by the disclosures. And 19 percent of the adolescents who confessed that they had been abused regretted making the disclosures. In general, however, confession seems to be a surprisingly beneficial act.

ALL WORK AND NO PLAY MAKES JACK A DULL BOY

To me, the most frightening scene in the movie *The Shining* was the one in which actress Shelley Duvall, concerned that her husband (Jack Nicholson) was going crazy, approached the desk at which he had spent several months supposedly writing a novel. There she found hundreds of pages containing nothing but the sentence, "All work and no play makes Jack a dull boy" typed thousands of times on a manual typewriter. I've always wondered who did all that typing! And I've also wondered about the truth of the proverb. Once again, we're also faced with contradictory bits of folk wisdom that urge us to work until we drop: "Rest makes rusty." "Labor warms, sloth harms." "Labor is itself a pleasure."

Is too much work, without the balance of leisure activity ("play"), actually harmful? Research suggests that the answer is yes, with one possible exception: if you love your work—in other words, if you've been able to make your *avocation* your *vocation*—then work may provide you with some of the benefits of play.

In the 1940s, anthropologist Adam Curle pointed out that the distinction between work and leisure seems to be an unfortunate product of modern society. In many traditional cultures, he wrote, "there is not even a word for work." Work and play "are all of a piece," part of the integrated structure of daily living. But modern society has created the need for people to earn a living, an endeavor that can be difficult and can easily get out of hand. Hence, the modern pursuit of "leisure time" and "balance"—correctives for the desperate measures people take to pay their bills.

Study after study confirms the dangers of overwork. It may or may not make you a dull person, but it clearly dulls your mind. For example, recent research on fire fighters by Peter Knauth, Ph.D., shows that long work shifts increase reaction time and lower alertness. And studies with emergency room physicians show that overwork increases errors and impedes judgment. Indeed, a Hollywood cameraman, coming off an 18-hour work shift, made news recently when he lost control of his car and died in a crash.

Conversely, leisure activities have been shown in numerous studies by researchers Howard and Diane Tinsley, Virginia Lewis, and others, to relieve stress, improve mood, increase life satisfaction, and even boost the immune system.

Curiously, the hard-driven "type A" personalities among us are not necessarily Dull Jacks. According to a recent study of more than 300 college students by Robert A. Hicks, Ph.D., and his colleagues, type-A students claim to engage in considerably more leisure activities than their relaxed, type-B counterparts. Type As may simply live "more intensely" than type Bs, whether they're on the job or goofing off.

The distinction between work and play is, to some extent, arbitrary. But it's clear that if you spend too much time doing things you don't want to do, your performance, health, and sense of well-being will suffer.

BOYS WILL BE BOYS

The widely held (though politically incorrect) belief that boys are predisposed from birth to feel, learn, and perform differently from girls is strongly supported by research. For example, boys are, on average, considerably more aggressive than girls. They are left-handed more frequently than girls and tend to be better at math and at spatial rotation tasks. Girls, meanwhile, may perform certain kinds of memory tasks better. They also start talking earlier than boys, and, at the playground, they're more likely to imitate boys than boys are to imitate girls. And boys tend to listen more with their right ear, while girls tend to listen with both ears equally. These findings generally hold up cross-culturally, which suggests that they are at least somewhat independent of environmental influences. Upbringing plays an important role in gender differences, of course—even in the first days after birth, parents treat boy babies differently from girls—but converging evidence from psychology, neuroscience, and evolutionary biology suggests that many gender differences are actually programmed from birth, if not from conception.

Since the brain is the mechanism that generates behavior, where we find behavioral differences, we should also find neurological differences. Indeed, recent research suggests a host of differences between male and female brains. For example, although, on average, male brains are larger than female brains, the hemispheres of the brain seem to be better connected in females, which may help explain why females are more sensitive and emotional than males.

Behavior is also driven by hormones. Here, too, there are significant gender differences. From birth, testosterone levels are higher in males, which helps to account for males' aggressiveness. June Reinisch, Ph.D., then at Indiana University, studied boys and girls whose mothers had been exposed to antimiscarriage drugs that mimic testosterone. Not surprisingly, she found that these children of both sexes were considerably more aggressive than their counterparts with normal testosterone levels. But even among the exposed children, the boys were more aggressive than the girls.

So boys will indeed be boys (and, by implication, girls will be girls). But this is only true "on average." Male and female traits overlap considerably, which means that a particular male could be more emotional than most females and a particular female could be better at math than most males. To be fair, you have to go case by case.

EARLY TO BED, AND EARLY TO RISE, MAKES A MAN HEALTHY, WEALTHY, AND WISE

This proverb, often attributed to Ben Franklin, actually seems to have originated in the late 1400s, and Franklin may have lifted it from a collection of adages published in 1656. Historical trivia aside, research on sleep suggests that the proverb gives sound advice—but only because our culture is out-of-synch with the biology of nearly half the population.

Here's how it works: it's long been known that the body has natural rhythms. Those that occur on a 24-hour cycle are called "circadian" and include cycles of temperature change, wakefulness, and eating. For most people, these cycles are highly resistant to change. This much you probably have heard, but what you might not know is that there are two distinctly different circadian rhythm patterns. "Larks"—who show what researchers call "morningness" (honest!)—are people whose cycles peak early in the day. Not surprisingly, larks awaken early and start the day strong. "Owls"— people inclined toward "eveningness"—peak late in the day. In both cases, the peaks are associated with better performance on memory tasks, quicker reaction times, heightened alertness, and cheerful moods. Some people are extreme larks or owls, others are moderates, and a few fit neither category.

There's a problem here, especially if, like me, you're an extreme owl. The trouble is that many important human activities—business meetings, job interviews, weddings, classes, and so on—are conducted during daylight hours, when larks have a distinct advantage. Not surprisingly, owls spend much of their time griping about how out-of-synch they seem to be. A 1978 study of college students by Wilse B. Webb, Ph.D., and Michael H. Bonnet, Ph.D., of the University of Florida, paints a grim picture for people like me: "Larks reported waking up when they expected to, waking up feeling more rested, and waking up more easily than the owls." Larks also reported having "fewer worries" and getting "more adequate sleep," and they awakened feeling physically better than owls. The differences were even greater, moreover, when owls tried to adapt to the lark sleep pattern. What's more, these problems can impair not only owls' sense of restedness but also their bank account; a study of Navy personnel suggests that people who sleep well make considerably more money than people who sleep poorly.

The long and short of it is that if your biorhythms allow you easily to "go to bed with the lamb and rise with the lark" (another old proverb), you may indeed end up with more money, better health, and more life satisfaction—but only because your internal clock is more in-synch with the stock exchange.

SPARE THE ROD AND SPOIL THE CHILD

A recent headline in my local newspaper proclaimed, "Spanking Backfires, Latest Study Says." I cringe when I see stories like this, because I believe they ultimately harm many children. People have come to confuse discipline with "abuse," which is quite a different beast. "Discipline"—whether in the form of "time outs," reprimands, or spankings—is absolutely necessary for parenting. Extensive research by

psychologist Diana Baumrind, Ph.D., and others, has shown that permissive parenting produces children who can't handle independence and are unable to behave in a socially responsible manner. A great many social problems that we face today may be the inadvertent product of a generation of well-meaning, misinformed, overly-permissive parents.

However, if all you provide is discipline, without affection and emotional support—the "authoritarian" parenting style—you can damage your children. Offspring of authoritarian parents tend to be hostile and defiant, and, like the victims of permissive parents, they too have trouble with independence.

The most effective parenting style involves both a high level of discipline and ample affection and support. That's the best approach for producing children who are self-reliant, socially responsible, and successful in their own relationships, research shows.

In the latest anti-spanking study, published in August by University of New Hampshire sociologist Murray Straus, Ph.D., children between the ages of 6 to 9 who were spanked more than three times a week displayed more misbehavior two years later. Doesn't this show that spanking causes misbehavior? Not at all. Correlational studies are difficult to interpret. Perhaps without those spankings, the kids would have been even worse off. It's also possible that many of these spankings were unnecessary or excessive, and that it was this inappropriate discipline that sparked the later misbehavior.

Conversely, at least eight studies with younger kids show that spanking can indeed improve behavior. The age of the child, in fact, is probably important. Children under the age of six seem to regard spanking as a parent's right. But older kids may view it as an act of aggression, and in such cases spanking's effects may not be so benign.

Punishment, verbal or physical, applied in moderation and with the right timing, is a powerful teaching tool. It should not be the first or the only tool that a parent uses, but it has its place.

TRUTH À LA CARTE

But what about the restaurant debate? Does absence make the heart grow fonder or not? Alas, not enough research has been conducted to shed much light on this question. We do know that "out of sight, out of mind" is true when we're fresh from the womb; young babies will behave as if a toy has vanished into thin air when the toy is moved out of sight. But our memories quickly improve. Research conducted by Julia Vormbrock, Ph.D., and others, shows that children grow more fond of their caregivers when they're separated from them—at least for a few days. After two weeks of separation, however, most children become "detached," reports Vormbrock.

Psychologist Robert Pelligrini, Ph.D., once asked 720 young adults about separation, and two-thirds said that "absence makes the heart grow fonder" seemed more true than "out of sight, out of mind." A poll, however, doesn't tell us much about the truth of the matter. To settle things, we'll need an experiment. Hmmm. First we'll need 100 couples, whom we'll give various tests of "fondness." Then we'll assign, at random, half of the couples to a Control Group and half to an Absence Group. Next we'll separate the partners in each couple in our Absence Group by, say, 1,000 miles for six months—somehow providing jobs, housing, and social support for every person we relocate. Finally, we'll readminister our fondness tests

---

Rating the Proverbs

Here's a quick rundown on how well some other common proverbs measure up to research findings:

★★★★★	Looks good
★★★★	Some evidence supports it
★★★	Not clear
★★	Some evidence casts doubt
★	Scrap heap

"Once bitten, twice shy." Behind almost every dog or cat phobia, there's a bite or scratch. ★★★★★

"Practice makes perfect." Even the brain-injured can often learn new material with sufficient repetition. ★★★★

"Misery loves company." Depressed people often shun company, which unfortunately is part of the problem. ★★

"Two heads are better than one." Teams or groups typically produce better solutions than individuals do. ★★★★

"Cold hands, warm heart." Cold hands, poor circulation. See your physician. ★

"Every cloud has a silver lining." Not really, but therapy techniques like cognitive restructuring can get you to think so, and that can get you through the day. ★★★

"Old habits die hard." When we fail at a task, we tend to resort to old behavior patterns, even those from childhood. ★★★★

"You can't teach an old dog new tricks." You'll feel better, think more clearly, and may even live longer if you keep learning throughout life. ★★

"Familiarity breeds contempt." People tend to like what's familiar. ★

"Blood will tell." For better or worse, genes really do set limits on both physical characteristics and behavior. ★★★★

"A woman's place is in the home." Only when artificial barriers keep her there. ★

"When the cat's away, the mice will play." Kids and employees tend to slack off when their parents or supervisors are out of sight. ★★★★

"There's no accounting for tastes." Until you look at upbringing, biochemistry, evolutionary influences, and so on. ★★

to all 100 couples. If we find significantly greater levels of fondness in the separated couples than in the unseparated couples, we'll have strong support for the idea that absence makes the heart grow fonder.

Any volunteers? What? You would never subject yourself to such an absurd procedure? Well, fortunately, no one would ever conduct such research, either.

And that's the bottom line: the behavioral sciences can provide useful insights about how we should lead our lives, but there are limits to the kind of research that can be conducted with people. Folk wisdom may be flawed, but, in some instances, it's all we've got or will ever have. So don't put all your eggs in one basket.

CRITICAL THINKING QUESTIONS

1. A number of proverbs are rated in the box at the end of the article. Select one of the proverbs, and design a study that would test its validity.
2. Select one of the proverbs referred to in Question 1, and find a study that has been conducted on the topic. Summarize the results.
3. In addition to the folk wisdom mentioned in the article, what are other examples of common-sense ideas that contradict one another?
4. Many people rely on folk wisdom to guide their actions or explain certain situations. Is doing so ineffective or even dangerous? Or does folk wisdom (or common sense) still play a useful role in helping people manage their lives? Summarize the pros and cons of relying on folk wisdom as a guide to behavior.

ARTICLE 2 _____

Have you ever participated in a social psychology experiment? What were you thinking while you were participating? Were you accepting of the situation and the explanation you were given by the researcher, or were you trying to figure out the real purpose of the experiment? If you were doing the latter, you would be in good company, as many people have come to associate psychological research (and in particular, social psychology research) with the use of deception.

Deception has always been a staple in the research conducted in the field. But what exactly is *deception?* Is it simply another term for *lying?* In practice, deception in research can be located on a continuum from simply withholding from the subjects the true nature of the experiment to actively creating a cover story to try to keep the subjects from determining the actual purpose of the study. Deception is largely based on the assumption that if subjects knew the true nature of the experiment (the hypothesis being tested, that is), then they would not act naturally and hence contaminate the results.

This next classic article by Herbert C. Kelman explores the use of deception in social psychological experiments. After discussing some of the ethical issues involved in the use of deception, Kelman goes on to suggest how the use of deception should be handled, as well as alternatives to deception. In the years since the publication of this article in 1967, many changes in the ethical guidelines for the treatment of human subjects have been made. For example, it is now standard policy for institutions to have ethical review boards for the approval of any study involving human subjects. Nonetheless, deception in one form or another is still a common feature in social psychological research.

Human Use of Human Subjects

The Problem of Deception in Social Psychological Experiments[1]

■ Herbert C. Kelman

Though there is often good reason for deceiving Ss in social psychological experiments, widespread use of such procedures has serious (a) ethical implications (involving not only the possibility of harm to S, but also the quality of the E-S relationship), (b) methodological implications (relating to the decreasing naïveté of Ss), and (c) implications for the future of the discipline. To deal with these problems, it is necessary (a) to increase active awareness of the negative implications of deception and use it only when clearly justified, not as a matter of course; (b) to explore ways of counteracting and minimizing negative consequences of deception when it is used; and (c) to develop new experimental techniques that dispense with deception and rely on S's positive motivations.

In 1954, in the pages of the *American Psychologist*, Edgar Vinacke raised a series of questions about experiments—particularly in the area of small groups—in which "the psychologist conceals the true purpose and conditions of the experiment, or positively misinforms the subjects, or exposes them to painful, embarrassing, or worse, experiences, without the subjects' knowledge of what is going on [p. 155]." He summed up his concerns by asking, "What . . . is the proper balance between the interests of science and the thoughtful treatment of the persons who, innocently, supply the data? [p. 155]." Little effort has been made in the intervening years to seek answers to the questions he raised. During these same years, however, the problem of deception in social psychological experiments has taken on increasingly serious proportions.[2]

The problem is actually broader, extending beyond the walls of the laboratory. It arises, for example, in various field studies in which investigators enroll as members of a group that has special interest for them so that they can observe its operations from the inside. The pervasiveness of the problem becomes even more apparent when we consider that deception is built into most of our measurement devices, since it is important to keep the respondent unaware of the personality or attitude dimension that we wish to explore. For the present purposes, however, primarily the problem of deception in the context of the social psychological experiment will be discussed.

The use of deception has become more and more extensive, and it is now a commonplace and almost standard feature of social psychological experiments. Deception has been turned into a game, often played with great skill and virtuosity. A considerable amount of the creativity and ingenuity of social psychologists is invested in the development of increasingly elaborate deception situations. Within a single experiment, deception may be built upon deception in a delicately complex structure. The literature now contains a fair number of studies in which second- or even third-order deception was employed.

One well-known experiment (Festinger & Carlsmith, 1959), for example, involved a whole progression of deceptions. After the subjects had gone through an experimental task, the investigator made it clear—through word and gesture—that the experiment was over and that he would now "like to explain what this has been all about so you'll have some idea of why you were doing this [p. 205]." This explanation was false, however, and was designed to serve as a basis for the true experimental manipulation. The manipulation itself involved asking subjects to serve as the experimenter's accomplices. The task of the "accomplice" was to tell the next "subject" that the experiment in which he had just participated (which

was in fact a rather boring experience) had been interesting and enjoyable. He was also asked to be on call for unspecified future occasions on which his services as accomplice might be needed because "the regular fellow couldn't make it, and we had a subject scheduled [p. 205]." These newly recruited "accomplices," of course, were the true subjects, while the "subjects" were the experimenter's true accomplices. For their presumed services as "accomplices," the true subjects were paid in advance—half of them receiving $1, and half $20. When they completed their service, however, the investigators added injury to insult by asking them to return their hard-earned cash. Thus, in this one study, in addition to receiving the usual misinformation about the purpose of the experiment, the subject was given feedback that was really an experimental manipulation, was asked to be an accomplice who was really a subject, and was given a $20 bill that was really a will-o'-the-wisp. One wonders how much further in this direction we can go. Where will it all end?

It is easy to view this problem with alarm, but it is much more difficult to formulate an unambiguous position on the problem. As a working experimental social psycholgist, I cannot conceive the issue in absolutist terms. I am too well aware of the fact that there are good reasons for using deception in many experiments. There are many significant problems that probably cannot be investigated without the use of deception, at least not at the present level of development of our experimental methodology. Thus, we are always confronted with a conflict of values. If we regard the acquisition of scientific knowledge about human behavior as a positive value, and if an experiment using deception constitutes a significant contribution in such knowledge which could not very well be achieved by other means, then we cannot unequivocally rule out this experiment. The question for us is not simply whether it does or does not use deception, but whether the amount and type of deception are justified by the significance of the study and the unavailability of alternative (that is, deception-free) procedures.

I have expressed special concern about second-order deceptions, for example, the procedure of letting a person believe that he is acting as experimenter or as the experimenter's accomplice when he is in fact serving as the subject. Such a procedure undermines the relationship between experimenter and subject even further than simple misinformation about the purposes of the experiment; deception does not merely take place *within* the experiment, but encompasses the whole definition of the relationship between the parties involved. Deception that takes place while the person is within the role of subject for which he has contracted can, to some degree, be isolated, but deception about the very nature of the contract itself is more likely to suffuse the experimenter-subject relationship as a whole and to remove the possibility of mutual trust. Thus, I would be inclined to take a more absolutist stand with regard to such second-order deceptions—but even here the issue turns out to be more complicated. I am stopped short when I think, for example, of the ingenious studies on experimenter bias by Rosenthal and his associates (e.g., Rosenthal & Fode, 1963; Rosenthal, Persinger, Vikan-Kline, & Fode, 1963; Rosenthal, Persinger, Vikan-Kline, & Mulry, 1963). These experiments employed second-order deception in that subjects were led to believe that they were the experimenters. Since these were experiments about experiments, however, it is very hard to conceive of any alternative procedures that the investigators might have used. There is no question in my mind that these are significant studies; they provide fundamental inputs to present efforts at reexamining the social psychology of the experiment. These studies, then, help to underline even further the point that we are confronted with a conflict of values that cannot be resolved by fiat.

I hope it is clear from these remarks that my purpose in focusing on this problem is not to single out specific studies performed by some of my colleagues and to point a finger at them. Indeed, the finger points at me as well. I too have used deception, and have known the joys of applying my skills and ingenuity to the creation of elaborate experimental situations that the subjects would not be able to decode. I am now making active attempts to find alternatives to deception, but still I have not forsworn the use of deception under any and all circumstances. The questions I am raising, then, are addressed to myself as well as to my colleagues. They are questions with which all of us who are committed to social psychology must come to grips, lest we leave their resolution

to others who have no understanding of what we are trying to accomplish.

What concerns me most is not so much that deception is used, but precisely that it is used without question. It has now become standard operating procedure in the social psychologist's laboratory. I sometimes feel that we are training a generation of students who do not know that there is any other way of doing experiments in our field—who feel that deception is as much de rigueur as significance at the .05 level. Too often deception is used not as a last resort, but as a matter of course. Our attitude seems to be that if you can deceive, why tell the truth? It is this unquestioning acceptance, this routinization of deception, that really concerns me.

I would like to turn now to a review of the bases for my concern with the problem of deception, and then suggest some possible approaches for dealing with it.

IMPLICATIONS OF THE USE OF DECEPTION IN SOCIAL PSYCHOLOGICAL EXPERIMENTS

My concern about the use of deception is based on three considerations: the ethical implications of such procedures, their methodological implications, and their implications for the future of social psychology.

1. *Ethical implications.* Ethical problems of a rather obvious nature arise in the experiments in which deception has potentially harmful consequences for the subject. Take, for example, the brilliant experiment by Mulder and Stemerding (1963) on the effects of threat on attraction to the group and need for strong leadership. In this study—one of the very rare examples of an experiment conducted in a natural setting—independent food merchants in a number of Dutch towns were brought together for group meetings, in the course of which they were informed that a large organization was planning to open up a series of supermarkets in the Netherlands. In the High Threat condition, subjects were told that there was a high probability that their town would be selected as a site for such markets, and that the advent of these markets would cause a considerable drop in their business. On the advice of the executives of the shopkeepers' organizations, who had helped to

arrange the group meetings, the investigators did not reveal the experimental manipulations to their subjects. I have been worried about these Dutch merchants ever since I heard about this study for the first time. Did some of them go out of business in anticipation of the heavy competition? Do some of them have an anxiety reaction every time they see a bulldozer? Chances are that they soon forgot about this threat (unless, of course, supermarkets actually did move into town) and that it became just one of the many little moments of anxiety that must occur in every shopkeeper's life. Do we have a right, however, to add to life's little anxieties and to risk the possibility of more extensive anxiety purely for the purposes of our experiments, particularly since deception deprives the subject of the opportunity to choose whether or not he wishes to expose himself to the risks that might be entailed?

The studies by Bramel (1962, 1963) and Bergin (1962) provide examples of another type of potentially harmful effects arising from the use of deception. In the Bramel studies, male undergraduates were led to believe that they were homosexually aroused by photographs of men. In the Bergin study, subjects of both sexes were given discrepant information about their level of masculinity or femininity; in one experimental condition, this information was presumably based on an elaborate series of psychological tests in which the subjects had participated. In all of these studies, the deception was explained to the subject at the end of the experiment. One wonders, however, whether such explanation removes the possibility of harmful effects. For many persons in this age group, sexual identity is still a live and sensitive issue, and the self-doubts generated by the laboratory experience may take on a life of their own and linger on for some time to come.

Yet another illustration of potentially harmful effects of deception can be found in Milgram's (1963, 1965) studies of obedience. In these experiments, the subject was led to believe that he was participating in a learning study and was instructed to administer increasingly severe shocks to another person who after a while began to protest vehemently. In fact, of course, the victim was an accomplice of the experimenter and did not receive any shocks. Depending on the conditions, sizable proportions of the subjects

obeyed the experimenter's instructions and continued to shock the other person up to the maximum level, which they believed to be extremely painful. Both obedient and defiant subjects exhibited a great deal of stress in this situation. The complexities of the issues surrounding the use of deception become quite apparent when one reads the exchange between Baumrind (1964) and Milgram (1964) about the ethical implications of the obedience research. There is clearly room for disagreement, among honorable people, about the evaluation of this research from an ethical point of view. Yet, there is good reason to believe that at least some of the obedient subjects came away from this experience with a lower self-esteem, having to live with the realization that they were willing to yield to destructive authority to the point of inflicting extreme pain on a fellow human being. The fact that this may have provided, in Milgram's (1964) words, "an opportunity to learn something of importance about themselves, and more generally, about the conditions of human action [p. 850]" is beside the point. If this were a lesson from life, it would indeed constitute an instructive confrontation and provide a valuable insight. But do we, for the purpose of experimentation, have the right to provide such potentially disturbing insights to subjects who do not know that this is what they are coming for? A similar question can be raised about the Asch (1951) experiments on group pressure, although the stressfulness of the situation and the implications for the person's self-concept were less intense in that context.

While the present paper is specifically focused on social psychological experiments, the problem of deception and its possibly harmful effects arises in other areas of psychological experimentation as well. Dramatic illustrations are provided by two studies in which subjects were exposed, for experimental purposes, to extremely stressful conditions. In an experiment designed to study the establishment of a conditioned response in a situation that is traumatic but not painful, Campbell, Sanderson, and Laverty (1964) induced—through the use of a drug—a temporary interruption of respiration in their subjects. "This has no permanently harmful physical consequences but is nonetheless a severe stress which is not in itself painful . . . [p. 628]." The subjects' reports confirmed that this was a "horrific" experience for them. "All the subjects in the standard series said that they thought they were dying [p. 631]." Of course the subjects, "male alcoholic patients who volunteered for the experiment when they were told that it was connected with a possible therapy for alcoholism [p. 629]," were not warned in advance about the effect of the drug, since this information would have reduced the traumatic impact of the experience.[3] In a series of studies on the effects of psychological stress, Berkun, Bialek, Kern, and Yagi (1962) devised a number of ingenious experimental situations designed to convince the subject that his life was actually in danger. In one situation, the subjects, a group of Army recruits, were actually "passengers aboard an apparently stricken plane which was being forced to 'ditch' or crash-land [p. 4]." In another experiment, an isolated subject in a desolate area learned that a sudden emergency had arisen (accidental nuclear radiation in the area, or a sudden forest fire, or misdirected artillery shells—depending on the experimental condition) and that he could be rescued only if he reported his position over his radio transmitter, "which has quite suddenly failed [p. 7]." In yet another situation, the subject was led to believe that he was responsible for an explosion that seriously injured another soldier. As the authors pointed out, reactions in these situations are more likely to approximate reactions to combat experiences or to naturally occurring disasters than are reactions to various laboratory stresses, but is the experimenter justified in exposing his subjects to such extreme threats?

So far, I have been speaking of experiments in which deception has potentially harmful consequences. I am equally concerned, however, about the less obvious cases, in which there is little danger of harmful effects, at least in the conventional sense of the term. Serious ethical issues are raised by deception per se and the kind of use of human beings that it implies. In our other interhuman relationships, most of us would never think of doing the kinds of things that we do to our subjects—exposing others to lies and tricks, deliberately misleading them about the purposes of the interaction or withholding pertinent information, making promises or giving assurances that we intend to disregard. We would view such behavior as a violation of the respect to which all fellow humans are entitled and of the whole basis

of our relationship with them. Yet we seem to forget that the experimenter-subject relationship—whatever else it is—is a *real* interhuman relationship, in which we have responsibility toward the subject as another human being whose dignity we must preserve. The discontinuity between the experimenter's behavior in everyday life and his behavior in the laboratory is so marked that one wonders why there has been so little concern with this problem, and what mechanisms have allowed us to ignore it to such an extent. I am reminded, in this connection, of the intriguing phenomenon of the "holiness of sin," which characterizes certain messianic movements as well as other movements of the true-believer variety. Behavior that would normally be unacceptable actually takes on an aura of virtue in such movements through a redefinition of the situation in which the behavior takes place and thus of the context for evaluating it. A similar mechanism seems to be involved in our attitude toward the psychological experiment. We tend to regard it as a situation that is not quite real, that can be isolated from the rest of life like a play performed on stage, and to which, therefore, the usual criteria for ethical interpersonal conduct become irrelevant. Behavior is judged entirely in the context of the experiment's scientific contribution and, in this context, deception—which is normally unacceptable—can indeed be seen as a positive good.

The broader ethical problem brought into play by the very use of deception becomes even more important when we view it in the light of present historical forces. We are living in an age of mass societies in which the transformation of man into an object to be manipulated at will occurs "on a mass scale, in a systematic way, and under the aegis of specialized institutions deliberately assigned to this task [Kelman, 1965]." In institutionalizing the use of deception in psychological experiments, we are, then, contributing to a historical trend that threatens values most of us cherish.

2. *Methodological implications.* A second source of my concern about the use of deception is my increasing doubt about its adequacy as a methodology for social psychology.

A basic assumption in the use of deception is that a subject's awareness of the conditions that we are trying to create and of the phenomena that we wish to study would affect his behavior in such a way that we could not draw valid conclusions from it. For example, if we are interested in studying the effects of failure on conformity, we must create a situation in which the subjects actually feel that they have failed, and in which they can be kept unaware of our interest in observing conformity. In short, it is important to keep our subjects naïve about the purposes of the experiment so that they can respond to the experimental inductions spontaneously.

How long, however, will it be possible for us to find naïve subjects? Among college students, it is already very difficult. They may not know the exact purpose of the particular experiment in which they are participating, but at least they know, typically, that it is *not* what the experimenter says it is. Orne (1962) pointed out that the use of deception "on the part of psychologists is so widely known in the college population that even if a psychologist is honest with the subject, more often than not he will be distrusted." As one subject pithily put it, "'Psychologists always lie!'" Orne added that "This bit of paranoia has some support in reality [pp. 778–779]." There are, of course, other sources of human subjects that have not been tapped, and we could turn to them in our quest for naïveté. But even there it is only a matter of time. As word about psychological experiments gets around in whatever network we happen to be using, sophistication is bound to increase. I wonder, therefore, whether there is any future in the use of deception.

If the subject in a deception experiment knows what the experimenter is trying to conceal from him and what he is really after in the study, the value of the deception is obviously nullified. Generally, however, even the relatively sophisticated subject does not know the exact purpose of the experiment; he only has suspicions, which may approximate the true purpose of the experiment to a greater or lesser degree. Whether or not he knows the *true* purpose of the experiment, he is likely to make an effort to figure out its purpose, since he does not believe what the experimenter tells him, and therefore he is likely to operate in the situation in terms of his own hypothesis of what is involved. This may, in line with Orne's (1962) analysis, lead him to do what he thinks the experimenter wants him to do. Conversely, if he resents the experimenter's attempt to deceive him, he may try to

throw a monkey wrench into the works; I would not be surprised if this kind of Schweikian game among subjects became a fairly well-established part of the culture of sophisticated campuses. Whichever course the subject uses, however, he is operating in terms of his own conception of the nature of the situation, rather than in terms of the conception that the experimenter is trying to induce. In short, the experimenter can no longer assume that the conditions that he is trying to create are the ones that actually define the situation for the subject. Thus, the use of deception, while it is designed to give the experimenter control over the subject's perceptions and motivations, may actually produce an unspecifiable mixture of intended and unintended stimuli that make it difficult to know just what the subject is responding to.

The tendency for subjects to react to unintended cues—to features of the situation that are not part of the experimenter's design—is by no means restricted to experiments that involve deception. This problem has concerned students of the interview situation for some time, and more recently it has been analyzed in detail in the writings and research of Riecken, Rosenthal, Orne, and Mills. Subjects enter the experiment with their own aims, including attainment of certain rewards, divination of the experimenter's true purposes, and favorable self-presentation (Riecken, 1962). They are therefore responsive to demand characteristics of the situation (Orne, 1962), to unintended communications of the experimenter's expectations (Rosenthal, 1963), and to the role of the experimenter within the social system that experimenter and subject jointly constitute (Mills, 1962). In any experiment, then, the subject goes beyond the description of the situation and the experimental manipulation introduced by the investigator, makes his own interpretation of the situation, and acts accordingly.

For several reasons, however, the use of deception especially encourages the subject to dismiss the stated purposes of the experiment and to search for alternative interpretations of his own. First, the continued use of deception establishes the reputation of psychologists as people who cannot be believed. Thus, the desire "to penetrate the experimenter's inscrutability and discover the rationale of the experiment [Riecken, 1962, p. 34]" becomes especially strong. Generally, these efforts are motivated by the subject's desire to meet the expectations of the experimenter and of the situation.

They may also be motivated, however, as I have already mentioned, by a desire to outwit the experimenter and to beat him at his own game, in a spirit of genuine hostility or playful one-upmanship. Second, a situation involving the use of deception is inevitably highly ambiguous since a great deal of information relevant to understanding the structure of the situation must be withheld from the subject. Thus, the subject is especially motivated to try to figure things out and likely to develop idiosyncratic interpretations. Third, the use of deception, by its very nature, causes the experimenter to transmit contradictory messages to the subject. In his verbal instructions and explanations he says one thing about the purposes of the experiment; but in the experimental situation that he has created, in the manipulations that he has introduced, and probably in covert cues that he emits, he says another thing. This again makes it imperative for the subject to seek his own interpretation of the situation.

I would argue, then, that deception increases the subject's tendency to operate in terms of his private definition of the situation, differing (in random or systematic fashion) from the definition that the experimenter is trying to impose; moreover, it makes it more difficult to evaluate or minimize the effects of this tendency. Whether or not I am right in this judgment, it can, at the very least, be said that the use of deception does not resolve or reduce the unintended effects of the experiment as a social situation in which the subject pursues his private aims. Since the assumptions that the subject is naïve and that he sees the situation as the experimenter wishes him to see it are unwarranted, the use of deception no longer has any special obvious advantages over other experimental approaches. I am not suggesting that there may not be occasions when deception may still be the most effective procedure to use from a methodological point of view. But since it raises at least as many methodological problems as any other type of procedure does, we have every reason to explore alternative approaches and to extend our methodological inquiries to the question of the effects of using deception.

3. *Implications for the future of social psychology.* My third concern about the use of deception is based on its long-run implications for our discipline and combines both the ethical and methodological considerations that I have already raised. There is something disturbing about the idea of relying on massive decep-

tion as the basis for developing a field of inquiry. Can one really build a discipline on a foundation of such research?

From a long-range point of view, there is obviously something self-defeating about the use of deception. As we continue to carry out research of this kind, our potential subjects become more and more sophisticated, and we become less and less able to meet the conditions that our experimental procedures require. Moreover, as we continue to carry out research of this kind, our potential subjects become increasingly distrustful of us, and our future relations with them are likely to be undermined. Thus, we are confronted with the anomalous circumstance that the more research we do, the more difficult and questionable it becomes.

The use of deception also involves a contradiction between our experimental procedures and our long-range aims as scientists and teachers. In order to be able to carry out our experiments, we are concerned with maintaining the naïveté of the population from which we hope to draw our subjects. We are all familiar with the experimenter's anxious concern that the introductory course might cover the autokinetic phenomenon, need achievement, or the Asch situation before he has had a chance to complete his experimental runs. This perfectly understandable desire to keep procedures secret goes counter to the traditional desire of the scientist and teacher to inform and enlighten the public. To be sure, experimenters are interested only in temporary secrecy, but it is not inconceivable that at some time in the future they might be using certain procedures on a regular basis with large segments of the population and thus prefer to keep the public permanently naïve. It is perhaps not too fanciful to imagine, for the long run, the possible emergence of a special class, in possession of secret knowledge—a possibility that is clearly antagonistic to the principle of open communication to which we, as scientists and intellectuals, are so fervently committed.

DEALING WITH THE PROBLEM OF DECEPTION IN SOCIAL PSYCHOLOGICAL EXPERIMENTS

If my concerns about the use of deception are justified, what are some of the ways in which we, as experimental social psychologists, can deal with them? I would like to suggest three steps that we can take: increase our active awareness of the problem, explore ways of counteracting and minimizing the negative effects of deception, and give careful attention to the development of new experimental techniques that dispense with the use of deception.

1. *Active awareness of the problem.* I have already stressed that I would not propose the complete elimination of deception under all circumstances, in view of the genuine conflict of values with which the experimenter is confronted. What is crucial, however, is that we always ask ourselves the question whether deception, in the given case, is necessary and justified. How we answer the question is less important than the fact that we ask it. What we must be wary of is the tendency to dismiss the question as irrelevant and to accept deception as a matter of course. Active awareness of the problem is thus in itself part of the solution for it makes the use of deception a matter for discussion, deliberation, investigation, and choice. Active awareness means that, in any given case, we will try to balance the value of an experiment that uses deception against its questionable or potentially harmful effects. If we engage in this process honestly, we are likely to find that there are many occasions when we or our students can forego the use of deception—either because deception is not necessary (that is, alternative procedures that are equally good or better are available), because the importance of the study does not warrant the use of an ethically questionable procedure, or because the type of deception involved is too extreme (in terms of the possibility of harmful effects or of seriously undermining the experimenter-subject relationship).

2. *Counteracting and minimizing the negative effects of deception.* If we do use deception, it is essential that we find ways of counteracting and minimizing its negative effects. Sensitizing the apprentice researcher to this necessity is at least as fundamental as any other part of research training.

In those experiments in which deception carries the potential of harmful effects (in the more usual sense of the term), there is an obvious requirement to build protections into every phase of the process. Subjects must be selected in a way that will exclude individuals who are especially vulnerable; the potentially harmful manipulation (such as the induction of stress) must be kept at a moderate level of intensity; the experimenter must be sensitive to danger signals in the reactions of his subjects and be prepared to deal with crises when they arise; and, at the conclusion of the session, the experimenter must take time not only to reassure the subject, but also to help him work through his feelings about the experience to whatever degree may be required. In general, the principle that a subject ought not to leave the laboratory with greater anxiety or lower self-esteem than he came with is a good one to follow. I would go beyond it to argue that the subject should in some positive way be enriched by the experience, that is, he should come away from it with the feeling that he has learned something, understood something, or grown in some way. This, of course, adds special importance to the kind of feedback that is given to the subject at the end of the experimental session.

Postexperimental feedback is, of course, the primary way of counteracting negative effects in those experiments in which the issue is deception as such, rather than possible threats to the subject's well-being. If we do deceive the subject, then it is our obligation to give him a full and detailed explanation of what we have done and of our reasons for using this type of procedure. I do not want to be absolutist about this, but I would suggest it as a good rule of thumb to follow: Think very carefully before undertaking an experiment whose purposes you feel unable to reveal to the subjects even after they have completed the experimental session. It is, of course not enough to give the subject a perfunctory feedback, just to do one's duty. Postexperimental explanations should be worked out with as much detail as other aspects of the procedure and, in general, some thought ought to be given to ways of making them meaningful and instructive for the subject and helpful for rebuilding his relationship with the experimenter. I feel very strongly that to accomplish these purposes, we must keep the feedback itself inviolate and under no circumstance give the subject false feedback or pretend to be giving him feedback while we are in fact introducing another experimental manipulation. If we hope to maintain any kind of trust in our relationship with potential subjects, there must be no ambiguity that the statement "The experiment is over and I shall explain to you what it was all about" means precisely that and nothing else. If subjects have reason to suspect even that statement, then we have lost the whole basis for a decent human relationship with our subjects and all hope for future cooperation from them.

3. *Development of new experimental techniques.* My third and final suggestion is that we invest some of the creativity and ingenuity, now devoted to the construction of elaborate deceptions, in the search for alternative experimental techniques that do not rely on the use of deception. The kind of techniques that I have in mind would be based on the principle of eliciting the subject's positive motivations to contribute to the experimental enterprise. They would draw on the subject's active participation and involvement in the proceedings and encourage him to cooperate in making the experiment a success—not by giving the results he thinks the experimenter wants, but by conscientiously taking the roles and carrying out the tasks that the experimenter assigns to him. In short, the kind of techniques I have in mind would be designed to involve the subject as an active participant in a joint effort with the experimenter.

Perhaps the most promising source of alternative experimental approaches are procedures using some sort of role playing. I have been impressed, for example, with the role playing that I have observed in the context of the Inter-Nation Simulation (Guetzkow, Alger, Brody, Noel, & Snyder, 1963), a laboratory procedure involving a simulated world in which the subjects take the roles of decision-makers of various nations. This situation seems to create a high level of emotional involvement and to elicit motivations that have a real-life quality to them. Moreover, within this situation—which is highly complex and generally permits only gross experimental manipulations—it is possible to test specific theoretical hypotheses by using data based on repeated measurements as interaction between the simulated nations develops. Thus, a study carried out at the Western Behavioral Sciences Institute provided, as an extra, some interesting opportunities for testing hypotheses derived from balance theory, by the use of mutual ratings made by decision-makers of Nations A, B, and C, before and after A shifted from an alliance with B to an alliance with C.

A completely different type of role playing was used effectively by Rosenberg and Abelson (1960) in their studies of cognitive dilemmas. In my own research program, we have been exploring different kinds of role-playing procedures with varying degrees of success. In one study, the major manipulation consisted in informing subjects that the experiment to which they had just committed themselves would require them (depending on the condition) either to receive shocks from a fellow subject, or to administer shocks to a fellow subject. We used a regular deception procedure, but with a difference: We told the subjects before the session started that what was to follow was make-believe, but that we wanted them to react as if they really found themselves in this situation. I might mention that some subjects, not surprisingly, did not accept as true the information that this was all make-believe and wanted to know when they should show up for the shock experiment to which they had committed themselves. I have some questions about the effectiveness of this particular procedure. It did not do enough to create a high level of involvement, and it turned out to be very complex since it asked subjects to role-play subjects, not people. In this sense, it might have given us the worst of both worlds, but I still think it is worth some further exploration. In another experiment, we were interested in creating differently structured attitudes about an organization by feeding different kinds of information to two groups of subjects. These groups were then asked to take specific actions in support of the organization, and we measured attitude changes resulting from these actions. In the first part of the experiment, the subjects were clearly informed that the organization and the information that we were feeding to them were fictitious, and that we were simply trying to simulate the conditions under which attitudes about new organizations are typically formed. In the second part of the experiment, the subjects were told that we were interested in studying the effects of action in support of an organization on attitudes toward it, and they were asked (in groups of five) to role-play a strategy meeting of leaders of the fictitious organization. The results of this study were very encouraging. While there is obviously a great deal that we need to know about the meaning of this situation to the subjects, they did react differentially to the experimental manipulations and these reactions followed an orderly pattern, despite the fact that they knew it was all make-believe.

There are other types of procedures, in addition to role playing, that are worth exploring. For example, one might design field experiments in which, with the full cooperation of the subjects, specific experimental variations are introduced. The advantages of dealing with motivations at a real-life level of intensity might well outweigh the disadvantages of subjects' knowing the general purpose of the experiment. At the other extreme of ambitiousness, one might explore the effects of modifying standard experimental procedures slightly by informing the subject at the beginning of the experiment that he will not be receiving full information about what is going on, but asking him to suspend judgment until the experiment is over.

Whatever alternative approach we try, there is no doubt that it will have its own problems and complexities. Procedures effective for some purposes may be quite ineffective for others, and it may well turn out that for certain kinds of problems there is no adequate substitute for the use of deception. But there *are* alternative procedures that, for many purposes, may be as effective or even more effective than procedures built on deception. These approaches often involve a radically different set of assumptions about the role of the subject in the experiment: They require us to *use* the subject's motivation to cooperate rather than to bypass it; they may even call for increasing the sophistication of potential subjects, rather than maintaining their naïveté. My only plea is that we devote some of our energies to active exploration of these alternative approaches.

REFERENCES

Asch, S. E. Effects of group pressure upon the modification and distortion of judgments. In H. Guetzkow (Ed.), *Groups, leadership, and men.* Pittsburgh: Carnegie Press, 1951. Pp. 117–190.

Baumrind, D. Some thoughts on ethics of research: After reading Milgram's "Behavioral Study of Obedience." *American Psychologist,* 1964, **19**, 421–423.

Bergin, A. E. The effect of dissonant persuasive communications upon changes in a self-referring attitude. *Journal of Personality,* 1962, **30**, 423–438.

Berkun, M. M., Bialek, H. M., Kern, R. P., & Yagi, K. Experimental studies of psychological stress in man. *Psychological Monographs,* 1962, **76**(15, Whole No. 534).

Bramel, D. A dissonance theory approach to defensive projection. *Journal of Abnormal and Social Psychology,* 1962, **64**, 121–129.

Bramel, D. Selection of a target for defensive projection. *Journal of Abnormal and Social Psychology,* 1963, **66**, 318–324.

Campbell, D., Sanderson, R. E., & Laverty, S. G. Characteristics of a conditioned response in human subjects during extinction trials following a single traumatic conditioning trial. *Journal of Abnormal and Social Psychology,* 1964, **68**, 627–639.

Festinger, L., & Carlsmith, J. M. Cognitive consequences of forced compliance. *Journal of Abnormal and Social Psychology,* 1959, **58**, 203–210.

Guetzkow, H., Alger, C. F., Brody, R. A., Noel, R. C., & Snyder, R. C. *Simulation in international relations.* Englewood Cliffs, N.J.: Prentice-Hall, 1963.

Kelman, H. C. Manipulation of human behavior: An ethical dilemma for the social scientist. *Journal of Social Issues,* 1965, **21**(2), 31–46.

Milgram, S. Behavioral study of obedience. *Journal of Abnormal and Social Psychology,* 1963, **67**, 371–378.

Milgram, S. Issues in the study of obedience: A reply to Baumrind. *American Psychologist,* 1964, **19**, 848–852.

Milgram, S. Some conditions of obedience and disobedience to authority. *Human Relations,* 1965, **18**, 57–76.

Mills, T. M. A sleeper variable in small groups research: The experimenter. *Pacific Sociological Review,* 1962, **5**, 21–28.

Mulder, M., & Stemerding, A. Threat, attraction to group, and need for strong leadership. *Human Relations,* 1963, **16**, 317–334.

Orne, M. T. On the social psychology of the psychological experiment: With particular reference to demand characteristics and their implications. *American Psychologist,* 1962, **17**, 776–783.

Riecken, H. W. A program for research on experiments in social psychology. In N. F. Washburne (Ed.), *Decisions, values and groups.* Vol. 2. New York: Pergamon Press, 1962. Pp. 25–41.

Rosenberg, M. J., & Abelson, R. P. An analysis of cognitive balancing. In M. J. Rosenberg et al., *Attitude organization and change.* New Haven: Yale University Press, 1960. Pp. 112–163.

Rosenthal, R. On the social psychology of the psychological experiment: The experimenter's hypothesis as unintended determinant of experimental results. *American Scientist,* 1963, **51**, 268–283.

Rosenthal, R., & Fode, K. L. Psychology of the scientist: V. Three experiments in experimenter bias. *Psychological Reports,* 1963, **12**, 491–511. (Monogr. Suppl. 3-V12)

Rosenthal, R., Persinger, G. W., Vikan-Kline, L., & Fode, K. L. The effect of early data returns on data subsequently obtained by outcome-biased experimenters. *Sociometry,* 1963, **26**, 487–498.

Rosenthal, R., Persinger, G. W., Vikan-Kline, L., & Mulry, R. C. The role of the research assistant in the mediation of experimenter bias. *Journal of Personality,* 1963, **31**, 313–335.

Vinacke, W. E. Deceiving experimental subjects. *American Psychologist,* 1954, **9**, 155.

ENDNOTES

1. Paper read at the symposium on "Ethical and Methodological Problems in Social Psychological Experiments," held at the meetings of the American Psychological Association in Chicago, September 3, 1965. This paper is a product of a research program on social influence and behavior change supported by United States Public Health Service Research Grant MH-07280 from the National Institute of Mental Health.

2. In focusing on deception in *social* psychological experiments, I do not wish to give the impression that there is no serious problem elsewhere. Deception is widely used in most studies involving human subjects and gives rise to issues similar to those discussed in this paper. Some examples of the use of deception in other areas of psychological experimentation will be presented later in this paper.

3. The authors reported, however, that some of their other subjects were physicians familiar with the drug; "they did not suppose they were dying but, even though they knew in a general way what to expect, they too said that the experience was extremely harrowing [p. 632]." Thus, conceivably, the purposes of the experiment might have been achieved even if the subjects had been told to expect the temporary interruption of breathing.

CRITICAL THINKING QUESTIONS

1. Which of the studies mentioned in the article involves the greatest ethical issues? Why? Select one of the studies cited in this article, and suggest an alternative to the type of deception that was employed.

2. Should the use of deception be banned? Why or why not? If not, under what conditions should it be allowed? What impact would such a limitation have on social psychological research? Defend your position.

3. Who should determine what constitutes an ethically appropriate experiment? Professors? Students? Outside laypeople? Explain your answer. What would be the ideal composition of a board charged with reviewing research proposals? Why?

4. Obtain a copy of the current "American Psychological Association Guide for the Ethical Treatment of Human Subjects." Review these guidelines, considering how comprehensive they are. What criteria should be used in determining what is in the best interests of the subjects of an experiment?

5. What do you think of Kelman's position on "second-order" deception? Do you agree that it is of even greater concern than standard ("first-order") deception practices? Why or why not?

6. What do you think of Kelman's suggestions for the development of new experimental techniques as an alternative to deception? Find a research study that tried such a technique in lieu of deception. Alternatively, find a research study reported in this book of readings and suggest an alternative to the deception that was used. In either case, what might be lost and what might be gained by not deceiving subjects? Explain your answer.

ADDITIONAL RELATED READINGS

Benson, E. S. (2006). All that's gold does not glitter: How the Golden Fleece tarnished psychological science. *Observer, 19*(6), 13–20.

Pittenger, D. J. (2002). Deception in research: Distinctions and solutions from the perspective of utilitarianism. *Ethics and Behavior, 12*(2), 117–142.

*ARTICLE 3*_____

Anyone who reads a newspaper or magazine or watches the news constantly encounters the results of one study or another reporting what people think about certain issues (the war in Iraq, for example) or what factors are most associated with certain behaviors (that violent video games increase real-life aggressive tendencies, for example). Often we hear only the conclusions of a particular study but not necessarily the details of what the study involved.

Unfortunately, as the saying goes, "The devil is in the details." Knowing exactly what was done in a study or who was surveyed in an opinion poll is important in determining how much confidence (if any) we can have in the reported findings. While it might be assumed that anyone conducting research knows how to do so properly and thus minimize problems, such is not always the case. Even well-intentioned researchers may have methodological issues in their studies that may impact their findings.

To acquire a true appreciation of the complexities of conducting valid research, it is usually necessary to take a course or courses in research methodology and statistics; however, not everyone will have the opportunity to do so. Yet to be an intelligent consumer of the research results we routinely encounter in our lives, some understanding of the issues pertaining to research studies is important.

The following article, published by the American Psychological Association, provides suggestions for how to become a wise consumer of psychological research. Understanding these concepts will help you maximize your appreciation of the remaining articles in this book as well as the research results you see reported in your daily life.

How to Be a Wise Consumer of Psychological Research

It is difficult to turn the pages of a newspaper without coming across a story that makes an important claim about human nature. News stories report the latest findings regarding what causes divorce, how men and women differ psychologically, or how work-related stress influences physical illness. Other stories summarize the results of surveys designed to tell us how people will vote in an upcoming election or what proportion of Americans routinely wear seat belts. Flip to the advertisements and you will be exposed to claims about everything from how to improve your memory by listening to subliminal tapes to how to become more popular. Being able to evaluate research claims objectively is an important skill. Separating the scientific wheat from the chaff can influence how you vote, whether you adopt a new diet, or whether you decide to get professional help for a child with a learning disorder. With this in mind, this short essay is devoted to the topic of being a wise consumer of psychological research. As consumers of both products and ideas, we all need to know the difference between carefully conducted and poorly conducted research. **This essay can help you evaluate research-based claims and make you a better consumer of many of the products and services that shape your daily life.**

SHOW ME THE DATA! LOOKING AT EVIDENCE

Perhaps the most important lesson about being a wise consumer of psychological research is that, from a scientific perspective, all claims require **evidence,** not just opinions. Scientists who evaluate research claims behave like ideal jury members who are asked to evaluate claims made by prosecuting attorneys. They begin with the skeptical assumption that all claims are false (the defendant is innocent until proven guilty; the diet plan is ineffective; testosterone plays no role in aggression). Only after considering the strengths and weaknesses of the evidence relevant to a claim do jurors and scientists decide whether to accept the claims of those doing the claiming (for example, prosecuting attorneys, advertisers, scientists). This decision to accept or reject a claim is best made by paying careful attention to the methods that served as the basis for a specific claim. Behavioral scientists have hundreds of tools in their methodological toolboxes, but as it turns out, two of these tools turn out to be much more important than any others. Understanding the nature and purpose of these two tools is thus the first step to becoming an educated consumer of psychological research. In short, sound research methods lead to more valid research conclusions. The two tools that lie at the heart of sound research methods are random sampling and experimental manipulation based on random assignment.

SAYS WHO? RANDOM SAMPLING

When behavioral scientists want to assess the attitudes or preferences of very large groups of people (e.g., American voters, Asian-American college students, human beings), they face a seemingly insurmountable problem. It is usually impossible to ask every member of a very large group what he or she thinks, feels, or does. However, behavioral scientists have solved this tricky problem by developing a technique called **random sampling.** When survey researchers use random sampling, they select a very small proportion of the people from within a very large sample (e.g., 1,000 out of 50 million registered voters). They then **estimate** what the entire population is like on the basis of the responses of those sampled. The key to getting

an accurate estimate is the use of random sampling. Random sampling refers to selecting people from a population so that everyone in the entire population (e.g., all registered voters in the U.S.) has an equal chance of being selected. This turns out to be an incredibly powerful technique. If every person in a group of 50 million voters really does have an equal chance of being selected into a national survey, then the results of the survey based on 1,000 people will almost always prove to resemble the results for the total population.

An excellent example of the importance of random sampling can be found in the 1936 U.S. Presidential election. Prior to that election, the *Literary Digest* sent postcards to more than 10 million Americans, asking them to report who they planned to vote for in the upcoming election. Among the 2 million Americans who returned the postcards, Alf Landon was the overwhelming favorite. In contrast, a much smaller survey conducted by the recently-formed Gallup group yielded very different results. Based on the responses of only a few thousand likely voters, the Gallup poll suggested that Franklin D. Roosevelt would be the winner. If you pull a dime out of your pocket, and look to see whose face is there, you'll see that the Gallup pollsters were correct. FDR won in a landslide, and Alf Landon faded into obscurity. How did the Gallup poll, based on many fewer people outperform the enormous *Literary Digest* poll? The Gallup pollsters came very close to performing a true random sample of likely voters. In contrast, the *Literary Digest* sampled people by taking names from automobile registrations and telephone listings. In 1936, people who owned cars and phones were usually pretty wealthy—and wealthy people overwhelming preferred Alf Landon.

The lesson of the *Literary Digest* error is that whenever you hear the results of any survey, you should ask yourself how the surveyed people were sampled. Were those sampled really like the pool of people (e.g., American voters, African American children) whose attitudes and behavior the researcher would like to describe?

Even when a researcher makes careful use of random sampling, it is also useful to pay attention to a different form of sampling bias, known as **non-response bias.** If only a small percentage of randomly sampled people agree to respond to a survey, it is quite likely that those who did respond will be different than those who refused. Modern pollsters have long mastered the science of random sampling. These days, most of the error in most scientific polls is based on the fact that it can be hard to get very high response rates (or hard to know who to sample in the first place). For example, if you randomly sampled all those eligible to vote in a state gubernatorial race, and you only got a 30% response rate, you would have to worry about whether those who refused to be surveyed would vote the same way as the eager 30% who agreed. Moreover, even if everyone agreed to be surveyed, you'd have to worry about whether the sub sample of all eligible voters who actually showed up at the polls on election day had the same preferences as those who either didn't bother to vote or were unable to do so.

It is also important to note that random sampling helps you describe only the population of people from whom you sampled (and not other populations). For example, if researchers randomly sampled registered voters, but only did so in North Carolina, they might get a great idea of what North Carolinians believe, but it would be very risky to generalize these results to other Americans. This is why people sometimes criticize the results of surveys taken of college students, who differ markedly from older adults. On the other hand, if surveyors wanted to know the opinions of college students, it would make little sense to sample anyone else. The key issue might be exactly which college students. A random sample of 1,000 American college students would tell us much more than a random sample of 1,000 students at Vassar College. Of course, if we cared only about Vassar College students, we would want to sample Vassarians at random. The key issue in sampling is to pay careful attention to who was sampled and to make certain that those sampled are the same kind of people about whom a researcher has made a claim (a claim about what the evidence shows).

HOW TO ASK WHY: EXPERIMENTAL MANIPULATIONS AND RANDOM ASSIGNMENT

When a researcher moves from descriptive research to experimental research, random sampling is still important, but it begins to take a back seat to a sec-

ond major technique. This second technique is random assignment, and it is the cornerstone of the experimental method. Unlike random sampling, which is a technique for deciding who to study, **random assignment** can take place only **after people** have already been selected into a study. Random assignment is a technique for assigning people to different specific conditions in an experiment, and random assignment occurs only when everyone in the study has an equal chance of serving in any specific condition. In the same way that random sampling guarantees that the people sampled in a study will be as similar as possible to those who were not sampled, random assignment guarantees that those assigned to one experimental condition will be as similar as possible to those assigned to a different condition. This is crucial because the whole idea of an experiment is to identify two identical groups of people and then to **manipulate** something. One group gets an experimental treatment, and one does not. If the group that gets the treatment (e.g., a drug, exposure to a violent videogame) behaves differently than the control group that did not get the treatment, we can attribute the difference to the treatment—but only if we can rest assured that the two groups were similar prior to the treatment.

Another way to put this is that if we wish to identify the causes of human behavior, we must usually perform experiments in which we manipulate one thing, or a few factors, at a time. We can only do this by making use of random assignment. Suppose a researcher at Cornell University developed a new technique for teaching foreign language. If the researcher could do so, he might persuade all of his colleagues in the Spanish department to start using this new technique. After a year of instruction using the new technique, suppose that the professor documented that the average student who completed one year of Spanish at Cornell performed well above the national average in a test of Spanish fluency (relative to students at other universities who had also completed a year of Spanish). Can we attribute this performance advantage to the new instruction technique? Given how difficult it is to get admitted to Cornell in the first place, it is likely that students at Cornell would have performed well above the national norm even if they had been taught using a new technique. If the researcher really wanted to know if his teaching technique was superior, he would have needed to randomly assign some Cornell students to receive the new form of instruction while randomly assigning others to receive a traditional form of instruction (this would be hard to do, but that is a detail).

Consider a more important question. Do seatbelts save lives? One way to find out would be to obtain records of thousands of serious automobile accidents. To simplify things, suppose a researcher focused exclusively on drivers (rather than passengers) and found an accurate way to determine whether drivers were wearing their seatbelts at the time of each crash. The researcher then obtained accurate records of whether the driver in each crash survived. Imagine that drivers wearing seatbelts were much more likely to have survived. Can we safely assume that seatbelts are the reason? Not on the basis of this study alone. The problem is that, for ethical reasons, the people in this hypothetical study were not randomly assigned to different seatbelt conditions. As it turns out, those who do and do not routinely wear seatbelts differ in many important ways. Compared with habitual non-users of seatbelts, habitual users are older, more educated, and less likely to speed or drink and drive. These additional factors are also likely to influence survival in a serious accident, and they are all confounded with seatbelt use. On the basis of this study and this study alone, we cannot tell whether it is seatbelts or other safe driving practices that are responsible for the greater survival rates among seatbelt users.

If we were to conduct a large-scale experiment on seatbelt use (by determining habitual seatbelt use on the basis of coin flips), we could completely eliminate all of these confounds in one simple step. Random assignment would create two identical groups of people, exactly half of whom were forced to use seatbelts at all times, and exactly half of whom were forbidden from doing so during the experimental period. Of course, this hypothetical experiment would be unethical. Thus, researchers interested in seatbelt use have had to do a lot of other things to document the important role that seatbelts play in saving people's lives (including laboratory crash tests and studies that used sophistical statistical techniques to separate the effects of seatbelt use from other effects). The point is not that seatbelts don't save lives. They clearly do. The point is that it has taken a lot of time and effort to document this fact because of the impossibility of

conducting an experiment on this topic. If you want to conduct a single study to figure out what causes something, you will almost always need to conduct an experiment in which you make use of random assignment. As a consumer of psychological research, you must thus ask yourself whether a research claim was based on the results of a careful experiment, or whether a researcher may have compared two groups of people who differed in more than one way at the beginning of the study.

LONGITUDINAL RESEARCH

Sometimes a researcher can bypass the use of random assignment by comparing people with themselves—by conducting a **longitudinal study** or a study with a **pretest** and a **post-test**. Although such studies can be very informative, these studies often come with their own special kinds of confounds. Many of these confounds boil down to the fact that people can and do change over time, for many reasons. For example, consider GRE prep courses. When a student who scores poorly on the GRE takes a preparation course and then takes the GRE again, such a student will often do better the second time around, sometimes a lot better! This would seem to show that the prep course is effective. However, another very effective way to improve the performance of a group of students who have recently performed poorly on a test is to give them the test again without any intervention. In most cases, such students will do better on the test the second time around (including a different version of the same test). (The reason why low scorers tend to improve in the absence of training is known as "regression toward the mean", but its details are beyond the scope of this short essay.) The key issue is that it is always important to have a control group if you want to assess the impact of a treatment.

SOME FINAL THOUGHTS

There are many other ways in which research can go astray. Did Dr. Snittle word his survey questions fairly? Were participants reporting their attitudes honestly? Did those carrying out the research bias answers by subtly communicating to participants what they hoped to find? Was the size of the sample large enough to draw meaningful comparisons? For example, if you read that 4 out of 5 doctors use Brand X, were only five doctors surveyed? Were those who conducted the research strongly motivated to produce a specific result? For example, if those studying the effects of a drug were paid by a pharmaceutical company to do the research, could this conflict of interest distort the way they collect or interpret their data? The list continues. Specific issues such as these aside, however, the two concerns that should come to mind first when evaluating any research claim have to do with proper sampling and proper experimental control. First, were those studied truly representative of the people about whom we would like to draw conclusions? Second, did the researchers isolate the variables they studied by disentangling them from other confounded variables? It is not always easy to get answers to these questions, but if you get in the habit of asking them you will gradually become a better shopper for psychological truths.

CRITICAL THINKING QUESTIONS

1. Opinion surveys often are conducted via telephone. The technology of communication has changed considerably in recent times (e.g., cell phones, voice mail, etc.). Do you think these technological changes have affected who may or may not be sampled for a given study or who may choose to respond to a given survey? Explain.

2. The term *external validity* refers to how generalizable the results of one particular study are to other settings. A large number of social psychology experiments tend to use college students as subjects. Is this a problem? Why or why not?

3. Develop a list of what you consider the most important questions social psychology should try to answer. As you go through the course, keep track of which of these questions have been investigated and what the findings were. If a question you listed has not been investigated, consider why that may be the case.

4. Find the results of a study related to a topic in social psychology that has been reported in a recent newspaper or magazine. Based on the points raised in this article, what questions should you ask about the study as a wise consumer of psychological research? What information that you consider important in reaching valid conclusions is not reported in the article?

5. Apply the concepts raised in this article to one or more of the studies described in Article 2, "Human Use of Human Subjects."

CHAPTER INTEGRATION QUESTIONS

1. All three articles in this chapter relate to aspects of research: why relying on common sense is not always accurate, the problems of deception in research, and how to be a wise consumer of psychological research. Identify one or more themes common to all three articles.

2. Based on these articles, what are the major issues confronting an individual embarking on a career in social psychology research?

3. In *How to Lie with Statistics,* Darrell Huff states, "Statistics are like people. Torture them enough and they will tell you anything." What does this quotation mean to you? Do you agree or disagree with it? Why?

Chapter Two

SOCIAL PERCEPTION

HOW DO WE form impressions of other people? What information do we use in forming those impressions? How important are first impressions? How do we make judgments about why people act the way they do? These are some of the questions addressed by the readings in this chapter on social perception.

When we interact with another person, we are literally bombarded with information. What the person looks like, what he or she is saying, and how he or she is acting comprise but a fraction of the information available to us that we may use in forming an impression of the individual. One judgment we may make about another individual concerns his or her overall character. In other words, we want to know how honest, trustworthy, likeable, or good the person is. But exactly what are we looking for? And are some of us better than others at making accurate judgments?

One topic of study in this area is how long it takes for us to form an impression of someone. Do we do so almost immediately, or do we hold off until we know more about him or her? Furthermore, how accurate are our first impressions? Is a first impression formed after less than a minute of interaction with a stranger any less accurate than an impression formed after knowing someone for a much longer period of time? These and other questions pertaining to the power of first impressions are examined in Article 4, "The Once-Over: Can You Trust First Impressions?"

Another topic of interest is whether all the information available about someone is equally relevant in forming our impressions of him or her. In other words, are some factors more important than others? Article 5, "The Warm-Cold Variable in First Impressions of Persons," examines some of the important factors that influence our judgments of other people. This classic article is a fine example of the power of first impressions and the impact that they have on how we relate to others.

Finally, Article 6, "Detecting Lies in Children and Adults," offers a contemporary look at research on one particular aspect of impression formation: the ability to detect when someone is lying. The article examines people's ability to detect lies in children and adults. Despite the obvious interest any adult would have in detecting lies in children (ask any parent about this statement), surprisingly few studies have been done on this topic.

ARTICLE 4 _____

What information do we use in forming impressions of other people? When meeting someone for the first time, we rely on a variety of information, such as how he or she acts, looks, and dresses, and what he or she says. Some of this information is nonverbal. We pay a lot of attention to facial expressions, for example, as well as body postures and movements. Most of us have some sort of intuitive rules for decoding nonverbal behavior. For example, what does it mean when someone is standing upright with his or her arms folded across the chest? Is that person being defensive? Not very warm and open? Some popularizations of psychology maintain that certain nonverbal cues have specific meanings, such as in the example just given. However, the example used also might mean nothing more than that the person was cold or that he or she habitually stands that way. Regardless of any supposedly clearcut meanings of nonverbal behavior, we all have our own intuitive means for making judgments about the people we meet.

Although we may have confidence in our own judgments, the concept known as the *fundamental attribution error* suggests that we only see what we want to see. According to this concept, we have a basic tendency to make global, personality generalizations based upon observations made in specific situations. For example, if we meet someone at a party who seems warm, outgoing, and confident, we assume that this is what his or her personality is like in other situations, as well. In other words, we think that we know the real person and ignore or downplay the fact that he or she may act quite differently in other situations. Worse yet, once we form this initial impression, it may be hard to change, since we may persist in only seeing what is consistent with our initial judgment.

So, how long does it take for us to make a judgment about someone? An hour? Fifteen minutes? Two seconds? The following article by Carlin Flora discusses research that shows that people make judgments about others in a remarkably short period of time. Furthermore, these quick judgments tend to be amazingly similar to those made by people interacting over a much longer time period or even by trained interviewers. But the question is: How accurate are the judgments made by *any* of these people?

The Once-Over

Can You Trust First Impressions?

■ Carlin Flora

Bill and Hillary Clinton often tell the story of how they met: They locked eyes across Yale's law library, until Hillary broke the silent flirtation and marched straight over to Bill. "Look, if you're going to keep staring at me, and I'm going to keep staring back, we might as well be introduced. I'm Hillary Rodham. What's your name?" Bill has said he couldn't remember his own name. It was quite a first impression, one so powerful that it sparked a few chapters of U.S. history.

Initial encounters are emotionally concentrated events that can overwhelm us—even convince us that the room is spinning. We walk away from them with a first impression that is like a Polaroid picture—a

Reprinted from *Psychology Today*, 2004 (May/June), *37*, 60–66. Reprinted with permission from *Psychology Today* magazine. Copyright © 2004 (Sussex Publishers, Inc.).

head-to-toe image that develops instantly and never entirely fades. Often, that snapshot captures important elements of the truth.

Consider one study in which untrained subjects were shown 20- to 32-second videotaped segments of job applicants greeting interviewers. The subjects then rated the applicants on attributes such as self-assurance and likability. Surprisingly, their assessments were very close to those of trained interviewers who spent at least 20 minutes with each applicant. What semblance of a person—one with a distinct appearance, history and complex personality—could have been captured in such a fleeting moment?

The answer lies in part in how the brain takes first-impression Polaroids—creating a composite of all the signals given off by a new experience. Psychologists agree that snap judgments are a holistic phenomenon in which clues (mellifluous voice, Rolex watch, soggy handshake, hunched shoulders) hit us all at once and form an impression larger than their sum.

We do search for one particular sign on a new face: a smile. "We can pick up a smile from 30 meters away," says Paul Ekman, professor of psychology at the University of California Medical School in San Francisco, and a pioneer of research on facial expressions. "A smile lets us know that we're likely to get a positive reception, and it's hard not to reciprocate."

By the time we flash that return grin, our Polaroid shutter will have already closed. Just three seconds are sufficient to make a conclusion about fresh acquaintances. Nalini Ambady, professor of psychology at Tufts University in Medford, Massachusetts, studies first impressions carved from brief exposure to another person's behavior, what she calls "thin slices" of experience. She says humans have developed the ability to quickly decide whether a new person will hurt or enrich us—judgments that had lifesaving ramifications in an earlier era.

She believes that thin slices are generated in the most primitive area of the brain, where feelings are also processed, which accounts for the emotional punch of some first encounters. Immediate distrust of a certain car salesman or affinity for a prospective roommate originates in the deepest corners of the mind.

The ability to interpret thin slices evolved as a way for our ancestors to protect themselves in an eat-or-be-eaten world, whereas modern-day threats to sur-vival often come in the form of paperwork (dwindling stock portfolios) or intricate social rituals (impending divorce). The degree to which thin slices of experience help us navigate modern encounters—from hitchhikers to blind dates—is up for debate.

Ekman says that people excel at reading facial expressions quickly, but only when a countenance is genuine. Most people cannot tell if someone is feigning an emotion, he says, "unless their eyes have been trained to spot very subtle expressions that leak through." Consider anger: When we are boiling mad, our lips narrow—an expression we can't make on demand when we're pretending.

And the accuracy of a snap judgment always depends on what exactly we're sizing up. Ekman doesn't think we can use a thin slice of behavior to judge, say, if someone is smart enough to be our study partner or generous enough to lend us a bus token. "But we can pretty easily distinguish one emotion from another, particularly if it's on the face for a second or more." Spending more time with a genuine person, he says, won't yield a more accurate sense of that person's emotional state.

First impressions are not merely hardwired reactions—we are also taught how to judge others, holding our thin slices up to the light of social stereotypes. Brian Nosek, professor of psychology at the University of Virginia, studies the implicit attitudes that enter into our calculations. Just because someone carries an ACLU membership card or makes a point to invite their senior-citizen friends to dance-club outings doesn't mean they don't have prejudices bubbling under the surface. Nosek and colleagues administer a quick online test that reveals the beliefs people either can't or won't report.

Called the Implicit Association Test, it asks participants to pair concepts, such as "young" with "good," or "elderly" with "good." If, in some part of his mind, "old" is more closely related to "bad" than to "good," the test taker will respond more quickly to the first pairing of words than to the second. In versions of these tests, small differences in response times are used to determine if someone is biased toward youth over the elderly, African-Americans over Caucasians or for President Bush over President Kennedy. "When I took the test," says Nosek, "I showed a bias toward whites. I was shocked. We

Street-Corner Psychologists: From Store Manager to Police Officer,
Certain Professions Rely on Making the Right Snap Judgment

—Jeff Grossman, Neil Parmar, Jammie Salagubang, and Susan A. Smith

Jeff Ayers, novelty-store manager

To spot a thief, check for eye contact, says New York-based Ayers. Persistent looking around or eyes that dart from left to right should raise suspicion. Ayers also watches people with "forced body language." They pace purposefully up and down aisles. "Sometimes the best-dressed [are the culprits]; they're on a shopping spree with someone else's credit card. The ones I can't [pick out] are those I've been friendly with. One guy would jibber-jabber, then bend down to tie his shoes and stick $300 worth of stuff in his bag."

Gerald Scott, police officer

Scott has been a New York City police officer for 10 years. He says he can easily spot bad apples on the street because they "tend to stay in a certain space for long periods of time. They're not really doing anything, they're just watching everybody. They're never reading the paper or anything. They're worried about everything going on around them. Just look at their eyes. There's a lot of nervousness. You can tell they're trying to figure out if you're a cop or not."

Eric McMullen, cardsharp

In the gritty gambling locales of Harlem, McMullen is better known as "DOC," or the Dealer of Cards. "If I don't cheat, I don't eat," says the amateur magician turned master cardsharp. "Amateurs have shifty eyes. They look around the table and try to talk to everyone. Let's say the sharp wants to switch the whole deck. He'll get a little fidgety—that's a telltale sign for cheating." Subtlety is the secret behind flawless moves. "Always make gestures and jokes, look people in the eye and don't look at the deck."

John Breen, retired detective

"I'm not claiming to be Sherlock Holmes, but there are a number of behavioral interviewing techniques taught in the police academy that can help tell you when someone is lying," says Breen, a former police lieutenant in Arizona. "A suspect might put her hand up to her mouth or she may cross her arms over her chest. Whereas someone who is more receptive, open and forthcoming won't cross her arms. But you can't take that as gospel. You have to [measure up] the individual and determine what her normal reactions might be."

Sudha Chinniah, high-end salesperson

"You can never tell who's going to spend on clothing," says Chinniah, who works at the Bergdorf Goodman department store in New York. But "how you look is an extension of [how you feel]. The wealthiest guy may be dressed casually, but he carries himself with confidence. A customer's wallet, watch and shoes approximate her financial background. Right now there's a trend toward slim shoes with elongated toes, which defines a customer who's absolutely current."

David Boyle, county prosecutor

Every nuance counts for a trial lawyer, who must quickly convince a group of strangers that his version of the facts is the truth. "Everything you do is being judged—the way you dress, the way you talk," says Boyle, a prosecutor in Walton County, Georgia. If he wants jurors to listen to a friendly witness, Boyle positions himself at the far end of the jury box, forcing the witness to look straight at the jury and speak loud enough for everyone to hear. During harmful testimony, he'll study his files or consult with his partner to indicate complete disinterest.

call it unconsciousness-raising, in contrast to the consciousness-raising of the 1960s."

As subtle as implicit attitudes are, they can cause serious real-world damage. If an angry person stumbles upon someone of a different race or religion, he is likely to perceive that person negatively, according to recent research. Anger incites instinctive prejudiced responses toward "outsiders," a finding that has

How to Make a Great First Impression

Curb Conversational Narcissism
He's talking about his new Subaru, which reminds you of the battle you waged—and won—with that smarmy Hertz-rental-car dealer in Miami last month. This "faux segue" is a big no-no, says psychologist and business consultant Valerie White. "We are tempted to share impressive things about ourselves, but the one idea you should keep in mind is 'How am I making the other person feel?'" Actively encourage others to talk about themselves, and respond genuinely—without bringing it back to you.

Don't Betray Your Anxiety
"If you're not quick-witted or well-versed in certain subjects, you can still make a great impression," White says. Just focus on the other person. This in turn will take the pressure off you. However, avoid interrogating a new acquaintance. If you're jittery, control movements such as leg twitching. And remember to speak slowly—nervousness makes us talk too fast.

Fake a Sunny Mood
"Be yourself" is solid first-impression advice from cognitive scientists and self-help gurus alike. But it's worth suppressing a bad mood when you meet someone new. While you know you are just experiencing a momentary state, a new acquaintance will take you for a full-time complainer. "There is a contagion effect," says White. "A bad mood will bring the other person down, too. Try to start off well, and then share what's bothering you."

The Eyes Have It
If you want to get to know a stranger, break with body language conventions by catching her eye for more than a second. When you first meet someone, author and lecturer Nicholas Boothman says, focus on your eye contact, your smile and your posture. "If you notice somebody's eye color, and you say 'great' to yourself, you will actually be smiling, and you will give off a super mood."

Get in Sync
Adjusting your posture, voice, words and gestures to match those of a new acquaintance is critical, says Boothman, because we are attracted to others who are just like us. "People respond when you speak at their pace," agrees White. To establish an instant rapport, mirror your new friend's head nods and tilts.

Use Flattery, Sparingly
"People like to be flattered," says White. "Even if they suspect you are brownnosing, they still like it." But use flattery judiciously—focus on the other person's accomplishments or achievements. This works best when a person believes you don't say ingratiating things to just anyone.

The Do-Over
You arrive at a party fuming over a parking ticket. A cheery guest introduces herself, but you brush her off and head for the bar. You've made a bad impression, but you can recover if you demonstrate self-awareness, says White. Pull her aside and say, "I wasn't myself earlier." Show your sense of humor: "I see you met my evil twin." And remember to cut others slack if they make a bad impression on you.

important implications for people in law enforcement and security.

Certain physical features consistently prompt our brains to take first-impression Polaroids with a distorting filter. People who have a "baby face," characterized by a round shape, large eyes and small nose and chin, give off the impression of trustworthiness and naiveté—on average, a false assumption. A pretty face also leads us astray: Our tendency is to perceive beautiful people as healthier and just plain better than others.

Leslie Zebrowitz, professor of psychology at Brandeis University in Massachusetts, argues that we overgeneralize in the presence of baby mugs and homely visages. Humans are hardwired to recognize a baby as an innocent, weak creature who requires protection. By the same token, mating with someone who is severely deformed, and thereby unattractive, may keep your DNA from spreading far and wide. But we overgeneralize these potentially helpful built-in responses, coddling adults with babyish miens who in fact don't need our care and shunning unattractive people who may not meet our standards of beauty but certainly don't pose an imminent threat to our gene pool.

Zebrowitz has found that many baby-faced grownups, particularly young men, overcompensate for misperceptions by cultivating tougher-than-average personalities in an attempt to ward off cheek-pinching aunts. Think of the sweet-faced rapper Eminem, who never cracks a smile, or the supermodel-juggling, hard-partying actor Leonardo DiCaprio.

Not every observer is equally likely to draw unwarranted conclusions about a smooth-cheeked man or a woman with stunning, symmetrical features. People who spend time cultivating relationships are more likely to make accurate snap judgments.

"A good judge of personality isn't just someone who is smarter—it's someone who gets out and spends time with people," says David Funder, a professor of psychology at the University of California at Riverside, who believes in the overall accuracy of snap judgments. Funder has found that two observers often reach a consensus about a third person, and the assessments are accurate in that they match the third person's assessment of himself. "We're often fooled, of course, but we're more often right."

On the other side of the equation, some people are simpler to capture at first glance than others. "The people who are easiest to judge are the most mentally healthy," says Randy Colvin, associate professor of psychology at Northeastern University in Boston. "With mentally healthy individuals," Colvin theorizes, "exterior behavior mimics their internal views of themselves. What you see is what you get."

LEARN MORE ABOUT IT

First Impressions Valerie White and Ann Demarais *(Bantam, 2004)*

Emotions Revealed: Recognizing Faces and Feelings to Improve Communication and Emotional Life Paul Ekman *(Times Books, 2003)*

How to Make People Like You in 90 Seconds or Less Nicholas Boothman *(Workman, 2000)*

Implicit Association Test (https://implicit.harvard.edu .implicit/)

CRITICAL THINKING QUESTIONS

1. In everyday situations, what can be done to help minimize the power of first impressions? Or is it even possible not to *form* first impressions? Defend your position with data regarding impression formation and impression management.

2. What advice have you received from others about how to make a good first impression? How consistent (or inconsistent) is that advice with the information contained in this article?

3. How might the findings in this article about the power of first impressions be applicable to jury trials? Dating situations? Job interviews? Is the process involved in forming a first impression fundamentally the same in all situations, or does it depend on the context in which the impression is being made? Defend your position.

4. Is it feasible to teach people to be more aware of the first impressions they make? Is it possible to teach people how to interpret such impressions more accurately? How might either or both of these goals be accomplished? Explain your answers.

5. "You cannot *not* communicate." Discuss what this statement means in terms of impression formation.

ARTICLE 5 _____

A variety of sources of information may be available for use in forming an impression of a person. However, that does not mean that all of the information will be used or hold equal value. Some sources of information may carry more weight than others. For example, we may notice how the person acts, or we may have heard something about him or her from someone else. How do we use this information to develop an impression of the person?

Building on the classic work of S. E. Asch, Harold H. Kelley examines what can be called a *central organizing trait,* one that is important in influencing the impressions that we form. By examining the effect of changing just one adjective in describing a person (i.e., *warm* versus *cold*), the study demonstrates that this initial difference influenced how the subjects actually rated the person. Even more interesting is that these differences in initial impression carried over into how the subjects interacted with the person. The implication is that perhaps our initial impressions lead us to act in certain ways toward others, perhaps creating a self-fulfilling prophecy by giving us what we expected to see in the first place.

The Warm-Cold Variable in First Impressions of Persons

■ Harold H. Kelley

This experiment is one of several studies of first impressions (3), the purpose of the series being to investigate the stability of early judgments, their determinants, and the relation of such judgments to the behavior of the person making them. In interpreting the data from several nonexperimental studies on the stability of first impressions, it proved to be necessary to postulate inner-observer variables which contribute to the impression and which remain relatively constant through time. Also some evidence was obtained which directly demonstrated the existence of these variables and their nature. The present experiment was designed to determine the effects of one kind of inner-observer variable, specifically, *expectations* about the stimulus person which the observer brings to the exposure situation.

That prior information or labels attached to a stimulus person make a difference in observers' first impressions is almost too obvious to require demonstration. The expectations resulting from such preinformation may restrict, modify, or accentuate the impressions he will have. The crucial question is: What changes in perception will accompany a given expectation? Studies of stereotyping, for example, that of Katz and Braly (2), indicate that from an ethnic label such as "German" or "Negro," a number of perceptions follow which are culturally determined. The present study finds its main significance in relation to a study by Asch (1) which demonstrates that certain crucial labels can transform the entire impression of the person, leading to attributions which are related to the label on a broad cultural basis or even, perhaps, on an autochthonous basis.

Asch read to his subjects a list of adjectives which purportedly described a particular person. He then asked them to characterize that person. He found that the inclusion in the list of what he called *central* qualities, such as "warm" as opposed to "cold," produced a widespread change in the entire impression. This effect was not adequately explained by the halo effect since it did not extend indiscriminately in a positive or negative direction to all characteristics. Rather, it differentially transformed the other qualities, for example, by changing their relative importance in the total impression. Peripheral qualities (such as "polite" versus "blunt") did not produce effects as strong as those produced by the central qualities.[1]

The present study tested the effects of such central qualities upon the early impressions of *real* persons, the same qualities, "warm" vs. "cold," being used. They were introduced as preinformation about the stimulus person before his actual appearance; so presumably they operated as expectations rather than as part of the stimulus pattern during the exposure period. In addition, information was obtained about the effects of the expectations upon the observers' behavior toward the stimulus person. An earlier study in this series has indicated that the more incompatible the observer initially perceived the stimulus person to be, the less the observer initiated interaction with him thereafter. The second purpose of the present experiment, then, was to provide a better controlled study of this relationship.

No previous studies reported in the literature have dealt with the importance of first impressions for behavior. The most relevant data are found in the sociometric literature, where there are scattered studies of the relation between choices among children having some prior acquaintance and their interaction behavior. For an example, see the study by Newstetter, Feldstein, and Newcomb (8).

PROCEDURE

The experiment was performed in three sections of a psychology course (Economics 70) at the Massachusetts Institute of Technology.[2] The three sections provided 23, 16, and 16 subjects respectively. All 55 subjects were men, most of them in their third college year. In each class the stimulus person (also a male) was completely unknown to the subjects before the experimental period. One person served as stimulus person in two sections, and a second person took this role in the third section. In each case the stimulus person was introduced by the experimenter, who posed as a representative of the course instructors and who gave the following statement:

> Your regular instructor is out of town today, and since we of Economics 70 are interested in the general problem of how various classes react to different instructors, we're going to have an instructor today

you've never had before, Mr. ____. Then, at the end of the period, I want you to fill out some forms about him. In order to give you some idea of what he's like, we've had a person who knows him write up a little biographical note about him. I'll pass this out to you now and you can read it before he arrives. Please read these to yourselves and don't talk about this among yourselves until the class is over so that he won't get wind of what's going on.

Two kinds of these notes were distributed, the two being identical except that in one the stimulus person was described among other things as being "rather cold" whereas in the other form the phrase "very warm" was substituted. The content of the "rather cold" version is as follows:

> Mr. ____ is a graduate student in the Department of Economics and Social Science here at M.I.T. He has had three semesters of teaching experience in psychology at another college. This is his first semester teaching Ec. 70. He is 26 years old, a veteran, and married. People who know him consider him to be a rather cold person, industrious, critical, practical, and determined.

The two types of preinformation were distributed randomly within each of the three classes and in such a manner that the students were not aware that two kinds of information were being given out. The stimulus person then appeared and led the class in a twenty-minute discussion. During this time the experimenter kept a record of how often each student participated in the discussion. Since the discussion was almost totally leader-centered, this participation record indicates the number of times each student initiated verbal interaction with the instructor. After the discussion period, the stimulus person left the room, and the experimenter gave the following instructions:

> Now, I'd like to get your impression of Mr. ____. This is not a test of you and can in no way affect your grade in this course. This material will not be identified as belonging to particular persons and will be kept strictly confidential. It will be of most value to us if you are completely honest in your evaluation of Mr. ____. Also, please understand that what you put down will not be used against him or cause him to lose his job or anything like that. This is not a test of him but merely a study of how different classes react to different instructors.

The subjects then wrote free descriptions of the stimulus person and finally rated him on a set of 15 rating scales.

RESULTS AND DISCUSSION

1. *Influence of warm-cold variable on first impressions.* The differences in the ratings produced by the warm-cold variable were consistent from one section to another even where different stimulus persons were used. Consequently, the data from the three sections were combined by equating means (the S.D.'s were approximately equal) and the results for the total group are presented in Table 1. Also in this table is presented that part of Asch's data which refers to the qualities included in our rating scales. From this table it is quite clear that those given the "warm" preinformation consistently rated the stimulus person more favorably than those given the "cold" preinformation. Summarizing

the statistically significant differences, the "warm" subjects rated the stimulus person as more considerate of others, more informal, more sociable, more popular, better natured, more humorous, and more humane. These findings are very similar to Asch's for the characteristics common to both studies. He found more frequent attribution to his hypothetical "warm" personalities of sociability, popularity, good naturedness, generosity, humorousness, and humaneness. So these data strongly support his finding that such a central quality as "warmth" can greatly influence the total impression of a personality. This effect is found to be operative in the perception of real persons.

This general favorableness in the perceptions of the "warm" observers as compared with the "cold" ones indicates that something like a halo effect may have been operating in these ratings. Although his data are not completely persuasive on this point, Asch was convinced that such a general effect was *not* operating

TABLE 1 / Comparison of "Warm" and "Cold" Observers in Terms of Average Ratings Given Stimulus Persons

Item	Low End of Rating Scale	High End of Rating Scale	Average Rating Warm N = 7	Average Rating Cold N = 28	Level of Significance of Warm-Cold Difference	Asch's Data: Per Cent of Group Assigning Quality at Low End of Our Rating Scale* Warm	Asch's Data: Per Cent of Group Assigning Quality at Low End of Our Rating Scale* Cold
1	Knows his stuff	Doesn't know his stuff	3.5	4.6			
2	Considerate of others	Self-centered	6.3	9.6	1%		
3†	Informal	Formal	6.3	9.6	1%		
4†	Modest	Proud	9.4	10.6			
5	Sociable	Unsociable	5.6	10.4	1%	91%	38%
6	Self-assured	Uncertain of himself	8.4	9.1			
7	High intelligence	Low intelligence	4.8	5.1			
8	Popular	Unpopular	4.0	7.4	1%	84%	28%
9†	Good natured	Irritable	9.4	12.0	5%	94%	17%
10	Generous	Ungenerous	8.2	9.6		91%	08%
11	Humorous	Humorless	8.3	11.7	1%	77%	13%
12	Important	Insignificant	6.5	8.6		88%	99%
13†	Humane	Ruthless	8.6	11.0	5%	86%	31%
14†	Submissive	Dominant	13.2	14.5			
15	Will go far	Will not get ahead	4.2	5.8			

*Given for all qualities common to Asch's list and this set of rating scales.

†These scales were reversed when presented to the subjects.

in his study. Closer inspection of the present data makes it clear that the "warm-cold" effect cannot be explained altogether on the basis of simple halo effect. In Table 1 it is evident that the "warm-cold" variable produced differential effects from one rating scale to another. The size of this effect seems to depend upon the closeness of relation between the specific dimension of any given rating scale and the central quality of "warmth" or "coldness." Even though the rating of intelligence may be influenced by a halo effect, it is not influenced to the same degree to which considerateness is. It seems to make sense to view such strongly influenced items as considerateness, informality, good naturedness, and humaneness as dynamically more closely related to warmth and hence more perceived in terms of this relation than in terms of a general positive or negative feeling toward the stimulus person. If first impressions are normally made in terms of such general dimensions as "warmth" and "coldness," the power they give the observer in making predictions and specific evaluations about such disparate behavior characteristics as formality and considerateness is considerable (even though these predictions may be incorrect or misleading).

The free report impression data were analyzed for only one of the sections. In general, there were few sizable differences between the "warm" and "cold" observers. The "warm" observers attributed more nervousness, more sincerity, and more industriousness to the stimulus person. Although the frequencies of comparable qualities are very low because of the great variety of descriptions produced by the observers, there is considerable agreement with the rating scale data.

Two important phenomena are illustrated in these free description protocols, the first of them having been noted by Asch. *Firstly,* the characteristics of the stimulus person are interpreted in terms of the precognition of warmth or coldness. For example, a "warm" observer writes about a rather shy and retiring stimulus person as follows: "He makes friends slowly but they are lasting friendships when formed." In another instance, several "cold" observers described him as being, ". . . intolerant: would be angry if you disagree with his view. . ."; while several "warm" observers put the same thing this way: "Unyielding in principle, not easily influenced or swayed from his original attitude." *Secondly,* the preinformation about the stimulus per-

son's warmth or coldness is evaluated and interpreted in the light of the direct behavioral data about him. For example, "He has a slight inferiority complex which leads to his coldness," and "His conscientiousness and industriousness might be mistaken for coldness." Examples of these two phenomena occurred rather infrequently, and there was no way to evaluate the relative strengths of these countertendencies. Certainly some such evaluation is necessary to determine the conditions under which behavior which is contrary to a stereotyped label resists distortion and leads to rejection of the label.

A comparison of the data from the two different stimulus persons is pertinent to the last point in so far as it indicates the interaction between the properties of the stimulus person and the label. The fact that the warm-cold variable generally produced differences in the same direction for the two stimulus persons, even though they are very different in personality, behavior, and mannerisms, indicates the strength of this variable. However, there were some exceptions to this tendency as well as marked differences in the *degree* to which the experimental variable was able to produce differences. For example, stimulus person A typically appears to be anything but lacking in self-esteem and on rating scale 4 he was generally at the "proud" end of the scale. Although the "warm" observers tended to rate him as they did the other stimulus person (i.e., more "modest"), the difference between the "warm" and "cold" means for stimulus person A is very small and not significant as it is for stimulus person B. Similarly, stimulus person B was seen as "unpopular" and "humorless," which agrees with his typical classroom behavior. Again the "warm" observers rated him more favorably on these items, but their ratings were not significantly different from those of the "cold" observers, as was true for the other stimulus person. Thus we see that the strength or compellingness of various qualities of the stimulus person must be reckoned with. The stimulus is not passive to the forces arising from the label but actively resists distortion and may severely limit the degree of influence exerted by the preinformation.[3]

2. *Influence of warm-cold variable on interaction with the stimulus person.* In the analysis of the frequency with which the various students took part in the discussion led by the stimulus person, a larger

proportion of those given the "warm" preinformation participated than of those given the "cold" preinformation. Fifty-six per cent of the "warm" subjects entered the discussion, whereas only 32 per cent of the "cold" subjects did so. Thus the expectation of warmth not only produced more favorable early perceptions of the stimulus person but led to greater initiation of interaction with him. This relation is a low one, significant at between the 5 per cent and 10 percent level of confidence, but it is in line with the general principle that social perception serves to guide and steer the person's behavior in his social environment.

As would be expected from the foregoing findings, there was also a relation between the favorableness of the impression and whether or not the person participated in the discussion. Although any single item yielded only a small and insignificant relation to participation, when a number are combined the trend becomes clear cut. For example, when we combine the seven items which were influenced to a statistically significant degree by the warm-cold variable, the total score bears considerable relation to participation, the relationship being significant as well beyond the 1 per cent level. A larger proportion of those having favorable total impressions participated than of those having unfavorable impressions, the bi-serial correlation between these variables being .34. Although this relation may be interpreted in several ways, it seems most likely that the unfavorable perception led to a curtailment of interaction. Support for this comes from one of the other studies in this series (3). There it was found that those persons having unfavorable impressions of the instructor at the end of the first class meeting tended less often to initiate interactions with him in the succeeding four meetings than did those having favorable first impressions. There was also some tendency in the same study for those persons who interacted least with the instructor to change least in their judgments of him from the first to later impressions.

It will be noted that these relations lend some support to the autistic hostility hypothesis proposed by Newcomb (7). This hypothesis suggests that the possession of an initially hostile attitude toward a person leads to a restriction of communication and contact with him which in turn serves to preserve the hostile attitude by preventing the acquisition of data which could correct it. The present data indicate that a restriction of interaction is associated with unfavorable preinformation and an unfavorable perception. The data from the other study support this result and also indicate the correctness of the second part of the hypothesis, that restricted interaction reduces the likelihood of change in the attitude.

What makes these findings more significant is that they appear in the context of a discussion class where there are numerous *induced* and *own* forces to enter the discussion and to interact with the instructor. It seems likely that the effects predicted by Newcomb's hypothesis would be much more marked in a setting where such forces were not present.

SUMMARY

The warm-cold variable had been found by Asch to produce large differences in the impressions of personality formed from a list of adjectives. In this study the same variable was introduced in the form of expectations about a real person and was found to produce similar differences in first impressions of him in a classroom setting. In addition, the differences in first impressions produced by the different expectations were shown to influence the observers' behavior toward the stimulus person. Those observers given the favorable expectation (who, consequently, had a favorable impression of the stimulus person) tended to interact more with him than did those given the unfavorable expectation.

REFERENCES

1. Asch, S. E., Forming impressions of personality. *J. Abnorm. Soc. Psychol.,* 1946, 41, 258–290.
2. Katz, D., and Braly, K. W. Verbal stereotypes and racial prejudice. In Newcomb, T. M. and Hartley, E. L. (eds.), *Readings in social psychology.* New York: Holt, 1947. Pp. 204–210.
3. Kelley, H. H. First impressions in interpersonal relations. Ph.D. thesis, Massachusetts Institute of Technology, Cambridge, Mass. Sept., 1948.
4. Krech, D., and Crutchfield, R. S. *Theory and problems of social psychology.* New York, McGraw-Hill, 1948.
5. Luchins, A. S. Forming impressions of personality: A critique. *J. Abnorm. Soc. Psychol.,* 1948, 43, 318–325.

6. Mensch, I. N., and Wishner, J. Asch on "Forming impressions of personality": further evidence. *J. Personal.*, 1947, 16, 188–191.

7. Newcomb, T. M. Autistic hostility and social reality. *Hum. Relations.*, 1947, 1, 69–86.

8. Newstetter, W. I., Feldstein, M. H., and Newcomb, T. M. *Group adjustment: A study in experimental sociology.* Cleveland: Western Reserve University, 1938.

ENDNOTES

1. Since the present experiment was carried out, Mensch and Wishner (6) have repeated a number of Asch's experiments because of dissatisfaction with his sex and geographic distribution. Their data substantiate Asch's very closely. Also, Luchins (5) has criticized Asch's experiments for their artificial methodology, repeated some of them, and challenged some of the kinds of interpretations Asch made from his data. Luchins also briefly reports some tantalizing conclusions from a number of studies of first impressions of actual persons.

2. Professor Mason Haire, now of the University of California, provided valuable advice and help in executing the experiment.

3. We must raise an important question here: Would there be a tendency for "warm" observers to distort the perception in the favorable direction regardless of how much the stimulus deviated from the expectation? Future research should test the following hypothesis, which is suggested by Gestalt perception theory (4, pp. 95–98): If the stimulus differs but slightly from the expectation, the perception will tend to be *assimilated* to the expectation; however, if the difference between the stimulus and expectation is too great, the perception will occur by contrast to the expectation and will be distorted in the opposite direction.

CRITICAL THINKING QUESTIONS

1. Reread the information that was presented to the subjects to manipulate the warm-cold variable. The manipulation obviously produced a significant effect on the subjects' subsequent evaluations of the teacher. Do you feel that the manipulation was realistic? For example, how realistic is it to have a guest teacher described as "rather cold" in a brief biographical sketch? Could this particular manipulation have resulted in any experimental demand characteristics? Address the issue of the relative importance of experimental versus mundane realism as it pertains to this study.

2. How long lasting do you think first impressions are? For example, would they persist over the course of a semester or even longer? How could you test this?

3. What are the practical implications of this study? If you were working in a setting where you were interviewing and hiring applicants for a job, how could you use this information to help you make better, more accurate decisions?

4. The warm-cold information was provided by the instructor of the course, a person who presumably had high credibility. Do you think the credibility of the source of the information would affect how influenced the individuals were? How could you test this?

ADDITIONAL RELATED READINGS

Denrell, J. (2005). Why most people disapprove of me: Experience sampling in impression formation. *Psychological Review, 112*(4), 951–978.

Pontari, B. A., & Schlenker, B. R. (2004). Providing and withholding impression management support for romantic partners: Gender of the audience matters. *Journal of Experimental Social Psychology, 40*(1), 41–51.

ARTICLE 6_____

As discussed in Article 4 on first impressions, we use a variety of information in forming judgments of other people. Yet this process also seems to occur quite quickly. In fact, as that article points out, we often draw conclusions about people we meet in as little as three seconds!

Some of the information that we use in forming initial impressions of people is based on stereotypes of what they look like or whom they remind us of, but even more information is obtained from watching their nonverbal cues. Why is this the case? Simply put, many of the things that people do are under their direct control. For example, the words that we choose to speak are subject to our conscious influence and hence can be readily manipulated. But our nonverbal behavior, such as the body movements that accompany our words, are somewhat less under conscious control. Furthermore, while we are better able to select the words we speak, we may be less aware of—and thus able to control—changes in our speech patterns (known as *paralanguage*), such as pausing, pitch of voice, and rate of speech. An observer may give the nonverbal and paralanguage cues more weight than what we actually say because those cues may seem a more honest reflection of what we are really all about.

One obvious practical application of the use of nonverbal and paralanguage cues is to detect deception. Being able to tell when someone is lying to us has real advantages. Research suggests that lying is a fairly common part of human interaction. Occasionally, these falsehoods take the form of bold-faced lies, such as making up a story to get out of trouble for something we have done. More commonly, however, we use so-called white lies to skirt the truth and perhaps not hurt someone's feelings ("Yes, dear, I really loved the vacuum cleaner you gave me for Christmas").

But how accurate are most of us in detecting such deceptions? Furthermore, are trained professionals, such as police and customs agents, better at detecting deception than the average person? Are women better than men at detecting lies, and does it make a difference if we are trying to detect lies in children or in adults?

The following article by Robin S. Edelstein, Tanya L. Luten, Paul Ekman, and Gail S. Goodman describes a study that examined the detection of lies in both children and adults. In fact, little research has been conducted on detecting lying in children or on the question of whether some people are better than others at detecting lies, regardless if the liar is a child or an adult.

Detecting Lies in Children and Adults

■ Robin S. Edelstein, Tanya L. Luten, Paul Ekman, and Gail S. Goodman

ABSTRACT

In this study, observers' abilities to detect lies in children and adults were examined. Adult participants observed videotaped interviews of both children and adults either lying or telling the truth about having been touched by a male research assistant. As hypothesized, observers detected children's lies more accurately than adults' lies;

Springer / *Law and Human Behavior, 30,* 2006, 1–10, Detecting lies in children and adults, by R. S. Edelstein, T. L. Luten, P. Ekman, and G. S. Goodman. Copyright © 2006 Springer Publishing. With kind permission from Springer Science and Business Media.

however, adults' truthful statements were detected more accurately than were children's. Further analyses revealed that observers were biased toward judging adults' but not children's statements as truthful. Finally, consistent with the notion that there are stable individual differences in the ability to detect lies, observers who were highly accurate in detecting children's lies were similarly accurate in detecting adults' lies. Implications of these findings for understanding lie-detection accuracy are discussed, as are potential applications to the forensic context.

INTRODUCTION

Both legal professionals and psychologists have an interest in the study of lie detection. In a legal setting, jurors, police officers, and attorneys are among those entrusted with the responsibility of determining when others are telling the truth. Accordingly, how people detect lies in others, and how accurately they do so, are questions of considerable forensic importance (Frank & Ekman, 2004). These questions have also interested psychologists, in part, because of our human desire to know when we are being lied to, be it by our children, spouses, colleagues, or others.

Despite this interest in lie-detection, relatively few studies have examined adults' abilities to detect children's ties. Just like adults, children may be called upon by legal professionals to recount events that may or may not have happened, and fact-finders must determine the veracity of their statements. Children's statements may be particularly influential in cases where physical evidence of a crime is lacking, such as in many cases of child sexual abuse. Yet, relatively little is currently known about how accurate people are at determining when children are lying. The goal of this study was to redress this gap in the literature by examining adults' abilities to detect lies in children and adults. In addition, we were interested in the extent to which lie-detection abilities were generalizable across targets, that is, whether individuals who were particularly accurate in detecting adults' lies would be similarly accurate in detecting children's lies.

How Accurate Are People at Detecting Lies?

For purposes of this study, lying is defined as a deliberate falsification, in which the target has not been forewarned of the speaker's intention to lie (Ekman, 1997; Ekman, 2001). This is in contrast to other forms of deception (e.g., by magicians or poker players) in which the target is notified, either implicitly or explicitly, that misinformation may be provided. Findings from studies of lie detection indicate that, on average, people's accuracy in detecting adults' lies rarely exceeds that which would be expected by chance (Ekman, O'Sullivan. Friesen, & Scherer, 1991; Malone & DePaulo, 2001; Vrij & Baxter, 1999). These results may reflect adult liars' ability to conceal indicators of deception, observers' inability to perceive cues exhibited by liars, or both. Moreover, insofar as these findings can be extended to the forensic context, they suggest that it may be particularly difficult to distinguish witnesses who are lying from those who are telling the truth.

Developmental research suggests that as children get older, their understanding of deception improves and they become increasingly able to deceive others (DePaulo, Stone, & Lassiter, 1985; Lewis, 1993; Talwar & Lee, 2002; Wilson, Smith, & Ross, 2003). Although it has been hypothesized that young children's lies should therefore be more readily detectable compared to those of adults, few studies have directly addressed this issue. There is some evidence that adult observers are highly accurate in their detection of truth and lies in first graders (Morency & Krauss, 1982), whereas accuracy scores for fourth and fifth graders are somewhat lower (Allen & Atkinson, 1978; Orcutt, Goodman, Tobey, Batterman-Faunce, & Thomas, 2001; Westcott, Davies, Graham, & Clifford, 1991).

For instance, in one study, college students assessed the truthfulness of 32 children (ages 7–8 and 10–11 years) who were videotaped either lying or telling the truth about a visit to a natural history museum (Westcott et al., 1991). Participants' overall ability to detect children's lies was only slightly above chance (59%), a rate comparable to that found in studies concerning adults' lies. Accuracy was higher, however, when younger children and boys were being assessed. Results also suggested a truth bias, such that participants were more likely to judge the children to be telling the truth than to be lying.

Although these findings suggest that lie-detection accuracy decreases with the age of the target, to our knowledge only one published study has compared untrained observers' accuracy in detecting lies among child versus adult targets (Feldman, Jenkins, & Popoola, 1979). Feldman et al. (1979) investigated adults' ability to tell when third graders, seventh graders, and adults were lying about a drink's taste. These researchers found that participants were better able to identify when third graders were lying than when either seventh graders or adults were lying. There was no significant difference between participants' lie-detection accuracy for seventh graders and adults. These findings suggest that, at least by the seventh grade (i.e., approximately age 12), children have become proficient enough in controlling their nonverbal behavior to hide indicators of lying.

It is important to note that these findings may be limited in their generalizability to the forensic context. That is, children in these studies told relatively innocuous lies (e.g., about a visit to a museum), which may differ from the kinds of lies told, for instance, during police investigations or criminal trials. In the present study, children, aged 5–7, and adults were asked to lie about being touched by a male research assistant. This particular lie was chosen because of its possible forensic implications; for instance, sexual abuse allegations often involve (potentially false) accusations of inappropriate touching. On the basis of prior research, we hypothesized that observers would be more accurate when detecting the lies of children than those of adults.

Are There Stable Individual Differences in the Ability to Detect Lies?

Although most observers rarely exceed chance accuracy when detecting lies, there is some evidence that certain groups of individuals (i.e., Secret Service and CIA agents, police officers, sheriffs, and "deception-interested" psychologists) can detect lies at significantly higher rates (e.g., Ekman & O'Sullivan, 1991; Ekman, O'Sullivan, & Frank, 1999; Mann, Vrij, & Bull, 2004). Individuals who are highly accurate when distinguishing truth from lies also tend to score high on tests measuring the ability to recognize microexpressions of emotion (facial expressions present for only a quarter of a second) (Ekman & Friesen, 1969), a finding that has been replicated many times,

including in the United States, England, and Canada (Ekman, 2001). These findings suggest that, under certain circumstances, liars may exhibit behavioral cues that the trained (or experienced) perceiver can use to determine the veracity of their statements.

These findings also suggest that there are relatively stable individual differences in the ability to detect lies. Insofar as lie-detection success is a stable characteristic of an individual, it may be related to other abilities, such as skill in "reading" others' emotions. Along these lines, studies have been conducted to examine whether detection accuracy is associated with the ability to interpret nonverbal behaviors (Littlepage, Maddox, & Pineault, 1985; Littlepage, McKinnie, & Pineault, 1983) or with other personality factors, such as self-monitoring (Kraut & Poe, 1980) or social anxiety (DePaulo & Tang, 1994). Most of these studies have found no relation between personal abilities and detection accuracy (but see DePaulo & Tang, 1994).

There is some evidence, however, that observers' ability to detect lies in one target is related to their ability to detect lies in another target. Frank and Ekman (1997), for instance, compared individuals' detection abilities across two different types of lies (i.e., a false opinion scenario, in which participants had to lie about a strongly held opinion, and a crime scenario). Results indicated that the ability to detect lies in one scenario was positively related to the ability to detect lies in the other scenario (see also Frank & Ekman, 2004), suggesting that lie-detection abilities may generalize across situations and may therefore reflect a relatively stable individual difference or ability. Following this line of reasoning, we hypothesized that observers who were accurate in their detection of adults' lies would be similarly accurate in their detection of children's lies.

METHOD

Observers

Participants (i.e., observers) were 144 undergraduate students, ranging in age from 17 to 34 years ($M = 20.3$ years, $SD = 2.30$). Fifty-eight percent of the sample was female. Approximately 80% of observers described themselves as U.S. citizens, and 67% reported that their first language was English. The ethnic composition of the sample was 38% Asian American, 32% Caucasian–non-Hispanic, 11% Hispanic, 4% African American, and 15% of various other descents. Students participated in exchange for course credit.

Materials

Videotaped Interviews   Observers were shown two series of videotaped interviews, one of adults and one of children. All interviews were approximately 5 min in duration. The videotape of adults included individual interviews with five men and five women between the ages of 18 and 24 years. The videotape of children included five male and five female children between the ages of 5 and 7 years. For each interview, the videocamera was positioned to provide a close-up head-on-view of the child's or adult's face and upper torso as he or she sat next to an interviewer behind a desk. The interviewer, who was blind to the experimental hypotheses and whether the interviewees were lying or telling the truth, was also visible on the videotape. The videocamera was concealed from the liars/truthtellers, although they had been informed that a video recording would be taken.

Both children and adults were interviewed about a play session that had occurred in a university laboratory with a male research assistant named Kris. During the session, which involved a single child or adult at a time, Kris touched half of the participants on their bare stomach, nose, and neck (in the context of a game). Approximately 2 weeks later (M = 11.5 days), participants returned to the laboratory for a standardized interview about their interaction with Kris. The same 30-question interview was used for both children and adults. The interview began with a series of open-ended questions (e.g., "Tell me what happened when you came here last time"). However, the majority of questions were closed-ended and focused primarily on whether participants had been touched by Kris (e.g., "Did the man touch your nose?," "Did he touch your stomach?").

Participants who were touched on their bare stomach, nose, and neck during the play session were asked to answer all questions truthfully. Participants who were *not* touched on their bare stomach, nose, and neck during the play session were asked to lie during their interviews, that is, to say that Kris had touched them on the bare stomach, nose, and neck, when he had not done so. Children and adults who were instructed to lie were told to pretend that they were actors/actresses and to be as convincing in their lies as possible.

Procedure

Observers viewed the videotaped interviews in small groups of approximately 20 people. Two versions of the child and adult videotapes were created, varying in the order of interview presentation. Both order of presentation (i.e., child vs. adult) and videotape version were counterbalanced across groups. After obtaining informed consent, observers were given a rating sheet with the age of each liar or truthteller indicated next to the corresponding item number, and an instruction sheet describing the interview scenario. Observers were instructed that after watching each interview they were to indicate on the rating sheet whether or not they thought the person had been lying. Observers were not told how many interviewees were lying or telling the truth.

A practice interview was shown to familiarize observers with the video format and the rating sheet. Observers were not given feedback as to whether the practice person was lying or telling the truth. The rest of the interviews per age group (child vs. adult) were then shown. After each interview, observers were given a chance to make their judgments before the videotape continued. The same procedure was repeated for the second videotape.

Results

Observers' accuracy was determined by computing the proportion of interviews correctly identified (i.e., truth vs. lie). Separate scores were calculated for the child and adult interviews. Preliminary analyses indicated that the order of video presentation (i.e., whether child or adult targets were viewed first) and video version were unrelated to detection accuracy; thus, neither is considered further.[1]

Detection Accuracy   On average, observers accurately evaluated 50% of both child, M = .50, SD = .18, *range* = .10–.90, and adult, M = .50, SD = .19, range = .10–.90, targets. Accuracy was unrelated to observer age, gender, or ethnicity. To determine if accuracy varied according to whether the targets were lying or telling the truth, a 2 (target age: child vs. adult) × 2 (honesty condition: truth vs. lie) repeated-measures analysis of variance (ANOVA) was conducted, with the proportion of targets correctly identified serving as the dependent variable. The means from this analysis are presented in Table 1. Results revealed a significant main effect of honesty condition, $F(1, 143) = 12.17$, $p = .001$, $\eta_p^2 = .08$, and a significant interaction between target age and honesty condition, $F(1, 143) = 47.14$, $p < .001$, $\eta_p^2 = .25$. Simple effects analyses indicated that participants were significantly more accurate in detecting adults' versus children's truthtelling, $F(1, 143) = 19.02$, $p < .001$, $\eta_p^2 = .12$, and, as predicted, children's versus adults' lying, $F(1, 143) = 24.51$, $p < .001$, $\eta_p^2 = .15$.[2]

Signal Detection Analyses Although proportion accuracy is typically used to assess lie-detection success (Malone & DePaulo, 2001), an important limitation of the analyses just presented is their failure to consider truth and lie judgments simultaneously. That is, because 50% of the targets in this study lied about their experience and 50% told the truth, chance performance (i.e., 50% accuracy) could result if observers judged all targets to be telling the truth (or to be lying). Alternatively, 50% accuracy could be obtained if a participant performed at chance on *both* truthful and untruthful interviews. This limitation is addressed by signal detection analysis (Green & Swets, 1966; Swets, Dawes, & Monahan, 2000), which provides a measure of *discrimination* (*d'*) between two groups of items (i.e., honest and dishonest

reports, for purposes of the present study). Higher *d'* scores reflect better discrimination abilities; a *d'* score of zero indicates chance performance.

Signal detection analysis also provides information about observers' biases (*β*) in making these determinations. For example, are observers more likely to think that children are lying compared to adults, or vice versa? For purposes of this study, a positive *β* score reflects a tendency to judge targets as lying, whereas a negative score reflects a bias toward "truth" judgments; a *β* score of zero indicates the absence of bias.

The d' Scores The *d'* scores in this study ranged from −2.12 to +2.12 and were unrelated to observer age, gender, and ethnicity. A repeated-measures ANOVA revealed that there was no significant difference in observers' ability to discriminate between truth and lies for child, $M = .001$, $SD = .96$, versus adult targets, $M = .006$, $SD = 1.04$. Note that, on average, participants were at chance when discriminating between truth and lies for both child and adult targets.

β Scores *β* scores ranged from −1.0 to +1.0, and were not significantly related to observers' age and ethnicity. Because preliminary analyses indicated that bias was related to participant gender, a 2 (gender) × 2 (target age: child vs. adult) ANOVA was conducted. Results revealed main effects of both gender, $F(1, 142) = 4.68$, $p < .05$, $\eta_p^2 = .03$, and age, $F(1, 142) = 35.57$, $p < .001$, $\eta_p^2 = .20$. As can be seen in Table 2, participants were relatively unbiased when evaluating children's statements, but were biased to judge adults' statements as truthful. Women were also more likely than men to make "truth" judgments. The interaction between gender and target age was nonsignificant.

Relation between Accuracy with Adults and with Children The second goal of this study was to determine whether the ability to detect lies in children is related to the ability to detect lies in adults. Results were consistent with the hypothesis that lie-detection ability is a generalizable skill: The correlation between observers' overall detection-accuracy scores for adults and children was significant, $r = .39$, $p < .001$, as was that between *d'* scores for adults and children, $r = .40$,

TABLE 1 / Mean Proportion Accuracy Scores for Child and Adult Targets According to Honesty Condition

Honesty Condition	Target Age	
	Children	Adults
Truth	.48 (.26)	.59 (.25)
Lie	.52 (.23)	.41 (.23)

Note: N = 144. Standard deviations are given in parentheses.

TABLE 2 / Bias (β) Scores for Child versus Adult Targets

Gender	Target Age		
	Child	Adult	Mean
Male	.10 (.44)	−.11 (.46)	−.01 (.33)
Female	.04 (.29)	−.28 (.41)	−.12 (.28)
Mean	.06 (.36)	−.21 (.44)	−0.7 (.31)

Note: N = 144. Standard deviations are given in parentheses. Negative scores indicate a bias toward "truth" responses, whereas positive scores indicate a bias toward "lie" responses.

$p < .001$. Thus, observers who were accurate in detecting truth and lies in adults were also likely to be accurate in detecting truth and lies in children. In addition, bias scores for children and adults were significantly related, $r = .18$, $n = 144$, $p < .05$, suggesting that observers were somewhat consistent in their tendency to favor "truth" or "lie" judgments.

DISCUSSION

This study was designed to investigate adults' abilities to detect lies in children and adults. We had two primary goals: First, we examined the hypothesis that adults are more accurate in detecting children's compared to adults' lies. Second, we considered the relation between accuracy of lie detection for child and adult targets.

How Accurate Were Observers at Detecting Lies?

Overall lie-detection accuracy in this study was 50% for both children's and adults' statements. This finding is consistent with previous research, which indicates that untrained observers rarely exceed chance performance in lie detection (Ekman et al., 1991; Malone & DePaulo, 2001).

On the basis of the previous research, which suggests that the ability to deceive others develops with age (DePaulo et al., 1985; Talwar & Lee, 2002), we hypothesized that children's lies would be more accurately detected than those of adults. This hypothesis was partially supported: Observers were significantly more accurate when detecting children's versus adults' lies. However, the opposite pattern emerged for truthtelling determinations: Observers were more accurate when assessing adults' compared to children's truthtelling. Moreover, accuracy was above chance only for the adult truthful interviews, whereas accuracy for the adult untruthful interviews was significantly below chance.

That observers were more accurate in determining children's compared to adults' lying, with the reverse pattern evident for truthtelling, suggests that observers may be biased in making these determinations. Indeed, signal detection analyses indicated that observers were more likely to make "truth" judgments when evaluating adult interviews, but were equally likely to make "truth" or "lie" judgments when evaluating child interviews. Moreover, analysis of d' scores revealed no significant differences in observers' ability to discriminate between adults' versus children's truthful and untruthful statements. Although very few prior studies of lie detection have incorporated signal detection analyses (Malone & DePaulo, 2001), findings from the present study highlight the importance of using such measures, which simultaneously consider accuracy for both truthful and untruthful statements. It is possible that previous findings, indicating greater lie-detection accuracy for younger versus older child targets, similarly reflect response biases rather than the actual behavior of the targets (or the skill of the observers).

The truth bias uncovered in this study is consistent with previous research on lie detection in adults (DePaulo, Charlton, Cooper, Lindsay, & Muhlenbruck, 1997; Malone & DePaulo, 2001; Vrij & Baxter, 1999) and children (Westcott et al., 1991). Of note, however, Ekman et al. (Ekman & O'Sullivan, 1991; Ekman et al., 1999) found the opposite pattern of results among (predominantly male) law enforcement officers; these individuals appeared to be biased toward judging adult targets as untruthful. Thus, a truthtelling bias may be evident primarily among laypersons, such as college students, or at least among those who are judging people they know are not suspected of a crime.

The findings of Ekman et al.(Ekman & O'Sullivan, 1991; Ekman et al., 1999) may also reflect the small percentage of women in law enforcement. In the present study, female observers were more likely than male observers to believe both children and adults. This finding is consistent with research on jurors' perceptions of child sexual abuse victims (Bottoms & Goodman, 1994; Castelli, Goodman, & Ghetti, in press; Golding, Sanchez, & Sego, 1997; McCauley & Parker, 2001) and adult rape victims (Frazier & Borgida, 1988). In these studies, female mock jurors are more likely than their male counterparts to find both children's and adults' statements credible.

Further research is necessary to better understand why observers were more likely to believe adults than children in this study, and to examine the source of observers' biases. It is also important to examine whether this bias generalizes to forensic settings: To the extent that judges, jurors, or attorneys are predisposed to believe that adults (but not children) are telling the truth, children may be perceived as less credible when recounting their experiences, simply because of their age. Manipulating the conditions under which observers make their judgments (i.e., resulting in more or less conservative decisions) could elucidate factors that contribute to these biases.

It is important to note that, as in most studies of lie detection, our findings are generalizable only to instances of deliberate falsification. Lies told under different circumstances (e.g., as the result of overly suggestive or coercive interview procedures) may differ in the ease with which they can be detected by observers.

Are There Stable Individual Differences in the Ability to Detect Lies?

As argued by Frank and Ekman (1997), if the ability to detect lies is a relatively stable and generalizable skill, detection accuracy should be correlated across situations in which lies are being told. Although in the present study only one situation (i.e., lying about being touched) was employed, two groups of targets (i.e., children and adults) were involved. Thus, observers' accuracy across these two groups could be compared.

Consistent with the hypothesis that lie-detection abilities are generalizable, we found that observers' abilities to detect lies in children were strongly related to their abilities to detect lies in adults. Although the

average observer was at chance when discriminating between true and false statements, those who were highly accurate (or inaccurate) with one group of targets were also highly accurate (or inaccurate) with the other group. This finding suggests that some observers may be especially skilled at determining the veracity of others' statements. Future research may uncover particular skills or personality characteristics that may be important for detection success, for example, empathy, sensitivity to social cues, or conscientiousness. Moreover, further research focused on highly accurate observers may identify specific behavioral or verbal cues indicative of lying (e.g., facial expressions) (Frank & Ekman, 2004); such information could be useful for training police officers, judges, or other individuals involved in judging the veracity of children's and adults' statements.

Note that previous research has generally failed to find a relation between observers' abilities to detect lies in one individual and their abilities to detect lies in another individual (Kraut, 1978). Ekman (2001) has argued that these findings are due in part to the "low-stakes" nature of the lies being detected. That is, when people are telling relatively innocuous lies, they tend not to be concealing strong negative emotions that could betray their true feelings. Indeed, when Frank and Ekman (1997) compared individuals' detection abilities across two different types of "high-stakes" lies (i.e., a false opinion scenario and a crime scenario), both with considerable rewards and punishments at stake, they found that the ability to detect lies in one scenario was positively related to the ability to detect lies in the other scenario (see also Frank & Ekman, 2004). It is possible that the correlation obtained in the present study between detection accuracy for child and adult targets similarly reflects the nature of the lies being told: Targets were asked to lie about being touched by a male research assistant, which may be more anxiety-provoking than being asked to lie, for instance, about visiting a museum or the taste of a drink. Cues indicative of lying may thus have been more detectable, at least to some observers, in the present study than in previous research. More generally, insofar as lies told in a forensic context (e.g., about having committed a crime) are similarly anxiety-provoking, it is possible that such lies would be more easily detectable, particularly to skilled or

experienced observers, than those told in most laboratory studies of lie-detection (Frank & Ekman,
2004). If so, the implications for the courtroom are
far-reaching. For example, some jurors may be particularly skilled at detecting high-stakes lies when a witness takes the stand. It would be of interest in future
research to determine if such jurors have any greater
sway in juror decision-making.

CONCLUSIONS

In summary, this study extends previous research
on lie detection in several ways. First, our findings provide some support for the prediction that
children's lies are more easily detected than those of
adults. Second, our results indicate that observers
may be biased to judge adults' (but not children's)
statements as truthful, at least in the context of the
present study. Third, women were more likely than
men to show this truth bias. The source and extent
of these biases deserve attention in future research.
Finally, results from this study are consistent with
those of Frank and Ekman (1997) in suggesting that
some individuals are particularly skilled at detecting
lies. A closer examination of the personality characteristics of highly accurate observers, and the strategies they use to detect lies, may lead to a better
understanding of the specific skills involved in lie
detection.

REFERENCES

Allen, V. L., & Atkinson, M. L. (1978). Encoding of
nonverbal behavior by high-achieving and low-achiev-
ing children. *Journal of Educational Psychology, 70,*
298–305.

Bottoms, B. L., & Goodman, G. S. (1994). Perceptions of
children's credibility in sexual assault cases. *Journal of
Applied Social Psychology, 24,* 702–732.

Castelli, P., Goodman, G. S., & Ghetti, S. (2005). Effects
of age and leading questions on children's credibility.
Journal of Applied Social Psychology, 35, 297–319.

DePaulo, B. M., Charlton, K., Cooper, H., Lindsay, J. L.,
& Muhlenbruck, L. (1997). The accuracy–confidence
correlation in the detection of deception. *Personality and
Social Psychology Review, 1,* 346–357.

DePaulo, B. M., Stone, J. L., & Lassiter, G. D. (1985).
Deceiving and detecting deceit. In B. Schlenker (Ed.),
The self and social life (pp. 323–370). New York:
McGraw Hill.

DePaulo, B. M., & Tang, J. (1994). Social anxiety and
social judgment: the example of detecting deception.
Journal of Research in Personality, 28, 142–153.

Ekman, P. (1997). Lying and deception. In N. L. Stein, P. A.
Ornstein, B. Tversky, & C. Brainerd (eds.), *Memory for
everyday and emotional events* (pp. 333–348). Mahwah,
NJ: Erlbaum.

Ekman, P. (2001). *Telling lies: clues to deceit in the market-
place, marriage, and politics.* New York: Norton.

Ekman, P., & Friesen, W. V. (1969). Nonverbal leakage and
clues to deception. *Psychiatry, 32,* 88–105.

Ekman, P., & O'Sullivan, M. (1991). Who can catch a liar?
American Psychologist, 46, 913–920.

Ekman, P., O'Sullivan, M., & Frank, M. G. (1999). A few
can catch a liar. *Psychological Science, 10,* 263–266.

Ekman, P., O'Sullivan, M., Friesen, W. V., & Scherer, K. R.
(1991). Face, voice, and body in detecting deceit. *Journal of Nonverbal Behavior, 15,* 125–135.

Feldman, R. S., Jenkins, L., & Popoola, O. (1979). Detection of deception in adults and children via facial expressions. *Child Development, 50,* 350–355.

Frank, M. G., & Ekman, P. (1997). Appearing truthful
generalizes across different deceptive situations. *Journal
of Personality and Social Psychology, 86,* 486–495.

Frank, M. G., & Ekman, P. (2004). Nonverbal detection
of deception in forensic context. In W. T. O'Donohue
& E. R. Levensky (eds.), *Handbook of forensic psychology*
(pp. 635–653). San Diego, CA: Elsevier.

Frank, M. G., & Ekman, P. (2004). The ability to detect
deceit generalizes across different types of high-stakes
lies. *Journal of Personality and Social Psychology, 72,*
1429–1439.

Frazier, P., & Borgida, E. (1988). Juror common understanding and the admissibility of rape trauma syndrome evidence in court. *Law and Human Behavior, 12,* 101–122.

Golding, J. M., Sanchez, R. P., & Sego, S. A. (1997). The
believability of hearsay testimony in a child sexual assault
trial. *Law and Human Behavior, 21,* 299–325.

Green, D. M., & Swets, J. A. (1966). *Signal detection theory
and psychophysics.* New York: Wiley.

Kraut, R. E. (1978). Verbal and nonverbal cues in the perception of lying. *Journal of Personality and Social Psychology, 36,* 380–391.

Kraut, R. E., & Poe, D. (1980). On the line: the deception
judgments of customs inspectors and laymen. *Journal of
Personality and Social Psychology, 39,* 784–798.

Lewis, M. (1993). The development of deception. In M.
Lewis & C. Saarni (eds.), *Lying and deception in everyday
life* (pp. 90–105). New York: Guilford Press.

Litlepage, G. E., Maddox, J., & Pineault, M. A. (1985). Recognition of discrepant nonverbal messages and detection of deception. *Perceptual and Motor Skills, 60,* 119–124.

Littlepage, G. E., McKinnie, R., & Pineault, M. A. (1983). Relationship between nonverbal sensitivities and detection of deception. *Perceptual and Motor Skills, 57,* 651–657.

Malone, B. E., & DePaulo, B. M. (2001). Measuring sensitivity to deception. In J. A. Hall & F. J. Bernieri (eds.), *Interpersonal sensitivity* (pp. 103–124). Mahwah, NJ: Erlbaum.

Mann, S., Vrij, A., & Bull, R. (2004). Detecting true lies: police officers' ability to detect suspects' lies. *Journal of Applied Psychology, 89,* 137–149.

McCauley, M. R., & Parker, J. R. (2001). When will a child be believed? The impact of the victim's age and juror's gender on children's credibility and verdict in a sexual-abuse case. *Child Abuse and Neglect, 25,* 523–539.

Morency, N. L., & Krauss, R. M. (1982). The nonverbal encoding and decoding of affect in first and fifth graders. In R. S. Feldman (Ed.), *Development of nonverbal behavioral skill* (pp. 181–199). New York: Springer-Verlag.

Orcutt, H. K., Goodman, G. S., Tobey, A. E., Batterman-Faunce, J. M., & Thomas, S. (2001). Detecting deception in children's testimony: factfinders' abilities to reach the truth in open court and closed-circuit trials. *Law and Human Behavior, 25,* 339–372.

Swets, J. A., Dawes, R. M., & Monahan, J. (2000). Psychological science can improve diagnostic decisions. *Psychological Science in the Public Interest, 1,* 1–26.

Talwar, V., & Lee, K. (2002). Development of lying to conceal a transgression: children's control of expressive behavior during verbal deception. *International Journal of Behavioral Development, 26,* 436–444.

Vrij, A., & Baxter, M. (1999). Accuracy and confidence in detecting truth and lies in elaborations and denials: truth bias, lie bias and individual differences. *Expert Evidence, 7,* 25–36.

Westcott, H., Davies, G., Graham, M., & Clifford, B. (1991). Adults' perceptions of children's videotaped truthful and deceptive statements. *Children and Society, 5,* 123–135.

Wilson, A. E., Smith, M. D., & Ross, H. S. (2003). The nature and effects of young children's lies. *Social Development, 12,* 21–45.

ENDNOTES

1. Although accuracy was unrelated to videotape order (i.e., child vs. adult targets viewed first), there was a general tendency for accuracy to decrease across interviews, particularly for adult targets in the lying condition. It is possible that these targets were more consistent in their statements, which made them appear more believable, or that observers were less attentive to later targets. When analyses were reconducted using only the first three targets viewed in each category (i.e., child and adult targets lying and telling the truth: 12 targets in total), the pattern of results obtained was virtually identical to that reported here.

2. Accuracy for individual targets ranged from 32 to 77% for the truthtelling child targets, 20 to 79% for the lying child targets, 45 to 84% for the adult truthtelling targets, and 17 to 72% for the adult lying targets.

CRITICAL THINKING QUESTIONS

1. Compare the conclusions in this article with those presented in Article 4. What similarities do you see in their findings? What differences? Can any of the information presented in this article (Article 6) be generalized to the issues of impression formation presented in Article 4 or vice versa? Explain your answer.

2. What implications does the information presented in this article have for situations such as therapy sessions and courtroom proceedings? For instance, is it feasible to teach people to be more aware of the nonverbal and verbal messages they send when they are lying or telling the truth? Can people learn how to interpret such messages more accurately? How might either or both of these goals be accomplished? Explain your answers.

3. This study found a bias in observers judging adults as truthful but not children, especially in female observers. What may be the reasons for this? What are the implications of this finding for real-world settings?

4. Why are some people more accurate than others in detecting lies in both children and adults? How can the information in Article 4 relate to this question? Be specific in your answer.

5. How useful are the findings of the present study for detecting deception in real-world settings? Include in your answer the implications for both forensic and nonforensic settings.

CHAPTER INTEGRATION QUESTIONS

1. Do any common themes emerge from the three articles in this chapter? If so, what are they?

2. Using the information from these articles, what advice could you give on how to make the most positive first impression on others? Also, how can we more accurately form first impressions of other people?

3. Spanish philosopher Santayana wrote, "People often see what they believe rather than believe what they see." What does this quotation mean to you? Do you agree or disagree with it? Why?

4. How can you relate the Santayana quotation to the chapter themes that you identified in Question 1?

Chapter Three

SOCIAL COGNITION

THE WORLD AROUND us presents a complex array of information. Due simply to sheer volume, it is humanly impossible to pay attention to all the information available to us. So, given all of this information, how do we make sense of it? This chapter on social cognition examines some of the ways that people process information about themselves and others in order to make judgments.

A major interest of social psychologists is how people mentally process the information they receive. Decisions are not always based on a thorough analysis of the information at hand. Instead, people sometimes rely on mental shortcuts or intuition in reaching decisions. These mental shortcuts, or *heuristics,* are commonly employed strategies that people use for making sense of the world. The problem is, these mental strategies often get us into trouble by shading how we interpret events in the world around us. Article 7, "Some Systematic Biases of Everyday Judgment," examines how heuristics and other forms of cognitive bias may hinder effective decision making.

Social cognition also deals with how we make sense of ourselves. One interesting line of research has addressed the relationship between cognition and emotion. Specifically, do our mental processes influence what we feel, or do our feelings shape our mental processes? Article 8, "Cognitive, Social, and Physiological Determinants of Emotional State," is a classic investigation of the relationship between thought processes and emotion. The methods and findings of the study make interesting reading, but its implications are even more important: Is it possible to change the emotions we experience simply by changing the cognitive labels that we attach to them?

The last article in this chapter returns to the question of how we come to understand the world around us. Specifically, Article 9, "Pluralistic Ignorance and Hooking Up," looks at the discrepancy between what people personally believe is acceptable behavior and what they erroneously think others are actually doing. This false sense that "everyone else is doing it" may have important implications for individual behavior.

ARTICLE 7 _____

Social cognition is concerned with the processes that people use to make sense of the social world. One finding from research in this area is that people tend to be *cognitive misers;* that is, all things being equal, people prefer to think as little as possible in reaching decisions. To help them achieve this goal, they employ cognitive strategies such as *heuristics* (i.e., mental shortcuts for understanding the world).

For example, why are some people afraid of flying? If you asked them whether they know that statistics show that airplane travel actually is safer than other modes of transportation, the majority undoubtedly would say that yes, they know that. Yet their fear persists. Why? One contributing factor may be the *availability heuristic,* a mental shortcut that involves judging the probability of something happening by how easily it comes to mind. We all can vividly recall the images of airplane crashes that appear in the media every time an accident occurs. The pictures are terrifying, so they readily come to mind. Even though automobile accidents are more common, how often do we see detailed (and repeated) images of car crashes? Rarely. So even though airplane crashes occur much less frequently than fatal automobile accidents, it is easier to recall images of the former. Hence, we have a greater tendency to fear them, as well.

We use many types of heuristics to help us explain and understand our world. What all of these mental shortcuts do, however, are create biases in how we interpret the events around us. Many of these biases involve inconsequential events, and no harm comes from believing them. But in other situations, using this biased information processing to make important decisions about our lives may lead to problems.

The following article by Thomas Gilovich examines some of the biases in everyday judgment that cloud our ability for accurate, critical thinking.

Some Systematic Biases of Everyday Judgment

■ Thomas Gilovich

Skeptics have long thought that everyday judgment and reasoning are biased in predictable ways. Psychological research on the subject conducted during the past quarter century largely confirms these suspicions. Two types of explanations are typically offered for the dubious beliefs that are dissected in *Skeptical Inquirer.* On one hand, there are motivational causes: Some beliefs are comforting, and so people embrace that comfort and convince themselves that a questionable proposition is true. Many types of religious beliefs, for example, are often explained this way. On the other hand, there are cognitive causes: faulty processes of reasoning and judgment that lead people to misevaluate the evidence of their everyday experience. The skeptical community is convinced that everyday judgment and reasoning leave much to be desired.

Why are skeptics so unimpressed with the reasoning abilities and habits of the average person? Until recently, this pessimism was based on simple observation, often by those with a particularly keen eye for the foibles of human nature. Thus, skeptics often cite such thinkers as Francis Bacon, who stated:

> . . . *all superstition is much the same whether it be that of astrology, dreams, omens, retributive judgment, or the like . . . [in that] the deluded believers*

Reprinted from *The Skeptical Inquirer,* March 13, 1997, *21*(2), p. 31. Copyright © 1997, CSICOP, Inc. www.CSICOP.org. Reprinted with permission.

observe events which are fulfilled, but neglect or pass over their failure, though it be much more common. (Bacon 1899/1620)

John Stuart Mill and Bertrand Russell are two other classic scholars who, along with Bacon, are often quoted for their trenchant observations on the shortcomings of human judgment. It is also common to see similar quotes of more recent vintage—in *Skeptical Inquirer* and elsewhere—from the likes of Richard Feynman, Stephen Jay Gould, and Carl Sagan. During the past twenty-five years, a great deal of psychological research has dealt specifically with the quality of everyday reasoning, and so it is now possible to go beyond simple observation and arrive at a truly rigorous assessment of the shortcomings of everyday judgment. In so doing, we can determine whether or not these scholars we all admire are correct. Do people misevaluate evidence in the very ways and for the very reasons that Bacon, Russell, and others have claimed? Let us look at the research record and see.

THE "COMPARED TO WHAT?" PROBLEM

Some of the common claims about the fallibility of human reasoning stand up well to empirical scrutiny. For example, it is commonly argued that people have difficulty with what might be called the "compared to what" problem. That is, people are often overly impressed with an absolute statistic without recognizing that its true import can only be assessed by comparison to some relevant baseline.

For instance, a 1986 article in *Discover* magazine (cited in Dawes 1988) urges readers who fly in airplanes to "know where the exits are and rehearse in your mind exactly how to get to them." Why? The article approvingly notes that someone who interviewed almost two hundred survivors of fatal airline accidents found that ". . . more than 90% had their escape routes mentally mapped out beforehand." Good for them, but note that whoever did the study cannot interview anyone who perished in an airplane crash. Air travel being as scary as it is to so many people, perhaps 90 percent or more of those who died in airline crashes rehearsed their escape routes as well. Ninety percent sounds impressive because it is so close to 100 percent. But without a more pertinent comparison, it really does not mean much.

Similarly, people are often impressed that, say, 30 percent of all infertile couples who adopt a child subsequently conceive. That is great news for that 30 percent to be sure, but what percentage of those who do not adopt likewise conceive? People likewise draw broad conclusions from a cancer patient who goes into remission after steadfastly practicing mental imagery. Again, excellent news for that individual, but might the cancer have gone into remission even if the person had not practiced mental imagery?

This problem of failing to invoke a relevant baseline of comparison is particularly common when the class of data that requires inspection is inherently difficult to collect. Consider, for example, the commonly expressed opinion, "I can always tell that someone is wearing a hairpiece." Are such claims to be believed, or is it just that one can tell that someone is wearing a hairpiece . . . when it is obvious that he is wearing a hairpiece? After all, how can one tell whether some have gone undetected? The goal of a good hairpiece is to fool the public, and so the example is one of those cases in which the confirmations speak loudly while the disconfirmations remain silent.

A similar asymmetry should give pause to those who have extreme confidence in their "gaydar," or their ability to detect whether someone is gay. Here, too, the confirmations announce themselves. When a person for whatever reason "seems gay" and it is later determined that he is, it is a salient triumph for one's skill at detection. But people who elude one's gaydar rarely go out of their way to announce, "By the way, I fooled you: I'm gay."

At any rate, the notion that people have difficulty invoking relevant comparisons has received support from psychological research. Studies of everyday reasoning have shown that the logic and necessity of control groups, for example, is often lost on a large segment of even the educated population (Boring 1954; Einhorn and Hogarth 1978; Nisbett and Ross 1980).

THE "SEEK AND YE SHALL FIND" PROBLEM

Another common claim that stands up well to empirical research is the idea that people do not assess hypotheses even-handedly. Rather, they tend to seek out confirmatory evidence for what they suspect to be true, a tendency that has the effect of "seek and ye shall find." A biased search for confirmatory information frequently turns up more apparent support for a hypothesis than is justified.

This phenomenon has been demonstrated in numerous experiments explicitly designed to assess people's hypothesis-testing strategies (Skov and Sherman 1986; Snyder and Swann 1978). But it is so pervasive that it can also be seen in studies designed with an entirely different agenda in mind. One of my personal favorites is a study in which participants were given the following information (Shafir 1993):

Imagine that you serve on the jury of an only-child sole-custody case following a relatively messy divorce. The facts of the case are complicated by ambiguous economic, social, and emotional considerations, and you decide to base your decision entirely on the following few observations. To which parent would you award sole custody of the child?

Parent A:
average income
average health
average working hours
reasonable rapport with the child
relatively stable social life

Parent B:
above-average income
minor health problems
lots of work-related travel
very close relationship with the child
extremely active social life

Faced with this version of the problem, the majority of respondents chose to award custody to Parent B, the "mixed bag" parent who offers several advantages (above-average income), but also some disadvantages (health problems), in comparison to Parent A. In another version of the problem, however, a different group is asked to which parent they would deny custody of the child. Here, too, a majority selects Parent B. Parent B, then, is paradoxically deemed both more and less worthy of caring for the child.

The result is paradoxical, that is, unless one takes into account people's tendencies to seek out confirming information. Asked which parent should be awarded the child, people look primarily for positive qualities that warrant being awarded the child—looking less vigilantly for negative characteristics that would lead one to favor the other parent. When asked which parent should be denied custody, on the other hand, people look primarily for negative qualities that would disqualify a parent. A decision to award or deny, of course, should be based on a comparison of the positive and negative characteristics of the two parents, but the way the question is framed channels respondents down a narrower path in which they focus on information that would confirm the type of verdict they are asked to render.

The same logic often rears its head when people test certain suppositions or hypotheses. Rumors of some dark conspiracy, for example, can lead people to search disproportionately for evidence that supports the plot and neglect evidence that contradicts it.

THE SELECTIVE MEMORY PROBLEM

A third commonly sounded complaint about everyday human thought is that people are more inclined to remember information that fits their expectations than information at variance with their expectations. Charles Darwin, for example, said that he took great care to record any observation that was inconsistent with his theories because "I had found by experience that such facts and thoughts were far more apt to escape from the memory than favourable ones" (cited in Clark 1984).

This particular criticism of the average person's cognitive faculties is in need of revision. Memory research has shown that often people have the easiest time recalling information that is inconsistent with their expectations or preferences (Bargh and Thein 1985; Srull and Wyer 1989). A little reflection indicates that this is particularly true of those "near misses" in life that become indelibly etched in the brain. The novelist Nicholson Baker (1991) provides a perfect illustration:

[I] told her my terrible story of coming in second in the spelling bee in second grade by spelling keep "c-e-e-p" after successfully tossing off microphone, and how for two or three years afterward I was pained every time a yellow garbage truck drove by on Highland Avenue and I saw the capitals printed on it, "Help

*Keep Our City Clean," with that impossible irratio-
nal K that had made me lose so humiliatingly. . . .*

Baker's account, of course, is only an anecdote, possibly an apocryphal one at that. But it is one that,
as mentioned above, receives support from more systematic studies. In one study, for example, individuals who had bet on professional football games were
later asked to recall as much as they could about the
various bets they had made (Gilovich 1983). They
recalled significantly more information about their
losses—outcomes they most likely did not expect to
have happen and certainly did not prefer to have happen (see Figure 1).

Thus, the simple idea that people remember best
that which they expect or prefer needs modification.
Still, there is something appealing and seemingly
true about the idea, and it should not be discarded
prematurely. When considering people's belief in
the accuracy of psychic forecasts, for example, it certainly seems to be fed by selective memory for successful predictions. How then can we reconcile this
idea with the finding that often inconsistent information is better recalled? Perhaps the solution lies in
considering when an event is eventful. With respect
to their capacity to grab attention, some events are
one-sided and others two-sided. Two-sided events are
those that stand out and psychologically register as
events regardless of how they turn out. If you bet on
a sporting event or an election result, for example,

either outcome—a win or a loss—has emotional
significance and is therefore likely to emerge from
the stream of everyday experience and register as an
event. For these events, it is doubtful that confirmatory information is typically better remembered than
disconfirmatory information.

In contrast, suppose you believe that "the telephone always rings when I'm in the shower." The
potentially relevant events here are one-sided. If the
phone happens to ring while showering, it will certainly register as an event, as you experience great
stress in deciding whether to answer it, and you run
dripping wet to the phone only to discover that it is
someone from AT&T asking if you are satisfied with
your long-distance carrier. When the phone does not
ring when you are in the shower, on the other hand, it
is a non-event. Nothing happened. Thus, with respect
to the belief that the phone always rings while you
are in the shower, the events are inherently one-sided:
Only the confirmations stand out.

Perhaps it is these one-sided events to which Bacon's
and Darwin's comments best apply. For one-sided
events, as I discuss below, it is often the outcomes consistent with expectations that stand out and are more
likely to be remembered. For two-sided events, on the
other hand, the two types of outcomes are likely to be
equally memorable; or, on occasion, events inconsistent with expectations may be more memorable.

But what determines whether an event is one-
or two-sided? There are doubtless several factors.
Let's consider two of them in the context of psychic predictions. First, events relevant to psychic
predictions are inherently one-sided in the sense
that such predictions are disconfirmed not by any
specific event, but by their accumulated failure to
be confirmed. Thus, the relevant comparison here
is between confirmations and non-confirmations,
or between events and non-events. It is no surprise,
surely, that events are typically more memorable
than non-events.

In one test of this idea, a group of college students
read a diary purportedly written by another student,
who described herself as having an interest in the
prophetic nature of dreams (Madey 1993). To test
whether there was any validity to dream prophecy,
she decided to record each night's dreams and keep
a record of significant events in her life, and later

**FIGURE 1 / Gamblers' Recall of Information
about Bets Won and Lost. (From Gilovich 1983.)**

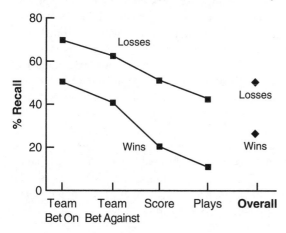

determine if there was any connection between the two. Half of the dreams (e.g., "I saw lots of people being happy") were later followed by events that could be seen as fulfilling ("My professor cancelled our final, which produced cheers throughout the class"). The other half went unfulfilled.

After reading the entire diary and completing a brief "filler" task, the participants were asked to recall as many of the dreams as they could. As Figure 2 shows, they recalled many more of the prophecies that were fulfilled than those that were not (see Figure 2). This result is hardly a surprise, of course, because the fulfillment of a prophecy reminds one of the original prediction, whereas a failure to fulfill it is often a non-event. The relevant outcomes are therefore inherently one-sided, and the confirmations are more easily recalled. The end result is that the broader belief in question—in this case, dream prophecy—receives spurious support.

The events relevant to psychic predictions are one-sided in another way as well. Psychic predictions are notoriously vague about when the prophesied events are supposed to occur. "A serious misfortune will befall a powerful leader" is a more common prophecy than "The President will be assassinated on March 15th." Such predictions are temporally unfocused, in that there is no specific moment to which interested parties are to direct their attention. For such predictions, confirmatory events are once again more likely to stand out because confirmations are more likely to prompt a recollection of the original prophecy. The events relevant to temporally unfocused expectations, then, tend to be one-sided, with the confirmations typically more salient and memorable than disconfirmations.

Temporally focused expectations, on the other hand, are those for which the timing of the decisive outcome is known in advance. If one expects a particular team to win the Super Bowl, for example, one knows precisely when that expectation will be confirmed or refuted—at the end of the game. As a result, the events relevant to temporally focused expectations tend to be two-sided because one's attention is focused on the decisive moment, and both outcomes are likely to be noticed and remembered.

In one study that examined the memory implications of temporally focused and unfocused expectations, participants were asked to read the diary of a student who, as part of an ESP experiment, was required to try to prophesy an otherwise unpredictable event every week for several weeks (Madey and Gilovich 1993). The diary included the student's weekly prophecy as well as various passages describing events from that week. There were two groups of participants in the experiment. In the temporally unfocused condition, the prophecies made no mention of when the prophesied event was likely to occur ("I have a feeling that I will get into an argument with my Psychology research group"). In the temporally focused condition, the prediction identified a precise day on which the event was to occur ("I have a feeling that I will get into an argument with my Psychology research group on Friday"). For each group, half of the prophecies were confirmed (e.g., "Our professor assigned us to research groups, and we immediately disagreed over our topic") and half were disconfirmed (e.g., "Our professor assigned us to research groups, and we immediately came to a unanimous decision on our topic"). Whether confirmed or disconfirmed, the relevant event was described in the diary entry for the day prophesied in the temporally focused condition. After reading the diary and completing a short distracter task, the participants were asked to recall as many prophecies and relevant events as they could.

FIGURE 2 / Participants' Recall of Dream Prophecies That Were Either Confirmed or Unconfirmed. (Adapted from Madey 1993.)

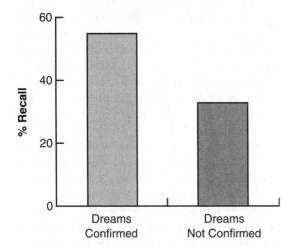

Knowing when the prophesied events were likely to occur helped the respondents' memories, but only for those prophecies that were disconfirmed (see Figure 3). Confirmatory events were readily recalled whether temporally focused or not. Disconfirmations, on the other hand, were rarely recalled unless they disconfirmed a temporally focused prediction. When one considers that most psychic predictions are temporally unfocused, the result, once again, is that the evidence for psychic predictions can appear more substantial than it is.

CONCLUSION

There is, of course, much more psychological research on the quality of everyday judgment than that reviewed here (see, for example, Baron 1988; Dawes 1988; Gilovich 1991; Nisbett and Ross 1980; Kahneman, Slovic, and Tversky 1982). But even this brief review is sufficient to make it clear that some of the reputed biases of everyday judgment turn out to be real, verifiable shortcomings. Systematic research by

FIGURE 3 / Participants' Recall of Prophecies That Were Confirmed or Disconfirmed, as a Function of Whether or Not the Prophecies Specified When the Critical Events Were to Occur. (Adapted from Madey and Gilovich 1993.)

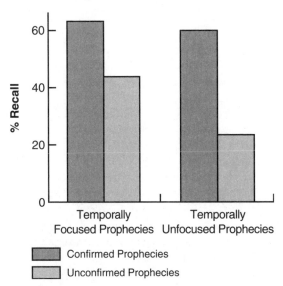

and large supports the suspicions of much of the skeptical community that everyday judgment is not to be trusted completely. At one level, this should not come as a surprise: It is precisely because everyday judgment cannot be trusted that the inferential safeguards known as the scientific method were developed. It is unfortunate that those safeguards are not more widely taught or more generally appreciated.

REFERENCES

Bacon, F. 1899. *Advancement of Learning and the Novum Organum* (rev. ed.). New York: Colonial Press. (Original work published 1620).

Baker, N. 1991. *Room Temperature.* New York: Vintage.

Bargh, J. A., and R. D. Thein. 1985. Individual construct accessibility, person memory, and the recall-judgment link: The case of information overload. *Journal of Personality and Social Psychology* 49: 1129–1146.

Baron, J. 1988. *Thinking and Deciding.* New York: Cambridge University Press.

Boring, E. G. 1954. The nature and history of experimental control. *American Journal of Psychology* 67: 573–589.

Clark, R. W. 1984. *The Survival of Charles Darwin: A Biography of a Man and an Idea.* New York: Random House.

Dawes, R. M. 1988. *Rational Choice in an Uncertain World.* San Diego, Calif.: Harcourt Brace Jovanovich.

Einhorn, H. J., and R. M. Hogarth. 1978. Confidence in judgment: Persistence in the illusion of validity. *Psychological Review* 85: 395–416.

Gilovich, T. 1983. Biased evaluation and persistence in gambling. *Journal of Personality and Social Psychology* 44: 1110–1126.

———.1991. *How We Know What Isn't So: The Fallibility of Human Reason in Everyday Life.* New York: Free Press.

Kahneman, D., P. Slovic, and A. Tversky. 1982. *Judgment under Uncertainty: Heuristics and Biases.* Cambridge: Cambridge University Press.

Madey, S. F. 1993. Memory for expectancy-consistent and expectancy-inconsistent information: An investigation of one-sided and two-sided events. Unpublished doctoral dissertation, Cornell University.

Madey, S. F., and T. Gilovich. 1993. Effect of temporal focus on the recall of expectancy-consistent and expectancy-inconsistent information. *Journal of Personality and Social Psychology* 65: 458–468.

Nisbett, R. E., and L. Ross. 1980. *Human Inference: Strategies and Shortcomings of Social Judgment.* Englewood Cliffs, N.J.: Prentice-Hall.

Shafir, E. 1993. Choosing versus rejecting: Why some options are both better and worse than others. *Memory and Cognition* 21: 546–556.

Skov, R. B., and S. J. Sherman. 1986. Information-gathering processes: Diagnosticity, hypothesis-confirmatory strategies, and perceived hypothesis confirmation. *Journal of Experimental Social Psychology* 22: 93–121.

Synder, M., and W. B. Swann. 1978. Hypothesis-testing processes in social interaction. *Journal of Personality and Social Psychology* 36: 1202–1212.

Srull, T. K., and R. S. Wyer. 1989. Person memory and judgment. *Psychological Review* 9: 58–83.

CRITICAL THINKING QUESTIONS

1. Find sources from various media that illustrate the "compared to what" problem discussed in the article. Discuss how your examples illustrate erroneous reasoning.

2. The article states that "Studies of everyday reasoning have shown that the logic and necessity of control groups, for example, is often lost on a large segment of even the educated population." Explain what is meant by the "logic and necessity of control groups."

3. Do you agree or disagree with the concept expressed in the quote in Question 2 that many people have poor critical-thinking skills? If you agree, what suggestions do you have for how people can handle life's issues most effectively? If you disagree, defend your position.

4. Give a personal example of some sort of biased thinking that you have witnessed. What bias or biases were involved?

5. Check your horoscope at the beginning of the day to see what it says is in store for you. Then record events at the end of the day that either confirm or disconfirm the predictions in your horoscope. Use the information contained in the article to discuss your findings.

ARTICLE 8

How do you know what emotion you are experiencing? Ask that question of someone who has just learned that he or she has won the lottery, and the answer would undoubtedly be "thrilled," "excited," "overjoyed," or some such adjective to describe a very positive emotional state. Ask if it is actually anger that the winner is feeling, and he or she probably would look at you as if you were crazy. But how does that person *know* what emotion he or she is feeling?

The work that follows by Schachter and Singer is a classic study that addresses what determines a person's emotional state. Briefly, the authors' findings suggest that what we call *emotion* is partly due to some sort of physiological arousal. However, what we feel is also determined by the cognitive label that we attach to that physiological arousal. According to this approach, a person who experiences some sort of physiological arousal might subjectively experience one of two very different emotional states, either anger or euphoria, depending on how he or she labeled the experience. The article discusses the process as well as some of the conditions that result when this process occurs.

While reading the article, think of its implications: Is cognition a necessary part of emotion? Without it, what (if anything) would we feel? What about newborn children? Since their cognitive abilities are not yet fully developed, does that mean that they don't experience emotions?

Cognitive, Social, and Physiological Determinants of Emotional State[1]

■ Stanley Schachter and Jerome E. Singer

The problem of which cues, internal or external, permit a person to label and identify his own emotional state has been with us since the days that James (1890) first tendered his doctrine that "the bodily changes follow directly the perception of the exciting fact, and that our feeling of the same changes as they occur *is* the emotion" (p. 449). Since we are aware of a variety of feeling and emotion states, it should follow from James' proposition that the various emotions will be accompanied by a variety of differentiable bodily states. Following James' pronouncement, a formidable number of studies were undertaken in search of the physiological differentiators of the emotions. The results, in these early days, were almost uniformly negative. All of the emotional states experimentally manipulated were characterized by a general pattern of excitation of the sympathetic nervous system but there appeared

to be no clear-cut physiological discriminators of the various emotions. This pattern of results was so consistent from experiment to experiment that Cannon (1929) offered, as one of the crucial criticisms of the James-Lange theory, the fact that "the same visceral changes occur in very different emotional states and in non-emotional states" (p. 351).

More recent work, however, has given some indication that there may be differentiators. Ax (1953) and Schachter (1957) studied fear and anger. On a large number of indices both of these states were characterized by a similarly high level of autonomic activation but on several indices they did differ in the degree of activation. Wolf and Wolff (1947) studied a subject with a gastric fistula and were able to distinguish two patterns in the physiological responses of the stomach wall. It should be noted, though, that for

Reprinted from *Psychological Review*, 1962, *69*, 379–399.

many months they studied their subject during and following a great variety of moods and emotions and were able to distinguish only two patterns.

Whether or not there are physiological distinctions among the various emotional states must be considered an open question. Recent work might be taken to indicate that such differences are at best rather subtle and that the variety of emotion, mood, and feeling states are by no means matched by an equal variety of visceral patterns.

This rather ambiguous situation has led Ruckmick (1936), Hunt, Cole, and Reis (1958), Schachter (1959) and others to suggest that cognitive factors may be major determinants of emotional states. Granted a general pattern of sympathetic excitation as characteristic of emotional states, granted that there may be some differences in pattern from state to state, it is suggested that one labels, interprets, and identifies this stirred-up state in terms of the characteristics of the precipitating situation and one's apperceptive mass. This suggests, then, that an emotional state may be considered a function of a state of physiological arousal[2] and of a cognition appropriate to this state of arousal. The cognition, in a sense, exerts a steering function. Cognitions arising from the immediate situation as interpreted by past experience provide the framework within which one understands and labels his feelings. It is the cognition which determines whether the state of physiological arousal will be labeled as "anger," "joy," "fear," or whatever.

In order to examine the implications of this formulation let us consider the fashion in which these two elements, a state of physiological arousal and cognitive factors, would interact in a variety of situations. In most emotion inducing situations, of course, the two factors are completely interrelated. Imagine a man walking alone down a dark alley; a figure with a gun suddenly appears. The perception-cognition "figure with a gun" in some fashion initiates a state of physiological arousal; this state of arousal is interpreted in terms of knowledge about dark alleys and guns and the state of arousal is labeled "fear." Similarly a student who unexpectedly learns that he has made Phi Beta Kappa may experience a state of arousal which he will label "joy."

Let us now consider circumstances in which these two elements, the physiological and the cognitive,

are, to some extent, independent. First, is the state of physiological arousal alone sufficient to induce an emotion? Best evidence indicates that it is not. Marañon[3] (1924), in a fascinating study (which was replicated by Cantril & Hunt, 1932, and Landis & Hunt, 1932), injected 210 of his patients with the sympathomimetic agent adrenalin and then simply asked them to introspect. Seventy-one percent of his subjects simply reported their physical symptoms with no emotional overtones; 29% of the subjects responded in an apparently emotional fashion. Of these the great majority described their feelings in a fashion that Marañon labeled "cold" or "as if" emotions, that is, they made statements such as "I feel *as if* I were afraid" or "*as if* I were awaiting a great happiness." This is a sort of emotional "déjà vu" experience; these subjects are neither happy nor afraid, they feel "as if" they were. Finally a very few cases apparently reported a genuine emotional experience. However, in order to produce this reaction in most of these few cases, Marañon (1924) points out:

> One must suggest a memory with strong affective force but not so strong as to produce an emotion in the normal state. For example, in several cases we spoke to our patients before the injection of their sick children or dead parents and they responded calmly to this topic. The same topic presented later, during the adrenal commotion, was sufficient to trigger emotion. This adrenal commotion places the subject in a situation of "affective imminence." (pp. 307–308)

Apparently, then, to produce a genuinely emotional reaction to adrenalin, Marañon was forced to provide such subjects with an appropriate cognition.

Though Marañon (1924) is not explicit on his procedure, it is clear that his subjects knew that they were receiving an injection and in all likelihood knew that they were receiving adrenalin and probably had some order of familiarity with its effects. In short, though they underwent the pattern of sympathetic discharge common to strong emotional states, at the same time they had a completely appropriate cognition or explanation as to why they felt this way. This, we would suggest, is the reason so few of Marañon's subjects reported any emotional experience.

Consider now a person in a state of physiological arousal for which no immediately explanatory or appropriate cognitions are available. Such a state could result were one covertly to inject a subject with adrenalin or, unknown to him, feed the subject a sympathomimetic drug such as ephedrine. Under such conditions a subject would be aware of palpitations, tremor, face flushing, and most of the battery of symptoms associated with a discharge of the sympathetic nervous system. In contrast to Marañon's (1924) subjects he would, at the same time, be utterly unaware of why he felt this way. What would be the consequence of such a state?

Schachter (1959) has suggested that precisely such a state would lead to the arousal of "evaluative needs" (Festinger, 1954), that is, pressures would act on an individual in such a state to understand and label his bodily feelings. His bodily state grossly resembles the condition in which it has been at times of emotional excitement. How would he label his present feelings? It is suggested, of course, that he will label his feelings in terms of his knowledge of the immediate situation.[4] Should he at the time be with a beautiful woman, he might decide that he was wildly in love or sexually excited. Should he be at a gay party, he might, by comparing himself to others, decide that he was extremely happy and euphoric. Should he be arguing with his wife, he might explode in fury and hatred. Or, should the situation be completely inappropriate, he could decide that he was excited about something that had recently happened to him or, simply, that he was sick. In any case, it is our basic assumption that emotional states are a function of the interaction of such cognitive factors with a state of physiological arousal.

This line of thought, then, leads to the following propositions:

1. Given a state of physiological arousal for which an individual has no immediate explanation, he will "label" this state and describe his feelings in terms of the cognitions available to him. To the extent that cognitive factors are potent determiners of emotional states, it could be anticipated that precisely the same state of physiological arousal could be labeled "joy" or "fury" or "jealousy" or any of a great diversity of emotional labels depending on the cognitive aspects of the situation.

2. Given a state of physiological arousal for which an individual has a completely appropriate explanation (e.g., "I feel this way because I have just received an injection of adrenalin") no evaluative needs will arise and the individual is unlikely to label his feelings in terms of the alternative cognitions available.

Finally, consider a condition in which emotion inducing cognitions are present but there is no state of physiological arousal. For example, an individual might be completely aware that he is in great danger but for some reason (drug or surgical) remain in a state of physiological quiescence. Does he experience the emotion "fear"? Our formulation of emotion as a joint function of a state of physiological arousal and an appropriate cognition, would, of course, suggest that he does not, which leads to our final proposition.

3. Given the same cognitive circumstances, the individual will react emotionally or describe his feelings as emotions only to the extent that he experiences a state of physiological arousal.[5]

PROCEDURE

The experimental test of these propositions requires (a) the experimental manipulation of a state of physiological arousal, (b) the manipulation of the extent to which the subject has an appropriate or proper explanation of his bodily state, and (c) the creation of situations from which explanatory cognitions may be derived.

In order to satisfy the first two experimental requirements, the experiment was cast in the framework of a study of the effects of vitamin supplements on vision. As soon as a subject arrived, he was taken to a private room and told by the experimenter:

> *In this experiment we would like to make various tests of your vision. We are particularly interested in how certain vitamin compounds and vitamin supplements affect the visual skills. In particular, we want to find out how the vitamin compound called "Suproxin" affects your vision.*
>
> *What we would like to do, then, if we can get your permission, is to give you a small injection of Suproxin. The injection itself is mild and harmless; however, since some people do object to being injected we don't want to talk you into anything. Would you mind receiving a Suproxin injection?*

If the subject agrees to the injection (and all but 1 of 185 subjects did) the experimenter continues with instructions we shall describe shortly, then leaves the room. In a few minutes a physician enters the room, briefly repeats the experimenter's instructions, takes the subject's pulse and then injects him with Suproxin.

Depending upon condition, the subject receives one of two forms of Suproxin—epinephrine or a placebo.

Epinephrine or adrenalin is a sympathomimetic drug whose effects, with minor exceptions, are almost a perfect mimicry of a discharge of the sympathetic nervous system. Shortly after injection systolic blood pressure increases markedly, heart rate increases somewhat, cutaneous blood flow decreases, while muscle and cerebral blood flow increase, blood sugar and lactic acid concentration increase, and respiration rate increases slightly. As far as the subject is concerned the major subjective symptoms are palpitation, tremor, and sometimes a feeling of flushing and accelerated breathing. With a subcutaneous injection (in the dosage administered to our subjects), such effects usually begin within 3–5 minutes of injection and last anywhere from 10 minutes to an hour. For most subjects these effects are dissipated within 15–20 minutes after injection.

Subjects receiving epinephrine received a subcutaneous injection of 1/2 cubic centimeter of a 1:1000 solution of Winthrop Laboratory's Suprarenin, a saline solution of epinephrine bitartrate.

Subjects in the placebo condition received a subcutaneous injection of 1/2 cubic centimeter of saline solution. This is, of course, completely neutral material with no side effects at all.

Manipulating an Appropriate Explanation

By "appropriate" we refer to the extent to which the subject has an authoritative, unequivocal explanation of his bodily condition. Thus, a subject who had been informed by the physician that as a direct consequence of the injection he would feel palpitations, tremor, etc. would be considered to have a completely appropriate explanation. A subject who had been informed only that the injection would have no side effects would have no appropriate explanation of his state. This dimension of appropriateness was manipulated in three experimental conditions which shall be called: Epinephrine Informed (Epi Inf), Epinephrine Ignorant (Epi Ign), and Epinephrine Misinformed (Epi Mis).

Immediately after the subject had agreed to the injection and before the physician entered the room, the experimenter's spiel in each of these conditions went as follows:

Epinephrine Informed. *I should also tell you that some of our subjects have experienced side effects from the Suproxin. These side effects are transitory, that is, they will only last for about 15 or 20 minutes. What will probably happen is that your hand will start to shake, your heart will start to pound, and your face may get warm and flushed. Again these are side effects lasting about 15 or 20 minutes.*

While the physician was giving the injection, she told the subject that the injection was mild and harmless and repeated this description of the symptoms that the subject could expect as a consequence of the shot. In this condition, then, subjects have a completely appropriate explanation of their bodily state. They know precisely what they will feel and why.

Epinephrine Ignorant

In this condition, when the subject agreed to the injection, the experimenter said nothing more relevant to side effects and simply left the room. While the physician was giving the injection, she told the subject that the injection was mild and harmless and would have no side effects. In this condition, then, the subject has no experimentally provided explanation for his bodily state.

Epinephrine Misinformed. *I should also tell you that some of our subjects have experienced side effects from the Suproxin. These side effects are transitory, that is, they will only last for about 15 or 20 minutes. What will probably happen is that your feet will feel numb, you will have an itching sensation over parts of your body, and you may get a slight headache. Again these are side effects lasting 15 or 20 minutes.*

And again, the physician repeated these symptoms while injecting the subject.

None of these symptoms, of course, are consequences of an injection of epinephrine and, in effect, these instructions provide the subject with a completely inappropriate explanation of his bodily feelings. This condition was introduced as a control condition of sorts. It seemed possible that the description of side effects in the Epi Inf condition might turn the subject introspective, self-examining, possibly slightly troubled. Differences on the dependent variable between the Epi Inf and Epi Ign conditions might, then, be due to such factors rather than to differences in appropriateness. The false symptoms in the Epi Mis condition should similarly turn the subject introspective, etc., but the instructions in this condition do not provide an appropriate explanation of the subject's state.

Subjects in all of the above conditions were injected with epinephrine. Finally, there was a placebo condition in which subjects, who were injected with saline solution, were given precisely the same treatment as subjects in the Epi Ign condition.

Producing an Emotion Inducing Cognition

Our initial hypothesis has suggested that given a state of physiological arousal for which the individual has no adequate explanation, cognitive factors can lead the individual to describe his feelings with any of a diversity of emotional labels. In order to test this hypothesis, it was decided to manipulate emotional states which can be considered quite different—euphoria and anger.

There are, of course, many ways to induce such states. In our own program of research, we have concentrated on social determinants of emotional states and have been able to demonstrate in other studies that people do evaluate their own feelings by comparing themselves with others around them (Schachter 1959; Wrightsman 1960). In this experiment we have attempted again to manipulate emotional state by social means. In one set of conditions, the subject is placed together with a stooge who has been trained to act euphorically. In a second set of conditions the subject is with a stooge trained to act in an angry fashion.

Euphoria

Immediately[6] after the subject had been injected, the physician left the room and the experimenter returned with a stooge whom he introduced as another subject, then said:

Both of you have had the Suproxin shot and you'll both be taking the same tests of vision. What I ask you to do now is just wait for 20 minutes. The reason

for this is simply that we have to allow 20 minutes for the Suproxin to get from the injection site into the bloodstream. At the end of 20 minutes when we are certain that most of the Suproxin has been absorbed into the bloodstream, we'll begin the tests of vision.

The room in which this was said had been deliberately put into a state of mild disarray. As he was leaving, the experimenter apologetically added:

The only other thing I should do is to apologize for the condition of the room. I just didn't have time to clean it up. So, if you need any scratch paper or rubber bands or pencils, help yourself. I'll be back in 20 minutes to begin the vision tests.

As soon as the experimenter had left, the stooge introduced himself again, made a series of standard icebreaker comments, and then launched his routine. For observation purposes, the stooge's act was broken into a series of standard units, demarcated by a change in activity or a standard comment. In sequence, the units of the stooge's routine were the following:

1. Stooge reaches for a piece of paper and starts doodling saying, "They said we could use this for scratch, didn't they?" He doodles a fish for some 30 seconds, then says:
2. "This scrap paper isn't even much good for doodling" and crumples paper and attempts to throw it into wastebasket in far corner of the room. He misses but this leads him into a "basketball game." He crumples up other sheets of paper, shoots a few baskets, says "Two points" occasionally. He gets up and does a jump shot saying, "The old jump shot is really on today."
3. If the subject has not joined in, the stooge throws a paper basketball to the subject saying, "Here, you try it."
4. Stooge continues his game saying, "The trouble with paper basketballs is that you don't really have any control."
5. Stooge continues basketball, then gives it up saying, "This is one of my good days. I feel like a kid again. I think I'll make a plane." He makes a paper airplane saying, "I guess I'll make one of the longer ones."
6. Stooge flies plane. Gets up and retrieves plane. Flies again, etc.
7. Stooge throws plane at subject.

8. Stooge, flying plane, says, "Even when I was a kid, I was never much good at this."
9. Stooge tears off part of plane saying, "Maybe this plane can't fly but at least it's good for something." He wads up paper and making a slingshot of a rubber band begins to shoot the paper.
10. Shooting, the stooge says, "They [paper ammunition] really go better if you make them long. They don't work right if you wad them up."
11. While shooting, stooge notices a sloppy pile of manila folders on a table. He builds a tower of these folders, then goes to the opposite end of the room to shoot at the tower.
12. He misses several times, then hits and cheers as the tower falls. He goes over to pick up the folders.
13. While picking up, he notices, behind a portable blackboard, a pair of hula hoops which have been covered with black tape with a few wires sticking out of the tape. He reaches for these, taking one for himself and putting the other aside but within reaching distance of the subject. The stooge tries the hula hoop, saying, "This isn't as easy as it looks."
14. Stooge twirls hoop wildly on arm, saying, "Hey, look at this—this is great."
15. Stooge replaces the hula hoop and sits down with his feet on the table. Shortly thereafter the experimenter returns to the room.

This routine was completely standard, though its pace, of course, varied depending upon the subject's reaction, the extent to which he entered into this bedlam and the extent to which he initiated activities of his own. The only variations from this standard routine were those forced by the subject. Should the subject originate some nonsense of his own and request the stooge to join in, he would do so. And, he would, of course, respond to any comments initiated by the subject.

Subjects in each of the three "appropriateness" conditions and in the placebo condition were submitted to this setup. The stooge, of course, never knew in which condition any particular subject fell.

Anger

Immediately after the injection, the experimenter brought a stooge into the subject's room, introduced the two and after explaining the necessity for a 20 minute delay for "the Suproxin to get from the injection site into the bloodstream" he continued, "We would like you to use these 20 minutes to answer these questionnaires." Then handing out the questionnaires, he concludes with, "I'll be back in 20 minutes to pick up the questionnaires and begin the tests of vision."

Before looking at the questionnaire, the stooge says to the subject,

I really wanted to come for an experiment today, but I think it's unfair for them to give you shots. At least, they should have told us about the shots when they called us; you hate to refuse, once you're here already.

The questionnaires, five pages long, start off innocently requesting face sheet information and then grow increasingly personal and insulting. The stooge, sitting directly opposite the subject, paces his own answers so that at all times subject and stooge are working on the same question. At regular points in the questionnaire, the stooge makes a series of standardized comments about the questions. His comments start off innocently enough, grow increasingly querulous, and finally he ends up in a rage. In sequence, he makes the following comments.

1. Before answering any items, he leafs quickly through the questionnaire saying, "Boy, this is a long one."
2. Question 7 on the questionnaire requests, "List the foods that you would eat in a typical day." The stooge comments, "Oh for Pete's sake, what did I have for breakfast this morning?"
3. Question 9 asks, "Do you ever hear bells? _____ How often? _____" The stooge remarks, "Look at Question 9. How ridiculous can you get? I hear bells every time I change classes."
4. Question 13 requests, "List the childhood diseases you have had and the age at which you had them" to which the stooge remarks, "I get annoyed at this childhood disease question. I can't remember what childhood diseases I had, and especially at what age. Can you?"
5. Question 17 asks, "What is your father's average annual income?" and the stooge says, "This really irritates me. It's none of their business what my father makes. I'm leaving that blank."
6. Question 25 presents a long series of items such as "Does not bathe or wash regularly," "Seems

to need psychiatric care," etc. and requests the respondent to write down for which member of his immediate family each item seems most applicable. The question specifically prohibits the answer "None" and each item must be answered. The stooge says, "I'll be damned if I'll fill out Number 25. 'Does not bathe or wash regularly'— that's a real insult." He then angrily crosses out the entire item.

7. Question 28 reads: "How many times each week do you have sexual intercourse?" 0–1 _____ 2–3 _____ 4–6 _____ 7 and over _____. The stooge bites out, "The hell with it! I don't have to tell them all this."

8. The stooge sits sullenly for a few moments then he rips up his questionnaire, crumples the pieces and hurls them to the floor, saying, "I'm not wasting any more time. I'm getting my books and leaving" and he stamps out of the room.

9. The questionnaire continues for eight more questions ending with: "With how many men (other than your father) has your mother had extramarital relationships?" 4 and under _____; 5–9 _____; 10 and over _____.

Subjects in the Epi Ign, Epi Inf and Placebo conditions were run through this "anger" inducing sequence. The stooge, again, did not know to which condition the subject had been assigned.

In summary, this is a seven condition experiment which, for two different emotional states, allows us (a) to evaluate the effects of "appropriateness" on emotional inducibility and (b) to begin to evaluate the effects of sympathetic activation on emotional inducibility. In schematic form the conditions are the following:

Euphoria	*Anger*
Epi Inf	Epi Inf
Epi Ign	Epi Ign
Epi Mis	Placebo
Placebo	

The Epi Mis condition was not run in the Anger sequence. This was originally conceived as a control condition and it was felt that its inclusion in the Euphoria conditions alone would suffice as a means of evaluating the possible artifactual effect of the Epi Inf instructions.

Measurement

Two types of measures of emotional state were obtained. Standardized observation through a one-way mirror was the technique used to assess the subject's behavior. To what extent did he act euphoric or angry? Such behavior can be considered in a way as a "semi-private" index of mood for as far as the subject was concerned, his emotional behavior could be known only to the other person in the room—presumably another student. The second type of measure was self-report in which, on a variety of scales, the subject indicated his mood of the moment. Such measures can be considered "public" indices of mood for they would, of course, be available to the experimenter and his associates.

Observation

Euphoria

For each of the first 14 units of the stooge's standardized routine an observer kept a running chronicle of what the subject did and said. For each unit the observer coded the subject's behavior in one or more of the following categories:

Category 1: Joins in activity. If the subject entered into the stooge activities, e.g., if he made or flew airplanes, threw paper basketballs, hula hooped, etc., his behavior was coded in this category.

Category 2: Initiates new activity. A subject was so coded if he gave indications of creative euphoria, that is, if, on his own, he initiated behavior outside of the stooge's routine. Instances of such behavior would be the subject who threw open the window and, laughing, hurled paper basketballs at passersby; or, the subject who jumped on a table and spun one hula hoop on his leg and the other on his neck.

Categories 3 and 4: Ignores or watches stooge. Subjects who paid flatly no attention to the stooge or who, with or without comment, simply watched the stooge without joining in his activity were coded in these categories.

For any particular unit of behavior, the subject's behavior was coded in one or more of these categories. To test reliability of coding two observers independently coded two experimental sessions. The observers agreed completely on the coding of 88% of the units.

Anger

For each of the units of stooge behavior, an observer recorded the subject's responses and coded them according to the following category scheme:

Category 1: Agrees. In response to the stooge the subject makes a comment indicating that he agrees with the stooge's standardized comment or that he, too, is irked by a particular item on the questionnaire. For example, a subject who responded to the stooge's comment on the "father's income" question by saying, "I don't like that kind of personal question either" would be so coded (scored +2).

Category 2: Disagrees. In response to the stooge's comment, the subject makes a comment which indicates that he disagrees with the stooge's meaning or mood; e.g., in response to the stooge's comment on the "father's income" question, such a subject might say, "Take it easy, they probably have a good reason for wanting the information" (scored −2).

Category 3: Neutral. A noncommittal or irrelevant response to the stooge's remark (scored 0).

Category 4: Initiates agreement or disagreement. With no instigation by the stooge, a subject, so coded, would have volunteered a remark indicating that he felt the same way or, alternatively, quite differently than the stooge. Examples would be "Boy I hate this kind of thing" or "I'm enjoying this" (scored +2 or −2).

Category 5: Watches. The subject makes no verbal response to the stooge's comment but simply looks directly at him (scored 0).

Category 6: Ignores. The subject makes no verbal response to the stooge's comment nor does he look at him; the subject, paying no attention at all to the stooge, simply works at his own questionnaire (scored −1).

A subject was scored in one or more of these categories for each unit of stooge behavior. To test reliability, two observers independently coded three experimental sessions. In order to get a behavioral index of anger, observation protocol was scored according to the values presented in parentheses after each of the above definitions of categories. In a unit-by-unit comparison, the two observers agreed completely on the scoring of 71% of the units jointly observed. The scores of the two observers differed by a value of 1 or less for 88% of the units coded and

in not a single case did the two observers differ in the direction of their scoring of a unit.

Self-Report of Mood and Physical Condition

When the subject's session with the stooge was completed, the experimenter returned to the room, took pulses and said:

Before we proceed with the vision tests, there is one other kind of information which we must have. We have found, as you can probably imagine, that there are many things beside Suproxin that affect how well you see in our tests. How hungry you are, how tired you are, and even the mood you're in at the time—whether you feel happy or irritated at the time of testing will affect how well you see. To understand the data we collect on you, then, we must be able to figure out which effects are due to causes such as these and which are caused by Suproxin.

The only way we can get such information about your physical and emotional state is to have you tell us. I'll hand out these questionnaires and ask you to answer them as accurately as possible. Obviously our data on the vision tests will only be as accurate as your description of your mental and physical state.

In keeping with this spiel, the questionnaire that the experimenter passed out contained a number of mock questions about hunger, fatigue, etc., as well as questions of more immediate relevance to the experiment. To measure mood or emotional state the following two were the crucial questions:

1. How irritated, angry or annoyed would you say you feel at present?

I don't feel at all irritated or angry	I feel a little irritated and angry	I feel quite irritated and angry	I feel very irritated and angry	I feel extremely irritated and angry
(0)	(1)	(2)	(3)	(4)

2. How good or happy would you say you feel at present?

I don't feel at all happy or good	I feel a little happy and good	I feel quite happy and good	I feel very happy and good	I feel extremely happy and good
(0)	(1)	(2)	(3)	(4)

To measure the physical effects of epinephrine and determine whether or not the injection had been successful in producing the necessary bodily state, the following questions were asked:

1. Have you experienced any palpitation (consciousness of your own heart beat)?

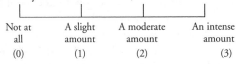

Not at all	A slight amount	A moderate amount	An intense amount
(0)	(1)	(2)	(3)

2. Did you feel any tremor (involuntary shaking of the hands, arms or legs)?

Not at all	A slight amount	A moderate amount	An intense amount
(0)	(1)	(2)	(3)

To measure possible effects of the instructions in the Epi Mis condition, the following questions were asked:

1. Did you feel any numbness in your feet?
2. Did you feel any itching sensation?
3. Did you experience any feeling of headache?

To all three of these questions was attached a four-point scale running from "Not at all" to "An intense amount."

In addition to these scales, the subjects were asked to answer two open-end questions on other physical or emotional sensations they may have experienced during the experimental session. A final measure of bodily state was pulse rate which was taken by the physician or the experimenter at two times—immediately before the injection and immediately after the session with the stooge.

When the subjects had completed these questionnaires, the experimenter announced that the experiment was over, explained the deception and its necessity in detail, answered any questions, and swore the subjects to secrecy. Finally, the subjects answered a brief questionnaire about their experiences, if any, with adrenalin and their previous knowledge or suspicion of the experimental setup. There was no indication that any of the subjects had known about the experiment beforehand but 11 subjects were so extremely suspicious of some crucial feature of the experiment that their data were automatically discarded.

Subjects

The subjects were all male, college students taking classes in introductory psychology at the University of Minnesota. Some 90% of the students in these classes volunteer for a subject pool for which they receive two extra points on their final exam for every hour that they serve as experimental subjects. For this study the records of all potential subjects were cleared with the Student Health Service in order to insure that no harmful effects would result from the injections.

Evaluation of the Experimental Design

The ideal test of our propositions would require circumstances which our experiment is far from realizing. First, the proposition that: "A state of physiological arousal for which an individual has no immediate explanation will lead him to label this state in terms of the cognitions available to him" obviously requires conditions under which the subject does not and cannot have a proper explanation of his bodily state. Though we toyed with such fantasies as ventilating the experimental room with vaporized adrenalin, reality forced us to rely on the disguised injection of Suproxin—a technique which was far from ideal for no matter what the experimenter told them, some subjects would inevitably attribute their feelings to the injection. To the extent that subjects did so, differences between the several appropriateness conditions should be attenuated.

Second, the proposition that: "Given the same cognitive circumstances the individual will react emotionally only to the extent that he experiences a state of physiological arousal" requires for its ideal test the manipulation of states of physiological arousal and of physiological quiescence. Though there is no question that epinephrine effectively produces a state of arousal, there is also no question that a placebo does not prevent physiological arousal. To the extent that the experimental situation effectively produces sympathetic stimulation in placebo subjects, the proposition is difficult to test, for such a factor would attenuate differences between epinephrine and placebo subjects.

Both of these factors, then, can be expected to interfere with the test of our several propositions. In presenting the results of this study, we shall first present condition by condition results and then evaluate the effect of these two factors on experimental differences.

RESULTS

Effects of the Injections on Bodily State

Let us examine first the success of the injections at producing the bodily state required to examine the propositions at test. Does the injection of epinephrine produce symptoms of sympathetic discharge as compared with the placebo injection? Relevant data are presented in Table 1 where it can be immediately seen that on all items subjects who were in epinephrine conditions show considerably more evidence of sympathetic activation than do subjects in placebo conditions. In all epineprine conditions pulse rate increases significantly when compared with the decrease characteristic of the placebo conditions. On the scales it is clear that epinephrine subjects experience considerably more palpitation and tremor than do placebo subjects. In all possible comparisons on these symptoms, the mean scores of subjects in any of the epinephrine conditions are greater than the corresponding scores in the placebo conditions at better than the .001 level of significance. Examination of the absolute values of these scores makes it quite clear that subjects in epinephrine conditions were, indeed, in a state of physiological arousal, while most subjects in placebo conditions were in a relative state of physiological quiescence.

The epinephrine injection, of course, did not work with equal effectiveness for all subjects; indeed for a few subjects it did not work at all. Such subjects reported almost no palpitation or tremor, showed no increase in pulse and described no other relevant physical symptoms. Since for such subjects the necessary experimental conditions were not established, they were automatically excluded from the data and all further tabular presentations will not include such subjects. Table 1, however, does include the data of these subjects. There were four such subjects in euphoria conditions and one of them in anger conditions.

In order to evaluate further data on Epi Mis subjects it is necessary to note the results of the "numbness," "itching," and "headache" scales also presented in Table 1. Clearly the subjects in the Epi Mis condition do not differ on these scales from subjects in any of the other experimental conditions.

Effects of the Manipulations on Emotional State

Euphoria

Self-Report The effects of the several manipulations on emotional state in the euphoria conditions are presented in Table 2. The scores recorded in this table are derived, for each subject, by subtracting the value of the point he checks on the irritation scale from the value of the point he checks on the happiness scale. Thus, if a subject were to check the point "I feel a little irritated and angry" on the irritation scale and

TABLE 1 / Effects of the Injections on Bodily State

| Condition | N | Pulse | | Self-Rating of | | | | |
		Pre	Post	Palpitation	Tremor	Numbness	Itching	Headache
Euphoria								
Epi Inf	27	85.7	88.6	1.20	1.43	0	0.16	0.32
Epi Ign	26	84.6	85.6	1.83	1.76	0.15	0	0.55
Epi Mis	26	82.9	86.0	1.27	2.00	0.06	0.08	0.23
Placebo	26	80.4	77.1	0.29	0.21	0.09	0	0.27
Anger								
Epi Inf	23	85.9	92.4	1.26	1.41	0.17	0	0.11
Epi Ign	23	85.0	96.8	1.44	1.78	0	0.06	0.21
Placebo	23	84.5	79.6	0.59	0.24	0.14	0.06	0.06

TABLE 2 / Self-Report of Emotional State in the Euphoria Conditions

Condition	N	Self-Report Scales	Comparison	p
Epi Inf	25	0.98	Epi Inf vs. Epi Mis	< .01
Epi Ign	25	1.78	Epi Inf vs. Epi Ign	.02
Epi Mis	25	1.90	Placebo vs. Epi Mis, Ign, or Inf	ns
Placebo	26	1.61		

All *p* values reported throughout paper are two-tailed.

the point "I feel very happy and good" on the happiness scale, his score would be +2. The higher the positive value, the happier and better the subject reports himself as feeling. Though we employ an index for expositional simplicity, it should be noted that the two components of the index each yield results completely consistent with those obtained by use of this index.

Let us examine first the effects of the appropriateness instructions. Comparison of the scores for the Epi Mis and Epi Inf conditions makes it immediately clear that the experimental differences are not due to artifacts resulting from the informed instructions. In both conditions the subject was warned to expect a variety of symptoms as a consequence of the injection. In the Epi Mis condition, where the symptoms were inappropriate to the subject's bodily state the self-report score is almost twice that in the Epi Inf condition where the symptoms were completely appropriate to the subject's bodily state. It is reasonable, then, to attribute differences between informed subjects and those in other conditions to differences in manipulated appropriateness rather than to artifacts such as introspectiveness or self-examination.

It is clear that, consistent with expectations, subjects were more susceptible to the stooge's mood and consequently more euphoric when they had no explanation of their own bodily states than when they did. The means of both the Epi Ign and Epi Mis conditions are considerably greater than the mean of the Epi Inf condition.

It is of interest to note that Epi Mis subjects are somewhat more euphoric than are Epi Ign subjects. This pattern repeats itself in other data shortly to be presented. We would attribute this difference to differences in the appropriateness dimension. Though, as in the Epi Ign condition, a subject is not provided with an explanation of his bodily state, it is, of course, possible that he will provide one for himself which is not derived from his interaction with the stooge. Most reasonably he could decide for himself that he feels this way because of the injection. To the extent that he does so he should be less susceptible to the stooge. It seems probable that he would be less likely to hit on such an explanation in the Epi Mis condition than in the Epi Ign condition for in the Epi Mis condition both the experimenter and the doctor have told him that the effects of the injection would be quite different from what he actually feels. The effect of such instructions is probably to make it more difficult for the subject himself to hit on the alternative explanation described above. There is some evidence to support this analysis. In open-end questions in which subjects described their own mood and state, 28% of the subjects in the Epi Ign condition made some connection between the injection and their bodily state compared with the 16% of subjects in the Epi Mis condition who did so. It could be considered, then, that these three conditions fall along a dimension of appropriateness, with the Epi Inf condition at one extreme and the Epi Mis condition at the other.

Comparing the placebo to the epinephrine conditions, we note a pattern which will repeat itself throughout the data. Placebo subjects are less euphoric than either Epi Mis or Epi Ign subjects but somewhat more euphoric than Epi Inf subjects. These differences are not, however, statistically significant. We shall consider the epinephrine-placebo comparisons in detail in a later section of this paper following the presentation of additional relevant data. For the moment, it is clear that, by self-report manipulating appropriateness has had a very strong effect on euphoria.

Behavior Let us next examine the extent to which the subject's behavior was affected by the experimental manipulations. To the extent that his mood has been affected, one should expect that the subject will join in the stooge's whirl of manic activity and initiate similar activities of his own. The relevant data are presented in Table 3. The column labeled "Activity index" presents summary figures on the extent to which the subject joined in the stooge's activity. This is a weighted index which reflects both the nature of the activities in which the subject engaged and the amount of time he was active. The index was devised by assigning the following weights to the subject's activities: 5—hula hooping; 4—shooting with slingshot; 3—paper airplanes; 2—paper basketballs; 1—doodling; 0—does nothing. Pretest scaling on 15 college students ordered these activities with respect to the degree of euphoria they represented. Arbitrary weights were assigned so that the wilder the activity, the heavier the weight. These weights are multiplied by an estimate of the amount of time the subject spent in each activity and the summed products make up the activity index for each subject. This index may be considered a measure of behavioral euphoria. It should be noted that the same between-condition relationships hold for the two components of this index as for the index itself.

TABLE 3 / Behavioral Indications of Emotional State in the Euphoria Conditions

Condition	N	Activity Index	Mean Number of Acts Initiated
Epi Inf	25	12.72	.20
Epi Ign	25	18.28	.56
Epi Mis	25	22.56	.84
Placebo	26	16.00	.54

p value

Comparison	Activity Index	Initiates
Epi Inf vs. Epi Mis	.05	.03
Epi Inf vs. Ipi Ign	ns	.08
Plac vs. Epi Mis. Ign. or Inf	ns	ns

Tested by χ^2 comparison of the proportion of subjects in each condition initiating new acts.

The column labeled "Mean number of acts initiated" presents the data on the extent to which the subject deviates from the stooge's routine and initiates euphoric activities of his own.

On both behavioral indices, we find precisely the same pattern of relationships as those obtained with self-reports. Epi Mis subjects behave somewhat more euphorically than do Epi Ign subjects who in turn behave more euphorically than do Epi Inf subjects. On all measures, then, there is consistent evidence that a subject will take over the stooge's euphoric mood to the extent that he has no other explanation of his bodily state.

Again it should be noted that on these behavioral indices, Epi Ign and Epi Mis subjects are somewhat more euphoric than placebo subjects but not significantly so.

Anger

Self-Report Before presenting data for the anger conditions, one point must be made about the anger manipulation. In the situation devised, anger, if manifested, is most likely to be directed at the experimenter and his annoyingly personal questionnaire. As we subsequently discovered, this was rather unfortunate, for the subjects, who had volunteered for the experiment for extra points on their final exam, simply refused to endanger these points by publicly blowing up, admitting their irritation to the experimenter's face or spoiling the questionnaire. Though as the reader will see, the subjects were quite willing to manifest anger when they were alone with the stooge, they hesitated to do so on material (self-ratings of mood and questionnaire) that the experimenter might see and only after the purposes of the experiment had been revealed were many of these subjects willing to admit to the experimenter that they had been irked or irritated.

This experimentally unfortunate situation pretty much forces us to rely on the behavioral indices derived from observation of the subject's presumably private interaction with the stooge. We do, however, present data on the self-report scales in Table 4. These figures are derived in the same way as the figures presented in Table 2 for the euphoria conditions, that is, the value checked on the irritation scale is subtracted from the

TABLE 4 / Self-Report of Emotional State in the Anger Conditions

Condition	N	Self-Report Scales	Comparison	p
Epi Inf	22	1.91	Epi Inf vs. Epi Ign	.08
Epi Ign	23	1.39	Placebo vs. Epi Ign or Inf	ns
Placebo	23	1.63		

value checked on the happiness scale. Though, for the reasons stated above, the absolute magnitude of these figures (all positive) is relatively meaningless, we can, of course, compare condition means within the set of anger conditions. With the happiness-irritation index employed, we should, of course, anticipate precisely the reverse results from those obtained in the euphoria conditions; that is, the Epi Inf subjects in the anger conditions should again be less susceptible to the stooge's mood and should, therefore, describe themselves as in a somewhat happier frame of mind than subjects in the Epi Ign condition. This is the case; the Epi Inf subjects average 1.91 on the self-report scales while the Epi Ign subjects average 1.39.

Evaluating the effects of the injections, we note again that, as anticipated, Epi Ign subjects are somewhat less happy than Placebo subjects but, once more, this is not a significant difference.

Behavior The subject's responses to the stooge, during the period when both were filling out their questionnaires, were systematically coded to provide a behavioral index of anger. The coding scheme and the numerical values attached to each of the categories have been described in the methodology section. To arrive at an "Anger index" the numerical value assigned to a subject's responses to the stooge is summed together for the several units of stooge behavior. In the coding scheme used, a positive value to this index indicates that the subject agrees with the stooge's comment and is growing angry. A negative

value indicates that the subject either disagrees with the stooge or ignores him.

The relevant data are presented in Table 5. For this analysis, the stooge's routine has been divided into two phases—the first two units of his behavior (the "long" questionnaire and "What did I have for breakfast?") are considered essentially neutral revealing nothing of the stooge's mood; all of the following units are considered "angry" units for they begin with an irritated remark about the "bells" question and end with the stooge's fury as he rips up his questionnaire and stomps out of the room. For the neutral units, agreement or disagreement with the stooge's remarks is, of course, meaningless as an index of mood and we should anticipate no difference between conditions. As can be seen in Table 5, this is the case.

For the angry units, we must, of course, anticipate that subjects in the Epi Ign condition will be angrier than subjects in the Epi Inf condition. This is indeed the case. The Anger index for the Epi Ign condition is positive and large, indicating that these subjects have become angry, while in the Epi Inf condition the Anger index is slightly negative in value indicating that these subjects have failed to catch the stooge's mood at all. It seems clear that providing the subject with an appropriate explanation of his bodily state greatly reduces his tendency to interpret his state in terms of the cognitions provided by the stooge's angry behavior.

TABLE 5 / Behavioral Indications of Emotional State in the Anger Conditions

Condition	N	Neutral Units	Anger Units
Epi Inf	22	+0.07	−0.18
Epi Ign	23	+0.30	+2.28
Placebo	22[a]	−0.09	+0.79

Comparison for Anger Units	p
Epi Inf vs. Epi Ign	< .01
Epi Ign vs. Placebo	< .05
Placebo vs. Epi Inf	ns

[a]For one subject in this condition the sound system went dead and the observer could not, of course, code his reactions.

Finally, on this behavioral index, it can be seen that subjects in the Epi Ign condition are significantly angrier than subjects in the Placebo condition. Behaviorally, at least, the injection of epinephrine appears to have led subjects to an angrier state than comparable subjects who received placebo shots.

Conformation of Data to Theoretical Expectations

Now that the basic data of this study have been presented, let us examine closely the extent to which they conform to theoretical expectations. If our hypotheses are correct and if this experimental design provided a perfect test for these hypotheses, it should be anticipated that in the euphoria conditions the degree of experimentally produced euphoria should vary in the following fashion:

$$\text{Epi Mis} \geq \text{Epi Ign} > \text{Epi Inf} = \text{Placebo}$$

And in the anger conditions, anger should conform to the following pattern:

$$\text{Epi Ign} > \text{Epi Inf} = \text{Placebo}$$

In both sets of conditions, it is the case that emotional level in the Epi Mis and Epi Ign conditions is considerably greater than that achieved in the corresponding Epi Inf conditions. The results for the Placebo condition, however, are ambiguous for consistently the Placebo subjects fall between the Epi Ign and the Epi Inf subjects. This is a particularly troubling pattern for it makes it impossible to evaluate unequivocally the effects of the state of physiological arousal and indeed raises serious questions about our entire theoretical structure. Though the emotional level is consistently greater in the Epi Mis and Epi Ign conditions than in the Placebo condition, this difference is significant at acceptable probability levels only in the anger conditions.

In order to explore the problem further, let us examine the experimental factors identified earlier, which might have acted to restrain the emotional level in the Epi Ign and Epi Mis conditions. As was pointed out earlier, the ideal test of our first two hypotheses requires an experimental setup in which the subject has flatly no way of evaluating his state of physiological arousal other than by means of the experimentally provided cognitions. Had it been pos-

sible to physiologically produce a state of sympathetic activation by means other than injection, one could have approached this experimental ideal more closely than in the present setup. As it stands, however, there is always a reasonable alternative cognition available to the aroused subject—he feels the way he does because of the injection. To the extent that the subject seizes on such an explanation of his bodily state, we should expect that he will be uninfluenced by the stooge. Evidence presented in Table 6 for the anger condition and in Table 7 for the euphoria conditions indicates that this is, indeed, the case.

As mentioned earlier, some of the Epi Ign and Epi Mis subjects in their answers to the open-end questions clearly attributed their physical state to the injection, e.g., "the shot gave me the shivers." In Tables 6 and 7 such subjects are labeled "Self-informed." In Table 6 it can be seen that the self-informed subjects are considerably less angry than are the remaining subjects; indeed, they are not angry at all. With these self-informed subjects eliminated the difference between the Epi Ign and the Placebo conditions is significant at the .01 level of significance.

Precisely the same pattern is evident in Table 7 for the euphoria conditions. In both the Epi Mis and the Epi Ign conditions, the self-informed subjects have considerably lower activity indices than do the remaining subjects. Eliminating self-informed subjects, comparison of both of these conditions with the Placebo condition yields a difference significant at the .03 level of significance. It should be noted, too, that the self-informed subjects have much the same score on the activity index as do the experimental Epi Inf subjects (Table 3).

It would appear, then, that the experimental procedure of injecting the subjects, by providing an

TABLE 6 / The Effects of Attributing Bodily State to the Injection on Anger in the Anger Epi Ign Condition

Condition	N	Index	Anger p
Self-informed subjects	3	−1.67	*ns*
Others	20	+2.88	*ns*
Self-informed vs. Others			.05

TABLE 7 / The Effects of Attributing Bodily State to the Injection on Euphoria in the Euphoria Epi Ign and Epi Mis Conditions

Epi Ign			
	N	Activity Index	p
Self-informed subjects	8	11.63	ns
Others	17	21.14	ns
Self-informed vs. Others			.05

Epi Mis			
	N	Activity Index	p
Self-informed subjects	5	12.40	ns
Others	20	25.10	ns
Self-informed vs. Others			.10

alternative cognition, has, to some extent, obscured the effects of epinephrine. When account is taken of this artifact, the evidence is good that the state of physiological arousal is a necessary component of an emotional experience for when self-informed subjects are removed, epinephrine subjects give consistent indications of greater emotionality than do placebo subjects.

Let us examine next the fact that consistently the emotional level, both reported and behavioral, in Placebo conditions is greater than that in the Epi Inf conditions. Theoretically, of course, it should be expected that the two conditions will be equally low, for by assuming that emotional state is a joint function of a state of physiological arousal and of the appropriateness of a cognition we are, in effect, assuming a multiplicative function, so that if either component is at zero, emotional level is at zero. As noted earlier this expectation should hold if we can be sure that there is no sympathetic activation in the Placebo conditions. This assumption, of course, is completely unrealistic for the injection of placebo does not prevent sympathetic activation. The experimental situations were fairly dramatic and certainly some of the placebo sub-

jects gave indications of physiological arousal. If our general line of reasoning is correct, it should be anticipated that the emotional level of subjects who give indications of sympathetic activity will be greater than that of subjects who do not. The relevant evidence is presented in Tables 8 and 9.

As an index of sympathetic activation we shall use the most direct and unequivocal measure available— change in pulse rate. It can be seen in Table 1 that the predominant pattern in the Placebo condition is a decrease in pulse rate. We shall assume, therefore, that those subjects whose pulse increases or remains the same give indications of sympathetic activity while those subjects whose pulse decreases do not. In Table 8, for the euphoria condition, it is immediately clear that subjects who give indications of sympathetic activity are considerably more euphoric than are subjects who show no sympathetic activity. This relationship is, of course, confounded by the fact that euphoric subjects are considerably more active than non-euphoric subjects—a factor which independent of mood could elevate pulse rate. However, no such factor operates in the anger condition where angry subjects are neither more active nor talkative than calm subjects. It can be seen in Table 9 that Placebo subjects who show signs of sympathetic activation give indications of considerably more anger than do subjects who show no such signs. Conforming to expectation, sympathetic activation accompanies an increase in emotional level.

It should be noted, too, that the emotional levels of subjects showing no signs of sympathetic activity are quite comparable to the emotional level of subjects in the parallel Epi Inf conditions (see Tables 3

TABLE 8 / Sympathetic Activation and Euphoria in the Euphoria Placebo Condition

Subjects Whose:	N	Activity Index	p
Pulse decreased	14	10.67	ns
Pulse increased or remained same	12	23.17	ns
Pulse decrease vs. pulse increase or same			.02

TABLE 9 / Sympathetic Activation and Anger in Anger Placebo Condition

Subjects Whose:	N^a	Activity Index	p
Pulse decreased	13	+0.15	*ns*
Pulse increased or remained same	8	+1.69	*ns*
Pulse decrease vs. pulse increase or same			.01

[a]*N* reduced by two cases owing to failure of sound system in one case and experimenter's failure to take pulse in another.

and 5). The similarity of these sets of scores and their uniformly low level of indicated emotionality would certainly make it appear that both factors are essential to an emotional state. When either the level of sympathetic arousal is low or a completely appropriate cognition is available, the level of emotionality is low.

DISCUSSION

Let us summarize the major findings of this experiment and examine the extent to which they support the propositions offered in the introduction of this paper. It has been suggested, first, that given a state of physiological arousal for which an individual has no explanation, he will label this state in terms of the cognitions available to him. This implies, of course, that by manipulating the cognitions of an individual in such a state we can manipulate his feelings in diverse directions. Experimental results support this proposition for following the injection of epinephrine, those subjects who had no explanation for the bodily state thus produced, gave behavioral and self-report indications that they had been readily manipulable into the disparate feeling states of euphoria and anger.

From this first proposition, it must follow that given a state of physiological arousal for which the individual has a completely satisfactory explanation, he will not label this state in terms of the alternative cognitions available. Experimental evidence strongly supports this expectation. In those conditions in which subjects were injected with epinephrine and told precisely what they would feel and why,

they proved relatively immune to any effects of the manipulated cognitions. In the anger condition, such subjects did not report or show anger; in the euphoria condition, such subjects reported themselves as far less happy than subjects with an identical bodily state but no adequate knowledge of why they felt they way they did.

Finally, it has been suggested that given constant cognitive circumstances, an individual will react emotionally only to the extent that he experiences a state of physiological arousal. Without taking account of experimental artifacts, the evidence in support of this proposition is consistent but tentative. When the effects of "self-informing" tendencies in epinephrine subjects and of "self-arousing" tendencies in placebo subjects are partialed out, the evidence strongly supports the proposition.

The pattern of data, then, falls neatly in line with theoretical expectations. However, the fact that we were forced, to some extent, to rely on internal analyses in order to partial out the effects of experimental artifacts inevitably makes our conclusions somewhat tentative. In order to further test these propositions on the interaction of cognitive and physiological determinants of emotional state, a series of additional experiments, published elsewhere, was designed to rule out or overcome the operation of these artifacts. In the first of these, Schachter and Wheeler (1962) extended the range of manipulated sympathetic activation by employing three experimental groups—epinephrine, placebo, and a group injected with the sympatholytic agent, chlorpromazine. Laughter at a slapstick movie was the dependent variable and the evidence is good that amusement is a direct function of manipulated sympathetic activation.

In order to make the epinephrine-placebo comparison under conditions which would rule out the operation of any self-informing tendency, two experiments were conducted on rats. In one of these Singer (1961) demonstrated that under fear inducing conditions, manipulated by the simultaneous presentation of a loud bell, a buzzer, and a bright flashing light, rats injected with epinephrine were considerably more frightened than rats injected with a placebo. Epinephrine-injected rats defecated, urinated, and trembled more than did placebo-injected rats. In nonfear control conditions, there were no differences between epinephrine and placebo groups, neither group giving any indication of fear. In another study, Latané and Schachter (1962) demonstrated that rats injected with epinephrine were notably more capable of avoidance learning than were rats injected with a placebo. Using a modified Miller-Mowrer shuttle-box, these investigators found that during an experimental period involving 200 massed trials, 15 rats injected with epinephrine avoided shock an average of 101.2 trials while 15 placebo-injected rats averaged only 37.3 avoidances.

Taken together, this body of studies does give strong support to the propositions which generated these experimental tests. Given a state of sympathetic activation, for which no immediately appropriate explanation is available, human subjects can be readily manipulated into states of euphoria, anger, and amusement. Varying the intensity of sympathetic activation serves to vary the intensity of a variety of emotional states in both rats and human subjects.

Let us examine the implications of these findings and of this line of thought for problems in the general area of the physiology of the emotions. We have noted in the introduction that the numerous studies on physiological differentiators of emotional states have, viewed en masse, yielded quite inconclusive results. Most, though not all, of these studies have indicated no differences among the various emotional states. Since as human beings, rather than as scientists, we have no difficulty identifying, labeling, and distinguishing among our feelings, the results of these studies have long seemed rather puzzling and paradoxical. Perhaps because of this, there has been a persistent tendency to discount such results as due to ignorance or methodological inadequacy and to pay far more attention to the very few studies which demonstrate *some* sort of physiological differences among emotional states than to the very many studies which indicate no differences at all. It is conceivable, however, that these results should be taken at face value and that emotional states may, indeed, be generally characterized by a high level of sympathetic activation with few if any physiological distinguishers among the many emotional states. If this is correct, the findings of the present study may help to resolve the problem. Obviously this study does *not* rule out the possibility of physiological differences among the emotional states. It is the case, however, that given precisely the same state of epinephrine-induced sympathetic acti-

vation, we have, by means of cognitive manipulations, been able to produce in our subjects the very disparate states of euphoria and anger. It may indeed be the case that cognitive factors are major determiners of the emotional labels we apply to a common state of sympathetic arousal.

Let us ask next whether our results are specific to the state of sympathetic activation or if they are generalizable to other states of physiological arousal. It is clear that from our experiments proper, it is impossible to answer the question for our studies have been concerned largely with the effects of an epinephrine created state of sympathetic arousal. We would suggest, however, that our conclusions are generalizable to almost any pronounced internal state for which no appropriate explanation is available. This suggestion receives some support from the experiences of Nowlis and Nowlis (1956) in their program of research on the effects of drugs on mood. In their work the Nowlises typically administer a drug to groups of four subjects who are physically in one another's presence and free to interact. The Nowlises describe some of their results with these groups as follows:

> *At first we used the same drug for all 4 men. In those sessions seconal, when compared with placebo, increased the checking of such words as expansive, forceful, courageous, daring, elated, and impulsive. In our first statistical analysis we were confronted with the stubborn fact that when the same drug is given to all 4 men in a group, the N that has to be entered into the analysis is 1, not 4. This increases the cost of an already expensive experiment by a considerable factor, but it cannot be denied that the effects of these drugs may be and often are quite contagious. Our first attempted solution was to run tests on groups in which each man had a different drug during the same session, such as 1 on seconal, 1 on benzedrine, 1 on dramamine, and 1 on placebo. What does seconal do? Cooped up with, say, the egotistical benzedrine partner, the withdrawn, indifferent dramamine partner, and the slightly bored lactose man, the seconal subject reports that he is distractible, dizzy, drifting, glum, defiant, languid, sluggish, discouraged, dull, gloomy, lazy, and slow! This is not the report of mood that we got when all 4 men were on seconal. It thus appears that the moods of the partners do definitely influence the effect of seconal. (p. 350)*

It is not completely clear from this description whether this "contagion" of mood is more marked in drug than in placebo groups, but should this be the case, these results would certainly support the suggestion that our findings are generalizable to internal states other than that produced by an injection of epinephrine.

Finally, let us consider the implications of our formulation and data for alternative conceptualizations of emotion. Perhaps the most popular current conception of emotion is in terms of "activation theory" in the sense employed by Lindsley (1951) and Woodworth and Schlosberg (1958). As we understand this theory, it suggests that emotional states should be considered as at one end of a continuum of activation which is defined in terms of degree of autonomic arousal and of electroencephalographic measures of activation. The results of the experiment described in this paper do, of course, suggest that such a formulation is not completely adequate. It is possible to have very high degrees of activation without a subject either appearing to be or describing himself as "emotional." Cognitive factors appear to be indispensable elements in any formulation of emotion.

SUMMARY

It is suggested that emotional states may be considered a function of a state of physiological arousal and of a cognition appropriate to this state of arousal. From this follows these propositions:

1. Given a state of physiological arousal for which an individual has no immediate explanation, he will label this state and describe his feelings in terms of the cognitions available to him. To the extent that cognitive factors are potent determiners of emotional states, it should be anticipated that precisely the same state of physiological arousal could be labeled "joy" or "fury" or "jealousy" or any of a great diversity of emotional labels depending on the cognitive aspects of the situation.

2. Given a state of physiological arousal for which an individual has a completely appropriate explanation, no evaluative needs will arise and the individual is unlikely to label his feelings in terms of the alternative cognitions available.

3. Given the same cognitive circumstances, the individual will react emotionally or describe his feelings as emotions only to the extent that he experiences a state of physiological arousal.

An experiment is described which, together with the results of other studies, supports these propositions.

REFERENCES

Ax, A. F. Physiological differentiation of emotional states. *Psychosom. Med.,* 1953, *15,* 435–442.

Cannon, W. B. *Bodily changes in pain, hunger, fear and rage.* (2nd ed.) New York: Appleton, 1929.

Cantril, H., & Hunt, W. A. Emotional effects produced by the injection of adrenalin. *Amer. J. Psychol.,* 1932, *44,* 300–307.

Festinger, L. A theory of social comparison processes. *Hum. Relat.,* 1954, *7,* 114–140.

Hunt, J. McV., Cole, M. W., & Reis, E. E. Situational cues distinguishing anger, fear, and sorrow. *Amer. J. Psychol.,* 1958, *71,* 136–151.

James, W. *The principles of psychology.* New York: Holt, 1890.

Landis, C., & Hunt, W. A. Adrenalin and emotion. *Psychol. Rev.,* 1932, *39,* 467–485.

Latané, B., & Schachter, S. Adrenalin and avoidance learning. *J. Comp. Physiol. Psychol.,* 1962, *65,* 369–372.

Lindsley, D. B. Emotion. In S. S. Stevens (Ed.), *Handbook of experimental psychology.* New York: Wiley, 1951. Pp. 473–516.

Marañon, G. Contribution à l'étude de l'action émotive de l'adrénaline. *Rev. Francaise Endocrinol.,* 1924, *2,* 301–325.

Nowlis, V., & Nowlis, H. H. The description and analysis of mood. *Ann. N. Y. Acad. Sci.,* 1956, *65,* 345–355.

Ruckmick, C. A. *The psychology of feeling and emotion.* New York: McGraw-Hill, 1936.

Schachter, J. Pain, fear, and anger in hypertensives and normotensives: A psychophysiologic study. *Psychosom. Med.,* 1957, *19,* 17–29.

Schachter, S. *The psychology of affiliation.* Stanford, CA: Stanford Univer. Press, 1959.

Schachter, S., & Wheeler, L. Epinephrine, chlorpromazine, and amusement. *J. Abnorm. Soc. Psychol.,* 1962, *65,* 121–128.

Singer, J. E. The effects of epinephrine, chlorpromazine and dibenzyline upon the fright responses of rats under stress and non-stress conditions. Unpublished doctoral dissertation, University of Minnesota, 1961.

Wolf, S., & Wolff, H. G. *Human gastric function.* New York: Oxford Univer. Press, 1947.

Woodworth, R. S., & Schlosberg, H. *Experimental psychology.* New York: Holt, 1958.

Wrightsman, L. S. Effects of waiting with others on changes in level of felt anxiety. *J. Abnorm. Soc. Psychol.,* 1960, *61,* 216–222.

ENDNOTES

1. This experiment is part of a program of research on cognitive and physiological determinants of emotional state which is being conducted at the Department of Social Psychology at Columbia University under PHS Research Grant M-2584 from the National Institute of Mental Health, United States Public Health Service. This experiment was conducted at the Laboratory for Research in Social Relations at the University of Minnesota.

   The authors wish to thank Jean Carlin and Ruth Hase, the physicians in the study, and Bibb Latané and Leonard Weller who were the paid participants.

2. Though our experiments are concerned exclusively with the physiological changes produced by the injection of adrenalin, which appear to be primarily the result of sympathetic excitation, the term physiological arousal is used in preference to the more specific "excitation of the sympathetic nervous system" because there are indications, to be discussed later, that this formulation is applicable to a variety of bodily states.

3. Translated copies of Marañon's (1924) paper may be obtained by writing to the senior author.

4. This suggestion is not new for several psychologists have suggested that situational factors should be considered the chief differentiators of the emotions. Hunt, Cole, and Reis (1958) probably make this point most explicitly in their study distinguishing among fear, anger, and sorrow in terms of situational characteristics.

5. In his critique of the James-Lange theory of emotion, Cannon (1929) also makes the point that sympathectomized animals and patients do seem to manifest emotional behavior. This criticism is, of course, as applicable to the above proposition as it was to the James-Lange formulation. We shall discuss the issues involved in later papers.

6. It was, of course, imperative that the sequence with the stooge begin before the subject felt his first symptoms for otherwise the subject would be virtually forced to interpret his feelings in terms of events preceding the stooge's entrance. Pretests had indicated that, for most subjects, epinephrine-caused symptoms began within 3–5 minutes after injection. A deliberate attempt was made then to bring in the stooge within 1 minute after the subject's injection.

CRITICAL THINKING QUESTIONS

1. In order to conduct the experiment, the researchers deceived the subjects. What ethical issues are involved in this type of research? The obvious deception was not telling the subjects the true nature of the experiment. Does the use of injections of a drug that had a physiological impact on the subjects prompt additional ethical considerations? Explain your answer.

2. This study examines the effects of just one drug, epinephrine, which has excitatory effects on people. Would you expect a similar pattern of results for other classes of drugs? Why or why not? Which ones might be interesting to study?

3. What might the implications of this study be for people who use drugs in a social setting? Would the feelings that they associate with using drugs be due to how others around them responded? Explain your answer. How could you test this possibility?

4. Do you think it is possible to change the emotion you are experiencing by changing the label of the emotion? For example, if you were afraid of public speaking, could you change your emotion from a negative one (fear) to a positive one (excitement) by changing the label given to your physiological arousal? Have you had any personal experience with something like this that may have occurred or a situation when you were aware of how other people influenced how you interpreted the situation? Explain your answer.

ADDITIONAL RELATED READINGS

Lazarus, R. S. (1984). On the primacy of cognition. *American Psychologist, 39,* 124–129.

Zajonc, R. B. (1984). On the primacy of affect. *American Psychologist, 39,* 117–123.

ARTICLE 9 _____

"But everyone is doing it!" Most parents of adolescents have heard this argument as to why they should let their children do something they don't think the children should do. But is everyone else really doing "it," whatever that may be? As it turns out, the most important factor that may influence our behavior is not whether others are really doing it but whether we *believe* they are doing it.

How we go about making sense of the complex social world around us is the domain of social cognition. In making decisions, we tend to use a combination of both rational and less-than-rational (though not necessarily irrational) methods. For example, in trying to make a decision about a very important topic, we may use a very rational and fairly logical approach. Making two columns and listing the pros and cons of a certain decision would be an example of doing this. However, this type of approach takes time and effort. In most situations, we are willing to invest neither the time nor the effort to make decisions in such a manner. Instead, we rely on a variety of mental shortcuts, called *heuristics,* to help in decision making. For instance, if you believe there is a lot of drinking at your school, you may tend to remember more easily situations that confirm your belief rather than situations that do not. This *confirmation bias,* in turn, both confirms our initial beliefs (even if they aren't actually correct) and makes them even stronger.

In deciding how to act and how to live our lives, we rely on our own internal understanding of the world around us. If you are like most people, however, you probably also are somewhat influenced by what we *believe* others are thinking or doing. Based on prior beliefs or a few initial experiences, we may develop a certain notion as to what others are thinking or doing. This notion, in turn, may lead us to notice only the events that confirm our beliefs (the confirmation bias). However, it also may be the case that our beliefs about what others are thinking or doing may not actually be correct. Yet if we think that our beliefs about others are true, we may be tempted to act according to those beliefs, whether or not they are in fact true. In other words, we will do it because (we think) everyone else is doing it.

Pluralistic ignorance is the concept that describes having a false belief as to what is normative. That is, we think that everyone else endorses a given idea or behavior when that may not really be the case. The following article by Tracy A. Lambert, Arnold S. Kahn, and Kevin J. Apple examines pluralistic ignorance as it relates to the sexual behavior of college students and discusses how holding false beliefs may impact students' actual sexual behavior.

Pluralistic Ignorance and Hooking Up

■ Tracy A. Lambert, Arnold S. Kahn, and Kevin J. Apple

ABSTRACT

"Hooking up"—when two people agree to engage in sexual behavior for which there is no future commitment—has become popular on college campuses. In this study we examined the extent to which pluralistic ignorance affects hooking up. One hundred thirty-six female and 128 male college students answered questions regarding

Reprinted from *Journal of Sex Research,* 2003, *40,* 129–133. Copyright © 2003 Society for the Scientific Study of Sex. Reprinted with permission.

their own comfort and their perceived peers' comfort in engaging in a variety of sexual behaviors while hooking up. We hypothesized and found that both women and men rated their peers as being more comfortable engaging in these behaviors than they rated themselves. Men expressed more comfort than did women in engaging in these behaviors, and both sexes overestimated the other gender comfort with hooking up behaviors. Pluralistic ignorance appears to apply to hooking up on college campuses, and we explore some potential consequences of pluralistic ignorance in this context.

Although one-night stands and uncommitted sexual behaviors are not a recent phenomenon, past research has focused on personality traits, attitudes, and individual differences in willingness to engage in such behaviors (e.g., Gerrard, 1980; Gerrard & Gibbons, 1982; Simpson & Gangestad, 1991; Snyder, Simpson, & Gangestad, 1986). The tacit assumption in this past research was that sexual behaviors within a committed and loving relationship were unproblematic, but that unloving, uncommitted sexual relations had to be explained. However, today on college campuses across the United States what was once viewed as problematic has now become normative, and students refer to this process as "hooking up."

Hooking up occurs when two people who are casual acquaintances or who have just met that evening at a bar or party agree to engage in some forms of sexual behavior for which there will likely be no future commitment (Boswell & Spade, 1996; Kahn et al., 2000; Paul, McManus, & Hayes, 2000). The couple typically does not communicate what sexual behaviors they will or will not engage in, and frequently both parties have been drinking alcohol (Kahn et al., 2000; Paul et al., 2000). Paul et al. (2000) found that 78% of women and men on the campus being studied had engaged in hooking up at least once. In the Kahn et al. (2000) sample of college students, 86% of the women and 88% of the men indicated they had hooked up. Almost one half (47%) of the men and one third of the women in the Paul et al. sample engaged in sexual intercourse during the hookup, and Kahn et al. found that their sample believed petting below the waist, oral sex, and sexual intercourse occurred with some regularity in the process of hooking up.

Pluralistic ignorance, a concept first coined by Floyd Allport (1924, 1933), exists when, within a group of individuals, each person believes his or her private attitudes, beliefs, or judgments are discrepant from the norm displayed by the public behavior of others. Therefore, each group member, wishing to be seen as a desirable member of the group, publicly conforms to the norm, each believing he or she is the only one in the group experiencing conflict between his or her private attitude and his or her public behavior. Group members believe that most others in their group, especially those who are popular and opinion leaders (Katz & Lazarsfeld, 1955), actually endorse the norm and want to behave that way, while they themselves privately feel they are going along with the norm because of a desire to fit in with the group and exemplify the norm (Prentice & Miller, 1993, 1996). In this study we examined the extent to which pluralistic ignorance might be related to U.S. college students' comfort levels with sexual behaviors involved in hooking up. Consistent with the premise of pluralistic ignorance, we hypothesized that college students would perceive others as having a greater comfort level engaging in a variety of sexual behaviors than they themselves would have.

Prentice and Miller (1993) demonstrated pluralistic ignorance among college students in the area of alcohol consumption. On a campus where heavy alcohol use was the perceived norm, Prentice and Miller found that students estimated both the average student and their friends to have less discomfort with the level of alcohol consumption on campus than they reported for themselves. Furthermore, for male but not female students, they found greater consistency between respondents' comfort levels with alcohol consumption and the perceived norm and between respondents' reported drinking levels and the perceived norm at the end of the semester than at the beginning of the semester. Although correlational in nature, these results suggest that over time, male students may have changed their attitudes and behaviors to bring them more in line with the perceived norm. Perkins and Berkowitz (1986) reported similar findings with regard to the discrepancy between college students' own comfort with the amount of drinking at the university and what they estimated to be the general campus attitude.

Although pluralistic ignorance was originally conceptualized as a discrepancy between public behavior and private beliefs (Miller & McFarland, 1987), others have used the concept to refer to situations in which there is not direct evidence of behavioral similarity (e.g., Fields & Schuman, 1976; O'Gorman & Garry, 1976). More recently, Cohen and Shotland (1996) invoked the concept of pluralistic ignorance in a variety of dating situations for which public scrutiny was absent. They found that both men and women believed that the average other person of their sex had more liberal sexual expectations than they set for themselves, both sexes believing the average other person of their sex would expect sexual intercourse much sooner in a relationship than they themselves would expect it. When asked whether a same-sex peer would expect to have sexual intercourse with a person with whom they were emotionally involved but for whom they felt no physical attraction, both men and women believed the average man and woman would expect sexual intercourse, while only approximately 50% of the participants would expect sex themselves in such a relationship, and an even smaller percentage reported having had sex in such a relationship. Finally, when there was neither emotional nor physical attraction to a partner, few women or men expected that they would have sexual intercourse with the partner, but believed the average man and woman would indeed expect sexual intercourse.

Pluralistic ignorance might have consequences when beliefs about the norm condone intimate sexual behaviors. In the process of hooking up, pluralistic ignorance may lead one or both sexual partners to act according to the perceived norm rather than to their own convictions. There is a large literature showing that men have more liberal attitudes towards sexual behaviors and expect sexual intercourse sooner in a relationship than do women (Cohen & Shotland, 1996; Knox & Wilson, 1981; Oliver & Hyde, 1993) and that men are much more receptive than are women to offers of sexual intercourse (Clark & Hatfield, 1989). Byers and Lewis (1988) found that disagreements among dating partners on the desired level of sexual behavior was almost always in the direction of the male partner wanting a higher level of sexual intimacy than that desired by the female partner. Thus, it is possible that many men go into

hooking-up situations hoping to engage in more intimate sexual behaviors than are desired by their female partners. Because men are expected to initiate sexual activity (DeLamater, 1987; Peplau & Gordon, 1985), it is possible that in the process of hooking up, some women will experience unwanted sexual advances and possibly even sexual assault or rape.

In their research on hooking up, Kahn et al. (2000) asked 92 female and 50 male college students if they had ever had a "really terrible hooking up experience." Nearly one half of the women (42%) and the men (46%) indicated they had had such an experience. A "terrible experience" for the men was usually due to the women wanting a relationship or to the use of too much alcohol or drugs; none mentioned pressure to go further than they desired. However, nearly one half of the women (48.3%) who reported having a terrible hooking-up experience indicated that they were pressured to go further than they had wanted to go. They gave responses such as "I hooked up with a guy who didn't understand the meaning of 'no'" and "I didn't want to—he did—he wouldn't back off." These women may have experienced sexual assault during a hook up but did not label their experiences as such because they believed the behaviors to be normative. In addition, 10.3% of the women and 11.1% of the men in this sample said the hook up was terrible because they had gone too far without mentioning pressure from partner. Going too far might have been the consequence of pluralistic ignorance, conforming to a presumed norm.

The present study sought to extend the findings of Cohen and Shotland (1996), which were restricted to expectations of sexual intercourse in dating situations, to the area of hooking up. Further, we wanted to examine whether pluralistic ignorance occurred with other sexual behaviors besides sexual intercourse. Based on the research on pluralistic ignorance and gender differences in expected sexual behaviors, we hypothesized that both male and female students would see other students as more comfortable with various hooking-up behaviors than they were themselves. Although we expected individuals would vary in their own comfort levels with various hooking-up behaviors, we expected they would believe other students to be uniformly more comfortable engaging in those behaviors than they were themselves.

Furthermore, consistent with previous literature, we hypothesized that men would be significantly more comfortable than women with engaging in all hooking-up behaviors. Finally, we hypothesized that due to pluralistic ignorance, both women and men would overestimate the other gender's comfort with all hooking-up behaviors.

METHOD

Participants

One hundred seventy-five female and 152 male undergraduate students from a midsized residential southeastern public university that has few nontraditional students served as participants for the study. The convenience sample represented a moderately even distribution of year in school: for first years, $n = 79$ (41 females, 38 males); for sophomores, $n = 70$ (37 females, 33 males); for juniors, $n = 84$ (45 females, 39 males); and for seniors, $n = 93$ (52 females, 41 males). A female experimenter approached students as they entered the university library and asked them to volunteer to answer some questions about hooking up and sexual behaviors as part of her senior honors project. She approached other students in their residence halls. No differences appeared between these two samples for any of the dependent measures. Analyses concerning pluralistic ignorance and comfort with hooking up are based on the data from 136 women (77.7%) and 128 men (84.2%) who indicated that they had hooked up.

Materials and Procedure

The questionnaire consisted of questions developed by the authors to examine student attitudes toward hooking up. On the first page, students read that the investigator was interested in "students' attitudes and behaviors with regard to dating and 'hooking up'," and hooking up was defined as "a sexual encounter between two people who may or may not know each other well, but who usually are not seriously dating." Participants also signed an informed consent form, which indicated all information would be anonymous and confidential. To insure anonymity and encourage honest responding, the only demographic informa-

tion obtained was the participant's year in school. We made no attempt to determine sexual orientation or marital status; however, on this residential campus the overwhelming majority of students come to the university directly from high school, identify themselves as heterosexual, and have never been married (James Madison University Office of Institutional Research, 2001–2002). Participants were told they were not required to complete the survey if they became uncomfortable.

Students who said they had hooked up were instructed to continue to the next page. We constructed 11-point scales modeled after those used by Prentice and Miller (1993) on which 3 points were labeled: 1 = very uncomfortable, 6 = neutral, and 11 = very comfortable. Participants responded to the question "How comfortable are you with the amount of hooking up that goes on at [school name]?" They then responded to the question "How comfortable are you with engaging in the following activities during a hook up?" with regard to "petting above the waist," "petting below the waist," "oral sex," and "sexual intercourse." Participants used the same scales in response to the questions "How comfortable do you think the average female student is with the amount of hooking up that goes on at [school name]" and "How comfortable do you think the average female student is with engaging in the following activities during a hook up?" Finally, they responded to the questions "How comfortable do you think the average male student is with the amount of hooking up that goes on at [school name]?" and "How comfortable do you think the average male student is with engaging in the following activities during a hook up?"

Students who indicated that they had never hooked up were asked to skip to a different page of the survey, which contained questions regarding why they did not hook up and whether or not they believed that there was a relationship between hooking up and sexual assault. This part of the questionnaire was included so that all participants would work on the survey for approximately the same amount of time without knowing who had or had not hooked up.

Participants completed the questionnaire privately, usually within a short distance of the researcher. Those participating at the library placed their completed questionnaires in a large box, and those participating in their residence hall placed completed question-naires in a large envelope. When they were finished, participants were encouraged to ask questions and discuss the questionnaire with the researcher, who provided them with a debriefing statement and a list of campus resources for sexual assault.

RESULTS

We tested the hypothesis that students would experi-ence pluralistic ignorance regarding hooking up with a 2 (Gender) × 2 (Target: self or other) ANOVA, with target as a within-subjects variable. As hypothesized, participants demonstrated pluralistic ignorance by evaluating their own comfort level with the amount of hooking up, $M = 7.08$, $SD = 2.31$, significantly lower than their estimate of a same-sex peer's com-fort level, $M = 7.75$, $SD = 2.08$, $F(1, 262) = 24.24$, $p < .0001$, partial $[[eta].sup.2] = .085$. Participants believed that other college students were more com-fortable with the amount of hooking up than were they. This main effect of target was qualified by a significant gender by target: interaction, $F(1,262) = 7.55$, partial $[[eta].sup.2] = .028$, $p < .01$. Both men and women showed the same pattern of overestimat-ing their peers' comfort levels; however, the pattern was more pronounced among the male students ($[9.01.sub.peer]$ vs. $[7.95.sub.self]$), $t(127) = 4.68$, $p < .0001$, $d = .502$, than among the female students ($[6.57.sub.peer]$ vs. $[6.26.sub.self]$), $t(135) = 1.85$, $p < .05$, one-tailed, $d = .185$. Table 1 presents these means and standard deviations.

A dependent t test for equality of variances revealed that participants showed significantly less variabil-ity in their ratings of peer comfort level in hooking up than in their self-ratings, $t(262) = 1.96$, $p < .05$, one-tailed. When rating their own comfort levels, the standard deviation in participants' responses was 2.31. However, the standard deviation significantly decreased to 2.08 when participants estimated their peers' comfort with hooking up. This decrease in variability when estimating others' comfort provides some evidence for an illusion of universality. That is, participants showed greater uniformity in their beliefs about others' comfort levels compared to their own actual comfort level.

We used multivariate analysis of variance (MANOVA) to examine the hypothesis regarding men's and women's own comfort levels with vari-ous sexual behaviors, with participant gender as the between-subjects variable. Men reported signifi-cantly greater comfort with these behaviors than did women, $F(4, 259) = 35.17$, $p < .0001$, par-tial $[[eta].sup.2] = .352$. Table 2 shows that men's greater comfort occurred with all four hooking-up behaviors.

We tested the hypothesis that both men and women would overestimate the other gender's comfort with hooking-up behaviors using two separate MANO-VAS. The first examined the men's estimates of the average woman's comfort, and the second examined the women's estimates of the average man's comfort. To evaluate the accuracy of these estimates, the com-fort estimates were compared with the means of the actual comfort ratings of these hooking-up behaviors. Both the men, $F(4, 259) = 7.82$, $p < .0001$, partial 112 = .108, and the women, $F(4, 259) = 16.25$, $p < .0001$, partial 112 = .201, significantly overestimated the other gender's actual comfort levels with various hooking-up behaviors. As shown in Table 3, this over-

TABLE 1 / Ratings of Own and Average Same-Sex Student's Comfort with Hooking Up

Measure	Self M (SD)	Average Student M (SD)
Women	6.26 (1.79)	6.57 (1.63)
Men	7.95 (2.48)	9.01 (1.74)

Note: Ratings were made on 11-point scales (1 = *not at all comfortable* and 11 = *very comfortable*).

TABLE 2 / Ratings of Men and Women's Own Comfort with Hooking-Up Behaviors

	Men M (SD)	Women M (SD)
Petting above the waist	9.12 (2.47)	7.29 (2.68)
Petting below the waist	8.42 (2.60)	5.13 (2.73)
Oral sex	7.56 (3.05)	3.49 (2.63)
Sexual intercourse	5.65 (3.57)	2.15 (2.31)

TABLE 3 / Differences Between Each Gender's Own Comfort Level with Hooking-Up Behaviors and Estimates of the Other Gender's Comfort Levels

	Women's Estimate of Men M (SD)	Men's Actual Comfort Level M (SD)	Men's Estimate of Women M (SD)	Women's Actual Comfort Level M (SD)
Petting above the waist	9.80 (1.45)	9.12 (2.47)	7.73 (1.92)	7.29 (2.68)
Petting below the waist	9.30 (1.67)	8.42 (2.60)	6.38 (2.07)	5.13 (2.73)
Oral sex	8.61 (1.93)	7.56 (3.04)	5.49 (2.19)	3.49 (2.62)
Sexual intercourse	7.62 (2.24)	5.65 (3.57)	4.28 (2.36)	2.15 (2.31)

estimation occurred for both sexes on each of the four hooking-up behaviors.

DISCUSSION

Cohen and Shotland (1996) found evidence of pluralistic ignorance regarding expectations of sexual intercourse on a date. The current research extended these findings to other sexual behaviors, and did so in the context of hooking up. We found that both women and men reported less comfort with their perceived norm of hooking up than they believed was experienced by their same-sex peers, with men showing a greater difference between self- and peer-ratings than women. In addition, both men and women believed members of the other gender experienced greater comfort with hooking-up behaviors than members of the other gender actually reported. Men were less comfortable with engaging in hooking-up behaviors than women believed them to be, and women were less comfortable with engaging in hooking-up behaviors than men believed them to be. These findings appear to be due to pluralistic ignorance: Hooking up has become the norm for heterosexual sexual relationships on this campus, and since the great majority of students do in fact hook up, it appears that most students believe that others are comfortable—more comfortable than they are themselves—with engaging in a variety of uncommitted sexual behaviors. It is likely that most students believe others engage in these hooking-up behaviors primarily because they enjoy doing so, while they see themselves engaging in these behaviors primarily due to peer pressure.

Consistent with other pluralistic ignorance research (e.g., Prentice & Miller, 1993), this study showed evidence of an illusion of universality. The students failed to appreciate the extent to which others have different comfort levels with hooking-up behaviors. That is, students wrongly assumed that the attitudes of others about hooking up were more homogenous than they actually were.

Similar to other researchers (Cohen & Shotland, 1996; Knox & Wilson, 1981; Oliver & Hyde, 1993), we found that men expressed greater comfort than did women with sexually intimate hooking-up behaviors. In the context of hooking up, this could lead to serious consequences. Our study suggests that men believe women are more comfortable engaging in these behaviors than in fact they are, and also that women believe other women are more comfortable engaging in these behaviors than they are themselves. As a consequence, some men may pressure women to engage in intimate sexual behaviors, and some women may engage in these behaviors or resist only weakly because they believe they are unique in feeling discomfort about engaging in them. In this context it is possible for a woman to experience sexual assault but not interpret the behavior as such, believing it to be normative behavior with which her peers are comfortable.

"Most of Us" is a campaign implemented on many college campuses in an attempt to reveal pluralistic ignorance about alcohol consumption among college students (DeJong & Langford, 2002; Haines, 1998). The campaign is based on providing students with statistical evidence about actual student attitudes and behaviors regarding alcohol consumption. The goal of the campaign is to show that pluralistic ignorance exists regarding college students' heavy alcohol consumption, and that most students prefer to drink less than what is commonly perceived to be the norm. Considering the results of this study, we propose that a similar campaign highlighting students' beliefs about and comfort levels with sexual behaviors while hooking up might help reduce pluralistic ignorance about hooking up.

REFERENCES

Allport, E. H. (1924). *Social psychology.* Boston: Houghton Mifflin.

Allport, F. H. (1933). *Institutional behavior.* Chapel Hill: University of North Carolina Press.

Boswell, A., & Spade, J. (1996). Fraternities and collegiate rape culture. *Gender and Society, 10,* 133–147.

Byers, S., & Lewis, K. (1988). Dating couples' disagreements over the desired level of sexual intimacy. *The Journal of Sex Research, 24,* 15–29.

Clark, R. D., & Hatfield, E. (1989). Gender differences in receptivity to sexual offers. *Journal of Psychology and Human Sexuality, 2,* 39–55.

Cohen, L. L., & Shotland, R. L. (1996). Timing of first sexual intercourse in a relationship: Expectation, experiences, and perceptions of others. *The Journal of Sex Research, 33,* 291–299.

DeLamater, J. (1987). *Gender differences in sexual scenarios.* In K. Kelley (Ed.), Females, males, and sexuality (pp. 127–139). Albany, NY: SUNY Press.

DeJong, W., & Langford, L. A. (2002). Typology for campus-based alcohol prevention: Moving toward environmental management strategies. *Journal of Studies on Alcohol Supplement, 14,* 140–147.

Fields, J. M., & Schuman, H. (1976). Public beliefs and the beliefs of the public. *Public Opinion Quarterly, 40,* 427–448.

Gerrard, M. (1980). Sex guilt and attitudes towards sex in sexually active and inactive female college students. *Journal of Personality Assessment, 44,* 258–261.

Gerrard, M., & Gibbons, F. X. (1982). Sexual experience, sex guilt, and sexual moral reasoning. *Journal of Personality, 50,* 345–359.

Haines, M. (1998). Social norms: A wellness model for health promotion in higher education. *Wellness Management, 14*(4), 1–8.

James Madison University Office of Institutional Research (2001–2002). Retrieved February 22, 2003, from http://www.jmu.edu/instresrch/statsum/2001_02/2001-02toc.htm

Kahn, A. S., Fricker, K., Hoffman, J., Lambert, T., Tripp, M., Childress, K., et al. (2000, August). Hooking up: Dangerous new dating methods? In A. S. Kahn (Chair), *Sex, unwanted sex, and sexual assault on college campuses.* Symposium conducted at the annual Meeting of the American Psychological Association, Washington, DC.

Katz, E., & Lazarsfeld, P. E. (1955). *Personal influence: The part played by people in the flow of mass communication.* Glencoe, IL: Free Press.

Knox, D., & Wilson, K. (1981). Dating behaviors of university students. *Family Relations, 30,* 255–258.

Miller, T. D., & McFarland, C. (1987). Pluralistic ignorance: When similarity is interpreted as dissimilarity. *Journal of Personality and Social Psychology, 53,* 298–305.

O'Gorman, H. J., & Garry, S. L. (1976). Pluralistic ignorance: A replication and extension. *Public Opinion Quarterly, 40,* 449–458.

Oliver, M. B., & Hyde, J. S., (1993). Gender differences in sexuality: A meta-analysis. *Psychological Bulletin, 114,* 129–151.

Paul, E. L., McManus, B., & Hayes, A. (2000). "Hookups": Characteristics and correlates of college students' spontaneous and anonymous sexual experiences. *The Journal of Sex Research, 37,* 76–88.

Peplau, L. A., & Gordon, S. L. (1985). Women and men in love: Gender differences in close heterosexual relationships. In V. E. O'Leary, R. K. Unger, & B. S. Wallston (Eds.), *Women, gender, and social psychology* (pp. 257–292). Hillsdale, NJ: Lawrence Erlbaum Associates.

Perkins, H. W., & Berkowitz, A. D. (1986). Perceiving the community norms of alcohol use among students: Some research implications for campus alcohol education programming. *International Journal of the Addictions, 21,* 961–976.

Prentice, D. A., & Miller, D. T. (1993). Pluralistic ignorance and alcohol use on campus: Some consequences of misperceiving the social norm. *Journal of Personality and Social Psychology, 64,* 243–256.

Prentice, D. A., & Miller, D. T. (1996). Pluralistic ignorance and the perpetuation of social norms by unwitting actors. In M. P. Zanna (Ed.), *Advances in experimental social psychology* (Vol. 28, pp. 161–209). San Diego, CA: Academic Press.

Simpson, J. A., & Gangestad, S. W. (1991). Individual differences socio-sexuality: Evidence for convergent and discriminant validity. *Journal of Personality and Social Psychology, 60,* 870–883.

Snyder, M., Simpson, J. A., & Gangestad, S. (1986). Personality and sexual relations. *Journal of Personality and Social Psychology, 51,* 181–190.

This paper is based on an honors thesis by the first author under the direction of the second author. We wish to thank Steven Wise for his statistical assistance.

CRITICAL THINKING QUESTIONS

1. The authors of the article mention how a "Most of Us" campaign has been implemented on some college campuses to reduce drinking by exposing the pluralistic ignorance students may have about how much their peers really drink. Do you think such a campaign would be useful for pluralistic ignorance pertaining to "hooking up"? Why or why not? If there were such a campaign, what information should be included in it?

2. Besides that related to alcohol consumption and sexual behaviors, what other types of pluralistic ignorance may be operating among college students? Explain.

3. Upon reflection, can you think of times you have used a confirmation bias (mentioned in the introduction to this article) while ignoring examples of situations that did not confirm your beliefs? Explain.

4. How might the media be playing a role in promoting pluralistic ignorance? Think of examples of stories that may contribute to the sense that "everyone is doing it." Discuss the implications of the media's role.

5. Can the effects of pluralistic ignorance on people's private beliefs and behaviors somehow be minimized? For example, suppose you were a parent and didn't want your child to be unduly influenced by the misperceived norms of what others actually were doing. What would you do? Explain your answer.

CHAPTER INTEGRATION QUESTIONS

1. What do you see as a common theme or themes across all of the articles in this chapter?

2. Mark Twain said, "My life has been filled with terrible misfortunes—most of which never happened. Life does not consist mainly—or even largely—of facts and happenings. It consists mainly of the storm of thoughts that is forever blowing through one's head." What does this quotation mean to you? Do you agree or disagree with it? Defend your answer.

3. Relate the quotation from Twain to the overall theme or themes that you identified for this chapter in Question 1.

Chapter Four

ATTITUDES

THE STUDY OF attitudes is considered by many social psychologists to be the core issue in understanding human behavior. How we act in any given situation is the product of the attitudes that we have formed, which in turn are based on the experiences we have had.

Whether or not we believe that attitudes constitute the core of social psychology, the study of attitudes and attitude change has been prominent in social psychological research from the beginning. Part of this interest has been theoretically driven. How attitudes are formed and how they can be changed, as well as what factors make some attitudes so resistant to change, are but a few of the topics that theorists have studied. However, there is also a more pragmatic, applied reason for this interest in attitudes: Principles of attitude change and attitude measurement have a direct bearing on several major industries and even psychotherapy. For example, survey organizations and advertising agencies focus on attitudes, measuring what they are, how they change over time, as well as how best to change them. Likewise, a major goal of both therapy and health promotion might be viewed as modifying people's dysfunctional or health-endangering attitudes and behaviors. Theoretical research often has provided the foundation for the principles applied by clinicians, health professionals, and advertisers.

The readings in this chapter relate to various aspects of attitudes. Article 10, " Don't Even Think about It!" examines the issue of taboos as being a prime example of deeply held attitudes. How are taboos formed? Why are they maintained? How are they changed?

Article 11, "Cognitive Consequences of Forced Compliance," is a classic demonstration of a powerful theoretical model in social psychology known as *cognitive dissonance*. It is an excellent example of how common-sense predictions often are exactly opposite of what actually occurs.

Finally, Article 12, "Self-Esteem, Trivialization, and Attitude Change," is a contemporary article that elaborates on the concept of cognitive dissonance presented in Article 11. Article 12 provides insight into the direction dissonance research has gone since it was first presented over 50 years ago and how such a concept is continually tested and refined over time.

ARTICLE 10

Obviously, attitudes are formed in a great variety of ways. Some are the result of direct experience. For instance, we meet someone from a certain country and, based on that limited experience, form an attitude (or stereotype) about people from that country. In other words, we generalize our experience to form an attitude. In many other cases, however, we do not experience the person, situation, or event directly but rather indirectly. These so-called *secondhand attitudes* are the result of information we received from someone else, such as our parents or friends. In fact, this kind of information is a major source of our beliefs.

The number of attitudes that people hold can be virtually limitless; however, some attitudes are held more strongly than others. The strength of these attitudes often can be seen most clearly by their absence. That is, what topics do we never discuss? What would we never admit, or what would we never do? In other words, what are our *taboos?* A taboo involves the three elements that comprise all attitudes: First, there is a *cognitive* or *belief* component, which is what we believe is or should be true. Additionally, there is an *affective* or *emotional* component to the taboo. We not only believe something to be true, we also feel very strongly about it. Just the idea of the taboo being violated may fill us with disgust. Finally, the taboo involves a *behavior tendency;* we strongly tend to avoid doing things that violate our taboo belief and affective components.

Many taboos are shared among people in a culture, while others are unique to individuals. Thus, most people in a given society tend to believe that it is acceptable to eat certain foods while other foods are off limits. Sometimes, taboos are more unique, such as beliefs that certain topics should never be mentioned to certain people. In all cases, taboos serve to set limits (sometimes, severe limits) on what we believe, feel, and do.

The following article by Michael Ventura examines the topic of taboos, including their origins and the impact that they have on our daily lives. After reading the article, you may agree with the author that we are not really as free as we would like to believe, despite the fact that freedom is a central concept in American culture.

Don't Even Think about It!

■ Michael Ventura

Taboos come in all sizes. Big taboos: when I was a kid in the Italian neighborhoods of Brooklyn, to insult someone's mother meant a brutal fight—the kind of fight no one interferes with until one of the combatants goes down and stays down. Little taboos: until the sixties, it was an insult to use someone's first name without asking or being offered permission. Personal taboos: Cyrano de Bergerac would not tolerate the mention of his enormous nose. Taboos peculiar to one city: in Brooklyn (again), when the Dodgers were still at Ebbets Field, if you rooted for the Yankees you kept it to yourself unless you wanted a brawl. Taboos, big or small, are always about having to respect somebody's (often irrational) boundary—or else.

There are taboos shared within one family: my father did not feel free to speak to us of his grandmother's suicide until his father died. Taboos within intellectual elites: try putting a serious metaphysical or spiritual slant on a "think-piece" (as we call them in the trade) written for the *New York Times,* the *Washington Post,* or most big name magazines—it won't be printed. Taboos in the corporate and legal worlds: if you're male, you had best wear suits of somber colors, or you're not likely to be taken seriously; if you're female, you have to strike a very uneasy balance between the attractive and the prim, and even then you might not be taken seriously. Cultural taboos: in the Jim Crow days in the South, a black man who spoke with familiarity to a white woman might be beaten, driven out of town, or (as was not uncommon) lynched.

Unclassifiable taboos: in Afghanistan, as I write this, it is a sin—punishable by beatings and imprisonment—to fly a kite. Sexual taboos: there are few communities on this planet where two men can walk down a street holding hands without being harassed or even arrested; in Afghanistan (a great place for taboos these days) the Taliban would stone them to death. Gender taboos: how many American corporations (or institutions of any kind) promote women to power? National taboos: until the seventies, a divorced person could not run for major public office in America (it wasn't until 1981 that our first and only divorced president, Ronald Reagan, took office); today, no professed atheist would dare try for the presidency. And most readers of this article probably approve, as I do, of this comparatively recent taboo: even the most rabid bigot must avoid saying "nigger," "spic," or "kike" during, say, a job interview—and the most macho sexist must avoid words like "broad."

Notice that nearly all of our taboos, big and small, public and intimate, involve silence—keeping one's silence, or paying a price for not keeping it. Yet keeping silent has its own price: for then silence begins to fill the heart, until silence becomes the heart—a heart swelling with restraint until it bursts in frustration, anger, even madness.

The taboos hardest on the soul are those which fester in our intimacies—taboos known only to the people involved, taboos that can make us feel alone even with those to whom we're closest. One of the deep pains of marriage—one that also plagues brothers and sisters, parents and children, even close friends—is that as we grow more intimate, certain silences often become more necessary. We discover taboo areas, both in ourselves and in the other, that cannot be transgressed without paying an awful price. If we speak of

them, we may endanger the relationship; but if we do not speak, if we do not violate the taboo, the relationship may become static and tense, until the silence takes on a life of its own. Such silences are corrosive. They eat at the innards of intimacy until, often, the silence itself causes the very rupture or break-up that we've tried to avoid by keeping silent.

THE CANNIBAL IN US ALL

You may measure how many taboos constrict you, how many taboos you've surrendered to—at home, at parties, at work, with your lover or your family—by how much of yourself you must suppress. You may measure your life, in these realms, by what you cannot say, do, admit—cannot and must not, and for no better reason than that your actions or words would disrupt your established order. By this measure, most of us are living within as complex and strictured a system of taboos as the aborigines who gave us the word in the first place. You can see how fitting it is that the word "taboo" comes from a part of the world where cannibalism is said to be practiced to this day: the islands off eastern Australia—Polynesia, New Zealand, Melanesia. Until 1777, when Captain James Cook published an account of his first world voyage, Europe and colonial America had many taboos but no word that precisely meant taboo. Cook introduced this useful word to the West. Its instant popularity, quick assimilation into most European languages, and constant usage since, are testimony to how much of our lives the word describes. Before the word came to us, we'd ostracized, coerced, exiled, tormented, and murdered each other for myriad infractions (as we still do), but we never had a satisfying, precise word for our reasons.

We needed cannibals to give us a word to describe our behavior, so how "civilized" are we, really? We do things differently from those cannibals, on the surface, but is the nature of what we do all that different? We don't cook each other for ceremonial dinners, at least not physically (though therapists can testify that our ceremonial seasons, like Christmas and Thanksgiving, draw lots of business—something's cooking). But we stockpile weapons that can cook the entire world, and we organize our national priorities around their "necessity," and it's a national political taboo to seriously cut spending for those planet-cookers. If that's "progress," it's lost on me. In China it's taboo to be a Christian, in Israel it's taboo to be a Moslem, in Syria it's taboo to be a Jew, in much of the United States it's still taboo to be an atheist, while in American academia it's taboo to be deeply religious. Our headlines are full of this stuff. So it's hardly surprising that a cannibal's word still describes much of our behavior.

I'm not denying the necessity of every society to set limits and invent taboos (some rational, some not) simply in order to get on with the day—and to try to contain the constant, crazy, never-to-be-escaped longings that blossom in our sleep and distract or compel us while awake. Such longings are why even a comparatively tiny desert tribe like the ancient Hebrews needed commandments and laws against coveting each other's wives, stealing, killing, committing incest. That tribe hadn't seen violent, sexy movies, hadn't listened to rock 'n' roll, hadn't been bombarded with ads featuring half-naked models, and hadn't watched too much TV. They didn't need to. Like us, they had their hearts, desires, and dreams to instruct them how to be very, very naughty. The taboo underlying all others is that we must not live by the dictates of our irrational hearts—as though we haven't forgiven each other, or ourselves, for having hearts.

If there's a taboo against something, it's usually because a considerable number of people desire to do it. The very taboos that we employ to protect us from each other and ourselves, are a map of our secret natures. When you know a culture's taboos (or an individual's, or a family's) you know its secrets—you know what it really wants.

FAVORITE TABOOS

It's hard to keep a human being from his or her desire, taboo or not. We've always been very clever, very resourceful, when it comes to sneaking around our taboos. The Aztecs killed virgins and called it religion. The Europeans enslaved blacks and called it economics. Americans tease each other sexually and call it fashion.

If we can't kill and screw and steal and betray to our heart's desire, and, in general, violate every taboo in sight—well, we can at least watch other people do it. Or read about it. Or listen to it. As we have done, since ancient times, through every form of religion and entertainment. The appeal of taboos and our inability to escape our longing for transgression (whether or not we ourselves transgress) are why so many people who call themselves honest and law-abiding spend so much time with movies, operas, soaps, garish trials, novels, songs, Biblical tales, tribal myths, folk stories, and Shakespeare—virtually all of which, both the great and the trivial, are about those who dare to violate taboos. It's a little unsettling when you think about it: the very stuff we say we most object to is the fundamental material of what we call culture.

That's one reason that fundamentalists of all religions are so hostile to the arts. But fundamentalists partake of taboos in the sneakiest fashion of all. Senator Jesse Helms led the fight against the National Endowment for the Arts because he couldn't get the (vastly overrated) homosexual art of Robert Mapplethorpe or the most extreme performance artists out of his mind—he didn't and doesn't want to. He, like all fundamentalists, will vigorously oppose such art and all it stands for until he dies, because his very opposition gives him permission to concentrate on taboo acts. The Taliban of Afghanistan will ride around in jeeps toting guns, searching out any woman who dares show an inch of facial skin or wear white socks (Taliban boys consider white socks provocative), and when they find such a woman they'll jail and beat her—because their so-called righteousness gives them permission to obsess on their taboos. Pat Robertson and his ilk will fuss and rage about any moral "deviation," any taboo violation they can find, because that's the only way they can give themselves permission to entertain the taboos. They get to not have their taboo cake, yet eat it too.

We are all guilty of this to some extent. Why else have outlaws from Antigone to Robin Hood to Jesse James to John Gotti become folk heroes? Oedipus killed his father and slept with his mother, and we've been performing that play for 2500 years because he is the ultimate violator of our deepest taboos. Aristotle said we watch such plays for "catharsis," to purge our desires and fears in a moment of revelation. Baloney. Ideas like "catharsis" are an intellectual game, to glossy-up our sins. What's closer to the truth is that we need Oedipus to stand in for us. We can't have changed much in 2500 years, if we still keep him alive in our hearts to enact our darkest taboos for us. Clearly, the very survival of Oedipus as an instantly recognizable name tells us that we still want to kill our fathers and screw our mothers (or vice versa).

A COUNTRY OF BROKEN TABOOS

Taboos are a special paradox for Americans. However much we may long for tradition and order, our longings are subverted by the inescapable fact that our country was founded upon a break with tradition and a challenge to order—which is to say, the United States was founded upon the violation of taboos. Specifically, this country was founded upon the violation of Europe's most suffocating taboo: its feudal suppression (still enforced in 1776, when America declared its independence) of the voices of the common people. We were the first nation on earth to write into law that any human being has the right to say anything, and that even the government is (theoretically) not allowed to silence you.

At the time, Europe was a continent of state-enforced religions, where royalty's word was law and all other words could be crushed by law. (Again: taboo was a matter of enforced silence.) We were the first nation to postulate verbal freedom for everyone. All our other freedoms depend upon verbal freedom; no matter how badly and how often we've failed that ideal, it still remains our ideal.

Once we broke Europe's verbal taboos, it was only a matter of time before other traditional taboos fell too. As the writer Albert Murray has put it, Americans could not afford piety in their new homeland: "You can't be over respectful of established forms; you're trying to get through the wilderness of Kentucky." Thus, from the moment the Pilgrims landed, our famous puritanism faced an inherent contradiction. How could we domesticate the wilderness of this continent; how could peasants and rejects and "commoners" form a strong and viable nation; how could we develop all the new social forms and technologies necessary to blend all the disparate peoples who came here—without violating those same Puritan taboos which are so ingrained, to this day, in our national character?

It can't be over-emphasized that America's fundamental stance against both the taboos of Europe and the taboos of our own Puritans, was our insistence upon freedom of speech. America led the attack against silence. And it is through that freedom, the freedom to break the silence, that we've destroyed so many other taboos. Especially during the last 40 years, we've broken the silence that surrounded ancient taboos of enormous significance. Incest, child abuse, wife-battering, homosexuality, and some (by no means all) forms of racial and gender oppression, are not merely spoken of, and spoken against, they're shouted about from the rooftops. Many breathe easier because of this inevitable result of free speech. In certain sections of our large cities, for the first time in modern history, gay people can live openly and without fear. The feminist movement has made previously forbidden or hidden behaviors both speakable and doable. The National Organization of Women can rail against the Promise Keepers all they want (and they have some good reasons), but when you get a million working-class guys crying and hugging in public, the stoic mask of the American male has definitely cracked. And I'm old enough to remember when it was shocking for women to speak about wanting a career. Now virtually all affluent young women are expected to want a career.

Fifty years ago, not one important world or national leader was black. Now there are more people of color in positions of influence than ever. Bad marriages can be dissolved without social stigma. Children born out of wedlock are not damned as "bastards" for something that wasn't their fault. And those of us who've experienced incest and abuse have finally found a voice, and through our voices we've achieved a certain amount of liberation from shame and pain.

These boons are rooted in our decidedly un-Puritan freedom of speech. But we left those Puritans behind a long time ago—for the breaking of silence is the fundamental political basis of our nation, and no taboo is safe when people have the right to speak.

KEEPER OF YOUR SILENCE

In the process, though, we've lost the sanctity of silence. We've lost the sense of dark but sacred power inherent in sex, in nature, even in crime. Perhaps that is the price of our new freedoms.

It's also true that by breaking the silence we've thrown ourselves into a state of confusion. The old taboos formed part of society's structure. Without them, that structure has undeniably weakened. We are faced with shoring up the weakened parts, inventing new ways of being together that have pattern and order—for we cannot live without some pattern and order—but aren't so restrictive. Without sexual taboos, for instance, what are the social boundaries between men and women? When are they breached? What is offensive? Nobody's sure. Everybody's making mistakes. This is so excruciating that many are

In Search of the Last Taboo

There is no "last taboo," according to Michael Ventura. But there certainly are a lot of contenders, scattered like clues in a treasure hunt for the heart of our culture. Here, an assortment of last taboos "discovered" by the media in the past few years.

"What a great story: **Incest**. The last taboo!"—*Esquire,* on Kathryn Harrison's memoir *The Kiss*

"'The very word is a room-emptier,' Tina Brown wrote in her editor's note when, in 1991, Gail Sheehy broke the silence with a story in *Vanity* Fair. . . . **Menopause** may be the last taboo."
—*Fort Lauderdale Sun-Sentinel*

"The last taboo for women is not, as Gail Sheehy would have it, menopause, but **facial hair.**"
—*New York Times*

"At a time when this is the last taboo, Moreton depicts **erections**."—*Sunday Telegraph,* describing sculptor Nicholas Moreton's work

"Virtually no representations of **faith** are seen on television, it's the last taboo."—*Columbus Dispatch*

"Anything with **sex with underage kids** is the last taboo."—*Toronto Star*

"The last taboo: an openly **homosexual** actor playing a **heterosexual** lead."—*Boston Globe*

"With sexual mores gone the way of Madonna, **picking up the tab** has become the last taboo for women."—*Philadelphia Inquirer*

"Most Americans, if they think about **class** at all (it may be our last taboo subject), would surely describe themselves as middle class regardless of a petty detail like income."—*Los Angeles Times Syndicate*

"The Last Taboo Is **Age**: Why Are We Afraid of It?"—headline in the *Philadelphia Inquirer*

"Smash the last taboo! [Timothy] Leary says he's planning the first . . . **interactive suicide.**"
—*Washington Post*

"**Money** is the last taboo."—*Calgary Herald*

"**Menstruation** may be the last taboo."—*Manchester Guardian Weekly*

"The real last taboo is that of **privacy and dignity.**"—*Montreal Gazette*

"And then there's **bisexuality,** the last taboo among lesbians."—*Los Angeles Times*

"I think **personal smells** are one of the last taboos."—*The Observer*

"Television's last taboo, long after f-words and pumping bottoms became commonplace, was the **full-frontal vomit**. Now, even that last shred of inhibition has gone, and every drama . . . [has] a character heaving his guts all over the camera."—*The (London) Mail*

"**Tanning**. The last taboo. If you're tan, then your IQ must be lower than the SPF of the sunscreen you'd be using if you had any brains."—*Los Angeles Times*

nostalgic for some of the old taboos. But once a taboo is broken, then for good or ill it's very hard, perhaps impossible, to reinstate it.

But there is another, subtler confusion: yes, enormous taboos have fallen, but many taboos, equally important, remain. And, both as individuals and as a society, we're strained enough, confused enough, by the results of doing away with so many taboos in so short a time, that maybe we're not terribly eager for our remaining taboos to fall. We may sincerely desire that, but maybe we're tired, fed up, scared. Many people would rather our taboos remain intact for a couple of generations while we get our act together again, and perhaps they have a point. But the price of taboo remains what it's always been: silence and constriction.

What do we see, when we pass each other on the street, but many faces molded by the price paid for keeping the silences of the taboos that remain—spirits confined within their own, and their society's, silences? Even this brief essay on our public and intimate strictures is enough to demonstrate that we are still a primitive race, bounded by fear and prejudice, with taboos looming in every direction—no matter how much we like to brag and/or bitch that modern life is liberating us from all the old boundaries. The word taboo still says much more about us than most prefer to admit.

What is the keeper of your silence? The answer to that question is your own guide to your personal taboos. How must you confine yourself in order to get through your day at the job, or to be acceptable in your social circle? The answer to that is your map of your society's taboos. What makes you most afraid to speak? What desire, what word, what possibility, freezes and fevers you at the same time, making any sincere communication out of the question? What makes you vanish into your secret? That's your taboo, baby. You're still in the room, maybe even still smiling, still talking, but not really—what's really happened is that you've vanished down some hole in yourself, and you'll stay there until you're sure the threat to your taboo is gone and it's safe to come out again. If, that is, you've ever come out in the first place. Some never have.

What utterance, what hint, what insinuation, can quiet a room of family or friends? What makes people change the subject? What makes those at a dinner party dismiss a remark as though it wasn't said, or dismiss a person as though he or she wasn't really there? We've all seen conversations suddenly go dead, and just as suddenly divert around a particular person or subject, leaving them behind in the dead space, because something has been said or implied that skirts a silently shared taboo. If that happens to you often, don't kid yourself that you're living in a "free" society. Because you're only as free as your freedom from taboos—not on some grand abstract level, but in your day-to-day life.

It is probably inherent in the human condition that there are no "last" taboos. Or perhaps it just feels that way because we have such a long way to go. But at least we can know where to look: right in front of our eyes, in the recesses of our speechlessness, in the depths of our silences. And there is nothing for it but to confront the keepers of our silence. Either that, or to submit to being lost, as most of us silently are, without admitting it to each other or to ourselves—lost in a maze of taboos.

CRITICAL THINKING QUESTIONS

1. What do you believe are the five strongest and most universally held taboos in your culture? What would be the sanctions for someone who violated these taboos? Why do these taboos remain so strong, and what function may each serve? Explain your answers.

2. Discuss two beliefs or behaviors that have been considered taboo in your lifetime but are not any longer. When and why did each of these taboos disappear? Is there any particular reason each disappeared when it did rather than, say, 50 years before? Explain your answers.

3. Name two current taboos that you do not believe will be considered taboos 20 years from now. What will it take to eliminate each of these taboos? In your opinion, what are the effects of eliminating taboos? Discuss the positive versus negative effects.

4. Do you hold any personal taboos (as opposed to cultural taboos)? For example, are there certain topics that you cannot discuss or things that you cannot do with certain people yet can with others? Discuss what you believe are the origins, functions, and impacts of these personal taboos on you and on the people affected by them.

ARTICLE 11 _____

Suppose someone asked you to publicly say something that contradicted your privately held beliefs and then offered you either a small reward (say, $1) or a large reward ($20) for doing so. Under which of those conditions would you be most likely to actually change your privately held belief to bring it more into the realm of what you just said? If you guessed that would be most likely to happen in the $20 condition, you would have guessed wrong.

A major theory in social psychology is known as *cognitive dissonance.* Briefly stated, this theory says that people feel a tension when they are aware of an inconsistency either between two attitudes or between an attitude and a behavior. Moreover, the theory asserts that such tension produces some type of change to reduce the state of dissonance. The resulting outcome often is counterintuitive to what common sense would predict. The exact conditions under which cognitive dissonance operates and how it is reduced have been investigated in many experiments over the years.

The following article by Leon Festinger and James M. Carlsmith is *the* classic study on dissonance theory. The hypothesis being tested is a simple yet powerful and non-obvious one. Aside from the outcomes, of particular interest is the elaborate design of the experiment. While reading the article, put yourself in the shoes of the subjects and try to imagine how their thinking might account for the obtained results.

Cognitive Consequences of Forced Compliance

■ Leon Festinger and James M. Carlsmith

What happens to a person's private opinion if he is forced to do or say something contrary to that opinion? Only recently has there been any experimental work related to this question. Two studies reported by Janis and King (1954; 1956) clearly showed that, at least under some conditions, the private opinion changes so as to bring it into closer correspondence with the overt behavior the person was forced to perform. Specifically, they showed that if a person is forced to improvise a speech supporting a point of view with which he disagrees, his private opinion moves toward the position advocated in the speech. The observed opinion change is greater than for persons who only hear the speech or for persons who read a prepared speech with emphasis solely on elocution and manner of delivery. The authors of these two studies explain their results mainly in terms of mental rehearsal and thinking up new arguments. In this way, they propose, the person who is forced to improvise a speech convinces himself. They present some evidence, which is not altogether conclusive, in support of this explanation. We will have more to say concerning this explanation in discussing the results of our experiment.

Kelman (1953) tried to pursue the matter further. He reasoned that if the person is induced to make an overt statement contrary to his private opinion by the offer of some reward, then the greater the reward offered, the greater should be the subsequent opinion change. His data, however, did not support this idea. He found, rather, that a large reward produced less subsequent opinion change than did a smaller reward. Actually, this finding by Kelman is consistent with the theory we will outline below but, for a number of reasons, is not conclusive. One of the major weaknesses of the data is that not all subjects in the experiment made an overt statement contrary to their private opinion in order to obtain the offered

Reprinted from *Journal of Abnormal and Social Psychology,* 1959, *58,* 203–210.

reward. What is more, as one might expect, the percentage of subjects who complied increased as the size of the offered reward increased. Thus, with self-selection of who did and who did not make the required overt statement and with varying percentages of subjects in the different conditions who did make the required statement, no interpretation of the data can be unequivocal.

Recently, Festinger (1957) proposed a theory concerning cognitive dissonance from which come a number of derivations about opinion change following forced compliance. Since these derivations are stated in detail by Festinger (1957, Ch. 4), we will here give only a brief outline of the reasoning.

Let us consider a person who privately holds opinion "X" but has, as a result of pressure brought to bear on him, publicly stated that he believes "not X."

1. This person has two cognitions which, psychologically, do not fit together: one of these is the knowledge that he believes "X," the other the knowledge that he has publicly stated that he believes "not X." If no factors other than his private opinion are considered, it would follow, at least in our culture, that if he believes "X" he would publicly state "X." Hence, his cognition of his private belief is dissonant with his cognition concerning his actual public statement.

2. Similarly, the knowledge that he has said "not X" is consonant with (does fit together with) those cognitive elements corresponding to the reasons, pressures, promises of rewards and/or threats of punishment which induced him to say "not X."

3. In evaluating the total magnitude of dissonance, one must take account of both dissonances and consonances. Let us think of the sum of all the dissonances involving some particular cognition as "D" and the sum of all the consonances as "C." Then we might think of the total magnitude of dissonance as being a function of "D" divided by "D" plus "C."

Let us then see what can be said about the total magnitude of dissonance in a person created by the knowledge that he said "not X" and really believes "X." With everything else held constant, this total magnitude of dissonance would decrease as the number and importance of the pressures which induced him to say "not X" increased. Thus, if the overt behavior was

brought about by, say, offers of reward or threats of punishment, the magnitude of dissonance is maximal if these promised rewards or threatened punishments were just barely sufficient to induce the person to say "not X." From this point on, as the promised rewards or threatened punishment become larger, the magnitude of dissonance becomes smaller.

4. One way in which the dissonance can be reduced is for the person to change his private opinion so as to bring it into correspondence with what he has said. One would consequently expect to observe such opinion change after a person has been forced or induced to say something contrary to his private opinion. Furthermore, since the pressure to reduce dissonance will be a function of the magnitude of the dissonance, the observed opinion change should be greatest when the pressure used to elicit the overt behavior is just sufficient to do it.

The present experiment was designed to test this derivation under controlled, laboratory conditions. In the experiment we varied the amount of reward used to force persons to make a statement contrary to their private views. The prediction [from 3 and 4 above] is that the larger the reward given to the subject, the smaller will be the subsequent opinion change.

PROCEDURE

Seventy-one male students in the introductory psychology course at Stanford University were used in the experiment. In this course, students are required to spend a certain number of hours as subjects (Ss) in experiments. They choose among the available experiments by signing their names on a sheet posted on the bulletin board which states the nature of the experiment. The present experiment was listed as a two-hour experiment dealing with "Measures of Performance."

During the first week of the course, when the requirement of serving in experiments was announced and explained to the students, the instructor also told them about a study that the psychology department was conducting. He explained that, since they were required to serve in experiments, the department was conducting a study to evaluate these experiments in order to be able to improve them in the future. They were told that a sample of students would be interviewed after having served as *S*s. They were urged to cooperate in these interviews by being completely frank and honest. The importance of this announcement will become clear shortly. It enabled us to measure the opinions of our *S*s in a context not directly connected with our experiment and in which we could reasonably expect frank and honest expressions of opinion.

When the *S* arrived for the experiment on "Measures of Performance" he had to wait for a few minutes in the secretary's office. The experimenter (*E*) then came in, introduced himself to the *S* and, together, they walked into the laboratory room where the *E* said:

> This experiment usually takes a little over an hour but, of course, we had to schedule it for two hours. Since we have that extra time, the introductory psychology people asked if they could interview some of our subjects. *[Offhand and conversationally.] Did they announce that in class? I gather that they're interviewing some people who have been in experiments. I don't know much about it. Anyhow, they may want to interview you when you're through here.*

With no further introduction or explanation the *S* was shown the first task, which involved putting 12 spools onto a tray, emptying the tray, refilling it with spools, and so on. He was told to use one hand and to work at his own speed. He did this for one-half hour. The *E* then removed the tray and spools and placed in front of the *S* a board containing 48 square pegs. His task was to turn each peg a quarter turn clockwise, then another quarter turn, and so on. He was told again to use one hand and to work at his own speed. The *S* worked at this task for another half hour.

While the *S* was working on these tasks, the *E* sat, with a stop watch in his hand, busily making notations on a sheet of paper. He did so in order to make it convincing that this was what the *E* was interested in and that these tasks, and how the *S* worked on them, was the total experiment. From our point of view the experiment had hardly started. The hour which the *S* spent working on the repetitive, monotonous tasks was intended to provide, for each *S* uniformly, an experience about which he would have a somewhat negative opinion.

After the half hour on the second task was over, the *E* conspicuously set the stop watch back to zero,

put it away, pushed his chair back, lit a cigarette, and said:

> O.K. Well, that's all we have in the experiment itself. I'd like to explain what this has been all about so you'll have some idea of why you were doing this. *[E pauses.]* Well, the way the experiment is set up is this. There are actually two groups in the experiment. In one, the group you were in, we bring the subject in and give him essentially no introduction to the experiment. That is, all we tell him is what he needs to know in order to do the tasks, and he has no idea of what the experiment is all about, or what it's going to be like, or anything like that. But in the other group, we have a student that we've hired that works for us regularly, and what I do is take him into the next room where the subject is waiting—the same room you were waiting in before—and I introduce him as if he had just finished being a subject in the experiment. That is, I say: "This is so-and-so, who's just finished the experiment and I've asked him to tell you a little of what it's about before you start." The fellow who works for us then, in conversation with the next subject, makes these points: *[The E then produced a sheet headed "For Group B" which had written on it: It was very enjoyable, I had a lot of fun, I enjoyed myself, it was very interesting, it was intriguing, it was exciting. The E showed this to the S and then proceeded with his false explanation of the purpose of the experiment.]* Now, of course, we have this student do this, because if the experimenter does it, it doesn't look as realistic, and what we're interested in doing is comparing how these two groups do on the experiment—the one with this previous expectation about the experiment, and the other, like yourself, with essentially none.

Up to this point the procedure was identical for *S*s in all conditions. From this point on they diverged somewhat. Three conditions were run, Control, One Dollar, and Twenty Dollars, as follows:

Control Condition

The *E* continued:

> Is that fairly clear? *[Pause.]* Look, that fellow *[looks at watch]* I was telling you about from the introductory

psychology class said he would get here a couple of minutes from now. Would you mind waiting to see if he wants to talk to you? Fine. Why don't we go into the other room to wait? [The E left the S in the secretary's office for four minutes. He then returned and said:] O.K. Let's check and see if he does want to talk to you.

One and Twenty Dollar Conditions

The E continued:

Is that fairly clear how it is set up and what we're trying to do? [Pause.] Now, I also have a sort of strange thing to ask you. The thing is this. [Long pause, some confusion and uncertainty in the following, with a degree of embarrassment on the part of the E. The manner of the E contrasted strongly with the preceding unhesitant and assured false explanation of the experiment. The point was to make it seem to the S that this was the first time the E had done this and that he felt unsure of himself.] The fellow who normally does this for us couldn't do it today—he just phoned in, and something or other came up for him—so we've been looking around for someone that we could hire to do it for us. You see, we've got another subject waiting [looks at watch] who is supposed to be in that other condition. Now Professor _____, who is in charge of this experiment, suggested that perhaps we could take a chance on your doing it for us. I'll tell you what we had in mind: the thing is, if you could do it for us now, then of course you would know how to do it, and if something like this should ever come up again, that is, the regular fellow couldn't make it, and we had a subject scheduled, it would be very reassuring to us to know that we had somebody else we could call on who knew how to do it. So, if you would be willing to do this for us, we'd like to hire you to do it now and then be on call in the future, if something like this should ever happen again. We can pay you a dollar (twenty dollars) for doing this for us, that is, for doing it now and then being on call. Do you think you could do that for us?

If the S hesitated, the E said things like, "It will only take a few minutes," "The regular person is pretty reliable; this is the first time he has missed,"

or "If we needed you we could phone you a day or two in advance; if you couldn't make it, of course, we wouldn't expect you to come." After the S agreed to do it, the E gave him the previously mentioned sheet of paper headed "For Group B" and asked him to read it through again. The E then paid the S one dollar (twenty dollars), made out a hand-written receipt form, and asked the S to sign it. He then said:

O.K., the way we'll do it is this. As I said, the next subject should be here by now. I think the next one is a girl. I'll take you into the next room and introduce you to her, saying that you've just finished the experiment and that we've asked you to tell her a little about it. And what we want you to do is just sit down and get into a conversation with her and try to get across the points on that sheet of paper. I'll leave you alone and come back after a couple of minutes. O.K.?

The E then took the S into the secretary's office where he had previously waited and where the next S was waiting. (The secretary had left the office.) He introduced the girl and the S to one another saying that the S had just finished the experiment and would tell her something about it. He then left saying he would return in a couple of minutes. The girl, an undergraduate hired for this role, said little until the S made some positive remarks about the experiment and then said that she was surprised because a friend of hers had taken the experiment the week before and had told her that it was boring and that she ought to try to get out of it. Most Ss responded by saying something like "Oh, no, it's really very interesting. I'm sure you'll enjoy it." The girl listened quietly after this, accepting and agreeing to everything the S told her. The discussion between the S and the girl was recorded on a hidden tape recorder.

After two minutes the E returned, asked the girl to go into the experimental room, thanked the S for talking to the girl, wrote down his phone number to continue the fiction that we might call on him again in the future and then said: "Look, could we check and see if that fellow from introductory psychology wants to talk to you?"

From this point on, the procedure for all three conditions was once more identical. As the E and the S started to walk to the office where the interviewer was, the *E* said: "Thanks very much for working on those tasks for us. I hope you did enjoy it. Most of our subjects tell us afterward that they found it quite interesting. You get a chance to see how you react to the tasks and so forth." This short persuasive communication was made in all conditions in exactly the same way. The reason for doing it, theoretically, was to make it easier for anyone who wanted to persuade himself that the tasks had been, indeed, enjoyable.

When they arrived at the interviewer's office, the *E* asked the interviewer whether or not he wanted to talk to the *S*. The interviewer said yes, the *E* shook hands with the *S*, said good-bye, and left. The interviewer, of course, was always kept in complete ignorance of which condition the *S* was in. The interview consisted of four questions, on each of which the *S* was first encouraged to talk about the matter and was then asked to rate his opinion or reaction on an 11-point scale. The questions are as follows:

1. Were the tasks interesting and enjoyable? In what way? In what way were they not? Would you rate how you feel about them on a scale from −5 to +5 where −5 means they were extremely dull and boring, +5 means they were extremely interesting and enjoyable, and zero means they were neutral, neither interesting nor uninteresting.

2. Did the experiment give you an opportunity to learn about your own ability to perform these tasks? In what way? In what way not? Would you rate how you feel about this on a scale from 0 to 10 where 0 means you learned nothing and 10 means you learned a great deal.

3. From what you know about the experiment and the tasks involved in it, would you say the experiment was measuring anything important? That is, do you think the results may have scientific value? In what way? In what way not? Would you rate your opinion on this matter on a scale from 0 to 10 where 0 means the results have no scientific value or importance and 10 means they have a great deal of value and importance.

4. Would you have any desire to participate in another similar experiment? Why? Why not? Would you rate your desire to participate in a similar experiment again on a scale from −5 to +5, where −5 means you would definitely dislike to participate, +5 means

you would definitely like to participate, and 0 means you have no particular feeling about it one way or the other.

As may be seen, the questions varied in how directly relevant they were to what the *S* had told the girl. This point will be discussed further in connection with the results.

At the close of the interview the *S* was asked what he thought the experiment was about and, following this, was asked directly whether or not he was suspicious of anything and, if so, what he was suspicious of. When the interview was over, the interviewer brought the *S* back to the experimental room where the *E* was waiting together with the girl who had posed as the waiting *S*. (In the control condition, of course, the girl was not there.) The true purpose of the experiment was then explained to the *S* in detail, and the reasons for each of the various steps in the experiment were explained carefully in relation to the true purpose. All experimental *S*s in both One Dollar and Twenty Dollar conditions were asked, after this explanation, to return the money they had been given. All *S*s, without exception, were quite willing to return the money.

The data from 11 of the 71 *S*s in the experiment had to be discarded for the following reasons:

1. Five *S*s (three in the One Dollar and two in the Twenty Dollar condition) indicated in the interview that they were suspicious about having been paid to tell the girl the experiment was fun and suspected that that was the real purpose of the experiment.

2. Two *S*s (both in the One Dollar condition) told the girl that they had been hired, that the experiment was really boring but they were supposed to say it was fun.

3. Three *S*s (one in the One Dollar and two in the Twenty Dollar condition) refused to take the money and refused to be hired.

4. One *S* (in the One Dollar condition), immediately after having talked to the girl, demanded her phone number saying he would call her and explain things, and also told the *E* he wanted to wait until she was finished so he could tell her about it.

These 11 *Ss* were, of course, run through the total experiment anyhow and the experiment was explained to them afterwards. Their data, however, are not included in the analysis.

Summary of Design

There remain, for analysis, 20 *Ss* in each of the three conditions. Let us review these briefly: 1. *Control condition.* These *Ss* were treated identically in all respects to the *Ss* in the experimental conditions, except that they were never asked to, and never did, tell the waiting girl that the experimental tasks were enjoyable and lots of fun. 2. *One Dollar condition.* These *Ss* were hired for one dollar to tell a waiting *S* that tasks, which were really rather dull and boring, were interesting, enjoyable, and lots of fun. 3. *Twenty Dollar condition.* These *Ss* were hired for twenty dollars to do the same thing.

RESULTS

The major results of the experiment are summarized in Table 1 which lists, separately for each of the three experimental conditions, the average rating which the *Ss* gave at the end of each question on the interview. We will discuss each of the questions on the interview separately, because they were intended to measure different things. One other point before we proceed to examine the data. In all the comparisons, the Control condition should be regarded as a baseline from which to evaluate the results in the other two conditions. The Control condition gives us, essentially, the reactions of *Ss* to the tasks and their opinions about the experiment as falsely explained to them, without the experimental introduction of dissonance. The data from the other conditions may be viewed, in a sense, as changes from this baseline.

How Enjoyable the Tasks Were

The average ratings on this question, presented in the first row of figures in Table 1, are the results most important to the experiment. These results are the ones most directly relevant to the specific dissonance which was experimentally created. It will be recalled that the tasks were purposely arranged to be rather

TABLE 1 / Average Ratings on Interview Questions for Each Condition

Question on Interview	Experimental Condition		
	Control (*N* = 20)	One Dollar (*N* = 20)	Twenty Dollars (*N* = 20)
How enjoyable tasks were (rated from −5 to +5)	−.45	+1.35	−.05
How much they learned (rated from 0 to 10)	3.08	2.80	3.15
Scientific importance (rated from 0 to 10)	5.60	6.45	5.18
Participate in similar exp. (rated from −5 to +5)	−.62	+1.20	−.25

boring and monotonous. And, indeed, in the Control condition the average rating was −.45, somewhat on the negative side of the neutral point.

In the other two conditions, however, the *Ss* told someone that these tasks were interesting and enjoyable. The resulting dissonance could, of course, most directly be reduced by persuading themselves that the tasks were, indeed, interesting and enjoyable. In the One Dollar condition, since the magnitude of dissonance was high, the pressure to reduce this dissonance would also be high. In this condition, the average rating was +1.35, considerably on the positive side and significantly different from the Control condition at the .02 level[1] (*t* = 2.48).

In the Twenty Dollar condition, where less dissonance was created experimentally because of the greater importance of the consonant relations, there is correspondingly less evidence of dissonance reduction. The average rating in this condition is only −.05, slightly and not significantly higher than the Control condition. The difference between the One Dollar and Twenty Dollar conditions is significant at the .03 level (*t* = 2.22). In short, when an *S* was induced, by offer of reward, to say something contrary to his private opinion, this private opinion tended to change so as to correspond more closely with what he had said. The greater the reward offered (beyond what was necessary to elicit the behavior) the smaller was the effect.

Desire to Participate in a Similar Experiment

The results from this question are shown in the last row of Table 1. This question is less directly related to the dissonance that was experimentally created for the *Ss*. Certainly, the more interesting and enjoyable they felt the tasks were, the greater would be their desire to participate in a similar experiment. But other factors would enter also. Hence, one would expect the results on this question to be very similar to the results on "how enjoyable the tasks were" but weaker. Actually, the results, as may be seen in the table, are in exactly the same direction, and the magnitude of the mean differences is fully as large as on the first question. The variability is greater, however, and the differences do not yield high levels of statistical significance. The difference between the One Dollar condition (+1.20) and the Control condition (–.62) is significant at the .08 level ($t = 1.78$). The difference between the One Dollar condition and the Twenty Dollar condition (–.25) reaches only the .15 level of significance ($t = 1.46$).

The Scientific Importance of the Experiment

This question was included because there was a chance that differences might emerge. There are, after all, other ways in which the experimentally created dissonance could be reduced. For example, one way would be for the *S* to magnify for himself the value of the reward he obtained. This, however, was unlikely in this experiment because money was used for the reward and it is undoubtedly difficult to convince oneself that one dollar is more than it really is. There is another possible way, however. The *Ss* were given a very good reason, in addition to being paid, for saying what they did to the waiting girl. The *Ss* were told it was necessary for the experiment. The dissonance could, consequently, be reduced by magnifying the importance of this cognition. The more scientifically important they considered the experiment to be, the less was the total magnitude of dissonance. It is possible, then, that the results on this question, shown

in the third row of figures in Table 1, might reflect dissonance reduction.

The results are weakly in line with what one would expect if the dissonance were somewhat reduced in this manner. The One Dollar condition is higher than the other two. The difference between the One and Twenty Dollar conditions reaches the .08 level of significance on a two-tailed test ($t = 1.79$). The difference between the One Dollar and Control conditions is not impressive at all ($t = 1.21$). The result that the Twenty Dollar condition is actually lower than the Control condition is undoubtedly a matter of chance ($t = 0.58$).

How Much They Learned from the Experiment

The results on this question are shown in the second row of figures in Table 1. The question was included because, as far as we could see, it had nothing to do with the dissonance that was experimentally created and could not be used for dissonance reduction. One would then expect no differences at all among the three conditions. We felt it was important to show that the effect was not a completely general one but was specific to the content of the dissonance which was created. As can be readily seen in Table 1, there are only negligible differences among conditions. The highest t value for any of these differences is only 0.48.

DISCUSSION OF A POSSIBLE ALTERNATIVE EXPLANATION

We mentioned in the introduction that Janis and King (1954; 1956) in explaining their findings, proposed an explanation in terms of the self-convincing effect of mental rehearsal and thinking up new arguments by the person who had to improvise a speech. Kelman (1953), in the previously mentioned study, in attempting to explain the unexpected finding that the persons who complied in the moderate reward condition changed their opinion more than in the high reward condition, also proposed the same kind of explanation. If the results of our experiment are to be taken as strong corroboration of the theory of cognitive dissonance, this possible alternative explanation must be dealt with.

Specifically, as applied to our results, this alternative explanation would maintain that perhaps, for some reason, the *S*s in the One Dollar condition worked harder at telling the waiting girl that the tasks were fun and enjoyable. That is, in the One Dollar condition they may have rehearsed it more mentally, thought up more ways of saying it, may have said it more convincingly, and so on. Why this might have been the case is, of course, not immediately apparent. One might expect that, in the Twenty Dollar condition, having been paid more, they would try to do a better job of it than in the One Dollar condition. But nevertheless, the possibility exists that the *S*s in the One Dollar condition may have improvised more.

Because of the desirability of investigating this possible alternative explanation, we recorded on a tape recorder the conversation between each *S* and the girl. These recordings were transcribed and then rated, by two independent raters, on five dimensions. The ratings were, of course done in ignorance of which condition each *S* was in. The reliabilities of these ratings, that is, the correlations between the two independent raters, ranged from .61 to .88, with an average reliability of .71. The five ratings were:

1. The content of what the *S* said *before* the girl made the remark that her friend told her it was boring. The stronger the *S*'s positive statements about the tasks, and the more ways in which he said they were interesting and enjoyable, the higher the rating.
2. The content of what the *S* said *after* the girl made the above-mentioned remark. This was rated in the same way as for the content before the remark.
3. A similar rating of the overall content of what the *S* said.
4. A rating of how persuasive and convincing the *S* was in what he said and the way in which he said it.
5. A rating of the amount of time in the discussion that the *S* spent discussing the tasks as opposed to going off into irrelevant things.

The mean ratings for the One Dollar and Twenty Dollar conditions, averaging the ratings of the two independent raters, are presented in Table 2. It is clear from examining the table that, in all cases, the Twenty Dollar condition is slightly higher. The differences are

TABLE 2 / Average Ratings of Discussion between Subject and Girl

Dimensions Rated	Condition		
	One Dollar	Twenty Dollars	Value of *t*
Content before remark by girl (rated from 0 to 5)	2.26	2.62	1.08
Content after remark by girl (rated from 0 to 5)	1.63	1.75	0.11
Over-all content (rated from 0 to 5)	1.89	2.19	1.08
Persuasiveness and conviction (rated from 0 to 10)	4.79	5.50	0.99
Time spent on topic (rated from 0 to 10)	6.74	8.19	1.80

small, however, and only on the rating of "amount of time" does the difference between the two conditions even approach significance. We are certainly justified in concluding that the *S*s in the One Dollar condition did not improvise more nor act more convincingly. Hence, the alternative explanation discussed above cannot account for the findings.

SUMMARY

Recently, Festinger (1957) has proposed a theory concerning cognitive dissonance. Two derivations from this theory are tested here. These are:

1. If a person is induced to do or say something which is contrary to his private opinion, there will be a tendency for him to change his opinion so as to bring it into correspondence with what he has done or said.
2. The larger the pressure used to elicit the overt behavior (beyond the minimum needed to elicit it) the weaker will be the above-mentioned tendency.

A laboratory experiment was designed to test these derivations. Subjects were subjected to a boring experience and then paid to tell someone that the experience had been interesting and enjoyable. The amount of money paid the subject was varied. The private opinions of the subjects concerning the experiences were then determined.

The results strongly corroborate the theory that was tested.

REFERENCES

Festinger, L. *A theory of cognitive dissonance.* Evanston, Ill.: Row Peterson, 1957.

Janis, I. L., & King, B. T. The influence of role-playing on opinion change. *Journal of Abnormal and Social Psychology,* 1954, *49,* 211–218.

Kelman, H. Attitude change as a function of response restriction. *Human Relations,* 1953, *6,* 185–214.

King, B. T., & Janis, I. L. Comparison of the effectiveness of improvised versus non-improvised role-playing in producing opinion changes. *Human Relations,* 1956, *9,* 177–186.

ENDNOTE

1. All statistical tests referred to in this paper are two-tailed.

CRITICAL THINKING QUESTIONS

1. Using the concept of dissonance theory, select an attitude or belief that you might want to change and design a procedure that could be effective in producing change in the desired direction.
2. This study was cited in Article 2 as an example of some of the ethical issues in social psychological research. What do you see as the ethical issues present in this experiment? Do you see any alternative to deception in this type of study? Why or why not?
3. Based on personal experience, have you ever suspected that cognitive dissonance was operating in some change that came about in your own attitudes? Elaborate on how that may have occurred.
4. Festinger and Carlsmith discuss a possible alternative explanation for the obtained results. What is your position on this alternative explanation? Discuss any other possible explanations for the findings of the study.
5. Might cognitive dissonance be operating in many real-life situations? For example, consider the initiation process (known as *hazing*) used in some social groups, such as fraternities, or the procedures used in the military as part of basic training. How might cognitive dissonance be operating in these or other situations to account for the outcomes of the experience?

ADDITIONAL RELATED READINGS

Gosing, P., Denizeau, M., & Oberle, D. (2006). Denial of responsibility: A new mode of dissonance reduction. *Journal of Personality and Social Psychology, 90*(5), 722–733.

Maikovich, A. K. (2006). A new understanding of terrorism using *cognitive dissonance* principles. *Journal for the Theory of Social Behaviour, 35*(4), 373–397.

ARTICLE 12 _____

In the years since publication of Festinger and Carlsmith's classic study (Article 11), many experiments have been done to test dissonance theory and to elaborate on the conditions necessary for its operation. As it turns out, there are many different causes of dissonance. For example, dissonance may be aroused when an individual puts a great deal of effort into a given activity, as though he or she needs to justify expending so much effort to obtain a certain goal. This is sort of a "suffering leads to liking" effect. Dissonance will also likely be aroused when an individual has the freedom to choose whether to do (or not do) something. There is little reason to experience dissonance when you are forced to do something. You know why you did it: Someone *made* you do it. Finally, issues such as self-esteem may influence the arousal (and subsequent reduction) of cognitive dissonance. People with high levels of self-esteem may actually be *more* likely to engage in dissonance reduction than those with low levels of self-esteem when they see their behavior as inconsistent with their beliefs.

The central premise of cognitive dissonance theory is that people are motivated to avoid or reduce any tension produced by a perceived inconsistency between two attitudes or between an attitude and a behavior. So, what would happen when someone encounters a persuasive argument that is contrary to his or her own privately held beliefs? Dissonance theory suggests that this person will be motivated to reduce the internal tension generated by that perceived inconsistency, which can be accomplished in several ways. For example, he or she simply might not pay attention to the opposing viewpoint, distort the message to make it more consistent with his or her own beliefs, or avoid the message altogether.

The following article by Marie-Amélie Martinie and Valérie Fointiat examines the role of two factors, self-esteem and trivialization, in dissonance reduction. This article is an excellent example of the contemporary exploration of dissonance theory and a good illustration of the elaboration of research concepts over time. Specifically, when we look at the findings described in the original demonstration of cognitive dissonance, as found in Article 11, the conclusions seem fairly straightforward. (For instance, freely engaging in a behavior that runs counter to a privately held belief will result in changing the belief to bring it more in line with the expressed behavior.) The present article effectively demonstrates the ongoing quest to explore the underlying mechanisms of dissonance and the conditions under which it does and does not occur.

Self-Esteem, Trivialization, and Attitude Change

■ Marie-Amélie Martinie[1] and Valérie Fointiat[2]

The aim of this study was to investigate the relationship between trivialization and self-esteem. Low-self-esteem participants were expected to reduce cognitive dissonance by trivialization. In this experiment, dissonance was aroused by having participants write a counter-attitudinal essay. In the post-experimental phase, both the participants' attitude and trivialization were measured. The order of presentation of the variables was manipulated (attitude first vs. trivialization first). The results showed that participants with low self-esteem did not change their attitude and trivialized. These results limit the scope of the self-consistency view proposing that only participants with high self-esteem feel dissonance.

Most research on cognitive dissonance theory (Festinger, 1957) has been conducted using the forced-compliance paradigm, where participants freely agree to execute a counter-attitudinal or counter-motivational behavior. Execution of this act generates a state of psychological discomfort called cognitive dissonance. According to Festinger, individuals will be driven to reduce or eliminate this negative affective state. The reduction process takes place by means of an *a posteriori* rationalization of the behavior, which can take on two forms: cognitive rationalization or act rationalization. Cognitive rationalization consists of modifying one's attitude to agree with the performed action (i.e., attitude change: Festinger & Carlsmith, 1959); act rationalization consists of agreeing to perform a second act that is consistent with the first but more costly (i.e., act rationalization: Joule, 1986; Fointiat, 1996, 1998).

In 1957, Festinger noted another mode of dissonance reduction, trivialization. Neither the attitude nor the behavior is changed, but the importance granted to that attitude and/or behavior is modified. In their pioneering research, Simon, Greenberg, and Brehm (1995) measured trivialization regarding the general category of action, the issue to which the attitude pertained, the specific counter-attitudinal action, and the behavior if it had been pro-attitudinal, using four 9-point scales ranging from "not at all important" to "extremely important". In their first study, the participants wrote a counter-attitudinal essay. Only half of the participants were given the opportunity to agree or refuse to perform this act. The initial attitude was made salient, and thus resistant to change, by having half the participants think about their attitude before writing the essay. In the post-experimental phase, the attitude toward the essay and trivialization were measured. The results showed that the free-choice participants did not change attitudes but trivialized if the initial attitude was salient. In their second study, Simon et al. examined attitude change and trivialization as two alternate modes for reducing dissonance. They manipulated the presentation order of the dependent variables (attitude first vs. trivialization first) and choice (high choice vs. low choice). The results showed that the high-choice participants used the first reduction mode made available. They changed their attitude but did not trivialize if the attitude was measured first; they did not change their attitude but trivialized if trivialization was measured first. In their third study—based on self-affirmation theory (Steele & Liu, 1983), wherein dissonance can be reduced by reaffirmation of the central values of the self (i.e., self-affirmation)—Simon et al. tested trivialization after self-affirmation. After counter-attitudinal essay writing, only half of the participants were given the opportunity to affirm an important aspect of the self (self-affirmation vs. no self-affirmation). In the post-experimental phase, attitude and trivialization were measured. The results showed that following self-affirmation, participants did not change their attitude but trivialized.

Martinie, M.-A., & Fointiat, V. (2006). Self-esteem, trivialization, and attitude change. *Swiss Journal of Psychology, 65,* 221–225. Copyright © 2006 Verlag Hans Huber. Reprinted with permission.

More recently, Martinie and Joule (2000a, 2000b) looked at trivialization in a particular case of forced compliance: misattribution of aroused dissonance. In the misattribution situation, participants could attribute their dissonance to a perturbing environmental factor (i.e., stimulating drugs, photographs of war or erotic scenes). Classically, attitude change is no longer observed in this situation (Zanna & Cooper, 1974). However, the participants did use trivialization (Martinie & Joule, 2000a, 2000b). Finally, Michel and Fointiat (2003) looked at dissonance reduction and consistency. Consistency exists when exhibited attitudes or behaviors are compatible with each other (Channouf & Mangard, 1997; Jouffre, Py, & Somat, 2001). In their study, Michel and Fointiat found that inconsistent individuals trivialized more than consistent ones. To reduce dissonance, the latter changed their attitude.

As a whole, the results of these studies demonstrate the properties of the dissonance drive (e.g., Fazio & Cooper, 1983; Kiesler & Pallak, 1976; Wicklund & Brehm, 1976) and the alternate reduction-mode model: A participant who reduces dissonance by using one mode will not be inclined to use another mode (e.g., Beauvois, Joule, & Brunetti, 1993; Fointiat, 1998).

As Festinger (1957) and later Elliot and Devine (1994) argued, attitude change serves to alleviate psychological discomfort. However, not all authors interpret attitude change in the same way. For some (Bern, 1967), it results from an inference-making process; for others (Alexander & Knight, 1971; Joseph, Gaes, Tedeschi, & Cunningham, 1979; Tedeschi, Schlenker, & Bonoma, 1971), attitude change is nothing more than a pretence aimed at strengthening and protecting a positive identity in front of others. For self-consistency theorists (Aronson, 1969, 1972, 1992; Thibodeau & Aronson, 1992), attitude change allows people to maintain self-esteem by preserving two central elements of the self: good morals and competency. Aronson (1968) claimed that ". . . if dissonance exists it is because the individual's behavior is inconsistent with his self-concept" (p. 23). Individuals with low self-esteem are thought to feel less dissonance than individuals with high self-esteem because the dissonant act does not threaten their self-integrity (Aronson & Carlsmith, 1962;

Aronson & Mettee, 1968). The results of studies by Glass (1964) and Gibbons, Eggleston, and Benthin (1997) are in line with this view. Glass' participants, all opposed to using electric shocks on humans, first took a personality test. The experimenter gave them positive or negative feedback about the test. The feedback was used to manipulate their self-concept. Then, in a learning situation, the participants had to administer an electric shock to a peer whenever he or she made a mistake. In the post-experimental phase, the participants had to evaluate the peer. The results showed that participants rated the peer more negatively in the positive self-concept condition than in the negative self-concept condition. The negative peer evaluation served as a justification for administering the electric shocks and thus reduced dissonance. In a study on individuals who failed to stop smoking (dissonance situation), Gibbons et al. found that participants with low self-esteem did not change their perception of the risks of smoking, whereas high-self-esteem participants did.

For the advocates of "the new look" (Cooper & Fazio, 1984), two conditions are necessary for dissonance arousal: (1) the individual must feel free to execute the behavior that has negative consequences on oneself or others, and (2) the consequences must be foreseeable before the irrevocable act is carried out. In sum, the self does not enter into dissonance arousal. However, in a study by Holland, Meertens, and Van Vugt (2002), self-esteem was found to have an effect on dissonance reduction via self-justification strategies (internal vs. external). The participants in this study were persons who used their car as a means of transportation. Self-esteem was measured in the pre-experimental phase. Two months later, the participants received a letter informing them of an upcoming telephone interview. For one third of the participants, the letter was about the advantages of public transportation (safe, fast, timesaving) and the disadvantages of private transportation. This message induced what is called hedonistic dissonance, a result of the negative consequences of an act for the self. For the second third, the letter brought out the negative effects of private transportation on the environment and public health. This message induced what is called moral dissonance, a result of the negative consequences of an act for others. For the final third, the letter simply informed the participants about the telephone interview (control group). One week later, all participants were asked on the telephone to answer a self-justification questionnaire containing internal and external justifications. The results indicated that participants with low self-esteem had a tendency to rely more on external self-justifications in the moral-dissonance situation than in the hedonistic one. Participants with high self-esteem did not use a self-justification strategy. For Holland et al., these results are consistent with self-affirmation theory: "According to self-affirmation theory (Steele & Liu, 1983), high-self-esteem individuals should react less defensively to dissonance inductions because they retain more affirmational resources" (p. 1719).

The findings of the Holland et al. (2002) study suggest that the dissonance reduction process depends both on self-esteem and, for participants with low self-esteem, on the type of dissonance. The present article tests for trivialization among individuals with low self-esteem. Unlike Aronson (1969), we hypothesized that individuals with low self-esteem would feel dissonance and reduce it by trivialization.

METHOD

The pre-experimental phase was used to measure the self-esteem of the participants in the experimental group. In the experimental phase, all participants wrote a counter-attitudinal essay. The choice to write or not to write the essay was given to participants in the experimental conditions, but not in the control condition. In the post-experimental phase, attitude and trivialization were measured. The order of appearance of the dependent variables was manipulated (attitude first vs. trivialization first).

Aside from a dissonance effect (Festinger & Carlsmith, 1959) and a self-consistency effect (Thibodeau & Aronson, 1992) on the attitude measure, participants with low self-esteem were expected to reduce dissonance by trivialization. By virtue of the drive properties of dissonance (e.g., Fazio & Cooper, 1983) and the alternate reduction-mode model (Beauvois et al., 1993), it was also hypothesized that participants with high self-esteem would use the first available mode of dissonance reduction. More specifically, they were expected to change their attitude if attitude was

measured before trivialization, and to trivialize if trivialization was measured before attitude.

Participants

A total of 170 students at the University of Poitiers, France, who were not studying psychology took part in the experiment. Three participants refused to write the counter-attitudinal essay (two in the experimental conditions and one in the control condition).

Procedure

Phase 1 Self-esteem was measured on Rosenberg's scale (validated by Vallieres & Vallerand, 1990). Based on the distribution of the self-esteem scores, the participants were divided into three groups: high self-esteem, moderate self-esteem, and low self-esteem. Only the two extreme groups were retained for the study: high self-esteem and low self-esteem. There were 51 participants in the low-self-esteem group (with scores from 36 to 57), 50 in the high-self-esteem group (scores 70–90), and 20 in the control group.

Phase 2 All participants had to write an essay in favor of selective admission to universities (counter-attitudinal essay).[1] Participants in the experimental groups, but not in the control group, were given the opportunity to agree or refuse to write the counter-attitudinal essay.

Measures

Attitude The participants used a 9-point scale (1 = totally against, 9 = totally for) to rate themselves on the following item:

> *"What is your personal opinion about selective admission to universities?"*

Trivialization The participants used a 9-point scale (1 = not important at all, 9 = very important) to rate themselves on the following four items: "When you defend a position you disagree with, how important is it to you?" "For you, how important is the issue of selective admission to universities?" "If I asked you to write down arguments against selective admission to universities, how important would you say it was?" "How important do you feel your arguments in favor of selective admission to universities are?"

The order of appearance of the two dependent variables was manipulated. The experimental participants were randomly assigned to the attitude-first condition or the trivialization-first condition. For the control participants, attitude was measured first, then trivialization.

RESULTS

Attitude

As expected, a significant dissonance effect was found. Participants with high self-esteem in the attitude-first condition changed their attitude more, $M = 4.28$, $SD = 2.35$, than participants in the control condition, $M = 2.00$, $SD = 0.46$, $F(1, 116) = 14.65$, $p < .01$, $d = 1.82$.[2] There was also a significant self-consistency effect. High-self-esteem participants in the attitude-first condition changed their attitude more, $M = 4.28$, $SD = 2.35$, than low-self-esteem participants in the attitude-first and trivialization-first conditions, $M = 3.19$, $SD = 1.74$, and $M = 3.33$, $SD = 2.35$, respectively, $F(1, 116) = 4.5$, $p < .01$, $d = .75$ and $.62$, respectively. The mean value of the high-self-esteem participants in the trivialization-first condition, in comparison, was 3.68.

Trivialization

Like in Martinie and Joule (2000b), a trivialization index was calculated by summing the ratings on the four items. As expected, participants with low self-esteem in the attitude-first and trivialization-first conditions trivialized more, $M = 23.95$, $SD = 3.44$, and $M = 24.06$, $SD = 3.96$, respectively, than did control-condition participants, $M = 26.85$, $SD = 0.83$, $F(1, 116) = 8.56$, $p < .01$, $d = 1.97$ and 1.69, respectively. Low-self-esteem participants in the attitude-first and trivialization-first conditions trivialized more, $M = 23.95$, $SD = 3.44$, and $M = 24.06$, $SD = 3.96$, respectively, than the high-self-esteem participants in the attitude-first condition, $M = 26.71$, $SD = 3.11$, $F(1, 116) = 9.75$, $p < .01$, $d = 1.5$, and 1.14, respectively.

In line with the drive properties of dissonance, participants with high self-esteem in the trivialization-first condition trivialized more, $M = 24.72$, $SD = 3.43$, than did participants in the attitude-first condition, $M = 26.71$, $SD = 3.11$, $F(1, 116) = 3.62$, $p < .05$, $d = 1.10$. However, contrary to the alternate reduction-mode model, participants with high self-esteem did not differ from each other on the attitude measure. Their attitudes were just as favorable in the trivialization-first condition, $M = 3.681$, $SD = 2.05$, as in the attitude-first condition, $M = 4.28$, $SD = 2.35$, $F(1, 116) = 1.08$, *ns*.

DISCUSSION

Our results support the dissonance effect on attitude: High-self-esteem participants in the experimental conditions changed their attitude more than participants in the non-dissonance condition (control group). In line with the self-consistency theory (Thibodeau & Aronson, 1992), low-self-esteem participants did not undergo an attitude change compared to high-self-esteem participants given the opportunity to change their attitude first. In line with our own hypotheses, low-self-esteem participants reduced dissonance by means of trivialization rather than attitude change.

It was also hypothesized that participants with high self-esteem would use only one dissonance-reduction mode. This hypothesis was partially refuted: While these participants changed their attitude without trivializing when attitude was measured before trivialization, they trivialized *and* changed their attitude when trivialization came before attitude.

As a whole, our results limit the scope of the self-consistency view that individuals with high self-esteem feel dissonance more than individuals with low self-esteem (Thibodeau & Aronson, 1992). On the other hand, they are consistent with Holland et al.'s (2002) view that self-esteem is a moderator of dissonance-reduction strategies. This is precisely what was observed in our study: Participants with high self-esteem trivialized and/or changed attitudes, whereas participants with low self-esteem trivialized. Thus, in line with Cooper and Fazio (1984), the self does not enter into dissonance generation, and in line with Holland et al., the self orients the dissonance-reduction process.

As suggested by earlier results on trivialization (Simon et al., 1995; Martinie & Joule, 2000a, 2000b; Michel & Fointiat, 2003), a trivialization effect was obtained when attitude change was hindered or non-operational. An analysis of the correlation between the trivialization index and attitude change showed that the more participants trivialized, the less their attitude changed. However, participants with high self-esteem used both of these dissonance-reduction modes when trivialization was the first mode available to them. The observed complementarity of the two modes does not cast doubt on the drive property of dissonance (e.g., Fazio & Cooper, 1983; Kiesler & Pallak, 1976; Wicklund & Brehm, 1976). It seems that if the entire amount of dissonance is not completely eliminated by way of the drive properties of dissonance, a supplementary mode will be used to eliminate the remaining dissonance (e.g., Aronson, Blanton, & Cooper, 1995; Cook, Pallak, Storms, & McCaul, 1977).

Thus, trivialization alone appears to be insufficient for reducing dissonance in individuals with high self-esteem, perhaps because undermining the importance of one's own acts and/or attitudes is inconsistent with high self-esteem. The opposite reasoning can be applied to individuals with low self-esteem: Attributing a positive value to compliant behavior, i.e., attitude change (Beauvois & Joule, 1996), is probably inconsistent with low self-esteem, whereas trivializing would be consistent with it.

AUTHOR NOTE

We would like to thank two anonymous reviewers for their constructive criticism.

REFERENCES

Alexander, C. N., & Knight, G. (1971). Situated identities and social psychological experimentation. *Sociometry, 34,* 65–82.

Aronson, E. (1968). Progress and problems. In R. E. Abelson, E. Aronson, W. J. McGuire, T. M. Newcomb, M. J. Rosenberg, & P. H. Tannenbaum (Eds.), *Theories of cognitive consistency: A sourcebook* (pp. 5–27). Chicago: Rand McNally.

Aronson, E. (1969). The theory of cognitive dissonance: A current perspective. In L. Berkowitz (Ed.), *Advances in experimental social psychology* (pp. 1–34). New York: American Press.

Aronson, E. (1972). *The social animal.* New York: Freeman.

Aronson, E. (1992). The return of the repressed: Dissonance theory makes a comeback. *Psychological Inquiry, 3,* 303–311.

Aronson, E., & Carlsmith, J. M. (1962). Performance expectancy as a determinant of actual performance. *Journal of Abnormal and Social Psychology, 65,* 178–182.

Aronson, E., & Mettee, D. R. (1968). Dishonest behavior as a function of differential levels of induced self-esteem. *Journal of Personality and Social Psychology, 9,* 121–127.

Aronson, J., Blanton, H., & Cooper, J. (1995). From dissonance to disidentification: Selectivity in the self-affirmation process. *Journal of Personality and Social Psychology, 68,* 986–996.

Beauvois, J. L., & Joule, R. V. (1996). *A radical dissonance theory.* London: Taylor and Francis.

Beauvois, J. L., Joule R. V., & Brunetti, F. (1993). Cognitive rationalization and act rationalization in escalation of commitment. *Basic and Applied Social Psychology, 14,* 1–17.

Bem, D. J. (1967). Self-perception: An alternative interpretation of cognitive dissonance phenomena. *Journal of Personality and Social Psychology, 74,* 183–200.

Channouf, H., & Mangard, C. (1997). Les aspects socio-normatifs de la consistance cognitive. *Cahiers Internationaux de Psychologie Sociale, 36,* 28–45.

Cook, D. A., Pallak, M. S., Storms, M. D., & McCaul, K. D. (1977). The effect of compliance on attitude change and behavior change. *Personality and Social Psychology Bulletin, 3,* 71–74.

Cooper, J., & Fazio, R. H. (1984). A new look at dissonance. In L. Berkowitz (Ed.), *Advances in experimental social psychology* (pp. 229–262). Hillsdale, NJ: Erlbaum.

Elliot, A. J., & Devine, P. G. (1994). On the motivational nature of cognitive dissonance: Dissonance as psychological discomfort. *Journal of Personality and Social Psychology, 67,* 382–394.

Fazio, R. H., & Cooper, J. (1983). Arousal in the dissonance process. In J. T. Caccioppo, R. E. Petty (Eds.), *Social psychopysiology* (pp. 122–151). New York: Academic Press.

Festinger, L. (1957). *A theory of cognitive dissonance.* Evanston, IL: Row, Peterson.

Festinger, L., & Carlsmith, J. M. (1959). Cognitive consequence of forced compliance. *Journal of Abnormal Social Psychology, 58,* 203–210.

Fointiat, V. (1996). Rationalisation cognitive versus rationalisation en acte dans le paradigme de la fausse attribution de l' éveil de la dissonance. *Les Cahiers Internationaux de Psychologie Sociale, 3,* 10–21.

Fointiat, V. (1998). Rationalization in act and problematic behaviour justification. *European Journal of Social Psychology, 28,* 471–474.

Glass, D. C. (1964). Changes in liking as a mean of reducing cognitive discrepancies between self-esteem and aggression. *Journal of Personality, 32,* 531–549.

Gibbons, F. X., Eggleston, T. J., & Benthin, A. C. (1997). Cognitive reactions to smoking relapse: The reciprocal relation between dissonance and self-esteem. *Journal of Personality and Social Psychology, 72,* 184–195.

Holland, R. W., Meertens, R. M., & Van Vugt, M. (2002). Dissonance on the road: Self-esteem as a moderator of internal and external self-justification strategies. *Personality and Social Psychology Bulletin, 28,* 1713–1724.

Joseph, J. M., Gaes, G. G., Tedeschi, J. T., & Cunningham, M. R. (1979). Impression management effects in the forced compliance situation. *The Journal of Social Psychology, 107,* 89–98.

Jouffre, S., Py, J., & Somat, A. (2001). Norme d' internalité, norme de consistence et clairvoyance normative. *International Review of Social Psychology, 14,* 121–164.

Joule, R. V. (1986). *Rationalisation et engagement dans la soumission librement consentie.* Doctoral dissertation, Université des Sciences Humaines, Grenoble.

Kiesler, C. A., & Pallak, M. S. (1976). Arousal properties of dissonance manipulations. *Psychological Bulletin, 83,* 1014–1025.

Martinie, M. A., & Joule, R. V. (2000a). Rationalisation cognitive, trivialisation et rationalisation en acte clans le paradigme de la fausse attribution. In J. L. Beauvois, R. V. Joule, J. M. Monteil (Eds.), *Perspectives cognitives et conduites sociales* (pp. 41–61). Neuchâtel et Paris: Delachaux & Niestlé.

Martinie, M. A., & Joule, R. V. (2000b). Trivialisation et rationalisation en acte dans le paradigme de la fausse attribution: Deux voies alternatives de réduction de la dissonance. *Revue Internationale de Psychologie Sociale, 13,* 93–114.

Michel, S., & Fointiat, V. (2003). Trivialisation versus rationalisation cognitive: Quand l'adhésion à la norme de consistance guide le choix du mode de réduction de la dissonance. *Cahiers Internationaux de Psychologie Sociale, 56,* 58–63.

Tedeschi, J. T., Schlenker, B. R., & Bonoma, T. V. (1971). Cognitive dissonance: Private rationalization or public spectacle? *American Psychologist, 8,* 685–695.

Thibodeau, R., & Aronson, E. (1992). Taking a closer look: Re-asserting the role of the self-concept in dissonance theory. *Personality and Social Psychology Bulletin, 18,* 591–602.

Steele, C. M., & Liu, T. J. (1983). Dissonance process as self-affirmation. *Journal of Personality and Social Psychology, 45,* 5–19.

Simon, L., Greenberg, G., & Brehm, J. (1995). Trivialization: The forgotten mode of dissonance reduction. *Journal of Personality and Social Psychology, 68,* 247–260.

Vallieres, E., & Vallerand, R. J. (1990). Traduction et validation canadienne-française de l'Echelle de l'Estime de Soi de Rosenberg. *International Journal of Psychology, 2,* 305–316.

Wicklund, R. A., & Brehm, J. W. (1976). *Perspectives on cognitive dissonance.* Hillsdale, NJ: Erlbaum.

Zanna, M. F., & Cooper, J. (1974). Dissonance and the pill: An attribution approach to studying the arousal properties of dissonance. *Journal of Personality and Social Psychology, 29,* 703–709.

ENDNOTES

1. In France, admission to state universities is open to all students who have obtained their "baccalauréat" (high school diploma).

2. The cut-off values for Cohen's *d* were .2 (small effect size), .5 (medium effect size), and .8 (large effect size).

CRITICAL THINKING QUESTIONS

1. This study found that individuals with low self-esteem used trivialization to reduce their dissonance, whereas those with high self-esteem used trivialization and/or attitude change to reduce their dissonance. How would minimizing the ability to use trivialization affect the dissonance reduction of either group? How could you go about minimizing someone's ability to trivialize an issue?

2. Can the results of the present study be used to produce dissonance and hence change in real-world applications? For example, suppose you want to reduce smoking by inducing dissonance in participants. Design a study for doing so, taking into account the issue of self-esteem.

3. Question 3 in Article 11 asked, "Based on personal experience, have you ever suspected that cognitive dissonance was operating in some change that came about in your own attitudes?" Elaborate on your answer by including information from the present article on the roles of self-esteem and trivialization in dissonance reduction.

4. According to this study, individuals with high self-esteem seem to change their attitudes more easily as a result of experiencing dissonance than those with low self-esteem. How might attitude change be promoted in people with low self-esteem? Explain.

CHAPTER INTEGRATION QUESTIONS

1. Articles 11 and 12 both dealt with aspects of cognitive dissonance. How does this concept also relate to the content of Article 10?

2. Integrate the findings of all three articles into one or two themes. Discuss the practical application of your theme or themes.

3. "Only the most intelligent and most stupid do not change," according to Confucius, a Chinese philosopher. In light of the information presented in this chapter on attitudes and attitude change, do you agree or disagree with this quotation? Be sure to defend your position.

Chapter Five

SOCIAL IDENTITY

THE MAJORITY OF readings that you will encounter in this book focus on what might be called *situational variables:* particular circumstances that elicit predictable patterns of behavior in people. But do all people respond the same way in identical situations? Of course not. We each bring to every situation a set of experiences and characteristics that may influence how we act. Certainly, each of us has had unique life experiences that may be influential; biological dispositions, perhaps present from birth, may also play a role in determining behavior. Another influential factor is the personality of the individual.

But what is *personality?* Many theories have been developed to try to explain what this concept means. Some are *global theories* of personality, which attempt a total comprehensive portrait of an individual (e.g., Freud's), while others are *microtheories,* focusing on narrower, more particular dimensions of personality. Certainly, one major part of personality is *social identity*—the part of personality that is our internalized representation of how we view ourselves as being part of our social world. Two major parts of social identity—the *self* and *gender identity*—are addressed in the readings in this chapter.

Article 13, "The Many Me's of the Self-Monitor," looks at the sense of self that each of us has and asks whether that is comprised of a single sense of self or perhaps a number of selves, depending on the situation.

Article 14, "The Measurement of Psychological Androgyny," is a classic article that challenges the common-sense wisdom that the most appropriate gender-typed behavior is for a male to be masculine and a female, feminine. Perhaps masculinity and femininity are not mutually exclusive ends of a continuum after all.

The contemporary reading found in Article 15, "Examining Masculinity Norms, Problem Drinking, and Athletic Involvement as Predictors of Sexual Aggression in College Men," revisits the concept of masculinity introduced in Article 14 and considers the role it may play in the sexual aggression of young males. Additionally, the article examines other factors that may be involved in sexually coercive behavior. Given the seriousness of this behavior, the implications of this research are of particular interest.

ARTICLE 13

Think about who you are. Do you have a stable sense of self, of knowing what you feel, believe, and want? Or do you have many selves, depending on when and in what situation you try to answer this question?

Now think about your behavior. Do you act consistently across many different situations? Or does your behavior depend on the specific situation in which you find yourself?

These questions are indeed intriguing. At one extreme may be individuals who consistently act the same way in every situation, even when doing so might not be appropriate. At the other extreme are people who modify their behavior to fit each situation, showing little consistency across contexts. These are the two extremes on a continuum of what is known as *self-monitoring*.

Self-monitoring refers to the extent to which an individual is aware of and able to control the impressions that he or she conveys to others. A high self-monitoring individual is very attuned to the situation and modifies his or her behavior according to the demands of the context. A low self-monitoring individual tends to behave more in accordance with internal dispositions than with the demands of the situation.

What are the consequences of these two styles of behaving? Does a high self-monitoring person actually have many different selves, while a low self-monitoring person has but a single self? The relationship between self-monitoring and the sense of self is but one of the issues addressed in the following article by Mark Snyder.

The Many Me's of the Self-Monitor

■ Mark Snyder

The image of myself which I try to create in my own mind in order that I may love myself is very different from the image which I try to create in the minds of others in order that they may love me.   —*W. H. Auden*

The concept of the self is one of the oldest and most enduring in psychological considerations of human nature. We generally assume that people are fairly consistent and stable beings: that a person who is generous in one situation is also likely to be generous in other situations, that one who is honest is honest most of the time, that a person who takes a liberal stance today will favor the liberal viewpoint tomorrow.

It's not always so: each of us, it appears, may have not one but many selves. Moreover, much as we might like to believe that the self is an integral feature of personal identity, it appears that, to a greater extent, the self is a product of the individual's relationships with

other people. Conventional wisdom to the contrary, there may be striking gaps and contradictions—as Auden suggests—between the public appearances and private realities of the self.

Psychologists refer to the strategies and techniques that people use to control the impressions they convey to others as "impression management." One of my own research interests has been to understand why some individuals are better at impression management than others. For it is clear that some people are particularly sensitive to the ways they express and present themselves in social situations—at parties, job interviews, professional meetings, in confrontations of all kinds where one might choose to create and maintain an appearance, with or without a specific purpose in mind. Indeed, I have found that such people have developed the ability to carefully monitor their own performances and to skillfully adjust their performances when signals from others tell them that they are not having the desired effect. I call such persons "high self-monitoring individuals," and I have developed a 25-item measure—the Self-Monitoring Scale—that has proved its ability to distinguish high self-monitoring individuals from low self-monitoring individuals (see box [p. 139]). Unlike the high self-monitoring individuals, low self-monitoring individuals are not so concerned about taking in such information; instead, they tend to express what they feel, rather than mold and tailor their behavior to fit the situation.

My work on self-monitoring and impression management grew out of a long-standing fascination with explorations of reality and illusion in literature and in the theater. I was struck by the contrast between the way things often appear to be and the reality that lurks beneath the surface—on the stage, in novels, and in people's actual lives. I wanted to know how this world of appearances in social relationships was built and maintained, as well as what its effects were on the individual personality. But I was also interested in exploring the older, more philosophical question of whether, beneath the various images of self that people project to others, there is a "real me." If we are all actors in many social situations, do we then retain in any sense an essential self, or are we really a variety of selves?

SKILLED IMPRESSION MANAGERS

There are striking and important differences in the extent to which people can and do control their self-presentation in social situations: some people engage in impression management more often—and with greater skill—than others. Professional actors, as well as many trial lawyers, are among the best at it. So are successful salespeople, confidence artists, and politicians. The onetime mayor of New York, Fiorello LaGuardia, was particularly skilled at adopting the expressive mannerisms of a variety of ethnic groups. In fact, he was so good at it that in watching silent films of his campaign speeches, it is easy to guess whose vote he was soliciting.

Of course, such highly skilled performances are the exception rather than the rule. And people differ in the extent to which they can and do exercise control over their self-presentations. It is high self-monitoring individuals among us who are particularly talented in this regard. When asked to describe high self-monitoring individuals, their friends say that they are good at learning which behavior is appropriate in social situations, have good self-control of their emotional expression, and can effectively use this ability to create the impression they want. They are particularly skilled at intentionally expressing and accurately communicating a wide variety of emotions both vocally and facially. As studies by Richard Lippa of California State University at Fullerton have shown, they are usually such polished actors that they can effectively adopt the mannerisms of a reserved, withdrawn, and introverted individual and then do an abrupt about-face and portray, just as convincingly, a friendly, outgoing, and extroverted personality.

High self-monitoring individuals are also quite likely to seek out information about appropriate patterns of self-presentation. They invest considerable effort in attempting to "read" and understand others. In an experiment I conducted with Tom Monson (then one of my graduate students), various cues were given to students involved in group discussions as to what was socially appropriate behavior in the situation. For example, some of them thought that their taped discussions would be played back to fellow students; in those circumstances, I assumed they would want their opinions to appear as autonomous as possible. Others believed that their discussions were completely private; there, I assumed they would be most concerned with maintaining harmony and agreement in the group. High self-monitoring individuals were keenly attentive to these differences; they conformed with the group when conformity was the most appropriate behavior and did not conform when they knew that the norms of the larger student audience would favor autonomy in the face of social pressure. Low self-monitoring individuals were virtually unaffected by the differences in social setting: presumably, their self-presentations were more accurate reflections of their personal attitudes and dispositions. Thus, as we might have guessed, people who are most skilled in the arts of impression management are also most likely to practice it.

Although high self-monitoring individuals are well skilled in the arts of impression management, we

Monitor Your Self

On the scale I have developed to measure self-monitoring, actors are usually high scorers, as are many obese people, who tend to be very sensitive about the way they appear to others. For much the same reason, politicians and trial lawyers would almost certainly be high scorers. Recent immigrants eager to assimilate, black freshmen in a predominantly white college, and military personnel stationed abroad are also likely to score high on the scale.

The Self-Monitoring Scale measures how concerned people are with the impression they are making on others, as well as their ability to control and modify their behavior to fit the situation. I believe that it defines a distinct domain of personality that is quite different from the traits probed by other standard scales.

Several studies show that skill at self-monitoring is not associated with exceptional intelligence or with a particular social class. Nor is it related, among other things, to being highly anxious or extremely self-conscious, to being an extrovert, or to having a strong need for approval. They may be somewhat power-oriented or Machiavellian, but high self-monitoring individuals do not necessarily have high scores on the "Mach" scale, a measure of Machiavellianism developed by Richard Christie of Columbia University. (Two items from the scale: "The best way to handle people is to tell them what they want" and "Anyone who completely trusts anyone else is asking for trouble.") The steely-eyes Machiavellians are more manipulative, detached, and amoral than high self-monitoring individuals.

The Self-Monitoring Scale describes a unique trait and has proved to be both statistically valid and reliable, in tests on various samples.

[Below] is a 10-item abbreviated version of the Self-Monitoring Scale that will give readers some idea of whether they are low or high self-monitoring individuals. If you would like to test your self-monitoring tendencies, follow the instructions and then consult the scoring key.

—M. S.

These statements concern personal reactions to a number of different situations. No two statements are exactly alike, so consider each statement carefully before answering. If a statement is true, or mostly true, as applied to you, circle the T. If a statement is false, or not usually true, as applied to you, circle the F.

1. I find it hard to imitate the behavior of other people.   T   F
2. I guess I put on a show to impress or entertain people.   T   F
3. I would probably make a good actor.   T   F
4. I sometimes appear to others to be experiencing deeper emotions than I actually am.   T   F
5. In a group of people I am rarely the center of attention.   T   F
6. In different situations and with different people, I often act like very different persons.   T   F
7. I can only argue for ideas I already believe.   T   F
8. In order to get along and be liked, I tend to be what people expect me to be rather than anything else.   T   F
9. I may deceive people by being friendly when I really dislike them.   T   F
10. I'm not always the person I appear to be.   T   F

SCORING: Give yourself one point for each of questions 1, 5 and 7 that you answered F. Give yourself one point for each of the remaining questions that you answered T. Add up your points. If you are a good judge of yourself and scored 7 or above, you are probably a high self-monitoring individual; 3 or below, you are probably a low self-monitoring individual.

should not automatically assume that they necessarily use these skills for deceptive or manipulative purposes. Indeed, in their relationships with friends and acquaintances, high self-monitoring individuals are eager to use their self-monitoring abilities to promote smooth social interactions.

We can find some clues to this motive in the way high self-monitoring individuals tend to react to, and cope with, unfamiliar and unstructured social settings. In a study done at the University of Wisconsin, psychologists William Ickes and Richard Barnes arranged for pairs of strangers to spend time together in a waiting room, ostensibly to wait for an experiment to begin. The researchers then recorded the verbal and nonverbal behavior of each pair over a five-minute period, using video and audio tapes. All possible pairings of same-sex undergraduates at high, moderate, and low levels of self-monitoring were represented. Researchers scrutinized the tapes for evidence of the impact of self-monitoring on spontaneous encounters between strangers.

In these meetings, as in so many other aspects of their lives, high self-monitoring individuals suffered little or no shyness. Soon after meeting the other person, they took an active and controlling role in the conversation. They were inclined to talk first and to initiate subsequent conversational sequences. They also felt, and were seen by their partners to have, a greater need to talk. Their partners also viewed them as having been the more directive member of the pair.

It was as if high self-monitoring individuals were particularly concerned about managing their behavior in order to create, encourage, and maintain a smooth flow of conversation. Perhaps this quality may help self-monitoring people to emerge as leaders in groups, organizations, and institutions.

DETECTING IMPRESSION MANAGEMENT IN OTHERS

High self-monitoring individuals are also adept at detecting impression management in others. To demonstrate this finely tuned ability, three communications researchers at the University of Minnesota made use of videotaped excerpts from the television program "To Tell the Truth." On this program, one of the three guest contestants (all male in the excerpts chosen for the study) is the "real Mr. X." The other two who claim to be the real Mr. X are, of course, lying. Participants in the study watched each excerpt and then tried to identify the real Mr. X. High self-monitoring individuals were much more accurate than their low self-monitoring counterparts in correctly identifying the real Mr. X and in seeing through the deception of the other two contestants.

Not only are high self-monitoring individuals able to see beyond the masks of deception successfully but they are also keenly attentive to the actions of other people as clues to their underlying intentions. E. E. Jones and Roy Baumeister of Princeton University

---

William James on the Roles We Play

A man has as many social selves as there are individuals who recognize him and carry an image of him in their mind. . . . But as the individuals who carry the images form naturally into classes, we may practically say that he has as many different social selves as there are distinct *groups* of persons about whose opinions he cares. He generally shows a different side of himself to each of these different groups. Many a youth who is demure enough before his parents and teachers swears and swaggers like a pirate among his "tough" young friends. We do not show ourselves to our children as to our club companions, to our masters and employers as to our intimate friends. From this there results what practically is a division of the man into several selves; and this may be a discordant splitting, as where one is afraid to let one set of his acquaintances know him as he is elsewhere; or it may be a perfectly harmonious division of labor, as where one tender to his children is stern to the soldiers or prisoners under his command.

—William James
The Principles of Psychology, 1890

had college students watch a videotaped discussion between two men who either agreed or disagreed with each other. The observers were aware that one man (the target person) had been instructed either to gain the affection or to win the respect of the other. Low self-monitoring observers tended to accept behavior at face value. They found themselves attracted to the agreeable person, whether or not he was attempting to ingratiate himself with his discussion partner. In contrast, high self-monitoring observers were acutely sensitive to the motivational context within which the target person operated. They liked the target better if he was disagreeable when trying to ingratiate himself. But when he sought respect, they were more attracted to him if he chose to be agreeable. Jones and Baumeister suggest that high self-monitoring observers regarded agreeableness as too blatant a ploy in gaining affection and autonomy as an equally obvious route to respect. Perhaps the high self-monitoring individuals felt that they themselves would have acted with greater subtlety and finesse.

Even more intriguing is Jones's and Baumeister's speculation—and I share their view—that high self-monitoring individuals prefer to live in a stable, predictable social environment populated by people whose actions consistently and accurately reflect their true attitudes and feelings. In such a world, the consistency and predictability of the actions of others would be of great benefit to those who tailor and manage their own self-presentation in social situations. From this perspective, it becomes quite understandable that high self-monitoring individuals may be especially fond of those who avoid strategic posturing. Furthermore, they actually may prefer as friends those comparatively low in self-monitoring.

How can we know when strangers and casual acquaintances are engaged in self-monitoring? Are there some channels of expression and communication that are more revealing than others about a person's true, inner "self," even when he or she is practicing impression management?

Both scientific and everyday observers of human behavior have suggested that nonverbal behavior—facial expressions, tone of voice, and body movements—reveals meaningful information about a person's attitudes, feelings, and motives. Often, people who engage in self-monitoring for deceptive purposes are less skilled at controlling their body's expressive movements. Accordingly, the body may be a more revealing source of information than the face for detecting those who engage in self-monitoring and impression management.

More than one experiment shows how nonverbal behavior can betray the true attitude of those attempting impression management. Shirley Weitz of the New School for Social Research reasoned that on college campuses where there are strong normative pressures supporting a tolerant and liberal value system, all students would avoid saying anything that would indicate racial prejudice—whether or not their private attitudes supported such behavior. In fact, she found that among "liberal" white males at Harvard University, the most prejudiced students (as determined by behavioral measures of actual attempts to avoid interaction with blacks) bent over backwards to *verbally* express liking and friendship for a black in a simulated interracial encounter. However, their *nonverbal* behaviors gave them away. Although the prejudiced students made every effort to say kind and favorable things, they continued to do so in a cool and distant tone of voice. It was as if they knew the words but not the music: they knew *what* to say, but not *how* to say it.

Another way that prejudice can be revealed is in the physical distance people maintain between themselves and the target of their prejudice. To demonstrate this phenomenon, psychologist Stephen Morin arranged for college students to be interviewed about their attitudes toward homosexuality. Half the interviewers wore "Gay and Proud" buttons and mentioned their association with the Association of Gay Psychologists. The rest wore no buttons and simply mentioned that they were graduate students working on theses. Without the students' knowledge, the distance they placed their chairs from the interviewer was measured while the interviews were going on. The measure of social distance proved to be highly revealing. When the student and the interviewer were of the same sex, students tended to establish almost a foot more distance between themselves and the apparently gay interviewers. They placed their chairs an average of 32 inches away from apparently gay interviewers, but only 22 inches away from apparently nongay interviewers. Interestingly, most of the students expressed tolerant, and at times favorable, attitudes toward gay people in general. However, the distances they chose to put between themselves and the interviewers they thought gay betrayed underlying negative attitudes.

IMPRESSION MANAGERS' DILEMMAS

The well-developed skills of high self-monitoring individuals ought to give them the flexibility to cope quickly and effectively with a diversity of social roles. They can choose with skill and grace the self-presentation appropriate to each of a wide variety of social situations. But what happens when the impression manager must effectively present a true and honest image to other people?

Consider the case of a woman on trial for a crime that she did not commit. Her task on the witness stand is to carefully present herself so that everything she does and says communicates to the jurors clearly and unambiguously her true innocence, so that they will vote for her acquittal. Chances are good, however, that members of the jury are somewhat skeptical of the defendant's claims of innocence. After all, they might reason to themselves, the district attorney would not have brought this case to trial were the state's case against her not a convincing one.

The defendant must carefully manage her verbal and nonverbal behaviors so as to ensure that even a skeptical jury forms a true impression of her innocence. In particular, she must avoid the pitfalls of an image that suggests that "she doth protest her innocence too much and therefore must be guilty." To the extent that our defendant skillfully practices the art of impression management, she will succeed in presenting herself to the jurors as the honest person that she truly is.

It often can take as much work to present a truthful image as to present a deceptive one. In fact, in this case, just being honest may not be enough when facing skeptical jurors who may bend over backwards to interpret any and all of the defendant's behavior— nervousness, for example—as a sign of guilt.

The message from research on impression management is a clear one. Some people are quite flexible in their self-presentation. What effects do these shifts in public appearance have on the more private reali-

ties of self-concept? In some circumstances, we are persuaded by our own appearances: we become the persons we appear to be. This phenomenon is particularly likely to occur when the image we present wins the approval and favor of those around us.

In an experiment conducted at Duke University by psychologists E. E. Jones, Kenneth Gergen, and Keith Davis, participants who had been instructed to win the approval of an interviewer presented very flattering images of themselves. Half the participants (chosen at random) then received favorable reactions from their interviewers; the rest did not. All the participants later were asked to estimate how accurately and honestly their self-descriptions had mirrored their true personalities.

Those who had won the favor of their interviewers considered their self-presentations to have been the most honest of all. One interpretation of this finding is that those people were operating with rather pragmatic definitions of self-concept: that which produced the most positive results was considered to be an accurate reflection of the inner self.

The reactions of other people can make it all the more likely that we become what we claim to be. Other people may accept our self-presentations at face value; they may then treat us as if we really were the way we pretend to be. For example, if I act as if I like Chris, chances are Chris will like me. Chris will probably treat me in a variety of friendly ways. As a result of Chris's friendliness, I may come to like Chris, even though I did not in the first place. The result, in this case, may be beneficial to both parties. In other circumstances, however, the skilled impression manager may pay an emotional price.

High self-monitoring orientation may be purchased at the cost of having one's actions reflect and communicate very little about one's private attitudes, feelings, and dispositions. In fact, as I have seen time and again in my research with my former graduate students Beth Tanke and Bill Swann, correspondence between private attitudes and public behavior is often minimal for high self-monitoring individuals. Evidently, the words and deeds of high self-monitoring individuals may reveal precious little information about their true inner feelings and attitudes.

Yet, it is almost a canon of modern psychology that a person's ability to reveal a "true self" to intimates is essential to emotional health. Sidney Jourard, one of the first psychologists to hold that view, believed that only through self-disclosure could we achieve self-discovery and self-knowledge: "Through my self-disclosure, I let others know my soul. They can know it, really know it, only as I make it known. In fact, I am beginning to suspect that I can't even know *my own soul* except as I disclose it. I suspect that I will know myself 'for real' at the exact moment that I have succeeded in making it known through my disclosure to another person."

Only low self-monitoring individuals may be willing or able to live their lives according to Jourard's prescriptions. By contrast, high self-monitoring individuals seem to embody Erving Goffman's view of human nature. For him, the world of appearances appears to be all, and the "soul" is illusory. Goffman defines social interactions as a theatrical performance in which each individual acts out a "line." A line is a set of carefully chosen verbal and nonverbal acts that express one's self. Each of us, in Goffman's view, seems to be merely the sum of our various performances.

What does this imply for the sense of self and identity associated with low and high self-monitoring individuals?

I believe that high self-monitoring individuals and low self-monitoring individuals have very different ideas about what constitutes a self and that their notions are quite well-suited to how they live. High self-monitoring individuals regard themselves as rather flexible and adaptive people who tailor their social behavior shrewdly and pragmatically to fit appropriate conditions. They believe that a person is whoever he appears to be in any particular situation: "I am me, the me I am right now." This self-image fits well with the way high self-monitoring individuals present themselves to the world. It allows them to act in ways that are consistent with how they believe they should act.

By contrast, low self-monitoring individuals have a firmer, more single-minded idea of what a self should be. They value and strive for congruence between "who they are" and "what they do" and regard their actions as faithful reflections of how they feel and think. For them, a self is a single identity that must not be compromised for other people or in certain situations. Indeed, this view of the self parallels the low self-monitoring individual's consistent and stable self-presentation.

What is important in understanding oneself and others, then, is not the elusive question of whether there is a quintessential self, but rather, understanding how different people define those attributes of their behavior and experience that they regard as "me." Theory and research on self-monitoring have attempted to chart the processes by which beliefs about the self are actively translated into patterns of social behavior that reflect self-conceptions. From this perspective, the processes of self-monitoring are the processes of self—a system of operating rules that translate self-knowledge into social behavior.

CRITICAL THINKING QUESTIONS

1. Self-monitoring can be measured along a continuum. What are the advantages and disadvantages for someone who scores very high on this dimension (i.e., a high self-monitoring individual)? Very low (i.e., a low self-monitoring individual)?

2. How might high versus low self-monitoring individuals act differently in an intimate situation such as dating? Give examples to support your answer.

3. How do you think differences in self-monitoring develop? In other words, why might some people be attuned to external factors while others are not? In your opinion, what level of self-monitoring might be best overall for healthy functioning? Explain your answers.

4. Articles 11 and 12 dealt with the concept of cognitive dissonance. Based on your understanding of the concept, do you think that dissonance arousal in a given situation may be influenced by the level of self-monitoring used by the person? How so?

ARTICLE 14

Let's do a quick exercise. Make a list of words or adjectives that you would use to describe someone that you think of as being feminine. Make another list of masculine descriptors. Next, compare the lists. Does one set of characteristics seem better than the other or just different? Could it be that the different stereotypical characteristics associated with masculinity and femininity might each be important, depending on the situation?

Masculine characteristics are generally considered *instrumental,* meaning that they are useful in task- or goal-oriented situations. Feminine characteristics tend to be more *expressive,* meaning that they focus more on the affective concern of the welfare of others. Typically, American society socializes its members to believe that males should act masculine and females, feminine and that each gender should suppress the characteristics of its opposite.

The following classic article by Sandra L. Bem postulates that when males are only allowed to act masculine and females are only allowed to act feminine, each gender is, in a sense, limited in what it can do. Masculine males are thus good in situations that call for instrumental, get-the-job-done traits, whereas feminine females are good in settings where concern for the feelings of others is important. But what about the person of either gender who has both masculine *and* feminine characteristics? Might he or she not be more adaptive and flexible to a greater variety of human experiences? In short, might not this person be better adjusted than the more rigidly defined masculine males and feminine females? Besides attempting to answer these questions, Bem's article is also a good example of how an instrument designed to measure a dimension of behavior characteristics is developed.

The Measurement of Psychological Androgyny[1]

■ Sandra L. Bem

This article describes the development of a new sex-role inventory that treats masculinity and femininity as two independent dimensions, thereby making it possible to characterize a person as masculine, feminine, or "androgynous" as a function of the difference between his or her endorsement of masculine and feminine personality characteristics. Normative data are presented, as well as the results of various psychometric analyses. The major findings of conceptual interest are: (a) the dimensions of masculinity and femininity are empirically as well as logically independent; (b) the concept of psychological androgyny is a reliable one; and (c) highly sex-typed scores do not reflect a general tendency to respond in a socially desirable direction, but rather a specific tendency to describe oneself in accordance with sex-typed standards of desirable behavior for men and women.

Both in psychology and in society at large, masculinity and femininity have long been conceptualized as bipolar ends of a single continuum; accordingly, a person has had to be either masculine or feminine, but not both. This sex-role dichotomy has served to obscure two very plausible hypotheses: first, that many individuals might be "androgynous"; that is, they might be *both* masculine and feminine, *both* assertive and yielding, *both* instrumental and expressive—depending on the situational appropriateness of these various behaviors; and conversely, that strongly sex-typed individuals might be seriously limited in the range of behaviors available to them as they move from situation to situation. According to both Kagan (1964) and Kohlberg (1966), the highly sex-typed individual is motivated to keep his behavior consistent with an internalized sex-role standard, a goal that he presumably accomplishes by suppressing any behavior that might be considered undesirable or inappropriate for his sex. Thus, whereas a narrowly masculine self-concept might inhibit behaviors that are stereotyped as feminine, and a narrowly feminine self-concept might inhibit behaviors that are stereotyped as masculine, a mixed, or androgynous, self-concept might allow an individual to freely engage in both "masculine" and "feminine" behaviors.

The current research program is seeking to explore these various hypotheses, as well as to provide construct validation for the concept of androgyny (Bem, 1974). Before the research could be initiated, however, it was first necessary to develop a new type of sex-role inventory, one that would not automatically build in an inverse relationship between masculinity and femininity. This article describes that inventory.

The Bem Sex-Role Inventory (BSRI) contains a number of features that distinguish it from other, commonly used, masculinity-femininity scales, for example, the Masculinity-Femininity scale of the California Psychological Inventory (Gough, 1957). First, it includes both a Masculinity scale and a Femininity scale, each of which contains 20 personality characteristics. These characteristics are listed in the first and second columns of Table 1, respectively. Second, because the BSRI was founded on a conception of the sex-typed person as someone who has internalized society's sex-typed standards of desirable behavior for men and women, these personality characteristics were selected as masculine or feminine on the basis of sex-typed social desirability and not on the basis of differential endorsement by males and females as most other inventories have done. That is, a characteristic qualified as masculine if it was judged to be more desirable in American society for a man than for a woman, and it qualified as feminine if it was judged to be more desirable for a woman than for a man. Third, the BSRI characterizes a person as masculine, feminine, or androgynous as a function of the difference between his or her endorsement of masculine and feminine personality characteristics. A person is

TABLE 1 / Sample of Items on the Masculinity, Femininity, and Social Desirability Scales of the BSRI

Masculine Items	Feminine Items	Neutral Items
Aggressive Competitive	Tender Affectionate	Friendly Conscientious

Note: This table includes only a few samples of the items found in the BSRI. For the full list of items in each category, see the original source.

Source: Reproduced by special permission of the Publisher, MIND GARDEN, Inc., 855 Oak Grove Ave., Suite 215, Menlo Park, CA 94025 USA www.mindgarden.com from the **Bem Sex Role Inventory** by Sandra Bem. Copyright 1978 by Consulting Psychologists Press, Inc. All rights reserved. Further reproduction is prohibited without the Publisher's written consent.

thus sex typed, whether masculine or feminine, to the extent that this difference score is high, the androgynous, to the extent that this difference score is low. Finally, the BSRI also includes a Social Desirability scale that is completely neutral with respect to sex. This scale now serves primarily to provide a neutral context for the Masculinity and Femininity scales, but it was utilized during the development of the BSRI to insure that the inventory would not simply be tapping a general tendency to endorse socially desirable traits. The 20 characteristics that make up this scale are listed in the third column of Table 1.

ITEM SELECTION

Both historically and cross-culturally, masculinity and femininity seem to have represented two complementary domains of *positive* traits and behaviors (Barry, Bacon, & Child, 1957; Erikson, 1964; Parsons & Bales, 1955). In general, masculinity has been associated with an instrumental orientation, a cognitive focus on "getting the job done"; and femininity has been associated with an expressive orientation, an affective concern for the welfare of others.

Accordingly, as a preliminary to item selection for the Masculinity and Femininity scales, a list was compiled of approximately 200 personality characteristics that seemed to the author and several students to be both positive in value and either masculine or feminine in tone. This list served as the pool from which the masculine and feminine characteristics were ultimately chosen. As a preliminary to item selection for the Social Desirability scale, an additional list was compiled of 200 characteristics that seemed to be neither masculine nor feminine in tone. Of these "neutral" characteristics, half were positive in value and half were negative.

Because the BSRI was designed to measure the extent to which a person divorces himself from those characteristics that might be considered more "appropriate" for the opposite sex, the final items were selected for the Masculinity and Femininity scales if they were judged to be more desirable in American society for one sex than for the other. Specifically, judges were asked to utilize a 7-point scale, ranging from 1 ("Not at all desirable") to 7 ("Extremely desirable"), in order to rate the desirability in American society of each of the approximately 400 personality characteristics mentioned above. (E.g., "In American society, how desirable is it for a man to be truthful?" "In American society, how desirable is it for a woman to be sincere?") Each individual judge was asked to rate the desirability of all 400 personality characteristics either "for a man" or "for a woman." No judge was asked to rate both. The judges consisted of 40 Stanford undergraduates who filled out the questionnaire during the winter of 1972 and an additional 60 who did so the following summer. In both samples, half of the judges were male and half were female.

A personality characteristic qualified as masculine if it was independently judged by both males and females in both samples to be significantly more desirable for a man than for a woman ($p < .05$).[2] Similarly,

a personality characteristic qualified as feminine if it was independently judged by both males and females in both samples to be significantly more desirable for a woman than for a man ($p < .05$). Of those characteristics that satisfied these criteria, 20 were selected for the Masculinity scale and 20 were selected for the Femininity scale (see the first and second columns of Table 1, respectively).

A personality characteristic qualified as neutral with respect to sex and hence eligible for the Social Desirability scale (a) if it was independently judged by both males and females to be no more desirable for one sex than for the other ($t < 1.2, p > .2$) and (b) if male and female judges did not differ significantly in their overall desirability judgments of that trait ($t < 1.2, p > .2$). Of those items that satisfied these several criteria, 10 positive and 10 negative personality characteristics were selected for the BSRI Social Desirability scale in accordance with Edwards' (1964) finding that an item must be quite positive or quite negative in tone if it is to evoke a social desirability response set. (The 20 neutral characteristics are shown in the third column of Table 1.)

After all of the individual items had been selected, mean desirability scores were computed for the masculine, feminine, and neutral items for each of the 100 judges. As shown in Table 2, for both males and females, the mean desirability of the masculine and feminine items was significantly higher for the "appropriate" sex than for the "inappropriate" sex, whereas the mean desirability of the neutral items was no higher for one sex than for the other. These results are, of course, a direct consequence of the criteria used for item selection.

TABLE 2 / Mean Social Desirability Ratings of the Masculine, Feminine, and Neutral Items

Item	Male Judges			Female Judges		
	Masculine Item	Feminine Item	Neutral Item	Masculine Item	Feminine Item	Neutral Item
For a man	5.59	3.63	4.00	5.83	3.74	3.94
For a woman	2.90	5.61	4.08	3.46	5.55	3.98
Difference	2.69	1.98	.08	2.37	1.81	.04
t	14.41*	12.13*	.17	10.22*	8.28*	.09

*$p < .001$.

TABLE 3 / Mean Social Desirability Ratings of the Masculine and Feminine Items for One's Own Sex

Item	Male Judges for a Man	Female Judges for a Woman
Masculine	5.59	3.46
Feminine	3.63	5.55
Difference	1.96	2.09
t	11.94*	8.88*

*$p < .001$.

Table 3 separates out the desirability ratings of the masculine and feminine items for male and female judges rating their *own* sex. These own-sex ratings seem to best represent the desirability of these various items as perceived by men and women when they are asked to describe *themselves* on the inventory. That is, the left-hand column of Table 3 represents the phenomenology of male subjects taking the test and the right-hand column represents the phenomenology of female subjects taking the test. As can be seen in Table 3, not only are "sex-appropriate" characteristics more desirable for both males and females than "sex-inappropriate" characteristics, but the phenomenologies of male and female subjects are almost perfectly symmetric: that is, men and women are nearly equal in their perceptions of the desirability of sex-appropriate characteristics, sex-inappropriate characteristics, and the difference between them ($t < 1$ in all three comparisons).

SCORING

The BSRI asks a person to indicate on a 7-point scale how well each of the 60 masculine, feminine, and neutral personality characteristics describes himself. The scale ranges from 1 ("Never or almost never true") to 7 ("Always or almost always true") and is labeled at each point. On the basis of his responses, each person receives three major scores: a Masculinity score, a Femininity score and, most important, an Androgyny score. In addition, a Social Desirability score can also be computed.

The Masculinity and Femininity scores indicate the extent to which a person endorses masculine and feminine personality characteristics as self-descriptive. Masculinity equals the mean self-rating for all endorsed masculine items, and Femininity equals the mean self-rating for all endorsed feminine items. Both can range from 1 to 7. It will be recalled that these two scores are logically independent. That is, the structure of the test does not constrain them in any way, and they are free to vary independently.

The Androgyny score reflects the relative amounts of masculinity and femininity that the person includes in his or her self-description, and, as such, it best characterizes the nature of the person's total sex role. Specifically, the Androgyny score is defined as Student's *t* ratio for the difference between a person's masculine and feminine self-endorsement; that is, the Androgyny score is the difference between an individual's masculinity and femininity normalized with respect to the standard deviations of his or her masculinity and femininity scores. The use of a *t* ratio as the index of androgyny—rather than a simple difference score—has two conceptual advantages: first, it allows us to ask whether a person's endorsement of masculine attributes differs significantly from his or her endorsement of feminine attributes and, if it does ($|t| \geq 2.025$, $df = 38$, $p < .05$), to classify that person as significantly sex typed; and second, it allows us to compare different populations in terms of the percentage of significantly sex-typed individuals present within each.[3]

It should be noted that the greater the absolute value of the Androgyny score, the more the person is sex typed or sex reversed, with high positive scores indicating femininity and high negative scores indicating masculinity. A "masculine" sex role thus represents not only the endorsement of masculine attributes but the simultaneous rejection of feminine attributes. Similarly, a "feminine" sex role represents not only the endorsement of feminine attributes but the simultaneous rejection of masculine attributes. In contrast, the closer the Androgyny score is to zero, the more the person is androgynous. An "androgynous" sex role thus represents the equal endorsement of both masculine and feminine attributes.

The Social Desirability score indicates the extent to which a person describes himself in a socially desirable direction on items that are neutral with respect to sex. It is scored by reversing the self-endorsement ratings for the 10 undesirable items and then calculating the subject's mean endorsement score across all 20 neutral personality characteristics. The Social Desirability score can thus range from 1 to 7, with 1 indicating a strong tendency to describe oneself in a socially undesirable direction and 7 indicating a strong tendency to describe oneself in a socially desirable direction.

PSYCHOMETRIC ANALYSES

Subjects

During the winter and spring of 1973, the BSRI was administered to 444 male and 279 female students in introductory psychology at Stanford University. It was also administered to an additional 117 male and 77 female paid volunteers at Foothill Junior College. The data that these students provided represent the normative data for the BSRI, and, unless explicitly noted, they serve as the basis for all of the analyses that follow.

Internal Consistency

In order to estimate the internal consistency of the BSRI, coefficient alpha was computed separately for the Masculinity, Femininity and Social Desirability scores of the subjects in each of the two normative samples. (Nunnally, 1967). The results showed all three scores to be highly reliable, both in the Stanford sample (Masculinity a = .86; Femininity a = .80; Social Desirability a = .75) and in the Foothill sample (Masculinity a = .86; Femininity a = .82; Social Desirability a = .70). Because the reliability of the Androgyny *t* ratio could not be calculated directly, coefficient alpha was computed for the highly correlated Androgyny difference score, Femininity-Masculinity, using the formula provided by Nunnally (1967) for linear combinations. The reliability of the Androgyny difference score was .85 for the Stanford sample and .86 for the Foothill sample.

Relationship between Masculinity and Femininity

As indicated earlier, the Masculinity and Femininity scores of the BSRI are logically independent. That is, the structure of the test does not constrain them in any way, and they are free to vary independently.

The results from the two normative samples reveal them to be empirically independent as well (Stanford male $r = .11$, female $r = -.14$; Foothill male $r = -.02$, female $r = -.07$). This finding vindicates the decision to design an inventory that would not artifactually force a negative correlation between masculinity and femininity.

Social Desirability Response Set

It will be recalled that a person is sex typed on the BSRI to the extent that his or her Androgyny score reflects the greater endorsement of "sex-appropriate" characteristics than of "sex-inappropriate" characteristics. However, because of the fact that the masculine and feminine items are all relatively desirable, even for the "inappropriate" sex, it is important to verify that the Androgyny score is not simply tapping a social desirability response set.

Accordingly, product-moment correlations were computed between the Social Desirability score and the Masculinity, Femininity, and Androgyny scores for the Stanford and Foothill samples separately. They were also computed between the Social Desirability score and the absolute value of the Androgyny score. These correlations are displayed in Table 4. As expected, both Masculinity and Femininity were correlated with Social Desirability. In contrast, the near-zero correlations between Androgyny and Social Desirability confirm that the Androgyny score is not measuring a general tendency to respond in a socially desirable direction. Rather, it is measuring a very specific tendency to describe oneself in accordance with sex-typed standards of desirable behavior for men and women.

Test-Retest Reliability

The BSRI was administered for a second time to 28 males and 28 females from the Stanford normative sample. The second administration took place approximately four weeks after the first. During this second administration, subjects were told that we were interested in how their responses on the test might vary over time, and they were explicitly instructed not to try to remember how they had responded previously. Product-moment correlations were computed between the first and second administrations for the Masculinity, Femininity, Androgyny, and Social

TABLE 4 / Correlation of Masculinity, Femininity, and Androgyny with Social Desirability

Sample	Masculinity with Social Desirability		Femininity with Social Desirability		Androgyny with Social Desirability		|Androgyny| with Social Desirability	
	Males	Females	Males	Females	Males	Females	Males	Females
Stanford	.42	.19	.28	.26	.12	.03	.08	−.10
Foothill	.23	.19	.15	.15	−.07	.06	−.12	−.09
Stanford and Foothill combined	.38	.19	.28	.22	.08	.04	.03	−.10

Desirability scores. All four scores proved to be highly reliable over the four-week interval (Masculinity $r = .90$; Femininity $r = .90$; Androgyny $r = .93$; Social Desirability $r = .89$).

Correlations with Other Measures of Masculinity-Femininity

During the second administration of the BSRI, subjects were also asked to fill out the Masculinity-Femininity scales of the California Psychological Inventory and the Guilford-Zimmerman Temperament Survey, both of which have been utilized rather frequently in previous research on sex roles. Table 5 presents the correlations between these two scales and the Masculinity, Femininity, and Androgyny scales of the BSRI. As can be seen in the table, the Guilford-Zimmerman scale is not at all correlated with any of the three scales of the BSRI, whereas the California Psychological Inventory is moderately correlated

TABLE 5 / Correlation of the Masculinity-Femininity Scales of the California Psychological Inventory (CPI) and Guilford-Zimmerman Scale with the Masculinity, Femininity, and Androgyny Scales of the BSRI

Scale	CPI		Guilford-Zimmerman	
	Males	Females	Males	Females
BSRI Masculinity	−.42	−.25	.11	.15
BSRI Femininity	.27	.25	.04	−.06
BSRI Androgyny	.50	.30	−.04	−.06

Note: The CPI scale is keyed in the feminine direction, whereas the Guilford-Zimmerman scale is keyed in the masculine direction.

with all three. It is not clear why the BSRI should be more highly correlated with the CPI than with the Guilford-Zimmerman scale, but the fact that none of the correlations is particularly high indicates that the BSRI is measuring an aspect of sex roles which is not directly tapped by either of these two scales.

NORMS

Table 6 presents the mean Masculinity, Femininity, and Social Desirability scores separately by sex for both the Stanford and the Foothill normative samples. It also presents means for both the Androgyny *t* ratio and the Androgyny difference score. As can be seen in the table, males scored significantly higher than females on the Masculinity scale, and females scored significantly higher than males on the Femininity scale in both samples. On the two measures of androgyny, males scored on the masculine side of zero and females scored on the feminine side of zero. This difference is significant in both samples and for both measures. On the Social Desirability scale, females scored significantly higher than males at Stanford but not at Foothill. It should be noted that the size of this sex difference is quite small, however, even in the Stanford sample.

Table 7 presents the percentage of subjects within each of the two normative samples who qualified as masculine, feminine, or androgynous as a function of the Androgyny *t* ratio. Subjects are classified as sex typed, whether masculine or feminine, if the androgyny *t* ratio reaches statistical significance ($|t| \geq 2.025$, $df = 38$, $p < .05$), and they are classified as androgynous if the absolute value of the *t* ratio is less than or equal to one. Table 7 also indicates the percentage of subjects who fall between these various cutoff points.

TABLE 6 / Sex Differences on the BSRI

Scale Score	Stanford University			Foothill Junior College		
	Males ($n = 444$)	Females ($n = 279$)	t	Males ($n = 117$)	Females ($n = 77$)	t
Masculinity						
M	4.97	4.57		4.96	4.55	
SD	.67	.69	7.62*	.71	.75	3.86*
Femininity						
M	4.44	5.01		4.62	5.08	
SD	.55	.52	13.88*	.64	.58	5.02*
Social Desirability						
M	4.91	5.08		4.88	4.89	
SD	.50	.50	4.40*	.50	.53	*ns*
Androgyny t Ratio						
M	−1.28	1.10		−.80	1.23	
SD	1.99	2.29	14.33*	2.23	2.42	5.98*
Androgyny Difference Score						
M	−0.53	.43		−.34	.53	
SD	.82	.93	14.28*	.97	.97	6.08*

*$p < .001$.

It should be noted that these cut-off points are somewhat arbitrary and that other investigators should feel free to adjust them in accordance with the characteristics of their particular subject populations.

CONCLUDING COMMENT

It is hoped that the development of the BSRI will encourage investigators in the areas of sex dif-ferences and sex roles to question the traditional assumption that it is the sex-typed individual who typifies mental health and to begin focusing on the behavioral and societal consequences of more flexible sex-role self-concepts. In a society where rigid sex-role differentiation has already outlived its utility, perhaps the androgynous person will come to define a more human standard of psychological health.

TABLE 7 / Percentage of Subjects in the Normative Samples Classified as Masculine, Feminine, or Androgynous

Item	Stanford University		Foothill Junior College	
	Males ($n = 444$)	Females ($n = 279$)	Males ($n = 117$)	Females ($n = 77$)
% feminine ($t \geq 2.025$)	6	34	9	40
% near feminine ($1 < t < 2.025$)	5	20	9	8
% androgynous ($−1 \leq t \leq +1$)	34	27	44	38
% near masculine ($−2.025 < t < −1$)	19	12	17	7
% masculine ($t \leq −2.025$)	36	8	22	8

REFERENCES

Barry, H., Bacon, M. K., & Child, I. L. A cross-cultural survey of some sex differences in socialization. *Journal of Abnormal and Social Psychology,* 1957, *55,* 327–332.

Bem, S. L. Sex-role adaptability: One consequence of psychological androgyny. *Journal of Personality and Social Psychology,* 1974, in press.

Edwards, A. L. The measurement of human motives by means of personality scales. In D. Levine (Ed.), *Nebraska symposium on motivation: 1964.* Lincoln: University of Nebraska Press, 1964.

Erikson, E. H. Inner and outer space: Reflections on womanhood. In R. J. Lifton (Ed.), *The woman in America.* Boston: Houghton Mifflin, 1964.

Gough, H. G. *Manual for the California Psychological Inventory.* Palo Alto, Calif.: Consulting Psychologists Press, 1957.

Kagan, J. Acquisition and significance of sex-typing and sex-role identity. In M. L. Hoffman & L. W. Hoffman (Eds.), *Review of child development research.* Vol. 1. New York: Russell Sage Foundation, 1964.

Kohlberg, L. A cognitive-developmental analysis of children's sex-role concepts and attitudes. In E. E. Maccoby (Ed.), *The development of sex differences.* Stanford, Calif.: Stanford University Press, 1966.

Nunnally, J. C. *Psychometric theory.* New York: McGraw-Hill, 1967.

Parsons, T., & Bales, R. F. *Family, socialization, and interaction process.* New York: Free Press of Glencoe, 1955.

ENDNOTES

1. This research was supported by IROIMH 21735 from the National Institute of Mental Health. The author is grateful to Carol Korula, Karen Rook, Jenny Jacobs, and Odile van Embden for their help in analyzing the data.

2. All significance levels in this article are based on two-tailed *t* tests.

3. A Statistical Package for the Social Sciences (SPSS) computer program for calculating individual *t* ratios is available on request from the author. In the absence of computer facilities, one can utilize the simple Androgyny difference score, Femininity-Masculinity, as the index of androgyny. Empirically, the two indices are virtually identical ($r = .98$), and one can approximate the *t*-ratio value by multiplying the Androgyny difference score by 2.322. This conversion factor was derived empirically from our combined normative sample of 917 students at two different colleges.

CRITICAL THINKING QUESTIONS

1. Examine the sample items in Table 1 that are categorized as masculine, feminine, or neutral. Since this article was written in 1974, these items were selected over three decades ago. Do you think that these items are still applicable today, or are some of them dated and perhaps even controversial? Have notions of masculinity and femininity changed over time? Explain.

2. The BSRI (Bem Self-Role Inventory) is a self-report instrument. Do you think the way someone describes his or her characteristics on paper is necessarily an accurate portrayal of the way he or she really acts? In what way? How could you test this possibility?

3. What do you think of the concept of *androgyny?* Would society be better off if more people were androgynous rather than being either masculine *or* feminine? Why or why not?

4. Based on the information in the article, describe specific situations where an androgynous individual might be better suited than either a masculine or feminine individual. In what, if any, situations would someone only capable of masculine behaviors be more appropriate? What about someone only capable of feminine behaviors? Explain your answers.

5. After reading the article, you should have a good grasp of the concept of androgyny. If you explained this concept to others, do you think that most people would agree that they would be better off if they were androgynous rather than either masculine or feminine? Why or why not?

ADDITIONAL RELATED READINGS

Cheng, C. (2005). Processes underlying gender-role flexibility: Do androgynous individuals know more or know how to cope? *Journal of Personality, 73*(3), 645–673.

Lefkowitz, E. S. (2006). Masculinity and femininity predict optimal mental health: A belated test of the Androgyny Hypothesis. *Journal of Personality Assessment, 87*(1), 65–101.

ARTICLE 15

Men's sexual aggression toward women is a major concern in most societies. One type of such sexual aggression that has received increased attention is date rape. What differentiates date rape from other forms of rape is that in date rape, the two individuals generally know each other, which means the possibility of consensual sex exists. The concern over the prevalence of date rape is so great that many college freshmen orientation programs now address it, both to increase awareness of the problem and to prevent its occurrence.

Why would a man force a woman to have sex with him? There are many reasons for this behavior, but they can be broadly classified as either *situational* or *dispositional*. *Situational factors* pertain to the circumstances surrounding the event—for instance, becoming highly intoxicated and having clouded judgment and/or lowered inhibitions. The relationship between intoxication and sexual aggression is well documented. *Dispositional factors,* on the other hand, include all of the personality factors that predispose people to act in certain ways. Unlike situational factors, which change with the specific situation, dispositional factors are relatively enduring.

There are many dispositional factors that may predispose someone to coercive sexual behavior. One such factor may be the belief in and adherence to certain concepts of masculinity. For example, believing that men should dominate women or that sexual behavior need not be connected to emotional involvement might predispose a man toward sexually coercive behavior.

The following article by Benjamin D. Locke and James R. Mahalik examines how certain masculinity norms, drinking patterns, and athletic involvement may predict sexual aggression in college men. In addition to the important implications this study has for college students, the article also is a good example of how concepts such as masculinity (discussed in the previous study, Article 14) are further investigated over time.

Examining Masculinity Norms, Problem Drinking, and Athletic Involvement as Predictors of Sexual Aggression in College Men

■ Benjamin D. Locke and James R. Mahalik

Male sexual aggression toward women is a serious social problem, particularly on college campuses. In this study, college men's sexually aggressive behavior and rape myth acceptance were examined using conformity to 11 masculine norms and 2 variables previously linked to sexual aggression: problem drinking and athletic involvement. Results indicated that men who use alcohol problematically and conform to specific masculine norms (i.e., having power over women, being a playboy, disdaining gay men, being dominant, being violent, and taking risks) tended to endorse rape myths and report sexually aggressive behavior. Additionally, men who reported higher levels of problematic alcohol use and risk taking were more likely to report sexually aggressive behavior without endorsing rape myths. Implications and recommendations are discussed.

Male sexual aggression against women is a serious social problem (Federal Bureau of Investigation, 1992; U.S. Census Bureau, 1999), particularly within the college population (e.g., Koss, Gidycz, & Wisniewski, 1987). Sexual aggression prevalence rates are known to vary greatly across cultures, with certain cultural beliefs and values contributing to "rape-prone" cultures (Sanday, 1981). Thus, male sexual aggression can be conceptualized as a combination of sexually aggressive behaviors (e.g., harassment, rape) and the cultural beliefs that support such behaviors, including rape myths, such as rape results from uncontrollable male passions (Schwendinger & Schwendinger, 1974).

Because men account for the overwhelming majority of arrests for sexual violence against women, and because many of the rape myths contain assumptions about masculinity and men's power over women, it seems logical to examine how masculinity may contribute to these concerns. Some of the earliest studies reported that traditional masculinity attitudes predict men's adherence to rape supportive beliefs (Bunting & Reeves, 1983) and aggressive sexual behaviors (Mosher & Anderson, 1986). More recent research has found men's traditional views of the male role related to attitudes supportive of date rape (Truman, Tokar, & Fischer, 1996) and rape myth acceptance (Davis & Liddell, 2002); further, men's beliefs and expectations about masculinity were the most powerful and consistent predictor of their sexual violence-supporting beliefs and behaviors (Good, Heppner, Hillenbrand-Gunn, & Wang, 1995).

However, only Rando, Rogers, and Brittan-Powell (1998) have examined masculinity as a multidimensional construct in relation to sexual violence, finding that one dimension of masculinity (i.e., restricting affection to other men) predicted college men's sexual aggression, whereas other masculinity factors (e.g., pursuing success) did not. We believe that extending this type of multidimensional approach to understanding masculinity as it relates to sexually aggressive behaviors and rape myth acceptance is important for two reasons. First, assuming that masculinity is a singular global construct ignores the multiple dimensions of masculinity identified in U.S. society. For example, gender theorists posit (David & Brannon, 1976) and researchers confirm (Thompson & Pleck, 1995) a large number of cultural beliefs about masculine gender roles (e.g., be a winner; be emotion-ally controlled; have power over women; disdain gay men), with as many as 11 distinct masculinity norms identified (Mahalik et al., 2003). Second, using a multidimensional conceptualization of masculinity allows for the potential of a more complex, interpretable, and practically applicable relationship between the components of masculinity and sexual aggression.

Given our emphasis on college men in this study, we think it important to examine masculinity in the context of other variables identified as predictors of men's sexual aggression in the college population. One such variable is alcohol use, which is reported to increase men's perception that female behavior is sexual in nature, decrease the perception of risk involved in sexual aggression, and increase the likelihood of sexual aggression (Fromme & Wendel, 1995; Koss & Gaines, 1993; Seto & Barbaree, 1995; Testa, Livingston, & Collins, 2000).

Some research also suggests that participation in collegiate athletics is related to sexual aggression in college men. For example, one study found male college athletes responsible for up to one third of sexual assaults on college campuses (Koss & Dinero, 1988), and others document a relationship between collegiate athletics and sexual aggression (Caron, Halteman, & Stacy, 1997; Koss & Gaines, 1993; Marchell, 1998). No research, however, has examined whether problematic alcohol use and participation in college athletics relate to rape myth acceptance.

The purpose of this study is to extend previous research by examining how sexually aggressive behavior and endorsement of rape myths are predicted by masculinity as a multidimensional construct, along with previously demonstrated predictors of sexual aggression in a college population. Specifically, we predicted that greater conformity to masculinity norms, higher levels of problematic alcohol use, and greater involvement with college athletics would relate to higher levels of self-reported sexual aggression and greater endorsement of rape myths.

METHOD

Participants

Two hundred fifty-four male college students from undergraduate classes and psychology subject pools at four colleges and universities in the northeastern and mid-Atlantic regions of the United States participated. They ranged from 18 to 28 years of age ($M = 19.70$, $SD = 1.60$) and were mostly White (232 White, 7 Asian, 4 Black, 3 Latino, 3 biracial, and 5 other), single (251 single, 1 married, and 1 same-sex committed relationship), and heterosexual (249 heterosexual, 2 gay, and 3 bisexual). Of the four colleges and universities from which participants were recruited, one was a private university enrolling 9,000 students with Division I athletics; one was a public university of 11,000 students with Division I athletics; one was a private college of 1,800 students with Division III athletics; and one was a public college of 1,700 students with Division III athletics.

Measures

The Illinois Rape Myth Acceptance Scale (IRMA; Payne, Lonsway, & Fitzgerald, 1999) was used to measure men's endorsement of myths about rape. The IRMA is composed of 45 items rated on a 7-point Likert-type scale, with higher scores indicating greater acceptance of rape myths. Regarding validity, Payne et al. (1999) reported that IRMA scores related to holding more traditional gender role stereotypes, endorsing an adversarial relationship between the genders, expressing hostile attitudes toward women, being accepting of interpersonal violence, and having less empathy for a hypothetical rape victim. Internal consistency for the overall scale was reported at .93 (Payne et al., 1999), with $\alpha = .95$ for the total IRMA score in this study.

To measure men's sexually aggressive behavior toward women, we used the Sexual Experiences Survey (SES; Koss & Gaines, 1993). The 11 items were designed to reflect the legal parameters of rape as well as lesser forms of sexual aggression, such as coercive sexuality (e.g., "Attempted sexual intercourse with a woman by threatening to use force"), on a 5-point scale ranging from *never* to *often*. Originally developed in the early 1980s (Koss & Gidycz, 1985; Koss & Oros, 1982), the measure was revised in 1987 (Koss et al., 1987) and again in 1993 (Koss & Gaines, 1993). Research has found consistent relationships between men's level of sexual aggression and the SES, and that men were more likely to admit to sexual aggression using the SES than in face-to-face interviews (see

Koss & Gidycz, 1985). Addressing reliability, research has reported internal consistency estimates of .89 for men, with a test–retest agreement of .93 after 1 week (Koss & Gidycz, 1985). In the current study, $\alpha = .69$ for the total SES score.

Problematic drinking was assessed using the Alcohol Use Disorders Identification test (AUDIT; Saunders, Aasland, Babor, De La Fuente, & Grant, 1993). The AUDIT is a 10-item self-report instrument, scored on a 5-point Likert scale, designed to identify individuals for whom the use of alcohol places them at risk for alcohol problems or who are experiencing such problems. The time reference of the AUDIT items is the past year, although a few items have no specific time reference. AUDIT total scores can range from 0 to 40. AUDIT scores are reported to relate significantly to other self-report screening tests for alcohol abuse, such as the Michigan Alcohol Screening Test, CAGE, and MacAndrew Scale (Bohn, Babor, & Kranzler, 1995; Hays, Merz, & Nicholas, 1995; Saunders et al., 1993). Research supports the AUDIT'S internal consistency as satisfactory (Barry & Fleming, 1993), with $\alpha = .86$ in this study.

To measure men's level of athletic involvement, we adopted procedures from Koss and Gaines's (1993) study to enable comparisons. Participants answered one item, in which they were asked to check all of the following descriptions that applied to them: (1) "I participate informally in sports," (2) "I participate in at least one club sport," (3) "I participate in a non-revenue producing varsity sport (NO tickets sold)," and (4) "I participate in a revenue producing varsity sport (tickets ARE sold)." A score of 0 was assigned if they checked none of the options, 1 if they participated informally, 2 if they participated in at least one club sport, 3 if they participated in a non-revenue-producing varsity sport, and 4 if they participated in a revenue-producing varsity sport.

To assess participants' conformity to masculine norms, we used the Conformity to Masculinity Norms Inventory (CMNI; Mahalik et al., 2003). The inventory consists of 94 items answered on a 4-point scale (0 = strongly disagree to 3 = strongly agree) and assesses conformity to an array of masculinity norms found in the dominant culture in U.S. society. Using factor analysis, Mahalik et al. (2003) identified 11 distinct factors, labeled Winning, Emotional Control, Risk Taking, Violence, Dominance, Playboy, Self-Reliance, Primacy of Work, Power Over Women, Disdain for Homosexuals, and Pursuit of Status. Mahalik et al. (2003) reported that CMNI scores significantly related to other masculinity measures; significantly and positively related to psychological distress, social dominance, aggression, and the desire to be more muscular; and significantly and negatively related to attitudes toward psychological help seeking. Internal consistency estimates ranged from .75 to .91 for the 11 masculinity norms, with test–retest over a 2–3 week period ranging from .76 to .95 (Mahalik et al., 2003). In this study, alphas ranged from .70 to .90 for the 11 masculinity norms.

Procedure

Data were collected via a Web-based survey containing the measures described above along with informed consent and debriefing pages. All participants were provided with a link to a page where they indicated their informed consent. This link directed them to the survey, which took approximately 45 min, after which participants were directed to a debriefing page. All participants received experimental credit.

RESULTS

Preliminary Analyses

The means, standard deviations, and intercorrelations for scores on the IRMA, the SES, the AUDIT, athletic involvement, and the 11 CMNI subscales are presented in Table 1. Tests of normality for the continuous variables indicated that only the SES was nonnormal. Taking the natural log as suggested by Tabachnick and Fidell (1989) for positively skewed variables improved its skewness from 1.11 to 0.33. This transformed variable is reported as the SES variable.

Main Analysis

To test the hypothesis that greater conformity to masculinity norms, higher levels of problematic alcohol use, and greater involvement with college athletics will relate to higher levels of sexual aggression

toward women and greater acceptance of rape myths, we conducted a canonical correlation analysis. Rape myth acceptance and sexually aggressive behavior formed one side of the model, and problem drinking, athletic involvement, and conformity to 11 masculinity norms formed the other side of the model. Results indicated that the model was significant and that two significant roots accounted for 45% of the total variance.

To identify significant associations with the variates on the two roots, we used a criterion of .40 as a cutoff score for the structure correlate's coefficients. The first root (Wilks's λ = .59), $F(26, 478)$ = 5.61, p < .01, was characterized by strong negative loadings on Rape Myth Acceptance, SES, and Power Over Women and moderate negative loadings on Problematic Alcohol Use, Risk Taking, Violence, Dominance, Playboy, and Disdain for Homosexuals (see Table 2). These structure coefficients suggest that college men who use alcohol problematically and conform to a set of specific masculine norms (having power over women, being a playboy, disdaining gay men, being dominant, being violent, and taking risks) tended to accept rape myths and engage in sexual aggression. This root accounted for 34% of the explained variance.

The second root (Wilks's λ = .89), $F(12, 240)$ = 2.53, p < .01, consisted of moderate positive loadings on SES, Problematic Alcohol Use, and Risk Taking and a moderate negative loading on Rape Myth Acceptance. This finding suggests that men who report higher levels of problematic alcohol use and conform more to the masculine norm of risk taking are more likely to engage in sexual aggression but less likely to endorse rape myths. This root accounted for 11% of the explained variance.

DISCUSSION

Results from the first root of the canonical analysis supported the hypothesized relationships between masculinity norms and problematic alcohol use as predictive of sexually aggressive behavior toward women and rape myth acceptance but did not support our hypothesis that athletic involvement would also predict these variables. Examining the specific masculinity norms, we found those reflecting power

TABLE 1 / Means, Standard Deviations, and Intercorrelations of Scores on the Illinois Rape Myth Acceptance Scale, Sexual Experiences Survey, AUDIT, Athletic Involvement, and 11 Masculinity Norms

Variable	M	SD	1	2	3	4	5	6	7	8	9	10	11	12	13	14	15
1. Rape Myth Acceptance Scale	64.70	31.60	—														
2. Sexual Experiences Survey	1.00	1.10	.22***	—													
3. AUDIT	11.22	5.63	.10	.32***	—												
4. Athletic involvement	1.32	1.06	.03	.07	.08	—											
5. Winning	16.40	5.05	.16*	.20**	.28***	.27***	—										
6. Emotional control	15.38	5.60	.16*	.03	.16*	−0.8	.18**	—									
7. Risk taking	16.50	3.84	.10	.27***	.26***	.10	.38***	.12	—								
8. Violence	12.43	3.68	.20**	.17*	.29***	.10	.37***	.21**	.39***	—							
9. Power over women	8.58	4.18	.41***	.33***	.33***	.02	.33***	.21**	.13*	.35***	—						
10. Dominance	5.74	1.80	.28***	.24***	.26***	.01	.49***	.14*	.22***	.22***	.37***	—					
11. Playboy	12.51	6.22	.26***	.37***	.41***	.04	.28***	.29***	.18**	.40***	.58***	.30***	—				
12. Self-reliance	6.77	2.92	.14*	.15*	.27***	−.01	.25***	.47***	.10	.08	.23***	.28***	.21**	—			
13. Primacy of work	9.00	3.31	.13*	.01	−.11	−.01	.06	.19**	−.05	−.01	.21**	.20**	.10	.18**	—		
14. Disdain for homosexuals	17.09	5.43	.33***	.21**	.23***	−.01	.28***	.20**	.08	.29***	.34***	.15*	.27**	.10	−.03	—	
15. Pursuit of status	11.66	2.53	.05	.16	.25***	−.04	.32***	−.05	.19**	.16**	.12	.31***	.12	−.03	.08	.23***	—

Note. N = 254. AUDIT = Alcohol Use Disorders Identification Test.
*p < .05. **p < .01. ***p < .001.

TABLE 2 / Structure Correlational Coefficients for Canonical Analysis for Significant Canonical Roots

Variable	Root 1	Root 2
Rape Myth Acceptance Scale	**−.79**	**−.62**
Sexual Experiences Survey	**−.78**	**.63**
Problematic alcohol use	**−.46**	**.53**
Athletic involvement	−.11	.09
Conformity to masculine norms		
Winning	−.39	.09
Emotional control	−.22	−.31
Risk taking	**−.40**	**.43**
Violence	**−.41**	−.05
Power over women	**−.81**	−.19
Dominance	**−.58**	−.08
Playboy	**−.68**	.27
Self-reliance	−.33	.01
Primacy of work	−.16	−.32
Disdain for homosexuals	**−.60**	−.27
Pursuit of status	−.22	.27

Note. N = 254. Boldface indicates coefficients above .40.

with women (i.e., Power Over Women and Playboy), interpersonal power (i.e., Dominance), and disdaining gay men (i.e., Disdain for Homosexuals) to be particularly strong predictors of sexual aggression and rape myth acceptance. Other norms were modest predictors (i.e., Risk Taking and Violence), and still others were not significant at all (i.e., Emotional Control, Primacy of Work, Pursuit of Status, Winning, and Self-Reliance).

These results extend the findings of previous research linking masculinity and sexual aggression toward women (i.e., Bunting & Reeves, 1983; Good et al., 1995; Mosher & Anderson, 1986; Rando et al., 1998; Truman et al., 1996) by identifying which masculine norms are predictive, and which are not predictive, of sexual aggression. The strongest links to men's sexual violence and acceptance of rape myths had to do with masculinity norms about taking action to control women (i.e., conforming to power over women norms), believing that emotional involvement in sexual relationships is not a good idea (i.e., conforming to playboy norms), and being uncomfortable or angry at gay men and not wanting to be perceived as homosexual (i.e., conforming to disdain for gay men norms). The masculine norms that were predictive of sexual aggression seem to be similar to the construct of hostile masculinity (i.e., a hostile orientation and gratification from controlling or dominating women) used by Malamuth and colleagues to predict coerciveness against women and sexual aggression (Malamuth, Heavey, & Linz, 1993; Malamuth, Linz, Heavey, Barnes, & Acker, 1995; Malamuth, Sockloskie, Koss, & Tanaka, 1991).

The results also highlight both problematic alcohol use and conformity to specific masculinity norms in relation to sexual aggression. Whereas previous research examined only one set of variables (i.e., problematic alcohol use or masculinity), our results suggest that both are important to consider when identifying factors associated with sexual aggression. For example, it may be that sexual aggression is impulsive behavior facilitated by problematic alcohol use for those men who construct masculinity as being powerful over women, dominant, a playboy, and disdaining gay men, whereas for men who construct masculinity as composed of other norms, problematic alcohol use may not facilitate sexual aggression.

Results from the second root of our analysis are more complex to interpret given that they describe college men who do not endorse rape myths but do report sexually aggressive behaviors along with moderate alcohol abuse and risk taking. The second root appears to relate to those who do not believe rape myths but who may become sexually aggressive after drinking or engaging in risky behaviors. Thus, the findings from both roots support the directions of our hypothesis regarding sexually aggressive behavior, but the results from the second root provide a more complex picture of rape myth acceptance in relation to the variables studied.

Results did not support our hypothesis that participation in athletics would be predictive of sexual aggression or rape myth acceptance, despite the fact that some studies have found male college athletes are responsible for up to a third of sexual assaults on college campuses (Koss & Dinero, 1988) and others have reported a relationship between athletic involvement and sexual aggression (Koss & Gaines, 1993).

This was true even though we used the same measure of athletic involvement as Koss and Gaines (1993).

Given the findings about masculinity and problematic alcohol use, prevention efforts might address the most salient masculinity norms identified in this study—in particular Power Over Women, Dominance, Playboy, and Disdain for Homosexuals—along with problematic alcohol use. Cognitive therapy techniques could be used to help men identify and challenge particular masculinity norms (e.g., patriarchal attitudes or devaluing women) that may constrain their own well-being as well as contribute to sexual aggression (see Mahalik, 1999).

We think such an approach might also be useful in reducing men's defensiveness to such interventions. Because men are likely to feel vilified when men in general are blamed for sexual aggression, professionals who target specific masculine norms to address in interventions (i.e., Power Over Women, Dominance, Playboy, and Disdain for Homosexuals) as opposed to blaming men or masculinity in general as sources of the problem may encounter less resistance from participants. These ideas are speculative, but they could be evaluated in future research examining outreach programming to reduce sexual aggression.

Several limitations are also noted for the study. Similar to other studies that have examined sexual aggression in college men, this study used a self-report format, and the data were correlational. Further, the survey was Web based, which may have either increased honest responses from participants, given the anonymity and encryption of their responses, or decreased honest responses, if participants were worried about Internet security. Also, participants were mostly White, their economic circumstances allowed them to attend college, and they were being educated in a college or university. Generalization of the findings to groups of men who differ from this group on variables such as class, race, and educational level should be made cautiously. Last, athletic involvement was measured with a single item. Even though it was face valid and adopted from Koss and Gaines's (1993) well-cited study, the single item raises some validity concerns that one should keep in mind when interpreting the results.

Future research should address these limitations by replicating the study in different populations. Researchers should also work to identify contextual variables that may support sexual aggression (e.g., social norms of groups to which men belong), examine causal contributions to sexual aggression and rape myth acceptance, and design and evaluate preventive interventions for men's sexual aggression. By doing so, we may develop a better understanding of the influences on men's sexual violence toward women and reduce the high rates of male sexual violence on campuses and in the larger society, thereby improving both women's and men's lives.

REFERENCES

Barry, K. L., & Fleming, M. F. (1993). The Alcohol Use Disorders Identification Test (AUDIT) and the SMAST-13: Predictive validity in a rural primary care sample. *Alcohol atul Alcoholism, 28,* 33–42.

Bohn, M. J., Babor, T. F., & Kranzler, H. R. (1995). The Alcohol Use Disorders Identification Test (AUDIT): Validation of a screening instrument for use in medical settings. *Journal of Studies on Alcohol, 56,* 423–432.

Bunting, A. B., & Reeves, J. B. (1983). Perceived male sex orientation and beliefs about rape. *Deviant Behavior, 4,* 281–295.

Caron, S. L., Halteman, W. A., & Stacy, C. (1997). Athletes and rape: Is there a connection? *Perceptual & Motor Skills, 85,* 1379–1393.

David, D., & Brannon, R. (1976). *The forty-nine percent majority: The male sex role.* Reading, MA: Addison Wesley.

Davis, T. L., & Liddell, D. L. (2002). Getting inside the house: The effectiveness of a rape prevention program for college fraternity men. *Journal of College Student Development, 43,* 35–50.

Federal Bureau of Investigation. (1992). *Crime in the United States.* Washington, DC: U.S. Department of Justice.

Fromme, K., & Wendel, J. (1995). Beliefs about the effects of alcohol on involvement in coercive and consenting sexual activities. *Journal of Applied Social Psychology, 25,* 2099–2117.

Good, G. E., Heppner, M. J., Hillenbrand-Gunn, T. L., & Wang, L. F. (1995). Sexual and psychological violence: An exploratory study of predictors in college men. *Journal of Men's Studies, 4,* 59–71.

Hays, R. D., Merz, J. F., & Nicholas, R. (1995). Response burden, reliability, and validity of the CAGE, Short MAST, and AUDIT alcohol screening measures. *Behavior Research Methods, Instruments, and Computers, 27,* 277–280.

Koss, M. P., & Dinero, T. E. (1988). Predictors of sexual aggression among a national sample of male college students. *Annals of the New York Academy of Sciences, 528,* 133–147.

Koss, M. P., & Gaines, J. A. (1993). The prediction of sexual aggression by alcohol use, athletic participation, and fraternity affiliation. *Journal of Interpersonal Violence, 8,* 94–108.

Koss, M. P., & Gidycz, C. A. (1985). Sexual Experiences Survey: Reliability and validity. *Journal of Consulting and Clinical Psychology, 53,* 422–423.

Koss, M. P., Gidycz, C. A., & Wisniewski, N. (1987). The scope of rape: Incidence and prevalence of sexual aggression and victimization in a national sample of higher education students. *Journal of Consulting and Clinical Psychology, 55,* 162–170.

Koss, M. P., & Oros, C. J. (1982). Sexual Experiences Survey: A research instrument investigating sexual aggression and victimization. *Journal of Consulting and Clinical Psychology, 50,* 455–457.

Mahalik, J. R. (1999). Incorporating a gender role strain perspective in assessing and treating men's cognitive distortions. *Professional Psychology: Research and Practice, 30,* 333–340.

Mahalik, J. R., Locke, B., Ludlow, L., Diemer, M., Scott, R. P. J., Gottfried, M., & Freitas, G. (2003). Development of the Conformity to Masculine Norms Inventory. *Psychology of Men and Masculinity, 4,* 3–25.

Malamuth, N. M., Heavey, C. L., & Linz, D. (1993). Predicting men's antisocial behavior against women: The interaction model of sexual aggression. In G. C. Nagayama Hall & R. Hirschman (Eds.), *Sexual aggression: Issues in etiology, assessment, and treatment. Series in applied psychology: Social issues and questions* (pp. 63–97). Philadelphia: Taylor & Francis.

Malamuth, N. M., Linz, D., Heavey, C. L., Barnes, G., & Acker, M. (1995). Using the confluence model of sexual aggression to predict men's conflict with women: A 10-year follow-up study. *Journal of Personality and Social Psychology, 69,* 353–369.

Malamuth, N. M., Sockloskie, R. J., Koss, M. P., & Tanaka, J. S. (1991). Characteristics of aggressors against women: Testing a model using a national sample of college students. *Journal of Consulting and Clinical Psychology, 59,* 670–681.

Marchell, T. C. (1998). Sexual and physical aggression against women by male college athletes. *Dissertation Abstracts International, 58*(11B), 6269.

Mosher, D. L., & Anderson, R. D. (1986). Macho personality, sexual aggression, and reactions to guided imagery of realistic rape. *Journal of Research in Personality, 20,* 77–94.

Payne, D. L., Lonsway, K. A., & Fitzgerald, L. F. (1999). Rape myth acceptance: Exploration of its structure and its measurement using the Illinois Rape Myth Acceptance Scale. *Journal of Research in Personality, 33,* 27–68.

Rando, R. A., Rogers, J. R., & Brittan-Powell, C. S. (1998). Gender role conflict and college men's sexually aggressive attitudes and behavior. *Journal of Mental Health Counseling, 20,* 359–369.

Sanday, P. R. (1981). The socio-cultural context of rape: A cross-cultural study. *Journal of Social Issues, 37,* 5–27.

Saunders, J. B., Aasland, O. G., Babor, T. F., De La Fuente, J. R., & Grant, M. (1993). Development of the Alcohol Use Disorders Identification Test (AUDIT): WHO Collaborative Project on Early Detection of Persons with Harmful Alcohol Consumption II. *Addiction, 88,* 791–814.

Schwendinger, J. R., & Schwendinger, H. (1974). Rape myths: In legal, theoretical, and everyday practice. *Crime and Social Justice, 1,* 18–26.

Seto, M. C., & Barbaree, H. E. (1995). The role of alcohol in sexual aggression. *Clinical Psychology Review, 1–5,* 545–566.

Tabachnick, B. G., & Fidell, L. S. (1989). *Using multivariate statistics* (2nd ed.). New York: HarperCollins.

Testa, M., Livingston, J. A., & Collins, R. L. (2000). The role of women's alcohol consumption in evaluation of vulnerability to sexual aggression. *Experimental and Clinical Psychopharmacology, 8,* 185–191.

Thompson, E. H., Jr., & Pleck, J. H. (1995). Masculinity ideologies: A review of research instrumentation on men and masculinities. In R. F. Levant & W. S. Pollack (Eds.), *A new psychology of men* (pp. 129–163). New York: Basic Books.

Truman, D. M., Tokar, D. M., & Fischer, A. R. (1996). Dimensions of masculinity: Relations to date rape supportive attitudes and sexual aggression in dating situations. *Journal of Counseling & Development, 74,* 555–562.

U.S. Census Bureau. (1999). *Statistical abstract of the United States.* Washington, DC: U.S. Government Printing Office.

CRITICAL THINKING QUESTIONS

1. How could you use the results of this study to design an intervention program that would lessen some males' acceptance of and predisposition for sexually coercive behavior toward females? Be specific and include a discussion of whether such an intervention would likely work.

2. The article suggests that predisposition toward sexual aggression is not part of masculinity per se but rather only of certain aspects of masculinity. Does this finding somehow make it easier to address the issue than when a more global concept of masculinity is used? Discuss.

3. This study used only male college students as subjects. Do you think the findings can be generalized to other male populations as well? Why or why not? Also, might some populations of males be even more likely to endorse the specific masculine beliefs identified in the study as associated with sexual aggression? Explain your response.

4. The study found that involvement in athletics was not a predictor of sexual aggression. Do you think athletes in certain sports might be more likely to have a sexually coercive disposition? If so, which sports and why?

5. Would someone who is androgynous (as discussed in Article 14) be less likely to engage in sexual aggression toward women? Why or why not?

6. Some victims of sexual assault do not report the incident to the authorities. There are many reasons for this, but might one of them be the nonreporters' acceptance of certain masculinity norms? For example, if a woman believes that men should dominate women, will she be less likely to report a sexual assault? Discuss.

CHAPTER INTEGRATION QUESTIONS

1. Articles 14 and 15 both dealt with the concept of gender, an aspect of the self, whereas Article 13 dealt with a different aspect of the self—namely, self-monitoring. How might the concept of self-monitoring be related to the concepts of masculinity, femininity, and androgyny?

2. Might different styles of self-monitoring be related to acceptance of males' sexual aggression toward women? Explain your reasoning.

3. Psychologist Nathaniel Branden said, "Of all the judgments we pass in life, none is as important as the one we pass on ourselves." Do you agree or disagree with this statement? Explain your reasoning. How does this statement relate to an overall theme in this chapter?

Chapter Six

PREJUDICE
AND DISCRIMINATION

PREJUDICE. THINK OF the implications of that word. It is so negative that even people who are highly prejudiced often are reluctant to use that term to describe themselves. Instead, prejudiced people may say that their opinions about members of certain groups are accurate and well founded, perhaps even that these groups deserve disdain.

Although the words *prejudice* and *discrimination* are often used interchangeably, they actually refer to two different things. *Prejudice* is an attitude, a set of beliefs about a member of a group based just on membership in that group. *Discrimination,* on the other hand, is a behavior, the differential treatment of a person based on membership in a particular group. You do not need to look far for the results of prejudiced attitudes and discriminatory behaviors: History is full of suffering that has been inflicted on people due solely to their membership in particular groups.

During the last several decades of the twentieth century, many great strides were made in the area of social justice. Overt discrimination against various groups was outlawed and, in many cases, was reduced significantly. Consider the overtly stated opinions of people that you hear from day to day. The amount of racism, for example, is less noticeable than it would have been only 20 or 30 years ago.

So, does this mean that the level of prejudiced thinking has, indeed, decreased over time? Not necessarily. It may be that people just *express* these prejudices more subtlety than they did in the past. In fact, prejudiced thinking may be rooted in how our minds process information. Article 16, "Why We Hate," examines how we acquire prejudices and how prejudices manifest themselves. It turns out that prejudice may be expressed in more subtle ways than most of us realize.

Article 17, "Attitudes vs. Actions," deals with the consistency between people's attitudes and behaviors, or, more specifically, the consistency between prejudice and discrimination. Do we always act in accordance with our prejudiced attitudes? Or do we sometimes contradict what we say we believe? This classic article was one of the first to address the issue of whether prejudice and discrimination necessarily occur together.

Finally, Article 18, "The Contact Hypothesis Revisited: Status Bias in the Reduction of Prejudice in the United States and Lebanon," addresses a consideration raised in Article 16: specifically, that it may be easier to reduce forms of overtly expressed prejudice (*explicit prejudice*) than it is to reduce underlying and more subtle forms of prejudice (*implicit prejudice*). Furthermore, the social status of the person holding the prejudice also may play a role in the reduction of prejudice.

ARTICLE 16

Just about anyone, by virtue of membership in a particular group, can be a target of prejudice and discrimination. The standard scenario is that a person is prejudged and reacted to not as an individual but as a member of some group, such that the presumed general characteristics of the group are automatically attributed to the individual. This process is known as *stereotyping*.

Stereotyping is an everyday fact of life. Although we may hope that we judge every person as an individual, the cognitive strategies we use to make sense of our would, as discussed in Chapter 3, suggest otherwise. In particular, when confronted with a member of an identifiable group, we may rely on a stereotype as a sort of decision-making shortcut, rather than consider the person on his or her own merits. How we feel about the person and how we treat him or her will be based on the stereotype, not the individual. As such, stereotypes frequently underlie prejudiced attitudes and discriminatory behaviors.

Are people less prejudiced today than in the past? In attempting to answer this question, it may be useful to distinguish between the various ways in which prejudice can be expressed. At one extreme are legalized forms of discrimination, such as the so-called Jim Crow laws of the past, which institutionalized discrimination against African Americans, and current laws that restrict women from combat roles in the U.S. military. At the other extreme are subtle types of differential treatment, such as how people are addressed and even how much eye contact they receive. While subtle, these types of behaviors may have a huge impact on the people against whom they are directed. Furthermore, while it is relatively easy to control what we say (e.g., not making racist remarks), it is much more difficult to control the nonverbal cues that may betray our underlying feelings (e.g., moving away from someone).

The following article by Margo Monteith and Jeffrey Winters examines research that indicates that prejudices are not only easily acquired but also may operate in a very subtle fashion. Perhaps part of the reason we acquire prejudices so readily is that we may be "wired" to make distinctions between *us* and *them*. Once acquired, these prejudices may operate in a very subtle manner, even when we are consciously *not* expressing any overt forms of bias. There is some good news, however: Even these subtle forms of prejudice can be reduced, given the right set of circumstances.

Why We Hate

■ Margo Monteith and Jeffrey Winters

Balbir Singh Sodhi was shot to death on September 15 in Mesa, Arizona. His killer claimed to be exacting revenge for the terrorist attacks of September 11. Upon his arrest, the murderer shouted, "I stand for America all the way." Though Sodhi wore a turban and could trace his ancestry to South Asia, he shared neither ethnicity nor religion with the suicide hijackers. Sodhi—who was killed at the gas station where he worked—died just for being different in a nation gripped with fear.

Reprinted from *Psychology Today,* 2002 (May/June), *35,* 44–50, 87. Reprinted with permission from *Psychology Today* magazine. Copyright © 2002 (Sussex Publishers, Inc.).

For Arab and Muslim Americans, the months after the terrorist attacks have been trying. They have been harassed at work and their property has been vandalized. An Arab San Francisco shop owner recalled with anger that his five-year-old daughter was taunted by name-callers. Classmates would yell "terrorist" as she walked by.

Public leaders from President George W. Bush on down have called for tolerance. But the Center for American-Islamic Relations in Washington, D.C., has tallied some 1,700 incidents of abuse against Muslims in the five months following September 11. Despite our better nature, it seems, fear of foreigners or other strange-seeming people comes out when we are under stress. That fear, known as xenophobia, seems almost hardwired into the human psyche.

Researchers are discovering the extent to which xenophobia can be easily—even arbitrarily—turned on. In just hours, we can be conditioned to fear or discriminate against those who differ from ourselves by characteristics as superficial as eye color. Even ideas we believe are just common sense can have deep xenophobic underpinnings. Research conducted this winter at Harvard reveals that even among people who claim to have no bias, the more strongly one supports the ethnic profiling of Arabs at airport-security checkpoints, the more hidden prejudice one has against Muslims.

But other research shows that when it comes to whom we fear and how we react, we do have a choice. We can, it seems, choose not to give in to our xenophobic tendencies.

THE MELTING POT

America prides itself on being a melting pot of cultures, but how we react to newcomers is often at odds with that self-image. A few years ago, psychologist Markus Kemmelmeier, Ph.D., now at the University of Nevada at Reno, stuck stamped letters under the windshield wipers of parked cars in a suburb of Detroit. Half were addressed to a fictitious Christian organization, half to a made-up Muslim group. Of all the letters, half had little stickers of the American flag.

Would the addresses and stickers affect the rate at which the letters would be mailed? Kemmelmeier wondered. Without the flag stickers, both sets of letters were mailed at the same rate, about 75 percent of the time. With the stickers, however, the rates changed: Almost all the Christian letters were forwarded but only half of the Muslim letters were mailed. "The flag is seen as a sacred object," Kemmelmeier says. "And it made people think about what it means to be a good American."

In short, the Muslims didn't make the cut.

Not mailing a letter seems like a small slight. Yet in the last century, there have been shocking examples of xenophobia in our own back yard. Perhaps the most famous in American history was the fear of the Japanese during World War II. This particular wave of hysteria lead to the rise of slurs and bigoted depictions in the media, and more alarmingly, the mass internment of 120,000 people of Japanese ancestry beginning in 1942. The internments have become a national embarrassment: Most of the Japanese held were American citizens, and there is little evidence that the imprisonments had any real strategic impact.

Today the targets of xenophobia—derived from the Greek word for *stranger*—aren't the Japanese. Instead, they are Muslim immigrants. Or Mexicans. Or Chinese. Or whichever group we have come to fear.

Just how arbitrary are these xenophobic feelings? Two famous public-school experiments show how easy it is to turn one "group" against another. In the late 1960s, California high school history teacher Ron Jones recruited students to participate in an exclusive new cultural program called "the Wave." Within weeks, these students were separating themselves from others and aggressively intimidating critics. Eventually, Jones confronted the students with the reality that they were unwitting participants in an experiment demonstrating the power of nationalist movements.

A few years later, a teacher in Iowa discovered how quickly group distinctions are made. The teacher, Jane Elliott, divided her class into two groups—those with blue eyes and those with brown or green eyes. The brown-eyed group received privileges and treats, while the blue-eyed students were denied rewards and told they were inferior. Within hours, the once-harmonious classroom became two camps, full of mutual fear and resentment. Yet, what is especially shocking is that the students were only in the third grade.

SOCIAL IDENTITY

The drive to completely and quickly divide the world into "us" and "them" is so powerful that it must surely come from some deep-seated need. The exact identity of that need, however, has been subject to debate. In the 1970s, the late Henri Tajfel, Ph.D., of the University of Bristol in England, and John Turner, Ph.D., now of the Australian National University, devised a theory to explain the psychology behind a range of prejudices and biases, not just xenophobia. Their theory was based, in part, on the desire to think highly of oneself. One way to lift your self-esteem is to be part of a distinctive group, like a winning team; another is to play up the qualities of your own group and denigrate the attributes of others so that you feel your group is better.

Tajfel and Turner called their insight "social identity theory," which has proved valuable for understanding how prejudices develop. Given even the slenderest of criteria, we naturally split people into two groups—an "in-group" and an "out-group." The categories can be of geopolitical importance—nationality, religion, race, language—or they can be as seemingly inconsequential as handedness, hair color or even height.

Once the division is made, the inferences and projections begin to occur. For one, we tend to think more highly of people in the in-group than those in the out-group, a belief based only on group identity. Also, a person tends to feel that others in the in-group are similar to one's self in ways that—although stereotypical—may have little to do with the original criteria used to split the groups. Someone with glasses may believe that other people who wear glasses are more voracious readers—even more intelligent—than those who don't, in spite of the fact that all he really knows is that they don't see very well. On the other hand, people in the out-group are believed to be less distinct and less complex than are cohorts in the in-group.

Although Tajfel and Turner found that identity and categorization were the root cause of social bias, other researchers have tried to find evolutionary explanations for discrimination. After all, in the distant past, people who shared cultural similarities were found to be more genetically related than those who did not. Therefore, favoring the in-group was a way of helping perpetuate one's genes. Evolutionary explanations seems appealing, since they rely on the simplest biological urges to drive complicated behavior. But this fact also makes them hard to prove. Ironically, there is ample evidence backing up the "softer" science behind social identity theory.

HIDDEN BIAS

Not many of us will admit to having strong racist or xenophobic biases. Even in cases where bias becomes public debate—such as the profiling of Arab Muslims at airport-security screenings—proponents of prejudice claim that they are merely promoting common sense. That reluctance to admit to bias makes the issue tricky to study.

To get around this problem, psychologists Anthony Greenwald, Ph.D., of the University of Washington in Seattle, and Mahzarin Banaji, Ph.D., of Harvard, developed the Implicit Association Test. The IAT is a simple test that measures reaction time: The subject sees various words or images projected on a screen, then classifies the images into one of two groups by pressing buttons. The words and images need not be racial or ethnic in nature—one group of researchers tested attitudes toward presidential candidates. The string of images is interspersed with words having either pleasant or unpleasant connotations, then the participant must group the words and images in various ways—Democrats are placed with unpleasant words, for instance.

The differences in reaction time are small but telling. Again and again, researchers found that subjects readily tie in-group images with pleasant words and out-group images with unpleasant words. One study compares such groups as whites and blacks, Jews and Christians, and young people and old people. And researchers found that if you identify yourself in one group, it's easier to pair images of that group with pleasant words—and easier to pair the opposite group with unpleasant imagery. This reveals the underlying biases and enables us to study how quickly they can form.

Really though, we need to know very little about a person to discriminate against him. One of the authors of this story, psychologist Margo Monteith, Ph.D., performed an IAT experiment comparing attitudes toward two sets of made-up names; one set was supposedly

"American," the other from the fictitious country of Marisat. Even though the subjects knew nothing about Marisat, they showed a consistent bias against it.

While this type of research may seem out in left field, other work may have more "real-world" applications. The Southern Poverty Law Center runs a Web version of the IAT that measures biases based on race, age and gender. Its survey has, for instance, found that respondents are far more likely to associate European faces, rather than Asian faces, with so-called American images. The implication being that Asians are seen as less "American" than Caucasians.

Similarly, Harvard's Banaji has studied the attitudes of people who favor the racial profiling of Arab Muslims to deter terrorism, and her results run contrary to the belief that such profiling is not driven by xenophobic fears. "We show that those who endorse racial profiling also score high on both explicit and implicit measures of prejudice toward Arab Muslims," Banaji says. "Endorsement of profiling is an indicator of level of prejudice."

BEYOND XENOPHOBIA

If categorization and bias come so easily, are people doomed to xenophobia and racism? It's pretty clear that we are susceptible to prejudice and that there is an unconscious desire to divide the world into "us" and "them." Fortunately, however, new research also shows that prejudices are fluid and that when we become conscious of our biases we can take active—and successful—steps to combat them.

Researchers have long known that when observing racially mixed groups, people are more likely to confuse the identity of two black individuals or two white ones, rather than a white with a black. But Leda Cosmides, Ph.D., and John Tooby, Ph.D., of the Center for Evolutionary Psychology at the University of California at Santa Barbara, and anthropologist Robert Kurzban, Ph.D., of the University of California at Los Angeles, wanted to test whether this was innate or whether it was just an artifact of how society groups individuals by race.

To do this, Cosmides and her colleagues made a video of two racially integrated basketball teams locked in conversation, then they showed it to study participants. As reported in the *Proceedings of the National Academy of Sciences,* the researchers discovered that subjects were more likely to confuse two players on the same team, regardless of race, rather than two players of the same race on opposite teams.

Cosmides says that this points to one way of attacking racism and xenophobia: changing the way society imposes group labels. American society divides people by race and by ethnicity; that's how lines of prejudice form. But simple steps, such as integrating the basketball teams, can reset mental divisions, rendering race and ethnicity less important.

This finding supports earlier research by psychologists Samuel Gaertner, Ph.D., of the University of Delaware in Newark, and John Dovidio, Ph.D., of Colgate University in Hamilton, New York. Gaertner and Dovidio have studied how bias changes when members of racially mixed groups must cooperate to accomplish shared goals. In situations where team members had to work together, bias could be reduced by significant amounts.

Monteith has also found that people who are concerned about their prejudices have the power to correct them. In experiments, she told subjects that they had performed poorly on tests that measured belief in stereotypes. She discovered that the worse a subject felt about her performance, the better she scored on subsequent tests. The guilt behind learning about their own prejudices made the subjects try harder not to be biased.

This suggests that the guilt of mistaking individuals for their group stereotype—such as falsely believing an Arab is a terrorist—can lead to the breakdown of the belief in that stereotype. Unfortunately, such stereotypes are reinforced so often that they can become ingrained. It is difficult to escape conventional wisdom and treat all people as individuals, rather than members of a group. But that seems to be the best way to avoid the trap of dividing the world in two—and discriminating against one part of humanity.

READ MORE ABOUT IT

Nobody Left to Hate: Teaching Compassion After Columbine, Elliot Aronson (W. H. Freeman and Company, 2000)

The Racist Mind: Portraits of American Neo-Nazis and Klansmen, Madonna Kolbenschlag (Penguin Books, 1996)

CRITICAL THINKING QUESTIONS

1. "Endorsement of profiling is an indicator of level of prejudice." React to this quote from the article. Be specific in your response.

2. Based on the information in this article, how would you answer someone who claims that he or she is not in the least bit prejudiced?

3. After reading this article, how optimistic or pessimistic are you that prejudice can be eliminated from society? Specifically, can people overcome prejudiced thinking? Give examples to support your position.

4. If you were a parent and wanted to minimize the formation of prejudiced thinking in your children, what would you do? Despite your good intentions, what might limit your ability to accomplish this? Explain your answers.

5. Many studies on prejudice involve asking subjects about their attitudes toward particular groups. What do the findings of this article suggest about the validity of such self-reporting techniques? What may be a more accurate way of assessing prejudiced attitudes? Explain your answer.

6. What role does the media play in reinforcing, creating, or changing prejudices? Give specific examples to bolster your premise.

ARTICLE 17———————————————

As mentioned in the introduction to this chapter, the terms *prejudice* and *discrimination* often are used interchangeably, but, in fact, they refer to two different concepts. Prejudice is an *attitude,* whereby a particular person is judged based solely on his or her membership in a particular group. Discrimination refers to the *behavior* of treating people differently based upon their membership in a group.

While the two terms do, indeed, refer to different things, do they occur together in the real world? It stands to reason that if you have negative beliefs about a particular group of people, then you would act in a negative fashion toward them. Or does it? Are we always consistent in our attitudes and behaviors?

Sometimes there is a strong consistency between what people say about their beliefs and how they act. For example, surveys are usually accurate in predicting outcomes of elections based upon asking people about their attitudes toward the candidates. In other cases, such consistency simply does not exist.

"Attitudes vs. Actions" is a classic work in the field that addresses the issue of attitude-behavior consistency. Before LaPiere's publication of this study in 1934, attitude research on prejudice involved asking respondents to give hypothetical responses to hypothetical situations (e.g., Would you serve a person of a given race at your restaurant?). LaPiere measured the number of times that a Chinese couple was actually refused lodging or food and then followed up with a questionnaire to the same establishments six months later, asking if they would serve Chinese persons. In doing so, LaPiere claimed to demonstrate the lack of consistency between what people say and what they actually do. Even though the study does have some methodological flaws, it is a good example of pioneering research in the field. It also provides an interesting microcosm of prejudice and discrimination issues that existed in the United States over a half-century ago.

Attitudes vs. Actions

■ Richard T. LaPiere

By definition, a social attitude is a behaviour pattern, anticipatory set or tendency, predisposition to specific adjustment to designated social situations, or, more simply, a conditioned response to social stimuli.[1] Terminological usage differs, but students who have concerned themselves with attitudes apparently agree that they are acquired out of social experience and provide the individual organism with some degree of preparation to adjust, in a well-defined way, to certain types of social situations if and when these situations arise. It would seem, therefore, that the totality of the social attitudes of a single individual would include all his socially acquired personality which is involved in the making of adjustments to other human beings.

But by derivation social attitudes are seldom more than a verbal response to a symbolic situation. For the conventional method of measuring social attitudes is to ask questions (usually in writing) which demand a verbal adjustment to an entirely symbolic situation. Because it is easy, cheap, and mechanical, the attitudinal questionnaire is rapidly becoming a major method of sociological and socio-psychological investigation.

The technique is simple. Thus from a hundred or a thousand responses to the question "Would you get up to give an Armenian woman your seat in a street-car?" the investigator derives the "attitude" of non-Armenian males toward Armenian females. Now the question may be constructed with elaborate skill and hidden with consumate cunning in a maze of supplementary or even irrelevant questions yet all that has been obtained is a symbolic response to a symbolic situation. The words "Armenian woman" do not constitute an Armenian woman of flesh and blood, who might be tall or squat, fat or thin, old or young, well or poorly dressed—who might, in fact, be a goddess or just another old and dirty hag. And the questionnaire response, whether it be "yes" or "no," is but a verbal reaction and this does not involve rising from the seat or stolidly avoiding the hurt eyes of the hypothetical woman and the derogatory stares of other street-car occupants. Yet, ignoring these limitations, the diligent investigator will jump briskly from his factual evidence to the unwarranted conclusion that he has measured the "anticipatory behavior patterns" of non-Armenian males toward Armenian females encountered on street cars. Usually he does not stop here, but proceeds to deduce certain general conclusions regarding the social relationships between Armenians and non-Armenians. Most of us have applied the questionnaire technique with greater caution, but not I fear with any greater certainty of success.

Some years ago I endeavored to obtain comparative data on the degree of French and English antipathy towards dark-skinned peoples.[2] The informal questionnaire technique was used, but, although the responses so obtained were exceedingly consistent, I supplemented them with what I then considered an index to overt behavior. The hypothesis as then stated *seemed* entirely logical. "Whatever our attitude on the validity of 'verbalization' may be, it must be recognized that any study of attitudes through direct questioning is open to serious objection, both because of the limitations of the sampling method and because in classifying attitudes the inaccuracy of human judgment is an inevitable variable. In this study, however, there is corroborating evidence on these attitudes in the policies adopted by hotel proprietors. Nothing could be used as a more accurate index of color prejudice than the admission or non-admission of colored people to hotels. For the proprietor must reflect the group attitude in his policy regardless of his own feelings in the matter. Since he determines what the group attitude is towards Negroes through the expression of that attitude in overt behavior and over a long period of actual experience, the results will be exceptionally free from those disturbing factors which inevitably affect the effort to study attitudes by direct questioning."

But at that time I overlooked the fact that what I was obtaining from the hotel proprietors was still a "verbalized" reaction to a symbolic situation. The response to a Negro's request for lodgings might have been an excellent index of the attitude of hotel patrons towards living in the same hotel as a Negro. Yet to ask the proprietor "Do you permit members of the Negro race to stay here?" does not, it appears, measure his potential response to an actual Negro.

All measurement of attitudes by the questionnaire technique proceeds on the assumption that there is a mechanical relationship between symbolic and non-symbolic behavior. It is simple enough to prove that there is no *necessary* correlation between speech and action, between response to words and to the realities they symbolize. A parrot can be taught to swear, a child to sing "Frankie and Johnny" in the Mae West manner. The words will have no meaning to either child or parrot. But to prove that there is no *necessary* relationship does not prove that such a relationship may not exist. There need be no relationship between what the hotel proprietor says he will do and what he actually does when confronted with a colored patron. Yet there may be. Certainly we are justified in assuming that the verbal response of the hotel proprietor would be more likely to indicate what he would actually do than would the verbal response of people whose personal feelings are less subordinated to economic expediency. However, the following study indicates that the reliability of even such responses is very small indeed.

Beginning in 1930 and continuing for two years thereafter, I had the good fortune to travel rather extensively with a young Chinese student and his wife.[3] Both were personable, charming, and quick to win the admiration and respect of those they had the opportunity to become intimate with. But they were foreign-born Chinese, a fact that could not be disguised. Knowing the general "attitude" of Americans towards the Chinese as indicated by the "social distance" studies which have been made, it was with considerable trepidation that I first approached a hotel clerk in their company. Perhaps the clerk's eyebrows lifted slightly, but he accommodated us without a show of hesitation. And this in the "best" hotel in a small town noted for its narrow and bigoted "attitude" towards Orientals. Two months later I passed that way again, phoned the hotel and asked if they would accommodate "an important Chinese gentleman." The reply was an unequivocal "No." That aroused my curiosity and led to this study.

In something like ten thousand miles of motor travel, twice across the United States, up and down the Pacific Coast, we met definite rejection from those asked to serve us just once. We were received at 66 hotels, auto camps, and "Tourist Homes," refused at one. We were served in 184 restaurants and cafes scattered throughout the country and treated with what I judged to be more than ordinary consideration in 72 of them. Accurate and detailed records were kept of all these instances. An effort, necessarily subjective, was made to evaluate the overt response of hotel clerks, bell boys, elevator operators, and waitresses to the presence of my Chinese friends. The factors entering into the situations were varied as far and as often as possible. Control was not, of course, as exacting as that required by laboratory experimentation. But it was as rigid as is humanly possible in human situations. For example, I did not take the "test" subjects into my confidence fearing that their behavior might become self-conscious and thus abnormally affect the response of others towards them. Whenever possible I let my Chinese friend negotiate for accommodations (while I concerned myself with the car or luggage) or sent them into a restaurant ahead of me. In this way I attempted to "factor" myself out. We sometimes patronized high-class establishments after a hard and dusty day on the road and stopped at inferior auto camps when in our most presentable condition.

In the end I was forced to conclude that those factors which most influenced the behavior of others towards the Chinese had nothing at all to do with race. Quality and condition of clothing, appearance of baggage (by which, it seems, hotel clerks are prone to base their quick evaluations), cleanliness and neatness were far more significant for person to person

reaction in the situations I was studying than skin pigmentation, straight black hair, slanting eyes, and flat noses. And yet an air of self-confidence might entirely offset the "unfavorable" impression made by dusty clothes and the usual disorder to appearance consequent upon some hundred miles of motor travel. A supercilious desk clerk in a hotel of noble aspirations could not refuse his master's hospitality to people who appeared to take their request as a perfectly normal and conventional thing, though they might look like tin-can tourists and two of them belong to the racial category "Oriental." On the other hand, I became rather adept at approaching hotel clerks with that peculiar crab-wise manner which is so effective in provoking a somewhat scornful disregard. And then a bland smile would serve to reverse the entire situation. Indeed, it appeared that a genial smile was the most effective password to acceptance. My Chinese friends were skillful smilers, which may account, in part, for the fact that we received but one rebuff in all our experience. Finally, I was impressed with the fact that even where some tension developed due to the strangeness for the Chinese it would evaporate immediately when they spoke in unaccented English.

The one instance in which we were refused accommodations is worth recording here. The place was a small California town, a rather inferior auto-camp into which we drove in a very dilapidated car piled with camp equipment. It was early evening, the light so dim that the proprietor found it somewhat difficult to decide the genus *voyageur* to which we belonged. I left the car and spoke to him. He hesitated, wavered, said he was not sure that he had two cabins, meanwhile edging towards our car. The realization that the two occupants were Orientals turned the balance or, more likely, gave him the excuse he was looking for. "No," he said, "I don't take Japs!" In a more pretentious establishment we secured accommodations, and with an extra flourish of hospitality.

To offset this one flat refusal were the many instances in which the physical peculiarities of the Chinese served to heighten curiosity. With few exceptions this curiosity was considerably hidden behind an exceptional interest in serving us. Of course, outside of the Pacific Coast region, New York, and Chicago, the Chinese physiognomy attracts attention. It is different, hence noticeable. But the principal effect this curiosity has upon the behavior of those who cater to the traveler's needs is to make them more attentive, more responsive, more reliable. A Chinese companion is to be recommended to the white traveling in his native land. Strange features when combined with "human" speech and action seems, at times, to heighten sympathetic response, perhaps on the same principle that makes us uncommonly sympathetic toward the dog that has a "human" expression in his face.

What I am trying to say is that in only one out of 251 instances in which we purchased goods or services necessitating intimate human relationships did the fact that my companions were Chinese adversely affect us. Factors entirely unassociated with race were, in the main, the determinant of significant variations in our reception. It would appear reasonable to conclude that the "attitude" of the American people, as reflected in the behavior of those who are for pecuniary reasons presumably most sensitive to the antipathies of their white clientele, is anything but negative towards the Chinese. In terms of "social distance" we might conclude that native Caucasians are not averse to residing in the same hotels, auto-camps, and "Tourist Homes" as Chinese and will with complacency accept the presence of Chinese at an adjoining table in restaurant or cafe. It does not follow that there is revealed a distinctly "positive" attitude towards the Chinese, that whites prefer the Chinese to other whites. But the facts as gathered certainly preclude the conclusion that there is an intense prejudice towards the Chinese.

Yet the existence of this prejudice, very intense, is proven by a conventional "attitude" study. To provide a comparison of symbolic reaction to symbolic social situations with actual reaction to real social situations, I "questionnaired" the establishments which we patronized during the two year period. Six months were permitted to lapse between the time I obtained the overt reaction and the symbolic. It was hoped that the effects of the actual experience with Chinese guests, adverse or otherwise, would have faded during the intervening time. To the hotel or restaurant a questionnaire was mailed with an accompanying letter purporting to be a special and personal plea for response. The questionnaires all asked the same question, "Will you accept members of the Chinese race as guests in your establishment?" Two types of questionnaire were used. In one this question was inserted among similar queries concerning Germans, French, Japanese, Russians, Armenians, Jews, Negroes, Italians, and Indians. In the other the pertinent question

TABLE 1 / Distribution of Results from Questionnaire Study of Establishment "Policy" Regarding Acceptance of Chinese as Guests

   Replies are to the question: "Will you accept members of the Chinese race as guests in your establishment?"

	Hotels, Etc. Visited		Hotels, Etc. Not Visited		Restaurants, Etc. Visited		Restaurants, Etc. Not Visited	
Total	47		32		81		96	
	1*	2*	1	2	1	2	1	2
Number replying	22	25	20	12	43	38	51	45
No	20	23	19	11	40	35	37	41
Undecided: depend upon circumstances	1	2	1	1	3	3	4	3
Yes	1	0	0	0	0	0	0	1

*Column (1) indicates in each case those responses to questionnaires which concerned Chinese only. The figures in column (2) are from the questionnaires in which the above was inserted among questions regarding Germans, French, Japanese, etc.

was unencumbered. With persistence, completed replies were obtained from 128 of the establishments we had visited; 81 restaurants and cafes and 47 hotels, auto-camps, and "Tourist Homes." In response to the relevant question 92 per cent of the former and 91 per cent of the latter replied "No." The remainder replied "Uncertain; depend upon circumstances." From the woman proprietor of a small auto-camp I received the only "Yes," accompanied by a chatty letter describing the nice visit she had had with a Chinese gentleman and his sweet wife during the previous summer.

A rather unflattering interpretation might be put upon the fact that those establishments who had provided for our needs so graciously were, some months later, verbally antagonistic towards hypothetical Chinese. To factor this experience out responses were secured from 32 hotels and 96 restaurants located in approximately the same regions, but uninfluenced by this particular experience with Oriental clients. In this, as in the former case, both types of questionnaires were used. The results indicate that neither the type of questionnaire nor the fact of previous experience had important bearing upon the symbolic response to symbolic social situations.

It is impossible to make direct comparison between the reactions secured through questionnaires and from actual experience. On the basis of the above data it would appear foolhardy for a Chinese to attempt to travel in the United States. And yet, as I have shown, actual experience indicates that the American people, as represented by the personnel of hotels, restaurants, etc., are not at all averse to fraternizing with Chinese within the limitations which apply to social relationships between Americans themselves. The evaluations which follow are undoubtedly subject to the criticism which any human judgment must withstand. But the fact is that, although they began their travels in this country with considerable trepidations, my Chinese friends soon lost all fear that they might receive a rebuff. At first somewhat timid and considerably dependent upon me for guidance and support, they came in time to feel fully self-reliant and would approach new social situations without the slightest hesitation.

The conventional questionnaire undoubtedly has significant value for the measurement of "political attitudes." The presidential polls conducted by the *Literary Digest* have proven that. But a "political attitude" is exactly what the questionnaire can be justly held to measure; a verbal response to a symbolic situation. Few citizens are ever faced with the necessity of adjusting themselves to the presence of the political leaders whom, periodically, they must vote for—or against. Especially is this true with regard to the president, and it is in relation to political attitudes towards presidential candidates that we have our best evidence. But while the questionnaire may indicate what the voter will do when he goes to vote, it does not and cannot reveal what he will do when he meets Candidate Jones on the street, in his office, at his club, on the golf course, or wherever two men may meet and adjust in some way one to the other.

The questionnaire is probably our only means of determining "religious attitudes." An honest answer to the question "Do you believe in God?" reveals all there is to be measured. "God" is a symbol; "belief" a verbal expression. So here, too, the questionnaire is efficacious. But if we would know the emotional responsiveness of a person to the spoken or written word "God" some other method of investigation must be used. And if we would know the extent to which that responsiveness restrains his behavior it is to his behavior that we must look, not to his questionnaire response. Ethical precepts are, I judge, something more than verbal professions. There would seem little to be gained from asking a man if his religious faith prevents him from committing sin. Of course it does—on paper. But "moral attitudes" must have a significance in the adjustment to actual situations or they are not worth the studying. Sitting at my desk in California I can predict with a high degree of certainty what an "average" business man in an average Mid-Western city will reply to the question "Would you engage in sexual intercourse with a prostitute in a Paris brothel?" Yet no one, least of all the man himself, can predict what he would actually do should he by some misfortune find himself face to face with the situation in question. His moral "attitudes" are no doubt already stamped into his personality. But just what those habits are which will be invoked to provide him with some sort of adjustment to this situation is quite indeterminate.

It is highly probable that when the "Southern Gentleman" says he will not permit Negroes to reside

TABLE 2 / Distribution of Results Obtained from Actual Experience in the Situation Symbolized in the Questionnaire Study

Conditions	Hotels, Etc.		Restaurants, Etc.	
	Accompanied by investigator	Chinese not so accompanied at inception of situation*	Accompanied by by investigator	Chinese not so accompanied at inception of situation
Total	55	12	165	19
Reception very much better than investigator would expect to have received had he been alone, but under otherwise similar circumstances	6	19	63	9
Reception different only to extent of heightened curiosity, such as investigator might have incurred were he alone but dressed in manner unconventional to region yet not incongruous	3	22	76	6
Reception "normal"	2	9	21	3
Reception perceptibly hesitant and not to be explained on other than "racial" grounds	1	3	4	1
Reception definitely, though temporarily, embarrassing	0	1	1	0
Not accepted	0	1	0	0

*When the investigator was not present at the inception of the situation the judgments were based upon what transpired after he joined the Chinese. Since intimately acquainted with them it is probable that errors in judgment were no more frequent under these conditions than when he was able to witness the inception as well as results of the situation.

in his neighborhood we have a verbal response to a symbolic situation which reflects the "attitudes" which would become operative in an actual situation. But there is no need to ask such a question of the true "Southern Gentleman." We knew it all the time. I am inclined to think that in most instances where the questionnaire does reveal non-symbolic attitudes the case is much the same. It is only when we cannot easily observe what people do in certain types of situations that the questionnaire is resorted to. But it is just here that the danger in the questionnaire technique arises. If Mr. A adjusts himself to Mr. B in a specified way we can deduce from his behavior that he has a certain

"attitude" towards Mr. B and, perhaps, all of Mr. B's class. But if no such overt adjustment is made it is impossible to discover what A's adjustment would be should the situation arise. A questionnaire will reveal what Mr. A writes or says when confronted with a certain combination of words. But not what he will do when he meets Mr. B. Mr. B is a great deal more than a series of words. He is a man and he acts. His action is not necessarily what Mr. A "imagines" it will be when he reacts verbally to the symbol "Mr. B."

No doubt a considerable part of the data which the social scientist deals with can be obtained by the questionnaire method. The census reports are based upon verbal questionnaires and I do not doubt their basic integrity. If we wish to know how many children a man has, his income, the size of his home, his age, and the condition of his parents, we can reasonably ask him. These things he has frequently and conventionally converted into verbal responses. He is competent to report upon them, and will do so accurately, unless indeed he wishes to do otherwise. A careful investigator could no doubt even find out by verbal means whether the man fights with his wife (frequently, infrequently, or not at all), though the neighbors would be a more reliable source. But we should not expect to obtain by the questionnaire method his "anticipatory set or tendency" to action should his wife pack up and go home to Mother, should Elder Son get into trouble with the neighbor's daughter, the President assume the status of a dictator, the Japanese take over the rest of China, or a Chinese gentleman come to pay a social call.

Only a verbal reaction to an entirely symbolic situation can be secured by the questionnaire. It may indicate what the responder would actually do when confronted with the situation symbolized in the question, but there is no assurance that it will. And so to call the response a reflection of a "social attitude" is to entirely disregard the definition commonly given for the phrase "attitude." If social attitudes are to be conceptualized as partially integrated habit sets which will become operative under specific circumstances and lead to a particular pattern of adjustment they must, in the main, be derived from a study of humans behaving in actual social situations. They must not be imputed on the basis of questionnaire data.

The questionnaire is cheap, easy, and mechanical. The study of human behavior is time consuming, intellectually fatiguing, and depends for its success upon the ability of the investigator. The former method gives quantitative results, the latter mainly qualitative. Quantitative measurements arc quantitatively accurate; qualitative evaluations are always subject to the errors of human judgment. Yet it would seem far more worth while to make a shrewd guess regarding that which is essential than to accurately measure that which is likely to prove quite irrelevant.

NOTES

1. See Daniel D. Droba, "Topical Summaries of Current Literature," *The American Journal of Sociology,* 1934, p. 513.
2. "Race Prejudice: France and England," *Social Forces,* September 1928, pp. 102–111.
3. The results of this study have been withheld until the present time out of consideration for their feelings.

CRITICAL THINKING QUESTIONS

1. A central thesis of the LaPiere article was that the method of directly asking people about their attitudes has certain limitations in terms of accuracy and consistency. What are these limitations? How could they be overcome, other than in the ways suggested by the author?
2. LaPiere maintained that there is little consistency between responses to attitude surveys and actual behavior. If that is the case, then what is the value (if any) of the multitude of attitude surveys that are regularly administered in the United States? Support your position.
3. Did the study involve any ethical issues? For example, what do you think about the fact that the author did not tell his Chinese friends that they were part of a study he was conducting? Are there any other ethical considerations? Explain your answers.
4. The article ended by making a distinction between *quantitative results,* such as those obtained by questionnaires, and *qualitative results,* such as those obtained by the author in his visits to the establishments. LaPiere obviously favors qualitative methods, arguing that although they are prone to errors of human judgment, such methods are preferred because it is better to "make a shrewd guess regarding what is essential than to accurately

measure that which is likely quite irrelevant." Are the results of attitude questionnaires "likely quite irrelevant"? Why or why not?

5. If you were to conduct the study, what methodological improvements would you make to reduce the subjectivity of the measures?

6. A major conclusion of the study was that responses to hypothetical questions do not necessarily predict actual behavior. Is this evidence for a lack of consistency between attitudes and behavior? In answering this, think of the specific methodology that was employed. Was there anything wrong with it, given the conclusions that were drawn? What methodology could be used to more directly assess the consistency between attitudes and behavior? Explain your answers.

7. LaPiere made the observation that factors such as clothing, cleanliness, and smiles were more important in determining whether the couple was served than was skin color. Design a study that would experimentally test this observation.

ADDITIONAL RELATED READINGS

Oswald, D. L. (2005). Understanding Anti-Arab reactions Post-9/11: The role of threats, social categories, and personal ideologies. *Journal of Applied Social Psychology, 35*(9), 1775–1799.

Pettigrew, T. F., Christ, O., Wagner, U., & Stellmacher, J. (2007). Direct and intergroup contact effects on prejudice: A normative interpretation. *International Journal of Intercultural Relations, 31*(4), 411–425.

*ARTICLE 18*_____

Why are people prejudiced? Any social psychology text will list a number of reasons that account for prejudiced attitudes and discriminatory behaviors. For example, social learning approaches will focus on the attitudes a person learns in his or her environment, particularly at home, to account for prejudice. The realistic group conflict approach will focus on the competition between groups for scarce resources as a cause of prejudice. Yet other approaches will try to identify a personality type that might be related to prejudice—for instance, the authoritarian personality.

Over the past several decades, the amount of overtly discriminatory behavior based on race has decreased significantly in the United States. This may be due to changes in laws that make certain previously accepted forms of discrimination illegal. It also may be due to changes in attitudes and beliefs regarding prejudice. Regardless, one thing that is certain is that in most quarters today, the expression of overt racism is not nearly as common as it might have been a half-century ago. But does that mean that racial prejudice has indeed decreased? Or has it perhaps just become more subtle?

In answering these questions, it may be useful to distinguish between *explicit* and *implicit* racial prejudice. *Explicit* racial prejudice refers to overt expressions of prejudice, of which we are consciously aware. Saying that you would never live next door to a person of a certain race is an example of explicit racial prejudice. *Implicit* racial prejudice, on the other hand, comprises more subtle forms of prejudice, which typically operate out of conscious awareness. Taking longer to respond to a member of another race and unconsciously associating a certain race with undesirable characteristics are both examples of implicit racial prejudice. A crucial distinction between explicit and implicit racial prejudice is that the former can be consciously controlled (and hence is subject to social desirability), whereas the latter is very difficult to control.

The following article by P. J. Henry and Curtis D. Hardin examines how contact with members of another group may impact both explicit and implicit prejudice. Previous research had found that equal-status contact tended to reduce prejudice. However, this study found that that may depend on what type of prejudice is being measured (implicit or explicit) as well as the status of the group holding the prejudice. This article also is of interest because it uses two distinctly different cultures and groups as subjects.

The Contact Hypothesis Revisited
Status Bias in the Reduction of Implicit Prejudice in the United States and Lebanon

■ P. J. Henry and Curtis D. Hardin

ABSTRACT

Although 50 years of research demonstrate that friendly intergroup contact reduces intergroup prejudice, the findings are based solely on self-reported, explicit prejudice. In two parallel experiments examining intergroup

Henry, P. J., & Hardin, C. D. (2006). The contact hypothesis revisited: Status bias in the reduction of implicit prejudice in the United States and Lebanon. *Psychological Science, 17*(10), 862–868. Copyright © 2006 by American Psychological Society. Reprinted with permission of Blackwell Publishers.

contact and prejudice—between Whites and Blacks in the United States (Experiment 1) and between Christians and Muslims in Lebanon (Experiment 2)—we examined whether intergroup status differences moderate contact effects on implicit prejudice, as well as explicit prejudice. Both experiments replicated the standard effect of contact on explicit prejudice. They also demonstrated that intergroup contact reduces implicit prejudice among low-status groups. In Experiment 1, the implicit prejudice of Blacks toward Whites (but not Whites toward Blacks) was reduced as a function of friendly contact. In Experiment 2, the implicit prejudice of Muslims toward Christians (but not Christians toward Muslims) was reduced as a function of friendly contact.

Friendly contact with out-groups is known to reduce prejudice when the contact involves close, equal-status interpersonal interactions (Allport, 1954; Pettigrew, 1998; Pettigrew & Tropp, 2006). However, this effect has been shown exclusively by examining what is now termed *explicit* prejudice—that is, feelings about out-groups that are consciously accessible, seemingly controllable, and self-reported. In recent years, an additional form of prejudice has been identified: *implicit* prejudice, which may not be always consciously accessible, may be difficult or impossible to control, and is typically captured using reaction time measures of cognitive association (e.g., Devine, 1989; Greenwald & Banaji, 1995). Despite decades of research documenting effects of contact on explicit prejudice, little is known about the relation between contact and implicit prejudice.

IMPLICIT AND EXPLICIT PREJUDICE

Numerous findings of null or weak correlations between implicit and explicit measures of prejudice have led some researchers to conclude that these two forms of prejudice are products of distinct cognitive processes (e.g., Devine, Plant, Amodio, Harmon-Jones, & Vance, 2002; Dovidio, Kawakami, & Gaertner, 2002; Fazio, Jackson, Dunton, & Williams, 1995; Greenwald & Banaji, 1995). For example, dual-process models of prejudice (e.g., Devine & Monteith, 1999) postulate that explicit prejudice is flexible, labile, motivated, and intelligently sensitive to situational cues, whereas implicit prejudice, as a consequence of

years of exposure to associations in the environment, is unintelligent, impervious to conscious control, and relatively stable (Brendl, Markman, & Messner, 2001; Devine, 1989; Karpinski & Hilton, 2001; Pelham et al., 2005; cf. Lowery, Hardin, & Sinclair, 2001). From this perspective, implicit prejudice reflects chronic exposure to social organization and culture and is therefore especially resistant to change.

Recent research has challenged the dual-process assumption that implicit prejudice is impervious to change by demonstrating that it can be reduced or even reversed by social context (reviewed in Blair, 2002). Research has also demonstrated that implicit prejudice may have some flexibility: Different situations in a culture of intergroup conflict and prejudice may well "call out" different implicit attitudes (e.g., Lowery et al., 2001). Nevertheless, to the degree that implicit prejudice more than explicit prejudice reflects aggregate intergroup-related experiences, and to the degree that these experiences disproportionately favor high-status groups in society, one might expect social status to moderate the degree to which intergroup contact reduces implicit prejudice.

STATUS DIFFERENCES AND IMPLICIT PREJUDICE

Broadly recognized social-status hierarchies are known to be reinforced by ideological thinking. For example, members of low-status groups often have beliefs that favor higher-status groups or otherwise legitimize existing differences in group status. Such beliefs have been referred to as "false consciousness" (Jost & Banaji, 1994), "legitimizing myths" (Sidanius & Pratto, 1999), and "legitimizing ideologies" (Major et al., 2002). Beliefs that favor high-status groups are involved in a variety of asymmetries in intergroup processes. For example, out-group favoritism is greater among low-status groups than among high-status groups (Clark & Clark, 1947; Hewstone & Ward, 1985; Hinkle & Brown, 1990; Jost & Burgess, 2000; Sachdev & Bourhis, 1987), and low-status groups endorse more negative in-group stereotypes than high-status groups do (Glick & Fiske, 2001; Jost & Banaji, 1994).

Implicit prejudice may be especially sensitive to social status. Expressions of implicit out-group prejudice may be smaller among members of low-status groups than among members of high-status groups (Jost, Pelham, & Carvallo, 2002; Rudman, Greenwald, Mellot, & Schwartz, 1999); members of low-status groups sometimes even exhibit an implicit preference for high-status groups over their own group (Ashburn-Nardo, Knowles, & Monteith, 2003; Rudman, Feinberg, & Fairchild, 2002). Prejudices commonly reflected from situation to situation, and aggregated in the broader society as status, not only may establish implicit prejudice, but also may regulate implicit prejudice change (as a function of, e.g., intergroup contact).

Given that high-status groups are generally favored in society by definition, and given empirical findings of asymmetry in the implicit prejudice of high- and low-status groups, one might expect corresponding asymmetries in the effect of intergroup contact on implicit prejudice. Specifically, it may be easier for friendly interpersonal contact to reduce implicit prejudice toward groups for whom positive associations are broadly represented in society, that is, high-status groups, and more difficult for friendly interpersonal contact to reduce implicit prejudice toward groups for whom positive associations are not as broadly represented in society, that is, lower-status groups.

THE CONTACT HYPOTHESIS AND EXPLICIT AND IMPLICIT PREJUDICE

In the present research, we investigated how social status may moderate the relation between friendly contact and both implicit and explicit prejudice. We explored three plausible outcomes. First, contact may reduce out-group prejudice toward high-status and low-status groups equivalently. Second, contact may reduce high-status groups' prejudice toward low-status groups more than it reduces low-status groups' prejudice toward high-status groups, an outcome we call *high-status enlightenment*. Indeed, a recent meta-analysis (Pettigrew & Tropp, 2006) of 698 studies on the contact hypothesis showed that contact had a greater effect on high-status groups' explicit prejudice than on low-status groups' explicit prejudice (this difference was small but statistically significant). Third, contact may reduce low-status groups' out-group prejudice toward high-status groups more than it reduces

high-status groups' out-group prejudice toward low-status groups, an outcome we call *low-status deference*. Low-status deference is implied by theories that postulate the general maintenance of favorable biases toward high-status groups (e.g., Jost & Banaji, 1994; Sidanius & Pratto, 1999). Although low-status deference is not commonly found in studies of explicit prejudice (Pettigrew & Tropp, 2006), implicit prejudice may be especially sensitive to broad social hierarchies (e.g., Banaji & Greenwald, 1994; Devine & Monteith, 1999; Greenwald & Banaji, 1995) and therefore may be more likely to show this outcome.

To explore the effects of status and contact on intergroup prejudice, we conducted two parallel studies of implicit and explicit prejudice, investigating two dimensions of status in two cultures in different parts of the world. Experiment 1 utilized a sample of Whites and Blacks living in the United States. Experiment 2 utilized a sample of Christians and Muslims living in Beirut, Lebanon. Although many people are familiar with racial prejudice in the United States, religious prejudice in Lebanon may be less familiar. Briefly, most people in Lebanon are either Muslim or Christian, and the two groups are about equal in number. The Lebanese Civil War, which lasted from approximately 1975 to 1991, involved many kinds of interreligious fighting, but largely reflected Muslim-Christian conflict. The war crippled the country and is estimated to have resulted in the deaths of more than 100,000 citizens. Interreligious conflict remains threatening today, 15 years after the war's end. Christians in Beirut have historically enjoyed greater status than Muslims, a perception corroborated in this research.

METHOD

In both experiments, participants completed measures of explicit and implicit intergroup prejudice after completing a series of questionnaires that assessed intergroup status and interpersonal contact.

Subjects

For Experiment 1, a sample of 128 White (103 women, 25 men) and 32 Black (26 women, 6 men) students was recruited from undergraduate psychology classrooms at DePaul University; the students received partial course credit for their participation. For Experiment 2, a sample of 46 Christian (20 women, 26 men) and 37 Muslim (25 women, 12 men) students from psychology classrooms at the American University of Beirut (AUB) were recruited as part of a class exercise.[1]

Materials and Procedure

Participants completed surveys that measured perceived status differences between groups in society, out-group contact, explicit prejudice, and implicit prejudice.

Measures of Status Participants judged groups' status on 9-point scales from 1, *low status,* to 9, *high status.* In Experiment 1, participants rated the status of Whites/European Americans and Blacks/African Americans. In Experiment 2, participants rated the social status of Christian groups (Catholic, Orthodox, and Maronite) and Muslim groups (Sunni and Shiite).

Measures of Out-Group Contact In Experiment 1, the first two questions asked, "How many friends do you have who are White/European American?" and "How many friends do you have who are Black/African American?" Response options were "none" (0), "some" (1), "many" (2), "most" (3), and "all" (4). The next two questions asked, "How close do you feel to your closest White/European American friend?" and "How close do you feel to your closest Black/ African American friend?" Response options for these questions were "extremely close" (5), "very close" (4), "moderately close" (3), "somewhat close" (2), "not very close" (1), and "I have no close White/European American [Black/African American] friends" (0). A final series of questions began with "How many romantic partners have you had in your life?" with response options of "zero," "one," "two," "three," and "more than three." This question was followed by two items asking, "How many people have you had a romantic involvement with who are White/European American?" and "How many people have you had a romantic involvement with who are Black/African American?" The response options for these final two questions were "none" (0), "one" (1), "some" (2), "most" (3), and

"all" (4).[2] In Experiment 2, the items were identical, except that "White/ European American" and "Black/ African American" were replaced by "Christian" and "Muslim."

Out-group contact was calculated by subtracting in-group contact from out-group contact for each of the three contact items. These difference scores were standardized and averaged, and yielded acceptable reliability ($\alpha = .76$ and .74 for Experiment 1 and Experiment 2, respectively). Scores were standardized across all participants in each experiment, rather than standardized within each group, to control for intergroup differences in out-group contact.

Explicit Prejudice: Social Distance In Experiment 1, social distance was measured by a set of items about interaction with Whites and an identical set about interaction with Blacks. All items had 9-point scales anchored at *strongly agree* (1) and *strongly disagree* (9). The questions were as follows:

- "I would marry or get involved in a long-term relationship with a White/European American [Black/African American]."
- "I would become close friends with a White/European American [Black/African American]."
- "I would work for someone who is a White/European American [Black/African American]."
- "I would invite a White/European American [Black/African American] over for dinner."
- "I would live next door to a White/European American [Black/African American]."
- "I would live on the same block as a White/European American [Black/African American]."

Experiment 2 used the same items, but replaced "White/European American" and "Black/African American" with "Christian" and "Muslim."

The items scaled well: In Experiment 1, Cronbach's α was .98 for the closeness-to-Whites scale and .94 for the closeness-to-Blacks scale. In Experiment 2, α was .93 for the closeness-to-Christians scale and .91 for the closeness-to-Muslims scale. In-group bias in Experiment 1 was calculated by subtracting scores on the closeness-to-Blacks scale from scores on the closeness-to-Whites scale for the White participants and by subtracting scores on the closeness-to-Whites scale from scores on the closeness-to-Blacks scale for the Black participants. In-group bias in Experiment 2 was calculated by subtracting scores on the closeness-to-Muslims scale from scores on the closeness-to-Christians scale for the Christian participants and by subtracting scores on the closeness-to-Christians scale from scores on the closeness-to-Muslims scale for the Muslim participants.[3]

Explicit Prejudice: Feelings Participants expressed explicit attitudes toward both their group and their respective out-group on standard feeling-thermometer scales. In Experiment 1, participants expressed feelings about "African Americans/Blacks" and "White people" using two feeling thermometers in which 0 was labeled *very unfavorable* and 100 was labeled *favorable.* In-group bias was calculated by subtracting the Black rating from the White rating for White participants and by subtracting the White rating from the Black rating for Black participants. In Experiment 2, participants expressed explicit attitudes toward Muslims and Christians with a single item for each: "How do you feel about Muslims [Christians] in general?" Responses were recorded on a 9-point scale from 1, *very cold,* to 9, *very warm.* In-group bias was calculated by subtracting the Muslim rating from the Christian rating for Christian participants and the Christian rating from the Muslim rating for Muslim participants (see footnote 3).

Implicit Prejudice We assessed implicit prejudice with the implicit association task (IAT)—a popular index of implicit attitudes that, like the classic Stroop (1935) procedure, uses an interference paradigm (e.g., Lowery et al., 2001). The IAT captures the degree to which positive versus negative associations to a given group facilitate category judgments. Implicit attitudes toward groups were captured by using names that were identifiably Black or White (Experiment 1) or names that were identifiably Christian or Muslim (Experiment 2), along with words known to be highly positive (e.g., *happy, clean*) or negative (e.g., *hate, dirty*). In two critical blocks, participants paired White (or Christian) names and positive words (e.g., check on the right side of a stimulus word) and Black (or Muslim) names and negative words (e.g., check on the left side of a stimulus word); in two other critical blocks, the required response paired White (or Christian) names with nega-

tive words and Black (or Muslim) names with positive words. In each block, participants were given 25 s to respond to as many names and words as possible. The degree of implicit out-group prejudice was indicated by the degree to which more items were completed when the out-group was paired with negative words than when the out-group was paired with positive words.

Participants completed the IAT in groups. In Experiment 1, four pages served as practice trials; each of these pages listed words from only one category (Black/African-American names, White/European American names, pleasant words, or unpleasant words). The following four pages presented the critical trials; both words and names were listed down the center column of each page (each page served as one 25-s block). There were two pro-Black pages, on which participants checked Black names and pleasant words on one side and White names and unpleasant words on the other side, and two pro-White pages, on which participants checked White names and pleasant words on one side and Black names and unpleasant words on the other side. Implicit out-group prejudice was calculated by subtracting the total score for the pro-Black blocks from the total score for the pro-White blocks for White participants and by subtracting the total score for the pro-White blocks from the total score for the pro-Black blocks for Black participants.

Experiment 2 replicated Experiment 1, replacing White and Black names with Christian and Muslim names. Implicit out-group prejudice was calculated by subtracting the total score for the pro-Muslim blocks from the total score for the pro-Christian blocks for the Christian participants and by subtracting the total score for the pro-Christian blocks from the total score for the pro-Muslim blocks for Muslim participants.

RESULTS

Perceived Intergroup Status

To test whether participants recognized status differences in their societies, we ran a 2 (participant group) × 2 (target group) mixed-measures analysis of variance (ANOVA), with status of the target groups measured within subjects for each experiment. In both experiments, participants corroborated common perceptions of the reigning status hierarchies. In Experiment 1, greater status was perceived for Whites ($M = 8.45$,

$SE = 0.071$) than for Blacks ($M = 4.47$, $SE = 0.194$), $F(1, 158) = 380.02$, $p_{rep} > .999$, $\eta^2 = .706$. The effect was equally strong for Whites and Blacks, as indicated by a nonsignificant interaction, $F(1, 158) < 1$. In Experiment 2, greater status was perceived for Christians ($M = 6.33$, $SD = 1.33$) than for Muslims ($M = 5.74$, $SD = 1.45$), $F(1, 76) = 10.09$, $p_{rep} = .984$, $\eta^2 = .117$. The effect was equally strong for Christians and Muslims, as indicated by a nonsignificant interaction, $F(1, 76) < 1$.

Intergroup Contact

In Experiment 1, difference scores for number of friends (in-group friends minus out-group friends) showed that Whites had relatively more in-group friends ($M = 1.70$, $SD = 0.88$) than Blacks did ($M = 0.97$, $SD = 1.31$), $t(158) = 3.79$, $p_{rep} = .996$. There were no differences between Blacks and Whites in the reported closeness of the closest in-group friend relative to the reported closeness of the closest out-group friend. Neither did Blacks and Whites differ in the number of in-group romantic relationships relative to the number of out-group romantic relationships ($ts < 1.2$). In Experiment 2, the reported closeness toward the closest in-group friend relative to the reported closeness toward the closest out-group friend was significantly greater for Christians ($M = 0.72$, $SD = 1.27$) compared with Muslims ($M = 0.11$, $SD = 0.94$), $t(81) = 2.43$, $p_{rep} = .937$. Christians and Muslims did not differ significantly in their difference scores for numbers of friends ($t = 1.04$) and romantic relationships ($t = 1.5$). We statistically controlled for the greater relative in-group friendships for Whites and Christians by standardizing these contact items across all participants rather than within group, so that any score for contact indicated the same amount of relative out-group contact for both groups in each study.

Contact and Explicit Prejudice

To examine the relation between friendly contact and explicit prejudice, we ran a series of regressions predicting social distance and intergroup feelings for each experiment (see Fig. 1). These analyses included main effects for contact (a continuous measure from more to less contact) and for participant's group membership (a dichotomous measure indicating higher vs.

lower status) and an interaction term that multiplied the centered contact measure by the participant's group membership (see Aiken & West, 1996).

In both experiments, greater contact was associated with reduced social distance from the out-group (Experiment 1: ($\beta = -.176$, $p_{rep} = .914$; Experiment 2: $\beta = -.541$, $p_{rep} > .999$) and with less negative feelings toward the out-group (Experiment 1: ($\beta = -.310$, $p_{rep} = .998$; Experiment 2: $\beta = -.422$, $p_{rep} = .998$). These results replicate the well-documented effect of contact on explicit out-group prejudice. In Experiment 1, Whites and Blacks expressed equal levels of out-group prejudice on both measures. In Experiment 2, Christians and Muslims expressed equal levels of out-group prejudice as measured by intergroup feelings, but the measure of social distance showed greater out-group prejudice among Christians than among Muslims (group main effect ($\beta = -.201$, $p_{rep} = .912$). We found no evidence of high-status enlightenment, which would have been indicated by significant group-by-contact interactions (all $ts < 1.4$).

Contact and Implicit Prejudice

To test the relation between friendly contact and implicit prejudice, we ran the same regressions with implicit prejudice, rather than explicit prejudice, as the outcome variable. As shown in the bottom graphs in Figure 1, although greater contact was associated with reduced out-group prejudice (Experiment 1: $\beta = -.208$, $p_{rep} = .961$; Experiment 2: $\beta = -.288$, $p_{rep} = .968$), high-status groups expressed greater in-group favoritism than low-status groups regardless of contact (Experiment 1: ($\beta = -.196$, $p_{rep} = .950$; Experiment 2: $\beta = -.326$, $p_{rep} = .984$), a result consistent with the literatures documenting general favoritism toward high-status groups. More important, both experiments demonstrated that intergroup contact reduced prejudice toward high-status groups more than prejudice toward low-status groups, as indicated by significant Group Status × Contact interactions (Experiment 1: ($\beta = -.209$, $p_{rep} = .918$; Experiment 2: $\beta = -.303$, $p_{rep} = .851$). This finding is reflected in the simple slopes shown in the bottom row of Figure 1. Whereas Blacks in the United States and Muslims in Lebanon exhibited a strong and statistically significant decrease in implicit out-group prejudice as a

FIGURE 1 / Results from Experiment 1 (left) and Experiment 2 (right). Pro-in-group social distance, pro-in-group feelings, and pro-in-group associations are graphed as a function of degree of contact and race (Experiment 1) or religion (Experiment 2). The figures plot regression-line slopes from 1 standard deviation below the mean to 1 standard deviation above the mean on the measure of contact. The center of the x-axis is the intercept (mean) for the slope. The standardized regression coefficient (β) for each slope is shown. IAT = implicit association task. The asterisks indicate statistical signficance, *p < .05, **p < .01, ***p < .001.

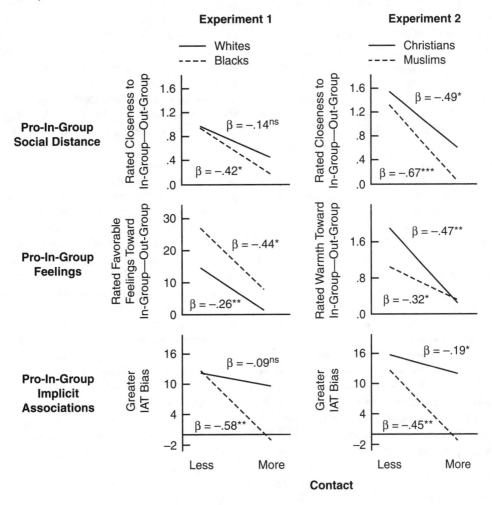

function of intergroup contact, Whites in the United States and Christians in Lebanon did not. This interaction reflects low-status deference and is congruent with the idea that intergroup contact facilitates positive implicit out-group attitudes to the extent that positive attitudes toward the out-group are broadly represented in society. Put another way, it is easier to generalize friendly intergroup experience to attitudes about high-status groups than to attitudes about low-status groups.

DISCUSSION

Prejudice research, including research on the contact hypothesis, is incomplete without taking into consideration broad intergroup status differences, as well as differences between explicit and implicit attitudes. We found that intergroup contact predicted reduced implicit prejudice toward out-groups, but only for the lower-status groups in our samples; that is, the results demonstrated low-status deference. These results obtained whether status involved Whites and Blacks in the United States or Christians and Muslims in Lebanon. The findings suggest that contact-induced changes in implicit prejudice are facilitated to the degree that they resonate with broadly recognized status differences. As regards explicit prejudice, although we were able to capture the general contact effect for both high- and low-status groups, we found no evidence of high-status enlightenment, which has been identified in a recent meta-analysis of contact studies (Tropp & Pettigrew, 2005). However, the high-status enlightenment shown in the meta-analysis was statistically significant but not dramatic (an average correlation of −.18 for minority status groups, compared with −.23 for majority status groups, an average difference of −.05), and was not found in many other past studies of the contact effect either. Further research is necessary to identify the conditions that elicit enlightenment and deference effects in explicit and implicit prejudice.

The dissociated effects of contact on implicit and explicit prejudice raise important new questions. In particular, why is there a status asymmetry in the relation between contact and implicit prejudice but not explicit prejudice? One possibility is suggested by the literature on power and interpersonal interactions, which demonstrates that low-power people are especially mindful in interactions with high-power people, whereas high-power people are especially heuristic and stereotypic in interactions with low-power people (Fiske, 1993; Keltner, Gruenfeld, & Anderson, 2003). Perhaps practice makes perfect: Over time, the effortful mindfulness of low-status people navigating common disadvantages in a hierarchical society may become automatized (Gollwitzer & Moskowitz, 1996; Moskowitz, 2001), eventuating in a kind of implicit accommodation toward high-status out-groups. In contrast, perhaps habitual inattention to members of low-status groups results in relatively little accommodation in the implicit attitude systems of members of high-status groups. Given the complex relations among status, contact, and prejudicial attitudes, further research is necessary to identify when

and how status moderates prejudice and intergroup relations.

An important caveat concerning causality is in order. Contact was measured, not manipulated, and consequently it is unclear whether contact caused the improvement in attitudes or whether more positive attitudes caused increased intimate contact. In reality, the relation between contact and attitudes is probably recursive, although our data cannot tease apart the causal relationships. However, the finding reported here is broadly congruent with research implicating friendship patterns in the dynamics of implicit prejudice. For example, adolescents engage in more negative implicit stereotyping about adolescents to the extent that they count adults as their friends (Gross & Hardin, in press).

The results presented here do not paint an optimistic picture regarding broad-based change in implicit prejudice toward low-status groups. Even friendship and romance with Blacks and Muslims were not associated with reduced implicit prejudice toward Blacks or Muslims in our experiments. Indeed, we found that Christians with the closest contact with Muslims, and Whites with the closest contact with Blacks, had the same amount of implicit prejudice as those with the least contact. These findings suggest that reducing common implicit prejudice toward low-status groups likely depends in part on broad, institutional, society-wide improvement in the actual status of low-status groups, which would likely elicit increasing proportions of situations that call out positive associations. However, given the surfeit of social contexts that so readily disadvantage Blacks and Muslims in the world today, including in Lebanon with its easy access to CNN and the global media, such changes remain a distant prospect.

REFERENCES

Aiken, L. S., & West, S. G. (1996). *Multiple regression: Testing and interpreting interactions.* Thousand Oaks, CA: Sage.

Allport, G. (1954). *The nature of prejudice.* Reading, MA: Addison-Wesley.

Ashburn-Nardo, L., Knowles, M. L., & Monteith, M. J. (2003). Black Americans' implicit racial associations and their implications for intergroup judgment. *Social Cognition, 21,* 61–87.

Banaji, M., & Greenwald, A. G. (1994). Implicit stereotyping and prejudice. In M. P. Zanna & J. M. Olson (Eds.), *The Ontario symposium: Col. 7. The psychology of prejudice* (pp. 55–76). Hillsdale, NJ: Erlbaum.

Blair, I. V. (2002). The malleability of automatic stereotypes and prejudice. *Personality and Social Psychology Bulletin, 6,* 242–261.

Brendl, C. M., Markman, A. B., & Messner, C. (2001). How do indirect measures of evaluation work? Evaluating the inference of prejudice in the Implicit Association Test. *Journal of Personality and Social Psychology, 81,* 760–773.

Clark, K. B., & Clark, M. P. (1947). Racial identification and preference in Negro children. In E. E. Maccoby, T. M. Newcomb, & E. L. Hartley (Eds.), *Readings in social psychology* (pp. 602–611). New York: Holt, Rinehart, & Winston.

Devine, P. G. (1989). Stereotypes and prejudice: Their automatic and controlled components. *Journal of Personality and Social Psychology, 56,* 5–18.

Devine, P. G., & Monteith, M. J. (1999). Automaticity and control in stereotyping. In S. Chaiken & Y. Trope (Eds.), *Dual-process theories in social psychology* (pp. 339–360). New York: Guilford Press.

Devine, P. G., Plant, E. A., Amodio, D. M., Harmon-Jones, E., & Vance, S. L. (2002). The regulation of explicit and implicit race bias: The role of motivations to respond without prejudice. *Journal of Personality and Social Psychology, 82,* 835–848.

Dovidio, J. F., Kawakami, K., & Gaertner, S. L. (2002). Implicit and explicit prejudice and interracial interaction. *Journal of Personality and Social Psychology, 82,* 62–68.

Fazio, R. H., Jackson, J. R., Dunton, B. C., & Williams, C. J. (1995). Variability in automatic activation as an unobtrusive measure of racial attitudes: A bona fide pipeline? *Journal of Personality and Social Psychology, 69,* 1013–1027.

Fiske, S. T. (1993). Controlling other people: The impact of power on stereotyping. *American Psychologist, 48,* 621–628.

Glick, P., & Fiske, S. T. (2001). An ambivalent alliance: Hostile and benevolent sexism as complementary justifications for gender inequality. *American Psychologist, 35,* 603–618.

Gollwitzer, P. M., & Moskowitz, G. B. (1996). Goal effects on action and cognition. In E. T. Higgins & A. W. Kruglanski (Eds.), *Social psychology: Handbook of basic principles* (pp. 361–399). New York: Guilford Press.

Greenwald, A. G., & Banaji, M. R. (1995). Implicit social cognition: Attitudes, self-esteem, and stereotypes. *Psychological Review, 102,* 4–27.

Gross, E. F., & Hardin, C. D. (in press). Implicit and explicit stereotyping of adolescents. *Social Justice Research.*

Hewstone, M., & Ward, C. (1985). Ethnocentrism and causal attribution in southeast Asia. *Journal of Personality and Social Psychology, 48,* 614–623.

Hinkle, S., & Brown, R. (1990). Intergroup comparisons and social identity: Some links and lacunae. In D. Abrams & M. A. Hogg (Eds.), *Social identity theory: Constructive and critical advances* (pp. 48–70). Hemel Hempstead, England: Harvester.

Jost, J. T., & Banaji, M. R. (1994). The role of stereotyping in system-justification and the producaion of false consciousness. *British Journal of Social Psychology, 33,* 1–27.

Jost, J. T., & Burgess, D. (2000). Attitudinal ambivalence and the conflict between group and system justification motives in low-status groups. *Personality and Social Psychology Bulletin, 26,* 293–305.

Jost, J. T., Pelham, B. W., & Carvallo, M. R. (2002). Nonconscious forms of system justification: Implicit and behavioral preferences for higher status groups. *Journal of Experimental Social Psychology, 38,* 586–602.

Karpinski, A., & Hilton, J. L. (2001). Attitudes and the Implicit Association Test. *Journal of Personality and Social Psychology, 81,* 774–788.

Keltner, D., Gruenfeld, D. H., & Anderson, C. (2003). Power, approach, and inhibition. *Psychological Review, 110,* 265–284.

Lowery, B. S., Hardin, C. D., & Sinclair, S. (2001). Social influence effects on automatic racial prejudice. *Journal of Personality and Social Psychology, 81,* 842–855.

Major, B., Gramzow, R. H., McCoy, S. K., Levin, S., Schmader, T., & Sidanius, J. (2002). Perceiving personal discrimination: The role of group status and legitimizing ideology. *Journal of Personality and Social Psychology, 82,* 269–282.

Moskowitz, G. B. (2001). Preconscious control and compensatory cognition. In G. B. Moskowitz (Ed.), *Cognitive social psychology: The Princeton symposium on the legacy and future of social cognition* (pp. 333–358). Hillsdale, NJ: Erlbaum.

Pelham, B. W., Koole, S. L., Hardin, C. D., Hetts, J. J., Seah, E., & DeHart, T. (2005). Gender moderates the relation between implicit and explicit self-esteem. *Journal of Experimental Social Psychology, 41,* 84–89.

Pettigrew, T. F. (1998). Intergroup contact theory. *Annual Review of Psychology, 49,* 65–85.

Pettigrew, T. F., & Tropp, L. R. (2006). A meta-analytic test of intergroup contact theory. *Journal of Personality and Social Psychology, 90,* 751–783.

Rudman, L. A., Feinberg, J., & Fairchild, K. (2002). Minority members' implicit attitudes: Automatic ingroup bias as a function of group status. *Social Cognition, 20,* 294–320.

Rudman, L. A., Greenwald, A. G., Mellot, D. S., & Schwartz, J. L. K. (1999). Measuring the automatic components of prejudice: Flexibility and generality of the Implicit Association Test. *Social Cognition, 17,* 437–465.

Sachdev, I., & Bourhis, R. Y. (1987). Status differentials and intergroup behavior. *European Journal of Social Psychology, 17,* 277–293.

Sidanius, J., & Pratto, E. (1999). *Social dominance: An intergroup theory of social hierarchy and oppression.* New York: Cambridge University Press.

Stroop, J. R. (1935). Studies of interference in serial verbal reactions. *Journal of Experimental Psychology, 18,* 643–662.

Tropp, L. R., & Pettigrew, T. F. (2005). Relationships between intergroup contact and prejudice among minority and majority status groups. *Psychological Science, 16,* 951–957.

ENDNOTES

1. AUB students are typically Lebanese. The study was conducted in English, the official language of instruction at AUB. Christians included students who identified themselves as Catholic, Orthodox, Protestant, or Maronite. Muslims included students who identified themselves as Sunni or Shiite.

2. For these questions, some participants who had had only one partner indicated "one," whereas others with only one partner indicated "all." Consequently, for consistency, those who indicated "one" were recoded as "all" for further analyses.

3. Difference scores were used to keep the measures parallel with the implicit association task, which requires difference scores in its computation. Nevertheless, the results are conceptually identical whether one uses the direct measures of out-group prejudice or difference scores.

CRITICAL THINKING QUESTIONS

1. This article used a particular methodology to measure implicit prejudice. In what other ways can implicit prejudice be manifested and/or measured? Be specific.

2. Using the information from this article and your own reasoning, describe how people can be made more aware of their implicit prejudices. How can implicit prejudices be reduced?

3. The article asks, "Why is there a status asymmetry in the relation between contact and implicit prejudice but not explicit prejudice?" Extend the discussion in the article by adding your own thoughts about why this may be the case.

4. This study offers the rather pessimistic conclusion that implicit prejudice toward low-status groups cannot be readily changed without actually raising the statuses of these groups. Do you agree or disagree with this conclusion? Explain your position.

5. Think of a real-life example of implicit prejudice—in other words, a situation where someone overtly said he or she was not prejudiced toward a particular group yet, in some unconscious way, betrayed his or her underlying prejudice. Describe the situation.

CHAPTER INTEGRATION QUESTIONS

1. Søren Kirkegaard, existential philosopher, said, "When you label me, you negate me." What does this quote mean to you? Explain.

2. How would you relate the Kirkegaard quote to each of the articles in this chapter?

3. Is there a common theme among the articles to which this quotation also applies? Discuss.

4. Have you ever felt that you were being judged based on having been assigned some label? Explain how this quotation may be applicable to experiences from your life.

Chapter Seven

INTERPERSONAL ATTRACTION

Do "BIRDS OF A FEATHER flock together," or do "Opposites attract"? Both of these folk wisdoms, as contradictory as they are, attempt to answer an age-old question: To whom are we attracted and why?

The research on *interpersonal attraction* has gone in various directions in an attempt to answer this question. *Attraction* here is defined not in the narrow sense of romantic attraction but as attraction to anyone with whom we may associate—a friend, a co-worker, or even a child. Many factors have been identified as important determinants of interpersonal attraction, but perhaps the most widely investigated factor (and the one with the most distressing findings) is that of *physical attractiveness.* Study after study seems to demonstrate that how someone looks is a major determinant of how he or she is viewed and treated by other people.

"Why I Hate Beauty," Article 19, examines how our perceptions of beauty have been markedly influenced by our almost constant exposure to media images of attractiveness. We are all aware of how we are confronted with very attractive people just about any time we look at television, watch a movie, or pick up a magazine. But what is the cumulative impact of our exposure to attractive people? This article explores the possibility that such exposure may not only have an impact on our satisfaction with our current partners but even on the possibility of our divorcing them later on.

Our judgment of physical attractiveness is not just limited to selecting potential partners, however. It may also influence what other characteristics we ascribe to people based solely on their looks. Article 20, "What Is Beautiful Is Good," is a classic demonstration of how positive stereotypes are associated with physical attractiveness. Given the pervasiveness of this physical attractiveness effect, it has real implications for how we deal with and judge others in our daily lives.

Article 21, "One Woman's Behavior Affects the Attractiveness of Others," likewise examines the impact of viewing attractive opposite-sex individuals on subjects' subsequent evaluations of their own partners' and more typical people's attractiveness. However, this study also examined how certain factors, such as smiling and acting friendly, may influence people. In turns out that men and women respond quite differently to these factors.

ARTICLE 19_____

Imagine that you are living a thousand years ago in just about any part of the world. If you were like the vast majority of people who lived then, you would be living in a small village and your exposure to other people would be pretty much limited to those living nearby. Without a means of rapid transportation, you most likely would not have ventured beyond a few miles of your birthplace during the course of your lifetime. Even if you were among the more adventurous of your group, you only may have traveled a few hundred miles, and even then, you mostly would have encountered people of similar background to your own. Given this situation, in deciding on a mate, to whom are you going to be most attracted? Will the looks of the other person matter? Research suggests that it will. But what will influence what you consider to be *beautiful?*

Our perceptions of what is beautiful are partly innate and partly learned. For example, research indicates that young infants, well before they have been exposed to media or cultural stereotypes of beauty, spend more time gazing at more attractive faces than less attractive faces. *Sociobiology,* the field that examines the biological or evolutionary underpinnings of our social behaviors, suggests that there is a biological reason we are drawn to attractive people. For example, in evolutionary terms, young, attractive women may suggest health and thus fertility to men seeking to carry on their genes. Sociobiological research even indicates that there are some universal factors associated with beauty, such as facial and body symmetry, which transcend specific cultural ideals of attractiveness. So, there may indeed be at least a partial biological reason as to why we have such a strong preference for beautiful people.

But what is considered physically attractive? While there may be some underlying biological reasons we prefer the more attractive to the less attractive, the specifics of what we may be attracted to are based on what we see around us. Take the opening scenario in the first paragraph. Living long ago, you most likely would have been exposed to a very small number of people in your lifetime. Given the diversity of human appearance, only a very small number of the people you may have encountered in your lifetime might be described as very physically attractive. So, what you as an individual might consider to be attractive would be based on the relative ratings of the people you saw around you. In other words, if you only very rarely (if ever) encountered a highly attractive person, you might consider the normal people surrounding you as more attractive than if you were constantly exposed to many highly attractive people.

Fast forward to the present time: The mass media has done many things to us and the world around us. One thing that it certainly has done, however, is to expose us to a large number of highly attractive people in ways that previously were simply not possible. On a daily basis, we are bombarded with images of young, highly attractive people, be it in advertising, the movies, or television shows. Moreover, people around the world get these same images of highly attractive people, over and over again.

Does this constant exposure to images of highly attractive people affect our perceptions of the real people around us? The following article by Michael Levine and Hara Estroff Marano suggests that it does. As the research described by the authors suggests, such constant exposure to mass media images of beauty actually may impact not only our choices of mates but also our satisfaction with our current mates and even the possibility of our divorcing them.

Why I Hate Beauty

■ Michael Levine with Hara Estroff Marano

Poets rave about beauty. Brave men have started wars over beauty. Women the world over strive for it. Scholars devote their lives to deconstructing our impulse to obtain it. Ordinary mortals erect temples to beauty. In just about every way imaginable, the world honors physical beauty. But I hate beauty.

I live in what is likely the beauty capital of the world and have the enviable fortune to work with some of the most beautiful women in it. With their smooth bodies and supple waists, these women are the very picture of youth and attractiveness. Not only are they exemplars of nature's design for detonating desire in men, but they stir yearnings for companionship that date back to ancestral mating dances. Still, beauty is driving me nuts, and although I'm a successful red-blooded American male, divorced and available, it is beauty alone that is keeping me single and lonely.

It is scant solace that science is on my side. I seem to have a confirmed case of the contrast effect. It doesn't make me any happier knowing it's afflicting lots of others too.

As an author of books on marketing, I have long known about the contrast effect. It is a principle of perception whereby the differences between two things are exaggerated depending on the order in which those things ore presented. If you lift a light object and then a heavy object, you will judge the second object heavier than if you had lifted it first or solo.

Psychologists Sara Gutierres, Ph.D., and Douglas Kenrick, Ph.D., both of Arizona State University, demonstrated that the contrast effect operates powerfully in the sphere of person-to-person attraction as well. In a series of studies over the past two decades, they have shown that, more than any of us might suspect, judgments of attractiveness (of ourselves and of others) depend on the situation in which we find ourselves. For example, a woman of average attractiveness seems a lot less attractive than she actually is if

a viewer has first seen a highly attractive woman. If a man is talking to a beautiful female at a cocktail party and is then joined by a less attractive one, the second woman will seem relatively unattractive.

The contrast principle also works in reverse. A woman of average attractiveness will seem more attractive than she is if she enters a room of unattractive women. In other words, context counts.

In their very first set of studies, which have been expanded and refined over the years to determine the exact circumstances under which the findings apply and their effects on both men and women, Gutierres and Kenrick asked male college dormitory residents to rate the photo of a potential blind date. (The photos had been previously rated by other males to be of average attractiveness.) If the men were watching an episode of *Charlie's Angels* when shown the photo, the blind date was rated less desirable than she was by males watching a different show. The initial impressions of romantic partners—women who were actually available to them and likely to be interested in them—were so adversely affected that the men didn't even want to bother.

Since these studies, the researchers have found that the contrast effect influences not only our evaluations of strangers but also our views of our own mates. And it sways self-assessments of attractiveness too.

Most recently, Kenrick and Gutierres discovered that women who are surrounded by other attractive women, whether in the flesh, in films or in photographs, rate themselves as less satisfied with their attractiveness—and less desirable as a marriage partner. "If there are a large number of desirable members of one's own sex available, one may regard one's own market value as lower," the researchers reported in the *Personality and Social Psychology Bulletin.*

If you had to pick ground zero for the contrast effect, it would be Hollywood. To feed the film industry's voracious appetite for attractive faces, it lures

Reprinted from *Psychology Today,* 2001 (July/August), *34,* 38–44. Reprinted with permission from *Psychology Today* magazine. Copyright © 2001 (Sussex Publishers, Inc.).

especially beautiful women from around the world. And for those who don't arrive already at the pinnacle of perfection, whole industries exist here to render it attainable, to reshape faces and bodies to the prevailing standard of attractiveness.

There's an extraordinarily high concentration of gorgeous females in Los Angeles, and courtesy of the usually balmy weather and lifestyle, they tend to be highly visible—and not just locally. The film and television industries project their images all over the world, not to mention all the supporting media dealing with celebrities and gossip that help keep them professionally viable.

As the head of a public relations agency, I work with these women day and night. You might expect that to make me feel good, as we normally like being around attractive people. But my exposure to extreme beauty is ruining my capacity to love the ordinarily beautiful women of the real world, women who are more likely to meet my needs for deep connection and partnership of the soul.

The contrast effect doesn't apply just to strangers men have yet to meet who might be most suitable for them. In ongoing studies, Gutierres and Kenrick have found that it also affects men's feelings about their current partner. Viewing pictures of attractive women weakens their commitment to their mates. Men rate themselves as being less in love with their partner after looking at *Playboy* centerfolds than they did before seeing the pictures of beautiful women.

This finding is all the more surprising because getting someone aroused normally boosts their attraction to their partner. But seeing beautiful models wiped out whatever effect the men might have experienced from being sexually aroused.

The strange thing is, being bombarded with visions of beautiful women (or for women, socially powerful men) doesn't make us think our partners are less physically attractive. It doesn't change our perception of our partner. Instead, by some sleight of mind, it distorts our idea of the pool of possibilities.

These images make us think there's a huge field of alternatives. It changes our estimate of the number of people who are available to us as potential mates. In changing our sense of the possibilities, it prods us to believe we could always do better, keeping us continually unsatisfied.

"The perception of the comparison pool is changed," says Gutierres. "In this context our partner doesn't look so great." Adds Kenrick: "You think, 'Yes, my partner's fine—but why do I have to settle for fine when there are just so many great people out there?'" All you have to do is turn on the TV or look at the covers of magazines in the supermarket checkout line to be convinced there are any number of incredibly beautiful women available.

Kenrick puts it in evolutionary perspective. Like us, he says, our ancestors were probably designed to make some estimation of the possible pool of alternatives and some estimation of their own worth relative to the possibilities.

The catch is they just didn't see that many people, and certainly not many beautiful people. They lived in a little village of maybe 30. Even if you counted distant third cousins, our ancestors might have been exposed to a grand total of 500 people in their lifetime. And among those 500, some were old, some were young, but very few were very attractive.

Today anyone who turns on the TV or looks at a magazine can easily see 500 beautiful people in an hour, certainly in an evening. "My pool includes the people I see in my everyday life," explains Kenrick. "I don't consciously think that the people I see through movies, TV and magazines are artificial. Still, seeing Juliette Binoche all the time registers in my brain."

Our minds have not caught up. They haven't evolved to correct for MTV. "Our research suggests that our brains don't discount the women on the cover of *Cosmo* even when subjects know these women are models. Subjects judge an average attractive woman as less desirable as a date after just having seen models," Kenrick says.

Part of the problem is we're built to selectively remember the really beautiful. They stand out. "That's what you're drawn to," says Kenrick. "It feels good on the brain." And any stimulus that's vivid becomes readily available to memory, encouraging you to overestimate the true frequency of beautiful women out there.

So the women men count as possibilities are not real possibilities for most of them. That leads to a lot of guys sitting at home alone with their fantasies of unobtainable supermodels, stuck in a secret, sorry state that makes them unable to access real love for real women. Or, as Kenrick finds, a lot of guys on college campuses whining, "There are no attractive women to date." Under a constant barrage of media images of beautiful women, these guys have an expectation of attractiveness that is unusually high—and that makes the real people around them, in whom they might really be interested, seem lackluster, even if they are quite good-looking.

The idea that beauty could make so many men so miserable has acquired hard-nosed mathematical proof. In the world of abstract logic, marriage is looked on as a basic matching problem with statistical underpinnings in game theory. Logic says that everybody wants to do as well as they possibly can in selecting a life partner. And when people apply varied criteria for choosing a mate, everybody ends up with a partner with whom they are more or less satisfied. Not everybody gets his or her No. 1 choice, but everybody winds up reasonably content.

But the world has changed since mathematicians first tackled the matching of people with mates in the early 1960s. Films, television and magazines have not only given beauty a commanding presence in our lives but have also helped standardize our vision of attractiveness. Enter Guido Caldarelli, Ph.D., of the University of Rome, and Andrea Capocci, Ph.D., of the University of Fribourg in Switzerland. Once they introduced into their mating equations what they call the "*Vogue* factor"—a measure of the influence of beauty—they found that people become dissatisfied with their sexual partners.

"When the concept of 'most beautiful' people in the world tends to be the same for everyone, it becomes more and more difficult to make more people happy," say the researchers. The same few beautiful people top everyone's list of desired partners— clearly an impossibility—and no one comes close to being matched with any of their choices. So people become unhappy with their partner possibilities.

Alas, it's not simply a theoretical issue. Sociologist Satoshi Kanazawa, Ph.D., finds that real-life consequences of the contrast effect exist, such as divorce. The contrast effect not only undermines marriages; it then keeps men single—and miserable.

Kanazawa, assistant professor of sociology at Indiana University of Pennsylvania, wondered: "If men found

themselves being less attracted to their mates after being exposed to eight or 16 pictures in a half-hour experiment, what would be the effect if that happened day in, day out, for 20 years?" It immediately occurred to him that high school and college teachers would be prime candidates for a study; they are constantly surrounded by young women in their reproductive prime. The only other occupation he could think of where the overwhelming majority of people men come in contact with are young women, was Hollywood movie directors, as well as producers and actors—a group not known for their stable marriages. But there was not an available body of data on them like there was on teachers, from a general population survey.

What Kanazawa found was summed up in the title of his report published last year in *Evolution and Human Behavior:* "Teaching May Be Hazardous to Your Marriage." Men are generally less likely to be currently divorced or separated than women, and overall teachers are particularly unlikely to be divorced or separated. But being a male teacher or professor wiped out that advantage. And not just any male teacher is at risk. Male kindergarten and grade school teachers were contentedly monogamous. "There appears to be something about male teachers who come in daily contact with teenage women that increases the likelihood of being currently divorced or separated," Kanazawa says. He adds that these men remain unmarried because any adult women they might meet and date after their divorce would pale in comparison to the pretty young things constantly around them.

"Most real-life divorces happen because one or the other spouse is dissatisfied with their mate," says Kanazawa. "The contrast effect can explain why men might unconsciously become dissatisfied. They don't know why they suddenly find their middle-aged wives not appealing anymore; their exposure to young women might be a reason."

It would be blissfully easy to point a finger and claim that such infatuation with the young and the beautiful is the fault of the media and its barrage of nubile bodies. But it would also be incorrect. They're just giving us what we are naturally interested in.

All the evidence indicates that we are wired to respond to beauty. It's more than a matter of mere aesthetics; beauty is nature's shorthand for healthy and fertile, for reproductive capacity, a visible cue that a woman has the kind of prime partner potential that will bestow good genes on future generations. One of the prime elements of beauty, for example, is symmetry of body features. Research suggests that symmetrical people are physically and psychologically healthier than their less symmetrical counterparts.

If we're now all reeling from a surfeit of images of attractiveness, well, it's a lot like our dietary love affair with sugar. "We want it. We need it. And our ancestors didn't have enough of it," observes Kenrick. "They were more concerned with starving. As a result, we have very hypersensitive detectors for it. And modern technology packages it and sends us doses that are way too large for our health."

There are, of course, beautiful women in other parts of the country. But L.A. is a mecca, attracting the most beautiful. Women don't look like this anywhere else in the country, and certainly not in the quantity they do here.

L.A. is an adopted city for me, as it is for many. Born in New York, I wonder from time to time what shape my life would have taken if I hadn't moved here in the 1970s. Whatever else, I would not have been saturated with the sight of so many beautiful women on a daily basis. But then I remember; these are the women whose images are broadcast all over the globe. While most people do not live in L.A., they visit it every day when they turn on the TV or go to the movies. It is safe to say that, to one degree or another, we all live in the shadow of the Hollywood sign.

CRITICAL THINKING QUESTIONS

1. This article suggests that we are exposed to very attractive people almost constantly in the media. What specific images of attractiveness are presented today in the media? Find media images of physical attractiveness from the 1950s and 1960s. What is the difference, if any, between the images presented then and the images presented now? Would the contrast effect work the same, regardless of the specific images of beauty being portrayed in the media? Explain.

2. Obesity among Americans recently has been described as a major health problem, second only to smoking as being preventable. At the same time, people have complained about the images of the very thin models and media figures that appear all around us. How do you reconcile this modeling of thinness as the ideal of beauty with the fact that Americans are increasingly overweight? In other words, why hasn't the media image of thinness resulted in people losing weight, when the opposite actually seems to have occurred? Explain.

3. This article deals with the issue of the contrast effect and how constant exposure to images of very attractive people may leave us less satisfied with our real-life peers. Besides beauty, what other images conveyed by the media may produce contrast effects, resulting in us being less happy with what we actually have and desirous of what we constantly see in the media?

4. Mass media images of beauty are disseminated worldwide via mechanisms such as movies and magazines. Many, but not all, of these images originate in the United States. Do you think the same contrast effect occurs in cultures that are very dissimilar to that of the United States? For that matter, would the same contrast effect occur even within the various subgroups that comprise the United States? Explain.

5. A common stereotype is that men rate the physical attractiveness of women as more important than women rate the physical attractiveness of men. In fact, much of the research on physical attractiveness focuses on the effects of female beauty on males. Design a study to determine how the contrast effect impacts females who are exposed to male media stereotypes of physical attractiveness.

ARTICLE 20

It may seem obvious that looks matter when it comes to dating and mate selection. While many people would argue that physical attractiveness is not the only thing that they look for in a potential partner, few would argue that they are oblivious to appearance. Furthermore, according to Article 19—which considered how people's beauty preferences might have biological roots—there is fairly strong agreement as to what features people find attractive.

So, what is life like for people who happen to have the features that others find attractive? Are their lives significantly different from those of individuals who do not possess such good looks? Furthermore, do looks have any impact on people's lives outside the areas of dating and mating popularity? For example, compared to a less attractive counterpart, will an attractive person more likely be successful in the work world? Be a better parent? Be a happier person overall? The following classic article by Karen Dion, Ellen Berscheid, and Elaine Walster was one of the first studies to investigate the "What is beautiful is good" effect. As indicated in the article, attractiveness may convey a great many benefits to those people who possess it.

What Is Beautiful Is Good[1]
■ Karen Dion, Ellen Berscheid, and Elaine Walster

A person's physical appearance, along with his sexual identity, is the personal characteristic that is most obvious and accessible to others in social interaction. The present experiment was designed to determine whether physically attractive stimulus persons, both male and female, are (a) assumed to possess more socially desirable personality traits than physically unattractive stimulus persons and (b) expected to lead better lives (e.g., be more competent husbands and wives, be more successful occupationally, etc.) than unattractive stimulus persons. Sex of Subject × Sex of Stimulus Person interactions along these dimensions also were investigated. The present results indicate a "what is beautiful is good" stereotype along the physical attractiveness dimension with no Sex of Judge × Sex of Stimulus interaction. The implications of such a stereotype on self-concept development and the course of social interaction are discussed.

A person's physical appearance, along with his sexual identity, is the personal characteristic most obvious and accessible to others in social interaction. It is perhaps for this reason that folk psychology has always contained a multitude of theorems which ostensibly permit the forecast of a person's character and personality simply from knowledge of his outward appearance. The line of deduction advanced by most physiognomic theories is simply that "What is beautiful is good . . . [Sappho, Fragments, No. 101]," and that "Physical beauty is the sign of an interior beauty, a spiritual and moral beauty . . . [Schiller, 1882]."

Several processes may operate to make the soothsayers' prophecies more logical and accurate than would appear at first glance. First, it is possible that a correlation between inward character and appearance exists because certain personality traits influence one's appearance. For example, a calm, relaxed person may develop fewer lines and wrinkles than a tense, irritable person. Second, cultural stereotypes about the kinds of personalities appropriate for beautiful or ugly people may mold the personalities of these individuals.

If casual acquaintances invariably assume that attractive individuals are more sincere, noble, and honest than unattractive persons, then attractive individuals should be habitually regarded with more respect than unattractive persons. Many have noted that one's self-concept develops from observing what others think about oneself. Thus, if the physically attractive person is consistently treated as a virtuous person, he may become one.

The above considerations pose several questions: (*a*) Do individuals in fact have stereotyped notions of the personality traits possessed by individuals of varying attractiveness? (*b*) To what extent are these stereotypes accurate? (*c*) What is the cause of the correlation between beauty and personality if, in fact, such a correlation exists?

Some observers, of course, deny that such stereotyping exists, and thus render Questions *b* and *c* irrelevant. Chief among these are rehabilitation workers (cf. Wright, 1960) whose clients possess facial and other physical disabilities. These researchers, however, may have a vested interest in believing that physical beauty is a relatively unimportant determinant of the opportunities an individual has available to him.

Perhaps more interestingly, it has been asserted that other researchers also have had a vested interest in retaining the belief that beauty is a peripheral characteristic. Aronson (1969), for example, has suggested that the fear that investigation might prove this assumption wrong has generally caused this to be a taboo area for social psychologists:

As an aside, I might mention that physical attractiveness is rarely investigated as an antecedent of liking—even though a casual observation (even by us experimental social psychologists) would indicate that we seem to react differently to beautiful women than to homely women. It is difficult to be certain why the effects of physical beauty have not been studied more systematically. It may be that, at some levels, we would hate to find evidence indicating that beautiful women are better liked than homely women—somehow this seems undemocratic. In a democracy we like to feel that with hard work and a good deal of motivation, a person can accomplish almost anything.

But, alas (most of us believe), hard work cannot make an ugly woman beautiful. Because of this suspicion perhaps most social psychologists implicitly prefer to believe that beauty is indeed only skin deep—and avoid the investigation of its social impact for fear they might learn otherwise [p. 160].

The present study was an attempt to determine if a physical attractiveness stereotype exists and, if so, to investigate the content of the stereotype along several dimensions. Specifically, it was designed to investigate (*a*) whether physically attractive stimulus persons, both male and female, are assumed to possess more *socially desirable personality traits* than unattractive persons and (*b*) whether they are expected to *lead better lives* than unattractive individuals. With respect to the latter, we wished to determine if physically attractive persons are generally expected to be better husbands and wives, better parents, and more successful socially and occupationally than less attractive persons.

Because it seemed possible that jealousy might attenuate these effects (if one is jealous of another, he may be reluctant to accord the other the status that he feels the other deserves), and since subjects might be expected to be more jealous of attractive stimulus persons of the same sex than of the opposite sex, we examined the Sex of Subject × Sex of Stimulus Person interactions along the dimensions described above.

METHOD

Subjects

Sixty students, 30 males and 30 females, who were enrolled in an introductory course in psychology at the University of Minnesota participated in this experiment. Each had agreed to participate in return for experimental points to be added to their final exam grade.

Procedure

When the subjects arrived at the designated rooms, they were introduced to the experiment as a study of accuracy in person perception. The experimenter stated that while psychological studies have shown that people do form detailed impressions of others on the basis of a very few cues, the variables determining the extent to which these early impressions are generally accurate have not yet been completely identified. The subjects were told that the purpose of the present study was to compare person perception accuracy of untrained college students with two other groups who had been trained in various interpersonal perception techniques, specifically graduate students in clinical psychology and clinical psychologists. The experimenter noted his belief that person perception accuracy is a general ability varying among people. Therefore, according to the experimenter, college students who are high on this ability may be as accurate as some professional clinicians when making first-impression judgments based on noninterview material.

The subjects were told that standard sets of photographs would be used as the basis for personality inferences. The individuals depicted in the photographs were said to be part of a group of college students currently enrolled at other universities who were participating in a longitudinal study of personality development scheduled to continue into adulthood. It would be possible, therefore, to assess the accuracy of each subject's judgments against information currently available on the stimulus persons and also against forthcoming information.

Stimulus Materials Following the introduction, each subject was given three envelopes. Each envelope contained one photo of a stimulus person of approximately the subject's own age. One of the three envelopes that the subject received contained a photograph of a physically attractive stimulus person; another contained a photograph of a person of average attractiveness; and the final envelope contained a photograph of a relatively unattractive stimulus person.[2] Half of our subjects received three pictures of girls; the remainder received pictures of boys.

To increase the generalizability of our findings and to insure that the general dimension of attractiveness was the characteristic responded to (rather than unique characteristics such as hair color, etc.), 12 different sets of three pictures each were prepared. Each subject received and rated only 1 set. Which 1 of the 12 sets of pictures the subject received, the order in

which each of the three envelopes in the set were presented, and the ratings made of the person depicted, were all randomly determined.

Dependent Variables The subjects were requested to record their judgments of the three stimulus persons in several booklets.[3] The first page of each booklet cautioned the subjects that this study was an investigation of accuracy of person perception and that we were not interested in the subjects' tact, politeness, or other factors usually important in social situations. It was stressed that it was important for the subject to rate the stimulus persons frankly.

The booklets tapped impressions of the stimulus person along several dimensions. First, the subjects were asked to open the first envelope and then to rate the person depicted on 27 different *personality traits* (which were arranged in random order).[4] The subjects' ratings were made on 6-point scales, the ends of which were labeled by polar opposites (i.e., exciting– dull). When these ratings had been computed, the subject was asked to open the second envelope, make ratings, and then open the third envelope.

In a subsequent booklet, the subjects were asked to assess the stimulus persons on five additional personality traits.[5] These ratings were made on a slightly different scale. The subjects were asked to indicate which stimulus person possessed the "most" and "least" of a given trait. The stimulus person thought to best represent a positive trait was assigned a score of 3; the stimulus person thought to possess an intermediate amount of the trait was assigned a score of 2; and the stimulus person thought to least represent the trait was assigned a score of 1.

In a previous experiment (see Endnote 3), a subset of items was selected to comprise an index of the *social desirability* of the personality traits assigned to the stimulus person. The subjects' ratings of each stimulus person on the appropriate items were simply summed to determine the extent to which the subject perceived each stimulus person as socially desirable.

In order to assess whether or not attractive persons are expected to lead happier and more successful lives than unattractive persons, the subjects were asked to estimate which of the stimulus persons would be most likely, and which least likely, to have a number of different life experiences. The subjects were reminded again that their estimates would eventually be checked for accuracy as the lives of the various stimulus persons evolved. The subjects' estimates of the stimulus person's probable life experiences formed indexes of the stimulus person's future happiness in four areas: (*a*) marital happiness (Which stimulus person is most likely to ever be divorced?); (*b*) parental happiness (Which stimulus person is most likely to be a good parent?); (*c*) social and professional happiness (Which stimulus person is most likely to experience deep personal fulfillment?); and (*d*) total happiness (sum of Indexes *a, b,* and *c*).

A fifth index, an occupational success index, was also obtained for each stimulus person. The subjects were asked to indicate which of the three stimulus persons would be most likely to engage in 30 different occupations. (The order in which the occupations were presented and the estimates made was randomized.) The 30 occupations had been chosen such that three status levels of 10 different general occupations were represented, three examples of which follow: Army sergeant (low status); Army captain (average status); Army colonel (high status). Each time a high-status occupation was foreseen for a stimulus person, the stimulus person was assigned a score of 3; when a moderate status occupation was foreseen, the stimulus person was assigned a score of 2; when a low-status occupation was foreseen, a score of 1 was assigned. The average status of occupations that a subject ascribed to a stimulus person constituted the score for that stimulus person in the occupational status index.

RESULTS AND DISCUSSION

Manipulation Check

It is clear that our manipulation of the relative attractiveness of the stimulus persons depicted was effective. The six unattractive stimulus persons were seen as less attractive than the average stimulus persons, who, in turn, were seen as less attractive than the six attractive stimulus persons. The stimulus persons' mean rankings on the attractiveness dimension were

1.12, 2.02, and 2.87, respectively. These differences were statistically significant ($F = 939.32$).[6]

Test of Hypotheses

It will be recalled that it was predicted that the subjects would attribute more socially desirable personality traits to attractive individuals than to average or unattractive individuals. It also was anticipated that jealousy might attenuate these effects. Since the subjects might be expected to be more jealous of stimulus persons of the same sex than of the opposite sex, we blocked both on sex of subject and sex of stimulus person. If jealousy attenuated the predicted main effect, a significant Sex of Subject × Sex of Stimulus Person interaction should be secured in addition to the main effect.

All tests for detection of linear trend and interaction were conducted via a multivariate analysis of variance. (This procedure is outlined in Hays, 1963.)

The means relevant to the hypothesis that attractive individuals will be perceived to possess more socially desirable personalities than others are reported in Table 1. Analyses reveal that attractive individuals were indeed judged to be more socially desirable than are unattractive ($F = 29.61$) persons. The Sex of Subject × Sex of Stimulus Person interaction was insignificant (interaction $F = .00$). Whether the rater was of the same or the opposite sex as the stimulus person, attractive stimulus persons were judged as more socially desirable.[7]

Furthermore, it was also hypothesized that the subjects would assume that attractive stimulus persons are likely to secure more prestigious jobs than those of lesser attractiveness, as well as experiencing happier marriages, being better parents, and enjoying more fulfilling social and occupational lives.

The means relevant to these predictions concerning the estimated future life experiences of individuals of varying degrees of physical attractiveness are also depicted in Table 1. As shown in the table, there was strong support for all of the preceding hypotheses save one. Attractive men and women were expected to attain more prestigious occupations than were those of lesser attractiveness ($F = 42.30$), and this expectation was expressed equally by raters of the same or

TABLE 1 / Traits Attributed to Various Stimulus Others

Trait Ascription[a]	Unattractive Stimulus Person	Average Stimulus Person	Attractive Stimulus Person
Social desirability of the stimulus person's personality	56.31	62.42	65.39
Occupational status of the stimulus person	1.70	2.02	2.25
Marital competence of the stimulus person	.37	.71	1.70
Parental competence of the stimulus person	3.91	4.55	3.54
Social and professional happiness of the stimulus person	5.28	6.34	6.37
Total happiness of the stimulus person	8.83	11.60	11.60
Likelihood of marriage	1.52	1.82	2.17

[a]The higher the number, the more socially desirable, the more prestigious an occupation, etc., the stimulus person is expected to possess.

the opposite sex as the stimulus person (interaction $F = .25$).

The subjects also assumed that attractive individuals would be more competent spouses and have happier marriages than those of lesser attractiveness ($F = 62.54$). (It might be noted that there is some evidence that this may be a correct perception. Kirkpatrick and Cotton (1951), reported that "well-adjusted" wives were more physically attractive than "badly adjusted" wives. "Adjustment," however, was assessed by friends' perceptions, which may have been affected by the stereotype evident here.)

According to the means reported in Table 1, it is clear that attractive individuals were not expected to be better parents ($F = 1.47$). In fact, attractive persons were rated somewhat lower than any other group of stimulus persons as potential parents, although no statistically significant differences were apparent.

As predicted, attractive stimulus persons were assumed to have better prospects for happy social and professional lives ($F = 21.97$). All in all, the attractive stimulus persons were expected to have more total happiness in their lives than those of lesser attractiveness ($F = 24.20$).

The preceding results did not appear to be attenuated by a jealousy effect (Sex of Subject × Stimulus Person interaction $Fs = .01, .07, .21$, and $.05$, respectively).

The subjects were also asked to estimate the likelihood that the various stimulus persons would marry early or marry at all. Responses were combined into a single index. It is evident that the subjects assumed that the attractive stimulus persons were more likely to find an acceptable partner than those of lesser attractiveness ($F = 35.84$). Attractive individuals were expected to marry earlier and to be less likely to remain single. Once again, these conclusions were reached by all subjects, regardless of whether they were of the same or opposite sex of the stimulus person (interaction $F = .01$).

The results suggest that a physical attractiveness stereotype exists and that its content is perfectly compatible with the "What is beautiful is good" thesis. Not only are physically attractive persons assumed to possess more socially desirable personalities than those of lesser attractiveness, but it is presumed that their lives will be happier and more successful.

The results also suggest that the physical attractiveness variable may have a number of implications for a variety of aspects of social interaction and influence. For example, it is clear that physically attractive individuals may have even more advantages in the dating market than has previously been assumed. In addition to an aesthetic advantage in marrying a beautiful spouse (cf. Josselin de Jong, 1952), potential marriage partners may also assume that the beautiful attract all of the world's fits and happiness. Thus, the lure of an riage partner should be strong indeed.

We do not know, of course, how well this stereotype stands up against contradictory information. Nor do we know the extent to which it determines the pattern of social interaction that develops with a person of a particular attractiveness level. Nevertheless, it would be odd if people did not behave toward others in accordance with this stereotype. Such behavior has been previously noted anecdotally. Monahan (1941) has observed that

> Even social workers accustomed to dealing with all types often find it difficult to think of a normal, pretty girl as being guilty of a crime. Most people, for some inexplicable reason, think of crime in terms of abnormality in appearance, and I must say that beautiful women are not often convicted [p. 103].

A host of other familiar social psychological dependent variables also should be affected in predictable ways.

In the above connection, it might be noted that if standards of physical attractiveness vary widely, knowledge of the content of the physical attractiveness stereotype would be of limited usefulness in predicting its effect on social interaction and the development of the self-concept. The present study was not designed to investigate the degree of variance in perceived beauty. (The physical attractiveness ratings of the stimulus materials were made by college students of a similar background to those who participated in this study.) Preliminary evidence (Cross & Cross, 1971) suggests that such differences in perceived beauty may not be as severe as some observers have suggested.

REFERENCES

Aronson, E. Some antecedents of interpersonal attraction. In W. J. Arnold & D. Levine (Eds.), *Nebraska Symposium on Motivation,* 1969, *17,* 143–177.

Cross, J. F., & Cross, J. Age, sex, race, and the perception of facial beauty. *Developmental Psychology,* 1971, *5,* 433–439.

Hays, W. L. *Statistics for psychologists.* New York: Holt, Rinehart & Winston, 1963.

Josselin de Jong, J. P. B. *Lévi-Strauss' theory on kinship and marriage.* Leiden, Holland: Brill, 1952.

Kirkpatrick, C., & Cotton, J. Physical attractiveness, age, and marital adjustment. *American Sociological Review,* 1951, *16,* 81–86.

Monahan, F. *Women in crime.* New York: Ives Washburn, 1941.

Schiller, J. C. F. *Essays, esthetical and philosophical, including the dissertation on the "Connexions between the animal and the spiritual in man."* London: Bell, 1882.

Wright, B. A. *Physical disability—A psychological approach.* New York: Harper & Row, 1960.

ENDNOTES

1. This research was financed in part by National Institute of Mental Health Grants MH 16729 to Berscheid and MH 16661 to Walster.

2. The physical attractiveness rating of each of the pictures was determined in a preliminary study. One hundred Minnesota undergraduates rated 50 yearbook pictures of persons of the opposite sex with respect to physical attractiveness. The criteria for choosing the 12 pictures to be used experimentally were (*a*) high-interrater agreement as to the physical attractiveness of the stimulus (the average interrater correlation for all of the pictures was .70); and (*b*) pictures chosen to represent the very attractive category and very unattractive category were not at the extreme ends of attractiveness.

3. A detailed report of the items included in these booklets is available. Order Document No. 01972 from the National Auxiliary Publication Service of the American Society for Information Science, c/o CCM Information Services, Inc., 909 3rd Avenue, New York, New York 10022. Remit in advance $5.00 for photocopies or $2.00 for microfiche and make checks payable to: Research and Microfilm Publications, Inc.

4. The subjects were asked how altruistic, conventional, self-assertive, exciting, stable, emotional, dependent, safe, interesting, genuine, sensitive, outgoing, sexually permissive, sincere, warm, sociable, competitive, obvious, kind, modest, strong, serious, sexually warm, simple, poised, bold, and sophisticated each stimulus person was.

5. The subjects rated stimulus persons on the following traits: friendliness, enthusiasm, physical attractiveness, social poise, and trustworthiness.

6. Throughout this report, $df = 1/55$.

7. Before running the preliminary experiment to determine the identity of traits usually associated with a socially desirable person (see Endnote 3), we had assumed that an exciting date, a nurturant person, and a person of good character would be perceived as quite different personality types. Conceptually, for example, we expected that an exciting date would be seen to require a person who was unpredictable, challenging, etc., while a nurturant person would be seen to be predictable and unthreatening. It became clear, however, that these distinctions were not ones which made sense to the subjects. There was almost total overlap between the traits chosen as representative of an exciting date, of a nurturant person, and a person of good or ethical character. All were strongly correlated with social desirability. Thus, attractive stimulus persons are assumed to be more exciting dates ($F = 39.97$), more nurturant individuals ($F = 13.96$), and to have better character ($F = 19.57$) than persons of lesser attractiveness.

CRITICAL THINKING QUESTIONS

1. The study used college students, presumably most of them ages 18 to 22. Do you think that the age of the subjects might influence the results? Why or why not?
2. The study used photographs as stimulus materials. Do you think that the "What is beautiful is good" effect also would occur in face-to-face encounters? Or might the judgments made in person somehow be different than those made by looking at photographs? How could you test this possibility?
3. The study indicated that physically attractive people are perceived as having more socially desirable traits and are expected to be more successful in life than their less attractive counterparts. Do you think that attractive people *actually* are more desirable and more successful in life? Why or why not?
4. This article suggests that ample positive attributions are made for attractive people. In what ways might being attractive actually be a liability, instead of an asset? Explain your reasoning.

ADDITIONAL RELATED READINGS

Riniolo, T. C., Johnson, K. C., Sherman, T. R., & Misso, J. A. (2006). Hot or not: Do professors perceived as physically attractive receive higher student evaluations? *Journal of General Psychology, 133*(1), 19–35.

Swami, V., Furnham, A., Georgiades, C., & Pang, L. (2007). Evaluating self and partner physical attractiveness. *Body Image, 4*(1), 97–101.

ARTICLE 21 _____

Both of the preceding articles looked at the important role that physical attractiveness plays in interpersonal attraction. Article 19 focused on the effects of constant media exposure to highly attractive people and the subsequent impact of such exposure on our perceptions of the people surrounding us. Article 20 demonstrated that we place great importance on physical attractiveness in deciding whom we want to date and that we associate all sorts of positive and desirable characteristics with people we find attractive. This "what is beautiful is good" effect may bestow significant benefits on people deemed physically attractive in a given society.

A great deal of the research that has investigated the relationship between physical attractiveness and attraction has used photographs of people as stimuli. In the typical research model, the subject views a photograph of an attractive or unattractive (or at least less attractive) stimulus person. Then either the subject is asked to make judgments about that stimulus person or the study determines how exposure to that stimulus person affects the subject's perceptions of his or her own partners or other real-world people.

However, when we encounter real people in the real world, their physical appearance is but one piece of the information available to us. Have you ever had the experience of seeing a very attractive person but, once you started to talk with him or her, found yourself not all that attracted? Or maybe you have, over time, become attracted to someone whom you found likeable but not physically attractive at first. Obviously, our being attracted to other individuals depends on more than just how they look.

The following article by Sandeep Mishra, Andrew Clark, and Martin Daly examines how factors other than physical attractiveness, such as how someone acts, may affect subjects' satisfaction with their own real-life partners and their judgments about other people around them.

One Woman's Behavior Affects the Attractiveness of Others

■ Sandeep Mishra, Andrew Clark, and Martin Daly

ABSTRACT

Previous research has shown that viewing photos of highly attractive women adversely affects men's evaluations of more typical women and of their own romantic partners. We could not replicate these results, but induced similar effects by showing participants an innocuous mock video interview of an opposite-sex stranger. Mated men's ratings of their partners and unattached men's ratings of other women were both lower if the interviewee had smiled and acted warmly than if she seemed uninterested, whereas women exhibited no such effects of watching a male interviewee. The results support the hypothesis that perceptions of attractiveness function to assist effective allocation of mating effort, not only in response to the relative quality of potential courtship targets but also in response to behavioral predictors of positive outcome.

This article was published in *Evolution and Human Behavior*, vol. 28, by S. Mishra, A. Clark, and M. Daly, "One woman's behavior affects the attractiveness of others," pp. 145–149, Copyright Elsevier 2007.

1. INTRODUCTION

In a series of studies, Kenrick and Gutierres (1980), Kenrick, Gutierres, and Goldberg (1989), and Kenrick, Neuberg, Zierk, and Krones (1994) have shown that looking at photographs of attractive women has an adverse effect on men's evaluations of more typical women and of their own female partners. Their interpretation of "contrast effects" is that the photographs are evolutionarily novel stimuli that "trick" mental processes whose function is local mate pool assessment, much as viewing pornography can trick men's psychophysiology into responses whose adaptive function resides in real sexual interactions.

This domain-specific interpretation is supported—against the alternative that such effects are consequences of basic perceptual processes regardless of content domain—by the fact that results are qualitatively and quantitatively different when women look at pictures of men. Whereas men's ratings of their partners were adversely affected by viewing attractive opposite-sex models, women's ratings of their partners were not, and an analogous effect could be induced in women, but not in men, by supplementing photographs with biographical information indicative of high dominance (Kenrick et al., 1989, 1994). This pattern of results was predicted on the basis of evolutionary theorizing and prior research (e.g., Buss, 1989), indicating that men attend to physical attractiveness in potential partners more than do women, and women attend to predictors of social and material success more than do men.

Whether an opposite-sex individual is an acceptable mate often depends on available alternatives, and even in species in which females are choosy and males are relatively indiscriminate, the latter still face the problem of adaptively allocating mating effort (e.g., Engqvist & Sauer, 2001). Clark (submitted for publication) has argued that the phenomenology of finding others more or less attractive functions to help people allocate mating effort effectively, and that a woman's attractiveness to a man should thus be influenced not only by her intrinsic attributes (her mate value) but also by cues indicative of whether courtship directed at her might succeed. In support of this argument, Clark has shown that watching a video of proceptive behavior apparently directed at the rater (smiling, touching one's hair, and generally exhibiting cues inviting further interaction) has an enduring positive effect on the viewer's perception of the actor's attractiveness. If this effect indeed mediates the reallocation of mating effort among potential targets, it may also be accompanied by contrast effects such as those reported by Kenrick et al., affecting the perceived attractiveness both of relationship partners and of anyone else who might, in principle, be an appropriate courtship target.

We report two experiments to test these ideas. First, we assessed whether the previously reported contrast effects of viewing attractive models versus art would hold up in our contemporary Canadian undergraduate sample. We then assessed whether the same effects could be induced by a video presenting cues of interaction with a proceptive opposite-sex person, in comparison to a control video of the same actor behaving unreceptively.

2. EXPERIMENT 1

2.1. Methods

Participants were 87 male and 66 female undergraduates (age: mean±S.D. = 19.1±2.3 years) who were enrolled in an introductory psychology course. Each participant was visually isolated while seated in front of a computer on which stimuli were presented and responses were recorded. Successive computer screens first posed biographic questions and then presented a series of 15 photographs, obtained from public domain Web sites, to be rated. For this task, participants were randomly assigned to one of two stimulus sets: (a) upper-body photographs of prerated highly attractive opposite-sex underwear models, obtained from men's and women's underwear catalogues, or (b) abstract art, consisting of simple patterns of colors. Participants were asked to rate the attractiveness of each photograph on a 6-point Likert scale (1 = *not attractive,* 6 = *very attractive*). To encourage careful scrutiny of the images, estimates of the painting's decade of creation or the model's age were also elicited.

One of the initial biographical questions was the respondent's current relationship status, and the answers determined which of two sets of further questions were asked after stimulus (model or art) presentation. Those who were currently "mated" ("dating one person exclusively," "living with boyfriend/girlfriend," or "living with husband/wife/partner") answered Question Set A, whereas those who were "unattached" ("dating not exclusively or "not dating or not in a relationship") answered Question Set B.

2.1.1. Question Set A: Judgments of Current Relationship Partner

Following Kenrick et al. (1994), mated participants (n = 51; 28 males and 23 females) rated their current partners on 17 attributes ("interesting," "romantic," "dominant," "intelligent," "physically attractive," "warm," "commanding," "understanding," "likable," "passionate," "powerful," "desirable to the opposite sex," "sexually attractive," "pleasant," "emotionally expressive," "natural leader," and "sociable") on a scale from 1 (not...) to 100 (very...).

2.1.2. Question Set B: Ratings of Unknown Students' Photographs

Unattached participants (n = 102; 59 males and 43 females) viewed a series of seven head-and-shoulder photographs of opposite-sex students from another university, which had been prerated as "average" (neither highly attractive nor unattractive) in a previous study. For each picture, participants first rated the attractiveness of the stimulus student on the same 6-point scale on which they had rated models or art, and then provided a second rating of whether the pictured person met the participant's threshold for a potential date on a 4-point Likert scale (1 = *far below threshold*, 2 = *below threshold*, 3 = *above threshold*, 4 = *far above threshold*).

2.2. Results

Both sexes rated the models more attractive than the abstract art (mean ratings of males: models = 4.7, art = 3.1, t_{85} = 10.49, p < .001; mean ratings of females: models = 3.7, art = 2.9, t_{64} = 4.59, p < .001), but this stimulus condition effect was more substantial in males [Sex × Stimulus Condition interaction: $F(1,149)$ = 30.71, p < .001].

2.2.1. Question Set A: Effects of Viewing Models versus Art on Evaluations of Relationship Partners

Following Kenrick et al. (1994), we ran 2 × 2 (Sex × Stimulus Set) analyses of variance (ANOVA) on an overall composite measure of partner evaluation, and averages for two subsets, namely, (a) sexual attractiveness, physical attractiveness, and desirability; and (b) dominant, commanding, powerful, and natural leader. None of the analyses yielded any significant effect (all ps > .1).

Exploratory 2 × 2 (Sex × Stimulus Set) ANOVA were conducted on the average ratings of relationship partners on all 17 items. Only one comparison provided any indication of anticipated contrast effects: a marginally significant Sex × Stimulus Condition interaction effect [$F(1,47)$ = 3.78, p = .06] indicates that men who had viewed models rated their partners as less physically attractive than those who had viewed art (mean: 79.8 vs. 90.8, respectively, t_{26} = 2.10, p < .05). Women exhibited no significant difference (mean: 90.0 vs. 85.8, respectively, p > .5). Because correlations among the ratings were highly variable and occasionally negative, we subjected them to principal components analysis (PCA) and ran similar ANOVA on the five significant factors obtained from the PCA, again without significant effects. With a Bonferonni a correction for multiple exploratory post hoc tests (α = .05/22 = .002), however, no significant differences remained.

2.2.2. Question Set B: Effects of Viewing Models versus Art on Evaluations of Opposite-Sex Strangers

After viewing experimental stimuli, unattached participants rated seven "average" opposite-sex faces with respect to attractiveness and their proximity to the rater's "dating threshold." Ratings of the seven stimuli were reduced to average values (Cronbach's α = .80 and .85 for the two measures), with results shown in Fig. 1.

For both sexes, ratings after viewing models were lower than after viewing art (attractiveness: men, t_{57} = 2.77, p < .01, women, t_{41} = 4.30, p < .001; dating threshold: men, t_{57} = 2.56, p = .01, women, t_{41} = 4.28, p < .001). A significant Sex × Stimulus Condition interaction effect [attractiveness measure: $F(1,98)$ = 4.81, p < .05; dating threshold: $F(1,98)$ = 4.99, p < .05] indicates that these contrast effects

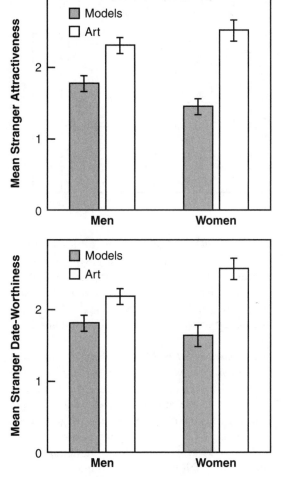

FIGURE 1 / Mean (±S.E.) ratings by unattached participants of "average" students' photos in Experiment 1 with respect to attractiveness (top panel) and position relative to the rater's "dating threshold" (bottom panel), after viewing either underwear models or abstract art.

induced by viewing attractive models were larger in women than in men.

3. EXPERIMENT 2

3.1. Methods

Participants were 72 male and 79 female undergraduates (age: mean±S.D. = 20.0±3.3 years) enrolled in a first-year psychology course. The procedure was identical to that of Experiment 1, except for differences in the stimuli seen between the initial biographical questions and the final rating tasks: instead of underwear models versus art, randomly assigned participants saw one of two short (101–120 s) videotaped mock interviews of a moderately attractive opposite-sex drama student, taken directly from Clark (submitted for publication).

Each pair of videos was shot in a single session and featured the same actor, identically groomed and dressed, facing the camera from the same distance and giving essentially the same answers to the same set of innocuous questions (e.g., "Why do you think is it important to vote?"). All answers were neutral and contained no potential confounding content, such as cues of parental investment willingness or ability. How the pair of videos differed was in the actor's affect. In one, the actor behaved proceptively: smiling, looking directly at the camera, and generally acting as if encouraging future interaction. In the other, the actor behaved unreceptively: never smiling, letting one's gaze wander, and sounding bored. Clark (submitted for publication) has verified that these videos are perceived as proceptive versus unreceptive, and that opposite-sex judges rated the male and female versions almost identically in this regard.

After viewing the mock interview, participants were asked to rate a still photograph of the actor (the same neutral-expression photograph regardless of which video had been seen) on a 6-point Likert scale (1 = *not attractive*, 6 = *very attractive*) and to estimate the actor's age. As in Experiment 1, participants then answered either Question Set A or Question Set B, depending on their responses to the current relationship status question (which had been asked before the video was seen).

3.2. Results

Participants of both sexes rated the actor's photograph significantly more attractive if they had just viewed the proceptive video rather than the unreceptive video: for men rating a female actor, the means were 4.2 and 2.8 (t_{70} = 5.27, p < .001); for women rating a male actor, the means were 3.5 and 3.0 ($t_{77} = 2.80$, $p < .01$). A significant Sex × Video Condition interaction [$F(1,147) = 6.35$, $p < .05$] indicates that actor receptivity had a stronger effect on men's ratings than on women's ratings. Actor receptivity had no effects on age estimates, and relationship status had no effects on attractiveness ratings.

3.2.1. Question Set A: Effects of Actor Receptivity on Evaluations of Relationship Partners

For mated participants ($n = 71$; 33 men, 38 women), we ran 2 × 2 (Sex × Stimulus Set) ANOVA on the average ratings of relationship partners on a composite measure of overall partner attractiveness, calculated by averaging ratings for all partner personality characteristics. In addition, the 17 rating scales were subjected to a PCA, and a 2 × 2 (Sex × Stimulus Set) ANOVA was run on the one significant factor, PCA Factor 1, on which all attributes loaded positively, except for "commanding" and "dominant." The attractiveness and dominance composite measures from Experiment 1 were not analyzed in Experiment 2, as the PCA did not highlight them as significant factors.

The results demonstrate the effects of actor receptivity on partner ratings, but only among males: men who had viewed the proceptive video downrated their partners on the composite measure of overall partner attractiveness ($\alpha = .80$) relative to those who had viewed the unreceptive video [Sex × Stimulus Condition interaction, $F(1,67) = 83.72$, $p < .001$; for men, $t_{31} = 2.97$, $p < .01$, for women, $t_{36} = 1.34$, $p > .1$]. The same significant pattern of results was apparent for PCA Factor 1.

Exploratory 2 × 2 (Sex × Stimulus Set) ANOVA were conducted on the ratings of relationship partners on all 17 items. The results also show the effects of actor receptivity on partner ratings only among males; Fig. 2 illustrates this effect with respect to mean partner ratings on the item "physically attractive" [Sex × Stimulus Condition interaction, $F(1,67) = 88.17$, $p < .001$; for men, $t_{31} = 2.94$, $p < .01$, for women, $t_{36} = 0.96$, $p > .3$]. The same significant pattern of results was apparent for several individual item ratings ("romantic," "intelligent," "physically attractive," "understanding," "likable," "sexually attractive," and "passionate").

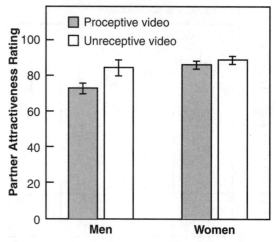

FIGURE 2 / Mean (±S.E.) ratings of the "physical attractiveness" of the raters' own relationship partners in Experiment 2, after viewing a mock video interview of an actor behaving either proceptively or unreceptively.

Because analyses of all 17 rating scales were exploratory and conducted post hoc, they were subject to a Bonferonni α correction for multiple tests α = .05/17 = .003). With this restriction, only the individual items "physically attractive," "understanding," "likable," and "sexually attractive" were statistically significant.

3.2.2. Question Set B: Effects of Actor Receptivity on Evaluations of Opposite-Sex Strangers

As in Experiment 1, unattached participants ($n = 80$; 39 men, 41 women) rated the attractiveness of seven "average" students, with the results presented in Fig. 3. A Sex × Stimulus Condition interaction was not significant [$F(1,76) = 0.744$, $p = .12$]. Because a nonsignificant interaction in ANOVA may mask important underlying simple effects, lower-level comparisons were conducted (Wahlsten, 1990, p. 117). Men's ratings were affected by which video they had observed (attractiveness: $t_{37} = 2.86$, $p < .01$; date worthiness: $t_{37} = 2.889$, $p < .01$); women's ratings were not affected (both measures: $t < 1.0$, $p > .3$).

4. DISCUSSION

Previous findings suggesting that males exhibit a contrast effect when rating romantic partners in response

FIGURE 3 / Mean (±S.E.) ratings by unattached participants of "average" students' photos in Experiment 2 with respect to attractiveness (top panel) and position relative to the rater's "dating threshold" (bottom panel), after viewing a mock video interview of an actor behaving either proceptively or unreceptively.

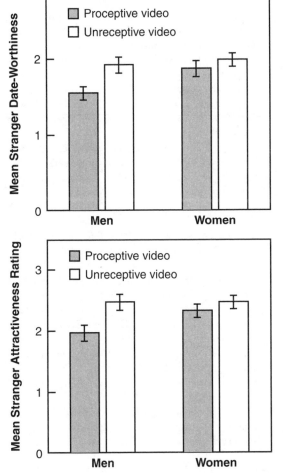

however, when male participants were exposed to proceptive females. Because proceptive behavior may aid in the adaptive allocation of mating effort and such signals may indicate an immediate potential mating opportunity, this contrast effect suggests that males shift preferences in order to allocate mating effort toward immediate courtship targets.

Participants of both sexes rated the videotaped actors as more attractive when they acted proceptively, replicating the results of Clark (submitted for publication), but men's ratings were more strongly affected than women's ratings and only men exhibited contrast effects by downrating other women and their own romantic partners. We expected this sex difference because signals of interest from the opposite sex are scarcer resources (of greater value) for men than for women. In mammals generally, the fitness of males is limited by the availability of willing partners to a much greater extent than is the fitness of females (Trivers, 1972), and human beings are no exception (e.g., Clark & Hatfield, 1989).

Kenrick et al. have interpreted their finding that viewing a series of attractive women diminishes the appeal of "average" women, as indicative of evaluative shifts in response to ancestral cues of the pool of potential mates. The contrast effects in our Experiment 2 extend the domain of such reactions to include evaluative shifts in response to cues of one particular woman's possible receptivity, thereby supporting the argument of Clark (submitted for publication) that finding others more or less attractive facilitates effective allocation of mating effort.

If only attractiveness had been rated by the unattached subjects, the contrast effects in Experiment 1 would have reflected nothing more than a subjective shift of rating scale anchors after seeing the models. However, the fact that these stimuli also influenced "date worthiness" suggests that such contrast effects could have behavioral consequences, at least in the short term. That the effect was larger in women than in men was unexpected and is surprising given that the men rated the opposite-sex models as more attractive than did the women. It is also contrary to the results of Kenrick et al. (1989, 1994), and whether this is because of subject pool differences or other factors is unclear. Because considerable evidence indicates that women are choosier about potential mates

to viewing photographs of attractive models (Kenrick et al., 1989, 1994) were not replicated in our Experiment 1. Men did not downrate their partners on a composite score of desirable attributes after viewing models, although a contrast effect was apparent for 1 of 17 attributes (physical attractiveness) before correcting for multiple comparisons. We did observe a contrast effect for composite scores in Experiment 2, than are men (Buss, 1989; Daly & Wilson, 1983; Kenrick, 1989), one might propose that men's ratings of date worthiness were relatively unaffected by the stimuli because men are chronically eager and relatively indiscriminate. This interpretation, however, is challenged by the fact that men did not, in general, rate "average" strangers as more dateworthy than did women and by the results of Experiment 2, in which similar contrast effects were produced by the videos, but only in men, as anticipated.

The fact that proceptivity influenced men's ratings of their partners on multiple dimensions, not just physical attractiveness, may speak of the specific characteristics that constitute proceptive behavior. A proceptive human female may be seen not only as attractive but also as warm, likable, pleasant, and sociable. If so, one would expect that mated male participants' ratings of their partners would be reduced in these multiple domains of judgment upon exposure to proceptive behavior, and this pattern of results is indeed what we observed.

Do the contrast effects observed here and in previous research have implications for social phenomena outside the laboratory? Kenrick and Gutierres (1980) suggested that men who are chronically exposed to attractive young women in their work might adopt unrealistically high standards and thus experience dissatisfaction with females available to them, a conjecture supported by the observation of Kanazawa and Still (2000) that male high school teachers and college professors have an unusually high incidence of divorce. Similarly, men exposed to depictions of women projecting proceptivity may experience inflated expectations of encountering receptive sexual partners. Media representations of proceptivity are probably not as salient as real-life encounters, but they may nonetheless have significant effects on social responses. Certainly, the psychology of *Homo sapiens* did not evolve in an environment laden with simulated social stimuli of the sort we experience today.

ACKNOWLEDGMENTS

We thank Paul Ramos for programming the experiments, and Martin Lalumiere, Christine Michell, Kelly Suschinsky, and Doug VanderLaan, for their useful advice and comments on drafts of the manuscript.

This research was supported by a Natural Sciences and Engineering Research Council of Canada grant to M. Daly.

REFERENCES

Buss, D. M. (1989). Sex differences in human mate preferences: Evolutionary hypotheses tested in 37 cultures. *Behavioral and Brain Sciences, 12,* 1–49.

Clark, A. P. (submitted for publication). Attracting interest: Displays of proceptivity increase the attractiveness of men and women.

Clark, R. D., & Hatfield, E. (1989). Gender differs in receptivity to sexual offers. *Journal of Psychology and Human Sexuality, 2,* 39–55.

Daly, M., & Wilson, M. (1983). *Sex, evolution, and behavior.* (2nd ed.) Belmont, CA: Wadsworth Publishing.

Engqvist, L., & Sauer, K. P. (2001). Strategic male mating effort and cryptic male choice in a scorpionfly *Proceedings of the Royal Society of London Series B, 268,* 729–735.

Kanazawa, S., & Still, M. C. (2000). Teaching may be hazardous to your marriage. *Evolution and Human Behavior, 21,* 185–190.

Kenrick, D. T. (1989). Bridging social psychology and sociobiology: The case of sexual attraction. In: R. W. Bell & N. J. Bell (Eds.), *Sociobiology and the social sciences* (pp. 5–23). Lubbock, TX: Texas Tech University Press.

Kenrick, D. T., & Gutierres, S. E. (1980). Contrast effects and judgments of physical attractiveness: When beauty becomes a social problem. *Journal of Personality and Social Psychology, 38,* 131–141.

Kenrick, D. T., Gutierres, S. E., & Goldberg, L. (1989). Influence of popular erotica on judgements of strangers, and mates. *Journal of Experimental Social Psychology, 25,* 159–167.

Kenrick, D. T., Neuberg, S. L., Zierk, K. L., & Krones, J. M. (1994). Evolution and social cognition: Contrast effects as a function of sex, dominance and physical attractiveness. *Personality and Social Psychology Bulletin, 20,* 210–217.

Trivers, R. L. (1972). Parental investment and sexual selection. In: B. Campbell (Ed.), *Sexual selection and the descent of man: 1871–1971* (pp. 136–179). Chicago: Aldine.

Wahlsten, D. (1990). Insensitivity of the analysis of variance to heredity–environment interaction. *Behavioral and Brain Sciences, 13,* 109–161.

CRITICAL THINKING QUESTIONS

1. This article discusses how evolutionary-based concepts may explain the differences between how men and women respond to opposite-sex individuals. For instance, men are influenced by physical attractiveness and perceived availability, whereas women are more influenced by displays of status and dominance. Discuss what you see as the pros and cons of this argument. What else might explain these effects, other than concepts from evolution?

2. The article mentions that males who work in environments where they are routinely exposed to young, attractive females (e.g., college professors) may have a higher divorce rate than males who do not work in such environments. This statement obviously is based on correlational data, which, by their nature, cannot establish cause-and-effect relationships. What explanations can be offered for this effect, other than the one suggested in the article? Discuss.

3. In this study, males were influenced by the perceived perceptivity (e.g., warm, likable, pleasant, sociable) of the female stimuli. Using the general concepts from this article and other studies reported in it, suggest whether a similar situation might arise for male viewers of pornography. In other words, will male viewers of pornography be less satisfied with their real-life partners than will nonviewers? Explain your reasoning.

4. This study (like most others) used college students as subjects, which means most of the subjects were in their late teens or early twenties. Would the same results likely be found using other age populations, say, males and females in their thirties, forties, fifties, or beyond? Explain your reasoning.

CHAPTER INTEGRATION QUESTIONS

1. All three articles in this chapter are concerned with the importance placed on physical attractiveness. Taken together, what implications do these articles have for how attractiveness affects us? Do the articles suggest how the impact of attractiveness can be minimized? If so, how?

2. What factors besides physical beauty may affect our attraction to other people? Might these factors, in turn, affect how physically attractive we find others? Explain.

3. "Beauty is in the eye of the beholder," according to an old proverb. In light of the information presented in the articles in this chapter, discuss whether this proverb is true or false or both.

Chapter Eight

CLOSE RELATIONSHIPS

OF ALL THE interactions that occur between human beings, perhaps none is more capable of producing such intense feelings as love. If we look at how often love is portrayed in the popular media, we get the definite impression that it is a major concern, almost a preoccupation, of most people. However, if we look at the literature in social psychology, we might get a very different impression. Until recently, the topic of love was largely ignored in the research literature.

A specific subject of interest to many people is the failure of love and the dissolution of relationships. Anyone who has been through a divorce or has witnessed its effects on someone close to them knows that the ending of a marriage is usually an extremely painful ordeal. Yet in spite of the pain involved in splitting up, nearly half of all marriages end up in divorce. What goes wrong? More importantly, what can be done earlier in a relationship to decrease the likelihood of divorce later on? Article 22, "Great Expectations," examines the types of unrealistic expectations that people today have for marriage as well as the origins of such beliefs. Perhaps having more realistic expectations for marriage is a key component to having a successful relationship.

After meeting someone who catches your attention, and then deciding that you would like to get to know him or her better, comes a big step: asking the person out. So you take the chance and ask for a date. Which response to your request would increase your liking of the recipient of your request the most: The person enthusiastically accepts your offer, or the person first plays "hard to get" and then later accepts your invitation? Much folk wisdom would suggest the value of not appearing too eager. But does that hard-to-get strategy actually work? Article 23, "Playing Hard to Get," is an amusing classic article that addresses this dating dilemma.

Finally, Article 24, "How Do I Love Thee? Let Me Count the Words," is a contemporary article that looks at how writing about one's relationship can impact not only the quality of the communication within the relationship but perhaps the stability of the relationship, as well. If this finding is indeed true, it may suggest a relatively easy way to enhance communication within relationships.

ARTICLE 22 _____

The high divorce rate in the United States is of social concern to a large number of Americans. Current statistics indicate that nearly half of all marriages will end in divorce. And while the number of divorces has decreased slightly in the last few years, it still remains around the 50% mark. Whether the high rates of divorce seen over the last few decades will remain the same, increase, or decrease remains to be seen. Nonetheless, the prevalence of divorce is certainly characteristic of contemporary U.S. society.

In spite of the 50/50 odds that a marriage will not last, nearly 95% of the adult U.S. population will marry at least once in their lifetimes. Marriage obviously holds a strong attraction for most people. Even among those who divorce, many will remarry, further pointing to the importance that most people place on the institution of marriage. It probably is a rare couple who marry with the thought that they will divorce. Indeed, most people take to heart the wedding vows of "For better or worse, in sickness and in health, until death do us part," believing that the dire divorce statistics apply to other couples, not them.

So, why has the divorce rate risen and continued to hover around the 50% mark? And for those married people today who have not divorced, are they less satisfied with their marriages than were their counterparts in the past? The answers to both of these questions are quite complex. However, one common denominator may lie in the reasons that people now have for getting married. If you are not married, take a moment and ask yourself (or someone else who is not married) why you want to get married. If you are married, why did you choose to do so? Chances are, the most common answer is for love, with the implication being that marriage provides people with unique happiness and satisfaction. Yet surveys of young adults a century ago found that the majority wanted to get married for much more pragmatic reasons, such as to have children and to own a home.

What does getting married for love (or happiness) have to do with the higher divorce rate? The problem is not marrying for love per se but rather entering a marriage with certain expectations. If a person marries for love and the love he or she experiences after marriage does not conform to his or her expectations, then the logical conclusion may be that he or she made a mistake. That is the thinking of many people today. We live in a culture that highly promotes individual happiness and fulfillment. Such an attitude suggests that individual happiness and fulfillment are paramount and should take precedence over all else. Thus, divorce is seen as an acceptable way to pursue individual happiness and fulfillment.

As mentioned earlier, a major part of the problem may be the unrealistic expectations that people today bring with them to marriage. These expectations may be impossible to meet and thus undoubtedly result in unhappiness in the relationship. The following article by Polly Shulman examines the types of unrealistic expectations that people today have for marriage as well as the sources of such expectations. Perhaps having more realistic views of courtship and marriage can provide a major antidote to the high rate of divorce.

Great Expectations

■ Polly Shulman

Marriage is dead! The twin vises of church and law have relaxed their grip on matrimony. We've been liberated from the grim obligation to stay in a poisonous or abusive marriage for the sake of the kids or for appearances. The divorce rate has stayed constant at nearly 50 percent for the last two decades. The ease with which we enter and dissolve unions makes marriage seem like a prime-time spectator sport, whether it's Britney Spears in Vegas or bimbos chasing after the Bachelor.

Long live the new marriage! We once prized the institution for the practical pairing of a cash-producing father and a home-building mother. Now we want it all—a partner who reflects our taste and status, who sees us for who we are, who loves us for all the "right" reasons, who helps us become the person we want to be. We've done away with a rigid social order, adopting instead an even more onerous obligation: the mandate to find a perfect match. Anything short of this ideal prompts us to ask: Is this all there is? Am I as happy as I should be? Could there be somebody out there who's better for me? As often as not, we answer yes to that last question and fall victim to our own great expectations.

That somebody is, of course, our soul mate, the man or woman who will counter our weaknesses, amplify our strengths and provide the unflagging support and respect that is the essence of a contemporary relationship. The reality is that few marriages or partnerships consistently live up to this ideal. The result is a commitment limbo, in which we care deeply for our partner but keep one stealthy foot out the door of our hearts. In so doing, we subject the relationship to constant review: Would I be happier, smarter, a *better person* with someone else? It's a painful modern quandary. "Nothing has produced more unhappiness than the concept of the soul mate," says Atlanta psychiatrist Frank Pittman.

Consider Jeremy, a social worker who married a businesswoman in his early twenties. He met another woman, a psychologist, at age 29, and after two agonizing years, left his wife for her. But it didn't work out—after four years of cohabitation, and her escalating pleas to marry, he walked out on her, as well. Jeremy now realizes that the relationship with his wife was solid and workable but thinks he couldn't have seen that 10 years ago, when he left her. "There was always someone better around the corner—and the safety and security of marriage morphed into boredom and stasis. The allure of willing and exciting females was too hard to resist," he admits. Now 42 and still single, Jeremy acknowledges, "I hurt others, and I hurt myself."

Like Jeremy, many of us either dodge the decision to commit or commit without fully relinquishing the right to keep looking—opting for an arrangement psychotherapist Terrence Real terms "stable ambiguity."

"You park on the border of the relationship, so you're in it but not of it," he says. There are a million ways to do that: You can be in a relationship but not be sure it's really the right one, have an eye open for a better deal or something on the side, choose someone impossible or far away.

Yet commitment and marriage offer real physical and financial rewards. Touting the benefits of marriage may sound like conservative policy rhetoric, but nonpartisan sociological research backs it up: Committed partners have it all over singles, at least on average. Married people are more financially stable, according to Linda Waite, a sociologist at the University of Chicago and a coauthor of *The Case for Marriage: Why Married People Are Happier, Healthier and Better Off.* Both married men and married women have more assets on average than singles; for women, the differential is huge.

The benefits go beyond the piggy bank. Married people, particularly men, tend to live longer than people who aren't married. Couples also live better: When people expect to stay together, says Waite, they pool their resources, increasing their individual standard of living. They also pool their expertise—in cooking say, or financial management. In general, women improve men's health by putting a stop to stupid bachelor tricks and bugging their husbands to exercise and eat their vegetables. Plus, people who aren't comparing their partners to someone else in bed have less trouble performing and are more emotionally satisfied with sex. The relationship doesn't have to be wonderful for life to get better, says Waite: The statistics hold true for mediocre marriages as well as for passionate ones.

The pragmatic benefits of partnership used to be foremost in our minds. The idea of marriage as a vehicle for self-fulfillment and happiness is relatively new, says Paul Amato, professor of sociology, demography and family studies at Penn State University. Surveys of high school and college students 50 or 60 years ago found that most wanted to get married in order to have children or own a home. Now, most report that they plan to get married for love. This increased emphasis on emotional fulfillment within marriage leaves couples ill-prepared for the realities they will probably face.

Because the early phase of a relationship is marked by excitement and idealization, "many romantic, passionate couples expect to have that excitement forever," says Barry McCarthy, a clinical psychologist and coauthor—with his wife, Emily McCarthy—of *Getting It Right the First Time: How to Build a Healthy Marriage.* Longing for the charged energy of the early days, people look elsewhere or split up.

Flagging passion is often interpreted as the death knell of a relationship. You begin to wonder whether you're really right for each other after all. You're comfortable together, but you don't really connect the way you used to. Wouldn't it be more honest—and braver—to just admit that it's not working and call it off? "People are made to feel that remaining in a marriage that doesn't make you blissfully happy is an act of existential cowardice," says Joshua Coleman, a San Francisco psychologist.

Coleman says that the constant cultural pressure to have it all—a great sex life, a wonderful family— has made people ashamed of their less-than-perfect relationships and question whether such unions are worth hanging on to. Feelings of dissatisfaction or disappointment are natural, but they can seem intol-

erable when standards are sky-high. "It's a recent historical event that people expect to get so much from individual partners," says Coleman, author of *Imperfect Harmony,* in which he advises couples in lackluster marriages to stick it out—especially if they have kids. "There's an enormous amount of pressure on marriages to live up to an unrealistic ideal."

Michaela, 28, was drawn to Bernardo, 30, in part because of their differences: She'd grown up in European boarding schools, he fought his way out of a New York City ghetto. "Our backgrounds made us more interesting to each other," says Michaela. "I was a spoiled brat and he'd been supporting himself from the age of 14, which I admired." Their first two years of marriage were rewarding, but their fights took a toll. "I felt that because he hadn't grown up in a normal family, he didn't grasp basic issues of courtesy and accountability," says Michaela. They were temperamental opposites: He was a screamer, and she was a sulker. She recalls, "After we fought, I needed to be drawn out of my corner, but he took that to mean that I was a cold bitch." Michaela reluctantly concluded that the two were incompatible.

In fact, argue psychologists and marital advocates, there's no such thing as true compatibility.

"Marriage is a disagreement machine," says Diane Sollee, founder of the Coalition for Marriage, Family and Couples Education. "All couples disagree about all the same things. We have a highly romanticized notion that if we were with the right person, we wouldn't fight." Discord springs eternal over money, kids, sex and leisure time, but psychologist John Gottman has shown that long-term, happily married couples disagree about these things just as much as couples who divorce.

"There is a mythology of 'the wrong person,'" agrees Pittman. "All marriages are incompatible. All marriages are between people from different families, people who have a different view of things. The magic is to develop binocular vision, to see life through your partner's eyes as well as through your own."

The realization that we're not going to get everything we want from a partner is not just sobering, it's downright miserable. But it is also a necessary step in building a mature relationship, according to Real, who has written about the subject in *How Can I Get Through to You: Closing the Intimacy Gap Between*

Men and Women. "The paradox of intimacy is that our ability to stay close rests on our ability to tolerate solitude inside a relationship," he says. "A central aspect of grown-up love is grief. All of us long for—and think we deserve—perfection."

We can hardly be blamed for striving for bliss and self-fulfillment in our romantic lives—our inalienable right to the pursuit of happiness is guaranteed in the first blueprint of American society.

This same respect for our own needs spurred the divorce-law reforms of the 1960s and 1970s. During that era, "The culture shifted to emphasize individual satisfaction, and marriage was part of that," explains Paul Amato, who has followed more than 2,000 families for 20 years in a long-term study of marriage and divorce. Amato says that this shift did some good by freeing people from abusive and intolerable marriages. But it had an unintended side effect: encouraging people to abandon relationships that may be worth salvaging.

In a society hell-bent on achievement and autonomy, working on a difficult relationship may get short shrift, says psychiatrist Peter Kramer, author of *Should You Leave?*

"So much of what we learn has to do with the self, the ego, rather than giving over the self to things like a relationship," Kramer says. In our competitive world, we're rewarded for our individual achievements rather than for how we help others. We value independence over cooperation, and sacrifices for values like loyalty and continuity seem foolish. "I think we get the divorce rate that we deserve as a culture."

The steadfast focus on our *own* potential may turn a partner into an accessory in the quest for self-actualization, says Maggie Robbins, a therapist in New York City. "We think that this person should reflect the beauty and perfection that is the inner me—or, more often, that this person should compensate for the yuckiness and mess that is the inner me," says Robbins. "This is what makes you tell your wife, 'Lose some weight—you're making me look bad,' not 'Lose some weight, you're at risk for diabetes.'"

Michaela was consistently embarrassed by Bernardo's behavior when they were among friends. "He'd become sullen and withdrawn—he had a shifty way of looking off to the side when he didn't want to talk. I felt like it reflected badly on me," she admits. Michaela left him and is now dating a wealthy entrepreneur. "I just thought there had to be someone else out there for me."

The urge to find a soul mate is not fueled just by notions of romantic manifest destiny. Trends in the workforce and in the media create a sense of limitless romantic possibility. According to Scott South, a demographer at SUNY-Albany, proximity to potential partners has a powerful effect on relationships. South and his colleagues found higher divorce rates among people living in communities or working in professions where they encounter lots of potential partners—people who match them in age, race and education level. "These results hold true not just for unhappy marriages but also for happy ones," says South.

The temptations aren't always living, breathing people. According to research by psychologists Sara Gutierres and Douglas Kenrick, both of Arizona State University, we find reasonably attractive people less appealing when we've just seen a hunk or a hottie—and we're bombarded daily by images of gorgeous models and actors. When we watch *Lord of the Rings,* Viggo Mortensen's kingly mien and Liv Tyler's elfin charm can make our husbands and wives look all too schlumpy.

Kramer sees a similar pull in the narratives that surround us. "The number of stories that tell us about other lives we could lead—in magazine articles, television shows, books—has increased enormously. We have an enormous reservoir of possibilities," says Kramer.

And these possibilities can drive us to despair. Too many choices have been shown to stymie consumers . . . and an array of alternative mates is no exception. In an era when marriages were difficult to dissolve, couples rated their marriages as more satisfying than do today's couples, for whom divorce is a clear option, according to the National Opinion Research Center at the University of Chicago.

While we expect marriage to be "happily ever after," the truth is that for most people, neither marriage nor divorce seem to have a decisive impact on happiness. Although Waite's research shows that married people are happier than their single counterparts, other studies have found that after a couple years of marriage, people are just about as happy (or unhappy) as they were before settling down. And assuming that marriage will automatically provide contentment is itself a surefire recipe for misery.

"Marriage is not supposed to make you happy. It is supposed to make you married," says Pittman. "When you are all the way in your marriage, you are free to do useful things, become a better person." A committed relationship allows you to drop pretenses and seductions, expose your weaknesses, be yourself—and know that you will be loved, warts and all. "A real relationship is the collision of my humanity and yours, in all its joy and limitations," says Real. "How partners handle that collision is what determines the quality of their relationship."

Such a down-to-earth view of marriage is hardly romantic, but that doesn't mean it's not profound: An authentic relationship with another person, says Pittman, is "one of the first steps toward connecting with the human condition—which is necessary if you're going to become fulfilled as a human being." If we accept these humble terms, the quest for a soul mate might just be a noble pursuit after all.

LEARN MORE ABOUT IT

101 Things I Wish I Knew When I Got Married   Linda and Charlie Bloom (New World Library, 2004)

CRITICAL THINKING QUESTIONS

1. "Nothing has produced more unhappiness than the concept of the soul mate." Discuss this quote from the article, giving specific examples to support why you do or do not agree with it.

2. Do an informal survey of people to find out what they think is the most important factor in a successful marriage. Chances are, "good communication" will most often be cited. How does this factor (or whatever factor your survey finds most important) relate to the information contained in the article? Discuss.

3. List five things that you learned from this article that may decrease your chance of getting divorced. Which of these factors would be the easiest to change or control? Which would be the most difficult? Explain your answers.

4. How are love and marriage portrayed in the movies? Identify specific films, and discuss each in terms of whether it portrays a realistic or unrealistic view of love and marriage. What, if any, problems are associated with the general media portrayals of love and marriage?

5. Article 19 discussed the concept of the contrast effect and how being exposed to very attractive people might make us less attracted to our actual partners. Beyond physical attractiveness, how else might the contrast effect be working to the detriment of successful marriages?

ARTICLE 23

Wanting to love and be loved is perhaps the most profound and universal human longing. As personal experience teaches us, love is not only a highly desired and sought after state but it also may actually be necessary for our very well-being. Yet exactly what love means and how it is expressed and felt may be something that differs in each of us.

Let's back up a step. Before talking about a deep and profound love for another person, what about the initial stages that may precede it? In other words, what factors are involved in the initial attraction to another potential romantic partner? People vary considerably in what they find attractive and desirable in another person, but there are common dimensions that seem to be fairly universal—the importance of physical attractiveness and certain personality traits such as intelligence, for instance.

Suppose that you have just met someone who has caught your attention. You are interested enough that you want to ask the person out on a date. Whether you are the iniator or the recipient of the request, a date often creates a set of mixed feelings. On one hand, the potential pleasure that one can have in a successful relationship is highly desirable. On the other hand, most people do not like rejection, and any such beginning also carries with it the possibility of an end.

All right, so he finally asks her out. (Although females certainly initiate dates, research still shows that males typically take this first step in U.S. culture.) How does she respond to his request? Obviously, she can say no. If she says yes, however, there are many ways that it can be said. Which do you think would be most favorably received by the man—someone who enthusiastically and without hesitation says "Yes. I thought you'd never ask" or someone who plays hard to get, ultimately accepting the invitation but only after some hesitation or convincing?

Folk advice going back thousands of years states that playing hard to get might be the way to proceed. As this classic article by Elaine Hatfield, G. William Walster, Jane Piliavin, and Lynn Schmidt indicates, however, that might not be the best advice to follow.

"Playing Hard to Get"

Understanding an Elusive Phenomenon

■ Elaine Hatfield, G. William Walster, Jane Piliavin, and Lynn Schmidt

According to folklore, the woman who is hard to get is a more desirable catch than the woman who is too eager for an alliance. Five experiments were conducted to demonstrate that individuals value hard-to-get dates more than easy-to-get ones. All five experiments failed. In Experiment VI, we finally gained an understanding of this elusive phenomenon. We proposed that two components contribute to a woman's desirability: (a) how hard the woman is for the subject to get and (b) how hard she is for other men to get. We predicted that the selectively hard-to-get woman (i.e., a woman who is easy for the subject to get but hard for all other men to get) would be preferred to either a uniformly hard-to-get woman, a uniformly easy-to-get woman, or a woman about which the subject has no information. This hypothesis received strong support. The reason for the popularity of the selec-

tive woman was evident. Men ascribe to her all of the assets of uniformly hard-to-get and the uniformly easy-to-get women and none of their liabilities.

According to folklore, the woman who is hard to get is a more desirable catch than is the woman who is overly eager for alliance. Socrates, Ovid, Terence, the *Kama Sutra,* and Dear Abby all agree that the person whose affection is easily won is unlikely to inspire passion in another. Ovid, for example, argued:

> *Fool, if you feel no need to guard your girl for her own sake, see that you guard her for mine, so I may want her the more. Easy things nobody wants, but what is forbidden is tempting. . . . Anyone who can love the wife of an indolent cuckold, I should suppose, would steal buckets of sand from the shore. (pp. 65–66)*

When we first began our investigation, we accepted cultural lore. We assumed that men would prefer a hard-to-get woman. Thus, we began our research by interviewing college men as to why they preferred hard-to-get women. Predictably, the men responded to experimenter demands. They explained that they preferred hard-to-get women because the elusive woman is almost inevitably a valuable woman. They pointed out that a woman can only afford to be "choosy" if she is popular—and a woman is popular for some reason. When a woman is hard to get, it is usually a tip-off that she is especially pretty, has a good personality, is sexy, etc. Men also were intrigued by the challenge that the elusive woman offered. One can spend a great deal of time fantasizing about what it would be like to date such a woman. Since the hard-to-get woman's desirability is well recognized, a man can gain prestige if he is seen with her.

An easy-to-get woman, on the other hand, spells trouble. She is probably desperate for a date. She is probably the kind of woman who will make too many demands on a person; she might want to get serious right away. Even worse, she might have a "disease."

In brief, nearly all interviewees agreed with our hypothesis that a hard-to-get woman is a valuable woman, and they could supply abundant justification for their prejudice. A few isolated men refused to cooperate. These dissenters noted that an elusive woman is not always more desirable than an available woman. Sometimes the hard-to-get woman is not only hard to get—she is *impossible* to get, because she is misanthropic and cold. Sometimes a woman is easy to get because she is a friendly, outgoing woman who boosts one's ego and insures that dates are "no hassle." We ignored the testimony of these deviant types.

We then conducted five experiments designed to demonstrate that an individual values a hard-to-get date more highly than an easy-to-get date. All five experiments failed.

THEORETICAL RATIONALE

Let us first review the theoretical rationale underlying these experiments.

In Walster, Walster, and Berscheid (1971) we argued that if playing hard to get does increase one's desirability, several psychological theories could account for this phenomenon:

1. Dissonance theory predicts that if a person must expend great energy to attain a goal, one is unusually appreciative of the goal (see Aronson and Mills, 1959; Gerard and Mathewson, 1966; Zimbardo, 1965). The hard-to-get date requires a suitor to expend more effort in her pursuit than he would normally expend. One way for the suitor to justify such unusual effort is by aggrandizing her.

2. According to learning theory, an elusive person should have two distinct advantages: (*a*) Frustration may increase drive—by waiting until the suitor has achieved a high sexual drive state, heightening his drive level by introducing momentary frustration, and then finally rewarding him, the hard-to-get woman can maximize the impact of the sexual reward she provides (see Kimball, 1961, for evidence that frustration does energize behavior and does increase the impact of appropriate rewards). (*b*) Elusiveness and value may be associated—individuals may have discovered through frequent experience that there is more competition for socially desirable dates than for undesirable partners. Thus, being "hard to get" comes to be associated with "value." As a consequence, the conditional stimulus (CS) of being hard to get generates a fractional antedating goal response and a fractional goal response, which leads to the conditioned response of liking.

3. In an extension of Schachterian theory, Walster (1971) argued that two components are necessary before an individual can experience passionate love; (*a*) He must be physiologically aroused; and (*b*) the setting must make it appropriate for him to conclude that his aroused feelings are due to love. On both counts, the person who plays hard to get might be expected to generate unusual passion. Frustration should increase the suitor's physiological arousal, and the association of "elusiveness" with "value" should increase the probability that the suitor will label his reaction to the other as "love."

From the preceding discussion, it is evident that several conceptually distinct variables may account for the hard-to-get phenomenon. In spite of the fact that we can suggest a plethora of reasons as to why the playing hard-to-get strategy might be an effective strategy, all five studies failed to provide any support for the contention that an elusive woman is a desirable woman. Two experiments failed to demonstrate that outside observers perceive a hard-to-get individual as especially "valuable." Three experiments failed to demonstrate that a suitor perceives a hard-to-get date as especially valuable.

Walster, Walster, and Berscheid (1971) conducted two experiments to test the hypothesis that teenagers would deduce that a hard-to-get boy or girl was more socially desirable than was a teenager whose affection could be easily obtained. In these experiments high school juniors and seniors were told that we were interested in finding out what kind of first impression various teenagers made on others. They were shown pictures and biographies of a couple. They were told how romantically interested the stimulus person (a boy or girl) was in his partner after they had met only four times. The stimulus person was said to have liked the partner "extremely much," to have provided no information to us, or to have liked the partner "not particularly much." The teenagers were then asked how socially desirable both teenagers seemed (i.e., how likable, how physically attractive, etc.). Walster, Walster, and Berscheid, of course, predicted that the more romantic interest the stimulus person expressed in a slight acquaintance, the less socially desirable that stimulus person would appear to an outside observer. The results were diametrically opposed to those pre-

dicted. The more romantic interest the stimulus person expressed in an acquaintance, the *more* socially desirable teenagers judged him to be. Restraint does not appear to buy respect. Instead, it appears that "All the world *does* love a lover."

Lyons, Walster, and Walster (1971) conducted a field study and a laboratory experiment in an attempt to demonstrate that men prefer a date who plays hard to get. Both experiments were conducted in the context of a computer matching service. Experiment III was a field experiment. Women who signed up for the computer matching program were contacted and hired as experimenters. They were then given precise instructions as to how to respond when their computer match called them for a date. Half of the time they were told to pause and think for 3 seconds before accepting the date. (These women were labeled "hard to get.") Half of the time they were told to accept the date immediately. (These women are labeled "easy to get.") The data indicated that elusiveness had no impact on the man's liking for his computer date.

Experiment IV was a laboratory experiment. In this experiment, Lyons et al. hypothesized that the knowledge that a woman is elusive gives one indirect evidence that she is socially desirable. Such indirect evidence should have the biggest impact when a man has no way of acquiring *direct* evidence about a coed's value or when he has little confidence in his own ability to assess value. When direct evidence is available, and the man possesses supreme confidence in his ability to make correct judgments, information about a woman's elusiveness should have little impact on a man's reaction to her. Lyons et al. thus predicted that when men lacked direct evidence as to a woman's desirability, a man's self-esteem and the woman's elusiveness should interact in determining his respect and liking for her. Lyons et al. measured males' self-esteem via Rosenberg's (1965) measure of self-esteem, Rosenfeld's (1964) measure of fear of rejection, and Berger's (1952) measure of self-acceptance.

The dating counselor then told subjects that the computer had assigned them a date. They were asked to telephone her from the office phone, invite her out, and then report their first impression of her. Presumably the pair would then go out on a date and eventually give us further information about how successful our computer matching techniques had been. Actually, all men were assigned a confederate as a date. Half of the time the woman played hard to get. When the man asked her out she replied:

> Mmm *[slight pause]* No, I've got a date then. It seems like I signed up for that Date Match thing a long time ago and I've met more people since then—I'm really pretty busy all this week.

She paused again. If the subject suggested another time, the confederate hesitated only slightly, then accepted. If he did not suggest another time, the confederate would take the initiative of suggesting: "How about some time next week—or just meeting for coffee in the Union some afternoon?" And again, she accepted the next invitation. Half of the time, in the easy-to-get condition, the confederate eagerly accepted the man's offer of a date.

Lyons et al. predicted that since men in this blind date setting lacked direct evidence as to a woman's desirability, low-self-esteem men should be more receptive to the hard-to-get woman than were high-self-esteem men. Although Lyons et al.'s manipulation checks indicate that their manipulations were successful and their self-esteem measure was reliable, their hypothesis was not confirmed. Elusiveness had no impact on liking, regardless of subject's self-esteem level.

Did we give up our hypothesis? Heavens no. After all, it had only been disconfirmed four times.

By Experiment V, we had decided that perhaps the hard-to-get hypothesis must be tested in a sexual setting. After all, the first theorist who advised a woman to play hard to get was Socrates; his pupil was Theodota, a prostitute. He advised:

> They will appreciate your favors most highly if you wait till they ask for them. The sweetest meats, you see, if served before they are wanted seem sour, and to those who had enough they are positively nauseating; but even poor fare is very welcome when offered to a hungry man. *[Theodota inquired]* And how can I make them hungry for my fare? *[Socrates' reply]* Why, in the first place, you must not offer it to them when they have had enough—but prompt them by behaving as a model of Propriety, by a show of reluctance to yield, and by holding back until they are as keen as can be; and then the same gifts are much more to

the recipient than when they're offered before they are desired. (see Xenophon, p. 48)

Walster, Walster, and Lambert (1971) thus proposed that a prostitute who states that she is selective in her choice of customers will be held in higher regard than will be the prostitute who admits that she is completely unselective in her choice of partners.

In this experiment, a prostitute served as the experimenter. When the customer arrived, she mixed a drink for him; then she delivered the experimental manipulation. Half of the time, in the hard-to-get condition, she stated, "Just because I see you this time it doesn't mean that you can have my phone number or see me again. I'm going to start school soon, so I won't have much time, so I'll only be able to see the people that I like the best." Half of the time, in the easy-to-get condition, she did not communicate this information. From this point on, the prostitute and the customer interacted in conventional ways.

The client's liking for the prostitute was determined in two ways: First, the prostitute estimated how much the client had seemed to like her. (Questions asked were, for example, How much did he seem to like you? Did he make arrangements to return? How much did he pay you?) Second, the experimenter recorded how many times within the next 30 days the client arranged to have sexual relations with her.

Once again we failed to confirm the hard-to-get hypothesis. If anything, those clients who were told that the prostitute did not take just anyone were *less* likely to call back and liked the prostitute less than did other clients.

At this point, we ruefully decided that we had been on the wrong track. We decided that perhaps all those practitioners who advise women to play hard to get are wrong. Or perhaps it is only under very special circumstances that it will benefit one to play hard to get.

Thus, we began again. We reinterviewed students—this time with an open mind. This time we asked men to tell us about the advantages *and* disadvantages of hard-to-get and easy-to-get women. This time replies were more informative. According to reports, choosing between a hard-to-get woman and an easy-to-get woman was like choosing between

Scylla and Charybdis—each woman was uniquely desirable and uniquely frightening.

Although the elusive woman was likely to be a popular prestige date, she presented certain problems. Since she was not particularly enthusiastic about you, she might stand you up or humiliate you in front of your friends. She was likely to be unfriendly, cold, and to possess inflexible standards.

The easy-to-get woman was certain to boost one's ego and to make a date a relaxing, enjoyable experience, but . . . Unfortunately, dating an easy woman was a risky business. Such a woman might be easy to get, but hard to get rid of. She might "get serious." Perhaps she would be so oversexed or overaffectionate in public that she would embarrass you. Your buddies might snicker when they saw you together. After all, they would know perfectly well why you were dating *her.*

The interlocking assets and difficulties envisioned when they attempted to decide which was better—a hard-to-get or an easy-to-get woman—gave us a clue as to why our previous experiments had not worked out. The assets and liabilities of the elusive and the easy dates had evidently generally balanced out. On the average, then, both types of women tended to be equally well liked. When a slight difference in liking did appear, it favored the easy-to-get woman.

It finally impinged on us that there are *two* components that are important determinants of how much a man likes a woman: (*a*) How hard or easy she is for him to get, and (*b*) how hard or easy she is for *other men* to get. So long as we were examining the desirability of women who were hard or easy for everyone to get, things balanced out. The minute we examined other possible configurations, it became evident that there is one type of woman who can transcend the limitations of the uniformly hard-to-get or the uniformly easy-to-get woman. If a woman has a reputation for being hard to get, but for some reason she is easy for the subject to get, she should be maximally appealing. Dating such a woman should insure one of great prestige; she is, after all, hard to get. Yet, since she is exceedingly available to the subject, the dating situation should be a relaxed, rewarding experience. Such a *selectively* hard-to-get woman possesses the assets of both the easy-to-get and the hard-to-get women, while avoiding all of their liabilities.

Thus, in Experiment VI, we hypothesized that a selectively hard-to-get woman (i.e., a woman who is easy for the subject to get but very hard for any other man to get) will be especially liked by her date. Women who are hard for everyone—including the subject—to get, or who are easy for everyone to get—or control women, about whom the subject had no information—will be liked a lesser amount.

METHOD

Subjects were 71 male summer students at the University of Wisconsin. They were recruited for a dating research project. This project was ostensibly designed to determine whether computer matching techniques are in fact more effective than is random matching. All participants were invited to come into the dating center in order to choose a date from a set of five potential dates.

When the subject arrived at the computer match office, he was handed folders containing background information on five women. Some of these women had supposedly been "randomly" matched with him; others had been "computer matched" with him. (He was not told which women were which.)

In reality, all five folders contained information about fictitious women. The first item in the folder was a "background questionnaire" on which the woman had presumably described herself. This questionnaire was similar to one the subject had completed when signing up for the match program. We attempted to make the five women's descriptions different enough to be believable, yet similar enough to minimize variance. Therefore, the way the five women described themselves was systematically varied. They claimed to be 18 or 19 years old; freshmen or sophomores; from a Wisconsin city, ranging in size from over 500,000 to under 50,000; 5 feet 2 inches to 5 feet 4 inches tall; Protestant, Catholic, Jewish or had no preference; graduated in the upper 10 to 50 percent of their high school class; and Caucasians who did not object to being matched with a person of another race. The women claimed to vary on a political spectrum from "left of center" through "moderate" to "near right of center"; to place little or no importance on politics and religion; and to like recent popular movies. Each woman listed four or five activities she liked to do on a first date (i.e., go to a movie, talk in a quiet place, etc.).

In addition to the background questionnaire, three of the five folders contained five "date selection forms." The experimenter explained that some of the women had already been able to come in, examine the background information of their matches, and indicate their first impression of them. Two of the subject's matches had not yet come in. Three of the women had already come in and evaluated the subject along with her four other matches. These women would have five date selection forms in their folders. The subject was shown the forms, which consisted of a scale ranging from "definitely do *not* want to date" (−10) to "definitely want to date" (+10). A check appeared on each scale. Presumably the check indicated how much the woman had liked a given date. (At this point, the subject was told his identification number. Since all dates were identified by numbers on the forms, this identification number enabled him to ascertain how each date had evaluated both him and her four other matches.)

The date selection forms allowed us to manipulate the elusiveness of the woman. One woman appeared to be uniformly hard to get. She indicated that though she was willing to date any of the men assigned to her, she was not enthusiastic about any of them. She rated all five of her date choices from +1 to +2, including the subject (who was rated 1.75).

One woman appeared to be uniformly easy to get. She indicated that she was enthusiastic about dating all five of the men assigned to her. She rated her desire to date all five of her date choices +7 to +9. This included the subject, who was rated 8.

One woman appeared to be easy for the subject to get but hard for anyone else to get (i.e., the selectively hard-to-get woman). She indicated minimal enthusiasm for four of her date choices, rating them from +2 to +3, and extreme enthusiasm (+8) for the subject.

Two women had no date selection forms in their folders (i.e., no information women).

Naturally, each woman appeared in each of the five conditions.

The experimenter asked the man to consider the folders, complete a "first impression questionnaire" for each woman, and then decide which *one* of the five women he wished to date. (The subject's rating of the dates constitute our verbal measure of liking; his

choice in a date constitutes our behavioral measure of liking.)

The experimenter explained that she was conducting a study of first impressions in conjunction with the dating research project. The study, she continued, was designed to learn more about how good people are at forming first impressions of others on the basis of rather limited information. She explained that filling out the forms would probably make it easier for the man to decide which one of the five women he wished to date.

The first impression questionnaire consisted of three sections:

Liking for Various Dates Two questions assessed subjects' liking for each woman: "If you went out with this girl, how well do you think you would get along?"—with possible responses ranging from "get along extremely well" (5) to "not get along at all" (1)—and "What was your overall impression of the girl?"—with possible responses ranging from "extremely favorable" (7) to "extremely unfavorable" (1). Scores on these two questions were summed to form an index of expressed liking. This index enables us to compare subjects' liking for each of the women.

Assets and Liabilities Ascribed to Various Dates We predicted that subjects would prefer the selective woman, because they would expect her to possess the good qualities of both the uniformly hard-to-get and the uniformly easy-to-get woman, while avoiding the bad qualities of both her rivals. Thus, the second section was designed to determine the extent to which subjects imputed good and bad qualities to the various dates.

This section was comprised of 10 pairs of polar opposites. Subjects were asked to rate how friendly–unfriendly, cold–warm, attractive–unattractive, easy-going–rigid, exciting–boring, shy–outgoing, fun-loving–dull, popular–unpopular, aggressive–passive, selective–nonselective each woman was. Ratings were made on a 7-point scale. The more desirable the trait ascribed to a woman, the higher the score she was given.

Liabilities Attributed to Easy-to-Get Women The third scale was designed to assess the extent to which subjects attributed selected negative attributes to each woman. The third scale consisted of six statements:

She would more than likely do something to embarrass me in public.

She probably would demand too much attention and affection from me.

She seems like the type who would be too dependent on me.

She might turn out to be too sexually promiscuous.

She probably would make me feel uneasy when I'm with her in a group.

She seems like the type who doesn't distinguish between the boys she dates. I probably would be "just another date."

Subjects were asked whether they anticipated any of the above difficulties in their relationship with each woman. They indicated their misgivings on a scale ranging from "certainly true of her" (1) to "certainly not true of her" (7).

The experimenter suggested that the subject carefully examine both the background questionnaires and the date selection forms of all potential dates in order to decide whom he wanted to date. Then she left the subject. (The experimenter was, of course, unaware of what date was in what folder.)

The experimenter did not return until the subject had completed the first impression questionnaires. Then she asked him which woman he had decided to date.

After his choice had been made, the experimenter questioned him as to what factors influenced his choice. Frequently men who chose the selectively easy-to-get woman said that "She chose me, and that made me feel really good" or "She seemed more selective than the others." The uniformly easy-to-get woman was often rejected by subjects who complained "She must be awfully hard up for a date—she really would take anyone." The uniformly hard-to-get woman was once described as a "challenge" but more often rejected as being "snotty" or "too picky."

At the end of the session, the experimenter debriefed the subject and then gave him the names of five actual dates who had been matched with him.

RESULTS

We predicted that the selectively hard-to-get woman (easy for me but hard for everyone else to get) would be liked more than women who were uniformly hard to get, uniformly easy to get, or neutral (the no information women). We had no prediction as to whether or not her three rivals would differ in attractiveness. The results strongly support our hypothesis.

Dating Choices

When we examine the men's choices in dates, we see that the selective woman is far more popular than any of her rivals. (See Table 1.) We conducted a chi-square test to determine whether or not men's choices in dates were randomly distributed. They were not ($\chi^2 = 69.5$, $df = 4$, $p < .001$). Nearly all subjects preferred to date the selective woman. When we compare the frequency with which her four rivals (combined) are chosen, we see that the selective woman does get far more than her share of dates ($\chi^2 = 68.03$, $df = 1$, $p < .001$).

We also conducted an analysis to determine whether or not the women who are uniformly hard to get, uniformly easy to get, or whose popularity is unknown, differed in popularity. We see that they did not ($\chi^2 = 2.86$, $df = 3$).

TABLE 1 / Men's Choices in a Date

Item	Selectively Hard to Get	Uniformly Hard to Get	Uniformly Easy to Get	No Information for No. 1	No Information for No. 2
Number of men choosing to date each woman	42	6	5	11	7

Liking for the Various Dates

Two questions tapped the men's romantic liking for the various dates: (*a*) "If you went out with this woman, how well do you think you'd get along?"; and (*b*) "What was your overall impression of the woman?" Scores on these two indexes were summed to form an index of liking. Possible scores ranged from 2 to 12.

A contrast was then set up to test our hypothesis that the selective woman will be preferred to her rivals. The contrast that tests this hypothesis is of the form $\Gamma_1 = 4\mu$ (selectively hard to get) − 1 (uniformly hard to get) − 2μ (neutral). We tested the hypothesis $\Gamma_1 = 0$ against the alternative hypothesis $\Gamma_1 \neq 0$. An explanation of this basically simple procedure may be found in Hays (1963). If our hypothesis is true, the preceding contrast should be large. If our hypothesis is false, the resulting contrast should not differ significantly from 0. The data again provide strong support for the hypothesis that the selective woman is better liked than her rivals ($F = 23.92$, $df = 1/70$, $p < .001$).

Additional Data Snooping

We also conducted a second set of contrasts to determine whether the rivals (i.e., the uniformly hard-to-get woman, the uniformly easy-to-get woman, and the control woman) were differentially liked. Using the procedure presented by Morrison (1967) in chapter 4, the data indicate that the rivals are differentially liked ($F = 4.43$, $df = 2/69$). As Table 2 indicates, the uniformly hard-to-get woman seems to be liked slightly less than the easy-to-get or control woman.

In any attempt to explore data, one must account for the fact that observing the data permits the researcher to capitalize on chance. Thus, one must use simultaneous testing methods so as not to spuriously inflate the probability of attaining statistical significance. In the present situation, we are interested in comparing the means of a number of dependent measures, namely the liking for the different women in the dating situation. To perform post hoc multiple comparisons in this situation, one can use a transformation of Hotelling's t^2 statistic, which is distributed as F. The procedure is directly analogous to Scheffé's multiple-comparison procedure for independent groups, except where one compares means of a number of dependent measures.

To make it abundantly clear that the main result is that the discriminating woman is better liked than each of the other rivals, we performed an additional post hoc analysis, pitting each of the rivals separately

TABLE 2 / Men's Reactions to Various Dates

Item	Type of Date			
	Selectively Hard to Get	Uniformly Hard to Get	Uniformly Easy to Get	No Information
Men's liking for dates	9.41[a]	7.90	8.53	8.58
Evaluation of women's assets and liabilities				
Selective[b]	5.23	4.39	2.85	4.30
Popular[b]	4.83	4.58	4.65	4.83
Friendly[c]	5.58	5.07	5.52	5.37
Warm[c]	5.15	4.51	4.99	4.79
Easy Going[c]	4.83	4.42	4.82	4.61
Problems expected in dating	5.23[d]	4.86	4.77	4.99

[a]The higher the number, the more liking the man is expressing for the date.
[b]Traits we expected to be ascribed to the selectively hard-to-get and the uniformly hard-to-get dates.
[c]Traits we expected to be ascribed to the selectively hard-to-get and the uniformly easy-to-get dates.
[d]The higher the number the *fewer* the problems the subject anticipates in dating.

against the discriminating woman. In these analyses, we see that the selective woman is better liked than the woman who is uniformly easy to get ($F = 3.99$, $df = 3/68$), than the woman who is uniformly hard to get ($F = 9.47$, $df = 3/68$), and finally, than the control women ($F = 4.93$, $df = 3/68$).

Thus, it is clear that although there are slight differences in the way rivals are liked, these differences are small, relative to the overwhelming attractiveness of the selective woman.

Assets and Liabilities Attributed to Dates

We can now attempt to ascertain *why* the selective woman is more popular than her rivals. Earlier, we argued that the selectively hard-to-get woman should occupy a unique position; she should be assumed to possess all of the virtues of her rivals, but none of their flaws.

The virtues and flaws that the subject ascribed to each woman were tapped by the polar–opposite scale. Subjects evaluated each woman on 10 characteristics.

We expected that subjects would associate two assets with a uniformly hard-to-get woman: Such a woman should be perceived to be both "selective" and "popular." Unfortunately, such a woman should also be assumed to possess three liabilities—she should be perceived to be "unfriendly," "cold," and "rigid." Subjects should ascribe exactly the opposite virtues and liabilities to the easy-to-get woman: Such a woman should possess the assets of "friendliness," "warmth," and "flexibility," and the liabilities of "unpopularity" and "lack of selectivity." The selective woman was expected to possess only assets: She should be perceived to be as "selective" and "popular" as the uniformly elusive woman, and as "friendly," "warm," and "easy-going" as the uniformly easy woman. A contrast was set up to test this specific hypothesis. (Once again, see Hays for the procedure.) This contrast indicates that our hypothesis is confirmed ($F = 62.43$, $df = 1/70$). The selective woman is rated most like the uniformly hard-to-get woman on the first two positive characteristics and most like the uniformly easy-to-get woman on the last three characteristics.

For the reader's interest, the subjects' ratings of all five women's assets and liabilities are presented in Table 2.

Comparing the Selective and the Easy Women

Scale 3 was designed to assess whether or not subjects anticipated fewer problems when they envisioned dating the selective woman than when they envisioned dating the uniformly easy-to-get woman. On the basis of pretest interviews, we compiled a list of many of the concerns men had about easy women (e.g., "She would more than likely do something to embarrass me in public.").

We, of course, predicted that subjects would experience more problems when contemplating dating the uniformly easy woman than when contemplating dating a woman who was easy for *them* to get, but hard for anyone else to get (i.e., the selective woman).

Men were asked to say whether or not they envisioned each of the difficulties were they to date each of the women. Possible replies varied from 1 (certainly true of her) to 7 (certainly not true of her). The subjects' evaluations of each woman were summed to form an index of anticipated difficulties. Possible scores ranged from 6 to 42.

A contrast was set up to determine whether the selective woman engendered less concern than the uniformly easy-to-get woman. The data indicate that she does ($F = 17.50$, $df = 1/70$). If the reader is interested in comparing concern engendered by each woman, these data are available in Table 2.

The data provide clear support for our hypotheses: The selective woman is strongly preferred to any of her rivals. The reason for her popularity is evident. Men ascribe to her all of the assets of the uniformly hard-to-get and the uniformly easy-to-get women, and none of their liabilities.

Thus, after five futile attempts to understand the "hard-to-get" phenomenon, it appears that we have finally gained an understanding of this process. It appears that a woman can intensify her desirability if she acquires a reputation for being hard-to-get and then, by her behavior, makes it clear to a selected romantic partner that she is attracted to him.

In retrospect, especially in view of the strongly supportive data, the logic underlying our predictions sounds compelling. In fact, after examining our data, a colleague who had helped design the five ill-fated experiments noted that, "That is exactly what I would have predicted" (given his economic view of man). Unfortunately, we are all better at postdiction than prediction.

REFERENCES

Aronson, E., and Mills, J. The effect of severity of initiation on liking for a group. *Journal of Abnormal and Social Psychology,* 1959, 67, 31–36.

Berger, E. M. The relation between expressed acceptance of self and expressed acceptance of others. *Journal of Abnormal and Social Psychology,* 1952, 47, 778–782.

Gerard, H. B. and Mathewson, G. C. The effects of severity of initiation and liking for a group: A replication. *Journal of Experimental Social Psychology,* 1966, 2, 278–287.

Hays, W. L. *Statistics for psychologists.* New York: Holt, Rinehart, 1963.

Kimball, G. A. *Hilgard and Marquis' conditioning and learning.* New York: Appleton-Century-Crofts, 1961.

Lyons, J., Walster, and Walster, G. W. Playing hard-to-get: An elusive phenomenon University of Wisconsin, Madison: Author, 1971. (Mimeo)

Morrison, D. F. *Multivariate statistical methods.* New York: McGraw-Hill, 1967.

Ovid. *The art of love.* Bloomington: University of Indiana Press, 1963.

Rosenberg, M. *Society and the adolescent self image.* Princeton, N.J.: Princeton University Press, 1965.

Rosenfeld, H. M. Social choice conceived as a level of aspiration. *Journal of Abnormal and Social Psychology,* 1964, 68, 491–499.

Walster, E. Passionate love. In B. I. Murstein (Ed.), *Theories of attraction and love.* New York: Springer, 1971.

Walster, E., Walster, G. W., and Berscheid, E. The efficacy of playing hard-to-get. *Journal of Experimental Education,* 1971, 39, 73–77.

Walster, G. W., and Lambert, P. Playing hard-to-get: A field study. University of Wisconsin, Madison: Author, 1971. (Mimeo)

Xenophon. *Memorabilia.* London: Heinemann, 1923.

Zimbardo, P. G. The effect of effort and improvisation on self persuasion produced by role-playing. *Journal of Experimental Social Psychology,* 1965, 1, 103–120.

This research was supported in part by National Science Foundation Grants GS 2932 and GS 30822X and in part by National Institute for Mental Health Grant MH 16661.

CRITICAL THINKING QUESTIONS

1. Nonsignificant results are difficult to interpret in research. For example, if a woman playing hard to get is not viewed differently from one playing "easy," is there really no difference? Why or why not? Or is it possible that the experimental manipulation (how playing hard to get or easy were varied in the study) was not strong enough to produce an effect? Discuss this possibility by examining how playing hard to get was manipulated in the first five experiments reported in this article.
2. Are ethical issues involved in any of the studies? In particular, what are your views of Study 5, which involved the services of a prostitute?
3. This study ultimately determined that selectively hard-to-get women were most preferred by the men. Do you think the reverse is true—that women most prefer selectively hard-to-get men? Why or why not?
4. Do you think that the results of this study could be generalized to the sexual arena (i.e., when it comes to sex, a selectively hard-to-get woman would be preferred over either a hard-to-get or easy-to-get woman)? Explain.

ADDITIONAL RELATED READINGS

Eastwick, P. W., Finkel, E. J., Mochon, D., & Ariely, D. (2007). Selective versus unselective romantic desire: Not all reciprocity is created equal. *Psychological Science, 18*(4), 317–319.

Simpson, J. A., Collins, A., Tran, S., & Haddon, K. C. (2007). Attachment and the experience and expression of emotions in romantic relationships: A developmental perspective. *Journal of Personality and Social Psychology, 92*(2), 355–367.

ARTICLE 24_____

What is *love?* The topic certainly has been and continues to be a popular one in the realm of philosophy, theology, and the arts. Yet in spite of the high value that people place on this experience, social scientists did not begin to investigate it until recently, for a variety of reasons. First and foremost is the subject matter itself. What, exactly, is *love?* How can we begin to define it, let alone measure it? Other reasons explain why the question was not addressed, as well. Many people think that the very importance of this feeling is why it should not be addressed. Perhaps love is supposed to be entirely private and best left alone.

But back to the question of what is *love*. You may know that you love someone based on the thoughts and feelings you have about him or her. But how does that person know that you love him or her? That person cannot tap directly into the private thoughts and feelings that you have for him or her. He or she can only infer that information from the ways that you act, whether in making certain gestures that are considered loving or by saying certain words.

But what exactly are the words that may help to foster a positive relationship? Is it enough just to say "I love you" often, or is it necessary to express other positive emotions and perhaps avoid expressing negative emotions? The following article by Richard B. Slatcher and James W. Pennebaker examines how a task such as writing expressively about one's relationship can affect communication within the relationship and the relationship itself.

How Do I Love Thee?
Let Me Count the Words
The Social Effects of Expressive Writing

■ Richard B. Slatcher and James W. Pennebaker

ABSTRACT

Writing about emotional experiences is associated with a host of positive outcomes. This study extended the expressive-writing paradigm to the realm of romantic relationships to examine the social effects of writing. For 3 consecutive days, one person from each of 86 dating couples either wrote about his or her deepest thoughts and feelings about the relationship or wrote about his or her daily activities. In the days before and after writing, instant messages were collected from the couples. Participants who wrote about their relationship were significantly more likely to still be dating their romantic partners 3 months later. Linguistic analyses of the instant messages revealed that participants and their partners used significantly more positive and negative emotion words in the days following the expressive-writing manipulation if the participants had written about their relationship than if they had written about their daily activities. Increases in positive emotion words partially mediated the relation between expressive writing and relationship stability.

Over the past two decades, multiple studies have demonstrated the positive benefits of expressive writing in domains as diverse as health, achievement, and

Slatcher, R. B., & Pennebaker, J. W. (2006). How do I love thee? Let me count the words: The social effects of expressive writing. *Psychological Science, 17*(8), 660–664. Copyright © 2006 by American Psychological Society. Reprinted with permission of Blackwell Publishers.

well-being. Most of these studies have used a relatively straightforward procedure in which participants write about their deepest thoughts and feelings about a particular topic for 20 min a day, 3 or 4 days in a row. The findings indicate that expressive writing can result in fewer doctor visits, fewer depressive symptoms, enhanced immune system functioning, better grades, and a host of other positive outcomes (for reviews, see Lepore & Smyth, 2002, and Smyth, 1998).

Researchers now are examining the social effects of expressive writing, working from the assumption that confronting conflicting or complex emotions or thoughts can facilitate social interactions. The preliminary findings suggest that expressive writing may be particularly beneficial for people in romantic relationships. For example, when people write expressively about recent relationship breakups, they are somewhat more likely than control participants to reunite with their partners (Lepore & Greenberg, 2002). Similarly, when married couples recovering from infidelity write emotionally expressive letters to each other, they experience reductions in depression, anger, and marital distress (Gordon, Baucom, & Snyder, 2004). The social effects of writing need not be limited to people recovering from a relationship breakup or to those whose relationship is in distress. People in healthy and committed romantic relationships also might benefit from expressive writing.

There are a number of ways in which one could measure the effects of expressive writing on the functioning of relationships. One way is to examine the impact of writing on relationship stability. Results from the few studies examining the social effects of expressive writing indicate that it may enhance relationship stability among couples in distress (Gordon et al., 2004; Lepore & Greenberg, 2002). Expressive writing could lead to improved stability for individuals in normal, healthy relationships as well.

Although previous studies have addressed the potential benefits of expressive writing for couples, none have examined the underlying mechanisms that might mediate writing's effects on relationship outcomes. One potential mediator is natural language use (Pennebaker & Graybeal, 2001; Sillars, Shellen, McIntosh, & Pomegranate, 1997). By measuring the words that people use with others in their social worlds, researchers can gain insight into the social changes that occur after expressive writing. The use of emotion words may

be particularly relevant. Positive emotion words—such as *happy* and *love*—and negative emotion words—such as *angry* and *nervous*—can reveal deeply felt emotions (Pennebaker, Mehl, & Niederhoffer, 2003; Twenge, Catanese, & Baumeister, 2003). Expressive writing provides an opportunity for reflection, and, accordingly, one would expect it to lead to increased emotional expressiveness with other people—reflected in increases in emotion words during social interactions. Such increases in emotion words might mediate higher-level changes in relationship functioning, such as improvements in relationship stability.

There are various ways to measure the words that people use. One technology—instant messaging (IM)—holds great promise. For many people (53 million adults, including 30% of all Internet users over the age of 40), IM is quickly replacing e-mail as a preferred mode of on-line dyadic communication (Shiu & Lenhart, 2004). Unlike e-mail, IM allows users to chat with each other so that a conversation can unfold in much the same way that spoken conversation does. The analysis of IM conversations can allow researchers to examine the ebb and flow of people's natural language use.

In the present study, we sought to investigate the social effects of expressive writing. Individuals in committed romantic relationships were randomly assigned either to write about their deepest thoughts and feelings about their relationship or to write about a superficial topic for 20 min a day, 3 days in a row. Three predictions were tested. First, we predicted that those who wrote about their relationship would be more likely to be dating their partners 3 months after the experiment. Second, we predicted that participants who wrote about their relationship would change in the way in which they communicated with their partners. Specifically, we expected those in this group to increase their use of positive and negative emotion words in their daily IM conversations. Finally, we predicted that changes in use of emotion words would mediate the relation between expressive writing and relationship stability.

METHOD

Participants

Eighty-six undergraduate psychology students (55 women, 31 men; mean age = 18.7, *SD* = 1.0) and their partners (31 women, 55 men; mean age = 19.3, SD = 1.6) were recruited on the basis that they were in a committed heterosexual romantic relationship and that they engaged in IM conversation with each other every day. The couples had been dating an average of 1.31 years (SD = 1.06).

Procedure

One member of each couple participated in the writing phase of the study. An experimenter met with participants individually or in small groups of 2 to 5 to give them an overview of the study. They were told that its purpose was to quantify the types of words that people use in writing and everyday interactions.

Participants were instructed to forward to a secure e-mail address all daily IM conversations between themselves and their partners during the 10 days of the study. Considerable effort was taken during the introductory session to reassure participants that their messages would be completely confidential.

Questionnaires assessing demographic information, relationship status, and relationship satisfaction were completed by participants and their partners online from home on the first day of the study. Satisfaction was measured using the Relationship Assessment Scale (RAS; Hendrick, 1988). The RAS consists of seven items, such as "In general, how satisfied are you with your relationship?" Ratings are made on a 7-point Likert scale.

Participants were randomly assigned to the experimental (n = 44) or control (n = 42) writing condition and were instructed to set aside 20 min per day on the fourth, fifth, and sixth days of the study for completion of the on-line writing exercises. Participants in the experimental condition were instructed to write about their deepest thoughts and feelings about their current romantic relationship, "to really let go and explore your very deepest emotions and thoughts about your relationship." Those in the control condition were instructed to write in detail about their daily activities—a standard control condition for expressive-writing studies. The purpose of the writing assignments was left intentionally vague to reduce the possibility of demand characteristics; participants were told that the writing assignments would be used to assess basic word use.

Three months later, participants completed a brief on-line questionnaire that assessed relationship status and satisfaction.

Linguistic Analysis

The IM conversations were analyzed using the Linguistic Inquiry and Word Count program (LIWC; Pennebaker, Francis, & Booth, 2001). All conversations from couples in both conditions were spell-checked prior to being submitted to LIWC. They were converted to text files, categorized by speaker (participant or partner), and subcategorized according to whether they dated from before or after the writing manipulation, resulting in a total of four separate IM text files per couple.

RESULTS

Relationship Stability and Language Use

Expressive writing was significantly related to the long-term stability of relationships, odds ratio = 3.09, p_{rep} = .95, Cohen's d = 0.54. Thirty-four participants (77%) in the experimental condition were still dating their partners at the 3-month follow-up mark, compared with 22 participants (52%) in the control condition. There were no significant differences in baseline relationship satisfaction between the conditions (experimental M = 6.21, SD = 0.63; control M = 6.01, SD = 0.66), nor was condition related to satisfaction at the 3-month follow-up (experimental M = 5.87, SD = 1.50; control M = 5.94, SD = 0.94). Note that the follow-up satisfaction measures are difficult to interpret because they were available only for couples still in their relationships.

Hierarchical linear modeling (HLM; Raudenbush & Bryk, 2002) was employed to analyze changes in use of emotion words within couples' IM conversations as a function of experimental condition. Initial analyses focused on the effects of expressive writing on positive emotion words in couples' conversations. Level 1 (individual-level) predictors were baseline use of positive emotion words and speaker (participant or partner). Only baseline use of positive emotion words was a significant Level 1 predictor, (β_1 = .51, p_{rep} > .99, d = 1.19. Level 2 (couple-level) predictors were gender of the participant, experimental condition, and a Gender × Condition interaction term. Only experimental condition was a significant Level 2 predictor, γ_{01} = .51, p_{rep} = .93, d = 0.46. Couples in the expressive-writing condition were more likely than those in the control condition to increase their use of positive emotion words with their romantic partners in the days following the manipulation. Additionally, participants and partners in the experimental condition increased their use of positive emotion words at similar rates as they communicated with each other via IM, even though only the participants were involved in the expressive-writing manipulation.

Next, the effect of expressive writing on negative emotion words was analyzed. Level 1 predictors were baseline use of negative emotion words, as well as the speaker variable. Only baseline use of negative emotion words was a significant Level 1 predictor, β_1 = .28, p_{rep} = .98, d = 0.46. Level 2 predictors were gender of the participant, experimental condition, and a Gender × Condition interaction term. Significant Level 2 predictors were experimental condition, γ_{01} = .54, p_{rep} = .98, d = 0.64, and the Gender × Condition interaction, γ_{02} = .52, p_{rep} = .97, d = 0.61. Compared with control couples, couples in the expressive-writing condition were more likely to increase their use of negative emotion words with their romantic partners in the days following the writing manipulation. This effect was moderated by the gender of the person in each couple who took part in the writing manipulation. Specifically, couples in which the male wrote about the relationship increased their use of negative emotion words significantly compared with control couples, whereas couples in which the female wrote about the relationship did not change in their use of negative emotion words compared with control couples.[1]

Mediation Effects of Changes in Use of Emotion Words

A strength of this design is that it allowed us to explore the degree to which measures of language may reflect the social psychological processes underlying the effects of expressive writing. Two sets of mediation analyses were conducted—one with positive emotion words as the potential mediator, the other with nega-

tive emotion words as the potential mediator. In both cases, the outcome measure was relationship stability at the 3-month follow-up. Means and standard deviations for couples' use of emotion words in their IM conversations are shown in Table 1.

Positive Emotion Words Experimental condition and use of positive emotion words before and after the writing manipulation were entered in separate steps into a logistic regression in which relationship stability was the dependent variable. Higher levels of postwriting positive emotion words were associated with higher levels of couple stability, odds ratio = 3.04, p_{rep} = .99, d = 0.95. After controlling for changes in positive emotion words, the effects of experimental condition on relationship stability were no longer significant, suggesting possible mediation. The results of a Sobel z test (Sobel, 1982) supported this analysis (z = 2.00, p_{rep} = .92). Thus, the salutary effects of writing about one's relationship were at least partially mediated by increases in use of positive emotion words in daily IM conversations.

TABLE 1 / Couples' Use of Emotion Words in Instant Messages as a Function of Time and Condition

Linguistic Dimension and Condition	Before the Writing Manipulation		After the Writing Manipulation	
	M	*SD*	*M*	*SD*
Positive emotion words				
Experimental condition	4.51	1.29	4.94	1.54
Control condition	4.39	1.42	4.31	1.36
Negative emotion words				
Experimental condition	1.84	0.61	2.36	0.96
Control condition	1.91	0.82	1.97	0.93

Note. Experimental condition n = 44; control condition n = 42.

Negative Emotion Words No relationship was found between increases in negative emotion words and couple stability ($p_{rep} < .50$). This also was the case in a separate analysis for just those couples in which the male was the participant. The effects of expressive writing on stability therefore were not mediated by changes in use of negative emotion words.

DISCUSSION

The relatively simple act of writing about their romantic relationship changed the way in which participants communicated with their partners in IM conversations; it also changed the way in which the partners communicated with the participants and improved relationship stability. Couples in the expressive-writing condition were more likely to increase their use of positive emotion words than were couples in the control condition; couples in the expressive-writing condition in which the male was the participant increased in their use of negative emotion words as well. Increases in positive emotion words partially mediated the association between writing and relationship stability.

Taken together, these findings shed light on processes underlying interactions in close relationships. In particular, the findings relating to increases in use of emotion words illuminate previous research (e.g., Butler et al., 2003; Gottman & Levenson, 2000; Laurenceau, Barrett, & Pietromonaco, 1998) suggesting that increased expression of positive emotions can result in better outcomes for relationships. This study is one of the first to go beyond self-reports to demonstrate that couples' increased emotional expressiveness may have the power to improve objective relationship outcomes.

An advantage of the current design is that it allows one to unobtrusively measure interpersonal processes underlying dyadic interactions. By analyzing the words that couples use in daily IM interactions, researchers can assess the extent to which the couples' language patterns are predictive of relationship quality and stability. Given the growth in electronic communication in recent years, IM technology may serve as a promising tool in examining real-time, on-line interactions in naturalistic settings.

That people may enhance their romantic relationships by simply writing down their thoughts and feelings about those relationships has clear implications for clinicians. The use of expressive writing as a tool for relationship enhancement could be applied to a broad range of relationships, including those in families, circles of friends, and even work groups. Expressive writing may serve to strengthen the relational connections of a broad array of social channels, particularly for persons who have not had extensive experience expressing emotions to others.

There are some potential limitations of this study. First, it is conceivable that the effects of writing on changes in word use may have been partially affected by demand characteristics. We believe that the emphasis on keeping the purpose of the study vague to participants and the fact that writing also influenced relationship stability make this an unlikely possibility. Second, it is unknown whether it was the act of writing itself that led to positive relationship outcomes, or whether simply directing people to mentally attend to and explore relationship issues would be equally beneficial; future studies should address this issue.

Unlike previous expressive-writing studies, this is the first to demonstrate some of the social processes that may underlie the effects of expressive writing. Further, this study points to the advantages gained in using current on-line technologies such as IM for psychological research. Such technologies now allow researchers to examine natural interactions in a relatively simple, inexpensive, and straightforward manner.

ACKNOWLEDGMENTS

Portions of this research were funded by a grant from the National Institutes of Health (MH52391). We would like to thank Greg Hixon, Amy Kaderka, and Girish Tembe for their assistance on this project and Amie Green, Timothy Loving, Matthew Newman, William Swann, and Simine Vazire for their helpful comments on an earlier draft of this article.

REFERENCES

Butler, E. A., Egloff, B., Wilhelm, F. H., Smith, N. C., Erickson, E. A., & Gross, J. J. (2003). The social consequences of expressive suppression. *Emotion, 3,* 48–67.

Gordon, K. C., Baucom, D. H., & Snyder, D. K. (2004). An integrative intervention for promoting recovery from extramarital affairs. *Journal of Marital and Family Therapy, 30,* 213–231.

Gottman, J. M., & Levenson, R. W. (2000). The timing of divorce: Predicting when a couple will divorce over a 14-year period. *Journal of Marriage and the Family, 62,* 737–745.

Hendrick, S. S. (1988). A generic measure of relationship satisfaction. *Journal of Marriage and the Family, 50,* 93–98.

Laurenceau, J.-P., Barrett, L. F., & Pietromonaco, P. R. (1998). Intimacy as an interpersonal process: The importance of self-disclosure, partner disclosure, and perceived partner responsiveness in interpersonal exchanges. *Journal of Personality and Social Psychology, 74,* 1238–1251.

Lepore, S. J., & Greenberg, M. A. (2002). Mending broken hearts: Effects of expressive writing on mood, cognitive processing, social adjustment and health following a relationship breakup. *Psychology and Health, 17,* 547–560.

Lepore, S. T., & Smyth, J. (2002). *The writing cure.* Washington, DC: American Psychological Association.

Pennebaker, J. W., Francis, M. E., & Booth, R. J. (2001). *Linguistic Inquiry and Word Count (LIWC).* Mahwah, NJ: Erlbaum.

Pennebaker, J. W., & Graybeal, A. (2001). Patterns of natural language use: Disclosure, personality, and social integration. *Current Directions in Psychological Science, 10,* 90–93.

Pennebaker, J. W., Mehl, M. R., & Niederhoffer, K. (2003). Psychological aspects of natural language use: Our words, our selves. *Annual Review of Psychology, 54,* 547–577.

Raudenbush, S. W., & Bryk, A. S. (2002). *Hierarchical linear models: Applications and data analysis methods* (2nd ed.). Newbury Park, CA: Sage.

Shiu, E., & Lenhart, A. (2004). *How Americans use instant messaging.* Retrieved October 14, 2005, from http://www.pewinternet.org/pdfs/PIP_Instantmessage_Report.pdf

Sillars, A. L., Shellen, W., McIntosh, A., & Pomegranate, M. A. (1997). Relational characteristics of language: Elaboration and differentiation in marital conversations. *Western Journal of Communication, 61,* 403–422.

Smyth, J. M. (1998). Written emotional expression: Effect sizes, outcome types, and moderating variables. *Journal of Consulting and Clinical Psychology, 66,* 174–184.

Sobel, M. E. (1982). Asymptotic intervals for indirect effects in structural equations models. In S. Leinhart (Ed.), *Sociological methodology 1982* (pp. 290–312). San Francisco: Jossey-Bass.

Twenge, J. M., Catanese, K. R., & Baumeister, R. F. (2003). Social exclusion and the deconstructed state: Time perception, meaninglessness, lethargy, lack of emotion, and self-awareness. *Journal of Personality and Social Psychology, 85,* 409–423.

Wegner, D. M. (1982, August). *When does the intimate group come to mind?* Paper presented at the annual meeting of the American Psychological Association, Washington, DC.

ENDNOTE

1. Exploratory analyses also were conducted on changes in use of first-person plural pronouns (e.g., *we, us, our*); no significant effects were found. Previous studies (e.g., Sillars et al., 1997; Wegner, 1982) have found positive correlations between relationship functioning and use of *we* when participants discussed their relationships with an interviewer. Note that this is a very different context from closed interactions between the two members of a couple, during which the use of we may not reflect intimacy between them (e.g., it may reflect condescension, emotional distancing, or the referencing of someone close outside the relationship).

CRITICAL THINKING QUESTIONS

1. This study found that through expressive writing, both male and female participants increased their use of positive emotion words, but males also increased their use of negative emotion words. Why may that be the case? Based on the results of this study, does it appear that increasing the use of any emotion words, whether positive or negative, is more important than just using positive emotion words? Explain.

2. Could simply talking about one's relationship each day have the same impact as writing about it? Why or why not? Design a study that would test this possibility.

3. The article suggests that the use of expressive writing could be applied to a broad range of relationships, even work groups. What might be the similarities and differences in using this technique in dating relationships versus other types of relationships?

4. The participants in the study knew that their IMs would be read by the experimenter. How might this have affected what they wrote? Explain why the enhanced use of emotion words occurred only in the experimental group and not in the control group.

CHAPTER INTEGRATION QUESTIONS

1. In a sense, the three articles in this chapter progress through the possible stages of a relationship, from the initial attraction ("playing hard to get") to communication in dating couples to divorce (but not in that order of article presentation). What similar themes run through these articles? Specifically, do any of the factors discussed about initial attraction and dating affect the likelihood of being divorced later on? Explain your answer.

2. What factors identified in the article on divorce may be useful in developing more satisfying relationships earlier on? Explain your answers.

3. In *Keeping the Love You Find: A Guide for Singles,* the author, Harville Hendrix, said, "Love is hard—life is hard—but it's the only game in town. It's a high-stakes game, because how well you play determines how you will thrive and grow. You might as well learn to play it as well as possible as soon as possible." What does this quotation mean to you? Do you agree or disagree with it? Explain.

Chapter Nine

SOCIAL INFLUENCE

SOCIAL INFLUENCE IS the process of inducing change in other people. Sometimes social change results from direct orders to do something, such as when a military officer gives an order to a subordinate. When this happens, we call it *obedience*. Basic to situations involving obedience is some sort of power, either real or imagined, that the person giving the orders has over the person obeying him or her.

Not all social influence is due to direct orders from people in positions of authority. Instead, we may simply ask that a person do something for us. *Compliance* is when a person does something just because he or she was asked to, not because the requestor had any type of power over him or her.

Finally, social influence also operates in a very subtle way when people follow *norms,* or generally expected ways of behaving in certain situations. For example, when you are in an elevator, what do you do? Most likely, you face forward and stare at the numbers. *Conformity* occurs in many situations where norms exist for proper behavior. In a sense, conformity is the lifeblood of a society, for without conformity to rules, society could not exist.

Among the studies that address situational influences on behavior—and, in particular, in bringing out negative behavior—the two most often mentioned are the Stanford prison experiment and Stanley Milgram's study on obedience. Article 25, "Revisiting the Stanford Prison Experiment: A Lesson in the Power of Situation," is written by the person who conducted this classic study, Philip G. Zimbardo. This article describes the study and also discusses the current relevance of the experiment.

Milgram's study—considered to be a classic work on obedience and perhaps one of the most widely known studies in the field of social psychology—is found in Article 26, "Behavioral Study of Obedience." This study intended to demonstrate experimentally that the average person could be induced to harm another person simply by being ordered to by someone in a position of authority. The large number of people in this study who fully obeyed the orders surprised everyone.

Finally, Article 27, "The Influence of Social Pressure and Black Clothing on Crime Judgements," examines how social pressure from a group may influence conformity and how even the clothing worn by the persons inducing the social pressure may impact conforming behavior. Building on the methodology of a classic experiment on conformity (i.e., the Asch line-judgment study), this article also demonstrates how research concepts are continually refined over the years.

ARTICLE 25 _____

When people read about a horrendous act that has been committed, they naturally think that the person who committed it is somehow deranged or inhuman. Sometimes that is indeed the case, as when a psychotic commits an act under orders he or she has supposedly received during hallucinations. Personal pathology and mental illness are certainly involved in many of the hideous acts that people commit. But are personality or psychological factors always the cause of such behavior? Is it possible that an otherwise normal individual may commit an abnormal, sick act not because there is something wrong with him or her but because of the situation he or she might be in?

History is full of examples of normal people who have committed abnormal acts. For example, warfare has often induced otherwise normal, nonviolent people not only to kill but also to commit atrocities. Yet the suggestion that somehow anyone placed in the same situation may act the same way is repugnant. It might be a lot more personally comforting to believe that people who do bad things are somehow different from us. We, after all, are good and certainly incapable of being mass murderers. Only other people who are either sick or are somehow overly conforming could do such things. In other words, we tend to attribute others' acts to their disposition—that is, some personality or other enduring trait causes them to act that way.

The work of Stanley Milgram, which appears in Article 26, is the classic study in the field of social psychology that suggested that perhaps individual characteristics (dispositions) are less responsible for people performing terrible acts than are the situations that produce such behavior. Another classic research study that rivals Milgram's obedience study is what has come to be known as the Stanford prison experiment. In the following article, researcher Philip G. Zimbardo describes this famous study and discusses the current relevance of the work.

Revisiting the Stanford Prison Experiment
A Lesson in the Power of Situation

■ Phillip G. Zimbardo

By the 1970s, psychologists had done a series of studies establishing the social power of groups. They showed, for example, that groups of strangers could persuade people to believe statements that were obviously false. Psychologists had also found that research participants were often willing to obey authority figures even when doing so violated their personal beliefs. The Yale studies by Stanley Milgram in 1963 demonstrated that a majority of ordinary citizens would continually shock an innocent man, even up to near-

lethal levels, if commanded to do so by someone acting as an authority. The "authority" figure in this case was merely a high-school biology teacher who wore a lab coat and acted in an official manner. The majority of people shocked their victims over and over again despite increasingly desperate pleas to stop.

In my own work, I wanted to explore the fictional notion from William Golding's *Lord of the Flies* about the power of anonymity to unleash violent behavior. In one experiment from 1969, female students who

Reprinted from *The Chronicle of Higher Education*, March 30, 2007, B6–B7. Reprinted with permission of Phillip G. Zimbardo.

were made to feel anonymous and given permission for aggression became significantly more hostile than students with their identities intact. Those and a host of other social-psychological studies were showing that human nature was more pliable than previously imagined and more responsive to situational pressures than we cared to acknowledge. In sum, these studies challenged the sacrosanct view that inner determinants of behavior—personality traits, morality, and religious upbringing—directed good people down righteous paths.

Missing from the body of social-science research at the time was the direct confrontation of good versus evil, of good people pitted against the forces inherent in bad situations. It was evident from everyday life that smart people made dumb decisions when they were engaged in mindless groupthink, as in the disastrous Bay of Pigs invasion by the smart guys in President John F. Kennedy's cabinet. It was also clear that smart people surrounding President Richard M. Nixon, like Henry A. Kissinger and Robert S. McNamara, escalated the Vietnam War when they knew, and later admitted, it was not winnable. They were caught up in the mental constraints of cognitive dissonance—the discomfort from holding two conflicting thoughts—and were unable to cut bait even though it was the only rational strategy to save lives and face. Those examples, however, with their different personalities, political agendas, and motives, complicated any simple conceptual attempt to understand what went wrong in these situations.

I decided that what was needed was to create a situation in a controlled experimental setting in which we could array on one side a host of variables, such as role-playing, coercive rules, power differentials, anonymity, group dynamics, and dehumanization. On the other side, we lined up a collection of the "best and brightest" of young college men in collective opposition to the might of a dominant system. Thus in 1971 was born the Stanford prison experiment, more akin to Greek drama than to university psychology study. I wanted to know who wins—good people or an evil situation—when they were brought into direct confrontation.

First we established that all 24 participants were physically and mentally healthy, with no history of crime or violence, so as to be sure that initially they were all "good apples." They were paid $15 a day to participate. Each of the student volunteers was randomly assigned to play the role of prisoner or guard in a setting designed to convey a sense of the psychology of imprisonment (in actuality, a mock prison set up in the basement of the Stanford psychology department). Dramatic realism infused the study. Palo Alto police agreed to "arrest" the prisoners and book them, and once at the prison, they were given identity numbers, stripped naked, and deloused. The prisoners wore large smocks with no underclothes and lived in the prison 24/7 for a planned two weeks; three sets of guards each patrolled eight-hour shifts. Throughout the experiment, I served as the prison "superintendent," assisted by two graduate students.

Initially nothing much happened as the students awkwardly tried out their assigned roles in their new uniforms. However, all that changed suddenly on the morning of the second day following a rebellion, when the prisoners barricaded themselves inside the cells by putting their beds against the door. Suddenly the guards perceived the prisoners as "dangerous"; they had to be dealt with harshly to demonstrate who was boss and who was powerless. At first, guard abuses were retaliation for taunts and disobedience. Over time, the guards became ever more abusive, and some even delighted in sadistically tormenting their prisoners. Though physical punishment was restricted, the guards on each shift were free to make up their own rules, and they invented a variety of psychological tactics to demonstrate their dominance over their powerless charges.

Nakedness was a common punishment, as was placing prisoners' heads in nylon stocking caps (to simulate shaved heads); chaining their legs; repeatedly waking them throughout the night for hourlong counts; and forcing them into humiliating "fun and games" activities. Let's go beyond those generalizations to review some of the actual behaviors that were enacted in the prison simulation. They are a lesson in "creative evil," in how certain social settings can transform intelligent young men into perpetrators of psychological abuse.

PRISON LOG, NIGHT 5

The prisoners, who have not broken down emotionally under the incessant stress the guards have been subjecting them to since their aborted rebellion on Day 2, wearily line up against the wall to recite their ID numbers and to demonstrate that they remember all 17 prisoner rules of engagement. It is the 1 a.m. count, the last one of the night before the morning shift comes on at 2 a.m. No matter how well the prisoners do, one of them gets singled out for punishment. They are yelled at, cursed out, and made to say abusive things to each other. "Tell him he's a prick," yells one guard. And each prisoner says that to the next guy in line. Then the sexual harassment that had started to bubble up the night before resumes as the testosterone flows freely in every direction.

"See that hole in the ground? Now do 25 push-ups [expletive] that hole! You hear me!" One after another, the prisoners obey like automatons as the guard shoves them down. After a brief consultation, our toughest guard (nicknamed "John Wayne" by the prisoners) and his sidekick devise a new sexual game. "OK, now pay attention. You three are going to be female camels. Get over here and bend over, touching your hands to the floor." When they do, their naked butts are exposed because they have no underwear beneath their smocks. John Wayne continues with obvious glee, "Now you two, you're male camels. Stand behind the female camels and *hump* them."

The guards all giggle at this double-entendre. Although their bodies never touch, the helpless prisoners begin to simulate sodomy by making thrusting motions. They are then dismissed back to their cells to get an hour of sleep before the next shift comes on, and the abuse continues.

By Day 5, five of the student prisoners have to be released early because of extreme stress. (Recall that each of them was physically healthy and psychologically stable less than a week before.) Most of those who remain adopt a zombielike attitude and posture, totally obedient to escalating guard demands.

TERMINATING THE TORMENT

I was forced to terminate the projected two-week-long study after only six days because it was running out of control. Dozens of people had come down to our "little shop of horrors," seen some of the abuse or its effects, and said nothing. A prison chaplain, parents, and friends had visited the prisoners, and

psychologists and others on the parole board saw a realistic prison simulation, an experiment in action, but did not challenge me to stop it. The one exception erupted just before the time of the prison-log notation on Night 5.

About halfway through the study, I had invited some psychologists who knew little about the experiment to interview the staff and participants, to get an outsiders' evaluation of how it was going. A former doctoral student of mine, Christina Maslach, a new assistant professor at the University of California at Berkeley, came down late Thursday night to have dinner with me. We had started dating recently and were becoming romantically involved. When she saw the prisoners lined up with bags over their heads, their legs chained, and guards shouting abuses at them while herding them to the toilet, she got upset and refused my suggestion to observe what was happening in this "crucible of human nature." Instead she ran out of the basement, and I followed, berating her for being overly sensitive and not realizing the important lessons taking place here.

"It is terrible what YOU are doing to those boys!" she yelled at me. Christina made evident in that one statement that human beings were suffering, not prisoners, not experimental subjects, not paid volunteers. And further, I was the one who was personally responsible for the horrors she had witnessed (and which she assumed were even worse when no outsider was looking). She also made clear that if this person I had become—the heartless superintendent of the Stanford prison—was the real me, not the caring, generous person she had come to like, she wanted nothing more to do with me.

That powerful jolt of reality snapped me back to my senses. I agreed that we had gone too far, that whatever was to be learned about situational power was already indelibly etched on our videos, data logs, and minds; there was no need to continue. I too had been transformed by my role in that situation to become a person that under any other circumstances I detest—an uncaring, authoritarian boss man. In retrospect, I believe that the main reason I did not end the study sooner resulted from the conflict created in me by my dual roles as principal investigator, and thus guardian of the research ethics of the experiment, and as the prison superintendent, eager to maintain the stability of my prison at all costs. I now realize that there should have been someone with authority above mine, someone in charge of oversight of the experiment, who surely would have blown the whistle earlier.

By the time Christina intervened, it was the middle of the night, so I had to make plans to terminate the next morning. The released prisoners and guards had to be called back and many logistics handled before I could say, "The Stanford prison experiment is officially closed." When I went back down to the basement, I witnessed the final scene of depravity, the "camel humping" episode. I was so glad that it would be the last such abuse I would see or be responsible for.

GOOD APPLES IN BAD BARRELS AND BAD BARREL MAKERS

The situational forces in that "bad barrel" had overwhelmed the goodness of most of those infected by their viral power. It is hard to imagine how a seeming game of "cops and robbers" played by college kids, with a few academics (our research team) watching, could have descended into what became a hellhole for many in that basement. How could a mock prison, an experimental simulation, become "a prison run by psychologists, not by the state," in the words of one suffering prisoner? How is it possible for "good personalities" to be so dominated by a "bad situation"? You had to be there to believe that human character could be so swiftly transformed in a matter of days— not only the traits of the students, but of me, a well-seasoned adult. Most of the visitors to our prison also fell under the spell. For example, individual sets of parents observing their son's haggard appearance after a few days of hard labor and long nights of disrupted sleep said they "did not want to make trouble" by taking their kid home or challenging the system. Instead they obeyed our authority and let some of their sons experience full-blown emotional meltdowns later on. We had created a dominating behavioral context whose power insidiously frayed the seemingly impervious values of compassion, fair play, and belief in a just world.

The situation won; humanity lost. Out the window went the moral upbringings of these young men,

as well as their middle-class civility. Power ailed, and unrestrained power became an aphrodisiac. Power without surveillance by higher authorities was a poisoned chalice that transformed character in unpredictable directions. I believe that most of us tend to be fascinated with evil not because of its consequences but because evil is a demonstration of power and domination over others.

CURRENT RELEVANCE

Such research is now in an ethical time capsule, since institutional review boards will not allow social scientists to repeat it (although experiments like it have been replicated on several TV shows and in artistic renditions). Nevertheless, the Stanford prison experiment is now more popular than ever in its 36-year history. A Google search of "experiment" reveals it to be fourth among some 132 million hits, and sixth among some 127 million hits on "prison." Some of this recent interest comes from the apparent similarities of the experiment's abuses with the images of depravity in Iraq's Abu Ghraib prison—of nakedness, bagged heads, and sexual humiliation.

Among the dozen investigations of the Abu Ghraib abuses, the one chaired by James R. Schlesinger, the former secretary of defense, boldly proclaims that the landmark Stanford study "provides a cautionary tale for all military detention operations." In contrasting the relatively benign environment of the Stanford prison experiment, the report makes evident that "in military detention operations, soldiers work under stressful combat conditions that are far from benign." The implication is that those combat conditions might be expected to generate even more extreme abuses of power than were observed in our mock prison experiment.

However, the Schlesinger report notes that military leaders did not heed that earlier warning in any way. They should have—a psychological perspective is essential to understanding the transformation of human character in response to special situational forces. "The potential for abusive treatment of detainees during the Global War on Terrorism was entirely predictable based on a fundamental understanding of the principles of social psychology coupled with an awareness of numerous known environmental risk factors," the report says. "Findings from the field of social psychology suggest that the conditions of war and the dynamics of detainee operations carry inherent risks for human mistreatment, and therefore must be approached with great caution and careful planning and training." (Unfortunately this vital conclusion is buried in an appendix.)

The Stanford prison experiment is but one of a host of studies in psychology that reveal the extent to which our behavior can be transformed from its usual set point to deviate in unimaginable ways, even to readily accepting a dehumanized conception of others, as "animals," and to accepting spurious rationales for why pain will be good for them.

The implications of this research for law are considerable, as legal scholars are beginning to recognize. The criminal-justice system, for instance, focuses primarily on individual defendants and their "state of mind" and largely ignores situational forces. The Model Penal Code states: "A person is not guilty of an offense unless his liability is based on conduct that includes a voluntary act or the omission to perform an act of which he is physically capable." As my own experiment revealed, and as a great deal of social-psychological research before and since has confirmed, we humans exaggerate the extent to which our actions are voluntary and rationally chosen—or, put differently, we all understate the power of the situation. My claim is not that individuals are incapable of criminal culpability; rather, it is that, like the horrible behavior brought out by my experiment in good, normal young men, the situation and the system creating it also must share in the responsibility for illegal and immoral behavior.

If the goals of the criminal system are simply to blame and punish individual perpetrators—to get our pound of flesh—then focusing almost exclusively on the individual defendant makes sense. If, however, the goal is actually to reduce the behavior that we now call "criminal" (and its resultant suffering), and to assign punishments that correspond with culpability, then the criminal-justice system is obligated, much as I was in the Stanford prison experiment, to confront the situation and our role in creating and perpetuating it. It is clear to most reasonable observers that the social experiment of imprisoning society's criminals for long terms is a failure on virtually all levels. By recognizing the situational determinants of behavior, we can move to a more productive public-health model of prevention and intervention, and away from the individualistic medical and religious "sin" model that has never worked since its inception during the Inquisition.

The critical message then is to be sensitive about our vulnerability to subtle but powerful situational forces and, by such awareness, be more able to overcome those forces. Group pressures, authority symbols, dehumanization of others, imposed anonymity, dominant ideologies that enable spurious ends to justify immoral means, lack of surveillance, and other situational forces can work to transform even some of the best of us into Mr. Hyde monsters, without the benefit of Dr. Jekyll's chemical elixir. We must be more aware of how situational variables can influence our behavior. Further, we must also be aware that veiled behind the power of the situation is the greater power of the system, which creates and maintains complicity at the highest military and governmental levels—with evil-inducing situations, like those at Abu Ghraib and Guantánamo Bay prisons.

CRITICAL THINKING QUESTIONS

1. What are the main implications of the Stanford prison experiment? Could anyone, including you, be induced to act in the same way as the prisoners or guards if put into the same situation? Do personality and perhaps free will really have nothing to do with how someone will act in such situations? Or is free will not really possible in such situations? Support your answers.

2. If bad behaviors can be induced by the techniques described in this article, does that mean that people should not be held responsible for the things they do? Would a defense of "It was the situation that made me do it" absolve an individual of personal responsibility for his or her actions? Explain your responses.

3. The article seems to suggest that given the right (or rather wrong) situation, it is fairly easy to bring out the worst in people. How could you prevent these negative effects? For example, would educating people about what happened in the Stanford prison experiment lessen the likelihood that such behaviors would recur in the future? Discuss.

4. Discuss the ethical issues surrounding the Stanford prison experiment.

5. As stated in the article, "The goals of the criminal justice system are simply to blame and punish individual perpetrators." Furthermore, "By recognizing the situational determinants of behavior, we can move to a more productive public-health model of prevention and intervention." Based on your understanding of the article, how might society and the criminal justice system be changed to address situational influences? Or is the focus on punishing individual perpetrators appropriate? Defend your position.

ARTICLE 26 _____

Stanley Milgram's article "Behavioral Study of Obedience" was one of his first describing a series of studies investigating the conditions that produce obedience to authority. This study, as well as Milgram's subsequent research, is truly classic. In fact, if you asked someone who has had only minimal exposure to the field of social psychology about landmark research, this study would perhaps come to mind.

Part of the widespread interest in Milgram's work is due to the implications it has. Basically, Milgram took a group of male volunteers from various backgrounds and ages and induced them to perform acts that appeared to harm another person. Nearly two-thirds of the subjects were fully obedient, continuing to give shocks even though it was apparent that they were harming the victim. Does that mean that just about anyone could be made to do the same? More importantly, while reading the article, keep in mind the actual situation confronting the subjects: What would have happened to them if they had refused to obey? Would the effect demonstrated by Milgram be greater for real-life situations, where there might be punishments for failing to obey?

Besides the implications of the research, Milgram's work on obedience also has attracted considerable interest over the years because of the ethical issues raised. When reading the article, try to put yourself in the shoes of the subjects: How would you feel if you volunteered for a study on learning and instead walked out of the experiment an hour later with the realization that you were willing to harm someone just because an authority figure told you to do so? Think about the ethical issues involved in the study, including the issue of debriefing subjects following an experiment.

Behavioral Study of Obedience
■ Stanley Milgram

This chapter describes a procedure for the study of destructive obedience in the laboratory. It consists of ordering a naive S to administer increasingly more severe punishment to a victim in the context of a learning experiment. Punishment is administered by means of a shock generator with thirty graded switches ranging from Slight Shock to Danger: Severe Shock. The victim is a confederate of the E. The primary dependent variable is the maximum shock the S is willing to administer before he refuses to continue further. Twenty-six Ss obeyed the experimental commands fully, and administered the highest shock on the generator. Fourteen Ss broke off the experiment at some point after the victim protested and refused to provide further answers. The procedure created extreme levels of nervous tension in some Ss. Profuse sweating, *trembling and stuttering were typical expressions of this emotional disturbance. One unexpected sign of tension—yet to be explained—was the regular occurrence of nervous laughter, which in some Ss developed into uncontrollable seizures. The variety of interesting behavioral dynamics observed in the experiment, the reality of the situation for the S, and the possibility of parametric variation within the framework of the procedure, point to the fruitfulness of further study.*

Obedience is as basic an element in the structure of social life as one can point to. Some system of authority is a requirement of all communal living, and it is only the man dwelling in isolation who is not forced to respond, through defiance or submission, to the

Reprinted from *Journal of Abnormal and Social Psychology,* 1963, *67,* 371–378. Copyright renewed 1991 by Alexandra Milgram. All rights reserved. Reprinted by permission.

commands of others. Obedience, as a determinant of behavior, is of particular relevance to our time. It has been reliably established that from 1933–1945 millions of innocent persons were systematically slaughtered on command. Gas chambers were built, death camps were guarded, daily quotas of corpses were produced with the same efficiency as the manufacture of appliances. These inhumane policies may have originated in the mind of a single person, but they could only be carried out on a massive scale if a very large number of persons obeyed orders.

Obedience is the psychological mechanism that links individual action to political purpose. It is the dispositional cement that binds men to systems of authority. Facts of recent history and observation in daily life suggest that for many persons obedience may be a deeply ingrained behavior tendency, indeed, a prepotent impulse overriding training in ethics, sympathy, and moral conduct. C. P. Snow (1961) points to its importance when he writes:

> When you think of the long and gloomy history of man, you will find more hideous crimes have been committed in the name of obedience than have ever been committed in the name of rebellion. If you doubt that, read William Shirer's "Rise and Fall of the Third Reich." The German Officer Corps were brought up in the most rigorous code of obedience . . . in the name of obedience they were party to, and assisted in, the most wicked large scale actions in the history of the world. (p. 24)

While the particular form of obedience dealt with in the present study has its antecedents in these episodes, it must not be thought all obedience entails acts of aggression against others. Obedience serves numerous productive functions. Indeed, the very life of society is predicated on its existence. Obedience may be ennobling and educative and refer to acts of charity and kindness, as well as to destruction.

GENERAL PROCEDURE

A procedure was devised which seems useful as a tool for studying obedience (Milgram, 1961). It consists of ordering a naive subject to administer electric shock to a victim. A simulated shock generator is used, with 30 clearly marked voltage levels that range

from 15 to 450 volts. The instrument bears verbal designations that range from Slight Shock to Danger: Severe Shock. The responses of the victim, who is a trained confederate of the experimenter, are standardized. The orders to administer shocks are given to the naive subject in the context of a "learning experiment" ostensibly set up to study the effects of punishment on memory. As the experiment proceeds the naive subject is commanded to administer increasingly more intense shocks to the victim, even to the point of reaching the level marked Danger: Severe Shock. Internal resistances become stronger, and at a certain point the subject refuses to go on with the experiment. Behavior prior to this rupture is considered "obedience," in that the subject complies with the commands of the experimenter. The point of rupture is the act of disobedience. A quantitative value is assigned to the subject's performance based on the maximum intensity shock he is willing to administer before he refuses to participate further. Thus for any particular subject and for any particular experimental condition the degree of obedience may be specified with a numerical value. The crux of the study is to systematically vary the factors believed to alter the degree of obedience to the experimental commands.

The technique allows important variables to be manipulated at several points in the experiment. One may vary aspects of the source of command, content and form of command, instrumentalities for its execution, target object, general social setting, etc. The problem, therefore, is not one of designing increasingly more numerous experimental conditions, but of selecting those that best illuminate the process of obedience from the sociopsychological standpoint.

RELATED STUDIES

The inquiry bears an important relation to philosophic analyses of obedience and authority (Arendt, 1958; Friedrich, 1958; Weber, 1947), an early experimental study of obedience by Frank (1944), studies in "authoritarianism" (Adorno, Frenkel-Brunswik, Levinson, and Sanford, 1950; Rokeach, 1961), and a recent series of analytic and empirical studies in social power (Cartwright, 1959). It owes much to the long concern with *suggestion* in social psychology, both in its normal forms (e.g., Binet, 1900) and in its clinical manifestations (Charcot, 1881). But it derives, in the first instance, from direct observation of a social fact; the individual who is commanded by a legitimate authority ordinarily obeys. Obedience comes easily and often. It is a ubiquitous and indispensable feature of social life.

METHOD

Subjects

The subjects were 40 males between the ages of 20 and 50, drawn from New Haven and the surrounding communities. Subjects were obtained by a newspaper advertisement and direct mail solicitation. Those who responded to the appeal believed they were to participate in a study of memory and learning at Yale University. A wide range of occupations is represented in the sample. Typical subjects were postal clerks, high school teachers, salesmen, engineers, and laborers. Subjects ranged in educational level from one who had not finished elementary school, to those who had doctorate and other professional degrees. They were paid $4.50 for their participation in the experiment. However, subjects were told that payment was simply for coming to the laboratory, and that the money was theirs no matter what happened after they arrived. Table 1 shows the proportion of age and occupational types assigned to the experimental condition.

Personnel and Locale

The experiment was conducted on the grounds of Yale University in the elegant interaction laboratory. (This detail is relevant to the perceived legitimacy of the experiment. In further variations, the experiment was dissociated from the university, with consequences for performance.) The role of experimenter was played by a 31-year-old high school teacher of biology. His manner was impassive, and his appearance somewhat stern throughout the experiment. He was dressed in a gray technician's coat. The victim was played by a 47-year-old accountant, trained for the role; he was of Irish-American stock, whom most observers found mild-mannered and likable.

Procedure

One naive subject and one victim (an accomplice) performed in each experiment. A pretext had to be devised that would justify the administration of electric shock by the naive subject. This was effectively accomplished by the cover story. After a general introduction on the presumed relation between punishment and learning, subjects were told:

> But actually, we know very little *about the effect of punishment on learning,* because almost no truly scientific studies have been made of it in human beings.
>
> For instance, we don't know how much *punishment is best for learning—and we don't know how much difference it makes as to who is giving the punishment, whether an adult learns best from a younger or an older person than himself—or many things of that sort.*
>
> So in this study we are bringing together a number of adults of different occupations and ages. And

TABLE 1 / Distribution of Age and Occupational Types in the Experiment

Occupations	20–29 Years *n*	30–39 Years *n*	40–50 Years *n*	Percentage of Total (Occupations)
Workers, skilled and unskilled	4	5	6	37.5
Sales, business, and white-collar	3	6	7	40.0
Professional	1	5	3	22.5
Percentage of total (age)	20	40	40	

Note: Total *n* = 40.

we're asking some of them to be teachers and some of them to be learners.

We want to find out just what effect different people have on each other as teachers and learners, and also what effect punishment will have on learning in this situation.

Therefore, I'm going to ask one of you to be the teacher here tonight and the other one to be the learner.

Does either of you have a preference?

Subjects then drew slips of paper from a hat to determine who would be the teacher and who would be the learner in the experiment. The drawing was rigged so that the naive subject was always the teacher and the accomplice always the learner. (Both slips contained the word "Teacher.") Immediately after the drawing the teacher and learner were taken to an adjacent room and the learner was strapped into an "electric chair" apparatus.

The experimenter explained that the straps were to prevent excessive movement while the learner was being shocked. The effect was to make it impossible for him to escape from the situation. An electrode was attached to the learner's wrist, and electrode paste was applied "to avoid blisters and burns." Subjects were told that the electrode was attached to the shock generator in the adjoining room.

In order to improve credibility the experimenter declared, in response to a question by the learner: "Although the shocks can be extremely painful, they cause no permanent tissue damage."

Learning Task The lesson administered by the subject was a paired-associate learning task. The subject read a series of word pairs to the learner, and then read the first word of the pair along with four terms. The learner was to indicate which of the four terms had originally been paired with the first word. He communicated his answer by pressing one of four switches in front of him, which in turn lit up one of four numbered quadrants in an answer-box located atop the shock generator.

Shock Generator The instrument panel consists of 30 lever switches set in a horizontal line. Each switch is clearly labeled with a voltage designation that ranges from 15 to 450 volts. There is a 15-volt incre-

ment from one switch to the next going from left to right. In addition, the following verbal designations are clearly indicated for groups of four switches going from left to right: Slight Shock, Moderate Shock, Strong Shock, Very Strong Shock, Intense Shock, Extreme Intensity Shock, Danger: Severe Shock. (Two switches after this last designation are simply marked XXX.)

Upon depressing a switch: a pilot light corresponding to each switch is illuminated in bright red; an electric buzzing is heard; an electric blue light, labeled "voltage energizer," flashes; the dial on the voltage meter swings to the right; various relay clicks are sounded.

The upper left-hand corner of the generator is labeled Shock Generator, Type ZLB, Dyson Instrument Company, Waltham, Mass. Output 15 Volts–450 Volts.

Details of the instrument were carefully handled to insure an appearance of authenticity. The panel was engraved by precision industrial engravers, and all components were of high quality. No subject in the experiment suspected that the instrument was merely a simulated shock generator.[1]

Sample Shock Each naive subject is given a sample shock on the shock generator, prior to beginning his run as teacher. This shock is always 45 volts, and is applied by pressing the third switch of the generator. The shock is applied to the wrist of the naive subject, and has its source in a 45-volt battery wired into the generator. This further convinces the subject of the authenticity of the generator.

Shock Instructions The subject is told to administer a shock to the learner each time he gives a wrong response. Moreover—and this is the key command—the subject is instructed to "move one lever higher on the shock generator each time the learner flashes a wrong answer." He is also instructed to announce the voltage level before administering a shock. This serves to continually remind subjects of the increasing intensity of shocks administered to the learner.

Preliminary and Regular Run Pretests revealed that the procedure of reading words and administering shocks requires some practice before it can be handled smoothly. Therefore, immediately preceding the regular run, the teacher is given a preliminary series of 10 words to read to the learner. There are 3 neutral words in the practice series (i.e., words that the learner answers correctly), so that shocks are administered for 7 of the words, with the maximum shock at 105 volts (moderate shock). Almost all subjects master the procedure by the time the preliminary run is over.

Subjects are then presented with a second list, and are told that the procedure is the same as for the first list; the experimenter adds, however:

When you get to the bottom of the list, repeat it over again, and continue giving shocks, until the learner has learned all the pairs correctly.

The experimenter instructs the subject to

start from 15 volts and increase the shock level one step each time the learner gives a wrong answer.

Feedback from the Victim   In all conditions the learner gives a predetermined set of responses to the word pair test, based on a schedule of approximately three wrong answers to one correct answer. In the present experimental condition no vocal response or other sign of protest is heard from the learner until Shock Level 300 is reached. When the 300-volt shock is administered, the learner pounds on the wall of the room in which he is bound to the electric chair. The pounding can be heard by the subject. From this point on, the learner's answers no longer appear on the four-way panel.

At this juncture, subjects ordinarily turn to the experimenter for guidance. The experimenter instructs the subject to treat the absence of a response as a wrong answer, and to shock the subject according to the usual schedule. He advises the subjects to allow 5–10 seconds before considering no response as a wrong answer, and to increase the shock level one step each time the learner fails to respond correctly. The learner's pounding is repeated after the 315-volt shock is administered; afterwards he is not heard from, nor do his answers reappear on the four-way signal box.

Experimenter Feedback   At various points in the experiment the subject may turn to the experi-

menter for advice on whether he should continue to administer shocks. Or he may indicate that he does not wish to go on. It was important to standardize the experimenter's responses to these inquiries and reactions.

If the subject indicated his unwillingness to go on, the experimenter responded with a sequence of "prods," using as many as necessary to bring the subject into line.

Prod 1: Please continue or Please go on.
Prod 2: The experiment requires that you continue.
Prod 3: It is absolutely essential that you continue.
Prod 4: You have no other choice, you must go on.

The prods were always made in sequence: Only if Prod 1 had been unsuccessful, could Prod 2 be used. If the subject refused to obey the experimenter after Prod 4, the experiment was terminated. The experimenter's tone of voice was at all times firm, but not impolite. The sequence was begun anew on each occasion that the subject balked or showed reluctance to follow orders.

Special Prods   If the subject asked if the learner was liable to suffer permanent physical injury, the experimenter said:

Although the shocks may be painful, there is no permanent tissue damage, so please go on. [Followed by Prods 2, 3, and 4 if necessary.]

If the subject said that the learner did not want to go on, the experimenter replied:

Whether the learner likes it or not, you must go on until he has learned all the word pairs correctly. So please go on. [Followed by Prods 2, 3, and 4 if necessary.]

Dependent Measures

The primary dependent measure for any subject is the maximum shock he administers before he refuses to go any further. In principle this may vary from 0 (for a subject who refuses to administer even the first shock) to 30 (for a subject who administers the highest shock on the generator). A subject who breaks off the experiment at any point prior to administering the thirtieth shock level is termed a *defiant* subject. One who complies with experimental commands fully, and proceeds to administer all shock levels commanded, is termed an *obedient* subject.

Further Records With few exceptions, experimental sessions were recorded on magnetic tape. Occasional photographs were taken through one-way mirrors. Notes were kept on any unusual behavior occurring during the course of the experiments. On occasion, additional observers were directed to write objective descriptions of the subjects' behavior. The latency and duration of shocks were measured by accurate timing devices.

Interview and Dehoax Following the experiment, subjects were interviewed; open-ended questions, projective measures, and attitude scales were employed. After the interview, procedures were undertaken to assure that the subject would leave the laboratory in a state of well being. A friendly reconciliation was arranged between the subject and the victim, and an effort was made to reduce any tensions that arose as a result of the experiment.

RESULTS

Preliminary Notions

Before giving an account of the experimental results, it is instructive to consider how persons predict others will perform when commanded to administer powerful shocks to another person. Fourteen Yale seniors, all psychology majors, were provided with a detailed description of the experimental situation. They were asked to reflect carefully on it, and to predict the behavior of 100 hypothetical subjects. More specifically, they were instructed to plot the distribution of obedience of "100 Americans of diverse occupations, and ranging in age from 20 to 50 years," who were placed in the experimental situation.

There was considerable agreement among the respondents on the expected behavior of hypothetical subjects. All respondents predicted that only an insignificant minority would go through to the end of the shock series. (The estimates ranged from 0 to 3 percent; i.e., the most "pessimistic" member of the class predicted that of 100 persons, 3 would continue through to the most potent shock available on the shock generator—450 volts.) The class mean was 1.2

percent. The question was also posed informally to colleagues of the author, and the most general feeling was that few if any subjects would go beyond the designation Very Strong Shock.

Result of Experiment 1

Subjects Accept Situation With few exceptions subjects were convinced of the reality of the experimental situation, that they were administering shocks to another person, and the most potent shocks were extremely painful. In the post-experimental interview subjects were asked: "How painful to the learner were the last few shocks that you administered to him?" Subjects were instructed to indicate their answers on a printed 14-point scale ranging from "Not at all painful" to "Extremely painful." The modal response was 14 (Extremely painful) with the mean at 13.42.

Signs of Extreme Tension Many subjects showed signs of nervousness in the experimental situation, and especially upon administering the more powerful shocks. In a large number of cases the degree of tension reached extremes that are rarely seen in sociopsychological laboratory studies. Subjects were observed to sweat, tremble, stutter, bite their lips, groan, and dig their fingernails into their flesh. These were characteristic rather than exceptional responses to the experiment.

One sign of tension was the regular occurrence of nervous laughing fits. Fourteen of the 40 subjects showed definite signs of nervous laughter and smiling. The laughter seemed entirely out of place, even bizarre. Full-blown, uncontrollable seizures were observed for 3 subjects. On one occasion we observed a seizure so violently convulsive that it was necessary to call a halt to the experiment. The subject, a 46-year-old encyclopedia salesman, was seriously embarrassed by his untoward and uncontrollable behavior. In the post-experimental interviews subjects took pains to point out that they were not sadistic types, and that the laughter did not mean they enjoyed shocking the victim.

Distribution of Scores It had been conjectured that persons would not, in general, agree to administer shocks beyond the level designated as Very Strong

Shock. The distribution of maximum shocks for this experiment is shown in Table 2. The obtained distribution of scores deviates radically from the prediction.

Upon command of the experimenter, each of the 40 subjects went beyond the expected breakoff point. No subject stopped prior to administering Shock Level 20. (At this level—300 volts—the victim kicks on the wall and no longer provides answers to the teacher's multiple-choice questions.)

Of the 40 subjects, 5 refused to obey the experimental commands beyond the 300-volt level. Four more subjects administered one further shock, and then refused to go on. Two broke off at the 330-volt level, and 1 each at 345, 360, and 375 volts. Thus a total of 14 subjects defied the experimenter. It is instructive to reprint their remarks at the point of defiance, as transcribed from the tape recordings:

> [0124] *I think he's trying to communicate, he's knocking . . . Well it's not fair to shock the guy . . . these are terrific volts. I don't think this is very humane . . . Oh, I can't go on with this; no, this isn't right. It's a hell of an experiment. The guy is suffering in there. No, I don't want to go on. This is crazy. [Subject refused to administer more shocks.]*

> [0123] *He's hanging in there. I'm gonna chicken out. I'd like to continue, but I can't do that to a man . . . I'm sorry I can't do that to a man. I'll hurt his heart. You take your check . . . No really, I couldn't do it.*

These subjects were frequently in a highly agitated and even angered state. Sometimes, verbal protest was at a minimum, and the subject simply got up from his chair in front of the shock generator, and indicated that he wished to leave the laboratory.

Of the 40 subjects, 26 obeyed the orders of the experimenter to the end, proceeding to punish the victim until they reached the most potent shock available on the shock generator. At that point, the experimenter called a halt to the session. (The maximum shock is labeled 450 volts, and is two steps beyond the designation: Danger: Severe Shock.) Although obedient subjects continued to administer shocks, they often did so under extreme stress. Some expressed reluctance to administer shocks beyond the 300-volt level, and displayed fears similar to those who defied the experimenter; yet they obeyed.

TABLE 2 / Distribution of Breakoff Points

Verbal Designation and Voltage Indication	Number of Subjects for Whom This Was Maximum Shock
Slight Shock	
15	
30	0
45	0
60	0
Moderate Shock	
75	0
90	0
105	0
120	0
Strong Shock	
135	0
150	0
165	0
180	0
Very Strong Shock	
195	0
210	0
225	0
240	0
Intense Shock	
255	0
270	0
285	0
300	5
Extreme Intensity Shock	
315	4
330	2
345	1
360	1
Danger: Severe Shock	
375	1
390	0
405	0
420	0
XXX	
435	0
450	26

After the maximum shocks had been delivered, and the experimenter called a halt to the proceedings, many obedient subjects heaved sighs of relief, mopped their brows, rubbed their fingers over their eyes, or nervously fumbled cigarettes. Some shook their heads, apparently in regret. Some subjects had remained calm throughout the experiment, and displayed only minimal signs of tension from beginning to end.

DISCUSSION

The experiment yielded two findings that were surprising. The first finding concerns the sheer strength of obedient tendencies manifested in this situation. Subjects have learned from childhood that it is a fundamental breach of moral conduct to hurt another person against his will. Yet, 26 subjects abandon this tenet in following the instructions of an authority who has no special powers to enforce his commands. To disobey would bring no material loss to the subject; no punishment would ensue. It is clear from the remarks and outward behavior of many participants that in punishing the victim they are often acting against their own values. Subjects often expressed deep disapproval of shocking a man in the face of his objections, and others denounced it as stupid and senseless. Yet the majority complied with the experimental commands. This outcome was surprising from two perspectives: first, from the standpoint of predictions made in the questionnaire described earlier. (Here, however, it is possible that the remoteness of the respondents from the actual situation, and the difficulty of conveying to them the concrete details of the experiment, could account for the serious underestimation of obedience.)

But the results were also unexpected to persons who observed the experiment in progress, through one-way mirrors. Observers often uttered expressions of disbelief upon seeing a subject administer more powerful shocks to the victim. These persons had a full acquaintance with the details of the situation, and yet systematically underestimated the amount of obedience that subjects would display.

The second unanticipated effect was the extraordinary tension generated by the procedures. One might suppose that a subject would simply break off or continue as his conscience dictated. Yet, this is very far from what happened. There were striking reactions of tension and emotional strain. One observer related:

I observed a mature and initially poised businessman enter the laboratory smiling and confident. Within 20 minutes he was reduced to a twitching, stuttering wreck, who was rapidly approaching a point of nervous collapse. He constantly pulled on his earlobe, and twisted his hands. At one point he pushed his fist into his forehead and muttered: "Oh God, let's stop it." And yet he continued to respond to every word of the experimenter and obeyed to the end.

Any understanding of the phenomenon of obedience must rest on an analysis of the particular conditions in which it occurs. The following features of the experiment go some distance in explaining the high amount of obedience observed in the situation.

1. The experiment is sponsored by and takes place on the grounds of an institution of unimpeachable reputation, Yale University. It may be reasonably presumed that the personnel are competent and reputable. The importance of this background authority is now being studied by conducting a series of experiments outside of New Haven, and without any visible ties to the university.

2. The experiment is, on the face of it, designed to attain a worthy purpose—advancement of knowledge about learning and memory. Obedience occurs not as an end in itself, but as an instrumental element in a situation that the subject construes as significant, and meaningful. He may not be able to see its full significance, but he may properly assume that the experimenter does.

3. The subject perceives that the victim has voluntarily submitted to the authority system of the experimenter. He is not (at first) an unwilling captive impressed for involuntary service. He has taken the trouble to come to the laboratory presumably to aid the experimental research. That he later becomes an involuntary subject does not alter the fact that, initially, he consented to participate without qualification. Thus he has in some degree incurred an obligation toward the experimenter.

4. The subject, too, has entered the experiment voluntarily, and perceives himself under obligation to aid the experimenter. He has made a commitment, and to disrupt the experiment is a repudiation of this initial promise of aid.

5. Certain features of the procedure strengthen the subject's sense of obligation to the experimenter.

For one, he has been paid for coming to the laboratory. In part this is canceled out by the experimenter's statement that:

Of course, as in all experiments, the money is yours simply for coming to the laboratory. From this point on, no matter what happens, the money is yours.[2]

6. From the subject's standpoint, the fact that he is the teacher and the other man the learner is purely a chance consequence (it is determined by drawing lots) and he, the subject, ran the same risk as the other man in being assigned the role of learner. Since the assignment of positions in the experiment was achieved by fair means, the learner is deprived of any basis of complaint on this count. (A similar situation obtains in Army units, in which—in the absence of volunteers—a particularly dangerous mission may be assigned by drawing lots, and the unlucky soldier is expected to bear his misfortune with sportsmanship.)

7. There is, at best, ambiguity with regard to the prerogatives of a psychologist and the corresponding rights of his subject. There is a vagueness of expectation concerning what a psychologist may require of his subject, and when he is overstepping acceptable limits. Moreover, the experiment occurs in a closed setting, and thus provides no opportunity for the subject to remove these ambiguities by discussion with others. There are few standards that seem directly applicable to the situation, which is a novel one for most subjects.

8. The subjects are assured that the shocks administered to the subject are "painful but not dangerous." Thus they assume that the discomfort caused the victim is momentary, while the scientific gains resulting from the experiment are enduring.

9. Through Shock Level 20 the victim continues to provide answers on the signal box. The subject may construe this as a sign that the victim is still willing to "play the game." It is only after Shock Level 20 that the victim repudiates the rules completely, refusing to answer further.

These features help to explain the high amount of obedience obtained in this experiment. Many of the arguments raised need not remain matters of speculation, but can be reduced to testable propositions to be confirmed or disproved by further experiments.[3]

The following features of the experiment concern the nature of the conflict which the subject faces.

10. The subject is placed in a position in which he must respond to the competing demands of two persons: the experimenter and the victim. The conflict must be resolved by meeting the demands of one or the other; satisfaction of the victim and the experimenter are mutually exclusive. Moreover, the resolution must take the form of a highly visible action, that of continuing to shock the victim or breaking off the experiment. Thus the subject is forced into a public conflict that does not permit any completely satisfactory solution.

11. While the demands of the experimenter carry the weight of scientific authority, the demands of the victim spring from his personal experience of pain and suffering. The two claims need not be regarded as equally pressing and legitimate. The experimenter seeks an abstract scientific datum; the victim cries out for relief from physical suffering caused by the subject's actions.

12. The experiment gives the subject little time for reflection. The conflict comes on rapidly. It is only minutes after the subject has been seated before the shock generator that the victim begins his protests. Moreover, the subject perceives that he has gone through but two-thirds of the shock levels at the time the subject's first protests are heard. Thus he understands that the conflict will have a persistent aspect to it, and may well become more intense as increasingly more powerful shocks are required. The rapidity with which the conflict descends on the subject, and his realization that it is predictably recurrent may well be sources of tension to him.

13. At a more general level, the conflict stems from the opposition of two deeply ingrained behavior dispositions: first, the disposition not to harm other people, and second, the tendency to obey those whom we perceive to be legitimate authorities.

REFERENCES

Adorno, T., Frenkel-Brunswik, Else, Levinson, D. J., and Sanford, R. N. *The authoritarian personality.* New York: Harper, 1950.

Arendt, H. What was authority? In C. J Friedrich (ed.), *Authority.* Cambridge: Harvard Univer. Press, 1958. Pp. 81–112.

Binet, A. *La suggestibilité.* Paris: Schleicher, 1900.

Buss, A. H. *The psychology of aggression.* New York: Wiley, 1961.

Cartwright, S. (ed.) *Studies in social power.* Ann Arbor: University of Michigan Institute for Social Research, 1959.

Charcot, J. M. *Oeuvres complètes.* Paris: Bureaux du Progrès Médical, 1881.

Frank, J. D. Experimental studies of personal pressure and resistance. *J. Gen. Psychol.* 1944, *30,* 23–64.

Freidrich, C. J. (ed.) *Authority.* Cambridge: Harvard Univer. Press, 1958.

Milgram, S. Dynamics of obedience. Washington: National Science Foundation, 25 January 1961. (Mimeo).

Milgram, S. Some conditions of obedience and disobedience to authority. *Hum. Relat.,* 1965, *18,* 57–76.

Rokeach, M. Authority, authoritarianism, and conformity. In I. A. Berg and B. M. Bass (eds.), *Conformity and deviation.* New York: Harper, 1961. Pp. 230–257.

Snow, C. P. Either-or. *Progressive,* 1961 (Feb.) 24.

Weber, M. *The theory of social and economic organization.* Oxford: Oxford Univer. Press, 1947.

ENDNOTES

1. A related technique, making use of a shock generator, was reported by Buss (1961) for the study of aggression in the laboratory. Despite the considerable similarity of technical detail in the experimental procedures, each investigator proceeded in ignorance of the other's work. Milgram provided plans and photographs of his shock generator, experimental procedure, and first results in a report to the National Science Foundation in January 1961. This report received only limited circulation. Buss reported his procedure six months later, but to a wider audience. Subsequently, technical information and reports were exchanged. The present article was first received in the editor's office on December 27, 1961; it was resubmitted with deletions on July 27, 1962.

2. Forty-three subjects, undergraduates at Yale University, were run in the experiment without payment. The results are very similar to those obtained with paid subjects.

3. A series of recently completed experiments employing the obedience paradigm is reported in Milgram (1965).

This research was supported by a grant (NSF G-17916) from the National Science Foundation. Exploratory studies conducted in 1960 were supported by a grant from the Higgins Fund at Yale University. The research assistance of Alan E. Elms and Jon Wayland is gratefully acknowledged.

CRITICAL THINKING QUESTIONS

1. What are the ethical implications of this study? In particular, are you satisfied that no lasting harm was done to the participants? Would the debriefing at the end of the experiment be sufficient to eliminate any long-term problems from participation in the study? What about short-term effects? Many of the subjects obviously suffered during the experiment. Was the infliction of this distress on the subjects justified? Support your answers. (*Note:* For a good discussion of the ethics of the study, see the Baumrind and Milgram articles cited below.)

2. What are the implications of this study for people accused of committing atrocities? Suppose that the results of this study had been known when the Nazi war criminals were put on trial in Nuremberg. Could the information have been used in their defense? Do the results remove some of the personal responsibility that people have for their actions? Explain your answers.

3. Subjects were paid a nominal amount for participation in the study. They were told that the money was theirs to keep simply because they showed up, regardless of what happened after they arrived. Do you think that this payment was partly responsible for the findings? Why or why not? Do you think that paying someone, no matter how small the amount, somehow changes the dynamics of the situation? Explain.

ADDITIONAL RELATED READINGS

Baumrind, D. (1964). Some thoughts on ethics of research after reading Milgram's "Behavioral study of obedience." *American Psychologist, 19,* 421–423.

Mastroianni, G. E. (2002). Milgram and the Holocaust: A reexamination. *Theoretical and Philosophical Psychology, 22*(2), 158–173.

Milgram, S. (1964). Issues in the study of obedience: A reply to Baumrind. *American Psychologist, 19,* 848–852.

ARTICLE 27

Conformity is a fact of life yet a behavior toward which we have decidedly ambivalent feelings. On the one hand, none of us like to think of ourselves as *conformist.* For most people, this word has a fairly negative connotation, suggesting people who mindlessly go along with the group rather than thinking for themselves. Even people who see themselves as nonconformist (such as in how they dress) often are just conforming to an alternative set of norms. Perhaps the best example of this is the teenager who dyes his hair blue because he wants to be "different in a conforming sort of way."

On the other hand, conformity is the very background of culture. How could we drive our cars, engage in social interactions, or do just about anything involving other people if we did not conform to what was expected of us in those situations? Without some level of conformity, total chaos would result. Even when we feel independent in the decisions we make, in fact, our choice is not *whether* to conform but rather which norms to conform to.

So, why is conformity such a vital part of the human experience? At a very basic level, it helps to promote survival of the group. After all, people are fundamentally social creatures, and without conformity, the daily interactions that make life possible would be impossible. But people conform for other reasons, as well. One such reason may be to obtain information about an otherwise ambiguous situation. For example, if you wanted to know the distance between Washington, DC, and New York City, you could look it up in a book. That information is a *fact:* an agreed upon, accepted piece of knowledge. As such, you need only to consult the proper source to find it.

But how much of social life is about readily determinable facts? Not much. Most of the situations and questions we face are not factual but rather matters of belief, custom, or opinion. Whom should I vote for? What is the right thing to do? What is the best way to live my life? The answers to questions such as these often come from other people. Thus, another reason we conform is because other people often are able to provide us with clues for how to behave, especially when the situation is otherwise ambiguous and we are unsure of what is expected of us.

People also conform to be accepted. If you have ever deviated from the norms or beliefs of a group to which you belong, you already know the intensely uncomfortable experience of being rejected or pressured by others in the group. To be accepted by the group, we must go along with them. Thus, we sometimes conform just to be accepted and to fit into a particular group.

One of the earliest influential studies on conformity was conducted by Soloman Asch in the 1950s. In his famous *line-judgment study,* groups of subjects, which included some confederates, were presented with a line as a stimulus and asked to select which of three other lines was the same length as the stimulus line. Preceding the judgment of the subject, one or four confederate subjects would give incorrect answers. The majority of subjects went along with an obviously incorrect group answer at least once. Overall, subjects expressed agreement with the wrong group response 37% of the time.

The following article by Aldert Vrij, Helen Pannell, and James Ost examines the use of social pressure in influencing judgments. This article also examines how the color of the clothing of the confederates in the experiment affected the conforming behaviors of the subjects.

The Influence of Social Pressure and Black Clothing on Crime Judgements

■ Aldert Vrij, Helen Pannell, and James Ost

ABSTRACT

The impact of (i) social pressure and (ii) colour of clothing on participants' crime judgements were examined. A total of 49 participants participated in small groups. They were read a crime report, and answered questions aloud about this report. Unknown to them, some group members were confederates and gave incorrect answers to some of the questions. In each session either one or four confederates were present who wore either dark or light clothing. Results revealed that participants gave numerous incorrect answers, with the most incorrect answers being given when (i) there were four confederates, and (ii) the confederates wore dark clothing.

INTRODUCTION

It is now half a century ago since Asch's (1951, 1955, 1956) classic conformity experiments were published in which he convincingly demonstrated that people's beliefs affect the beliefs of others. This effect of social influence has also been empirically illustrated in eyewitness testimony research. For example, in their eyewitness identification study, Baron, Vandello, & Brunsman (1996) asked people in groups of three (two of them were confederates) to identify a culprit in a line-up. Up to 50% of the participants conformed to the confederates' incorrect identifications.

Similar effects of social influence have also been found when slide-presented scenes (Roediger, Meade, & Bergman, 2001; Walther, Bless, Strack, Rachstraw, Wagner, & Werth, 2002) or stories (Betz, Skowronski, & Ostrom, 1996) are used as stimulus materials, and when participants are asked to make reality monitoring judgements (Hoffman, Granhag, Kwong, & Loftus, 2001). These effects also appear to be robust when examined with more ecologically valid stimulus material (Gabbert, Memon, & Allan, 2003; Wright, Self, & Justice, 2000). For example, Gabbert et al. (2003) found that 71% of witnesses to a video-presented staged crime incorporated nonwitnessed details provided by a co-witness into their own account.

The present experiment also examined the impact of social influence on people's judgements and we predicted that the presence of peer confederates who give incorrect answers would lead participants to conform (hypothesis 1). There are two reasons why people conform (Deutsch & Gerard, 1955): through informational influence, when people conform because they believe others are correct in their judgements; or through normative influence, when people conform because they fear the negative social consequences of appearing deviant. Usually, informative and normative influences operate jointly (Insko, Drenan, Solomon, Smith, & Wade, 1983).[1] Informational influence is more likely to occur when the questions are difficult to answer and participants are uncertain about the correct answers. In Asch's experiments, participants were conducting an easy task and, therefore, normative influence was most likely to occur. Indeed, although some of Asch's participants admitted that they came to agree with their group's erroneous judgements, normative influence was more prevalent as very few participants gave incorrect answers in the control condition where no incorrect information was provided by confederates. Moreover, when Asch asked participants to write their answers privately, their levels of conformity dropped sharply (Deutsch & Gerard, 1955). Our participants were not asked to complete a difficult task either, although the correct answers were probably less obvious than in Asch's experiments. We also expected normative influence to be prevalent and expected relatively few incorrect answers when the social pressure was low (hypothesis 2).

We also added a factor to the design that, to date, has not been investigated in the social influence literature: the impact of the colour of clothing the confederates were wearing. Frank and Gilovich (1988) were the first researchers to demonstrate the impact of the colour of clothing on impression formation. In their experiment, referees were shown a videotape of an American football match and were asked to make judgements about the actions of the defensive team. In one version the defensive team wore a black uniform and in the other version they wore a white uniform. The offensive team wore red in both versions. Apart from the colour of the uniforms, the two versions of the football match were kept constant. Results revealed that the referees were more inclined to penalise the defensive team when it was wearing a black uniform. To explain these findings, Frank and Gilovich (1988) pointed out that the colour black has a negative connotation, and that people often associate the colour black with meanness and aggressiveness. As a result they also see more aggressiveness or more malevolent intent in the actions of players wearing black uniforms. Obviously, black clothing will not make an aggressive impression in all situations. For example, it is unlikely that vicars will make an aggressive impression when they wear their black robes, neither will a mourning group of people at a funeral be seen as aggressors when they wear black clothing. However, the effect may occur in potentially aggressive settings. For example, Vrij (1997) found that undergraduates perceived a violent act as more aggressive when the violent person wore black clothing, and Vrij and Akehurst (1997) found that a woman who reported an alleged act of sexual harassment was perceived by undergraduates as more aggressive when she wore black clothing. Based on these findings it is plausible that people may appear more dominant when they wear black clothing, and we therefore predict that participants are more inclined to conform when the confederates wear black clothing (hypothesis 3). We also investigated participants' confidence ratings in the answers

they provided. We expected them (hypothesis 4) to be most confident in the condition with the least social pressure (i.e. the one confederate, light clothing condition, see Method).

METHOD

Participants

A total of 49 undergraduate students participated (27 males and 22 females). Their average age was 20.1 years.

Procedure

Participants were recruited at the University students' union and were asked to participate in a short psychology study. Those who were willing to participate were taken to a room in the students' union. The experiment was always conducted in a group consisting of five people. Hence, in the one-confederate condition (see below) four participants took part at a time, and in the four-confederate condition (see below) only one participant took part at a time. Confederates and participants were arranged in a circle. In the four-confederate condition, the participant was given a seat immediately to the right of the experimenter with confederates occupying the remaining seats. In the one-confederate condition, the confederate sat to the left of the experimenter and the participants occupied the remaining seats. In the one-confederate condition, the confederate made sure she seated herself in the designated place before the participants seated themselves. When four confederates were present, three were already seated in the middle three seats of the circle when the participant arrived. The fourth confederate accompanied the experimenter in order to reduce demand characteristics. The fourth confederate then ensured she occupied the seat to the left of the experimenter and the participant then had only the option of sitting in the seat to the experimenter's right.

First, all group members were asked to read and sign the informed consent form (confederates filled in these forms as well to reduce demand characteristics). The experimenter then read out the following instructions:

I will now read a short passage about a fictitious crime. Afterwards I will ask eight questions about what you have heard and will ask you to answer out loud one at a time when you are asked to do so.[2] Please do not ask any questions about the passage, as the answers you give must be based only on what you have heard. Please do not comment on or discuss the details of the passage or your answers with any other group member.

The experimenter then read the following crime details aloud:

One afternoon, a man burst in a jewellery shop stealing over £1000 worth of items. The shop owner described the man as being white with blonde hair, and aged about 25 years old. He wore blue jeans and a red sweater. Shortly after the robbery, police saw a man wearing a black tracksuit running towards a bus stop. He had brown hair and was about 45 years old.

The group were then asked the eight questions with the confederate to the experimenter's left being asked first and then working around the group in a clockwise direction so that the participant(s) were always asked after all the present confederates. Following each response, participants were required to rate their confidence in their own answer on a seven-point Likert scale (1 being not confident at all, 7 being very confident). Each question was asked individually, i.e. each group member answered question 1 (including the confidence rating) before question 2 was asked. Confederates gave correct answers to questions 1, 2 and 6, and incorrect answers to the remaining four questions. The following questions were asked and the answers and confidence ratings given by the confederates are mentioned between brackets (in the four-confederate condition, all four confederates gave the same answer to each question and the same confidence ratings): (1) According to the shop owner, what colour was the thief's hair? (blonde, 6); (2) How old was the thief in the shop owner's description? (25 years, 7); (3) How much money was the stolen jewellery worth? (£500, 7); (4) Based on the information given, do you think that the man the police saw running towards the bus stop was guilty or not guilty of the robbery? (guilty, 7); (5) What did the shop owner say the thief

was wearing? (beige trousers and green sweater, 7); (6) What was the man seen running towards a bus stop wearing? (black tracksuit, 6); (7) How old was the man seen running towards a bus stop shortly after the robbery? (30 years, 6); and (8) What colour was the hair of the man seen running towards a bus stop? (black, 7).

Questions to which the correct answers were given (questions 1, 2 and 6) are further referred to as "non-conformity questions". Presented in the text is the total accuracy score in answering these questions. Hence, one correct answer produces a 33% accuracy score, three correct answers a 100% accuracy score, etc. The answer given to question 4 is further referred to as the "verdict" question. Please note that the man the police saw running towards a bus stop did not match the description given by the shop owner, so that on the basis of the available evidence the participants could not possibly reach a "guilty" verdict. The confederates gave incorrect answers to the remaining four questions (3, 5, 7 and 8), and these questions are further referred to as "conformity questions". Presented in the text is the total accuracy score in answering these questions, and therefore, one correct answer produces a 25% accuracy score, four correct answers a 100% accuracy score, etc.

Independent Variables

There were three independent variables introduced in the experiment. The type of questions (conformity and non-conformity questions) has already been introduced above. Social pressure was manipulated with varying the number of confederates present in each group. In the low pressure condition one confederate was present and in the high pressure condition four confederates were present. All confederates were females. The third factor was the colour of clothing the confederates were wearing. They either wore dark clothing (further referred to as "black") or light clothing (further referred to as "white").

RESULTS

Although the suspect could not be found guilty on the basis of the available evidence, 30% of the

TABLE I / Guilty Verdicts and Accuracy Scores per Experimental Condition

	Guilty Verdicts	Correct/Incorrect Answers to Conformity Questions		Participants Who Answered All Conformity Questions Correctly
		Correct	Incorrect	
One confederate, black clothing	42%	79%	21%	50%
One confederate, white clothing	0%	92%	8%	75%
Four confederates, black clothing	40%	41%	59%	0%
Four confederates, white clothing	56%	53%	47%	10%

participants gave a guilty verdict. Also, incorrect answers were frequently given to the remaining questions, especially to the conformity questions. In total 31%[4] of the answers given to these questions were incorrect, and 61%[5] of the participants gave at least one incorrect answer to a conformity question. Table I provides a breakdown of the results as a function of experimental conditions. The guilty verdicts varied per condition and ranged from 0% (in the one confederate, white clothing condition) to 56% in the four confederates, white clothing condition. The percentage of incorrect answers given to the conformity questions was lowest in the one confederate, white clothing condition (92% correct and 8% incorrect answers) and highest in the four confederates, black clothing condition (41% correct and 59% incorrect answers). The majority of participants (75%) gave correct answers to all conformity questions in the one confederate, white clothing condition, whereas none of the participants answered all answers correctly in the four confederates, black clothing condition.

Guilty Verdicts[6]

In order to test the influence of clothing and social pressure on guilty verdicts, a log-linear analysis was carried out with guilty verdicts, social pressure and clothing as variables. The analysis revealed one effect, a guilty verdict × social pressure effect, $\chi^2(1, n = 47) = 4.28$, $p < 0.05$. More guilty verdicts (47%)

were given in the four-confederate condition than in the one-confederate condition (18%), supporting hypothesis 1. Table I shows that in the condition with the least social pressure (one confederate, white clothing condition) all participants gave the correct, not guilty, verdict, suggesting that the guilty verdict question was easy to answer. Therefore, normative influence is the most likely explanation for the above-mentioned effect, which supports hypothesis 2. Although the clothing effect was not significant, Table I suggests that clothing did have an impact but only in the low social pressure (i.e. one confederate) condition. In the high social pressure condition (when four confederates were present), the clothing had no impact on participants' guilt judgements (40% guilty verdicts when the four confederates wore black clothing and 56% guilty verdicts when they wore white clothing, $\chi^2(1, n = 19) = 0.50$, NS. However, in the low social pressure condition, colour of clothing did have an effect with many more guilty verdicts (42%) given when the confederate wore black clothing compared to when she wore white clothing (0%), $\chi^2(1, n = 28) = 9.98$, $p < 0.01$. This partially supports hypothesis 3.

In order to examine the effects of Clothing and Social Pressure on confidence expressed in the guilty/not guilty verdicts, an ANOVA was conducted with Clothing (black vs white) and Social Pressure (one vs four confederates) as factors and confidence as dependent variable. Only one effect, the Social Pressure × Clothing interaction effect, was significant, $F(1,43)$

TABLE II / Confidence in Guilty/Not Guilty Verdicts as a Function of Social Pressure and Clothing

| | No. of Confederates | | | |
| | One | | Four | |
Clothing	M	SD	M	SD
White	6.69[b]	0.7	6.00[a]	1.4
Black	5.50[a]	1.2	6.40[ab]	0.8

Note: Only cells with a different superscript differ significantly ($p < 0.05$) from each other.

$= 6.48$, $p < 0.05$, eta^2 $= 13\%$. The interaction effect is shown in Table II. Table II reveals that the highest confidence was expressed in the one confederate, white clothing condition (the condition where all participants reached a not guilty verdict). The confidence in this cell was significantly higher than the confidence in most other cells (see Table II). This supports hypothesis 4.

Accuracy and confidence in answering conformity and nonconformity questions. In order to examine the impact of clothing and social pressure on accuracy in answering conformity and non-conformity questions, an ANOVA was carried out utilising a mixed design with Type of Question (conformity vs non-conformity), Social Pressure (one vs four confederates) and Clothing (white vs black) as factors and accuracy as dependent variable. Type of Question was a within-subjects factor and Social Pressure and Clothing were between-subjects factors. The analysis revealed three significant effects, a main Type of Question effect, $F(1,45) = 41.70$, $p < 0.01$,

eta^2 $= 48\%$; a main Social Pressure effect, $F(1,45) = 14.24$, $p < 0.01$, eta^2 $= 24\%$; and a Type of Question × Social Pressure interaction effect, $F(1,45) = 28.92$, $p < 0.01$, eta^2 $= 39\%$. Since the higher order Type of Question × Social Pressure interaction effect is more informative than the Type of Question and Social Pressure main effects, only the interaction effect will be discussed. As can be seen in Table III, social pressure only had an effect on participants' answers to the conformity questions, with a considerably lower accuracy score (46%) when four confederates were present than when one confederate was present (87% accuracy). This difference regarding the conformity questions was significant, $F(1,47) = 36.85$, $p < 0.01$, eta^2 $= 44\%$, and supports hypothesis 1. Since a high percentage of questions were answered correctly in the one-confederate condition (87%), the findings suggest that the questions were relatively easy to answer and that participants were more prone to normative influence than to informational influence. This supports hypothesis 2.

TABLE III / Accuracy of Answers to Conformity and Non-Conformity Questions as a Function of Type of Question and Social Pressure

| | Questions | | | |
| | Non-Conformity | | Conformity | |
No. of Confederates	M	SD	M	SD
One	0.90	0.2	0.87	0.2
Four	0.94	0.2	0.46	0.3

TABLE IV / Accuracy of Answers to Conformity and Non-Conformity Questions as a Function of Type of Question and Clothing

	Questions			
	Non-Conformity		Conformity	
Clothing	M	SD	M	SD
White	0.91	0.2	0.77	0.3
Black	0.93	0.2	0.61	0.3

The Type of Question × Clothing effect almost reached significance, $F(1,45) = 3.70$, $p = 0.06$, eta^2 = 8%. This effect is displayed in Table IV. Table IV shows that, similar to the significant effect regarding Social Pressure, Clothing only had an effect on participants' responses to the conformity questions. Fewer replies (61%) to these questions were correct when the confederates wore black clothing than when they wore white clothing (77%), and this difference regarding conformity questions was significant, $F(1,47) = 3.61$, $p < 0.05$, one-tailed, eta^2 = 7%.[7] This supports hypothesis 3.

In order to examine the influence of social pressure and clothing on confidence in answering the conformity and non-conformity questions, a Type of Question × Social Pressure × Clothing ANOVA was conducted with confidence as dependent variable. The analysis revealed a significant main effect for Type of Question, $F(1,45) = 4.39$, $p < 0.05$, eta^2 = 9%. Par-

ticipants expressed higher confidence ($M = 6.58$, SD = 0.5) in their answers to the non-conformity questions than in their answers to the conformity questions ($M = 6.45$, SD = 0.5). The Social Pressure × Clothing interaction effect was also significant, $F(1,45) = 4.38$, $p < 0.05$, eta^2 = 9% and is displayed in Table V. Similar to the confidence regarding guilty/not guilty verdicts, the participants in the one confederate, white clothing condition expressed most confidence overall in the replies to their questions. This supports hypothesis 4. Perhaps more interesting is the level of confidence expressed when answering conformity questions as a function of clothing and social pressure. An ANOVA with Social Pressure and Clothing as factors and the level of confidence regarding conformity questions as dependent variable revealed that, again, highest confidence was expressed in the one confederate, white clothing condition (see Table VI). Participants' confidence in this condition was significantly higher than

TABLE V / Confidence in Replies to Conformity and Non-Conformity Questions as a Function of Social Pressure and Clothing

	No. of Confederates			
	One		Four	
Clothing	M	SD	M	SD
White	6.71[b]	0.3	6.41[ab]	0.2
Black	6.35[a]	0.6	6.51[ab]	0.2

Note: Only cells with a different superscript differ significantly ($p < 0.05$) from each other.

TABLE VI / Confidence in Replies to Conformity Questions as a Function of Social Pressure and Clothing

| | No. of Confederates | | | |
| | One | | Four | |
Clothing	M	SD	M	SD
White	6.79[b]	0.3	6.27[a]	0.4
Black	6.23[a]	0.7	6.36[a]	0.3

Note: Only cells with a different superscript differ significantly ($p < 0.05$) from each other.

the confidence expressed in the other cells (see Table VI). This supports hypothesis 4.

In order to explore whether accuracy and confidence were related to each other, a Pearson correlation was conducted between participants' accuracy regarding the conformity questions and their confidence in these answers. The correlation was significant, $r(49) = 0.29$, $p < 0.05$, indicating that as accuracy increased, confidence also increased.

DISCUSSION

The experiment clearly demonstrated that crime judgements could be influenced by the opinions of others. In the condition with the least social pressure (one confederate wearing light clothing) none of the participants reached a guilty verdict, whereas in the other conditions between 40 and 56% of the participants gave guilty verdicts. These percentages are high, given the fact that a guilty verdict could not have been given on the basis of the available evidence. Guilty verdicts were more likely to occur when there were four rather than one confederate expressing guilty verdicts. The colour of clothing the confederates were wearing did have an effect as well, but only in the one-confederate condition. Guilty verdicts were more likely to occur when the single confederate wore dark clothing rather than light clothing. In the four-confederate condition the colour of clothing had no impact, suggesting that in that situation, where the participants were confronted with four group members who gave a guilty verdict prior to the participant

was asked about his/her verdict, the presence of the others overshadowed the impact of the colour of their clothing. Although the colour of clothing effect was less powerful than the number of confederates effect, we believe it is noteworthy as people are likely to be less aware of this effect. That is, observers might well be aware that an individual group member who is confronted with a group opinion will be affected by that group opinion, but they may be less aware that the colour of clothing the other group members are wearing will also have an effect on the individual's opinion.

Apart from providing guilty and not guilty verdicts, participants were also asked factual questions about the crime. The results followed the verdict pattern described above. Participants were inclined to conform to incorrect answers, particularly when they were confronted with a group of people who expressed these incorrect opinions, and particularly when these people wore dark clothing.

Despite providing these erroneous answers and unjustified guilty verdicts, there is indirect evidence that participants were at least aware that something peculiar was going on, as (i) they expressed most confidence in their answers and verdicts when the least social pressure was available (in the one confederate, light clothing condition), and (ii) accuracy at answering questions was positively correlated with confidence in these answers. However, their diminished confidence when providing incorrect responses did not prevent them from giving these incorrect responses in the first place.

There are several explanations why dark clothing may have affected the participants' judgements. Perhaps participants were reluctant to disagree with confederates in dark clothing (normative influence) or, alternatively, dark clothing enhanced the believability of the confederates (informational influence). Also, a combination of both influences could have taken place. We are reluctant to suggest that dark clothing *per se* increased the believability of the confederate. In their colour of clothing experiment, Vrij & Akehurst (1997) measured the believability of a person wearing black or light clothing and found that dark clothing did not increase believability. However, there might have been an indirect effect.[8] Perhaps wearing dark clothing would have led to higher assertiveness of the confederates, which in turn may have enhanced their believability. There is evidence that wearing dark clothing affects someone's behaviour. Frank and Gilovich (1988), for example, demonstrated that wearing dark clothing led their participants to become more aggressive. With hindsight, it is unfortunate that we did not question participants about their reasons for conforming.

Perhaps another shortcoming of the study is that, because there were no incentives for participants, they may have been poorly motivated. However, given the nature of our experimental situation, we do not believe this to be the case. Our participants knew that they had to openly express their answers in front of fellow students, and in such situations people are typically motivated to perform well (Cottrell, Wack, Sekerak, & Rittle, 1968; Baron et al., 1996). Also, motivation was likely to be the same in all four conditions of the experiment and therefore cannot account for the differences we found between these four conditions.

In summary, the present experiment demonstrated that people could be influenced when making crime judgements by (i) social pressure and (ii) the colour of the clothing other people in their group are wearing. Regarding this colour of clothing effect, we would like to stress again that the effect is situational and therefore cannot be generalised to all contexts. For example, as mentioned above, mourners at a funeral are unlikely to appear dominant when they wear black clothing. It might even be the case that in other settings where authority figures wear white clothing, such as clinical settings, white clothing will be associated with dominance.[9] Future research could examine this.

NOTES

1. Indeed, McCloskey & Zaragoza (1985) suggested that the well known "misinformation effect" might in fact be a result of similar normative/informative social influence processes (which they refer to as "misinformation acceptance"), in which participants simply give the answer that they think the researcher wants to hear (Ainsworth, 1998).

2. This answering out loud was introduced to induce social pressure on the participants. However, it is likely to have a motivational effect as well due to evaluation apprehension (Cottrell, 1968), that is, participants are likely to do their best in the presence of others who are in the position to evaluate their performance.

3. In the four-confederate condition all confederates had to be of the same sex otherwise gender would have become a confounding variable in the Social Pressure conditions, that is, single gender in the one-confederate condition, and mixed gender in the four-confederate condition.

4. In most cases (68%) where participants gave incorrect answers to conformity questions, they gave the same answer as given by the confederate(s). In the remaining cases, they answered "I don't know" (10%) or they gave an incorrect, but different, answer (22%) than the confederate(s). Since all these answers are incorrect, we treat them all as incorrect answers in the further analyses. Question 1 resulted in 25% incorrect answers, question 5 in 22% incorrect answers, and questions 7 and 8 in, respectively, 39% and 37% incorrect answers.

5. Four percent answered all four conformity questions incorrectly, 12% gave one correct answer, 25% gave two, and 20% gave three correct answers.

6. Two participants (one in the four confederates, dark clothing condition, and one in the four confederates, light clothing condition) did not give a guilty or not guilty verdict, and were therefore dropped from these analyses.

7. The effects of Peer Pressure and Clothing on answering conformity questions occurred independently from each other, as the Peer Pressure × Clothing interaction effect regarding answering conformity questions was not significant, $F(1,45) = 0.01$, NS.

8. We are grateful to an anonymous reviewer for this suggestion.

9. We are grateful to an anonymous reviewer for this suggestion.

REFERENCES

Ainsworth, P. B. (1998). *Psychology, Law and Eyewitness Testimony.* Chichester: Wiley.

Asch, S. E. (1951). Effects of group pressure upon the modification and distortion of judgments. In H. Guetzkow (Ed.), *Groups, Leadership, and Men*. Pittsburgh, PA: Carnegie Press.

Asch, S. E. (1955). Opinions and social pressure. *Scientific American, 193,* 31–35.

Asch, S. E. (1956). Studies of independence and conformity: a minority of one against a unanimous majority. *Psychological Monographs, 70,* 416.

Baron, R. S., Vandello, J. A., & Brunsman, B. (1996). The forgotten variable in conformity research: impact of task importance on social influence. *Journal of Personality and Social Psychology, 71,* 915–927.

Betz, A. L., Skowronski, J. J., & Ostrom, T. M. (1996). Shared realities: social influence and stimulus memory. *Social Cognition, 14,* 113–140.

Cottrell, N. B., Wack, D. L., Sekerak, G. J., & Rittle, R. H. (1968). Social facilitation of dominant responses by the presence of an audience and the mere presence of others. *Journal of Personality and Social Psychology, 9,* 245–250.

Deutsch, M., & Gerard, H. B. (1955). A study of normative and informational social influences upon individual judgment. *Journal of Abnormal and Social Psychology, 51,* 629–636.

Frank, M. G., & Gilovich, T. (1988). The dark side of self- and social perception: black uniforms and aggression in professional sports. *Journal of Personality and Social Psychology, 54,* 74–85.

Gabbert, F., Memon, A., & Allan, K. (2003). Memory conformity: can eyewitnesses influence each other's memories for an event? *Applied Cognitive Psychology, 17,* 533–543.

Hoffman, H. G., Granhag, P. A., Kwong See, S. T., & Loftus, E. F. (2001). Social influences on reality monitoring decisions. *Memory and Cognition, 29,* 394–404.

Insko, C. A., Drenan, S., Solomon, M. R., Smith, R., & Wade, T. J. (1983). Conformity as a function of the consistency of positive self-evaluation with being liked and being right. *Journal of Experimental Social Psychology, 19,* 341–358.

McCloskey, M., & Zaragoza, M. (1985). Misleading post-event information and memory for events: argument and evidence against memory impairment hypotheses. *Journal of Experimental Psychology (General), 114,* 1–16.

Roediger, H. L. III, Meade, M. L., & Bergman, E. T. (2001). Social contagion of memory. *Psychonomic Bulletin and Review, 8,* 365–371.

Vrij, A. (1997). Wearing black clothes: the impact of offenders' and suspects' clothing on impression formation. *Applied Cognitive Psychology, 11,* 47–53.

Vrij, A., & Akehurst, L. (1997). The existence of a black clothing stereotype: the impact of a victim's black clothing on impression formation, Psychology. *Crime & Law, 3,* 227–237.

Walther, E., Bless, H., Strack, F., Rachstraw, P., Wagner, D., & Werth, L. (2002). Conformity effects in memory as a function of group size, dissenters and uncertainty. *Applied Cognitive Psychology, 16,* 793–810.

Wright, D. B., Self, G., & Justice, C. (2000). Memory conformity: exploring misinformation effects when presented by another person. *British Journal of Psychology, 91,* 189–202.

CRITICAL THINKING QUESTIONS

1. This study found that dark clothing influenced participants' judgments. What reasons beyond those mentioned in the article may explain why that was the case? Discuss the reasons.

2. The experimenter in the Milgram obedience study (Article 26) wore a white lab coat. Do you think the levels of obedience in that study would have been even higher if the experimenter had worn black? Why or why not? In what other situations could wearing white have a greater impact on conformity and obedience than wearing black? Explain.

3. Would the results found in this study apply to real-world jury deliberations? Why or why not? Address the similarities and differences between studies such as this one and the real-world situations they are meant to address.

4. Does the incidence of conformity vary from one culture to the next? Does it vary in different age groups? Find research studies that have examined these questions, and report their findings.

5. The article suggests that the color of the clothes worn by the confederates may have influenced their subsequent behavior toward the subjects in the experiment. Do you think people's behavior is influenced by the color of the clothes they are wearing? If yes, how so? Design a study that would test your hypothesis.

CHAPTER INTEGRATION QUESTIONS

1. President John F. Kennedy said, "Conformity is the jailer of freedom and the enemy of growth," and social manners writer Emily Post said, "To do exactly as your neighbors do is the only sensible rule." These two apparently contradictory quotations pertain to *conformity,* a type of social influence process. All of the articles in this chapter concern social influence processes. How do these quotes support or contradict these articles?

2. Develop an argument as to how *both* of the preceding quotes can be applied to the articles collectively. In other words, what theme from this chapter can you use to address this question?

3. Many of the chapters in this book have direct relevance in understanding a very dark period of human history: the Holocaust. Perhaps no topic is more germane in helping us understand how such a horror came to pass than that of social influence processes. How can some of the concepts on social influence be applied to how and why the Holocaust occurred? (You can find some useful information on this topic by visiting the website of the United States Holocaust Memorial Museum at www.ushmm.org. Click on "Online Exhibitions," some of which are permanent and some of which change, to address this topic.)

Chapter Ten

PROSOCIAL BEHAVIOR

H ELP. IT IS something that we all need at some time in our lives, and hopefully, it is something that we all give to others. Dramatic examples of helping or failing to help are not hard to find in the mass media. Consider the various published accounts of people needing help yet receiving none versus those of people who risk their own lives to help strangers.

Why do people help or not help? Is helpfulness a personality trait, so that some people are simply helpful individuals who give assistance in a variety of settings? Or does it have more to do with the specific situation, so that a person who helps in one situation is not necessarily more likely to help in another? Or perhaps these two factors somehow interact with one another, so that people with a certain type of personality in a certain type of situation are more likely to help than others.

Article 28, "Helping Others, Helping Ourselves," looks at the area of volunteerism and examines the various reasons people have for giving of themselves to others. The article examines the most common motivations for helping as well as the continuing question as to whether people ever help just for the sake of helping or if there is something in it for them, such as the good feeling that comes with it.

Article 29, "From Jerusalem to Jericho," is a classic example of a study that examines both situational and personality factors as influences on helping behavior. It turns out that both factors may be operating, with situational factors determining whether people will offer help in the first place and dispositional factors determining the nature of the helping response.

Finally, Article 30, "The Effect of Smiling on Helping Behavior: Smiling and Good Samaritan Behavior," looks at how one situational factor—having someone smile at you—may have an impact on your subsequent helping behavior. Does just being exposed to a smile, even if it isn't from the person you may be helping, increase your likelihood of helping?

E 28

Why do people help one another? Is their purpose pure altruism—that is, a totally unselfish concern for others without any personal benefits? Or do people help others because, in a sense, they also are doing it for themselves?

Questions like these have driven a good deal of research in social psychology that is focused on trying to determine the basic motivations for people engaging in prosocial acts. While these questions have not been definitively answered, several theories have been suggested for why people help.

The *empathy–altruism hypothesis* proposes that helpers are motivated solely by the desire to help someone in need of assistance. At the same time, the helper may feel good about having helped. Thus, the helper is deriving some personal benefit from having done a good deed. While the primary motivation may be to help another person, there also may be the secondary gain of feeling good about acting in a prosocial manner.

Another theoretical explanation for helping behavior is the *negative state relief model.* According to this model, when we see someone in distress or in need of help, we feel bad. In order to feel better, we help them. In other words, our underlying motivation for helping is to want to feel better about ourselves.

A third explanation for prosocial behavior is provided by the *empathic joy hypothesis.* It suggests that we are motivated to help others because it feels good to have a positive impact on the lives of others. How is this approach different from that of the empathy–altruism hypothesis? The empathy–altruism hypothesis includes the desire to help people in need just for the sake of helping them, whereas the empathic joy hypothesis maintains that our helping behavior is driven only by our own desire to feel good about ourselves.

You may notice that all three theories of helping behavior include at least some element of self-motivation. The model that most closely explains helping as being motivated purely by the desire to help is the empathy–altruism hypothesis. However, even that explanation suggests the possibility that while we may be motivated to help just for the sake of helping, we can also feel good about ourselves in the process.

The following article by Lea Winerman explores some of the reasons we help—in this case, specifically why people volunteer. While the focus of the article is on volunteerism, the theoretical explanations for helping discussed in this introduction apply to it, as well.

Helping Others, Helping Ourselves

■ Lea Winerman

Like many people who generally enjoy their careers, Dan Toporek nevertheless sometimes wondered if there were something missing—something else he could be doing to contribute to global improvement and well-being.

Instead of quitting his job, though, Toporek, the vice president of corporate communications for the travel Web site Travelocity, decided to put his company's name and resources to use. He and several co-workers convinced their bosses to launch a new program called Travel for Good to promote volunteer vacations.

On such vacations—sometimes called "volun-tourism"—people spend their trip time on activities like cleaning up national parks or building houses for Habitat for Humanity. And these vacations are becoming steadily more popular. One nonprofit service vacation organizer, GlobeAware, says that its registrations have increased 33 percent since 2000. Another—Earthwatch—has seen a 40 percent increase over the past several years.

Toporek and his colleagues spent many hours outside their regular workdays putting together the Travel for Good program, which includes a Web site that provides information about GlobeAware, Earthwatch and other groups, and competitive grant awards that will provide money for Travelocity employees and customers to take service vacations. The program launched in September.

"We've gotten a lot of employees involved in running it," Toporek says. "We're really excited, so we don't mind putting in the extra time."

This kind of behavior might be admirable—but, from a psychologist's point of view, it's also puzzling. Whether it be Toporek and his colleagues spending extra hours at work, or their customers who give up relaxation time on vacation, people who volunteer are doing work that promises them no obvious personal gain and may involve significant costs.

Yet in the United States, nearly one out of three adults regularly spends some time volunteering,

according to University of Minnesota psychologist Mark Snyder, PhD, who studies volunteerism. And in this season of gifts and giving—and of New Year's resolutions—volunteering may be on even more people's minds than usual.

"When I initially started thinking about this, I was struck by how much easier it was to come up with reasons why people shouldn't volunteer than why they should," Snyder says. "It's time consuming, it's stressful, it takes time away from your job or family or leisure." What is it, he began to ask, that propels so many people to donate their time, their energy and their efforts anyway?

MULTIPLE MOTIVES

Snyder and his colleagues have been working to answer that question for more than 20 years. In the mid-1980s, he and Claremont Graduate University psychologist Allen Omoto, PhD, began studying volunteers providing care for patients with HIV/AIDS.

"These people embodied all the details of volunteering," Snyder says. "They were developing an ongoing, helping relationship with a complete stranger. And it was with the backdrop of a lot of stress—working with someone who has a serious illness."

Omoto agrees, adding, "in the context of HIV there were particularly high costs [to volunteering], because of the prejudice and discrimination at that time."

Snyder, Omoto and their colleagues eventually surveyed volunteers who did all kinds of other community work too, as well as young, middle-aged and older volunteers.

Over the years, they've identified five primary motivations for volunteering:

■ **Values.** Volunteering to satisfy personal values or humanitarian concerns. For some people this can have a religious component.

■ **Community concern.** Volunteering to help a particular community, such as a neighborhood or ethnic group, to which you feel attached.

■ **Esteem enhancement.** Volunteering to feel better about yourself or escape other pressures.

■ **Understanding.** Volunteering to gain a better understanding of other people, cultures or places.

■ **Personal development.** Volunteering to challenge yourself, meet new people and make new friends, or further your career.

Different types of volunteers have slightly different levels of these motivations, according to Snyder. Younger volunteers, for example, are more likely to volunteer for career-related reasons, while older volunteers more often cite abstract ideas of good citizenship and contributing to their communities.

Still, Snyder says, "In many ways it's the similarities across types of volunteering that are striking."

Somewhat more recently, the researchers have begun to study the factors that help organizations hold on to volunteers. For example, in one study, published in 1998 in the *Journal of Personality and Social Psychology* (Vol. 74, No. 6, pages 1516–1530), psychologist E. Gil Clary, PhD, and Snyder surveyed 61 hospital volunteers about their motivations for volunteering, and then later about their experiences as a volunteer. They found that the people whose experiences best matched their motivations were more satisfied with the experience. Those same people also said that they'd be more likely to continue volunteering.

"People have an agenda when they volunteer—and that's in the best sense of the word," says Clary. "So outcomes depend on whether an organization can fulfill the volunteer's agenda."

Interestingly, the researchers have also found that people who have more seemingly "selfish" motivations—esteem enhancement, personal development and understanding—are more likely to stick with a volunteering organization longer than people with more "other focused" motivations, such as values, according to Omoto.

"It could be because the volunteering is more likely to satisfy those motivations," he says. "If your values say you should help people, you could probably always switch to another organization that also helps people."

Omoto and Snyder say that their research could help organizations that rely on volunteers. For example, if the organizations can figure out their volunteers' primary motives for volunteering, then they could tailor ads and other recruitment strategies to address those motivations—and they could try to steer the volunteers to activities most likely to satisfy them.

THEORETICAL UNDERPINNINGS

Psychologists who investigate the real-world motivations of real-life volunteers do so against the background of other researchers who study and discuss the theory of altruism.

These researchers are mainly concerned with whether altruism, as a concept, actually exists. Do people do altruistic things—including volunteering—because they are truly altruistic and selfless, or because they themselves receive some sort of benefit from every altruistic-seeming act?

University of Kansas psychologist Dan Batson, PhD, believes that true altruism exists as a motivational state with the goal of increasing another person's welfare. He theorizes that such selflessness is based on the empathy people feel for others. In a classic study, for example, he asked participants to watch as a confederate received fake "shocks" for failing a memory test. He found that when he asked people to imagine that person's pain, those who said that they felt compassion for the person also said they'd be willing to take several shocks on the person's behalf, even though they were allowed to leave the experiment at any time.

"We as humans are capable of a motive that has another's welfare as the ultimate goal," Batson says.

But Arizona State University psychology professor Robert Cialdini, PhD, disagrees. He says that while empathy does lead to increased helping, it does so not because of pure altruism but because thinking of another person's pain makes us sad, and one way to make ourselves feel better is to be helpful. Another possibility is that taking another person's perspective actually causes us to feel some overlap between ourselves and that other person, Cialdini says, and so we help them the way we would help ourselves.

As evidence for this, Cialdini has found that when participants are made to feel similar to another person—by giving them a fake electroencephalogram exam and telling them that they have sibling-like similar brain waves—and then are told to empathize with that person, they're more likely to help them. But when people don't feel similar to another person, they're less likely to help that person, even if they're instructed to empathize with them. "What we argue is that taking the perspective of another person can indeed lead to increased helping," Cialdini says. "But we don't assign it to a kind of pure altruism. We say that it's associated with a form of egoism, in which the self receives enhanced benefits." Certainly in the animal kingdom, egoism, it seems, is the driver of apparent altruism.

Most psychologists who study volunteerism say that although such theoretical arguments are important, they may not have much bearing on the practical question of why people volunteer.

"I don't doubt that, from a theoretical perspective, one can derive differences," Snyder says. "But in the real world, these things are intimately wrapped up. The same act of volunteering can have an altruistic component, reflecting a true concern for the welfare of others, but also an egoistic component, in that the volunteer receives clear benefits to the self. It's better to see the two feeding each other, rather than being in competition."

FURTHER READING

Batson, C. (1998). Altruism and prosocial behavior. In D. T. Gilbert, S. T. Fiske & G. Lindzey (Eds.), *The Handbook of Social Psychology, Vol. 2* (4th Ed., pp. 282–316). Boston: McGraw Hill.

Clary, E. G., & Snyder, S. (1999). The motivations to volunteer: Theoretical and practical considerations. *Current Direction in Psychological Science, 8,* 156–159.

Maner, J. et al (2002). The effects of perspective taking on motivations for helping: Still no evidence for altruism. *Personality and Social Psychology Bulletin, 28,* 1,601–1,610.

Omoto, A., & Snyder, S. (2002). Considerations of community: The context and process of volunteerism. *The American Behavioral Scientist, 45,* 846–847.

CRITICAL THINKING QUESTIONS

1. The article cites two different theories for why people help other people. Do you agree with Batson's position that true altruism exists, such that our only goal is to increase another person's welfare, or with Cialdini's position that we help others mainly because doing so makes us feel better about ourselves? Discuss your reasoning.

2. The article discusses five primary motivations for volunteering. Ask people you know who have volunteered their time to a project or cause why they did so. Do their stated reasons match any of the five motivational factors, or did they provide reasons other than those discussed in the article? Discuss your findings.

3. Explain how service organizations could use the information presented in this article not only to attract volunteers but also to keep volunteers coming back.

4. On a personal level, reflect on when you have helped someone (not necessarily in a volunteering situation). Why did you do it? Also reflect on a situation in which you did not help but later wished you had. Why didn't you help at that time? What factors influenced your behavior in each case? Are some of them mentioned in the article, or were there other factors operating? Explain your answers.

ARTICLE 29 _____

Many variables can potentially influence whether an individual will help someone in need. Some of these variables were discussed in the previous article. But what other factors may influence prosocial behavior?

Broadly speaking, two types of determinants can be considered. The first concerns *situational* factors: What circumstances surrounding the specific situation may affect helping behavior? The second variable concerns *dispositions:* To what extent are decisions to help due to relatively permanent personality factors? In other words, are some people more likely to help than others because of their unique personality makeup? Or does the situation, rather than personality, influence helping?

In "From Jerusalem to Jericho," John M. Darley and C. Daniel Batson examine both situational and dispositional variables in an experiment modeled after a biblical parable. Specifically, the study looks at helping as influenced by situational variables—whether the subjects were in a hurry and what they were thinking at the time—and dispositional variables—the religious orientations of the subjects. This classic article is interesting not only because of the methodology used but also because of the important implications of the results.

"From Jerusalem to Jericho"

A Study of Situational and Dispositional Variables in Helping Behavior

■ John M. Darley and C. Daniel Batson

The influence of several situational and personality variables on helping behavior was examined in an emergency situation suggested by the parable of the Good Samaritan. People going between two buildings encountered a shabbily dressed person slumped by the side of the road. Subjects in a hurry to reach their destination were more likely to pass by without stopping. Some subjects were going to give a short talk on the parable of the Good Samaritan, others on a nonhelping relevant topic; this made no significant difference in the likelihood of their giving the victim help. Religious personality variables did not predict whether an individual would help the victim or not. However, if a subject did stop to offer help, the character of the helping response was related to his type of religiosity.

Helping other people in distress is, among other things, an ethical act. That is, it is in act governed by ethical norms and precepts taught to children at home, in school, and in church. From Freudian and other personality theories, one would expect individual differences in internalization of these standards that would lead to differences between individuals in the likelihood with which they would help others. But recent research on bystander intervention in emergency situations (Bickman, 1969; Darley & Latané, 1968; Korte, 1969; but see also Schwartz & Clausen, 1970) has had bad luck in finding personality determinants of helping behavior. Although personality variables that one might expect to correlate with helping behavior have been measured (Machiavellianism, authoritarianism, social desirability, alienation, and social responsibility), these were not predictive of helping. Nor was this due to a generalized lack of predictability in the helping situation examined, since variations in the experimental situation, such as the availability of other people who might also help, produced marked changes in rates of helping behavior. These findings are reminiscent of Hartshorne and May's (1928) discovery that resistance to temptation, another ethically relevant act, did not seem to be a fixed characteristic of an individual. That is, a person who was likely to be honest in one situation was not particularly likely to be honest in the next (but see also Burton, 1963).

The rather disappointing correlation between the social psychologist's traditional set of personality variables and helping behavior in emergency situations suggests the need for a fresh perspective on possible predictors of helping and possible situations in which to test them. Therefore, for inspiration, we turned to the Bible, to what is perhaps the classical helping story in the Judeo-Christian tradition, the parable of the Good Samaritan. The parable proved of value in suggesting both personality and situational variables relevant to helping.

"And who is my neighbor?" Jesus replied, "A man was going down from Jerusalem to Jericho, and he fell among robbers, who stopped him and beat him, and departed, leaving him half dead. Now by chance a priest was going down the road; and when he saw him he passed by on the other side. So likewise a Levite, when he came to the place and saw him, passed by on the other side. But a Samaritan, as he journeyed, came to where he was; and when he saw him, he had compassion, and went to him and bound his wounds, pouring on oil and wine; then he set him on his own beast and brought him to an inn, and took care of him. And the next day he took out two dennarii and gave them to the innkeeper, saying, "Take care of him; and whatever more you spend, I will repay you when I come back." Which of these three, do you think, proved neighbor to him who fell among the robbers? He said, "The one who showed mercy on him." And Jesus said to him, "Go and do likewise." (Luke 10: 29–37 RSV)

To psychologists who reflect on the parable, it seems to suggest situational and personality differences between the nonhelpful priest and Levite and the helpful Samaritan. What might each have been thinking and doing when he came upon the robbery

victim on that desolate road? What sort of persons were they?

One can speculate on differences in thought. Both the priest and the Levite were religious functionaries who could be expected to have their minds occupied with religious matters. The priest's role in religious activities is obvious. The Levite's role, although less obvious, is equally important: The Levites were necessary participants in temple ceremonies. Much less can be said with any confidence about what the Samaritan might have been thinking, but, in contrast to the others, it was most likely not of a religious nature, for Samaritans were religious outcasts.

Not only was the Samaritan most likely thinking about more mundane matters than the priest and Levite, but, because he was socially less important, it seems likely that he was operating on a quite different time schedule. One can imagine the priest and Levite, prominent public figures, hurrying along with little black books full of meetings and appointments, glancing furtively at their sundials. In contrast, the Samaritan would likely have far fewer and less important people counting on him to be at a particular place at a particular time, and therefore might be expected to be in less of a hurry than the prominent priest or Levite.

In addition to these situational variables, one finds personality factors suggested as well. Central among these, and apparently basic to the point that Jesus was trying to make, is a distinction between types of religiosity. Both the priest and Levite are extremely "religious." But it seems to be precisely their type of religiosity that the parable challenges. At issue is the motivation for one's religion and ethical behavior. Jesus seems to feel that the religious leaders of his time, though certainly respected and upstanding citizens, may be "virtuous" for what it will get them, both in terms of the admiration of their fellowmen and in the eyes of God. New Testament scholar R. W. Funk (1966) noted that the Samaritan is at the other end of the spectrum:

The Samaritan does not love with side glances at God. The need of neighbor alone is made self-evident, and the Samaritan responds without other motivation. (pp. 218–219)

That is, the Samaritan is interpreted as responding spontaneously to the situation, not as being preoccupied with the abstract ethical or organizational do's and don'ts of religion as the priest and Levite would seem to be. This is not to say that the Samaritan is portrayed as irreligious. A major intent of the parable would seem to be to present the Samaritan as a religious and ethical example, but at the same time to contrast his type of religiosity with the more common conception of religiosity that the priest and Levite represent.

To summarize the variables suggested as affecting helping behavior by the parable, the situational variables include the content of one's thinking and the amount of hurry in one's journey. The major dispositional variable seems to be differing types of religiosity. Certainly these variables do not exhaust the list that could be elicited from the parable, but they do suggest several research hypotheses.

Hypothesis 1   The parable implies that people who encounter a situation possibly calling for a helping response while thinking religious and ethical thoughts will be no more likely to offer aid than persons thinking about something else. Such a hypothesis seems to run counter to a theory that focuses on norms as determining helping behavior because a normative account would predict that the increased salience of helping norms produced by thinking about religious and ethical examples would increase helping behavior.

Hypothesis 2   Persons encountering a possible helping situation when they are in a hurry will be less likely to offer aid than persons not in a hurry.

Hypothesis 3   Concerning types of religiosity, persons who are religious in a Samaritan-like fashion will help more frequently than those religious in a priest or Levite fashion.

Obviously, this last hypothesis is hardly operationalized as stated. Prior research by one of the investigators on types of religiosity (Batson, 1971), however, led us to differentiate three distinct ways of being religious: (a) for what it will gain one (cf. Freud, 1927, and perhaps the priest and Levite), (b) for its own intrinsic value (cf. Allport & Ross, 1967), and (c) as a response to and quest for meaning in one's everyday life (cf. Batson, 1971). Both of the latter conceptions would be proposed by their exponents as related to the more

Samaritanlike "true" religiosity. Therefore, depending on the theorist one follows, the third hypothesis may be stated like this: People (a) who are religious for intrinsic reasons (Allport & Ross, 1967) or (b) whose religion emerges out of questioning the meaning of their everyday lives (Batson, 1971) will be more likely to stop to offer help to the victim.

The parable of the Good Samaritan also suggested how we would measure people's helping behavior— their response to a stranger slumped by the side of one's path. The victim should appear somewhat ambiguous—dressed, possibly in need of help, but also possibly drunk or even potentially dangerous.

Further, the parable suggests a means by which the incident could be perceived as a real one rather than part of a psychological experiment in which one's behavior was under surveillance and might be shaped by demand characteristics (Orne, 1962), evaluation apprehension (Rosenberg, 1965), or other potentially artifactual determinants of helping behavior. The victim should be encountered not in the experimental context but on the road between various tasks.

METHOD

In order to examine the influence of these variables on helping behavior, seminary students were asked to participate in a study on religious education and vocations. In the first testing session, personality questionnaires concerning types of religiosity were administered. In a second individual session, the subject began experimental procedures in one building and was asked to report to another building for later procedures. While in transit, the subject passed a slumped "victim" planted in an alleyway. The dependent variable was whether and how the subject helped the victim. The independent variables were the degree to which the subject was told to hurry in reaching the other building and the talk he was to give when he arrived there. Some subjects were to give a talk on the jobs in which seminary students would be most effective, others, on the parable of the Good Samaritan.

Subjects

The subjects for the questionnaire administration were 67 students at Princeton Theological Seminary. Forty-seven of them, those who could be reached by telephone, were scheduled for the experiment. Of the 47, 7 subjects' data were not included in the analyses—3 because of contamination of the experimental procedures during their testing and 4 due to suspicion of the experimental situation. Each subject was paid $1 for the questionnaire session and $1.50 for the experimental session.

Personality Measures

Detailed discussion of the personality scales used may be found elsewhere (Batson, 1971), so the present discussion will be brief. The general personality construct under examination was religiosity. Various conceptions of religiosity have been offered in recent years based on different psychometric scales. The conception seeming to generate the most interest is the Allport and Ross (1967) distinction between "intrinsic" versus "extrinsic" religiosity (cf. also Allen & Spilka, 1967, on "committed" versus "consensual" religion). This bipolar conception of religiosity has been questioned by Brown (1964) and Batson (1971), who suggested three-dimensional analyses instead. Therefore, in the present research, types of religiosity were measured with three instruments which together provided six separate scales; (a) a *doctrinal orthodoxy* (D-O) scale patterned after that used by Glock and Stark (1966), scaling agreement with classic doctrines of Protestant theology; (b) the Allport-Ross *extrinsic* (AR-E) scale, measuring the use of religion as a means to an end rather than as an end in itself; (c) the All-port-Ross *intrinsic* (AR-I) scale, measuring the use of religion as an end in itself; (d) the *extrinsic external* scale of Batson's Religious Life Inventory (RELI-EE), designed to measure the influence of significant others and situations in generating one's religiosity; (e) the *extrinsic internal* scale of the Religious Life Inventory (RELI-EI), designed to measure the degree of "driveness" in one's religiosity; and (f) the *intrinsic* scale of the Religious Life Inventory (RELI-I), designed to measure the degree to which one's religiosity involves a questioning of the meaning of life arising out of one's interactions with his social environment. The order of presentation of the scales in the questionnaire was RELI, AR, D-O.

Consistent with prior research (Batson, 1971), a principal-component analysis of the total scale scores and individual items for the 67 seminarians produced a theoretically meaningful, orthogonally rotated three-component structure with the following loadings:

Religion as means received a single very high loading from AR-E (.903) and therefore was defined by Allport and Ross's (1967) conception of this scale as measuring religiosity as a means to other ends. This component also received moderate negative loadings from D-O (−.400) and AR-I (−.372) and a moderate positive loading from RELI-EE (.301).

Religion as an end received high loadings from RELI-EI (.874), RELI-EE (.725), AR-I (.768), and D-O (.704). Given this configuration, and again following Allport and Ross's conceptualization, this component seemed to involve religiosity as an end in itself with some intrinsic value.

Religion as quest received a single very high loading from RELI-I (.945) and a moderate loading from RELI-EE (.75). Following Batson, this component was conceived to involve religiosity emerging out of an individual's search for meaning in his personal and social world.

The three religious personality scales examined in the experimental research were constructed through the use of complete-estimation factor score coefficients from these three components.

Scheduling of Experimental Study

Since the incident requiring a helping response was staged outdoors, the entire experimental study was run in 3 days, December 14–16, 1970, between 10 A.M. and 4 P.M. A tight schedule was used in an attempt to maintain reasonably consistent weather and light conditions. Temperature fluctuation according to the *New York Times* for the 3 days during these hours was not more than 5 degrees Fahrenheit. No rain or snow fell, although the third day was cloudy, whereas the first two were sunny. Within days the subjects were randomly assigned to experimental conditions.[1]

Procedure

When a subject appeared for the experiment, an assistant (who was blind with respect to the personality scores) asked him to read a brief statement which explained that he was participating in a study of the vocational careers of seminary students. After developing the rationale for the study, the statement read:

What we have called you in for today is to provide us with some additional material which will give us a clearer picture of how you think than does the questionnaire material we have gathered thus far. Questionnaires are helpful, but tend to be somewhat oversimplified. Therefore, we would like to record a 3–5 minute talk you give based on the following passage. . . .

Variable 1: Message   In the task-relevant condition the passage read,

With increasing frequency the question is being asked: What jobs or professions do seminary students subsequently enjoy most, and in what jobs are they most effective? The answer to this question used to be so obvious that the question was not even asked. Seminary students were being trained for the ministry, and since both society at large and the seminary student himself had a relatively clear understanding of what made a "good" minister, there was no need even to raise the question of for what other jobs seminary experience seems to be an asset. Today, however, neither society nor many seminaries have a very clearly defined conception of what a "good" minister is or of what sorts of jobs and professions are the best context in which to minister. Many seminary students, apparently genuinely concerned with "ministering," seem to feel that it is impossible to minister in the professional clergy. Other students, no less concerned, find the clergy the most viable profession for ministry. But are there other jobs and/or professions for which seminary experience is an asset? And, indeed, how much of an asset is it for the professional ministry? Or, even more broadly, can one minister through an "establishment" job at all?

In the helping-relevant condition, the subject was given the parable of the Good Samaritan exactly as printed earlier in this article. Next, regardless of condition, all subjects were told,

You can say whatever you wish based on the passage. Because we are interested in how you think on your feet, you will not be allowed to use notes in giving the talk. Do you understand what you are to do? If not, the assistant will be glad to answer questions.

After a few minutes the assistant returned, asked if there were any questions, and then said:

Since they're rather tight on space in this building, we're using a free office in the building next door for recording the talks. Let me show you how to get there [draws and explains map on 3 × 5 card]. This is where Professor Steiner's laboratory is. If you go in this door [points at map], there's a secretary right here, and she'll direct you to the office we're using for recording. Another of Professor Steiner's assistants will set you up for recording your talk. Is the map clear?

Variable 2: Hurry   In the high-hurry condition the assistant then looked at his watch and said, "Oh, you're late. They were expecting you a few minutes ago. We'd better get moving. The assistant should be waiting for you so you'd better hurry. It shouldn't take but just a minute." In the intermediate-hurry condition he said, "The assistant is ready for you, so please go right over." In the low-hurry condition, he said, "It'll be a few minutes before they're ready for you, but you might as well head on over. If you have to wait over there, it shouldn't be long."

The Incident   When the subject passed through the alley, the victim was sitting slumped in a doorway, head down, eyes closed, not moving. As the subject went by, the victim coughed twice and groaned, keeping his head down. If the subject stopped and asked if something was wrong or offered to help, the victim, startled and somewhat groggy, said, "Oh, thank you [cough]. . . . No, it's all right. [Pause] I've got this respiratory condition [cough]. . . . The doctor's given me these pills to take, and I just took one. . . . If I just sit and rest for a few minutes I'll be O.K. . . . Thanks very much for stopping though [smiles weakly]." If the subject persisted, insisting on taking the victim inside the building, the victim allowed him to do so and thanked him.

Helping Ratings   The victim rated each subject on a scale of helping behavior as follows:

0 = failed to notice the victim as possibly in need at all; 1 = perceived the victim as possibly in need but did not offer aid; 2 = did not stop but helped

indirectly (e.g., by telling Steiner's assistant about the victim); 3 = stopped and asked if victim needed help; 4 = after stopping, insisted on taking the victim inside and then left him.

The victim was blind to the personality scale scores and experimental conditions of all subjects. At the suggestion of the victim, another category was added to the rating scales, based on his observations of the pilot subjects' behavior:

5 = after stopping, refused to leave the victim (after 3–5 minutes) and/or insisted on taking him somewhere outside experimental context (e.g., for coffee or to the infirmary).

(In some cases it was necessary to distinguish Category 0 from Category 1 by the postexperimental questionnaire and Category 2 from Category 1 on the report of the experimental assistant.)

This 6-point scale of helping behavior and a description of the victim were given to a panel of 10 judges (unacquainted with the research) who were asked to rank order the (unnumbered) categories in terms of "the amount of helping behavior displayed toward the person in the doorway." Of the 10, 1 judge reversed the order of Categories 0 and 1. Otherwise there was complete agreement with the ranking implied in the presentation of the scale above.

The Speech After passing through the alley and entering the door marked on the map, the subject entered a secretary's office. She introduced him to the assistant who gave the subject time to prepare and privately record his talk.

Helping Behavior Questionnaire After recording the talk, the subject was sent to another experimenter, who administered "an exploratory questionnaire on personal and social ethics." The questionnaire contained several initial questions about the interrelationship between social and personal ethics, and then asked three key questions: (a) "When was the last time you saw a person who seemed to be in need of help?" (b) "When was the last time you stopped to help someone in need?" (c) "Have you had experience helping persons in need? If so, outline briefly." These data were collected as a check on the victim's ratings

of whether subjects who did not stop perceived the situation in the alley as one possibly involving need or not.

When he returned, the experimenter reviewed the subject's questionnaire, and, if no mention was made of the situation in the alley, probed for reactions to it and then phased into an elaborate debriefing and discussion session.

Debriefing

In the debriefing, the subject was told the exact nature of the study, including the deception involved, and the reasons for the deception were explained. The subject's reactions to the victim and to the study in general were discussed. The role of situational determinants of helping behavior was explained in relation to this particular incident and to other experiences of the subject. All subjects seemed readily to understand the necessity for the deception, and none indicated any resentment of it. After debriefing, the subject was thanked for his time and paid, then he left.

RESULTS AND DISCUSSION

Overall Helping Behavior

The average amount of help that a subject offered the victim, by condition, is shown in Table 1. The unequal-N analysis of variance indicates that while the hurry variable was significantly ($F = 3.56$, $df = 2.34$, $p < .05$) related to helping behavior, the message variable was not. Subjects in a hurry were likely to offer less help than were subjects not in a hurry. Whether the subject was going to give a speech on the parable of the Good Samaritan or not did not significantly affect his helping behavior on this analysis.

Other studies have focused on the question of whether a person initiates helping action or not, rather than on scaled kinds of helping. The data from the present study can also be analyzed on the following terms: Of the 40 subjects, 16 (40%) offered some form of direct or indirect aid to the victim (Coding Categories 2–5), 24 (60%) did not (Coding Categories 0 and 1). The percentages of subjects who offered aid by situational variable were, for low hurry, 63%

TABLE 1 / Means and Analysis of Variance of Graded Helping Responses

	M			
	Hurry			Sum-mary
Message	Low	Medium	High	
Helping relevant	3.800	2.000	1.000	2.263
Task relevant	1.667	1.667	.500	1.333
Summary	3.000	1.818	.700	

Analysis of Variance				
Source	SS	df	MS	F
Message (A)	7.766	1	7.766	2.65
Hurry (B)	20.884	2	10.442	3.50*
A x B	5.237	2	2.619	.89
Error	99.633	34	2.930	

Note: $N = 40$.
*$p < .05$.

offered help, intermediate hurry 45%, and high hurry 10%, for helping-relevant message 53%, task-relevant message 29%. With regard to this more general question of whether help was offered or not, an unequal-N analysis of variance (arc sine transformation of percentages of helpers, with low- and intermediate-hurry conditions pooled) indicated that again only the hurry main effect was significantly ($F = 5.22$, $p < .05$) related to helping behavior; the subjects in a hurry were more likely to pass by the victim than were those in less of a hurry.

Reviewing the predictions in the light of these results, the second hypothesis, that the degree of hurry a person is in determines his helping behavior, was supported. The prediction involved in the first hypothesis concerning the message content was based on the parable. The parable itself seemed to suggest that thinking pious thoughts would not increase helping. Another and conflicting prediction might be produced by a norm salience theory. Thinking about the parable should make norms for helping salient and therefore produce more helping. The data, as hypothesized, are more congruent with the prediction drawn from the parable. A person going to speak on the parable of the Good Samaritan is not significantly more likely to stop to help a person by the side of the road than is a person going to talk about possible occupations for seminary graduates.

Since both situational hypotheses are confirmed, it is tempting to stop the analysis of these variables at this point. However, multiple regression analysis procedures were also used to analyze the relationship of all of the independent variables of the study and the helping behavior. In addition to often being more statistically powerful due to the use of more data information, multiple regression analysis has an advantage over analysis of variance in that it allows for a comparison of the relative effect of the various independent variables in accounting for variance in the dependent variable. Also, multiple regression analysis can compare the effects of continuous as well as nominal independent variables on both continuous and nominal dependent variables (through the use of point biserial correlations, *rpb*) and shows considerable robustness to violation of normality assumptions (Cohen, 1965, 1968). Table 2 reports the results of the multiple regression analysis using both help versus no help and the graded helping scale as dependent measures. In this table the overall equation *F*s show the *F* value of the entire regression equation as a particular row variable enters the equation. Individual variable *F*s were computed with all five independent variables in the equation. Although the two situational variables, hurry and message condition, correlated more highly with the dependent measure than any of the religious dispositional variables, only hurry was a significant predictor of whether one will help or not (column 1) or of the overall amount of help given (column 2). These results corroborate the findings of the analysis of variance.[2]

Notice also that neither form of the third hypothesis, that types of religiosity will predict helping, received support from these data. No correlation between the various measures of religiosity and any form of the dependent measure ever came near statistical significance, even though the multiple regression

TABLE 2 / Stepwise Multiple Regression Analysis

	Help vs. No Help					Graded Helping				
	Individual Variable		Overall Equation				Individual Variable		Variable Equation	
Step	r^a	F	R	F		Step	r	F	R	F
1. Hurry[b]	−.37	4.537*	.37	5.884*		1. Hurry	−.42	6.665*	.42	8.196**
2. Message[c]	.25	1.495	.41	3.834*		2. Message	.25	1.719	.46	5.083*
3. Religion as quest	−.03	.081	.42	2.521		3. Religion as quest	−.16	1.297	.50	3.897*
4. Religion as means	−.03	.003	.42	1.838*		4. Religion as means	−.08	.018	.50	2.848*
5. Religion as end	.06	.000	.42	1.430		5. Religion as end	−.07	.001	.50	2.213

Note: N = 40. Helping is the dependent variable. df = 1/34.
[a]Individual variable correlation coefficient is a point biserial where appropriate.
[b]Variables are listed in order of entry into stepwise regression equations.
[c]Helping-relevant message is positive.
*p < .05.
**p < .01.

analysis procedure is a powerful and not particularly conservative statistical test.

Personality Difference among Subjects Who Helped

To further investigate the possible influence of personality variables, analyses were carried out using only the data from subjects who offered some kind of help to the victim. Surprisingly (since the number of these subjects was small, only 16) when this was done, one religiosity variable seemed to be significantly related to the kind of helping behavior offered. (The situational variables had no significant effect.) Subjects high on the religion as quest dimension appear likely, when they stop for the victim, to offer help of a more tentative or incomplete nature than are subjects scoring low on this dimension (r = −.53, p < .05).

This result seemed unsettling for the thinking behind either form of Hypothesis 3. Not only do the data suggest that the Allport-Ross-based conception of religion as *end* does not predict the degree of helping, but the religion as quest component is a significant predictor of offering less help. This latter result seems counterintuitive and out of keeping with previous research (Batson, 1971), which found that this type of religiosity correlated positively with other

socially valued characteristics. Further data analysis, however, seemed to suggest a different interpretation of this result.

It will be remembered that one helping coding category was added at the suggestion of the victim after his observation of pilot subjects. The correlation of religious personality variables with helping behavior dichotomized between the added category (1) and all of the others (0) was examined. The correlation between religion as quest and this dichotomous helping scale was essentially unchanged (rpb = −.54, p < .05). Thus, the previously found correlation between the helping scale and religion as quest seems to reflect the tendency of those who score low on the quest dimension to offer help in the added helping category.

What does help in this added category represent? Within the context of the experiment, it represented an embarrassment. The victim's response to persistent offers of help was to assure the helper he was all right, had taken his medicine, just needed to rest for a minute or so, and, if ultimately necessary, to request the helper to leave. But the *super* helpers in this added category often would not leave until the final appeal was repeated several times by the victim (who was growing increasingly panicky at the possibility of the arrival of the next subject). Since it usually involved the subject's attempting to carry through a preset plan (e.g., taking the subject for a cup of coffee or revealing to him the strength to be found in Christ), and did not allow information from the victim to change that plan, we originally labeled this kind of helping as rigid—an interpretation supported by its increased likelihood among highly doctrinal orthodox subjects ($r = .63$, $p < .01$). It also seemed to have an inappropriate character. If this more extreme form of helping behavior is indeed effectively less helpful, then the second form of Hypothesis 3 does seem to gain support.

But perhaps it is the experimenters rather than the super helpers who are doing the inappropriate thing; perhaps the best characterization of this kind of helping is as different rather than as inappropriate. This kind of helper seems quickly to place a particular interpretation on the situation, and the helping response seems to follow naturally from this interpretation. All that can safely be said is that one style of helping that emerged in this experiment was directed toward the presumed underlying needs of the victim and was little modified by the victim's comments about his own needs. In contrast, another style was more tentative and seemed more responsive to the victim's statements of his need.

The former kind of helping was likely to be displayed by subjects who expressed strong doctrinal orthodoxy. Conversely, this fixed kind of helping was unlikely among subjects high on the religion as quest dimension. These latter subjects, who conceived their religion as involving an ongoing search for meaning in their personal and social world, seemed more responsive to the victim's immediate needs and more open to the victim's definitions of his own needs.

CONCLUSION AND IMPLICATIONS

A person not in a hurry may stop and offer help to a person in distress. A person in a hurry is likely to keep going. Ironically, he is likely to keep going even if he is hurrying to speak on the parable of the Good Samaritan, thus inadvertently confirming the point of the parable. (Indeed, on several occasions, a seminary student going to give his talk on the parable of the Good Samaritan literally stepped over the victim as he hurried on his way!)

Although the degree to which a person was in a hurry had a clearly significant effect on his likelihood of offering the victim help, whether he was going to give a sermon on the parable or on possible vocational roles of ministers did not. This lack of effect of sermon topic raises certain difficulties for an explanation of helping behavior involving helping norms and their salience. It is hard to think of a context in which norms concerning helping those in distress are more salient than for a person thinking about the Good Samaritan, and yet it did not significantly increase helping behavior. The results were in the direction suggested by the norm salience hypothesis, but they were not significant. The most accurate conclusion seems to be that salience of helping norms is a less strong determinant of helping behavior in the present situation than many, including the present authors, would expect.

Thinking about the Good Samaritan did not increase helping behavior, but being in a hurry decreased it. It is difficult not to conclude from this that the frequently cited explanation that ethics becomes a luxury as the speed of our daily lives increases is at least an accurate description. The picture that this explanation conveys is of a person seeing another, consciously noting his distress, and consciously choosing to leave him in distress. But perhaps this is not entirely accurate, for, when a person is in a hurry, something seems to happen that is akin to Tolman's (1948) concept of the "narrowing of the cognitive map." Our seminarians in a hurry noticed the victim in that in the postexperiment interview almost all mentioned him as, on reflection, possibly in need of help. But it seems that they often had not worked this out when they were near the victim. Either the interpretation of their visual picture as a person in distress or the empathic reactions usually associated with that interpretation had been deferred because they were hurrying. According to the reflections of some of the subjects, it would be inaccurate to say that they realized the victim's possible distress, then chose to ignore it; instead, because of the time pressures, they did not perceive the scene in the alley as an occasion for an ethical decision.

For other subjects it seems more accurate to conclude that they decided not to stop. They appeared aroused and anxious after the encounter in the alley. For these subjects, what were the elements of the choice that they were making? Why were the seminarians hurrying? Because the experimenter, *whom the subject was helping* was depending on him to get to a particular place quickly. In other words, he was in conflict between stopping to help the victim and continuing on his way to help the experimenter. And this is often true of people in a hurry; they hurry because somebody depends on their being somewhere. Conflict, rather than callousness, can explain their failure to stop.

Finally, as in other studies, personality variables were not useful in predicting whether a person helped or not. But in this study, unlike many previous ones, considerable variations were possible in the kinds of help given, and these variations did relate to personality measures—specifically to religiosity of the quest sort. The clear light of hindsight suggests that the dimension of kinds of helping would have been the appropriate place to look for personality differences all along; *whether* a person helps or not is an instant decision likely to be situationally controlled. How a person helps involves a more complex and considered number of decisions, including the time and scope to permit personality characteristics to shape them.

REFERENCES

Allen, R. O., & Spilka, B. Committed and consensual religion. A specification of religion-prejudice relationships. *Journal for the Scientific Study of Religion,* 1967, *6,* 191–206.

Allport, G. W., & Ross, J. M. Personal religious orientation and prejudice. *Journal of Personality and Social Psychology,* 1967, *5,* 432–443.

Batson, C. D. Creativity and religious development: Toward a structural-functional psychology of religion Unpublished doctoral dissertation, Princeton Theological Seminary, 1971.

Bickman, L. B. The effect of the presence of others on bystander intervention in an emergency. Unpublished doctoral dissertation, City College of the City University of New York, 1969.

Brown, L. B. Classifications of religious orientation. *Journal for the Scientific Study of Religion,* 1964, *4,* 91–99.

Burton, R. V. The generality of honesty reconsidered. *Psychological Review,* 1963, *70,* 481–499.

Cohen, J. Multiple regression as a general data-analytic system. *Psychological Bulletin,* 1968, *70,* 426–443.

Cohen, J. Some statistical issues in psychological research. In B. B. Wolman (Ed.), *Handbook of clinical psychology.* New York: McGraw-Hill, 1965.

Darley, J. M., & Latané, B. Bystander intervention in emergencies: Diffusion of responsibility. *Journal of Personality and Social Psychology,* 1968, *8,* 377–383.

Freud, S. *The future of an illusion.* New York: Liveright, 1953.

Funk, R. W. *Language, hermeneutic, and word of God.* New York: Harper & Row, 1966.

Glock, C. Y., & Stark, R. *Christian beliefs and anti-Semitism.* New York: Harper & Row, 1966.

Hartshorne, H., & May, M. A. *Studies in the nature of character.* Vol. 1. *Studies in deceit.* New York: Macmillan, 1928.

Korte, C. Group effects on help-giving in an emergency. *Proceedings of the 77th Annual Convention of the American Psychological Association,* 1969, *4,* 383–384. (Summary)

Orne, M. T. On the social psychology of the psychological experiment: With particular reference to demand characteristics and their implications. *American Psychologist,* 1962, *17,* 776–783.

Rosenberg, M. J. When dissonance fails: On eliminating evaluation apprehension from attitude measurement. *Journal of Personality and Social Psychology,* 1965, *1,* 28–42.

Schwartz, S. H., & Clausen, G. T. Responsibility, norms, and helping in an emergency. *Journal of Personality and Social Psychology,* 1970, *16,* 299–310.

Tolman, E. C. Cognitive maps in rats and men. *Psychological Review,* 1948, *55,* 189–208.

ENDNOTES

1. An error was made in randomizing that increased the number of subjects in the intermediate-hurry conditions. This worked against the prediction that was most highly confirmed (the hurry prediction) and made no difference to the message variable tests.

2. To check the legitimacy of the use of both analysis of variance and multiple regression analysis, parametric analyses, on this ordinal data, Kendall rank correlation coefficients were calculated between the helping scale and the five independent variables. As expected t approximated the correlation quite closely in each case and was significant for hurry only (hurry $\tau -.38, p < .001$).

For assistance in conducting this research thanks are due Robert Wells, Beverly Fisher, Mike Shafto, Peter Sheras, Richard Detweiler, and Karen Glasser. The research was funded by National Science Foundation Grant GS-2293.

CRITICAL THINKING QUESTIONS

1. Being prompted to think of the parable of the Good Samaritan did not increase the subjects' helping behavior in this study, but being in a hurry actually decreased it. Suppose that you are in the business of soliciting money for a worthy purpose. What strategies could you use to maximize the money you receive, based on the implications of this study? Explain.

2. *Rush hour,* as the name implies, describes a time of day when people are in a hurry to get to or from work. Do you think that people would be less likely to help someone in need during rush hour than at other times of the day? What about on weekends? Design a study to test this possibility, being sure to address any ethical issues that may be involved.

3. Reading about the Good Samaritan had no impact on subsequent helping behavior. Do you think that reading an article such as this one would change people's helping behavior? Why or why not? Specifically, now that you know that being in a hurry will decrease the likelihood of your giving help, do you think that this awareness will make you more likely to give help in the future, even if you are in a hurry? Why or why not? If simply telling someone about the Good Samaritan was not enough to improve people's helping behavior, what might be more effective?

ADDITIONAL RELATED READINGS

Bartlett, M. Y., & DeSteno, D. (2006). Gratitude and prosocial behavior: Helping when it costs you. *Psychological Science, 17*(4), 319–325.

McMahon, S. D., Wernsman, J., & Parnes, A. L. (2006). Understanding prosocial behavior: The impact of empathy and gender among African American adolescents. *Journal of Adolescent Health, 39*(1), 135–137.

ARTICLE 30

The literature on helping behavior indicates that quite a few situational factors can influence our tendency to help someone in need. For example, the previous article noted that being in a hurry significantly reduces the amount of helping we offer. Other factors—such as being exposed to enjoyable music and pleasant aromas and even being out on a beautiful, sunny day—all may increase the likelihood of helping behavior.

But what do many of these factors have in common? It could be that each of them puts us in a better mood, and in turn, we are more likely to help someone if we are in a good, rather than a neutral or bad, mood. Indeed, many previous studies have indicated that being in a good mood is more likely to lead to increased helping.

If you want to increase the likelihood that someone will offer you assistance, you can do many things to enhance his or her mood and hence helping. One such behavior, which is fairly easy to control, is smiling at the person. Research (and common sense) indicates that we respond more positively to a smiling person than to a person with a more neutral expression. We tend to view a smiling person as more attractive, more interesting, more intelligent, and, in general, as having more of a variety of positive traits. We also tend to behave more positively toward people who smile at us—for instance, by helping them more.

What is unique about the following article by Nicolas Gueguen and Marie-Agnes De Gail is that they look at the effect of smiling on helping behavior when the person smiling is *not* the one receiving help. In other words, they consider whether merely being exposed to someone smiling makes us more likely to help someone else later on. Perhaps the old adage "Smile and the world smiles with you" has important practical implications after all.

The Effect of Smiling on Helping Behavior
Smiling and Good Samaritan Behavior
■ Nicolas Gueguen and Marie-Agnes De Gail

Research has shown that a person receives more help when smiling. Nevertheless, this effect of smiling was only tested when the smiler was requesting help. An experiment was completed in which 8 confederates (4 young men and 4 young women) tested 800 passersby. In half of the cases, the confederate smiled at the passersby. A few seconds after this interaction, the passersby had the opportunity to help another confederate who dropped his/her computer diskettes on the ground. This research found that the previous smile of a stranger enhanced later helping behavior.

A positive mood induced by the smile of the first confederate could help to explain this result.

The positive effect of smiling on interpersonal attraction and perception is well established in the psychosocial literature. Adding a smile to the photograph of a face leads to more favorable perception of the target, and this effect was found on multiple personality dimensions. Lau (1982) reports finding that when smiling, a target was perceived to be more intelligent

N. Gueguen and M.-A. De Gail, The effect of smiling on helping behavior: Smiling and good Samaritan behavior, *Communication Reports*, 2003, *16*(2), 133–140. Copyright © 2003 by Western States Communication Association. Reprinted with permission.

than the same, nonsmiling, target. Otta, Pereira, Dela-vati, Pimentel and Pires (1993) report that they found that a smiling person receives more positive scores on the dimensions of leadership, optimism, sincerity, and kindness. A smile also enhances helping behavior toward the smiling person. Tidd and Lockard (1978) report that patrons in a bar give significantly larger tips to a waitress who approached them with a broad smile than to one with a minimal smile. In a similar vein, Solomon et al. (1981) report that a smiling con-federate in a large department store receives more help than a nonsmiling one.

The effect of smiling on helping behavior is well established, but the factors that explain this effect still remain in question. One possible explanation is that a positive perception of the solicitor, mediated by his/her smile, could predispose the subject to comply with his/her request. Research connecting perception of the solicitor with helping behavior has found that positive perceptions of the solicitor increases helping behavior (Takemura, 1993). For Tidd and Lockard (1978), who have found that a smile by a waitress enhanced her tips, the result was explained in terms of recipro-cal altruism. Patrons gave the waitress larger tips to reciprocate the better service of the waitress. For Solo-mon et al. (1981), the effect of smiling is explained in terms of anonymity. When a stranger smiles at the subject, he/she becomes identifiable and thus is more likely to receive help than is a control subject who did not smile and thus is more anonymous.

Even though these explanations of the effect of smiling on helping behavior are of interest, they have not been tested empirically. They also pre-suppose that smiling has an effect only in the interaction between the smiler and the recipient of the smile. Another possible explanation is that smiling enhances a positive mood that, in return, enhances helping behavior (Deutsch & Lamberti, 1986).

Many experimental studies report finding that positive mood activation when compared to neutral mood activation, increases helping behavior (Biz-man, Yinin, Ronco & Schachar, 1980; Forgas, 1997, 1998; Harris & Smith, 1975; Job, 1987; Levin & Isen, 1975; Rind, 1997; Weyant, 1978). This positive mood can be activated in many different ways and, most of the time, does not require elaborate means. A

false attribution of success or failure in a task leads to activation of a positive/negative mood that, in turn, affects helping behavior in a way that is congruent with the mood (Clark & Waddell, 1986). Finding a coin in a phone box or on the ground is sufficient to induce a positive mood that in return enhances altru-ism (Batson, Coke, Chard, Smith & Talaferro, 1979; Blevins & Murphy, 1974; Isen & Levin, 1972; Isen & Simmonds, 1978; Levin & Isen, 1975). To be offered a candy or a cookie brings about the same effect (Har-ris & Smith, 1975; Isen & Levin, 1972).

Some empirical studies also find that familiar environmental factors activate a positive mood and helping behavior. For instance, the amount of tips given by customers increases on sunny days (Cun-ningham, 1979). Further, Rind (1996) reports find-ing that even information about the weather, given by a waiter to customers who had not yet seen the color of the sky, is sufficient to make the waiter's tip vary, depending on whether he told them it was sunny or rainy. Even pleasant smells can enhance helping behavior. Pleasant ambient smells (e.g., bak-ing, cooking, roasting coffee) in a shopping mall lead passersby to provide change for a dollar to a same-sex confederate more readily than in the absence of such odors (Baron, 1997). A heavy perfume worn by a female-confederate led the passersby to help her in a more substantial way. Pleasant ambient music also has an important effect on helping behavior (Galizio & Hendricks, 1972).

Another way of inducing moods in participants consists of exposing them to pleasant versus unpleas-ant pictures or texts (Forgas, 1997, 1998). In this respect, it has been shown that a drawing may acti-vate a positive mood and, as a consequence, helping behavior. Drawing a smiling face on the bill increases the rate of tips granted to a waitress (Rind & Bordia, 1996). In the same way, a mere hand-made drawing of the sun, added at the bottom of the bill of cus-tomers having a drink outside a cafe, led them to up the waiter or waitress more frequently and in a much more substantial way (Gueguen & LeGoherel, 2000). Attaching a small card with a joke printed on it to the bill produced the same effects (Gueguen, 2002).

These studies seem to show that the effect of a positive mood on helping behavior is robust and is very easily obtained. It thus appears possible that the effect of smiling on helping is mediated by a positive mood. Kleinke and Walton (1982) have found that in an interaction with a confederate who was instructed to smile, participants reported significantly more positive feelings than in a control situation where the confederate was instructed to show a neutral expression. So, if the effect of smiling on helping behavior is mediated by a positive mood and not just by a positive perception of the smiler, then it might be expected that smiling would enhance helping behavior even when the solicitor is not the smiler. To test this hypothesis, an experiment was carried out in which subjects had the opportunity to help a confederate a few seconds after another confederate had smiled/not smiled to them.

METHOD

Participants

Eight hundred passersby (400 men and 400 women), aged approximately between 20 and 50, served as participants in this experiment. They were randomly selected from passersby who were walking in a supermarket of a medium-size city (more than 100,000 inhabitants) in a very attractive spot. This provincial town was Vannes, located in the west of France on the Breton Atlantic Coast.

Procedure

Eight individuals, 4 men and 4 women, aged 19–21 years old, served as confederates in this experiment. All of them were first-year students from the Department of Marketing at the University of Bretagne-Sud in Vannes and volunteered to participate as confederates in this experiment. Both the female and male confederates were selected by two other male and two other female evaluators who were asked to select confederates on their physical attractiveness. These evaluators were instructed to evaluate the attractiveness of student-photographs and to select people, males and females, with neutral attractiveness. After this, those selected were solicited to participate in the experiment, which they all agreed to do. The confederates were dressed casually and similarly to young

people of their age (t-shirts, jeans and light colored tennis shoes). Each confederate was instructed to set off down the stairs and look for the first participant, man or woman, aged between 20 to 50, who took the stairs. The confederate was instructed to look the participant in the eyes. If the participant returned the gaze, then he/she was instructed to smile (or not) at the subject and then to look in another direction. The smiling/not smiling condition was assigned randomly. Following this manipulation, a second confederate, who was blind to the smiling condition, appeared in front of the participant. This second confederate held a portfolio and a package of computer diskettes in one hand and two bags of food in the other. The confederate was instructed not to look the participant in the eyes because some studies have shown that gaze had an effect on compliance to a request (Brockner, Pressman, Cabitt, & Mora, 1982; Gueguen & Jacob, 2002). When the participant was two meters (6/7 feet) in front of the confederate, the confederate simulated a difficulty with his/her two grocery bags and accidentally dropped the diskettes on the ground. Still avoiding eye contact, the confederate bent down to collect the diskettes that had scattered all around him/her. An observer located not far away evaluated if the participant helped the confederate. Afterwards, the observer asked the first confederate to say if he/she had or had not smiled to the participant. The scene was then repeated until each confederate of each sex had tested 100 subjects (50 males and 50 females) in the two conditions (50 in the smile condition and 50 in the no-smile condition).

RESULTS

As no differences were found between the confederates $[X.\text{sup}.2]$ (7, 800) = 11.24, $p > .10$, the data were aggregated for the men and for the women confederates. The number of passersby who helped, according to their gender, the two confederates' genders and the experimental conditions, is presented in Table 1.

A log-linear statistical method was used to analyze our data. A significant effect for smiling was found, $[X.\text{sup}.2]$ (1, 799) = 9.16, $p < .005$. When the first confederate smiled, 29.5% of the passersby helped

TABLE 1 / Rate of Subjects (in %) Who Stopped and Helped According to the Smile Condition (Smile/No Smile) and Gender of the Confederates and the Participants[1]

	No Smile				Smile				
	First Confederate Male		First Confederate Female		First Confederate Male		First Confederate Female		Average 2nd Confederate
	Males	Females	Males	Females	Males	Females	Males	Females	
Second confederate male	16.0	20.0	12.0	22.0	12.0	40.0	28.0	36.0	23.3
Second confederate female	24.0	24.0	24.0	20.0	28.0	24.0	44.0	24.0	26.5
Average (1st confederate)	21.0		19.5		26.0		33.0		
Average (smile/no smile)		20.3				29.5			

[1]There are 50 subjects per case.

the second confederate whereas only 20.3% helped the second confederate in the nonsmiling condition. No significant effect of the first or of the second confederate's gender was found ($p > .20$ for both). Similarly, no significant effect of participant gender was found ($p > .20$). A 2 (smile/no smile) $\times$ 2 (1st male/female confederate) $\times$ 2 (2nd male/female confederate) $\times$ 2 (male/female participant) log-linear analysis revealed a significant interaction between the 2nd confederate's gender and the participant's gender, $[X.\text{sup}.2]$ (4, 796) = 17.81, $p < .001$. Results showed that male participants were more helpful toward female (30.0%) than male confederates (17.0%) whereas female participants were more helpful toward male (30.0%) than female confederates (23.0%). This was the only statistically significant interaction in this factorial analysis.

DISCUSSION

In the current experiment, female participants helped male confederates more readily than the female confederates, whereas male participants helped female confederates more often than male confederates. This pattern of results is congruent with previous studies (Bickman, 1974). This effect could be explained by traditional roles of self-presentation in opposite-sex behavior (Gruder & Cook, 1971; Harris & Bays, 1973). For these authors, a member of the opposite-sex would be helped more because the

helper wanted to look good in his/her eyes. Seduction motivation could explain why men helped women and why women helped men more favorably than solicitors of the same-sex as the requester.

Our results show that being smiled at by a stranger enhances subsequent helping behavior towards another person. These findings are congruent with the results found in the literature connecting smiling and helping behavior (Solomon et al., 1981; Tidd & Lockard, 1978) and confirm the influence of smiling on helping behavior in a new situation. Furthermore, these findings show that smiling enhances helping behavior toward a person who is not the smiler. These findings are congruent with other results concerning the effect of nonverbal behavior on helping behavior. Deutsch and Lamberti (1986) found that people were more likely to help a confederate who had dropped books if they had been socially rewarded by an experimenter a few minutes beforehand. In Deutsch and Lamberti's experiment, the social reward was manipulated by various nonverbal behaviors such as smiling and eye contact versus cold and distant facial expressions and no eye contact, and by different verbal behaviors such as pleasant conversation versus abrupt conversation. However, Deutsch and Lamberti's study amalgamated various nonverbal behaviors and the effect of simply smiling was not tested. Moreover, Deutsch and Lamberti tested the effects of positive and negative nonverbal behavior on subsequent helping behavior. In our experiment, smiling was the only nonverbal behavior manipulated and the effect of positive social behavior was compared to neutral social behavior. Our findings seem to support the hypothesis that smiling is sufficient to enhance subsequent helping behavior toward a confederate who was not the smiler.

Such an effect seems to support the idea that neither positive perceptions of the smiling confederate (Lau, 1982) nor reciprocal altruism (Tidd & Lockard, 1978) nor identification theory (Solomon et al., 1981) are complete theoretical explanations of the effect found in the present research. These explanations supposed that smiling had an effect only between the smiler and the participant, whereas our results show that smiling has an effect beyond this relationship. In the present experiment, the participant had no reason to reciprocate altruism towards the second confederate, no additional variable had affected his/her perception of the second confederate and the participant was clearly anonymous for the second confederate.

It therefore seems that another explanation must be evoked to explain these results. Kleinke and Walton (1982) have found that a smile by confederates enhanced positive perceptions but also induced a good feeling in the participant. Various studies have shown that nonverbal behavioral cues enhance positive mood in the target. Fisher, Rytting and Heslin (1976) have found that touch led the person who was touched to feel more positively. The same effect is found with gaze (Jourard & Friedman, 1970). These findings are congruent with the results found by Kleinke and Walton and confirm that nonverbal behavior affects mood. A host of previous studies have shown that positive mood is associated with altruism (Bizman, Yinin, Ronco & Schachar, 1980; Forgas, 1997, 1998; Harris & Smith, 1975; Job, 1987; Levin & Isen, 1975; Rind, 1997; Weyant, 1978). In the current experiment, then, it is possible that the effect of smiling by the first confederate on the participant's helping behavior towards the second confederate is mediated by a positive mood activated by this nonverbal behavior. Of course, this mood activation hypothesis needs to be further studied to substantiate its theoretical validity, and in order to produce clear understanding of the link between

affective states and smiling. An evaluation of the participants' moods by numerical scales should be introduced in these studies.

REFERENCES

Baron, R. (1997). The sweet smell of . . . helping: Effects of pleasant ambient fragrance on prosocial behavior in shopping malls. *Personality and Social Psychology Bulletin, 23*, 498–503.

Batson, D., Coke, J., Chard, F., Smith, D., & Talaferro, A. (1979). Generality of the "glow of goodwill": Effects of mood on helping and information acquisition. *Social Psychology Quarterly, 42*, 176–179.

Bickman, L. (1974). Sex and helping behavior. *The Journal of Social Psychology, 92*, 43–53.

Bizman, A., Yinin, Y., Ronco, B., & Schachar, T. (1980). Regaining self-esteem through helping behavior. *The Journal of Psychology, 105*, 203–209.

Blevins, G., & Murphy, T. (1974). Feeling good and helping: Further phonebooth findings. *Psychological Reports, 34*, 326.

Brockner, J., Pressman, B., Cabitt, J., & Moran, P. (1982). Nonverbal intimacy, sex, and compliance: A field study. *Journal of Nonverbal Behavior, 6*, 253–258.

Clark, M., & Waddell, B. (1986). Effects of mood on thoughts about helping, attraction and information acquisition. *Social Psychology Quarterly, 56*, 31–35.

Cunningham, M. R. (1979). Weather, mood and helping behavior: Quasi experiments with the sunshine Samaritan. *Journal of Personality and Social Psychology, 37*, 1947–1956.

Deutsch, F., & Lamberti, D. (1986). Does social approval increase helping? *Personality and Social Psychology Bulletin, 12*, 149–157.

Fisher, J., Rytting, M., & Heslin, R. (1976). Hands touching hands: Affective and evaluative effects of an interpersonal touch. *Sociometry, 39*, 416–421.

Forgas, J. P. (1997). Affect and strategic communication: The effects of mood on the production and interpretation of verbal requests. *Polish Psychological Bulletin, 28*, 145–173.

Forgas, J. P. (1998). Asking nicely? The effects of mood on responding to more or less polite requests. *Personality and Social Psychology Bulletin, 24*, 173–185.

Galizio, M., & Hendrick, C. (1972). Effect of musical accompaniment on attitude: The guitar as a prop for persuasion. *Journal of Applied Social Psychology, 2*, 350–359.

Gruder, C. L., & Cook, T. D. (1971). Sex, dependency, and helping. *Journal of Personality and Social Psychology, 19,* 290–294.

Gueguen, N. (2002). The effects of a joke on tipping when it is delivered at the same time as the bill. *Journal of Applied Social Psychology, 32,* 1955–1963.

Gueguen, N., & Jacob, C. (2002). Direct look versus evasive glance and compliance with a request. *The Journal of Social Psychology, 142,* 393–396.

Gueguen, N., & LeGoherel, P. (2000). Effect on barmen's tipping of drawing a sun on the bottom of customers' checks. *Psychological Reports, 87,* 223–226.

Harris, M., & Bays, G. (1973). Altruism and sex roles. *Psychological Reports, 32,* 1002.

Harris, M. B., & Smith, R. J. (1975). Mood and helping. *The Journal of Social Psychology, 91,* 215–221.

Isen, A., & Levin, P. (1972). Effect of feeling good on helping. *Journal of Personality and Social Psychology, 21,* 384–388.

Isen, A., & Simmonds, S. (1978). The effect of feeling good on a helping task that is incompatible with good mood. *Social Psychology Quarterly, 41,* 346–349.

Job, S. (1987). The effect of mood on helping behavior. *The Journal of Social Psychology, 127,* 323–328.

Jourard, S., & Friedman, R. (1970). Experimenter-subject "distance" and self-disclosure. *Journal of Personality and Social Psychology, 15,* 278–282.

Kleinke, C., & Walton J. (1982). Influence of reinforced smiling on affective responses in an interview. *Journal of Personality and Social Psychology, 42,* 557–565.

Lau, S. (1982). The effect of smiling on person perception. *The Journal of Social Psychology, 117,* 63–67.

Levin, P., & Isen, A. (1975). Further studies on the effect of feeling good on helping. *Sociometry, 38,* 141–147.

Otta, E., Pereira, B., Delavati, N., Pimentel, O., & Pires, C. (1993). The effects of smiling and of head tilting on person perception. *The Journal of Psychology, 128,* 323–331.

Rind, B. (1996). Effect of beliefs about weather conditions on tipping. *Journal of Applied Social Psychology, 26,* 137–147.

Rind, B. (1997). Effect of interest arousal on compliance with a request for help. *Basic and Applied Social Psychology, 19,* 49–59.

Rind, B., & Bordia, P. (1996). Effect on restaurant tipping of male and female servers drawing a happy, smiling face on backs of customers' checks. *Journal of Applied Social Psychology, 26,* 218–225.

Solomon, H., Zener-Solomon, L., Arnone, M., Maur, B., Reda, R., & Roth, E. (1981). Anonymity and helping. *The Journal of Social Psychology, 113,* 37–43.

Takemura, K. (1993). The effect of interpersonal sentiments on behavioral intention of helping behavior among Japanese students. *The Journal of Social Psychology, 133,* 675–681.

Tidd, K., & Lockard, J. (1978). Monetary significance of the affiliative smile: A case of reciprocal altruism. *Bulletin of the Psychonomic Society, 11,* 344–346.

Weyant, J. (1978). Effects of mood states, costs, and benefits of helping. *Journal of Personality and Social Psychology, 36,* 1169–1176.

CRITICAL THINKING QUESTIONS

1. The results reported in this article indicate that people were more likely to help someone else in need immediately after being exposed to someone else who smiled at them. How long do you think the effect of being exposed to a smile on subsequent helping behavior lasts? Just a few moments or much longer? Why? Design a study to determine how long the effects of smiling persist.

2. The present study demonstrated that being exposed to a smile resulted in a higher rate of helping another person in need. The study did not determine, however, if the mediating variable that results in increased helping is that the person being smiled at is in a better mood. What other possibilities might explain the results (i.e., other than that the subject was in a better mood)? Design a study to determine if being in a better mood, as opposed to some other reason, is responsible for increased helping behavior.

3. The confederates in this study all were college-aged students of average attractiveness and appearance. Could the age or appearance of who is doing the smiling affect the subsequent helping behavior? Explain your reasoning.

4. Besides the variables described in this article, what other factors may impact people's helping behavior? Explain why you think each may influence helping behavior.

CHAPTER INTEGRATION QUESTIONS

1. "The only thing that is necessary for the triumph of evil is for good men to do nothing," according to eighteenth-century political writer Edmund Burke. Discuss why you either agree or disagree with this statement.

2. Integrate the content of the three articles in this chapter to identify one or more themes regarding helping behavior. Can Burke's quote be used to help understand the theme or themes? Explain.

3. Besides the factors covered in the articles, what else might have an impact on helping behavior? Discuss.

Chapter Eleven

AGGRESSION

Pɪᴄᴋ ᴜᴘ ᴀ ᴄᴏᴘʏ of today's newspaper. How much of it concerns acts of violence, whether from war, terrorism, homicide, or domestic violence? Aggression seems to be a fairly common part of modern life.

Now think about your own experiences. Chances are, you have not directly experienced a murder or assault. But what other types of aggressive behavior have you witnessed? Have you seen verbal aggression, where the intention was to hurt another person's feelings? Have you experienced cruelty in one form or another, where pain was experienced, even though no blood was shed?

Must aggression be part of life? Is it simply human nature and consequently something that cannot be changed? Or is it possible that the amount of aggression in the world could be reduced, if not actually eliminated?

Article 31, "Bad Girls," reports on an alarming trend in the last few years in which rates of female aggression are increasing dramatically—in some cases, nearly equaling those of males. This article suggests that it may no longer be warranted to think of aggression as a male tendency.

In contrast, Article 32, "Transmission of Aggression through Imitation of Aggressive Models," represents one of the earliest studies demonstrating that aggression is learned and in particular that the violence portrayed on television may contribute to aggressiveness in children. Since many behavioral patterns, such as aggression, may be learned in childhood, knowledge about what contributes to aggression can be used to help reduce those very behaviors.

Finally, Article 33 provides a contemporary examination of whether exposure to guns increases testosterone levels and subsequent aggressive behavior. "Guns, Testosterone, and Aggression: An Experimental Test of a Mediational Hypothesis," tests the hypothesis that mere exposure to an aggressive stimulus, like a gun, is sufficient to increase aggression in subjects and that this exposure to a weapon also increases subjects' testosterone levels. Furthermore, the study examines the possibility that an increased level of testosterone may be the mediating factor in the higher levels of aggression in subjects exposed to the gun.

ARTICLE 31 _____

What causes aggression? Psychologists have asked that question for nearly a ⟨
In their search for an answer, several theoretical perspectives have emerged.

One such perspective holds that aggression is an innate tendency, something toward which people are biologically predisposed. This view, espoused by theorists such as Sigmund Freud, maintains that people periodically need to discharge a natural buildup of aggressive energy. Thus, human aggressiveness may be a normal and perhaps unavoidable fact of life.

A second view suggests that aggression is a drive to harm someone elicited by some external stimulus. In other words, certain external conditions, such as frustration, produce a tendency for people to want to harm or injure others.

Other theories of aggression maintain that aggressive behavior is purely the product of social learning. People are aggressive because they have *learned* how to be aggressive, perhaps by watching other people act in such a fashion.

If aggressive behavior is somehow a biological predisposition, we might expect a universal manifestation of its occurrence. For example, if males are naturally more aggressive than females, then this pattern should be relatively constant in varying cultures around the world. Furthermore, we might expect that the rates of aggression for males and females in a given culture would likewise be fairly constant, with males consistently acting more aggressively than females across different points in time.

Common-sense observations, as well as attention to media reports, certainly confirm the fact that men are more aggressive than women. Or are they? Perhaps male aggression is more likely to be noticed and reported than female aggression. Or maybe males are more likely to be punished than females who commit the same acts. The following article by Barry Yeoman presents strong evidence that the rates of female violence may be much higher than most people think. Moreover, the incidence of female aggression may be increasing at rates far exceeding those of males.

Bad Girls

■ Barry Yeoman

Sante Kimes doesn't exactly match the popular image of the career outlaw. A low-rent Elizabeth Taylor look-alike, the 64-year-old widow is partial to gaudy jewelry, thick perfume and towering black wigs, and to rid herself of her wattles, she got lipo-sculpture at a California clinic.

But beneath the big hair is a criminal whose rap sheet dates back almost four decades. In the mid-'80s, Kimes went to prison for enslaving a platoon of teenage maids from Mexico City. The women were forced to work 18-hour days without weekend breaks, and Kimes kept them in line by beating them with coat hangers and throwing them into searing showers. When one young woman declined to strip for an inspection, according to court records and news reports, Kimes attacked her with a hot iron.

Then came the apparent murders, for which Kimes is a principal suspect. A banker vanished after ɑ dinner appointment with her. A family friend was pulled out of a dumpster, a bullet in his head, after expressing his reservations about a real-estate scam involving Kimes and her husband. And last summer, New Yorkers were shocked by the disappearance of 82-year-old Irene Silverman, a diminutive former ballerina who was the landlady of Kimes' son. The Kimeses were allegedly trying to defraud Silverman out of her $4 million mansion—and then the retired dancer turned up missing. Kimes claims she's innocent.

What makes this gruesome crime spree hard to grasp is that Kimes, a former pinup model, doesn't fit any of our ruffian archetypes: the L.A. gang member, the Mafia hit man, the young street punk. She's now at an age when many women are described as grandmotherly. Most significantly, she's a woman. "Woman is the creator and fosterer of life; man has been the mechanizer and destroyer of life," anthropologist Ashley Montagu once said. "Women love the human race; men are on the whole hostile to it."

But our cultural assumptions may be off the mark. Witness the proliferation of female perpetrators like Kimes making headlines. The tabloids had a field day with Lorena Bobbitt, who amputated the penis of her sleeping husband. She in turn was eclipsed by Susan Smith, who drowned her two sons in a South Carolina lake. More recently came the murder last May of former Saturday Night Live actor Phil Hartman by his wife Brynn, who then turned around and shot herself.

The increase in female violence over the past century has been dramatic. When Auburn University sociologist Penelope Hanke, Ph.D., reviewed records from an Alabama prison from 1929 to 1985, she discovered that 95% of the cases where women murdered strangers occurred after 1970, along with 60% of slayings of friends and relatives. In another study of 460 female murderers, Illinois State University's Ralph Weisheit, Ph.D., Distinguished Professor of criminal justice, found that women were becoming more stereotypically male in their reasons for murdering. He revealed that robbery-murders accounted for 42% of the cases in 1983, compared to 18% in 1940. And even though males commit the vast majority of street violence, females seem to be catching up. "In 10 or 20 years, those statistics

should be equal," predicts Coramae Ritchey Mann, Ph.D., professor emerita of criminal justice at Indiana University.

The recent surge in crime among women illustrates that in spite of their stereotype as gentle nurturers, women have the natural capacity to be as violent as men, according to a growing number of experts. The difference, behavioral studies suggest, is that women need greater incentives to express that violence. Social changes over the years—especially the movement toward gender equality—have provided several.

Freda Adler, Ph.D., Distinguished Professor of criminal justice at Rutgers University, calls this the "liberation hypothesis." As the tightly constructed sex roles of previous years start to weaken, she says, women simply have more and more opportunities to break the law. "Women are more involved in what's going on in the world than they were a generation ago," she says. "You can't embezzle if you're not near funds. You can't get involved in a fight at the bar if you're not allowed in the bar."

VIOLENCE AT HOME

The most revolutionary discoveries about women and aggression involve violence toward loved ones. A preponderance of evidence shows that women can be just as ferocious as men. The most famous of these studies comes from Murray Straus, Ph.D., the founder and co-director of the University of New Hampshire's Family Research Laboratory. His National Family Violence Surveys, conducted in 1975 and 1985 with a total of 8,145 married and cohabiting couples, showed that 12.4% of women have assaulted their spouses, compared to 12.2% of men. When it comes to severe assaults, the numbers were 4.6% for women and 5% for men.

A 1999 study by the British Home Office, a government agency in the United Kingdom, found that 4.2% of men—the exact same figure as for women—had been assaulted by a partner in the previous year.

The patterns go back before marriage. Irene Frieze, Ph.D., remembers seeing studies that showed women to be more prone to violence in dating situations. "I didn't believe it," recalls Frieze, a professor of psychology and women's studies at the University of Pittsburgh. "I said, 'This can't be true. I'm going to do my

---

Really Bad Girls:
The violence that made headlines

For Love or Money

From 1896 to 1908, Belle Gunness killed between 16 and 49 people, including her stepdaughter, hired hands, lovers and husbands. When her homestead mysteriously burned in 1908, officials unearthed the bodies of 10 men and two women. Gunness escaped.

Sinister Sisters

"Sister Amy" Gilligan charged new patients $1,000 upon entry into the Archer Home for Elderly and Indigent Persons in Windsor, Connecticut, and then promptly dispatched them with arsenic, often tricking them into leaving her their insurance money. Arrested in 1916, Gilligan may have killed as many as 40 people in her care.

Angel Makers

Between 1911 and 1929, the Hungarian towns of Nagyrev and Tiszakurt saw the deaths of more than 100 people at the hands of women, led by village midwife Susanna Fazekas. She would boil flypaper and distribute the resulting poison to the women. Thirty-four women were put on trial; 18 went to prison; eight were executed. Fazekas killed herself with poison.

Brutal Brothel

For 10 years, sisters Delfine and Maria Gonzales ran a brothel on a ranch in central Mexico, torturing girls who resisted and killing those who fell ill, tried to run away or lost their looks. When police raided the ranch in 1964, the bodies of some 80 women were found buried, along with countless babies and 11 male migrant workers.

Smother Love

Over 13 years, Marybeth Tining killed nine of her own children while authorities held that the deaths were natural. "I smothered them each with a pillow," she said later, "because I'm not a good mother." In 1987, she was sentenced to 20 years to life, her husband still believing she was innocent.

Angel of Death

Waltraud Wagner used lethal injections, strangulation or drowning to kill between 49 and 300 elderly patients in an Austrian hospital in the mid-1980s. Wagner's motive, as one of her three conspirators put it: "The ones who got on my nerves were dispatched directly to a free bed with the good Lord." All four were sent to prison.

—*Sarah Blustain*

---

own study.'" Sure enough, of the college students she surveyed, 58% of women had assaulted their dates, compared to 55% of men.

When Frieze brought up her findings in her classes, the students weren't surprised. "One woman said, 'Well, it makes me feel strong and powerful when I hit my boyfriend.' They feel safe—that they can get away with this behavior—because the men have this moral code and they'll never strike back." The men, Frieze adds, don't take the violence seriously, because little of it causes serious injuries.

Straus admits that when it comes to the most brutal domestic assaults, the domain is still men's—they commit six times the number women do. "If by violence, you mean 'who's injured?,' then it's an overwhelmingly male crime," he says. That's why there's no great demand for battered men's shelters, and why a disproportionate number of wife beatings get reported to the police.

"You can't just equate numbers," says Ruth Brandwein, Ph.D., a social policy professor at the State University of New York at Stony Brook. "Women who engage in violence are often already in violent relationships. They are living under such unbearable tension that it gives them some control over when they're going to be abused."

VIOLENCE ON THE STREET

Except for high profile lawbreakers like Aileen Wuornos, the Florida prostitute who robbed and killed at least seven of her johns, most of the crime news involves male perpetrators. If a woman is involved, she's generally considered an accomplice to a man. When Bonnie and Clyde were killed in the 1930s, the *New York Times* headline read, "Barrow and woman slain in Louisiana trap!" Even Karla Faye Tucker, executed in Texas last year for a pickax slaying, was working in concert with her boyfriend.

According to the FBI's Uniform Crime Report, women made up only 15% of all those arrested for violent crimes in 1996, but the gap is closing. The statistics show that arrests of women for violent crimes increased 90% between 1985 and 1994, compared to 43% for men. The numbers hold up across many specific crimes: aggravated assault, other assault, and sex offenses other than rape and prostitution. Only in the case of murder did men widen their lead: a 13% rise for men compared to a 4% drop for women.

Indiana University's Mann believes that crime statistics are only now starting to catch up with reality. "Women are just as violent as men, and were often just getting away with the violence," she says.

"Now, with equal rights, the justice system is looking at females differently," explains Mann. "Whereas before they were excused or overlooked, now they are being apprehended."

A criminal defense lawyer admitted, "If she hasn't committed murder and she has children at home, she walks." A judge confided, "It's difficult to send a mature woman to prison. I keep thinking, 'Hey! She is somebody's mother!'"

Frank Julian, J.D., a professor of legal studies at Murray State University in Kentucky, cites a Florida-based study showing that men were 23% more likely to be imprisoned than women who committed the same crime, partly because of the sentencing recommendations of the probation officers. "Women

offenders were often viewed as suffering from psychological or emotional problems, or as victims of family problems, bad marriages or dependent relationships," Julian writes. "Men were more likely to have their cases judged in view of the seriousness of the offense committed, employment history and prior record."

IS VIOLENCE IN THE GENES?

In the 1960s, famed psychologist Albert Bandura conducted a series of experiments in which children watched adult models hitting inflatable Bobo dolls. The children were then offered the opportunity to imitate the behavior. Under normal circumstances, the boys knocked down the dolls far more often than the girls did. But when the models got rewarded for knocking down the Bobos, the children's behavior, changed—the boys and girls became almost equally aggressive.

That seems to suggest that males are innately more violent than females—but that women will resort to aggression when given an incentive. Which makes sense to Brenda Shook, Ph.D., a biological psychologist at Union Institute in Sacramento. "Females of all species will go to great lengths, including violence, to protect the young," says Shook. But among humans, the primary responsibility for defending the family—and thus preserving the family genes—went to the male.

But both biological and cultural theories of women's innate capacity for violence hinge on one major trigger. Says Freda Adler: "We're talking about socialization." And for time immemorial, males have been conditioned to be aggressive. Boys got G.I. Joes; girls got Barbies. Men were sent off to war; women bandaged their wounds.

But American girls have always gotten mixed messages. Our culture rewards a certain type of violence in women. "It is the height of femininity to slap a man's face," says Murray Straus. "It's drilled into them."

The groundwork for female violence, it seems, has been there all along. But what may have been a subtler message in a more genteel society has become a clearer directive. The media increasingly promote female violence: Weapon-wielding women are becoming commonplace in everything from Hollywood movies to Saturday morning cartoons.

Women also absorb the cultural norms aimed at everyone, and "this is a violent country," says Cora-mae Ritchey Mann. "There's no reason this wouldn't have rubbed off on them."

READ MORE ABOUT IT

When She Was Bad: Violent Women and the Myth of Innocence, Patricia Pearson (Viking, 1997).

Abused Men: The Hidden Side of Domestic Violence, Philip W. Cook (Praeger, 1997).

CRITICAL THINKING QUESTIONS

1. Interview someone who has worked or volunteered in a women's shelter. How does his or her report of the role of female aggression in domestic relationships confirm or differ from the information presented in the article?

2. Are "role models" of violent females more prevalent in the media today than they were 20 years ago? To test your hypothesis, sample four or five contemporary films as well as some released two decades ago.

3. Discuss the so-called liberation hypothesis discussed in the article. Develop your own list of reasons that may account for the increase in female aggression in recent years.

4. The article notes that women who commit the same aggressive acts as men may be less likely to be sentenced. What factors other than the actual crime may influence sentencing decisions? Explain your answers.

5. Survey your friends or fellow students regarding the use of aggression by males and females in dating relationships. Do you find results similar to those reported in the article? Explain.

ARTICLE 32

Think of the amount of time that a typical child spends in front of the television. Do you think that what that child sees on "the tube" influences his or her behavior to a great extent? Or is television more neutral—just entertainment with no lasting effects?

A major concern of parents and social psychologists alike is the impact of one particular aspect of television on children's subsequent behavior: aggression. If you have not done so in a long time, sit down and watch the Saturday morning cartoons or other programs shown after school or in the early evening, when children are most likely to be watching. How many of these programs involve some sort of violence? What are these shows teaching children, not only in terms of behaviors but also in terms of values?

The following article by Albert Bandura, Dorothea Ross, and Sheila A. Ross was one of the earliest studies to examine the impact of televised aggression on the behavior of children. In the more than 40 years since its publication, numerous other experiments have been conducted on the same topic. These studies strongly suggest that viewing televised aggression has a direct impact on the aggressive behavior of its viewers. The research by Bandura and his colleagues helped initiate this important line of research.

Transmission of Aggression through Imitation of Aggressive Models[1]

■ Albert Bandura, Dorothea Ross, and Sheila A. Ross[2]

A previous study, designed to account for the phenomenon of identification in terms of incidental learning, demonstrated that children readily imitated behavior exhibited by an adult model in the presence of the model (Bandura & Huston, 1961). A series of experiments by Blake (1958) and others (Grosser, Polansky, & Lippitt, 1951; Rosenblith, 1959; Schachter & Hall, 1952) have likewise shown that mere observation of responses of a model has a facilitating effect on subjects' reactions in the immediate social influence setting.

While these studies provide convincing evidence for the influence and control exerted on others by the behavior of a model, a more crucial test of imitative learning involves the generalization of imitative response patterns to new settings in which the model is absent.

In the experiment reported in this paper, children were exposed to aggressive and nonaggressive adult models and were then tested for amount of imitative learning in a new situation in the absence of the model. According to the prediction, subjects exposed to aggressive models would reproduce aggressive acts resembling those of their models and would differ in this respect both from subjects who observed nonaggressive models and from who had no prior exposure to any models. This hypothesis assumed that subjects had learned imitative habits as a result of prior reinforcement, and these tendencies would generalize to some extent to adult experimenters (Miller & Dollard, 1941).

It was further predicted that observation of subdued nonaggressive models would have a generalized inhibiting effect on the subjects' subsequent behavior, and this effect would be reflected in a difference between the nonaggressive and the control groups, with subjects in the latter group displaying significantly more aggression.

Hypotheses were also advanced concerning the influence of the sex of model and sex of subjects on

Reprinted from *Journal of Abnormal and Social Psychology,* 1961, *63,* 575–582.

imitation. Fauls and Smith (1956) have shown that preschool children perceive their parents as having distinct preferences regarding sex appropriate modes of behavior for their children. Their findings, as well as informal observation, suggest that parents reward imitation of sex appropriate behavior and discourage or punish sex inappropriate imitative responses, e.g., a male child is unlikely to receive much reward for performing female appropriate activities, such as cooking, or for adopting other aspects of the maternal role, but these same behaviors are typically welcomed if performed by females. As a result of differing reinforcement histories, tendencies to imitate male and female models thus acquire differential habit strength. One would expect, on this basis, subjects to imitate the behavior of a same-sex model to a greater degree than a model of the opposite sex.

Since aggression, however, is a highly masculine-typed behavior, boys should be more predisposed than girls toward imitating aggression, the difference being most marked for subjects exposed to the male aggressive model.

METHOD

Subjects

The subjects were 36 boys and 36 girls enrolled in the Stanford University Nursery School. They ranged in age from 37 to 69 months, with a mean age of 52 months.

Two adults, a male and a female, served in the role of model, and one female experimenter conducted the study for all 72 children.

Experimental Design

Subjects were divided into eight experimental groups of six subjects each and a control group consisting of 24 subjects. Half the experimental subjects were exposed to aggressive models and half were exposed to models that were subdued and nonaggressive in their behavior. These groups were further subdivided into male and female subjects. Half the subjects in the aggressive and nonaggressive conditions observed same-sex models, while the remaining subjects in each group viewed models of the opposite sex. The control group had no prior exposure to the adult

models and was tested only in the generalization situation.

It seemed reasonable to expect that the subjects' level of aggressiveness would be positively related to the readiness with which they imitated aggressive modes of behavior. Therefore, in order to increase the precision of treatment comparisons, subjects in the experimental and control groups were matched individually on the basis of ratings of their aggressive behavior in social interactions in the nursery school.

The subjects were rated on four five-point rating scales by the experimenter and a nursery school teacher, both of whom were well acquainted with the children. These scales measured the extent to which subjects displayed physical aggression, verbal aggression, aggression toward inanimate objects, and aggressive inhibition. The latter scale, which dealt with the subjects' tendency to inhibit aggressive reactions in the face of high instigation, provided a measure of aggression anxiety.

Fifty-one subjects were rated independently by both judges so as to permit an assessment of interrater agreement. The reliability of the composite aggression score, estimated by means of the Pearson product-moment correlation, was .89.

The composite score was obtained by summing the ratings on the four aggression scales; on the basis of these scores, subjects were arranged in triplets and assigned at random to one of two treatment conditions or to the control group.

Experimental Conditions

In the first step in the procedure subjects were brought individually by the experimenter to the experimental room and the model who was in the hallway outside the room was invited by the experimenter to come and join in the game. The experimenter then escorted the subject to one corner of the room, which was structured as the subject's play area. After seating the child at a small table, the experimenter demonstrated how the subject could design pictures with potato prints and picture stickers provided. The potato prints included a variety of geometrical forms; the stickers were attractive multicolor pictures of animals, flowers, and western figures to be pasted on a pastoral scene. These activities were selected since they had been established, by previous studies in the nursery school, as having high interest value for the children.

After having settled the subject in his corner, the experimenter escorted the model to the opposite corner of the room which contained a small table and chair, a tinker toy set, a mallet, and a 5-foot inflated Bobo doll. The experimenter explained that these were the materials provided for the model to play with and, after the model was seated, the experimenter left the experimental room.

With subjects in the *nonaggressive condition,* the model assembled the tinker toys in a quiet subdued manner totally ignoring the Bobo doll.

In contrast, with subjects in the *aggressive condition,* the model began by assembling the tinker toys but after approximately a minute had elapsed, the model turned to the Bobo doll and spent the remainder of the period aggressing toward it.

Imitative learning can be clearly demonstrated if a model performs sufficiently novel patterns of responses which are unlikely to occur independently of the observation of the behavior of a model and if a subject reproduces these behaviors in substantially identical form. For this reason, in addition to punching the Bobo doll, a response that is likely to be performed by children independently of a demonstration, the model exhibited distinctive aggressive acts which were to be scored as imitative responses. The model laid Bobo on its side, sat on it and punched it repeatedly in the nose. The model then raised the Bobo doll, picked up the mallet and struck the doll on the head. Following the mallet aggression, the model tossed the doll up in the air aggressively and kicked it about the room. This sequence of physically aggressive acts was repeated approximately three times, interspersed with verbally aggressive responses such as "Sock him in the nose . . . ," "Hit him down . . . ," "Throw him in the air . . . ," "Kick him . . . ," "Pow . . . ," and two nonaggressive comments, "He keeps coming back for more" and "He sure is a tough fella."

Thus in the exposure situation, subjects were provided with a diverting task which occupied their attention while at the same time insured observation of the model's behavior in the absence of any instructions to observe or to learn the responses in question. Since subjects could not perform the model's aggressive behavior, any learning that occurred was purely on an observational or covert basis.

At the end of 10 minutes, the experimenter entered the room, informed the subject that he would now go to another game room, and bid the model goodbye.

AGGRESSION AROUSAL

Subjects were tested for the amount of imitative learning in a different experimental room that was set off from the main nursery school building. The two experimental situations were thus clearly differentiated; in fact, many subjects were under the impression that they were no longer on the nursery school grounds.

Prior to the test for imitation, however, all subjects, experimental and control, were subjected to mild aggression arousal to insure that they were under some degree of instigation to aggression. The arousal experience was included for two main reasons. In the first place, observation of aggressive behavior exhibited by others tends to reduce the probability of aggression on the part of the observer (Rosenbaum & deCharms, 1960). Consequently, subjects in the aggressive condition, in relation both to the nonaggressive and control groups, would be under weaker instigation following exposure to the models. Second, if subjects in the nonaggressive condition expressed little aggression in the face of appropriate instigation, the presence of an inhibitory process would seem to be indicated.

Following the exposure experience, therefore, the experimenter brought the subject to an anteroom that contained these relatively attractive toys: a fire engine, a locomotive, a jet fighter plane, a cable car, a colorful spinning top, and a doll set complete with wardrobe, doll carriage, and baby crib. The experimenter explained that the toys were for the subject to play with but, as soon as the subject became sufficiently involved with the play material (usually in about 2 minutes), the experimenter remarked that these were her very best toys, that she did not let just anyone play with them, and that she had decided to reserve these toys for the other children. However, the subject could play with any of the toys that were in the next room. The experimenter and the subject then entered the adjoining experimental room.

It was necessary for the experimenter to remain in the room during the experimental session; otherwise a number of the children would either refuse to remain alone or would leave before the termination of the session. However, in order to minimize any influence her presence might have on the subject's behavior, the experimenter remained as inconspicuous as possible by busying herself with paper work at a desk in the far corner of the room and avoiding any interaction with the child.

Test for Delayed Imitation

The experimental room contained a variety of toys including some that could be used in imitative or non-imitative aggression, and others that tended to elicit predominantly nonaggressive forms of behavior. The aggressive toys included a 3-foot Bobo doll, a mallet and peg board, two dart guns, and a tether ball with a face painted on it which hung from the ceiling. The nonaggressive toys, on the other hand, included a tea set, crayons and coloring paper, a ball, two dolls, three bears, cars and trucks, and plastic farm animals.

In order to eliminate any variation in behavior due to mere placement of the toys in the room, the play material was arranged in a fixed order for each of the sessions.

The subject spent 20 minutes in this experimental room during which time his behavior was rated in terms of predetermined response categories by judges who observed the session through a one-way mirror in an adjoining observation room. The 20-minute session was divided into 5-second intervals by means of an electric interval timer, thus yielding a total number of 240 response units for each subject.

The male model scored the experimental sessions for all 72 children. Except for the cases in which he served as model, he did not have knowledge of the subjects' group assignments. In order to provide an estimate of interscorer agreement, the performances of half the subjects were also scored independently by a second observer. Thus one or the other of the two observers usually had no knowledge of the conditions to which the subjects were assigned. Since, however, all but two of the subjects in the aggressive condition performed the models' novel aggressive responses while subjects in the other conditions only rarely

exhibited such reactions, subjects who were exposed to the aggressive models could be readily identified through their distinctive behavior.

The responses scored involved highly specific concrete classes of behavior and yielded high interscorer reliabilities, the product-moment coefficients being in the .90s.

Response Measures

Three measures of imitation were obtained:

> *Imitation of physical aggression:* This category included acts of striking the Bobo doll with the mallet, sitting on the doll and punching it in the nose, kicking the doll, and tossing it in the air.
>
> *Imitative verbal aggression:* Subject repeats the phrases, "Sock him," "Hit him down," "Kick him," "Throw him in the air," or "Pow."
>
> *Imitative nonaggressive verbal responses:* Subject repeats, "He keeps coming back for more," or "He sure is a tough fella."

During the pretest, a number of the subjects imitated the essential components of the model's behavior but did not perform the complete act, or they directed the imitative aggressive response to some object other than the Bobo doll. Two responses of this type were therefore scored and were interpreted as partially imitative behavior.

> *Mallet aggression:* Subject strikes objects other than the Bobo doll aggressively with the mallet.
>
> *Sits on the Bobo doll:* Subject lays the Bobo doll on its side and sits on it, but does not aggress toward it.

The following additional nonimitative aggressive responses were scored:

> *Punched Bobo doll:* Subject strikes, slaps, or pushes the doll aggressively.
>
> *Nonimitative physical and verbal aggression:* This category included physically aggressive acts directed toward objects other than the Bobo doll and any hostile remarks except for those in the verbal imitation category; e.g., "Shoot the Bobo," "Cut him," "Stupid ball," "Knock over people," "Horses fighting, biting."

Aggressive gun play: Subject shoots darts or aims the guns and fires imaginary shots at objects in the room.

Ratings were also made of the number of behavior units in which subjects played nonaggressively or sat quietly and did not play with any of the material at all.

RESULT

Complete Imitation of Models' Behavior

Subjects in the aggression condition reproduced a good deal of physical and verbal aggressive behavior resembling that of the models, and their mean scores differed markedly from those of subjects in the non-aggressive and control groups who exhibited virtually no imitative aggression (see Table 1).

Since there were only a few scores for subjects in the nonaggressive and control conditions (approxi-

mately 70% of the subjects had zero scores), and the assumption of homogeneity of variance could not be made, the Friedman two-way analysis of variance by ranks was employed to test the significance of the obtained differences.

The prediction that exposure of subjects to aggressive models increases the probability of aggressive behavior is clearly confirmed (see Table 2). The main effect of treatment conditions is highly significant both for physical and verbal imitative aggression. Comparison of pairs of scores by the sign test shows that the obtained over-all differences were due almost entirely to the aggression displayed by subjects who had been exposed to the aggressive models. Their scores were significantly higher than those of either the nonaggressive or control groups, which did not differ from each other (Table 2).

Imitation was not confined to the model's aggressive responses. Approximately one-third of the sub-

TABLE 1 / Mean Aggression Scores for Experimental and Control Subjects

| Response Category | Experimental Groups | | | | Control Groups |
| | Aggressive | | Nonaggressive | | |
	F Model	M Model	F Model	M Model	
Imitative physical aggression					
Female subjects	5.5	7.2	2.5	0.0	1.2
Male subjects	12.4	25.8	0.2	1.5	2.0
Imitative verbal aggression					
Female subjects	13.7	2.0	0.3	0.0	0.7
Male subjects	4.3	12.7	1.1	0.0	1.7
Mallet aggression					
Female subjects	17.2	18.7	0.5	0.5	13.1
Male subjects	15.5	28.8	18.7	6.7	13.5
Punches Bobo doll					
Female subjects	6.3	16.5	5.8	4.3	11.7
Male subjects	18.9	11.9	15.6	14.8	15.7
Nonimitative aggression					
Female subjects	21.3	8.4	7.2	1.4	6.1
Male subjects	16.2	36.7	26.1	22.3	24.6
Aggressive gun play					
Female subjects	1.8	4.5	2.6	2.5	3.7
Male subjects	7.3	15.9	8.9	16.7	14.3

TABLE 2 / Significance of the Differences between Experimental and Control Groups in the Expression of Aggression

Response Category	χ^2_r	Q	P	Comparison of Pairs of Treatment Conditions		
				Aggressive vs. Nonaggressive _p_	Aggressive vs. Control _p_	Nonaggressive vs. Control _p_
Imitative responses						
Physical aggression	27.17		< .001	< .001	< .001	.09
Verbal aggression	9.17		< .02	.004	.048	.09
Nonaggressive verbal responses		17.50	< .001	.004	.004	ns
Partial imitation						
Mallet aggression	11.06		< .01	.026	ns	.005
Sits on Bobo		13.44	< .01	.018	.059	ns
Nonimitative aggression						
Punches Bobo doll	2.87		ns			
Physical and verbal	8.96		< .02	.026	ns	ns
Aggressive gun play	2.75		ns			

Note: ns = nonsignificant.

jects in the aggressive condition also repeated the model's nonaggressive verbal responses while none of the subjects in either the nonaggressive or control groups made such remarks. This difference, tested by means of the Cochran Q test, was significant well beyond the .001 level (Table 2).

Partial Imitation of Models' Behavior

Differences in the predicted direction were also obtained on the two measures of partial imitation.

Analysis of variance of scores based on the subjects' use of the mallet aggressively toward objects other than the Bobo doll reveals that treatment conditions are a statistically significant course of variation (Table 2). In addition, individual sign tests show that both the aggressive and the control groups, relative to subjects in the nonaggressive condition, produced significantly more mallet aggression, the difference being particularly marked with regard to female subjects. Girls who observed nonaggressive models performed a mean number of 0.5 mallet aggression responses as compared to mean values of 18.0 and

13.1 for girls in the aggressive and control groups, respectively.

Although subjects who observed aggressive models performed more mallet aggression ($M = 20.0$) than their controls ($M = 13.3$), the difference was not statistically significant.

With respect to the partially imitative response of sitting on the Bobo doll, the over-all group differences were significant beyond the .01 level (Table 2). Comparison of pairs of scores by the sign test procedure reveals that subjects in the aggressive group reproduced this aspect of the models' behavior to a greater extent than did the nonaggressive ($p = .018$) or the control ($p = .059$) subjects. The latter two groups, on the other hand, did not differ from each other.

Nonimitative Aggression

Analyses of variance of the remaining aggression measures (Table 2) show that treatment conditions did not influence the extent to which subjects engaged in aggressive gun play or punched the Bobo doll. The effect of conditions is highly significant

($\chi^2 r = 8.96$, $p < .02$), however, in the case of the subjects' expression of nominative physical and verbal aggression. Further comparison of treatment pairs reveals that the main source of the over-all difference was the aggressive and nonaggressive groups which differed significantly from each other (Table 2), with subjects exposed to the aggressive models displaying the greater amount of aggression.

Influence of Sex of Model and Sex of Subjects on Imitation

The hypothesis that boys are more prone than girls to imitate aggression exhibited by a model was only partially confirmed. *t* tests computed for subjects in the aggressive condition reveal that boys reproduced more imitative physical aggression than girls ($t = 2.50$, $p < .01$). The groups do not differ, however, in their imitation of verbal aggression.

The use of nonparametric tests, necessitated by the extremely skewed distributions of scores for subjects in the nonaggressive and control conditions, preclude an over-all test of the influence of sex of model per se, and of the various interactions between the main effects. Inspection of the means presented in Table 1 for subjects in the aggression condition, however, clearly suggests the possibility of a Sex × Model interaction. This interaction effect is much more consistent and pronounced for the male model than for the female model. Male subjects, for example, exhibited more physical ($t = 2.07$, $p < .05$) and verbal imitative aggression ($t = 2.51$, $p < .05$), more nonimitative aggression ($t = 3.15$, $p < .025$), and engaged in significantly more aggressive gun play ($t = 2.12$, $p < .05$) following exposure to the aggressive male model than the female subjects. In contrast, girls exposed to the female model performed considerably more imitative verbal aggression and more nonimitative aggression than did the boys (Table 1). The variances, however, were equally large and with only a small *N* in each cell the mean differences did not reach statistical significance.

Data for the nonaggressive and control subjects provide additional suggestive evidence that the behavior of the male model exerted a greater influence than the female model on the subjects' behavior in the generalization situation.

It will be recalled that, except for the greater amount of mallet aggression exhibited by the control subjects, no significant differences were obtained between the nonaggressive and control groups. The data indicate, however, that the absence of significant differences between these two groups was due primarily to the fact that subjects exposed to the nonaggressive female model did not differ from the controls on any of the measures of aggression. With respect to the male model, on the other hand, the differences between the groups are striking. Comparison of the sets of scores by means of the sign test reveals that, in relation to the control group, subjects exposed to the nonaggressive male model performed significantly less imitative physical aggression ($p = .06$), less imitative verbal aggression ($p = .002$), less mallet aggression ($p = .003$), less nonimitative physical and verbal aggression ($p = .03$) and they were less inclined to punch the Bobo doll ($p = .07$).

While the comparison of subgroups, when some of the over-all tests do not reach statistical significance, is likely to capitalize on chance differences, nevertheless the consistency of the findings adds support to the interpretation in terms of influence by the model.

Nonaggressive Behavior

With the exception of expected sex differences, Lindquist (1956) Type III analyses of variance of the nonaggressive response scores yielded few significant differences.

Female subjects spent more time than boys playing with dolls ($p < .001$), with the tea set ($p < .001$), and coloring ($p < .05$). The boys, on the other hand, devoted significantly more time than the girls to exploratory play with the guns ($p < .01$). No sex differences were found in respect to the subjects' use of the other stimulus objects, i.e., farm animals, cars, or tether ball.

Treatment conditions did produce significant differences on two measures of nonaggressive behavior that are worth mentioning. Subjects in the nonaggressive condition engaged in significantly more nonaggressive play with dolls than either subjects in the aggressive group ($t = 2.67$, $p < .02$), or in the control group ($t = 2.57$, $p < .02$).

Even more noteworthy is the finding that subjects who observed nonaggressive models spent more than twice as much time as subjects in aggressive condition ($t = 3.07$, $p < .01$) in simply sitting quietly without handling any of the play material.

DISCUSSION

Much current research on social learning is focused on the shaping of new behavior through rewarding and punishing consequences. Unless responses are emitted, however, they cannot be influenced. The results of this study provide strong evidence that observation of cues produced by the behavior of others is one effective means of eliciting certain forms of responses for which the original probability is very low or zero. Indeed, social imitation may hasten or short-cut the acquisition of new behaviors without the necessity of reinforcing successive approximations as suggested by Skinner (1953).

Thus subjects given an opportunity to observe aggressive models later reproduced a good deal of physical and verbal aggression (as well as nonaggressive responses) substantially identical with that of the model. In contrast, subjects who were exposed to nonaggressive models and those who had no previous exposure to any models only rarely performed such responses.

To the extent that observation of adult models displaying aggression communicates permissiveness for aggressive behavior, such exposure may serve to weaken inhibitory responses and thereby to increase the probability of aggressive reactions to subsequent frustrations. The fact, however, that subjects expressed their aggression in ways that clearly resembled the novel patterns exhibited by the models provides striking evidence for the occurrence of learning by imitation.

In the procedure employed by Miller and Dollard (1941) for establishing imitative behavior, adult or peer models performed discrimination responses following which they were consistently rewarded, and the subjects were similarly reinforced whenever they matched the leaders' choice responses. While these experiments have been widely accepted as demonstrations of learning by means of imitation, in fact, they simply involve a special case of discrimination learning in which the behavior of others serves as dis-criminative stimuli for responses that are already part of the subject's repertoire. Auditory or visual environmental cues could easily have been substituted for the social stimuli to facilitate the discrimination learning. In contrast, the process of imitation studied in the present experiment differed in several important respects from the one investigated by Miller and Dollard in that subjects learned to combine fractional responses into relatively complex novel patterns solely by observing the performance of social models without any opportunity to perform the models' behavior in the exposure setting, and without any reinforcers delivered either to the models or to the observers.

An adequate theory of the mechanisms underlying imitative learning is lacking. The explanations that have been offered (Logan, Olmsted, Rosner, Schwartz, & Stevens, 1955; Maccoby, 1959) assume that the imitator performs the model's responses covertly. If it can be assumed additionally that rewards and punishments are self-administered in conjunction with the covert responses, the process of imitative learning could be accounted for in terms of the same principles that govern instrumental trial-and-error learning. In the early stages of the developmental process, however, the range of component responses in the organism's repertoire is probably increased through a process of classical conditioning (Bandura & Huston, 1961; Mowrer, 1950).

The data provide some evidence that the male model influenced the subjects' behavior outside the exposure setting to a greater extent than was true for the female model. In the analyses of the Sex × Model interactions, for example, only the comparisons involving the male model yielded significant differences. Similarly, subjects exposed to the nonaggressive male model performed less aggressive behavior than the controls, whereas comparisons involving the female model were consistently nonsignificant.

In a study of learning by imitation, Rosenblith (1959) has likewise found male experimenters more effective than females in influencing children's behavior. Rosenblith advanced the tentative explanation that the school setting may involve some social deprivation in respect to adult males which, in turn, enhances the male's reward value.

The trends in the data yielded by the present study suggest an alternative explanation. In the case of a highly masculine-typed behavior such as physical aggression, there is a tendency for both male and female subjects to imitate the male model to a greater degree than the female model. On the other hand, in the case of verbal aggression, which is less clearly sex linked, the greatest amount of imitation occurs in relation to the same-sex model. These trends together with the finding that boys in relation to girls are in general more imitative of physical aggression but do not differ in imitation of verbal aggression, suggest that subjects may be differentially affected by the sex of the model but that predictions must take into account the degree to which the behavior in question is sex-typed.

The preceding discussion has assumed that maleness-femaleness rather than some other personal characteristics of the particular models involved, is the significant variable—an assumption that cannot be tested directly with the data at hand. It was clearly evident, however, particularly from boys' spontaneous remarks about the display of aggression by the female model, that some subjects at least were responding in terms of a sex discrimination and their prior learning about what is sex appropriate behavior (e.g., "Who is that lady? That's not the way for a lady to behave. Ladies are supposed to act like ladies. . . ." "You should have seen what that girl did in there. She was just acting like a man. I never saw a girl act like that before. She was punching and fighting but not swearing."). Aggression by the male model, on the other hand, was more likely to be seen as appropriate and approved by both the boys ("Al's a good socker, he beat up Bobo. I want to sock like Al.") and the girls ("That man is a strong fighter, he punched and punched and he could hit Bobo right down to the floor and if Bobo got up he said, 'Punch your nose.' He's a good fighter like Daddy.").

The finding that subjects exposed to the quiet models were more inhibited and unresponsive than subjects in the aggressive condition, together with the obtained difference on the aggression measures, suggests that exposure to inhibited models not only decreases the probability of occurrence of aggressive behavior but also generally restricts the range of behavior emitted by the subjects.

"Identification with aggressor" (Freud, 1946) or "defensive identification" (Mowrer, 1950), whereby a person presumably transforms himself from object to agent of aggression by adopting the attributes of an aggressive threatening model so as to allay anxiety, is widely accepted as an explanation of the imitative learning of aggression.

The development of aggressive modes of response by children of aggressively punitive adults, however, may simply reflect object displacement without involving any such mechanism of defensive identification. In studies of child training antecedents of aggressively antisocial adolescents (Bandura & Walters, 1959) and of young hyperaggressive boys (Bandura, 1960), the parents were found to be nonpermissive and punitive of aggression directed toward themselves. On the other hand, they actively encouraged and reinforced their sons' aggression toward persons outside the home. This pattern of differential reinforcement of aggressive behavior served to inhibit the boys' aggression toward the original instigators and fostered the displacement of aggression toward objects and situations eliciting much weaker inhibitory responses.

Moreover, the findings from an earlier study (Bandura & Huston, 1961), in which children imitated to an equal degree aggression exhibited by a nurturant and a nonnurturant model, together with the results of the present experiment in which subjects readily imitated aggressive models who were more or less neutral figures suggest that mere observation of aggression, regardless of the quality of the model-subject relationship, is a sufficient condition for producing imitative aggression in children. A comparative study of the subjects' imitation of aggressive models who are feared, who are liked and esteemed, or who are essentially neutral figures would throw some light on whether or not a more parsimonious theory than the one involved in "identification with the aggressor" can explain the modeling process.

SUMMARY

Twenty-four preschool children were assigned to each of three conditions. One experimental group observed aggressive adult models; a second observed inhibited nonaggressive models; while subjects in a control group had no prior exposure to the models. Half the subjects in the experimental conditions observed same-sex models and half viewed models of the opposite sex. Subjects were then tested for the amount of imitative as well as nonimitative aggression performed in a new situation in the absence of the models.

Comparison of the subjects' behavior in the generalization situation revealed that subjects exposed to aggressive models reproduced a good deal of aggression resembling that of the models, and that their mean scores differed markedly from those of subjects in the nonaggressive and control groups. Subjects in the aggressive condition also exhibited significantly more partially imitative and nonimitative aggressive behavior and were generally less inhibited in their behavior than subjects in the nonaggressive condition.

Imitation was found to be differentially influenced by the sex of the model with boys showing more aggression than girls following exposure to the male model, the difference being particularly marked on highly masculine-typed behavior.

Subjects who observed the nonaggressive models, especially the subdued male model, were generally less aggressive than their controls.

The implications of the findings based on this experiment and related studies for the psychoanalytic theory of identification with the aggressor were discussed.

REFERENCES

Bandura, A. Relationship of family patterns to child behavior disorders. Progress Report, 1960, Stanford University, Project No. M-1734, United States Public Health Service.

Bandura, A., & Huston, Aletha C. Identification as a process of incidental learning. *J. abnorm. soc. Psychol.*, 1961, *63*, 311–318.

Bandura, A., & Walters, R. H. *Adolescent aggression.* New York: Ronald, 1959.

Blake, R. R. The other person in the situation. In R. Tagiuri & L. Petrullo (Eds.), *Person perception and interpersonal behavior.* Stanford, Calif.: Stanford Univer. Press, 1958. Pp. 229–242.

Fauls, Lydia B., & Smith, W. D. Sex-role learning of five-year olds. *J. genet. Psychol.*, 1956, *89*, 105–117.

Freud, Anna. *The ego and the mechanisms of defense.* New York: International Univer. Press, 1946.

Grosser, D., Polansky, N., & Lippitt, R. A laboratory study of behavior contagion. *Hum. Relat.*, 1951, *4*, 115–142.

Lindquist, E. F. *Design and analysis of experiments.* Boston: Houghton Mifflin, 1956.

Logan, F., Olmsted, O. L., Rosner, B. S., Schwartz, R. D., & Stevens, C. M. *Behavior theory and social science.* New Haven: Yale Univer. Press, 1955.

Maccoby, Eleanor E. Role-taking in childhood and its consequences for social learning. *Child Develpm.*, 1959, *30*, 239–252.

Miller, N. E., & Dollard, J. *Social learning and imitation.* New Haven: Yale Univer. Press, 1941.

Mowrer, O. H. (Ed.) Identification: A link between learning theory and psychotherapy In, *Learning theory and personality dynamics.* New York: Ronald, 1950. Pp. 69–94.

Rosenbaum, M. E., & deCharms, R. Direct and vicarious reduction of hostility. *J. abnorm. soc. Psychol.*, 1960, *60*, 105–111.

Rosenblith, Judy F. Learning by imitation in kindergarten children. *Child Develpm.*, 1959, *30*, 69–80.

Schachter, S., & Hall, R. Group-derived restraints and audience persuasion. *Hum. Relat.*, 1952, *5*, 397–406.

Skinner, B. F. *Science and human behavior.* New York: Macmillan, 1953.

ENDNOTES

1. This investigation was supported by Research Grant M-4398 from the National Institute of Health, United States Public Health Service.

2. The authors wish to express their appreciation to Edith Dowley, Director, and Patricia Rowe, Head Teacher, Stanford University Nursery School for their assistance throughout this study.

CRITICAL THINKING QUESTIONS

1. Notice that the children's anger was aroused prior to their being placed in the situation where their aggression would be measured. Why was this done? What might have resulted had their anger not been aroused beforehand? Were there different effects, depending on whether the children experienced prior anger arousal? If so, then what are the implications for generalizing the results of this study to how violent television affects its young viewers? Explain your answers.

2. This study reported that the gender of the actor made a difference in how much physical aggression was imitated. It also mentioned that some of the children simply found it inappropriate for a female actor to act aggressively. Over 40 years have passed since publication of this study. Do you think children today would still see physical aggression by a female as inappropriate? Support your answer.

3. Analyze the content of television shows directed toward children (including cartoons) for aggression, examining the type of aggression (physical versus verbal) and the gender of the aggressive character. Relate the findings to Question 2, above.

4. Examine research conducted over the last three decades that documents the impact of televised aggression on children's behavior. Given these findings, what should be done? Should laws be passed to regulate the amount of violence shown on television? Or should this form of censorship be avoided? Explain. What other alternatives might exist to reverse or prevent the potential harm of observing violence on television?

ADDITIONAL RELATED READINGS

Coyne, S. M., & Archer, J. (2005). The relationship between indirect and physical aggression on television and real life. *Social Development, 14*(2), 324–338.

Selah-Shayovitis, R. (2006). Adolescent preferences for violence in television shows and music video clips. *International Journal of Adolescence and Youth, 13*(1–2), 99–112.

ARTICLE 33_____

An important area of research on aggression concerns its causes. Three general classes of theories have emerged: The first class, which can be called *instinct theories,* explains aggression as somehow rooted in biology. Thus, aggression stems from internally generated forces and is something that human beings are genetically programmed to do. A second type of theory, called *drive reduction,* essentially explains aggression as arising from forces outside the individual; for instance, experiencing frustration may produce readiness to engage in aggressive behavior. *Social learning* is the third theoretical explanation of aggression. Basically, this approach maintains that aggression, like many other complex social behaviors, is learned. It is not instinctive nor is it simply a reaction to a specific external event.

Each of these theoretical views attributes aggression to a different cause. It follows, then, that whichever theoretical explanation you adopt will influence how optimistic you are about the possible control of aggression. For example, if you believe that aggression is innate, a biological predisposition of sorts, then there is not much that can be done about it. It is simply human nature to be aggressive. However, if you believe that aggression is learned, then it is not inevitable that people be aggressive. After all, if aggressive behaviors can be learned, then nonaggressive behaviors can be learned, as well. And if aggression arises from forces outside the individual, then aggression can be reduced to the extent that one can control those outside forces.

A good deal of research has been done to establish that exposure to aggressive stimuli increases aggressive behavior. For example, a so-called weapons effect has been found, whereby merely being in the presence of a weapon increases aggressive behavior. The following contemporary article by Jennifer Klinesmith, Tim Kasser, and Francis T. McAndrew examines whether exposure to a gun increases aggression. In addition, this article looks at whether the presence of a gun also increases testosterone level and whether an increased level of testosterone might be a mediating factor in expressing aggressive behavior.

Guns, Testosterone, and Aggression
An Experimental Test of a Mediational Hypothesis
■ Jennifer Klinesmith, Tim Kasser, and Francis T. McAndrew

ABSTRACT

We tested whether interacting with a gun increased testosterone levels and later aggressive behavior. Thirty male college students provided a saliva sample (for testosterone assay), interacted with either a gun or a children's toy for 15 min, and then provided another saliva sample. Next, subjects added as much hot sauce as they wanted to a cup of water *they believed another subject would have to drink. Males who interacted with the gun showed significantly greater increases in testosterone and added more hot sauce to the water than did those who interacted with the children's toy. Moreover, increases in testosterone partially mediated the effects of interacting with the gun on this aggressive behavior.*

Klinesmith, J., Kasser, T., & McAndrew, F. T. (2006). Guns, testosterone, and aggression: An experimental test of a mediational hypothesis. *Psychological Science, 17*(7), 568–571. Copyright © 2006 by American Psychological Society. Reprinted with permission of Blackwell Publishers.

Substantial evidence suggests that aggression can be increased by the presence of weapons in the environment and by the hormone testosterone. Several studies show that the presence of aggressive environmental cues such as weapons can increase the accessibility of hostile, aggressive thoughts and lead to more aggressive behavior (Anderson, Benjamin, & Bartholow, 1998; Bartholow, Anderson, Carnagey, & Benjamin, 2005; Berkowitz & LePage, 1967; Bettencourt & Kernahan, 1997; Killias & Haas, 2002). Regarding testosterone, in animal species ranging from chickens to monkeys, the injection of this hormone increases aggressiveness and social dominance behavior, regardless of whether the animals are males or females (Ellis, 1986); in humans, however, the results are more mixed, with many laboratory and field studies revealing strong positive relations between testosterone and levels of restlessness, tenseness, and tendency toward violence (Archer, 1994; Campbell, Muncer, & Odber, 1997; Dabbs, Carr, Frady, & Riad, 1995; Dabbs, Jurkovic, & Frady, 1991) and other studies failing to replicate such effects (Archer, 1991; Archer, Birring, & Wu, 1998; O'Connor, Archer, Hair, & Wu, 2001; Rowe, Maughan, Worthman, Costello, & Angold, 2004).

Surprisingly, we were unable to find any studies that examined whether testosterone and the presence of a weapon might work together to increase aggressive behavior. Perhaps the presence of a stimulus such as a gun triggers increases in testosterone levels, which in turn increase aggressive behavior. Such a chain of events would be predicted by the *challenge hypothesis* developed by Wingfield, Hegner, Dufty, and Ball (1990) to explain aggressive behavior in male pair-bonded birds. According to this hypothesis, testosterone rises in response to situational cues that represent either a threat to a male's status or a signal that competition with other males is imminent; such increases in testosterone then facilitate whatever competitive behaviors (including potentially aggressive responses) are necessary for meeting the challenge. The challenge hypothesis has been supported by studies across a wide range of vertebrate species (Cavigelli & Pereira, 2000; Ferree, Wikelski, & Anderson, 2004; Hirschenhauser, Taborsky, Oliveira, Canario, & Oliveira, 2004; Muller & Wrangham, 2004); most studies in humans have focused on how males' testosterone levels rise and fall depending on success or

failure in competitions (Archer, 1991; Booth, Shelley, Mazur, Tharp, & Kittok,1989; Gladue, Boechler, & McCaul,1989; Mazur, Booth, & Dabbs,1992; Mazur & Lamb, 1980) or in response to insults (Cohen, Nisbett, Bowdle, & Schwarz, 1996; see Archer, 2006, for a review of the applicability of the challenge hypothesis to humans).

In this study, we examined whether the presence of a gun (vs. a control object) might act as a stimulus signaling competition and a threat to status; if so, according to the challenge hypothesis, it should cause increases in males' testosterone levels, which in turn should increase their aggressive behavior. We assessed males' testosterone levels both before and after interacting with a gun or a children's toy; to measure aggression, we adapted a method developed by Lieberman, Solomon, Greenberg, and McGregor (1999) that gives subjects the opportunity to anonymously put hot sauce in a cup of water that they believe another person will have to drink. We hypothesized that males who interacted with the gun would show both a greater increase in testosterone levels and more aggression than would males who interacted with the children's toy. We also hypothesized that changes in testosterone levels would be correlated with aggression levels and would indeed mediate the effects of interacting with a gun on later aggressive behavior.

METHOD

Subjects

Subjects were 30 male college students (age range: 18–22) who received extra course credit or a small monetary reward for their participation. All subjects were run during the afternoon or early evening.

Procedure and Materials

When recruited, subjects were informed that the study would examine taste sensitivity in males and that they would therefore need to provide saliva for hormone analysis; subjects were asked not to eat, drink, smoke, or brush their teeth for 1 hr prior to testing in order to minimize impurities in the saliva samples. When subjects arrived at the lab, a female experimenter confirmed that the subjects had indeed followed these instructions before she administered consent procedures. Next, participants provided an approximately 6-ml sample of saliva by spitting into a cup; this saliva was used to assess baseline, or Time 1, testosterone levels.

All subjects were then led into a room containing a television, a chair, and a table with an object and some paper on it. For experimental subjects, the object was a pellet gun identical in size, shape, and feel to a Desert Eagle automatic handgun; for control subjects, the object was the children's game Mouse Trap™. Subjects were told that the study was investigating whether taste sensitivity was associated with the attention to detail required for creating instructions concerning the object. Subjects were therefore asked to spend 15 min handling the object and writing a set of instructions about how to assemble and disassemble it; a drawing of the object was also provided for subjects to label the object's parts. The handgun and children's game were similar in number and complexity of parts.

After 15 min, the experimenter reentered the room, asked the subject to stop working on the instructions, and obtained a Time 2 saliva sample from the subject. The subject was told he would next perform the taste-sensitivity portion of the study. He was given a cup filled with 85 g of water and a single drop of Frank's Red Hot Sauce. The subject was told that the sample had been prepared by a previous subject, was instructed to take a sip of the sample, and was then asked to rate the taste of the sample on a scale provided.

The experimenter left and then returned with a tray containing a cup of 85 g of water, a nearly full bottle of Frank's Red Hot Sauce, and a lid. The subject was asked to prepare a sample for the next subject by placing as much hot sauce in the water as he wanted. He was assured that neither the person who drank it nor the experimenter would know how much hot sauce he had put in the water, as the lid was to be put on the cup after the hot sauce was added. The experimenter then left the room, and the subject signaled when he was finished adding the hot sauce. (Throughout this process, the gun or the game remained in the room.) The cup was then removed from the room, and the experimenter weighed it again to obtain a measure of the amount of hot

sauce, in grams, the subject had added to the water. This served as our primary measure of aggression (see Lieberman et al., 1999).

Because of the potentially arousing nature of the experiment, we wanted to ensure that all subjects were reasonably calm when they left the lab. Therefore, all subjects next watched a relaxing video of nature scenes and classical music. Given that subjects had been deceived, we next debriefed them, emphasizing that they should not feel badly about any aggressive behavior they exhibited. Interestingly, several subjects were disappointed when told that the sample of hot sauce and water they had prepared would not actually be given to the next subject. No subjects expressed suspicion as to the true nature of the study.

Testosterone Levels

Time 1 and Time 2 saliva samples were stored for 24 hr at room temperature, centrifuged, and then frozen at −20 °C until the time of the assay (Erikkson & Von Der Pahlen, 2002). The samples were then brought to room temperature, transferred to Eppendorf tubes, centrifuged for 15 min at 3,000 rpm to remove debris, and then assayed in duplicate using a commercially available microwell kit for testosterone level (Salimetrics, LLC, State College, PA). All samples were assayed in house in a single batch using a standard radioimmunoassay (RIA) procedure under the supervision of an experienced RIA technician; at both Time 1 and Time 2, the duplicates were averaged to yield our measures of testosterone level. The intra-assay coefficient of variation for subjects was 5.3%, and the sensitivity of the assay was less than 1.5 pg/ml from zero for men. Mean Time 1 and Time 2 testosterone levels were 222.59 pg/ml *(SD = 97.17)* and 253.92 pg/ml *(SD = 98.32),* respectively. We subtracted each subject's Time 1 level from his Time 2 level to obtain a measure of change in testosterone.

RESULTS

Our first hypothesis was confirmed: Subjects who interacted with the handgun showed a greater increase in testosterone from Time 1 to Time 2 (mean change = 62.05 pg/ml, *SD* = 48.86) than did those who interacted with the children's game (mean change = 0.68 pg/ml, SD = 28.57), $t(28)$ = –4.20, p_{rep} = .99, d = 1.53. Thus, interacting with the gun increased testosterone levels.

Our second hypothesis was also confirmed: Subjects who interacted with the gun added more hot sauce to the water (M = 13.61 g, SD = 8.35) than did those who interacted with the children's toy (M = 4.23 g, SD = 2.62), $t(28)$ = –4.16, p_{rep} = .99, d = 1.52. Thus, interacting with the gun increased aggressive behavior.

Our third hypothesis was also confirmed: The amount of hot sauce placed in the cup was positively correlated with changes in testosterone level (r = .64, p_{rep} = .99; R^2 = .41). Given that all three of Baron and Kenny's (1986) prerequisites for a mediational model were met, we next examined whether the size of the association between the predictor variable (i.e., gun vs. game) and the outcome variable (i.e., grams of hot sauce added) diminished once the effects of the purported mediating variable (i.e., changes in testosterone) were controlled. Indeed, the size of the correlation between group membership (experimental vs. control) and aggression dropped from r = –.62 (p_{rep} = .99) to pr = –.36 (p_{rep} = .91) after controlling for changes in testosterone. Finally, to more stringently test our mediational hypothesis, we computed Sobel's (1982) test for mediation, using the Web site developed by Preacher and Leonardelli (2001). As before, the evidence suggested that the effect of guns on aggression was significantly mediated by changes in testosterone levels, Sobel's test = 2.09, p_{rep} = .93.

DISCUSSION

Past research shows that both testosterone and exposure to guns are associated with aggressive behavior, but no studies, to our knowledge, have examined how the two factors might work together. The present results demonstrated that males who interacted with a gun showed a greater increase in testosterone levels and more aggressive behavior than did males who interacted with a children's toy. Mediational analyses suggested that part of the reason that guns increase aggression is that they cause increases in testosterone levels.

Such findings not only are consistent with the challenge hypothesis (Wingfield et al., 1990), but also provide new support for it both by examining a new type of "challenging" stimulus and by assessing later aggressive behavior. Additionally, the results provide evidence against some interpretations suggesting that experimental effects of guns on aggression are due to subtle demand characteristics. That is, it seems unlikely that subtle experimenter pressures could significantly increase subjects' testosterone levels; instead, it seems more reasonable to believe that the presence of the gun had this effect.

Future research could explore a variety of avenues for correcting some of the limitations of the present study. For example, would females' biological and behavioral responses to guns be similar to males'? Perhaps they would, as other female animals act more aggressively when injected with testosterone (Ellis, 1986). But perhaps they would not, as the types of evolutionary challenges faced by ancestral females were different from those faced by males, and thus females may react to guns differently than males. Another topic worthy of further study concerns the fact that subjects in this study only had the opportunity to aggress in an anonymous, rather indirect fashion against an unknown individual. Would the same pattern of results hold if the aggression was directed against a particular individual, or if there was a possibility of retribution from the victim? Finally, would past experience with guns moderate these effects? That is, would individuals who frequently handle guns (such as hunters or soldiers) respond similarly to those with little or no experience with weapons? Previous research (Bartholow et al., 2005) suggests that this may be the case, but a link with testosterone has yet to be established.

In sum, the present study replicates past research showing that exposure to guns may increase later interpersonal aggression, but further demonstrates that, at least for males, it does so in part by increasing testosterone levels. Such findings raise many of the usual questions about whether the presence of guns in modern society contributes to violent behavior. Although our study is clearly far from definitive, its results suggest that guns may indeed increase aggressiveness partially via changes in the hormone testosterone.

ACKNOWLEDGMENTS

We thank Heather Hoffmann, Janet Kirkley, Glen Normile, and Neil Schmitzer-Torbert for their assistance. This research was funded by a grant from the Richter Memorial Scholarship Program.

REFERENCES

Anderson, C. A., Benjamin, A. J., Jr., & Bartholow, B. D. (1998). Does the gun pull the trigger? Automatic priming effects of weapon pictures and weapon names. *Psychological Science, 9,* 308–314.

Archer, J. (1991). The influence of testosterone on human aggression. *British Journal of Psychology, 82,* 1–28.

Archer, J. (1994). Violence between men. In J. Archer (Ed.), *Male violence* (pp. 121–140). London: Routledge.

Archer, J. (2006). Testosterone and human aggression: An evaluation of the challenge hypothesis. *Neuroscience and Biobehavioral Reviews, 30,* 319–345.

Archer, J., Birring, S. S., & Wu, F. C. W. (1998). The association between testosterone and aggression among young men: Empirical findings and a meta-analysis. *Aggressive Behavior, 24,* 411–420.

Baron, R. M., & Kenny, D. A. (1986). The moderator-mediator variable distinction in social psychological research: Conceptual, strategic, and statistical considerations. *Journal of Personality and Social Psychology, 51,* 1173–1182.

Bartholow, B. D., Anderson, C. A., Carnagey, N. L., & Benjamin, A. J., Jr. (2005). Interactive effects of life experience and situational cues on aggression: The weapons priming effect in hunters and non-hunters. *Journal of Experimental Social Psychology, 41,* 48–60.

Berkowitz, L., & LePage, A. (1967). Weapons as aggression-eliciting stimuli. *Journal of Personality and Social Psychology, 7,* 202–207.

Bettencourt, B. A., & Kernahan, C. (1997). A meta-analysis of aggression in the presence of violent cues: Effects of gender differences and aversive provocation. *Aggressive Behavior, 23,* 447–456.

Booth, A., Shelley, G., Mazur, A., Tharp, G., & Kittok, R. (1989). Testosterone and winning and losing in human competition. *Hormones and Behavior, 23,* 556–571.

Campbell, A., Muncer, S., & Odber, J. (1997). Aggression and testosterone: Testing a bio-social model. *Aggressive Behavior, 23,* 229–238.

Cavigelli, S. A., & Pereira, M. E. (2000). Mating season aggression and fecal testosterone levels in male ring-tailed lemurs, *Lemur catta. Hormones and Behavior, 37,* 246–255.

Cohen, D., Nisbett, R. E., Bowdle, B. Y., & Schwarz, N. (1996). Insult, aggression, and the Southern culture of honor: An "experimental ethnography." *Journal of Personality and Social Psychology, 70,* 945–960.

Dabbs, J. M., Jr., Carr, T. S., Frady, R. L., & Riad, J. K. (1995). Testosterone, crime, and misbehavior among 692 male prison inmates. *Personality and Individual Differences, 18,* 627–633.

Dabbs, J. M., Jr., Jurkovic, G., & Frady, R. L. (1991). Salivary testosterone and cortisol among late adolescent male offenders. *Journal of Abnormal Child Psychology, 19,* 469–478.

Ellis, L. (1986). Evidence of neuroandrogenic etiology of sex roles from a combined analysis of human, nonhuman primate, and nonprimate mammalian studies. *Personality and Individual Differences, 7,* 519–552.

Erikkson, C. J., & Von Der Pahlen, B. (2002). Testosterone, dihydro-testosterone and cortisol in men with and without alcohol-related aggression. *Journal of Studies on Alcohol, 63,* 518–526.

Ferree, E. D., Wikelski, M. C., & Anderson, D. J. (2004). Hormonal correlates of siblicide in Nazca boobies: Support for the challenge hypothesis. *Hormones and Behavior, 46,* 655–662.

Gladue, B. A., Boechler, M., & McCaul, K. D. (1989). Hormonal response to competition in human males. *Aggressive Behavior, 15,* 409–422.

Hirschenhauser, K., Taborsky, M., Oliveira, T., Canario, A. V. M., & Oliveira, R. F. (2004). A test of the "challenge hypothesis" in cichlid fish: Simulated partner and territory intruder experiments. *Animal Behaviour, 68,* 741–750.

Killias, M., & Haas, H. (2002). The role of weapons in violent acts: Some results of a Swiss national cohort study. *Journal of Interpersonal Violence, 17,* 14–32.

Lieberman, J. D., Solomon, S., Greenberg, J., & McGregor, H. A. (1999). A hot new way to measure aggression: Hot sauce allocation. *Aggressive Behavior, 25,* 331–348.

Mazur, A., Booth, A., & Dabbs, J. M., Jr. (1992). Testosterone and chess competition. *Social Psychology Quarterly, 55,* 70–77.

Mazur, A., & Lamb, T. A. (1980). Testosterone, status, and mood in human males. *Hormones and Behavior, 14,* 236–246.

Muller, M. N., & Wrangham, R. W. (2004). Dominance, aggression, and testosterone in wild chimpanzees: A test of the 'challenge hypothesis.' *Animal Behaviour, 67,* 113–123.

O'Connor, D. B., Archer, J., Hair, W. H., & Wu, F. C. W. (2001). Exogenous testosterone, aggression, and mood in eugonadal and hypogonadal men. *Physiology and Behavior, 75,* 557–566.

Preacher, K. J., & Leonardelli, G. J. (2001, March). Calculation for the Sobel test: An interactive calculation tool for mediation tests. Retrieved September 2005 from http://www.unc.edu/~preacher/sobel/sobel.htm

Rowe, R., Maughan, B., Worthman, C. M., Costello, E. J., & Angold, A. (2004). Testosterone, antisocial behavior, and social dominance in boys: Pubertal development and biosocial interaction. *Biological Psychiatry, 55,* 546–552.

Sobel, M. E. (1982). Asymptotic intervals for indirect effects in structural equations models. In S. Leinhart (Ed.), *Sociological methodology 1982* (pp. 290–312). San Francisco: Jossey-Bass.

Wingfield, J. C., Hegner, R. E., Dufty, A. M., Jr., & Ball, G. F. (1990). The "challenge hypothesis": Theoretical implications for patterns of testosterone secretion, mating systems, and breeding strategies. *American Naturalist, 136,* 829–846.

CRITICAL THINKING QUESTIONS

1. The article speculates as to whether females will react to the presence of guns in the same way males did in this study. Do you think females and males will react similarly to the presence of guns? Be specific in discussing your response to this question.

2. Based on the conclusion from this study, might exposure to other aggressive stimuli also raise testosterone level and hence aggression? For example, would an effect similar to exposure to a gun be found for people watching a violent event, such as a boxing match? Discuss your reasoning and suggest a way to study your beliefs.

3. A concept known as *habituation* maintains that our response to a given stimulus is lessened with repeated exposure to it. Do you think this concept could apply to exposure to guns (i.e., that people who are regularly exposed to guns will have a different response than people who encounter them only infrequently)? Why or why not?

4. Examine your own assumptions about aggression. Do you believe that it is part of human nature (i.e., genetically or biologically determined), due to forces outside the individual (e.g., exposure to aggressive stimuli like guns), or due to learning and experience (e.g., family or cultural background)? How do your personal assumptions influence your view of the purpose of punishing criminals, in general, and the issue of capital punishment, in particular? Explain your answers.

CHAPTER INTEGRATION QUESTIONS——————

1. Revisit the introduction to Article 31, which outlines three theoretical perspectives on aggression. Considering the three articles in this chapter together, which theoretical perspective do you feel is most supported by the data? Why?

2. Based on the information from the three articles, can you recommend one or more ways to reduce the occurrence of aggression? Explain your answer.

3. One major concern facing the world today is *terrorism*. What insights, if any, can you draw from the articles in this chapter regarding the causes of and potential control of terrorism? What factors other than those discussed in the articles are important in understanding the causes and control of terrorism? Explain your answers.

Chapter Twelve

GROUP BEHAVIOR

HOW MUCH OF your life is spent interacting with people in some sort of group? If we use the simple definition of a *group* as "two or more individuals that have some unifying relationship," then most likely a significant amount of your time is spent in groups, whether informal (such as two friends trying to decide what to do on a Saturday night) or formal (a work group deciding on a course of action).

Research on group behavior has gone in many directions. The three articles selected for this chapter focus on some of the most commonly investigated topics. Article 34, "Groupthink," examines a set of circumstances found in certain types of groups that may lead them to make very poor decisions, even when they may be composed of very competent individuals. Since the conditions that may contribute to groupthink are not uncommon, the implications of the article for developing more effective groups are clearly important.

Article 35, "The Effect of Threat upon Interpersonal Bargaining," is a classic work. Think of these two possible situations: In the first situation, Party 1 has the potential to inflict harm on Party 2, but Party 2 cannot reciprocate. In the second situation, both parties have equal threat potential; that is, if Party 1 inflicts harm, Party 2 can reciprocate. Which situation would yield the best outcomes for *both* parties? As the article demonstrates, the answer is not what you might think.

Article 36, "Gender Differences in Cooperation and Competition: The Male-Warrior Hypothesis," explores how men and women might be different in terms of how and when they compete and cooperate. The article uses the logic of evolutionary psychology for generating its intriguing hypothesis. It may be that men have a greater focus on group activities than women do, and this, in turn, may be rooted in our genes.

ARTICLE 34

Let us suppose that you are in a position of authority. As such, you are called on to make some very important decisions. You want to make the best possible decisions, so you turn to other people for input. You assemble the best possible set of advisors—people distinguished by their abilities and knowledge. Before making a final decision, you meet with them to discuss the options.

Following such a procedure would seem to ensure that the decision you make will be a good one. After all, with your expert resources, how can you go wrong?

Actually, it is not very hard to imagine that the above procedure could go wrong. Working in a group, even when that group is composed of very competent individuals, does not guarantee quality decision making. To the contrary, as the following article by Irving L. Janis explains, groups may actually make some very poor decisions. The concept of *groupthink,* a term coined by Janis, explains how and why some groups come to make poor decisions, not only failing to recognize that these are poor decisions but actually convincing themselves more and more that these are good decisions. Considering the number of decisions that are made in groups, the process of groupthink, as well as the suggestions for how it can be minimized, are important indeed.

Groupthink

■ Irving L. Janis

The idea of "groupthink" occurred to me while reading Arthur M. Schlesinger's chapters on the Bay of Pigs in *A Thousand Days.* At first I was puzzled: How could bright men like John F. Kennedy and his advisers be taken in by such a stupid, patchwork plan as the one presented to them by the C.I.A. representatives? I began wondering if some psychological contagion of complacency might have interfered with their mental alertness.

I kept thinking about this notion until one day I found myself talking about it in a seminar I was conducting at Yale on the psychology of small groups. I suggested that the poor decision-making performance of those high officials might be akin to the lapses in judgment of ordinary citizens who become more concerned with retaining the approval of the fellow members of their work group than with coming up with good solutions to the tasks at hand.

When I re-read Schlesinger's account I was struck by many further observations that fit into exactly the pattern of concurrence-seeking that has impressed me in my research on other face-to-face groups when a "we" feeling of solidarity is running high. I concluded that a group process was subtly at work in Kennedy's team which prevented the members from debating the real issues posed by the C.I.A.'s plan and from carefully appraising its serious risks.

By now I was sufficiently fascinated by what I called the "groupthink" hypothesis to start looking into similar historic fiascoes. I selected for intensive analysis three that were made during the administrations of three other American presidents: Franklin D. Roosevelt (failure to be prepared for Pearl Harbor), Harry S. Truman (the invasion of North Korea) and Lyndon B. Johnson (escalation of the Vietnam war). Each decision was a group product, issuing from a series of meetings held by a small and cohesive group of government officials and advisers. In each case I found the same kind of detrimental group process that was at work in the Bay of Pigs decision.

In my earlier research with ordinary citizens I had been impressed by the effects—both unfavorable and favorable—of the social pressures that develop in cohesive groups: in infantry platoons, air crews, therapy groups, seminars and self-study or encounter groups. Members tend to evolve informal objectives to preserve friendly intra-group relations, and this becomes part of the hidden agenda at their meetings. When conducting research on groups of heavy smokers, for example, at a clinic established to help people stop smoking, I noticed a seemingly irrational tendency for the members to exert pressure on each other to increase their smoking as the time for the final meeting approached. This appeared to be a collusive effort to display mutual dependence and resistance to the termination of the sessions.

Sometimes, even long before the final separation, pressures toward uniformity subverted the fundamental purpose. At the second meeting of one group of smokers, consisting of 12 middle-class American men and women, two of the most dominant members took the position that heavy smoking was an almost incurable addiction. Most of the others soon agreed that nobody could be expected to cut down drastically. One man took issue with this consensus, arguing that he had stopped smoking since joining the group and that everyone else could do the same. His declaration was followed by an angry discussion. Most of the others ganged up against the man who was deviating from the consensus.

At the next meeting the deviant announced that he had made an important decision. "When I joined," he said, "I agreed to follow the two main rules required by the clinic—to make a conscientious effort to stop smoking, and to attend every meeting. But I have learned that you can only follow one of the rules, not both. I will continue to attend every meeting but I have gone back to smoking two packs a day and I won't make any effort to stop again until after the last meeting." Whereupon the other members applauded, welcoming him back to the fold.

No one mentioned that the whole point of the meetings was to help each person to cut down as rapidly as possible. As a psychological consultant to the group, I tried to call this to the members' attention and so did my collaborator, Dr. Michael Kahn. But the members ignored our comments and reiterated their consensus that heavy smoking was an addiction from which no one would be cured except by cutting down gradually over a long period of time.

This episode—an extreme form of groupthink—was only one manifestation of a general pattern that the group displayed. At every meeting the members were amiable, reasserted their warm feelings of solidarity and sought concurrence on every important topic, with no reappearance of the unpleasant bickering that would spoil the cozy atmosphere. This tendency could be maintained, however, only at the expense of ignoring realistic challenges—like those posed by the psychologists.

The term "groupthink" is of the same order as the words in the "newspeak" vocabulary that George Orwell uses in *1984*—a vocabulary with terms such as "doublethink" and "crimethink." By putting "groupthink" with those Orwellian words, I realize that it takes on an invidious connotation. This is intentional: groupthink refers to a deterioration of mental efficiency, reality testing and moral judgment that results from in-group pressures.

When I investigated the Bay of Pigs invasion and other fiascoes, I found that there were at least six major defects in decision-making which contributed to failures to solve problems adequately.

First, the group's discussions were limited to a few alternatives (often only two) without a survey of the full range of alternatives. Second, the members failed to re-examine their initial decision from the standpoint of non-obvious drawbacks that had not been originally considered. Third, they neglected courses of action initially evaluated as unsatisfactory; they almost never discussed whether they had overlooked any nonobvious gains.

Fourth, members made little or no attempt to obtain information from experts who could supply sound estimates of losses and gains to be expected from alternative courses. Fifth, selective bias was shown in the way the members reacted to information and judgments from experts, the media and outside critics; they were only interested in facts and opinions that supported their preferred policy. Finally, they spent little time deliberating how the policy might be hindered by bureaucratic inertia, sabotaged by political opponents or derailed by the accidents that happen to the best of well-laid plans. Consequently, they failed to work out contingency plans to cope with foreseeable setbacks that could endanger their success.

I was surprised by the extent to which the groups involved in these fiascoes adhered to group norms and pressures toward uniformity, even when their policy was working badly and had unintended consequences that disturbed the conscience of the members. Members consider loyalty to the group the highest form of morality. That loyalty requires each member to avoid raising controversial issues, questioning weak arguments or calling a halt to soft-headed thinking.

Paradoxically, soft-headed groups are likely to be extremely hard-hearted toward out-groups and enemies. In dealing with a rival nation, policy-makers constituting an amiable group find it relatively easy to authorize dehumanizing solutions such as large-scale bombings. An affable group of government officials is unlikely to pursue the difficult issues that arise when alternatives to a harsh military solution come up for discussion. Nor are they inclined to raise ethical issues that imply that this "fine group of ours, with its humanitarianism and its high-minded principles, could adopt a course that is inhumane and immoral."

The greater the threat to the self-esteem of the members of a cohesive group, the greater will be their inclination to resort to concurrence-seeking at the expense of critical thinking. Symptoms of groupthink will therefore be found most often when a decision poses a moral dilemma, especially if the most advantageous course requires the policy-makers to violate their own standards of humanitarian behavior. Each member is likely to become more dependent than ever on the in-group for maintaining his self-image as a decent human being and will therefore be more strongly motivated to maintain group unity by striving for concurrence.

Although it is risky to make huge inferential leaps from theory to practice, we should not be inhibited from drawing tentative inferences from these fiascoes. Perhaps the worst mistakes can be prevented if we take steps to avoid the circumstances in which groupthink is most likely to flourish. But all the prescriptive hypotheses that follow must be validated by systematic research before they can be applied with any confidence.

The leader of a policy-forming group should, for example, assign the role of critical evaluator to each member, encouraging the group to give high priority to airing objections and doubts. He should also be impartial at the outset, instead of stating his own preferences and expectations. He should limit his briefings to unbiased statements about the scope of the problem and the limitations of available resources.

The organization should routinely establish several independent planning and evaluation groups to work on the same policy question, each carrying out its deliberations under a different leader.

One or more qualified colleagues within the organization who are not core members of the policy-making group should be invited to each meeting and encouraged to challenge the views of the core members.

At every meeting, at least one member should be assigned the role of devil's advocate, to function like a good lawyer in challenging the testimony of those who advocate the majority position.

Whenever the policy issue involves relations with a rival nation, a sizable block of time should be spent surveying all warning signals from the rivals and constructing alternative scenarios.

After reaching a preliminary consensus the policy-making group should hold a "second chance" meeting at which all the members are expected to express their residual doubts and to rethink the entire issue. They might take as their model a statement made by Alfred P. Sloan, a former chairman of General Motors, at a meeting of policy-makers:

"Gentlemen, I take it we are all in complete agreement on the decision here. Then I propose we postpone further discussion until our next meeting to give ourselves time to develop disagreement and perhaps gain some understanding of what the decision is all about."

It might not be a bad idea for the second-chance meeting to take place in a relaxed atmosphere far from the executive suite, perhaps over drinks. According to a report by Herodotus dating from about 450 B.C., whenever the ancient Persians made a decision following sober deliberations, they would always reconsider the matter under the influence of wine. Tacitus claimed that during Roman times the Germans also had a custom of arriving at each decision twice—once sober, once drunk.

Some institutionalized form of allowing second thoughts to be freely expressed might be remarkably effective for breaking down a false sense of unanimity and related illusions, without endangering anyone's reputation or liver.

PEARL HARBOR: GENIALITY AND SECURITY

On the night of Dec. 6, 1941—just 12 hours before the Japanese struck—Admiral Husband E. Kimmel (Commander in Chief of the Pacific Fleet) attended a dinner party given by his old crony, Rear Admiral H. Fairfax Leary, and his wife. Other members of the in-group of naval commanders and their wives were also present. Seated next to Admiral Kimmel was Fanny Halsey, wife of Admiral Halsey, who had left Hawaii to take his task force to the Far East. Mrs. Halsey said that she was certain the Japanese were going to attack. "She was a brilliant woman," according to Captain Joel Bunkley, who described the party, "but everybody thought she was crazy."

Admiral Leary, at a naval inquiry in 1944, summarized the complacency at that dinner party and at the daily conferences held by Admiral Kimmel during the preceding weeks. When asked whether any thought had been given to the possibility of a surprise attack by the Japanese, he said, "We all felt that the contingency was remote . . . and the feeling strongly existed that the Fleet would have adequate warning of any chance of an air attack." The same attitude was epitomized in testimony given by Captain J. B. Earle, chief of staff, Fourteenth Naval District. "Somehow or other," he said, "we always felt that 'it couldn't happen here.'"

From the consistent testimony given by Admiral Kimmel's advisers, they all acted on the basis of an "unwarranted feeling of immunity from attack," though they had been given a series of impressive warnings that they should be prepared for war with Japan.

Most illuminating of the norm-setting behavior that contributed to the complacency of Kimmel's in-group is a brief exchange between Admiral Kimmel and Lieutenant Commander Layton. Perturbed by the loss of radio contact with the Japanese aircraft carriers, Admiral Kimmel asked Layton on Dec. 1, 1941, to check with the Far East Command for additional information. The next day, discussing the lost carriers again with Layton, he remarked jokingly: "What, you don't know where the carriers are? Do you mean to say that they could be rounding Diamond Head [at

Honolulu] and you wouldn't know it?" Layton said he hoped they would be sighted well before that.

This exchange implies an "atmosphere of geniality and security." Having relegated the Japanese threat to the category of laughing matters, the admiral was making it clear that he would be inclined to laugh derisively at anyone who thought otherwise. "I did not at any time suggest," Layton later acknowledged at a Congressional hearing, "that the Japanese carriers were under radio silence approaching Oahu. I wish I had."

But the admiral's foolish little joke may have induced Layton to remain silent about any vague, lingering doubts he may have had. Either man would risk the scornful laughter of the other—whether expressed to his face or behind his back—if he were to express second thoughts such as, "Seriously, though, shouldn't we do something about the slight possibility that those carriers might *really* be headed this way?" Because this ominous inference was never drawn, not a single reconnaissance plane was sent out to the north of the Hawaiian Islands, allowing the Japanese to win the incredible gamble they were taking in trying to send their aircraft carriers within bombing distance of Pearl Harbor without being detected.

That joking exchange was merely the visible part of a huge iceberg of solid faith in Pearl Harbor's invulnerability. If a few warm advocates of preparedness had been within the Navy group, steamed up by the accumulating warning signals, they might have been able to melt it. But they would certainly have had a cold reception. To urge a full alert would have required presenting unwelcome arguments that countered the myth of Pearl Harbor's impregnability. Anyone who was tempted to do so knew that he would be deviating from the group norm: the others were likely to consider him "crazy," just as the in-group regarded Mrs. Halsey at the dinner party on the eve of the disaster when she announced her deviant opinion that the Japanese would attack.

ESCALATION IN VIETNAM: HOW COULD IT HAPPEN?

A highly revealing episode occurred soon after Robert McNamara told a Senate committee some impressive facts about the ineffectiveness of the bombings. President Johnson made a number of bitter comments about McNamara's statement. "That military genius, McNamara, has gone dovish on me," he complained to one Senator. To someone in his White House staff he spoke even more heatedly, accusing McNamara of playing into the hands of the enemy. He drew the analogy of "a man trying to sell his house while one of his sons went to the prospective buyer to point out that there were leaks in the basement."

This strongly suggests that Johnson regarded his in-group of policy advisers as a family and its leading dissident member as an irresponsible son who was sabotaging the family's interest. Underlying this revealing imagery are two implicit assumptions that epitomize groupthink: We are a good group, so any deceitful acts that we perpetrate are fully justified. Anyone who is unwilling to distort the truth to help us is disloyal.

This is only one of the many examples of how groupthink was manifested in Johnson's inner circle.

A PERFECT FIASCO: THE BAY OF PIGS

Why did President Kennedy's main advisers, whom he had selected as core members of his team, fail to pursue the issues sufficiently to discover the shaky ground on which the faulty assumptions of the Cuban invasion plan rested? Why didn't they pose a barrage of penetrating and embarrassing questions to the representatives of the C.I.A. and the Joint Chiefs of Staff? Why were they taken in by the incomplete and inconsistent answers they were given in response to the relatively few critical questions they raised?

Schlesinger says that "for all the utter irrationality with which retrospect endowed the project, it had a certain queer logic at the time as it emerged from the bowels of government." Why? What was the source of the "queer logic" with which the plan was endowed? If the available accounts describe the deliberations accurately, many typical symptoms of groupthink can be discerned among the members of the Kennedy team: an illusion of invulnerability, a collective effort to rationalize their decision, an unquestioned belief in the group's inherent morality, a stereotyped view of enemy leaders as too evil to warrant genuine attempts to negotiate, and the emergence of self-appointed mind-guards.

Robert Kennedy, for example, who had been constantly informed about the Cuban invasion plan, asked Schlesinger privately why he was opposed. The President's brother listened coldly and then said: "You may be right or you may be wrong, but the President has made his mind up. Don't push it any further. Now is the time for everyone to help him all they can."

Here is a symptom of groupthink, displayed by a highly intelligent man whose ethical code committed him to freedom of dissent.

Robert Kennedy was functioning in a self-appointed role that I call being a "mind-guard." Just as a bodyguard protects the President and other high officials from physical harm, a mindguard protects them from thoughts that might damage their confidence in the soundness of the policies which they are about to launch.

CRITICAL THINKING QUESTIONS

1. How common is groupthink? Do you think that the conditions that give rise to groupthink are relatively rare or relatively common? Explain your answers. Cite additional examples of decisions that may have been influenced by groupthink.

2. Have you ever been involved in a group that experienced some sort of groupthink process? Describe the situation, and discuss the process in terms of groupthink.

3. If groupthink is common, then it would be useful if people were made aware of how it works. Should the conditions of groupthink, as well as how it can be prevented, be taught to leaders and potential leaders? How could this be accomplished?

4. The article gave some suggestions as to how groupthink could be prevented or at least minimized. Would all leaders be equally open to following these suggestions? Or might individual characteristics influence how open various leaders might be? How so?

ARTICLE 35

Whenever two or more individuals act as a group, a central part of the interaction may involve trying to reach some agreement about an issue or activity. When the group consists of individuals or nations, reaching agreement is often a major concern.

Bargaining is one form that such negotiations take. The bargaining may be about something small and be informal in style, such as a couple deciding on which movie to see, or it may be major and formal, such as two nations trying to reach an agreement on nuclear arms control. In either case, central to the bargaining is the belief by both parties that reaching a mutually agreed upon solution will possibly benefit both of them.

Two broad approaches to bargaining are cooperation and competition. In a *competitive* situation, individuals or groups view the situation in "win-lose" terms: I want to win, and it most likely will be at your expense. In a *cooperative* arrangement, the situation is more likely to be viewed as a "win-win" opportunity: We can both get something good out of this; neither one has to lose. Other things being equal, a cooperative strategy is more likely to ensure a good outcome for all concerned. But is that the strategy most likely to be used? Or do individuals and groups tend to use competitive strategies instead, even if it might not ultimately be in their best interest to do so?

The following classic contribution by Morton Deutsch and Robert M. Krauss examines the effect of threat on interpersonal bargaining. One major finding of the study is that the presence of threat, as well as whether only one or both parties are capable of threat, has a major impact on the outcome of the bargaining situation. Common sense might suggest that if my opponent has some threat that he or she can use against me, then I would better off having the same level of threat to use against him or her, rather than having no threat to retaliate with. The findings of the study do not confirm this expectation, however, and may suggest a rethinking of the use of threat and power in real-world negotiations.

The Effect of Threat upon Interpersonal Bargaining

■ Morton Deutsch and Robert M. Krauss

A bargain is defined in *Webster's Unabridged Dictionary* as "an agreement between parties settling what each shall give and receive in a transaction between them"; it is further specified that a bargain is "an agreement or compact viewed as advantageous or the reverse." When the term "agreement" is broadened to include tacit, informal agreements as well as explicit agreements, it is evident that bargains and the processes involved in arriving at bargains ("bargaining") are pervasive characteristics of social life.

The definition of bargain fits under sociological definitions of the term "social norm." In this light, the experimental study of the bargaining process and of bargaining outcomes provides a means for the laboratory study of the development of certain types of social norms. But unlike many other types of social situations, bargaining situations have certain distinctive features that make it relevant to consider the conditions that determine whether or not a social norm will develop as well as those that determine the nature

Reprinted from *Journal of Personality and Social Psychology,* 1960, *61,* 181–189.

of the social norm if it develops. Bargaining situations highlight the possibility that, even where cooperation would be mutually advantageous, shared purposes may not develop, agreement may not be reached, and interaction may be regulated antagonistically rather than normatively.

The essential features of a bargaining situation exist when:

1. Both parties perceive that there is the possibility of reaching an agreement in which each party would be better off, or no worse off, than if no agreement were reached.
2. Both parties perceive that there is more than one such agreement that could be reached.
3. Both parties perceive each other to have conflicting preferences or opposed interests with regard to the different agreements that might be reached.

Everyday examples of bargaining include such situations as: the buyer-seller relationship when the price is not fixed, the husband and wife who want to spend an evening out together but have conflicting preferences about where to go, union-management negotiations, drivers who meet at an intersection when there is no clear right of way, disarmament negotiations.

In terms of our prior conceptualization of cooperation and competition (Deutsch, 1949) bargaining is thus a situation in which the participants have mixed motives toward one another: on the one hand, each has interest in cooperating so that they reach an agreement; on the other hand, they have competitive interests concerning the nature of the agreement they reach. In effect, to reach agreement the cooperative interest of the bargainers must be strong enough to overcome their competitive interests. However, agreement is not only contingent upon the *motivational* balances of cooperative to competitive interests but also upon the situational and *cognitive* factors which facilitate or hinder the recognition or invention of a bargaining agreement that reduces the opposition of interest and enhances the mutuality of interest.[1]

These considerations lead to the formulation of two general, closely related propositions about the likelihood that a bargaining agreement will be reached.

1. Bargainers are more likely to reach an agreement, the stronger are their cooperative interests in comparison with their competitive interests.

2. Bargainers are more likely to reach an agreement, the more resources they have available for recognizing or inventing potential bargaining agreements and for communicating to one another once a potential agreement has been recognized or invented.

From these two basic propositions and additional hypotheses concerning conditions that determine the strengths of the cooperative and competitive interests and the amount of available resources, we believe it is possible to explain the ease or difficulty of arriving at a bargaining agreement. We shall not present a full statement of these hypotheses here but turn instead to a description of an experiment that relates to Proposition 1.

The experiment was concerned with the effect of the availability of threat upon bargaining in a two-person experimental bargaining game.[2] Threat is defined as the expression of an intention to do something detrimental to the interests of another. Our experiment was guided by two assumptions about threat:

1. If there is a conflict of interest and one person is able to threaten the other, he will tend to use the threat in an attempt to force the other person to yield. This tendency should be stronger, the more irreconcilable the conflict is perceived to be.
2. If a person uses threat in an attempt to intimidate another, the threatened person (if he considers himself to be of equal or superior status) would feel hostility toward the threatener and tend to respond with counterthreat and/or increased resistance to yielding. We qualify this assumption by stating that the tendency to resist should be greater, the greater the perceived probability and magnitude of detriment to the other and the less the perceived probability and magnitude of detriment to the potential resister from the anticipated resistance to yielding.

The second assumption is based upon the view that when resistance is not seen to be suicidal or useless, to allow oneself to be intimidated, particularly by someone who does not have the right to expect deferential behavior, is to suffer a loss of social face and, hence, of self-esteem: and that the culturally defined way of maintaining self-esteem in the face of attempted intimidation is to engage in a contest for supremacy vis-à-vis the power to intimidate or, minimally, to resist intimidation. Thus, in effect, the use of threat (and if it is available to be used, there will be a tendency to use it) should strengthen the competitive interests of the bargainers in relationship to one another by introducing or enhancing the competitive struggle for self-esteem. Hence, from Proposition 1, it follows that the availability of a means of threat should make it more difficult for the bargainers to reach agreement (providing that the threatened person has some means of resisting the threat). The preceding statement is relevant to the comparison of both of our experimental conditions of threat, bilateral and unilateral (described below), with our experimental condition of nonthreat. We hypothesize that a bargaining agreement is more likely to be achieved when neither party can threaten the other, than when one or both parties can threaten the other.

Consider now the situations of bilateral threat and unilateral threat. For several reasons, a situation of bilateral threat is probably less conducive to agreement than is a condition of unilateral threat. First, the sheer likelihood that a threat will be made is greater when two people rather than one have the means of making the threat. Secondly, once a threat

is made in the bilateral case it is likely to evoke counterthreat. Withdrawal of threat in the face of counterthreat probably involves more loss of face (for reasons analogous to those discussed in relation to yielding to intimidation) than does withdrawal of threat in the face of resistance to threat. Finally, in the unilateral case, although the person without the threat potential can resist and not yield to the threat, his position vis-à-vis the other is not so strong as the position of the threatened person in the bilateral case. In the unilateral case, the threatened person may have a worse outcome than the other whether he resists or yields; while in the bilateral case, the threatened person is sure to have a worse outcome if he yields but he may insure that he does not have a worse outcome if he does not yield.

METHOD

Procedure

Subjects (*Ss*) were asked to imagine that they were in charge of a trucking company, carrying merchandise over a road to a destination. For each trip completed they made $.60, minus their operating expenses. Operating expenses were calculated at the rate of one cent per second. So, for example, if it took 37 seconds to complete

FIGURE 1 / Subject's Road Map

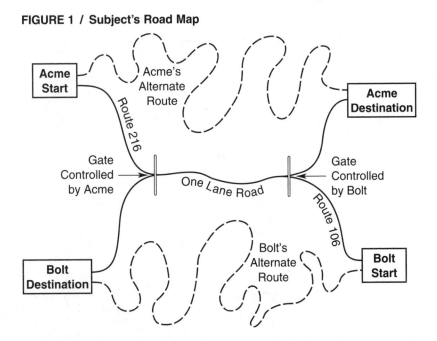

a particular trip, the player's profit would be $.60 – $.37 or a net profit of $.23 for that particular trip.

Each *S* was assigned a name, Acme or Bolt. As the "road map" (see Figure 1) indicates, both players start from separate points and go to separate destinations. At one point their paths cross. This is the section of road labeled "one lane road," which is only one lane wide, so that two trucks, heading in opposite directions, could not pass each other. If one backs up the other can go forward, or both can back up, or both can sit there head-on without moving.

There is another way for each *S* to reach the destination on the map, labeled the "alternate route." The two players' paths do not cross on this route, but the alternative is 56% longer than the main route. *Ss* were told that they could expect to lose at least $.10 each time they used the alternate route.

At either end of the one-lane section there is a gate that is under the control of the player to whose starting point it is closest. By closing the gate, one player can prevent the other from traveling over that section of the main route. The use of the gate provides the threat potential in this game. In the bilateral threat potential condition (Two Gates) both players had

gates under their control. In a second condition of unilateral threat (One Gate) Acme had control of a gate but Bolt did not. In a third condition (No Gates) neither player controlled a gate.

Ss played the game seated in separate booths placed so that they could not see each other but could see the experimenter (*E*). Each *S* had a "control panel" mounted on a 12" × 18" × 12" sloping-front cabinet (see Figure 2). The apparatus consisted essentially of a reversible impulse computer that was pulsed by a recycling timer. When the *S* wanted to move her truck forward she threw a key that closed a circuit pulsing the "add" coil of the impulse counter mounted on her control panel. As the counter cumulated, *S* was able to determine her "position" by relating the number on her counter to reference numbers that had been written in on her road map. Similarly, when she wished to reverse, she would throw a switch that activated the "subtract" coil of her counter, thus subtracting from the total on the counter each time the timer cycled.

S's counter was connected in parallel to counters on the other *S*'s panel and on *E*'s panel. Thus each player had two counters on her panel, one represent-

FIGURE 2 / Subject's Control Panel

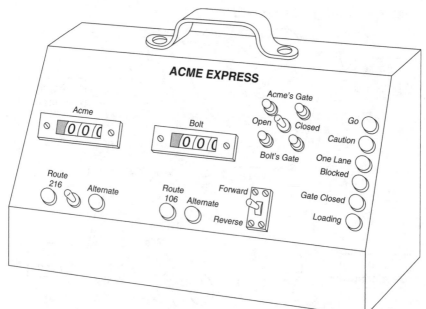

ing her own position and the other representing the other player's. Provision was made in construction of the apparatus to permit cutting the other player's counter out of the circuit, so that each S knew only the position of her own truck. This was done in the present experiment. Experiments now in progress are studying the effects of knowledge of the other person's position and other aspects of interpersonal communication upon the bargaining process.

The only time one player definitely knew the other player's position was when they had met head-on on the one-way section of road. This was indicated by a traffic light mounted on the panel. When this light was on, neither player could move forward unless the other moved back. The gates were controlled by toggle switches and panel-mounted indicator lights showed, for both Ss, whether each gate was open or closed.

The following "rules of the game" were stated to the Ss:

1. A player who started out on one route and wished to switch to the other route could only do so after first reversing and going back to the start position. Direct transfer from one route to the other was not permitted except at the start position.
2. In the conditions where Ss had gates, they were permitted to close the gates no matter where they were on the main route, so long as they were on the main route (i.e., they were not permitted to close the gate while on the alternate route or after having reached their destinations). However, Ss were permitted to open their gates at any point in the game.

Ss were taken through a number of practice exercises to familiarize them with the game. In the first trial they were made to meet head-on on the one-lane path; Acme was then told to back up until she was just off the one-lane path and Bolt was told to go forward. After Bolt had gone through the one-lane path, Acme was told to go forward. Each continued going forward until each arrived at her destination. The second practice trial was the same as the first except that Bolt rather than Acme backed up after meeting head-on. In the next practice trial, one of the players was made to wait just before the one-way path while the other traversed it and then was allowed to continue. In the next practice trial, one player was made to take

the alternate route and the other was made to take the main route. Finally, in the bilateral and unilateral threat conditions the use of the gate was illustrated (by having the player get on the main route, close the gate, and then go back and take the alternate route). The Ss were told explicitly, with emphasis, that they did *not* have to use the gate. Before each trial in the game the gate or gates were in the open position.

The instructions stressed an individualistic motivation orientation. Ss were told to try to earn as much money for themselves as possible and to have no interest in whether the other player made money or lost money. They were given $4.00 in poker chips to represent their working capital and told that after each trial they would be given "money" if they made a profit or that "money" would be taken from them if they lost (i.e., took more than 60 seconds to complete their trip). The profit or loss of each S was announced so that both Ss could hear the announcement after each trial. Each pair of Ss played a total of 20 trials; on all trials, they started off together. In other words each trial presented a repetition of the same bargaining problem. In cases where Ss lost their working capital before the 20 trials were completed, additional chips were given them. Ss were aware that their monetary winnings and losses were to be imaginary and that no money would change hands as a result of the experiment.

Subjects

Sixteen pairs of Ss were used in each of the three experimental conditions. The Ss were female clerical and supervisory personnel of the New Jersey Bell Telephone Company who volunteered to participate during their working day.[3] Their ages ranged from 20 to 39, with a mean of 26.2. All were naive to the purpose of the experiment. By staggering the arrival times and choosing girls from different locations, we were able to insure that the Ss did not know with whom they were playing.

Data Recorded

Several types of data were collected. We obtained a record of the profit or loss of each S on each trial. We also obtained a detailed recording of the actions taken by each S during the course of a trial. For this purpose, we used an Esterline-Angus model AW Operations Recorder which enabled us to obtain a "log" of each move each *S* made during the game (e.g., whether and when she took the main or alternate route; when she went forward, backward, or remained still; when she closed and opened the gate; when she arrived at her destination).

RESULTS[4]

The best single measure of the difficulty experienced by the bargainers in reaching an agreement is the sum of each pair's profits (or losses) on a given trial. The higher the sum of the payoffs to the two players on a given trial, the less time it took them to arrive at a procedure for sharing the one-lane path of the main route. (It was, of course, possible for one or both of the players to decide to take the alternate route so as to avoid a protracted stalemate during the process of bargaining. This, however, always results in at least a $.20 smaller joint payoff if only one player took the alternate route, than an optimally arrived at agreement concerning the use of the one-way path.) Figure 3 presents the medians of the summed payoffs (i.e., Acme's plus Bolt's) for all pairs in each of the three experimental conditions over the 20 trials.[5] These striking results indicate that agreement was least difficult to arrive at in the no threat condition, was more difficult to arrive at in the unilateral threat condition, and exceedingly difficult or impossible to arrive at in the bilateral threat condition (see also Table 1).

FIGURE 3 / Median Joint Payoff (Acme + Bolt) over Trials

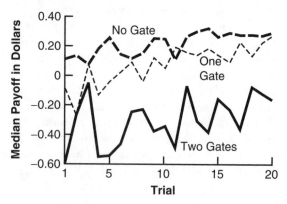

Examination of Figure 3 suggests that learning occurred during the 20 trials: the summed payoffs for pairs of *S*s tend to improve as the number of trials increases. This suggestion is confirmed by an analysis of variance of the slopes for the summed payoffs[6] over the 20 trials for each of the 16 pairs in each of the 3 experimental treatments. The results of this analysis indicate that the slopes are significantly greater than zero for the unilateral threat ($p < .01$) and the no threat ($p < .02$) conditions; for the bilateral threat condition, the slope does not reach statistical significance ($.10 < p < .20$). The data indicate that the pairs in the no threat condition started off at a fairly high level but, even so, showed some improvement over the 20 trials; the pairs in the unilateral threat condi-

TABLE 1 / Mean Payoffs Summated over the Twenty Trials

| | Means | | | Statistical Comparisons: *p* values[a] | | | |
| | (1) No Threat | (2) Unilateral Threat | (3) Bilateral Threat | | | | |
Variable				Overall	(1) vs. (2)	(1) vs. (3)	(2) vs. (3)
Summed Payoffs (Acme + Bolt)	203.31	−405.88	−875.12	.01	.01	.01	.05
Acme's Payoff	122.44	−118.56	−406.56	.01	.10	.01	.05
Bolt's Payoff	80.88	−287.31	−468.56	.01	.01	.01	.20
Absolute Differences in Payoff (A − B)	125.94	294.75	315.25	.05	.05	.01	*ns*

[a]Evaluation of the significance of overall variation between conditions is based on an *F* test with 2 and 45 *df*. Comparisons between treatments are based on a two-tailed *t* test.

FIGURE 4 / Acme's Median Payoff

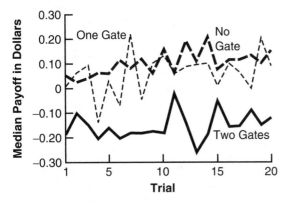

FIGURE 5 / Bolt's Median Payoff

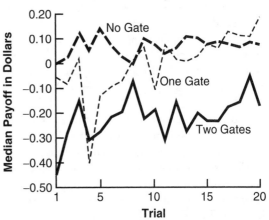

tion started off low and, having considerable opportunity for improvement, used their opportunity; the pairs in the bilateral threat condition, on the other hand, did not benefit markedly from repeated trials.

Figure 4 compares Acme's median profit in the three experimental conditions over the 20 trials; while Figure 5 compares Bolt's profit in the three conditions. (In the unilateral threat condition, it was Acme who controlled a gate and Bolt who did not.) Bolt's as well as Acme's outcome is somewhat better in the no threat condition than in the unilateral threat condition; Acme's, as well as Bolt's, outcome is clearly worst in the

bilateral threat condition (see Table 1 also). However, Figure 6 reveals that Acme does somewhat better than Bolt in the unilateral condition. Thus, if threat-potential exists within a bargaining relationship it is better to possess it oneself than to have the other party possess it. However, it is even better for neither party to possess it. Moreover, Figure 5 shows that Bolt is better off not having than having a gate even when Acme has a gate: Bolt tends to do better in the unilateral threat condition than in the bilateral threat condition.

The size of the absolute discrepancy between the payoffs of the two players in each pair provides a

FIGURE 6 / Acme's and Bolt's Median Payoffs in Unilateral Threat Condition

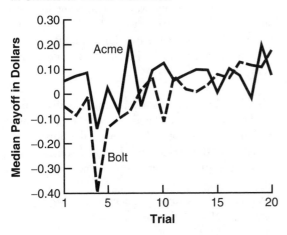

FIGURE 7 / Median Absolute Differences in Payoff

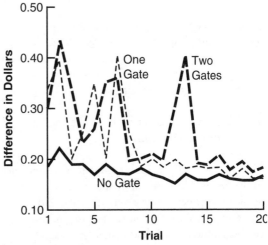

measure of the confusion or difficulty in predicting what the other player was going to do. Thus, a large absolute discrepancy might indicate that after one player had gone through the one-way path and left it open, the other player continued to wait; or it might indicate that one player continued to wait at a closed gate hoping the other player would open it quickly but the other player did not; etc. Figure 7 indicates that the discrepancy between players in the no threat condition is initially small and remains small for the 20 trials. For the players in both the bilateral and unilateral threat conditions, the discrepancy is initially relatively larger; but it decreases more noticeably in the unilateral threat condition by the tenth trial and, therefore, is consistently smaller than in the bilateral condition.

By way of concrete illustration, we present a synopsis of the game for one pair in each of three experimental treatments.

No Threat Condition

Trial 1   The players met in the center of the one-way section. After some back-and-forth movement Bolt reversed to the end of the one-way section, allowing Acme to pass through, and then proceeded forward herself.

Trial 2   They again met at the center of the one-way path. This time, after moving back and forth deadlocked for some time, Bolt reversed to "start" and took the alternate route to her destination, thus leaving Acme free to go through on the main route.

Trial 3   The players again met at the center of the one-way path. This time, however, Acme reversed to the beginning of the path, allowing Bolt to go through to her destination. Then Acme was able to proceed forward on the main route.

Trial 5   Both players elected to take the alternate route to their destinations.

Trial 7   Both players took the main route and met in the center. They waited, deadlocked, for a considerable time. Then Acme reversed to the end of the one-way path allowing Bolt to go through, then proceeded through to her destination.

Trials 10–20   Acme and Bolt fall into a pattern of alternating who is to go first on the one-way section. There is no deviation from this pattern.

The only other pattern that emerges in this condition is one in which one player dominates the other. That is, one player consistently goes first on the one-way section and the other player consistently yields.

Unilateral Threat Condition

Trial 1   Both players took the main route and met in the center of it. Acme immediately closed the gate, reversed to "start," and took the alternate route to her destination. Bolt waited for a few seconds, at the closed gate, then reversed and took the alternate route.

Trial 2   Both players took the main route and met in the center. After moving back and forth deadlocked for about 15 seconds, Bolt reversed to the beginning of the one-way path, allowed Acme to pass, and then proceeded forward to her destination.

Trial 3   Both players started out on the main route, meeting in the center. After moving back and forth deadlocked for a while, Acme closed her gate, reversed to "start," and took the alternate route. Bolt, meanwhile, waited at the closed gate. When Acme arrived at her destination she opened the gate, and Bolt went through to complete her trip.

Trial 5   Both players took the main route, meeting at the center of the one-way section. Acme immediately closed her gate, reversed, and took the alternate route. Bolt waited at the gate for about 10 seconds, then reversed and took the alternate route to her destination.

Trial 10   Both players took the main route and met in the center. Acme closed her gate, reversed, and took the alternate route. Bolt remained waiting at the closed gate. After Acme arrived at her destination, she opened the gate and Bolt completed her trip.

Trial 15   Acme took the main route to her destination and Bolt took the alternate route.

Trials 17–20 Both players took the main route and met in the center. Bolt waited a few seconds, then reversed to the end of the one-way section allowing Acme to go through. Then Bolt proceeded forward to her destination.

Other typical patterns that developed in this experimental condition included an alternating pattern similar to that described in the no threat condition, a dominating pattern in which Bolt would select the alternate route leaving Acme free to use the main route unobstructed, and a pattern in which Acme would close her gate and then take the alternate route, also forcing Bolt to take the alternate route.

Bilateral Threat Condition

Trial 1 Acme took the main route and Bolt took the alternate route.

Trial 2 Both players took the main route and met head-on. Bolt closed her gate. Acme waited a few seconds, then closed her gate, reversed to "start," then went forward again to the closed gate. Acme reversed and took the alternate route. Bolt again reversed, then started on the alternate route. Acme opened her gate and Bolt reversed to "start" and went to her destination on the main route.

Trial 3 Acme took the alternate route to her destination. Bolt took the main route and closed her gate before entering the one-way section.

Trial 5 Both players took the main route and met head-on. After about 10 seconds spent backing up and going forward, Acme closed her gate, reversed, and took the alternate route. After waiting a few seconds, Bolt did the same.

Trials 8–10 Both players started out on the main route, immediately closed their gates, reversed to "start," and took the alternate route to their destinations.

Trial 15 Both players started out on the main route and met head-on. After some jockeying for position,

Acme closed her gate, reversed, and took the alternate route to her destination. After waiting at the gate for a few seconds, Bolt reversed to "start" and took the alternate route to her destination.

Trials 19–20 Both players started out on the main route, immediately closed their gates, reversed to "start," and took the alternate routes to their destinations.

Other patterns that emerged in the bilateral threat condition included alternating first use of the one-way section, one player's dominating the other on first use of the one-way section, and another dominating pattern in which one player consistently took the main route while the other consistently took the alternate route.

DISCUSSION

From our view of bargaining as a situation in which both cooperative and competitive tendencies are present and acting upon the individual, it is relevant to inquire as to the conditions under which a stable agreement of any form develops. However, implicit in most economic models of bargaining (e.g., Stone, 1958; Zeuthen, 1930) is the assumption that the cooperative interests of the bargainers are sufficiently strong to insure that some form of mutually satisfactory agreement will be reached. For this reason, such models have focused upon the form of the agreement reached by the bargainers. Siegel and Fouraker (1960) report a series of bargaining experiments quite different in structure from ours in which only one of many pairs of *S*s were unable to reach agreement. Siegel and Fouraker explain this rather startling result as follows:

> *Apparently the disruptive forces which lead to the rupture of some negotiations were at least partially controlled in our sessions. . . .*
> *Some negotiations collapse when one party becomes incensed at the other, and henceforth strives to maximize his opponent's displeasure rather than his own satisfaction. . . . Since it is difficult to transmit insults by means of quantitative bids, such disequilibrating behavior was not induced in the present*

studies. If subjects were allowed more latitude in their communications and interactions, the possibility of an affront offense-punitive behavior sequence might be increased (p. 100).

In our experimental bargaining situation, the availability of threat clearly made it more difficult for bargainers to reach a mutually profitable agreement. These results, we believe, reflect psychological tendencies that are not confined to our bargaining situation: the tendency to use threat (if the means for threatening is available) in an attempt to force the other person to yield, when the other is seen as obstructing one's path; the tendency to respond with counterthreat or increased resistance to attempts at intimidation. How general are these tendencies? What conditions are likely to elicit them? Answers to these questions are necessary before our results can be generalized to other situations.

Dollard, Doob, Miller, Mowrer, and Sears (1939) have cited a variety of evidence to support the view that aggression (i.e., the use of threat) is a common reaction to a person who is seen as the agent of frustration. There seems to be little reason to doubt that the use of threat is a frequent reaction to interpersonal impasses. However, everyday observation indicates that threat does not inevitably occur when there is an interpersonal impasse. We would speculate that it is most likely to occur: when the threatener has no positive interest in the other person's welfare (he is either egocentrically or competitively related to the other); when the threatener believes that the other has no positive interest in his welfare; and when the threatener anticipates either that his threat will be effective or, if ineffective, will not worsen his situation because he expects the worst to happen if he does not use his threat. We suggest that these conditions were operative in our experiment; Ss were either egocentrically or competitively oriented to one another[7] and they felt that they would not be worse off by the use of threat.

Everyday observation suggests that the tendency to respond with counterthreat or increased resistance to attempts at intimidation is also a common occurrence. We believe that introducing threat into a bargaining situation affects the meaning of yielding. Although we have no data to support this interpretation directly, we will attempt to justify it on the basis of some additional assumptions.

Goffman (1955) has pointed out the pervasive significance of "face" in the maintenance of the social order. In this view, self-esteem is a socially validated system that grows out of the acceptance by others of the claim for deference, prestige, and recognition that a person presents in his behavior toward others. Since the rejection of such a claim would be perceived (by the recipient) as directed against his self-esteem, he must react against it rather than accept it in order to maintain the integrity of his self-esteem system.

One may view the behavior of our Ss as an attempt to make claims upon the other, an attempt to develop a set of shared expectations as to what each was entitled to. Why then did the Ss' reactions differ so markedly as a function of the availability of threat? The explanation lies, we believe, in the cultural interpretation of yielding (to a peer or subordinate) under duress, as compared to giving in without duress. The former, we believe, is perceived as a negatively valued form of behavior, with negative implications for the self-image of the person who so behaves. At least partly, this is so because the locus of causality is perceived to be outside the person's voluntary control. No such evaluation, however, need be placed on the behavior of one who "gives in" in a situation where no threat or duress is a factor. Rather, we should expect the culturally defined evaluation of such a person's behavior to be one of "reasonableness" or "maturity," because the source of the individual's behavior is perceived to lie within his own control.

Our discussion so far has suggested that the psychological factors which operate in our experimental bargaining situation are to be found in many real-life bargaining situations. However, it is well to recognize some unique features of our experimental game. First, the bargainers had no opportunity to communicate verbally with one another. Prior research on the role of communication in trust (Deutsch, 1958, 1960; Loomis, 1959) suggests that the opportunity for communication would have made reaching an agreement easier for individualistically-oriented bargainers. This same research (Deutsch, 1960) indicates, however, that communication may not be effective between competitively oriented bargainers. This possibility was expressed spontaneously by a number of our *Ss* in a post-game interview.

Another characteristic of our bargaining game is that the passage of time, without coming to an agreement, is costly to the players. There are, of course, bargaining situations in which lack of agreement may simply preserve the *status quo* without any worsening of the bargainers' respective situations. This is the case in the typical bilateral monopoly case, where the buyer and seller are unable to agree upon a price (e.g., see Siegel & Fouraker, 1960). In other sorts of bargaining situations, however, (e.g., labor-management negotiations during a strike, international negotiations during an expensive cold war) the passage of time may play an important role. In our experiment, we received the impression that the meaning of time changed as time passed without the bargainers reaching an agreement. Initially, the passage of time seemed to place the players under pressure to come to an agreement before their costs mounted sufficiently to destroy their profit. With the continued passage of time, however, their mounting losses strengthened their resolution not to yield to the other player. They comment: "I've lost so much, I'll be damned if I give in now. At least I'll have the satisfaction of doing better than she does." The mounting losses and continued deadlock seemed to change the game from a mixed motive into a predominantly competitive situation.

It is, of course, hazardous to generalize from a laboratory experiment to the complex problems of the real world. But our experiment and the theoretical ideas underlying it can perhaps serve to emphasize some notions which, otherwise, have an intrinsic plausibility. In brief, these are that there is more safety in cooperative than in competitive coexistence, that it is dangerous for bargainers to have weapons, and that it is possibly even more dangerous for a bargainer to have the capacity to retaliate in kind than not to have this capacity when the other bargainer has a weapon. This last statement assumes that the one who yields has more of his values preserved by accepting the agreement preferred by the other than by extended conflict. Of course, in some bargaining situations in the real world, the loss incurred by yielding may exceed the losses due to extended conflict.

SUMMARY

The nature of bargaining situations was discussed. Two general propositions about the conditions affecting the likelihood of a bargaining agreement were presented. The effects of the availability of threat upon interpersonal bargaining were investigated experimentally in a two-person bargaining game. Three experimental conditions were employed: no threat (neither player could threaten the other), unilateral threat (only one of the players had a means of threat available to her), and bilateral threat (both players could threaten each other). The results indicated that the difficulty in reaching an agreement and the amount of (imaginary) money lost, individually as well as collectively, was greatest in the bilateral and next greatest in the unilateral threat condition. Only in the no threat condition did the players make an overall profit. In the unilateral threat condition, the player with the threat capability did better than the player without the threat capability. However, comparing the bilateral and unilateral threat conditions, the results also indicate that when facing a player who had threat capability one was better off *not* having than having the capacity to retaliate in kind.

REFERENCES

Deutsch, M. A theory of cooperation and competition. *Hum. Relat.,* 1949, *2,* 129–152.

Deutsch, M. Trust and suspicion. *J. conflict Resolut.,* 1958, *2,* 265–279.

Deutsch, M. The effect of motivational orientation upon trust and suspicion. *Hum. Relat.,* 1960, *13,* 123–140.

Dollard, J., Doob, L. W., Miller, N. E., Mowrer, O. H., & Sears, R. H. *Frustration and aggression.* New Haven: Yale Univer. Press, 1939.

Goffman, E. On face-work, *Psychiatry,* 1955, *18,* 213–231.

Loomis, J. L. Communication, the development of trust and cooperative behavior. *Hum. Relat.,* 1959, *12,* 305–315.

Schelling, T. C. Bargaining, communication and limited war. *J. conflict Resolut.,* 1957, *1,* 19–38.

Schelling, T. C. The strategy of conflict: Prospectus for the reorientation of game theory. *J. conflict Resolut.,* 1958, *2,* 203–264.

Siegel, S., & Fouraker, L. E. *Bargaining and group decision making.* New York: McGraw-Hill, 1960.

Stone, J. J. An experiment in bargaining games. *Economet-rica,* 1958, *26,* 286–296.

Zeuthen, F. *Problems of monopoly and economic warfare.* London: Routledge, 1930.

NOTES

1. Schelling in a series of stimulating papers on bargaining (1957, 1958) has also stressed the "mixed motive" character of bargaining situations and has analyzed some of the cognitive factors which determine agreements.

2. The game was conceived and originated by M. Deutsch; R. M. Krauss designed and constructed the apparatus employed in the experiment.

3. We are indebted to the New Jersey Bell Telephone Company for their cooperation in providing *S*s and facilities for the experiment.

4. We are indebted to M. J. R. Healy for suggestions concerning the statistical analysis of our data.

5. Medians are used in graphic presentation of our results because the wide variability of means makes inspection cumbersome.

6. A logarithmic transformation of the summed payoffs on each trial for each pair was made before computing the slopes for a given pair.

7. A post-experimental questionnaire indicated that, in all three experimental conditions, the *S*s were most strongly motivated to win money, next most strongly motivated to do better than the other player, next most motivated to "have fun," and were very little or not at all motivated to help the other player.

CRITICAL THINKING QUESTIONS

1. For many years, the mutually assured destruction (MAD) policy defined U.S. nuclear strategy. That is, nuclear war was to be prevented by the threat of assured destruction of the aggressor nation. What might be the implications of this study for the nuclear policies of nations?

2. The best performance in this study was obtained in the no-threat condition; the unilateral threat condition, in turn, produced better results than the bilateral threat condition, which did the worst. To what extent are these findings generalizable to other situations? In some situations, might it be best to have bilateral threat instead of unilateral threat? What variables might be important in determining when each would be preferred? Explain.

3. In an area such as international relations, how can the existence of threat be reduced? What role may communication play in the process?

ADDITIONAL RELATED READINGS

Anderhub, V., Guth, W., & Marchand, N. (2004). Early or late conflict settlement in a variety of games—An experimental study. *Journal of Economic Psychology, 25*(2), 177–194.

Fehr, E., & Fischbacher, Ú. (2004). Third-party punishment and social norms. *Evolution and Human Behavior, 25*(2), 63–87.

ARTICLE 36

The previous classic piece, Article 35, dealt with the bargaining strategies people use in reaching agreements. *Cooperative behavior* can be viewed as a form of altruism, whereby we try to help others achieve their goals (although we may be helping ourselves, as well). *Competitive behavior,* on the other hand, tends to be more of a win–lose approach, whereby the other person or group is viewed as a rival and what they get is at our expense.

But where do these tendencies to compete or cooperate come from? Some psychologists might explain them as learned behaviors. Evolutionary psychologists, however, might explain these behaviors as rooted in our ancestral past (and hence, in our genes). The reasoning of this approach is that human history is rooted in intergroup conflict and warfare. In order for a group to survive, certain behaviors would have evolved that foster cooperation within the group as well as competition with (or in a sense, protection from) other groups. If these behavioral strategies were successful, then they would be passed along to future generations via genetics.

This evolution-based reasoning also would lead to some specific predictions for gender differences. Specifically, if warfare traditionally and almost exclusively has been the domain of men, then perhaps men will have evolved a greater focus on group issues (since warfare mostly is a group activity) and on group rivalry (again, something that is part of warfare). Women, on the other hand, might be more interpersonally oriented, rather than group oriented, due to their traditional focus on childrearing.

The following contemporary article by Mark Van Vugt, David De Cremer, and Dirk P. Janssen proposes and tests the *male-warrior hypothesis,* examining gender differences in cooperative and competitive situations. It is an interesting examination of some of the ideas derived from evolutionary theories.

Gender Differences in Cooperation and Competition
The Male-Warrior Hypothesis

Mark Van Vugt, David De Cremer, and Dirk P. Janssen

ABSTRACT

Evolutionary scientists argue that human cooperation is the product of a long history of competition among rival groups. There are various reasons to believe that this logic applies particularly to men. In three experiments, using a step-level public-goods task, we found that men contributed more to their group if their group was competing with other groups than if there was no intergroup competition. Female cooperation was relatively unaffected by intergroup competition. These findings suggest that men respond more strongly than women to intergroup threats. We speculate about the evolutionary origins of this gender difference and note some implications.

Van Vugt, M., De Cremer, D., & Janssen, D. P. (2007). Gender differences in cooperation and competition: The male-warrior hypothesis. *Psychological Science, 18*(1), 19–23. Copyright © 2007 by American Psychological Society. Reprinted with permission of Blackwell Publishers.

A tribe including many members who, from possessing in high degree the spirit of patriotism, fidelity, obedience, courage, and sympathy, were always ready to aid one another, and to sacrifice themselves for the common good, would be victorious over most other tribes, and this would be natural selection. (Darwin, 1871, p. 132)

Evolutionarily minded social scientists assert that human altruism and cooperation are the result of the species' unique history of intergroup conflict and warfare (Alexander, 1987; Buss, 1999; Campbell, 1975; Tooby & Cosmides, 1988). Social psychological research is consistent with this idea. Humans spontaneously make "us versus them" categorizations and quickly develop deep emotional attachments to groups even when membership is based on trivial criteria, like the flip of a coin (Brewer, 1979; Ostrom & Sedikides, 1992; Tajfel & Turner, 1979). Humans also readily discriminate against members of out-groups (Fiske, 2002) and engage in costly altruistic actions to defend their group (De Cremer & Van Vugt, 1999; Sherif, 1966).

We hypothesize that an ancestral history of frequent and violent intergroup conflict has shaped the social psychology and behavior of men in particular. Compared with women, men are more likely to engage in intergroup rivalry because for them the (reproductive) benefits, for example, in access to mates and prestige gains, sometimes outweigh the costs (Buss, 1999; Tooby & Cosmides, 1988). Indeed, research on traditional societies shows that tribal warfare is almost exclusively the domain of men, and that male warriors have more sexual partners and greater status within their community than other men do (Chagnon, 1988). A U.S. study on male street gangs revealed that gang members have above-average mating opportunities (Palmer & Tilley, 1995). Finally, recent experiments in social psychology have shown that whereas women are more interpersonally oriented, men are more group oriented (Baumeister & Sommer, 1997); men also recall group events better than women (Gabriel & Gardner, 1999), and men engage more frequently in competitive between-group interactions than women do (Pemberton, Insko, & Schopler, 1996).

Thus, there is some theoretical and empirical support for the idea that men's behaviors and cognitions are more intergroup oriented than women's. We refer to this idea as the *male-warrior hypothesis*. This general hypothesis leads to the prediction that men, more than women, increase their altruistic group contributions during intergroup competition. In this article, we report three experiments in which we tested the male-warrior hypothesis using a social-dilemma task.

EXPERIMENT 1

Design and Procedure

One hundred twenty undergraduate students at the University of Southampton, England, participated in this experiment (mean age = 20.1 years). Forty of the students (33%) were men. Participants were randomly assigned to one of two experimental conditions (competition: individual vs. group). They arrived at the laboratory in 6-person groups to participate in what was described as a group investment experiment. Each participant was placed in front of a computer in a separate cubicle, and all instructions were administered via the computer. The task was a step-level public-goods game. Each member of the group received an endowment of £2 (approximately $4), which could be kept for him- or herself or invested in the group, but not divided between the two options. If the group as a whole contributed £8 or more to the group fund (i.e., if at least 4 of 6 members contributed their £2), then each group member would receive £4, regardless of whether he or she made a contribution. But if the group failed to contribute £8, no bonuses were given out, and only the contributors would lose their £2 investment. Several practice sessions ensured that all participants understood these instructions.[1]

Participants were told that the study was running simultaneously at 10 different universities in England. The universities, which were individually named (e.g., Birmingham, Exeter, Oxford, Southampton), were chosen on the basis of data indicating which other universities students apply to before coming to Southampton. We assumed that these universities provided a salient intergroup comparison (for similar procedures, see Kramer & Brewer, 1984; Van Vugt & De Cremer, 1999). In the *group* condition, the instructions said that the study was investigating how well student groups at these different universities performed the task relative to one another.

In the *individual* condition, the participants also were told about these other participating universities, but the study was described as investigating how well students individually performed in such tasks. After receiving this information, participants decided whether or not to invest their £2 in the group. They were then debriefed, paid, and thanked for their efforts.

Results

We performed a logistic regression on the contribution decision, using a 2 (gender) × 2 (competition) design. There was no main effect for gender, $\chi^2(1, N = 120) = 2.05$, $p_{rep} = .77$, $\varphi = .13$, or for competition, $\chi^2(1, N = 120) = 0.16$, $p_{rep} = .36$, $\varphi = .03$. The predicted interaction between gender and competition was obtained, $\chi^2(1, N = 20) = 11.56$, $p_{rep} > .99$, $\varphi = .34$. The percentages (Fig. 1) show that, as predicted by our hypothesis, the men contributed more often in the group condition ($M = 92\%$, $SD = 27\%$) than in the individual condition ($M = 57\%$, $SD = 51\%$), $\chi^2(1, N = 40) = 7.03$, $p_{rep} > .95$, $\varphi = .42$. The percentage of female contributors was lower in the group condition ($M = 53\%$, $SD = 51\%$) than in the individual condition ($M = 78\%$, $SD = 42\%$), $\chi^2(1, N = 80) = 5.71$, $p_{rep} > .93$, $\varphi = .26$.

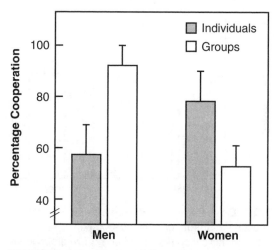

FIGURE 1 / Results from Experiment 1: Percentage of participants who cooperated, as a function of condition and gender. Error bars represent standard errors above the mean.

The results of Experiment 1 demonstrate that men become more altruistic when their group is competing with other groups. To establish the reliability of this finding, we conducted a replication experiment, in which we asked participants how much of their endowment they wished to contribute, rather than to make an all-or-nothing contribution, so as to obtain a finer measure of their cooperativeness.

EXPERIMENT 2

Design and Procedure

Ninety-three undergraduate students at the University of Southampton participated in this experiment. Forty-three (46%) were men. Participants were randomly assigned to one of two experimental conditions (competition: individual vs. group). The procedures and instructions were essentially the same as in the previous experiment, with the following exceptions. Each group member was given an endowment of £3 (300 pence), any amount of which could be invested in the group. The public good (a bonus of £5 for each member, regardless of his or her contribution) was provided if the sum of investments exceeded £12.

Results

We performed a 2 (gender) × 2 (competition) analysis of variance on the contribution level. There was a main effect of competition, $F(1, 89) = 10.81$, $p_{rep} > .99$, $\eta^2 = .108$, and a marginally significant main effect of gender, $F(1, 89) = 3.05$, $p_{rep} > .83$, $\eta^2 = .033$, with women ($M = 201.30$, $SD = 46.16$) contributing more than men ($M = 188.51$, $SD = 62.30$). This effect was qualified by the predicted Gender × Competition interaction, $F(1, 89) = 4.23$, $p_{rep} > .88$, $\eta^2 = .045$. The means (Fig. 2) show that, as predicted, men contributed more in the group condition ($M = 212.60$, $SD = 56.64$) than in the individual condition ($M = 155.06$, $SD = 54.96$), $F(1, 89) = 13.37$, $p_{rep} > .99$. For women, there was no difference between the group condition ($M = 209.25$, $SD = 33.65$) and the individual condition ($M = 196.00$, $SD = 52.77$), $F(1, 89) < 1$.

In a third experiment, we attempted to replicate this effect with iterated trials of the same public-goods task. We also examined a potential psychological mediator

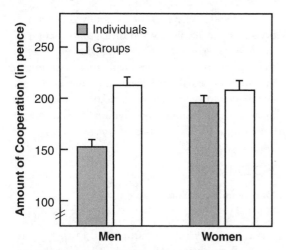

FIGURE 2 / Results from Experiment 2: Mean amount contributed (0–300 pence), as a function of condition and gender. Error bars represent standard errors above the mean.

of the impact of intergroup competition, group identification (Brewer, 1979; Tajfel & Turner, 1979).

EXPERIMENT 3

Design and Procedure

Ninety undergraduate students at the University of Southampton (mean age = 21 years) participated in this experiment. Forty-eight (53%) were men. Participants were randomly assigned to one of two experimental conditions (competition: individual vs. group), and the competition manipulation was the same as in the previous experiments. The dependent measure was the mean contribution level (0–300 pence) across six trials. Participants also answered a postexperiment questionnaire with five questions about their group identification (e.g., "I identify with the group I am in"), responding to each on a scale from 1, *not at all,* to 9, *very strongly* (Van Vugt & De Cremer, 1999). The group-identification measure had good reliability (α = .79).

Results

A 2 (gender) × 2 (competition) analysis of variance on the mean contribution level showed a main effect

of gender, $F(1, 86) = 6.67$, $p_{rep} > .93$, $\eta^2 = .072$, with women ($M = 235.45$, $SD = 50.05$) overall contributing more than men ($M = 197.13$, $SD = 88.98$).[2] There was also a significant main effect of competition, $F(1, 86) = 5.84$, $p_{rep} > .93$, $\eta^2 = .064$, qualified by the predicted Gender × Competition interaction, $F(1, 86) = 7.68$, $p_{rep} > .95$, $\eta^2 = .082$ (see Fig. 3, top panel). Men contributed more in the group condition ($M = 235.12$, $SD = 46.22$) than in the individual condition ($M = 159.13$, $SD = 105.02$), $F(1, 86) = 14.71$, $p_{rep} > .99$. Again, for women, there was no dif-

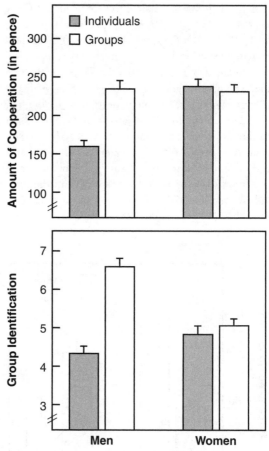

FIGURE 3 / Results from Experiment 3: Amount of cooperation (upper panel; 0–300 pence) and group identification (lower panel; 1 = low group identification, 9 = high group identification), as a function of condition and gender. Error bars represent standard errors above the mean.

ference between the group (M = 232.35, SD = 49.81) and individual (M = 237.56, SD = 51.13) conditions, $F(1, 86) < 1$.

Does group identification mediate the enhanced cooperation rates of men in response to an intergroup threat? A 2 (gender) × 2 (competition) analysis of the group-identification scale yielded no main effect for gender, $F(1, 86) = 1.63$, $p_{rep} > .72$, $\eta^2 = .019$, but there was an effect of competition, $F(1, 86) = 11.12$, $p_{rep} > .99$, $\eta^2 = .115$, which was qualified by a Gender × Competition interaction, $F(1, 86) = 7.11$, $p_{rep} > .95$, $\eta^2 = .076$. As predicted, men identified more strongly with the group in the group condition (M = 6.56, SD = 1.15) than in the individual condition (M = 4.27, SD = 2.07), $F(1, 86) = 19.74$, $p_{rep} > .99$. There was no such difference for women (Ms = 5.06 in the group condition vs. 4.80 in the individual condition, SDs = 1.54 and 2.12, respectively), $F(1, 86) < 1$ (see Fig. 3, lower panel).

We tested mediation for men and women separately using a bootstrap method, as suggested by Shrout and Bolger (2004) for small sample sizes. For men, competition predicted group identification, β = .573, $F(1, 46) = 22.45$, $p_{rep} > .99$. In a model with competition and group identification predicting cooperation, competition was no longer significant, β = .232, $F(1, 45) = 2.23$, $p_{rep} < .82$, $\Delta R^2 = -.036$. A bootstrap test with 1,000 replications indicated a significant indirect effect, β = .185, confidence interval = [.043,.409]. The nonsignificant final path from competition to cooperation suggests full mediation by group identification for men.[3] There was no mediation for women (β = –.060, n.s.). These results show that men's cooperative behavior increases during intergroup competition because an intergroup threat enhances males' group identification.

DISCUSSION

The results of three experiments show that men identify and cooperate more with their group under conditions of intergroup threat than where there is no threat, whereas women's cooperation is largely unaffected by this manipulation.[4] Our research thus supports the male-warrior hypothesis, the idea that men's social behavior and psychology are more strongly intergroup driven than women's.

This hypothesis accounts for some previously unexplained sex differences in cooperation, for example, the fact that men make more competitive choices in social dilemmas between groups than women do (cf. the group-discontinuity effect; see Wildschut, Pinter, Vevea, Insko, & Schopler, 2003). The male-warrior hypothesis also speaks to the broader social science literature. Male intergroup rivalries are a universal feature of human societies, in wars, civil conflicts, gang rivalries, and competitive team sports (Keegan, 1994; Palmer & Tilley, 1995; Pemberton et al., 1996). Compared with women, men engage more in risky, heroic forms of helping (Eagly & Crowley, 1986), identify more with large social units (Baumeister & Sommer, 1997; Gabriel & Gardner, 1999), and are higher in social-dominance orientation (Sidanius & Pratto, 2001). The anthropological literature reveals that tribal warfare is largely the domain of men (Chagnon, 1988). Finally, in humans' closest genetic relative, the chimpanzee, coalition formation in defending territory is primarily a male activity (Boehm, 1999; Wrangham & Peterson, 1996).

We do not mean to imply that men cooperate within their group only for intergroup reasons. Men also contribute to groups through providing food, trading, and rearing offspring (Kenrick, Li, & Butner, 2003). Nor do we mean to imply that women are completely insensitive to intergroup conflict, or do not contribute as much to group welfare as men do. On the contrary, women, on average, contributed more to the group than men across our three experiments. Our findings merely demonstrate that men respond more strongly than women to intergroup conflict.

These findings fit nicely with an evolutionary hypothesis about specific male intergroup adaptations—the male-warrior hypothesis—and such evolved intergroup traits are likely to be reinforced through cultural processes, for example, during childhood socialization (Eagly & Crowley, 1986). Women's social psychology is likely to be shaped more strongly by different kinds of needs, such as defending their offspring and creating supportive social networks (Taylor, Klein, Lewis, & Gruenewald, 2000). Investigating the way men and women respond differently to various group and individual threats is a fruitful avenue for further investigation.

Future research should also address various implications of the male-warrior hypothesis. One implication is that people should assign more weight to "intergroup" personality traits such as physical ability, fighting prowess, bravery, courage, and heroism when evaluating men than when evaluating women. Further, status in a group and, perhaps, attractiveness as a mate should be more strongly associated with contributions to intergroup activities for men than for women. Men should also generally be more interested than women in what might be considered intergroup hobbies and professions, like playing team sports, watching war movies, and joining the military.

We should note a limitation of our research, a limitation that is intrinsic to experimental public-goods research. Because the payoffs in our experiments were not substantial, we do not know if men in reality would be willing to take huge risks to defend their group. Yet the literature on warfare and suicide terrorism suggests that men are quite prepared to sacrifice themselves on behalf of their group (Atran, 2003; Keegan, 1994). Another limitation is that intergroup competition in our experiments was merely symbolic. As in most social-identity experiments, groups were not competing with each other for a tangible reward. Prestige battles between universities, however, are significant in Britain (and in the United States), and we therefore assume that our participants were genuinely affected by the manipulation.

To conclude, evolutionary scientists assert that humans' unique capacity to cooperate in large groups derives from a long history of intergroup conflict. Here we have argued that intergroup conflict has shaped the psychology and behavior of men in particular, and we have provided data to support this proposal. The male-warrior hypothesis deserves further attention from social and evolutionary scientists interested in understanding the roots of human altruism, cooperation, and intergroup aggression.

ACKNOWLEDGMENTS

We thank Ed Hagen, Constantine Sedikides, and the members of the Evolution and Social Sciences Group at the University of Kent for their helpful comments on an earlier version of this article.

ENDNOTES

1. The rational-choice prediction for the step-level public-goods game is that participants will contribute nothing. This game reflects a warlike situation in the sense that, depending on the size of members' contributions, the group either wins everything or loses everything.

2. There was a main effect of trial, $F(5, 430) = 8.83$, $p < .001$, $p_{rep} > .99$, $\eta^2 = .093$, revealing that group contributions decreased from Trial 1 to Trial 6. However, because gender and competition did not interact with trial, we do not discuss this factor further.

3. Alternative mediation tests produced essentially the same results, $z(Sobel) = 1.99$, $p_{rep} > .88$, and MacKinnon's $z_\alpha z_\beta = 10.58$, $p_{rep} > .93$.

4. Further research might shed light on the differences between the experiments in women's cooperation levels.

REFERENCES

Alexander, R. D. (1987). *The biology of moral systems.* London: Aldine.

Atran, S. (2003). The genesis of suicide terrorism. *Science, 299,* 1534–1539.

Baumeister, R. F., & Sommer, K. L. (1997). What do men want? Gender differences and the two spheres of belongingness. *Psychological Bulletin, 122,* 38–14.

Boehm, C. (1999). *Hierarchy in the forest.* London: Harvard University Press.

Brewer, M. B. (1979). Ingroup bias in the minimal intergroup situation: A cognitive-motivational analysis. *Psychological Bulletin, 86,* 307–324.

Buss, D. M. (1999). *Evolutionary psychology.* London: Allyn & Bacon.

Campbell, D. T. (1975). On the conflicts between biological and social evolution and between psychology and oral tradition. *American Psychologist, 30,* 1103–1126.

Chagnon, N. A. (1988). Life histories, blood revenge, and warfare in a tribal population. *Science, 239,* 985–992.

Darwin, C. (1871). *The descent of man and selection in relation to sex.* London: Murray.

De Cremer, D., & Van Vugt, M. (1999). Social identification effects in social dilemmas: A transformation of motives. *European Journal of Social Psychology, 29,* 871–893.

Eagly, A., & Crowley, M. (1986). Gender and helping behavior: A meta-analytic review of the social-psychological literature. *Psychological Bulletin, 100,* 283–308.

Fiske, S. T. (2002). What we now know about bias and intergroup conflict, the problem of the century. *Current Directions in Psychological Science, 11,* 123–128.

Gabriel, S., & Gardner, W. L. (1999). Are there his and hers types of interdependence? The implications of gender differences in collective versus relational interdependence for affect, behavior and cognition. *Journal of Personality and Social Psychology, 77,* 642–655.

Keegan, J. (1994). *A history of warfare.* New York: Random House.

Kenrick, D., Li, N. P., & Butner, J. (2003). Dynamical evolutionary psychology: Individual decision rules and emergent social norms. *Psychological Review, 110,* 3–28.

Kramer, R. M., & Brewer, M. B. (1984). Effects of group identity on resource rise in a simulated commons dilemma. *Journal of Personality and Social Psychology, 46,* 1044–1057.

Ostrom, T. M., & Sedikides, C. (1992). The outgroup homogeneity effect in natural and minimal groups. *Psychological Bulletin, 112,* 536–552.

Palmer, C. T., & Tilley, C. F. (1995). Sexual access to females as a motivation for joining gangs: An evolutionary approach. *Journal of Sex Research, 32,* 213–217.

Pemberton, M. B., Insko, C. A., & Schopler, J. (1996). Memory for and experience of differential competitive behavior of individuals and groups. *Journal of Personality and Social Psychology, 71,* 953–966.

Sherif, M. (1966). *In common predicament: Social psychology of intergroup conflict and cooperation.* Boston: Houghton Mifflin.

Shrout, P. E., & Bolger, N. (2004). Mediation in experimental and non-experimental studies: New procedures and recommendations. *Psychological Methods, 7,* 422–445.

Sidanius, J., & Pratto, F. (2001). *Social dominance.* Cambridge, England: Cambridge University Press.

Tajfel, H., & Turner, J. C. (1979). An integrative theory of intergroup conflict. In W. G. Austin & S. Worchel (Eds.), *The social psychology of intergroup relations* (pp. 33–47). Monterey, CA: Brooks/Cole.

Taylor, S. E., Klein, L. C., Lewis, B. P., & Gruenewald, R. A. R. (2000). Biobehavioral responses to stress in females: Tend-and-befriend not fight-or-flight. *Psychological Review, 107,* 413–429.

Tooby, J., & Cosmides, L. (1988). *The evolution of war and its cognitive foundations* (Institute for Evolutionary Studies Technical Report 88-1). Retrieved December 6, 2006, from http://www.psych.ucsb.edu/research/cep/papers/Evolofwar.pdf

Van Vugt, M., & De Cremer, D. (1999). Leadership in social dilemmas: The effects of group identification on collective actions to provide public goods. *Journal of Personality and Social Psychology, 76,* 587–599.

Wildschut, T., Pinter, B., Vevea, J. L., Insko, C. A., & Schopler, J. (2003). Beyond the group mind: A quantitative review of the interindividual-intergroup discontinuity effect. *Psychological Bulletin, 129,* 698–722.

Wrangham, R., & Peterson, D. (1996). *Demonic males: Apes and the origins of human violence.* London: Bloomsbury.

CRITICAL THINKING QUESTIONS

1. Restate the male-warrior hypothesis in your own words. Do you agree or disagree with it? Explain your reasoning.

2. If the male-warrior hypothesis is correct, what other behaviors and characteristics might you expect to find more in males than in females? If these differences do indeed exist, what, if any, explanations other than evolutionary concepts might account for these differences? Explain.

3. You undoubtedly have encountered other studies besides this one that use evolutionary-based explanations for social behavior. Do you agree or disagree with attributing human social behavior to evolutionary processes? Explain your reasoning.

4. Increasingly, women are a larger part of the armed forces in many nations. Based on the Discussion section of this article, what are the implications (if any) for females in the military? In other words, how would females be expected to act differently from their male counterparts? Defend your position.

CHAPTER INTEGRATION QUESTIONS

1. While the three articles in this chapter do not deal primarily with leadership per se, they all have implications for how leaders can affect the outcomes of group decisions. What are those implications?

2. Based on your own experience with working in groups, what factors other than those presented in the articles may influence the functioning and outcomes of groups? Explain why you think these factors are important.

3. Abraham Lincoln said, "Nearly all men can stand adversity, but if you want to test a man's character, give him power." Relate this quotation to a unifying theme or themes in the articles in this chapter.

Chapter Thirteen

BUSINESS PSYCHOLOGY

A MAJOR PART of your waking life will be spent at work. You may already be in a full-time position (or have been), or you may have had experience working at a part-time job. When you think about the work you are doing now or hope to do in the future, you may have many concerns. For instance, you may wonder how much money you will make. But you also may be concerned about whether you will enjoy what you do. If you become a manager and are responsible for other people's behavior, you also may be concerned with how best to utilize the human resources available for the benefit of the organization as well as that of the individual employee.

Social psychology has long been involved in the area of business, or *organizational*, psychology. Early work in the field looked at factors such as leadership style and how it may contribute to worker behavior. While work in that area has continued, the influence of social psychology has expanded into virtually all domains of work-related activities, including productivity, job satisfaction, and employee motivation, to name but a few. The articles in this chapter provide a sampling of the many ways in which social psychology contributes to our understanding of work behavior.

Article 37, "The Psychology of Voluntary Employee Turnover," examines the question of why people decide to leave a job (or conversely, why they choose to stay). The research and theories presented in this article build on concepts from social cognition, some of which were addressed in Chapter Three of this book. In addition to the theoretical importance of such research, there are obvious practical implications for employers and individuals, as well.

Article 38, "One More Time: How Do You Motivate Employees?" is a truly classic piece that examines the questions of what motivates people, what factors are involved in job satisfaction, and what conditions influence productivity. Your beliefs about what motivates you and others to work may change after you read this article.

Finally, Article 39, "Doing Better but Feeling Worse: Looking for the 'Best' Job Undermines Satisfaction," examines the strategies people use in making decisions such as which job to take. While certain decision-making strategies often result in obtaining a higher-paying job, for example, the same strategies, applied at the same times, may result in greater dissatisfaction with the job in the end. Given that you most likely are or will soon be searching for a job, the implications of these findings may be of personal relevance.

ARTICLE 37 _____

At the heart of any organization—whether a small, family-run business or a large, multi-national corporation—are its *people*. Perhaps nothing is more critical to the ultimate success or failure of an organization than the hiring of the best people for the appropriate jobs.

Most employers not only want to attract the best people to their organizations, but they also want to retain them. Employers often direct a great deal of resources at recruitment (finding the best person for the job). They also want to make sure that the right people, once hired, stay.

Job retention has been an important topic of research for organizational psychologists for some time. Much of the traditional research on job retention focused on issues such as job satisfaction, with the reasoning that if people have a high level of job satisfaction, they will stay where they are. Conversely, they will leave only if the job does not supply them with an expected level of satisfaction. In many ways, this finding coincides with common-sense reasoning: If we're happy doing what we're doing, why change?

But is low job satisfaction the only reason people leave? Or is it possible that some people, no matter how happy they are with their jobs, could decide to quit? Over the years, research on employee turnover has become more sophisticated in examining the many variables involved in such decisions. Much of this research has stemmed from an increased understanding of how humans make decisions in general (the issue of social cognition, addressed in Chapter Three).

The following article by Wendy S. Harman, Thomas W. Lee, Terence R. Mitchell, William Felps, and Bradley P. Owens considers recent research and theories that may help to explain why people leave and why people stay in organizations. Given the importance of employee retention, this is a topic of practical importance to most organizations.

The Psychology of Voluntary Employee Turnover

■ Wendy S. Harman, Thomas W. Lee, Terence R. Mitchell, William Felps, and Bradley P. Owens

ABSTRACT

Most research on voluntary turnover has focused on dissatisfaction-induced and rational decision-making processes, with some attention paid to external market influences. This focus leaves unexplained a large portion of the variance in why people choose to quit a job. Recently, however, researchers are considering the alternative ways that the turnover process is enacted, as well as what businesses can do to prevent turnover.

Turnover has been and remains an active area of theorizing and empirical research within the domain of organizational psychology. Older theories are being retested and modified, new theorizing is being introduced, and current research is providing better answers to the main research question: Why do people voluntarily leave a job? In this article, we selectively summarize the huge body of work on the psychology of

Harman, W. S., Lee, T. W., Mitchell, T. R., Felps, W., & Owens, B. P. (2007). The psychology of voluntary employee turnover. *Current Directions in Psychological Science, 16*(1), 51–54. Copyright © 2007 by American Psychological Society. Reprinted with permission of Blackwell Publishers.

voluntary turnover and present the current directions in turnover theory and research.

WHY PEOPLE LEAVE

Traditional research on turnover focuses on negative job attitudes (e.g., low levels of job satisfaction) as the cause of leaving. In their seminal work, March and Simon (1958) proposed a psychological explanation of turnover that is based on individuals' utility functions: When outcomes (such as pay or promotion opportunities) are too low relative to the employee's expectations, an employee becomes dissatisfied and motivated to leave the organization, increasing his or her "desirability of movement." Turnover, then, becomes a function of the extent of this desirability combined with the perceived ease of movement (i.e., number of perceived job alternatives). Much research and theorizing followed. Griffeth, Hom, and Gaertner (2000) reported that across the many intellectually rigorous models focusing on job satisfaction and perceived alternatives, the ability to predict voluntary turnover remained remarkably weak, with variance explained hovering around 5%.

In response to these disappointing findings, Lee and Mitchell (1994) used image theory from psychology (Beach & Mitchell, 1998) to develop their *unfolding model* of voluntary turnover. The unfolding model describes different psychological paths that people follow when they decide to leave an organization. The central contribution of this approach is that it shifted theorizing from an assumption that turnover is always an evaluative and rational process to a broader model of how decisions are actually made. This analysis revealed that although some decisions to quit are probably quite consistent with standards of expected-value rationality, a great many others are driven by more intuitive or routinized decision processes.

IMAGE THEORY AND THE UNFOLDING MODEL

Image theory is perhaps the most viable and elaborate alternative to the notion of decisions based on subjective expected utility. In contrast to the idea that people generally do or should make calculations that maxi-

mize utility, image theory suggests that some types of incoming information (e.g., a job offer) prompt a comparison of that information to three job-related images. As an automatic, though conscious, process, the individual first will compare the information with his or her value image (the person's set of important values regarding his or her job). Next, the individual will compare the incoming information with the trajectory image (the person's set of goals that motivate job behavior). Last, the individual will compare the information with the strategic image (the behavioral tactics and strategies that the person believes are effective in attaining job-related goals). Should the incoming information contain an alternative that passes this screening process (i.e., being compatible with the three images), the individual then compares the alternative with the status quo. Typically, the status quo wins and the person does nothing. Should the person have more than one alternative that passes the screening process, he or she will then conduct more rational cost/benefit analyses among alternatives.

The unfolding model labels incoming information that leads to image considerations as *shocks*. Shocks lead the person to consider leaving his or her job. The shock can be internal or external to the individual, and it can be negative (e.g., a fight with the boss), positive (e.g., winning the lottery), or neutral (e.g., an unanticipated job offer). Additionally, the social and cognitive context in which the shock occurs provides the *decision frame* or frame of reference within which the employee interprets the meaning of the shock.

The unfolding model introduces five paths (i.e., distinct sets of psychological processes) that lead to voluntary turnover (see Table 1). In the first path, the shock triggers a preexisting script. The person then engages the preexisting script and leaves without considering alternatives or his or her attachment to the organization. Suppose, for example, an employee has the following pregnancy script: If I become pregnant, then I will quit work to stay home with the new baby. Once the information about being pregnant is known, the script is enacted without further consideration. The decision is automatic because there is an existing script that dictates the decision. The second path also contains a shock that triggers leaving without the consideration of job alternatives. The difference is that, in this second case, there is no prior action

TABLE 1 / Paths by Which the Turnover Decision May Unfold Over Time

	Initiating Event	→	Cognitive/Emotional Process	→	Search Behavior	→	Quit Decision
Path 1	Shock (e.g., pregnancy)	→	Prompts quitting script enactment	→	None	→	Automatic
Path 2	Shock (e.g., unpleasant new boss)	→	Comparison of shock to images leads to high dissatisfaction	→	None	→	Fairly automatic
Path 3	Shock (e.g., unexpected job offer)	→	Comparison of shock to images leads to relative dissatisfaction	→	Search for alternatives	→	Deliberate
Path 4a	No shock	→	Accumulating dissatisfaction	→	None	→	Fairly automatic
Path 4b	No shock	→	Accumulating dissatisfaction	→	Search for alternatives	→	Deliberate

Note. Moving from left to right, paths 1–3 include an initiating event (shock) that leads to the quit decision. Paths 4a and 4b do not contain shocks; instead the process begins with accumulating dissatisfaction that leads to the turnover decision.

script. Instead, incoming information is interpreted as violating a person's value, goal, or strategic images, and leaving occurs without further deliberation. This process is fairly automatic; the question of leaving is decided once the individual decides that one or more image violations have occurred. An example of this path would be a situation in which a strongly disliked coworker gets promoted to be an individual's boss, violating that individual's belief that enjoyable work involves having a friendly relationship with the supervisor (strategy image violation), and the individual leaves without considering other job alternatives.

The third path in the unfolding model contains a shock that triggers an evaluation via the three images (values, trajectory, strategic) of the current job; if the information contained in the shock is not compatible with the images, the individual then considers leaving. This can lead to a deliberate search for job alternatives and certainly involves an evaluation of at least one alternative. For example, an unexpected job offer may prompt someone to compare the current job to the unexpected job offer. Paths 4a and 4b do not contain shocks. Path 4a describes a situation in which a person's job satisfaction becomes so low that he or she leaves without considering job alternatives. Path 4b is the more traditional view of turnover in

which low satisfaction leads to a deliberate search, evaluation of alternatives, an intention to leave, and subsequent turnover.

Several recent turnover studies have provided support for the unfolding model. To test the unfolding model, Lee, Mitchell, Wise, and Fireman (1996) used multiple case studies of a sample of nurses who had voluntarily quit their jobs. They found that of those sampled, 14% reported following the first decision path, 14% followed the second, 32% followed the third, 18% followed 4a, and 23% followed 4b (percentages are rounded). These findings provided preliminary evidence for the model and for the contention that people use these four distinct psychological processes when engaged in a turnover decision. Lee, Mitchell, Holtom, McDaniel, and Hill (1999) conducted a replication and extension using a sample of accountants from the Big 6 accounting firms. They reported substantial support for a slightly modified model, with 93% of the subjects fitting clearly into one of the four paths. Differences with respect to job type were uncovered when comparing the accountant sample with the sample of nurses from Lee et al. (1996). Nurses left significantly more often via paths 1, 2, and 4a than did the accountants, who left significantly more often by path 3. Other recent studies support the importance of job type in determining turnover path (Kammeyer-Mueller, Wanberg, Glomb, & Ahlburg, 2005; Maertz, Stevens, & Campion, 2003; Sims, Drasgow, & Fitzgerald, 2005).

Specific Contributions

The unfolding model moves traditional turnover theory away from a reliance on the rationalistic approaches of previous theories to a more descriptively accurate model grounded in current psychological thinking (e.g., image theory). As a consequence, the unfolding model makes a number of specific contributions. First, it introduces the notion of automated scripts into the turnover process (path 1). Second, the model incorporates shocks (positive, neutral, or negative) as catalysts to turnover (paths 1, 2, and 3). Third, in contrast to the traditional single sequential process, the multiple paths of the unfolding model allow for greater explanatory power with distinctive psychological processes in each path. Fourth, the model highlights the possibility that job satisfaction may have no influence on the decision to quit—that is, people who are satisfied still may leave (paths 1 and 3). Fifth, the relative speed of the quit decisions—immediate in paths 1 and 2 but slower in paths 3 and 4b—is introduced to the turnover literature. Sixth, and finally, the unfolding model allows for the possibility that turnover could happen even in the absence of job alternatives (paths 1, 2, and 4a). In sum, the unfolding model represents a major alternative to traditional theories of leaving.

WHY PEOPLE STAY

As we have reviewed, traditional turnover models hold that employees leave because of negative job attitudes and stay because of positive job attitudes. Accordingly, the vast majority of scholarly efforts presume that staying is simply the opposite of leaving (e.g., increase job satisfaction to retain employees), though this is not necessarily the case. Research by Rusbult, Farrell, and colleagues (1983, 1988) showed that turnover decisions are influenced by people's comparisons between the investments made in their job or organization, the rewards they receive, the quality of alternatives, and the costs associated with working for a particular organization—and these comparisons

change over time. As this research and the unfolding model suggest, employee retention issues are not simplistic. Mitchell, Holtom, Lee, Sablynski, and Erez (2001) proposed a construct called *job embeddedness* to explain why employees remain in an organization. Job embeddedness describes a web of forces that cause people to feel they cannot leave their job. The critical components to job embeddedness include the extent to which people are linked with others or to activities, the extent to which their jobs and communities fit with other aspects of their lives, and the ease with which their respective links can be broken—that is, what they would sacrifice if they left. These three dimensions are identified as *links, fit,* and *sacrifice,* respectively, and are concerned with both on-job and off-the-job experiences.

Links refers to formal and informal connections that a person has with other individuals and institutions. The more connected an individual is with the organization (e.g., belongs to workgroups) and with the community (e.g., affiliated with local clubs, interest groups, or churches), the more embedded he or she is. Fit is the individual's perceived compatibility with the organization and with the community. The employee's personal values and career goals need to be congruent with the larger organizational culture; this congruence allows the employee to feel tied personally and professionally to the organization. In addition, individuals need to feel as though they and their family also fit with the community in which they live. Again, the better the fit, the more likely the person is to stay. Sacrifice refers to the perceived cost of leaving. These costs may be material or psychological. Leaving may entail giving up the advantages associated with tenure (e.g., big office, vacation time), as well as the personal losses such as companionship with colleagues or perks unique to the organization. Community sacrifices are relevant only if the individual needs to move to a new location. The loss of the sense of belonging to a community (including giving up such things as tickets to the local football team, the home inhabited for 20 years) can influence the community sacrifice dimension.

The empirical evidence for job embeddedness is substantial. In a two-sample test of grocery employees and hospital workers, Mitchell et al. (2001) found that employees' self-rated embeddedness scores at time 1 predicted which employees had left the organization a year later at time 2. Additionally, the researchers found that overall job embeddedness predicts variance in turnover over and above that explained by the major variables in most turnover research (i.e., job satisfaction, organizational commitment, job search, and job alternatives). Further, Lee, Mitchell, Sablynski, Burton, and Holtom (2004) sought to extend the original formulation by considering on- and off-the-job embeddedness separately. These scholars reported that off-the-job embeddedness predicted absences and turnover (over and above that of job satisfaction and organizational commitment), whereas on-the-job embeddedness did not. Conversely, they also reported that on-the-job embeddedness predicted organizational citizenship behavior and in-role job performance (again, over and above satisfaction and commitment), whereas off-the-job embeddedness did not.

Specific Contributions

The job embeddedness construct makes two main contributions to the turnover literature. First, it significantly expands the scope of variables researchers consider when trying to understand why people remain in a job, such as the inclusion of nonattitudinal determinants of turnover like structural links to other people. Second, embeddedness includes consideration of off-the-job factors like fit with one's neighbors and community—a contribution that is more subtle and theoretical in nature. Job embeddedness is premised on the notion that many people rarely consider leaving their jobs because they are so immersed in their environments. This realistic understanding of human psychology can guide continued efforts to understand why people leave and why they stay.

FUTURE RESEARCH AND CONCLUSIONS

The unfolding model and the job embeddedness construct are significant advances in the turnover literature, but researchers still need to determine the basic science behind the models. It would be beneficial to integrate this work more fully with judgment and decision-making research regarding deliberate and automatic processes. For example, are there situational triggers that make people aware of quit options (e.g., other people leaving, changes outside of work)? This sort of basic perceptual research could greatly increase understanding of the actual phenomenon of quitting. In addition, research that addresses the intersection of the unfolding model and job embeddedness construct would be exceptionally helpful. For example, does job embeddedness buffer the effects of shocks from the unfolding model? Additionally, research looking into practical interventions that are informed by the theories would be valuable. For example, which types of shocks in the unfolding model are controllable by the organization, and how might organizations work to embed employees in the organization or community? Because many organizational psychologists work in applied settings, endeavoring to develop applications of this research could be particularly beneficial.

In closing, premised on psychologically grounded models of cognition and decision-making, both the unfolding model and the job embeddedness construct provide means of looking beyond job satisfaction to other factors important to the voluntary turnover process. We look forward to new work that builds on these tools.

RECOMMENDED READING

Lee, T. W., & Mitchell, T. R. (1994). (See References)

Lee, T. W., Mitchell, T. R., Sablynski, C. T., Burton, J. P., & Holtom, B. C. (2004). (See References)

Mitchell, T. R., Holtom, B. C., Lee, T. W., Sablynski, C. T., & Erez, M. (2001). (See References)

REFERENCES

Beach, L. R., & Mitchell, T. R. (1998). The basics of image theory. In L. R. Beach (Ed.), *Image theory: Theoretical and empirical foundations* (pp. 3–18). Hillsdale, NJ: Erlbaum.

Griffeth, R. W., Hom, P. W., & Gaertner, S. (2000). A meta-analysis of antecedents and correlates of employee turnover: Update, moderator tests, and research implications for the next millennium. *Journal of Management, 26,* 463–488.

Kammeyer-Mueller, J. D., Wanberg, C. R., Glomb, T. M., & Ahlburg, D. (2005). The role of temporal shifts in turnover processes: It's about time. *Journal of Applied Psychology, 90,* 644–658.

Lee, T. W., & Mitchell, T. R. (1994). An alternative approach: The unfolding model of voluntary employee turnover. *Academy of Management Review, 19,* 51–89.

Lee, T. W., Mitchell, T. R., Holtom, B. C., McDaniel, L. S., & Hill, J. W. (1999). The unfolding model of voluntary turnover: A replication and extension. *Academy of Management Journal, 42,* 450–462.

Lee, T. W., Mitchell, T. R., Sablynski, C. J., Burton, J. R., & Holtom, B. C. (2004). The effects of job embeddedness on organizational citizenship, job performance, volitional absences, and voluntary turnover. *Academy of Management Journal, 47,* 711–722.

Lee, T. W., Mitchell, T. R., Wise, L., & Fireman, S. (1996). An unfolding model of voluntary employee turnover. *Academy of Management Journal, 39,* 5–36.

Maertz, C. P., Stevens, M. J., & Campion, M. A. (2003). A turnover model for the Mexican maquiladoras. *Journal of Vocational Behavior, 63,* 111–135.

March, J. G., & Simon, H. A. (1958). *Organizations.* New York: Wiley.

Mitchell, T. R., Holtom, B. C., Lee, T. W., Sablynski, C. J., & Erez, M. (2001). Why people stay: Using job embeddedness to predict voluntary turnover. *Academy of Management Journal, 44,* 1102–1121.

Rusbult, C. E., & Farrell, D. (1983). A longitudinal test of the investments model: The impact on job satisfaction, job commitment, and turnover variations in rewards, costs, alternatives, and investments. *Journal of Applied Psychology, 68,* 429–438.

Rusbult, C. E., Farrell, D., Rogers, G., & Mainous, A. G. (1988). Impact of exchange variables on exit, voice, loyalty, and neglect: An integrative model of responses to declining job satisfaction. *Academy of Management Journal, 31,* 599–627.

Sims, C. S., Drasgow, F., & Fitzgerald, L. F. (2005). The effects of sexual harassment on turnover in the military: Time-dependent modeling. *Journal of Applied Psychology, 90,* 1141–1152.

CRITICAL THINKING QUESTIONS:

1. What concepts from social cognition and social perception (Chapters Three and Two of this book, respectively) may be used to explain how so-called shocks may induce a person to leave? Additionally, how might these concepts be used to help explain job embeddedness? Discuss your reasoning.

2. What factors that contribute to a sense of job embeddedness can be controlled (or at least somewhat managed) by an organization? How might they be addressed by an organization in a practical, realistic manner? Explain your reasoning.

3. How can organizations deal with and possibly control the shocks that lead to employee turnover? How might the shock be addressed by an organization in a practical, realistic manner? Explain your reasoning.

4. Leaving a job, whether for another job or not, is not exactly the same thing as dropping out of college or transferring to another school. Nonetheless, can the concepts of shocks and embeddedness be applied to leaving school? Explain.

5. Can the concepts of shocks and embeddedness be applied to why people stay or leave a relationship—for instance, a marriage? How so? Elaborate on your reasoning.

ARTICLE 38

Why do people work? Is it just to earn a living (or in some cases, to make a lot of money), or are there other reasons, too? If you look at the number of references in American culture to the "Monday morning blues" and "TGIF," you might get the impression that people would rather not work, if given a choice. Many people would consider it distinctly odd if someone expressed joy at the prospect of returning to work after a weekend off. Do most workers really feel that way? Is that the way it *should* be?

The question of what motivates people to work has been of major interest to industrial/organizational psychologists for quite some time. Ultimately concerned with productivity and profits, business has an obvious interest in trying to discover ways to increase employee motivation, since increased motivation is often viewed as synonymous with increased output. Different theories of motivation have been drawn from areas in the behavioral sciences, ranging from learning theory to humanistic theories of motivation. All seek to identify the factors that motivate people and how to implement these factors to increase motivation levels.

One person who has made significant contributions to the understanding of motivation in the workplace is Frederick Herzberg. In the following classic article, he presents an analysis of commonly used methods of motivation and why they don't work, followed by his own theory and research. Whether you fully accept the tenets and suggestions found in the article, it will most likely get you to reexamine your own assumptions about what motivates people to work.

One More Time
How Do You Motivate Employees?
■ Frederick Herzberg

KITA—the externally imposed attempt by management to "install a generator" in the employee—has been demonstrated to be a total failure, the author says. The absence of such "hygiene" factors as good supervisor-employee relations and liberal fringe benefits can make a worker unhappy, but their presence will not make him want to work harder. Essentially meaningless changes in the tasks that workers are assigned to do have not accomplished the desired objective either. The only way to motivate the employee is to give him challenging work in which he can assume responsibility. Frederick Herzberg, who is Professor and Chairman of the Psychology Department at Case Western Reserve University, has devoted many years to the study of motivation in the United States and abroad. He is the author of Work and Nature of Man *(World Publishing Company, 1966).*

How many articles, books, speeches, and workshops have pleaded plaintively, "How do I get an employee to do what I want him to do?"

The psychology of motivation is tremendously complex, and what has been unraveled with any degree of assurance is small indeed. But the dismal ratio of knowledge to speculation has not dampened the enthusiasm for new forms of snake oil that are constantly coming on the market, many of them with academic testimonials. Doubtless this article will have no depressing impact on the market for snake oil, but since the ideas expressed in it have been tested in many corporations and other organizations, it will help—I hope—to redress the imbalance in the aforementioned ratio.

"MOTIVATING" WITH KITA

In lectures to industry on the problem, I have found that the audiences are anxious for quick and practical answers, so I will begin with a straightforward, practical formula for moving people.

What is the simplest, surest, and most direct way of getting someone to do something? Ask him? But if he responds that he does not want to do it, then that calls for a psychological consultation to determine the reason for his obstinacy. Tell him? His response shows that he does not understand you, and now an expert in communication methods has to be brought in to show you how to get through to him. Give him a monetary incentive? I do not need to remind the reader of the complexity and difficulty involved in setting up and administering an incentive system. Show him? This means a costly training program. We need a simple way.

Every audience contains the "direct action" manager who shouts, "Kick him!" And this type of manager is right. The surest and least circumlocuted way of getting someone to do something is to kick him in the pants—give him what might be called the KITA.

There are various forms of KITA, and here are some of them:

Negative Physical KITA   This is a literal application of the term and was frequently used in the past. It has, however, three major drawbacks: (1) it is inelegant; (2) it contradicts the precious image of benevolence that most organizations cherish; and (3) since it is a physical attack it directly stimulates the autonomic nervous system, and this often results in negative feedback—the employee may just kick you in return. These factors give rise to certain taboos against negative physical KITA.

The psychologist has come to the rescue of those who are no longer permitted to use negative physical KITA. He has uncovered infinite sources of psychological vulnerabilities and the appropriate methods to play tunes on them. "He took my rug away"; "I wonder what he meant by that"; "The boss is always going around me"—these symptomatic expressions of ego sores that have been rubbed raw are the result of application of:

Negative Psychological KITA   This has several advantages over negative physical KITA. First, the cruelty is not visible; the bleeding is internal and comes much later. Second, since it affects the higher cortical centers of the brain with its inhibitory powers, it reduces the possibility of physical backlash. Third, since the number of psychological pains that a person can feel is almost infinite, the direction and site possibilities of the KITA are increased many times. Fourth, the person administering the kick can manage to be above it all and let the system accomplish the dirty work. Fifth, those who practice it receive some ego satisfaction (one-upmanship), whereas they would find drawing blood abhorrent. Finally, if the employee does complain, he can always be accused of being paranoid since there is no tangible evidence of an actual attack.

Now, what does negative KITA accomplish? If I kick you in the rear (physically or psychologically), who is motivated? I am motivated; you move! Negative KITA does not lead to motivation, but to movement. So:

Positive KITA   Let us consider motivation. If I say to you, "Do this for me or the company, and in return I will give you a reward, an incentive, more status, a promotion all the quid pro quos that exist in the industrial organization," am I motivating you? The overwhelming opinion I receive from management people is, "Yes, this is motivation."

I have a year-old Schnauzer. When it was a small puppy and I wanted it to move, I kicked it in the rear and it moved. Now that I have finished its obedience training, I hold up a dog biscuit when I want the Schnauzer to move. In this instance, who is motivated—I or the dog? The dog wants the biscuit, but it is I who want it to move. Again, I am the one who is motivated, and the dog is the one who moves. In this instance all I did was apply KITA frontally; I exerted a pull instead of a push. When industry wishes to use such positive KITAs, it has available an incredible number and variety of dog biscuits (jelly beans for humans) to wave in front of the employee to get him to jump.

Why is it that managerial audiences are quick to see that negative KITA is *not* motivation, while they are almost unanimous in their judgment that positive KITA *is* motivation? It is because negative KITA is rape, and positive KITA is seduction. But it is infinitely worse to be seduced than to be raped; the latter is an unfortunate occurrence, while the former signifies that you were a party to your own downfall. This is why positive KITA is so popular: it is a tradition; it is in the American way. The organization does not have to kick you; you kick yourself.

Myths about Motivation

Why is KITA not motivation? If I kick my dog (from the front or the back), he will move. And when I want him to move again, what must I do? I must kick him again. Similarly, I can charge a man's battery, and then recharge it, and recharge it again. But it is only when he has his own generator that we can talk about motivation. He then needs no outside stimulation. He *wants to* do it.

With this in mind, we can review some positive KITA personnel practices that were developed as attempts to instill "motivation":

1. *Reducing time spent at work*—This represents a marvelous way of motivating people to work— getting them off the job! We have reduced (formally and informally) the time spent on the job over the last 50 or 60 years until we are finally on the way to the "6½-day weekend." An interesting variant of this approach is the development of off-hour recreation programs. The philosophy here seems to be that those who play together, work together. The fact is that motivated people seek more hours of work, not fewer.

2. *Spiraling wages*—Have these motivated people? Yes, to seek the next wage increase. Some medievalists still can be heard to say that a good depression will get employees moving. They feel that if rising wages don't or won't do the job, perhaps reducing them will.

3. *Fringe benefits*—Industry has outdone the most welfare-minded of welfare states in dispensing cradle-to-the-grave succor. One company I know of had an informal "fringe benefit of the month club" going for a while. The cost of fringe benefits in this country has reached approximately 25% of the wage dollar, and we still cry for motivation.

People spend less time working for more money and more security than ever before, and the trend cannot be reversed. These benefits are no longer rewards; they are rights. A 6-day week is inhuman, a 10-hour day is exploitation, extended medical coverage is a basic decency, and stock options are the salvation of American initiative. Unless the ante is continuously raised, the psychological reaction of employees is that the company is turning back the clock.

When industry began to realize that both the economic nerve and the lazy nerve of their employees had insatiable appetites, it started to listen to the behavioral scientists who, more out of a humanist tradition than from scientific study, criticized management for not knowing how to deal with people. The next KITA easily followed.

4. *Human relations training*—Over 30 years of teaching and, in many instances, of practicing psychological approaches to handling people have resulted in costly human relations programs and, in the end, the same question: How do you motivate workers? Here, too, escalations have taken place. Thirty years ago it was necessary to request, "Please don't spit on the floor." Today the same admonition requires three "please"'s before the employee feels that his superior has demonstrated the psychologically proper attitudes toward him.

The failure of human relations training to produce motivation led to the conclusion that the supervisor or manager himself was not psychologically true to himself in his practice of interpersonal decency. So an advanced form of human relations KITA, sensitivity training, was unfolded.

5. *Sensitivity training*—Do you really, really understand yourself? Do you really, really, really trust the other man? Do you really, really, really, really cooperate? The failure of sensitivity training is now being explained, by those who have become opportunistic exploiters of the technique, as a failure to really (five times) conduct proper sensitivity training courses.

With the realization that there are only temporary gains from comfort and economic and interpersonal KITA, personnel managers concluded that the fault lay not in what they were doing, but in the employee's failure to appreciate what they were doing. This opened up the field of communications, a whole new area of "scientifically" sanctioned KITA.

6. *Communications*—The professor of communications was invited to join the faculty of management training programs and help in making employees understand what management was doing for them. House organs, briefing sessions, supervisory instruction on the importance of communication, and all sorts of propaganda have proliferated until today there is even an International Council of Industrial Editors. But no motivation resulted, and the obvious thought occurred that perhaps management was not hearing what the employees were saying. That led to the next KITA.

7. *Two-way communication*—Management ordered morale surveys, suggestion plans, and group participation programs. Then both employees and management were communicating and listening to each other more than ever, but without much improvement in motivation.

The behavioral scientists began to take another look at their conceptions and their data, and they took human relations one step further. A glimmer of truth was beginning to show through in the writings of the so-called higher-order-need psychologists. People, so they said, want to actualize themselves. Unfortunately, the "actualizing" psychologists got mixed up with the human relations psychologists, and a new KITA emerged.

8. *Job participation*—Though it may not have been the theoretical intention, job participation often became a "give them the big picture" approach. For example, if a man is tightening 10,000 nuts a day on an assembly line with a torque wrench, tell him he is building a Chevrolet. Another approach had the goal of giving the employee a *feeling* that he is determining, in some measure, what he does on his job. The goal was to provide a *sense* of achievement rather than a substantive achievement in his task. Real achievement, of course, requires a task that makes it possible.

But still there was no motivation. This led to the inevitable conclusion that the employees must be sick, and therefore to the next KITA.

9. *Employee counseling*—The initial use of this form of KITA in a systematic fashion can be credited to the Hawthorne experiment of the Western Electric Company during the early 1930's. At that time, it was found that the employees harbored irrational feelings that were interfering with the rational operation of the factory. Counseling in this instance was a means of letting the employees unburden themselves by talking to someone about their problems. Although the counseling techniques were primitive, the program was large indeed.

The counseling approach suffered as a result of experiences during World War II, when the programs themselves were found to be interfering with the operation of the organizations; the counselors had forgotten their role of benevolent listeners and were attempting to do something about the problems that they heard about. Psychological counseling, however, has managed to survive the negative impact of World War II experiences and today is beginning to flourish with renewed sophistication. But, alas, many of these programs, like all the others, do not seem to have lessened the pressure of demands to find out how to motivate workers.

Since KITA results only in short-term movement it is safe to predict that the cost of these programs will increase steadily and new varieties will be developed as old positive KITAs reach their satiation points.

HYGIENE VS. MOTIVATORS

Let me rephrase the perennial question this way: How do you install a generator in an employee? A brief review of my motivation-hygiene theory of job attitudes is required before theoretical and practical suggestions can be offered. The theory was first drawn from an examination of events in the lives of engineers and accountants. At least 16 other investigations, using a wide variety of populations (including some in the Communist countries), have since been completed, making the original research one of the most replicated studies in the field of job attitudes.

The findings of these studies, along with corroboration from many other investigations using different procedures, suggest that the factors involved in producing job satisfaction (and motivation) are separate and distinct from the factors that lead to job dissatisfaction. Since separate factors need to be considered, depending on whether job satisfaction or job dissatisfaction is being examined, it follows that these two feelings are not opposites of each other. The opposite of job satisfaction is not job dissatisfaction but, rather, *no* job satisfaction; and, similarly, the opposite of job dissatisfaction is not job satisfaction, but *no* job dissatisfaction.

Stating the concept presents a problem in semantics, for we normally think of satisfaction and dissatisfaction as opposites—i.e., what is not satisfying must be dissatisfying, and vice versa. But when it comes to understanding the behavior of people in their jobs, more than a play on words is involved.

Two different needs of man are involved here. One set of needs can be thought of as stemming from his animal nature—the built-in drive to avoid pain from the environment, plus all the learned drives which become conditioned to the basic biological needs. For example, hunger, a basic biological drive, makes it necessary to earn money, and then money becomes a specific drive. The other set of needs relates to that unique human characteristic, the ability to achieve and, through achievement, to experience psychological growth. The stimuli for the growth needs are tasks that induce growth; in the industrial setting, they are the *job content*. Contrariwise, the stimuli inducing pain-avoidance behavior are found in the *job environment*.

The growth or *motivator* factors that are intrinsic to the job are: achievement, recognition for achievement, the work itself, responsibility, and growth or advancement. The dissatisfaction-avoidance of *hygiene* (KITA) factors that are extrinsic to the job include: company policy and administration, supervision, interpersonal relationships, working conditions, salary, status, and security.

A composite of the factors that are involved in causing job satisfaction and job dissatisfaction, drawn from samples of 1,685 employees, is shown in Exhibit I. The results indicate that motivators were the primary cause of satisfaction, and hygiene factors the primary cause of unhappiness on the job. The employees, studied in 12 different investigations, included lower-level supervisors, professional women, agricultural administrators, men about to retire from management positions, hospital maintenance personnel, manufacturing supervisors, nurses, food handlers,

military officers, engineers, scientists, housekeepers, teachers, technicians, female assemblers, accountants, Finnish foremen, and Hungarian engineers.

They were asked what job events had occurred in their work that had led to extreme satisfaction or extreme dissatisfaction on their part. Their responses are broken down in the exhibit into percentages of total "positive" job events and of total "negative" job events. (The figures total more than 100% on both the "hygiene" and "motivators" sides because often at least two factors can be attributed to a single event; advancement, for instance, often accompanies assumption of responsibility.)

To illustrate, a typical response involving achievement that had a negative effect for the employee was, "I was unhappy because I didn't do the job successfully." A typical response in the small number of positive job events in the Company Policy and Administration grouping was, "I was happy because the company reorganized the section so that I didn't report any longer to the guy I didn't get along with."

As the lower right-hand part of the exhibit shows, of all the factors contributing to job satisfaction, 81% were motivators. And of all the factors contributing to the employees' dissatisfaction over their work, 69% involved hygiene elements.

Eternal Triangle

There are three general philosophies of personnel management. The first is based on organizational theory, the second on industrial engineering, and the third on behavioral science.

The organizational theorist believes that human needs are either so irrational or so varied and adjustable to specific situations that the major function of personnel management is to be as pragmatic as the occasion demands. If jobs are organized in a proper manner, he reasons, the result will be the most efficient job structure, and the most favorable job attitudes will follow as a matter of course.

The industrial engineer holds that man is mechanistically oriented and economically motivated and his needs are best met by attuning the individual to the most efficient work process. The goal of personnel management therefore should be to concoct the most appropriate incentive system and to design the specific

EXHIBIT I / Factors Affecting Job Attitudes, as Reported in 12 Investigations

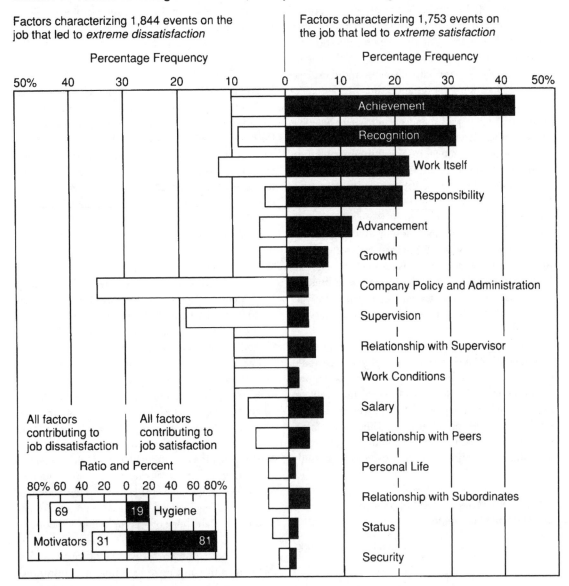

Factors characterizing 1,844 events on the job that led to *extreme dissatisfaction*

Factors characterizing 1,753 events on the job that led to *extreme satisfaction*

Percentage Frequency

Percentage Frequency

working conditions in a way that facilitates the most efficient use of the human machine. By structuring jobs in a manner that leads to the most efficient operation, the engineer believes that he can obtain the optimal organization of work and the proper work attitudes.

The behavioral scientist focuses on group sentiments, attitudes of individual employees, and the organization's social and psychological climate. According

to his persuasion, he emphasizes one or more of the various hygiene and motivator needs. His approach to personnel management generally emphasizes some form of human relations education, in the hope of instilling healthy employee attitudes and an organizational climate which he considers to be felicitous to human values. He believes that the proper attitudes will lead to efficient job and organizational structure.

There is always a lively debate as to the overall effectiveness of the approaches of the organizational theorist and the industrial engineer. Manifestly they have achieved much. But the nagging question for the behavioral scientist has been: What is the cost in human problems that eventually cause more expense to the organization—for instance, turnover, absenteeism, errors, violation of safety rules, strikes, restriction of output, higher wages, and greater fringe benefits? On the other hand, the behavioral scientist is hard put to document much manifest improvement in personnel management, using his approach.

The three philosophies can be depicted as a triangle as is done in Exhibit II, with each persuasion claiming the apex angle. The motivation-hygiene theory claims the same angle as industrial engineering but for opposite goals. Rather than rationalizing the work to increase efficiency, the theory suggests that work be *enriched* to bring about effective utilization of personnel. Such a systematic attempt to motivate employees by manipulating the motivator factors is just beginning.

The term *job enrichment* describes this embryonic movement. An older term, job enlargement, should be avoided because it is associated with past failures stemming from a misunderstanding of the problem. Job enrichment provides the opportunity for the employee's psychological growth, while job enlargement merely makes a job structurally bigger. Since scientific job enrichment is very new, this article only suggests the principles and practical steps that have recently emerged from several successful experiments in industry.

Job Loading

In attempting to enrich an employee's job, management often succeeds in reducing the man's personal contribution, rather than giving him an opportunity for growth in his accustomed job. Such an endeavor, which I shall call horizontal job loading (as opposed to vertical loading, or providing motivator factors), has been the problem of earlier job enlargement programs. This activity merely enlarges the meaninglessness of the job. Some examples of this approach, and their effect, are:

- Challenging the employee by increasing the amount of production expected of him. If he tightens 10,000 bolts a day, see if he can tighten 20,000 bolts a day. The arithmetic involved shows that multiplying zero by zero still equals zero.
- Adding another meaningless task to the existing one, usually some routine clerical activity. The arithmetic here is adding zero to zero.
- Rotating the assignments of a number of jobs that need to be enriched. This means washing dishes for a while, then washing silverware. The arithmetic is substituting one zero for another zero.
- Removing the most difficult parts of the assignment in order to free the worker to accomplish more of the less challenging assignments. This traditional industrial engineering approach amounts to subtraction in the hope of accomplishing addition.

These are common forms of horizontal loading that frequently come up in preliminary brainstorming sessions on job enrichment. The principles of vertical loading have not all been worked out as yet, and they remain rather general, but I have furnished seven useful starting points for consideration in Exhibit III.

A Successful Application

An example from a highly successful job enrichment experiment can illustrate the distinction between horizontal and vertical loading of a job. The subjects

EXHIBIT II / "Triangle" of Philosophies of Personnel Management

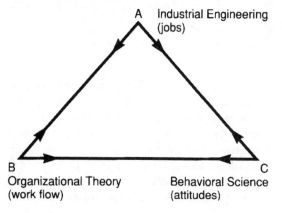

A   Industrial Engineering (jobs)

B   Organizational Theory (work flow)

C   Behavioral Science (attitudes)

EXHIBIT III / Principles of Vertical Job Loading

Principle	Motivators Involved
A. Removing some controls while retaining accountability	Responsibility and personal achievement
B. Increasing the accountability of individuals for own work	Responsibility and recognition
C. Giving a person a complete natural unit of work (module, division, area, and so on)	Responsibility, achievement, and recognition
D. Granting additional authority to an employee in his activity; job freedom	Responsibility, achievement, and recognition
E. Making periodic reports directly available to the worker himself rather than to the supervisor	Internal recognition
F. Introducing new and more difficult tasks not previously handled	Growth and learning
G. Assigning individuals specific or specialized tasks, enabling them to become experts	Responsibility, growth, and advancement

of this study were the stockholder correspondents employed by a very large corporation. Seemingly, the task required of these carefully selected and highly trained correspondents was quite complex and challenging. But almost all indexes of performance and job attitudes were low, and exit interviewing confirmed that the challenge of the job existed merely as words.

A job enrichment project was initiated in the form of an experiment with one group, designated as an achieving unit, having its job enriched by the principles described in Exhibit III. A control group continued to do its job in the traditional way. (There were also two "uncommitted" groups of correspondents formed to measure the so-called Hawthorne Effect—that is, to gauge whether productivity and attitudes toward the job changed artificially merely because employees sensed that the company was paying more attention to them in doing something different or novel. The results for these groups were substantially the same as for the control group, and for the sake of simplicity I do not deal with them in this summary.) No changes in hygiene were introduced for either group other than those that would have been made anyway, such as normal pay increases.

The changes for the achieving unit were introduced in the first two months, averaging one per week of the seven motivators listed in Exhibit III. At the end of six months the members of the achieving unit were found to be outperforming their counterparts in the control group, and in addition indicated a marked increase in their liking for their jobs. Other results showed that the achieving group had lower absenteeism and, subsequently, a much higher rate of promotion.

Exhibit IV illustrates the changes in performance, measured in February and March, before the study period began, and at the end of each month of the study period. The shareholder service index represents quality of letters, including accuracy of information, and speed of response to stockholders' letters of inquiry. The index of a current month was averaged into the average of the two prior months, which means that improvement was harder to obtain if the indexes of the previous months were low. The "achievers" were performing less well before the six-month period started, and their performance service index continued to decline after the introduction of the motivators, evidently because of uncertainty over their newly granted responsibilities. In the third month, however, performance improved, and soon the members of this group had reached a high level of accomplishment.

Exhibit V shows the two groups' attitudes toward their job, measured at the end of March, just before

EXHIBIT IV / Shareholder Service Index in Company Experiment (Three-Month Cumulative Average)

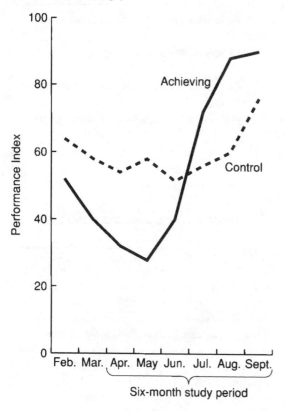

EXHIBIT V / Changes in Attitudes toward Tasks in Company Experiment (Changes in Mean Scores over Six-Month Period)

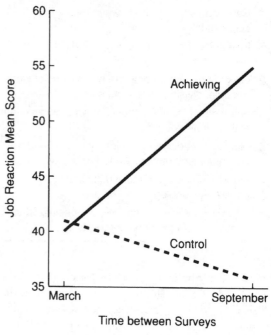

the first motivator was introduced, and again at the end of September. The correspondents were asked 16 questions, all involving motivation. A typical one was, "As you see it, how many opportunities do you feel that you have in your job for making worthwhile contributions?" The answers were scaled from 1 to 5, with 80 as the maximum possible score. The achievers became much more positive about their job, while the attitude of the control unit remained about the same (the drop is not statistically significant).

How was the job of these correspondents restructured? Exhibit VI lists the suggestions made that were deemed to be horizontal loading, and the actual vertical loading changes that were incorporated in the job of the achieving unit. The capital letters under "Principle" after "Vertical loading" refer to the corresponding letters in Exhibit III. The reader will note that the rejected forms of horizontal loading correspond

closely to the list of common manifestations of the phenomenon in Exhibit III, left column.

STEPS TO JOB ENRICHMENT

Now that the motivator idea has been described in practice, here are the steps that managers should take in instituting the principle with their employees:

1. Select those jobs in which (a) the investment in industrial engineering does not make changes too costly, (b) attitudes are poor, (c) hygiene is becoming very costly, and (d) motivation will make a difference in performance.

2. Approach these jobs with the conviction that they can be changed. Years of tradition have led managers to believe that the content of the jobs is sacrosanct and the only scope of action that they have is in ways of stimulating people.

EXHIBIT VI / Enlargement vs. Enrichment of Correspondents' Tasks in Company Experiment

Horizontal loading suggestions (rejected)	Vertical loading suggestions (adopted)	Principle
Firm quotas could be set for letters to be answered each day, using a rate which would be hard to reach.	Subject matter experts were appointed within each unit for other members of the unit to consult with before seeking supervisory help. (The supervisor had been answering all specialized and difficult questions.)	G
The women could type the letters themselves, as well as compose them, or take on any other clerical functions.	Correspondents signed their own names on letters. (The supervisor had been signing all letters.)	B
All difficult or complex inquiries could be channeled to a few women so that the remainder could achieve high rates of output. These jobs could be exchanged from time to time.	The work of the more experienced correspondents was proofread less frequently by supervisors and was done at the correspondents' desks, dropping verification from 100% to 10%. (Previously, all correspondents' letters had been checked by the supervisor.)	A
The women could be rotated through units handling different customers, and then sent back to their own units.	Production was discussed, but only in terms such as "a full day's work is expected." As time went on, this was no longer mentioned. (Before, the group had been constantly reminded of the number of letters that needed to be answered.)	D
	Outgoing mail went directly to the mailroom without going over supervisors' desks. (The letters had always been routed through the supervisors.)	A
	Correspondents were encouraged to answer letters in a more personalized way. (Reliance on the form-letter approach had been standard practice.)	C
	Each correspondent was held personally responsible for the quality and accuracy of letters. (This responsibility had been the province of the supervisor and the verifier.)	B, E

3. Brainstorm a list of changes that may enrich the jobs, without concern for their practicality.

4. Screen the list to eliminate suggestions that involve hygiene, rather than actual motivation.

5. Screen the list for generalities, such as "give them more responsibility," that are rarely followed in practice. This might seem obvious, but the motiva-tor words have never left industry; the substance has just been rationalized and organized out. Words like "responsibility," "growth," "achievement," and "chal-lenge," for example, have been elevated to the lyrics of the patriotic anthem for all organizations. It is the old problem typified by the pledge of allegiance to the flag being more important than contributions to

the country—of following the form, rather than the substance.

6. Screen the list to eliminate any *horizontal* loading suggestions.

7. Avoid direct participation by the employees whose jobs are to be enriched. Ideas they have expressed previously certainly constitute a valuable source for recommended changes, but their direct involvement contaminates the process with human relations *hygiene* and, more specifically, gives them only a *sense* of making a contribution. The job is to be changed, and it is the content that will produce the motivation, not attitudes about being involved or the challenge inherent in setting up a job. That process will be over shortly, and it is what the employees will be doing from then on that will determine their motivation. A sense of participation will result only in short-term movement.

8. In the initial attempts at job enrichment, set up a controlled experiment. At least two equivalent groups should be chosen, one an experimental unit in which the motivators are systematically introduced over a period of time, and the other one a control group in which no changes are made. For both groups, hygiene should be allowed to follow its natural course for the duration of the experiment. Pre- and post-installation tests of performance and job attitudes are necessary to evaluate the effectiveness of the job enrichment program. The attitude test must be limited to motivator items in order to divorce the employee's view of the job he is given from all the surrounding hygiene feelings that he might have.

9. Be prepared for a drop in performance in the experimental group the first few weeks. The changeover to a new job may lead to a temporary reduction in efficiency.

10. Expect your first-line supervisors to experience some anxiety and hostility over the changes you are making. The anxiety comes from their fear that the changes will result in poorer performance for their unit. Hostility will arise when the employees start assuming what the supervisors regard as their own responsibility for performance. The supervisor without checking duties to perform may then be left with little to do.

After a successful experiment however, the supervisor usually discovers the supervisory and managerial functions he has neglected, or which were never his because all his time was given over to checking the work of his subordinates. For example, in the R&D division of one large chemical company I know of, the supervisors of the laboratory assistants were theoretically responsible for their training and evaluation. These functions, however, had come to be performed in a routine, unsubstantial fashion. After the job enrichment program, during which the supervisors were not merely passive observers of the assistants' performance, the supervisors actually were devoting their time to reviewing performance and administering thorough training.

What has been called an employee-centered style of supervision will come about not through education of supervisors, but by changing the jobs that they do.

CONCLUDING NOTE

Job enrichment will not be a one-time proposition, but a continuous management function. The initial changes, however, should last for a very long period of time. There are a number of reasons for this:

- The changes should bring the job up to the level of challenge commensurate with the skill that was hired.
- Those who have still more ability eventually will be able to demonstrate it better and win promotion to higher-level jobs.
- The very nature of motivators, as opposed to hygiene factors, is that they have a much longer-term effect on employees' attitudes. Perhaps the job will have to be enriched again, but this will not occur as frequently as the need for hygiene.

Not all jobs can be enriched, nor do all jobs need to be enriched. If only a small percentage of the time and money that is now devoted to hygiene, however, were given to job enrichment efforts, the return in human satisfaction and economic gain would be one of the largest dividends that industry and society have ever reaped through their efforts at better personnel management.

The argument for job enrichment can be summed up quite simply: If you have someone on a job, use him. If you can't use him on the job, get rid of him, either via automation or by selecting someone with lesser ability. If you can't use him and you can't get rid of him, you will have a motivation problem.

NOTES

Readers of this article may be interested in "What Job Attitudes Tell About Motivation," by Lyman W. Porter and Edward E.

Lawler, III, *Harvard Business Review*, Vol. 46, January/February 1968, pp. 118–126.

Author's note: I should like to acknowledge the contributions that Robert Ford of the American Telephone and Telegraph Company has made to the ideas expressed in this paper, and in particular to the successful application of these ideas in improving work performance and the job satisfaction of employees.

CRITICAL THINKING QUESTIONS

1. Suppose we change the topic of the article from how to motivate *employees* to how to motivate *students.* Can Herzberg's principles of employee motivation be used in the academic environment? How? As part of this question, conduct a survey of students to identify what school factors lead to extreme satisfaction and extreme dissatisfaction. Classify these as hygiene or motivation factors.
2. Would the principles of successful job enrichment outlined by Herzberg apply equally to all employees in all situations? What individual- or work-related factors might mediate whether the principles will work?
3. Conduct an informal survey of people you know who work full time, asking them the same questions about job satisfaction and dissatisfaction outlined in the article. How well do your observations correspond with the information presented by Herzberg?
4. After reading an article such as this, why might some managers still be reluctant to undertake recommended changes? Are any of these concerns legitimate? Why or why not?

ADDITIONAL RELATED READINGS

Collier, J., & Esteban, R. (2007). Corporate social responsibility and employee commitment. *Business Ethics: A European Review, 16*(1), 19–33.

Elding, D. J., Tobias, A. M., & Walker, D. S. (2006). Towards a unified model of employee motivation. *Strategic Change, 15*(6), 295–304.

ARTICLE 39

For many of you reading this book, graduation is not far off. Although it still may be a few years away, that time will be here soon enough. For others, you may be in college after having been in the workforce full time. You may be returning to your former employer upon graduation, or you may be looking for a different type of position.

Deciding what to do for a living and where to work are major decisions for most people. After all, regardless of what we choose to do, we are going to spend a significant amount of time doing it. Consider what factors will be foremost in your mind when deciding where to work: How much money you will make? How happy you will be in that position? Some combination of these factors or other factors?

Industrial/organizational psychologists study a multitude of factors pertaining to the workplace. For example, a good deal of work has been done on practical issues of employment, such as reducing employee turnover, developing selection criteria to get the best fit between the person and the organization, and identifying the most effective styles of leadership and management, to name but a few. But what factors might predict satisfaction with a job before one even steps in the door?

One possibility might be the strategies people use in making decisions. It may be that some people exhaustively search all the possibilities to make sure they make the "right" decision, whereas other people may be satisfied with making a "good enough" decision.

The following article by Sheena S. Iyengar, Rachael E. Wells, and Barry Schwartz examines the decision-making strategies people use in looking for a job. More important is the authors' finding that although certain strategies may result, for example, in a higher-paying job, they also may lead to greater dissatisfaction with the job-search process and more unhappiness with the job ultimately selected. For anyone about to embark on a career search, the findings of this article will be of particular interest.

Doing Better but Feeling Worse
Looking for the "Best" Job Undermines Satisfaction
■ Sheena S. Iyengar, Rachael E. Wells, and Barry Schwartz

ABSTRACT

Expanding upon Simon's (1955) seminal theory, this investigation compared the choice-making strategies of maximizers and satisficers, finding that maximizing tendencies, although positively correlated with objectively better decision outcomes, are also associated with more negative subjective evaluations of these decision outcomes. Specifically, in the fall of their final year in school, students were administered a scale that measured maxi- *mizing tendencies and were then followed over the course of the year as they searched for jobs. Students with high maximizing tendencies secured jobs with 20% higher starting salaries than did students with low maximizing tendencies. However, maximizers were less satisfied than satisficers with the jobs they obtained, and experienced more negative affect throughout the job-search process. These effects were mediated by maximizers' greater*

Iyengar, S. S., Wells, R. E., & Schwartz, B. (2006). Doing better but feeling worse: Looking for the "best" job undermines satisfaction. *Psychological Science, 17*(2), 143–150. Copyright © 2006 by American Psychological Society. Reprinted with permission of Blackwell Publishers.

reliance on external sources of information and their fixation on realized and unrealized options during the search and selection process.

> Success is getting what you want. Happiness is wanting what you get.
>
> —American proverb

Half a century ago, Simon (1955, 1956, 1957) introduced an important distinction between maximizing and satisficing as choice-making strategies. To maximize is to seek the best and requires an exhaustive search of all possibilities. To satisfice is to seek "good enough," searching until encountering an option that crosses the threshold of acceptability. For example, compare the strategies of a maximizer versus a satisficer selecting a television show from choices available on 400 cable channels. The maximizer would channel-surf, exploring all the channels, spending so much time deciding on a show that little time would be left for viewing. The satisficer would most likely channel-surf until he or she encountered the first acceptable show, put down the remote control, and actually watch the show. Simon based his distinction on the idea that the limited information-processing capacities of organisms make maximizing impossible. In the modern world of almost unimaginable choice, this distinction is even more pertinent (see Iyengar & Lepper, 2000; Schwartz, 2004a, 2004b).

Expanding on Simon's classic theory, Schwartz et al. (2002) recently compared the decision-making processes of maximizers and satisficers, finding that people who exhibit maximizing tendencies, like the channel surfer just described, were less satisfied with their decision outcomes than their satisficing counterparts. The researchers asked participants about recent purchasing decisions and used a "maximization scale" to measure individual differences in maximizing tendencies. Their findings suggested that the experiences of maximizers differed from those of satisficers during the decision-making process and also later, when they evaluated their final decision outcome. Specifically, compared with satisficers, maximizers were more likely to engage in an exhaustive search of all available options and to compare their decisions with those of other people. Even though maximizers invested more time and effort during

the decision process and explored more options than satisficers—presumably in order to achieve greater satisfaction—they nonetheless felt worse about the outcomes that they achieved. Results showed that maximizing tendencies were positively correlated with regret, depression, and decision difficulty, and negatively correlated with happiness, life satisfaction, optimism, and satisfaction with decision outcomes.

Such differences in the subjective choice-making experiences of maximizers and satisficers are attributed to the fact that maximizers create a more onerous choice-making process for themselves. Initially, maximizers focus on increasing their choice sets by exploring multiple options, presumably because expanded choice sets allow for greater possibilities to seek out and find the elusive "best." Yet, as the number of options proliferates, cognitive limitations prevent decision makers from evaluating and comparing all options (Iyengar & Jiang, 2004; Iyengar & Lepper, 2000; Miller, 1956). Identifying the best becomes increasingly difficult, compelling maximizers to rely on external (often social) rather than internal standards to evaluate and select outcomes (Lyubomirsky & Ross, 1997). In addition, the inevitability of trade-offs among attractive options intensifies the sting of passing up one attractive alternative when choosing a more attractive one, and increases expectations for the quality and utility of the chosen alternative.

But do the very strategies that render maximizers less happy than satisficers with their decision outcomes also enable them to achieve decision outcomes that are objectively better? Perhaps there is utility associated with the strategic pursuit of real and imagined options and with the careful observation of other people's choice-making experiences—utility that may be reflected in the form of more effective deliberations and objectively better outcomes. Unlike prior investigations of the relation between maximizing tendencies and decision outcomes, the current investigation examined the effects of maximizing tendencies on both objective outcomes and the subjective experience of the decision maker throughout the process.

Thus, expanding on this nascent literature, the present study allowed us to test two hypotheses. The first was about the process of searching for choices and deciding which one to select. We hypothesized that compared with satisficers, maximizers invest more heavily in gathering information from external sources (thereby incurring search costs and perhaps prioritizing externally valued criteria) and fixate more on realized and unrealized options (thereby incurring opportunity costs). The second hypothesis involved decision outcomes. We hypothesized that these differences in the decision-making process contribute to more successful decision outcomes among maximizers than among satisficers, yet also result in maximizers' experiencing greater negative affect and reduced subjective well-being.

We chose to test these predictions within the consequential domain of graduating college students' job-search processes, which allowed us to examine the influence of maximizing tendencies on both actual and perceived decision outcomes, and afforded us the opportunity to examine reactions to the decision process as decisions were being made. Regardless of the finite number of offers made to job seekers, maximizers who are undertaking a job search face both the search costs and the raised expectations associated with contemplating an almost limitless set of employment possibilities. To determine how a maximizing orientation affects both the affective experiences and the objective outcomes of the job-search process, we measured the maximizing tendencies of participants from multiple institutions during the fall of their final year and subsequently followed them throughout their job search, measuring both how well they actually did and how well they thought they did. This methodology allowed us to test the following specific predictions: that compared with satisficers, maximizers would desire more options, plan to apply for more jobs, rely more on social comparison and other external sources of information, and obtain jobs with higher expected returns (i.e., salary), but also experience greater negative affect and less outcome satisfaction throughout the process and at the conclusion of their job search.

METHOD

Participants

Graduating students (predominantly undergraduate seniors) were recruited from 11 colleges and universi-

ties that varied in geographical region, university rank, and school size. The sample was 69.7% female. The median age of participants was 21 (range: 20–57), and 64% of participants were Caucasian, 26% Asian, and 10% of other racial-ethnic backgrounds. Participants majored in the social sciences (36%), arts and humanities (25%), engineering (16%), natural sciences and math (11%), and business (15%). At the first assessment (T1), 548 participants responded; response rates were 69.5% and 56% at the second and third assessments (T2 and T3), respectively. Five $200 prizes were raffled off among the participants who completed all three surveys.

Procedure

In November 2001 (T1), career services at the 11 participating institutions directed students who were just beginning their job searches (i.e., who had used career services in September through November) to our survey Web site. Via e-mail, we notified these participants of our follow-up on-line surveys in February 2002 (T2), as participants were completing applications, interviewing, and getting offers, and in May 2002 (T3), as they were accepting offers. Although it is difficult to calculate the percentage of students who chose to participate in the survey upon encountering the on-line advertisement, consultations with career-services staff provided us with numerical estimates of the total number of students who utilized career services in their job search within the given academic year. Given that the advertisement was available only to those students who were affiliated with career services between the months of September and November (approximately 25%), we calculated that response rates ranged from 17.4% to 53.2% across a sampling of participating institutions.

Measures

Maximizing Tendencies

At T1, participants completed 11 maximization items drawn from Schwartz et al. (2002; e.g., "When I am in the car listening to the radio, I often check other stations to see if something better is playing, even if I am relatively satisfied with what I'm listening to" and "When shopping, I have a hard time finding clothes that I really love"). Each item was rated on a scale from 1 (*strongly disagree*) to 9 (*strongly agree;* α = .6). Scores for the individual items were averaged to create a composite maximizing score. Overall, men (*n* = 166, *M* = 5.48) and women (*n* = 382, *M* = 5.10) from our sample population showed significantly higher maximizing tendencies than respondents in a recent national adult sample (Kliger & Schwartz, 2005; men: *n* = 3,261, *M* = 4.9; women: *n* = 4,692, *M* = 4.77), *t*(165) = 7.03, *p* < .0001, for men and *t*(381) = 6.28, *p* < .0001, for women. These differences may be at least partly attributable to the age difference between the two samples, as maximization tendencies have been found to be negatively correlated with age (Kliger & Schwartz, 2005). In our sample, maximizing tendencies were also significantly positively correlated with top-15 university rank, *r*(544) = .10, *p* < .05, and male gender, *r*(546) = .17, *p* < .0001, but not with any other demographic or control variable gathered.

Option Fixation

We used three measures to examine option fixation. At T1, we measured the number of options that participants pursued: "For approximately how many jobs do you anticipate applying?" Participants provided responses in numerical form. Note that the number of anticipated applications ranged from 1 to 1,000, exhibiting extreme right skewness (skew = 7.5) and kurtosis (69.0), and was therefore log-transformed. At T2, we measured participants' fixation on unrealized options: "I often fantasize about jobs that are quite different from the actual job(s) that I am pursuing." Responses were made on a scale from 1 (*strongly disagree*) to 9 (*strongly agree*). At T3, we measured participants' regret with the size of their choice set: "I wish I had pursued more options in my job search process." Responses were made on a scale from 1 (*not at all*) to 9 (*to a large extent*).

Reliance on External Influences

We created a single composite measure of five items (α = .70) to test reliance on external influences. At T1, participants were asked: "How much have you been using the services offered by the career services office at your school during the job search?" "To what extent have you consulted experts' ranking such as 'top compa-

nies,' 'fastest growing fields,' etc.?" "How much do you seek advice from your family regarding the job search (i.e., input, suggestions, etc.)?" and "To what extent do you compare your own job search process and results to those of your peers?" The question regarding peer comparison was repeated at T2. Participants responded on a scale from 1 (*very little*) to 9 (*very much*).

Job-Market Performance

At T2 and T3, participants were asked how many interviews they had received. In addition, at T3, they were asked how many job offers they had received and the annual salary (in dollars per year or hour) of the job offer they accepted. In the case of jobs with hourly wages, we determined how many hours per week participants were required to work and converted this information into an estimated annual salary.

Negative Affect

Participants' negative affect associated with the job-search process was measured at all three assessments. At T1 and T2, participants were asked, "To what extent does each of the following describe how you are generally feeling about the job search process?" The seven emotions listed were "pessimistic," "stressed," "tired," "anxious," "worried," "overwhelmed," and "depressed." Participants rated each emotion on a scale from 1 (*not at all*) to 9 (*extremely*) (T1 α = .86; T2 α = .89). At T3, the same question was repeated; however, three emotions were added (T3 α = .92): "regretful," "disappointed," and "frustrated." In addition, for participants who had accepted job offers, the question was modified to read: "To what extent does each of the following describe how you are feeling about the offer you accepted and your upcoming new job?" Composite measures for T1, T2, and T3 were constructed.

Outcome Satisfaction

Two items measured participants' satisfaction with their accepted job offers: "How satisfied are you with the offer you have accepted?" and "How confident are you that you made the right choice about where to work next year?" Responses were made on a scale from 1 (*not at all*) to 9 (*very satisfied/very confident;* α = .88). A score was obtained for each participant by averaging the responses to these two questions.

Demographics and Other Control Variables

We gathered information on age, sex, ethnicity, family income level, university affiliation and rank (as measured by U.S. News & World Report, 2001), geographic location, and academic major at T1. At T2, we collected information on overall grade point average (GPA). Participants were asked about their job-related activities (i.e., current stage in the job-search process) at all three assessments.

RESULTS

Preliminary Analysis

Table 1 reports the means and standard deviations as a function of maximizing status for all dependent measures, with maximizers and satisficers separated by a median split. Attrition analyses demonstrated that our initial sample differed demographically from the T2 and T3 samples: East Asians, children of foreign-born parents, and older students constituted a

TABLE 1 / Means and Standard Deviations for Maximizers and Satisficers

Dependent Variable	Maximizers	Satisficers
Anticipated applications[a]	20	10
Fixation on unrealized options	5.17 (2.55)	4.02 (2.47)
Regret with choice set size	5.09 (2.39)	4.52 (2.20)
Reliance on external influences	5.02 (1.65)	4.65 (1.62)
Salary (in $10K)	4.45 (1.34)	3.71 (1.35)
Negative affect (T1)	5.54 (1.56)	4.81 (1.59)
Negative affect (T2)	5.40 (1.67)	4.81 (1.83)
Negative affect (T3)	4.50 (1.82)	3.91 (1.78)
Outcome satisfaction	7.02 (1.78)	7.58 (1.55)

Note. Standard deviations are provided in parentheses. T1, T2, and T3 refer to the first, second, and third assessments, respectively.

[a]The scores reported for anticipated applications are medians, rather than means, and are only for students from universities not ranked within the top 15, as university rank interacted significantly with maximizing tendencies.

smaller proportion of both the T2 and T3 samples, and the proportion of participants who did not identify themselves with one specific ethnicity was larger at T3 than at T1. However, the T1, T2, and T3 samples did not differ as a function of the variables critical to our hypotheses (including maximizing score, log of the number of anticipated applications, fixation on unrealized options, regret with choice set size, and reliance on external influences). Further analyses revealed that compared with students who had not completed their job search at T3, those who had completed their search were significantly more likely to be business majors and less likely to be arts and humanities majors, were younger, had higher GPAs, came from wealthier socioeconomic backgrounds, and relied more heavily on external influences.[1] All regression analyses reported here controlled for gender, university rank, age, academic major, cumulative GPA (collected at T2), and whether a job offer had been accepted. See Tables 2 through 5 for full regression models including control variables. Note that, following Killeen (2005), in reporting the results of our regression analyses, we provide the probabilities of replicating our effects (denoted by p_{rep}), in addition to standard p values.

Main Effects for Maximizing Tendencies

As shown in Table 2, maximizing tendencies were positively correlated with increased option fixation, greater reliance on external influences, improved job-market performance, and more negative affective experiences. At T1, participants with greater maximizing tendencies anticipated applying for more jobs, $\beta = .13$, $t(537) = 2.35$, $p < .05$, $p_{rep} = .93$; however, this effect was attenuated among those attending high-ranked universities, $\beta = -.50$, $t(537) = -2.33$, $p < .05$, $p_{rep} = .93$. Among students in top-15 universities, the median for both maximizers and satisficers was 30, whereas in lower-ranked universities, the median was 20 for maximizers and 10 for satisficers. At T2, participants with greater maximizing tendencies fantasized more about jobs that they were not pursuing, $\beta = .23$, $t(372) = 4.48$, $p < .001$, $p_{rep} = .99$, such that every one-unit increase in maximizing was associated with a 0.59 increase in this measure. At T3, students with greater maximizing tendencies reported that they

TABLE 2 / Regression Models Predicting Mediator Variables

Variable	Logged Anticipated Applications	Fixation on Unrealized Options	Regret with Choice Set Size	Reliance on External Influences
Control Variables				
Female sex (0 = male, 1 = female)	.03	.00	.04	−.07
Top-15 university	.73**	.01	.02	.05
Age	.11*	−.00	.13*	−.17**
Business major	.25**	−.06	.05	.33**
Social sciences major	.24**	−.08	.02	.18
Science, math major	.03	−.16*	−.05	−.01
Engineering major	.21**	−.12	−.06	.11
Education major	−.01	−.04	.00	−.04
Arts, humanities major	.12	−.08	.08	−.04
Cumulative grade point average		−.09	−.18**	.02
Offer already accepted by point of DV measurement	−.09*	−.01	−.18**	.21**
Maximizing Variables				
Maximizing score	.13*	.23**	.18**	.17**
Maximizing Score × Top-15 University	−.50*			
Full-model R^2	.14	.08	.14	.28
ΔR^2 vs. control model	.01	.05	.03	.03
Model F ratio	7.06	2.60	3.34	11.28
Degrees of freedom	537	372	263	366
p_{rep}	.99	.98	.99	.99

Note. DV = dependent variable.

*$p < .05$. **$p < .01$.

wished that they had pursued still more options, $\beta = .18$, $t(263) = 2.96$, $p < .01$, $p_{rep} = .97$, such that every one-unit increase in maximizing was associated with a 0.40 increase in this measure. Additionally, students with greater maximizing tendencies were more reliant on external influences during T1 and T2 of the job-search process, $\beta = .17$, $t(366) = 3.63$, $p < .001$, $p_{rep} = .99$. Every one-unit increase in maximizing was associated with a 0.27 increase in this measure.

Indeed, job seekers with greater maximizing tendencies were offered an average of $7,430 more in salary than their satisficing counterparts, $\beta = .20$, $t(115) = 2.83$, $p < .01$, $p_{rep} = .96$, such that every one-unit increase in the maximizing composite score was associated with a $2,630 increase in the annual salary obtained (see Table 3). An analysis based on a median split of the maximizing scale showed that the mean salary of maximizing job seekers was $44,515, whereas that of satisficing job seekers was $37,085. This difference in salary between maximizing and satisficing job seekers was unaccounted for by the number of interviews or job offers received, as maximizing tendencies did not prove to be a significant predictor of either number of interviews (T2 Poisson regression: $\beta = .09$, $\chi^2 = 1.43$, n.s.; T3 Poisson regression: $\beta = .05$, $\chi^2 = 0.55$, n.s.) or offers obtained (T3 Poisson regression: $\beta = .09$, $\chi^2 = 1.80$, n.s.).

Greater maximizing tendencies were also associated with experiences of greater negative affect at all three assessments, T1: $\beta = .26$, $t(535) = 6.32$, $p < .001$, $p_{rep} = .99$; T2: $\beta = .18$, $t(365) = 3.56$, $p < .001$, $p_{rep} = .99$; T3: $\beta = .16$, $t(257) = 2.98$, $p < .01$, $p_{rep} = .97$ (see Table 4). Every one-unit increase in maximizing was associated with 0.40, 0.31, and 0.28 increases in negative affect at T1, T2, and T3, respectively. Participants with greater maximizing tendencies also

reported less satisfaction with their accepted job offers even with annual salary controlled, $\beta = -.28$, $t(115) = -2.92$, $p < .01$, $p_{rep} = .97$, such that every one-unit increase in maximizing was associated with a 0.43 decrease in reported satisfaction (see Table 5).

Mediators of Maximizing Tendencies

As shown in Tables 3 through 5, results suggest that the relation of maximizing tendencies with job-market performance and negative affective experience was mediated by a combination of reliance on external influences and option fixation. Reliance on external influences acted as a partial mediator of the effect

TABLE 3 / Regression Models Predicting Annual Salary of Accepted Job Offer

Variable	Salary: Initial Model	Salary: Mediator Model
Control Variables		
Female sex (0 = male, 1 = female)	−.16*	−.11
Top-15 university	.29**	.27**
Age	.06	.10
Business major	.11	.03
Social sciences major	−.00	.02
Science, math major	.08	.06
Engineering major	.32†	.36*
Arts, humanities major	−.28†	.20**
Cumulative grade point average	.19*	.15*
Maximizing Variable		
Maximizing score	.20**	.15*
Proposed Mediator		
Reliance on external influences		.27**
Full-model R^2	.49	.54
ΔR^2 vs. control model	.04	.09
ΔR^2 vs. previous model of same DV		.05
Model F ratio	10.22	11.29
Degrees of freedom	115	115
p_{rep}	.99	.99

Note. DV = dependent variable.

†$p < .10$. *$p < .05$. **$p < .01$.

TABLE 4 / Regression Models Predicting Negative Affective Experience

Variable	T1 Negative Affect: Initial Model	T1 Negative Affect: Mediator Model	T2 Negative Affect: Initial Model	T2 Negative Affect: Mediator Model	T2 Negative Affect: Controlling for T1 Negative Affect	T3 Negative Affect: Initial Model	T3 Negative Affect: Mediator Model	T3 Negative Affect: Controlling for T1 Negative Affect
Control Variables								
Female sex (0 = male, 1 = female)	.04	.04	−.01	−.01	−.02	−.04	−.04	−.07
Top-15 university	.11*	.03	.09†	.01	.01	−.03	−.05	−.08
Age	−.05	−.08†	−.10*	−.13**	−.06	.00	−.00	.01
Business major	.08	.01	−.00	−.02	−.02	.05	−.02	.02
Social sciences major	.08	.01	.02	.00	−.01	.12	.09	.08
Science, math major	−.01	−.02	.01	.06	.06	−.08	−.04	−.02
Engineering major	.06	.00	.05	.05	.05	.07	.09	.09
Education major	−.03	−.03	.05	.05	.03	.09	.10†	.06
Arts, humanities major	.08	.04	.04	.04	.01	.06	.07	.06
Cumulative grade point average	—	—	−.03	.01	.01	−.08	−.02	−.00
Offer already accepted by point of DV measurement	−.19*	−.16**	−.31**	−.30*	−.24**	−.53**	−.53**	−.52**
Maximizing Variable								
Maximizing score	.26**	.25**	.18**	.11*	.01	.16**	.06	.03
Proposed Mediators								
Logged anticipated applications		.29**		.21**	.04		.10†	.04
Fixation on unrealized options				.25**	.15**		.21**	.16**
Regret with choice set size								
Reliance on external influences							.18**	.11*
T1 negative affect					.59**			.31**
Full-model R^2	.13	.20	.14	.24	.52	.35	.42	.50
ΔR^2 vs. control model	.07	.14	.03	.13	.41	.02	.09	.17
ΔR^2 vs. previous model of same DV		.07		.10	.28		.07	.08
Model F ratio	6.98	10.97	4.70	8.07	25.75	11.18	11.85	15.16
Degrees of freedom	535	535	365	365	365	257	257	257
p_{rep}	.99	.99	.99	.99	.99	.99	.99	.99

Note. DV = dependent variable; T1, T2, and T3 = first, second, and third assessments, respectively.
†$p < .10$. *$p < .05$. **$p < .01$.

TABLE 5 / Regression Models Predicting Outcome Satisfaction

Variable	Outcome Satisfaction: Initial Model	Outcome Satisfaction: Mediator Model	Outcome Satisfaction: Controlling for T1 Negative Affect
Control Variables			
Female sex (0 = male, 1 = female)	.05	.08	.10
Top-15 university	−.05	−.04	−.02
Age	−.08	−.10	−.10
Business major	−.08	−.20	−.21
Social sciences major	−.04	−.17	−.16
Science, math major	.09	.02	.03
Engineering major	.04	−.14	−.14
Arts, humanities major	−.02	−.02	−.02
Cumulative grade point average	.20*	.02	.01
Salary (in $10K)	.12	.22†	.19
Maximizing Variable			
Maximizing score	−.28**	−.14	−.10
Proposed Mediators			
Fixation on unrealized options		−.27**	−.21*
Regret with choice set size		−.34**	−.31**
TI negative affect			−.23*
Full-model R^2	.16	.34	.38
ΔR^2 vs. control model	.07	.25	.29
ΔR^2 vs. previous model of same DV		.18	.03
Model F ratio	1.75	4.05	4.46
Degrees of freedom	115	115	115
p_{rep}	.85	.99	.99

Note. DV = dependent variable; T1 = first assessment.

†$p < .10$. *$p < .05$. **$p < .01$.

of maximizing on job-market performance, $\beta = .27$, $t(115) = 3.41$, $p < .01$, $p_{rep} = .98$. The positive correlational relation between maximizing and negative affect was observed to be partially mediated at T2 by logged anticipated applications, $\beta = .21$, $t(365) = 4.14$, $p < .001$, $p_{rep} = .99$, and fixation on unrealized options, $\beta = .25$, $t(365) = 5.15$, $p < .001$, $p_{rep} = .99$, and fully mediated at T3 by fixation on unrealized options, $\beta = .10$, $t(257) = 1.81$, $p < .10$, $p_{rep} = .85$; regret with choice set size, $\beta = .21$, $t(257) = 3.82$, $p < .001$, $p_{rep} = .99$; and reliance on external influences, $\beta = .18$, $t(257) = 3.01$, $p < .01$, $p_{rep} = .97$. In fact, the relation between maximizing tendencies and outcome satisfaction was also fully mediated by fixation on unrealized options, $\beta = −.27$, $t(115) = −2.81$, $p < .01$, $p_{rep} = .96$, and regret with choice set size, $\beta = −.34$,

$t(257) = -3.80$, $p < .001$, $p_{rep} = .99$. Even when T1 negative affective experience was included as a control in the regression models, similar results emerged.

DISCUSSION

Compared with satisficers, maximizers do better financially in their job search, but feel worse. In their quest for placement after graduation, students with greater maximizing tendencies not only pursue and fixate on realized and unrealized options to a greater degree, but also rely on more external sources of information than do more satisficing job seekers. These efforts result in higher payoffs: Maximizers earn starting salaries that are 20% higher than those of satisficers. Yet, despite their relative success, maximizers are less satisfied with the outcomes of their job search, and more pessimistic, stressed, tired, anxious, worried, overwhelmed, and depressed throughout the process. Why?

Perhaps maximizers are merely high achievers who have more past successes and superior credentials and have rightly learned to expect more of themselves. No matter how well they do, maximizers feel worse than satisficers because they fail to match these high expectations. Certainly, there is evidence to suggest that maximizers have histories of past success; we found significantly more maximizers in top-ranked universities than in other schools. However, there is also evidence to suggest that equating maximizing tendencies with capability oversimplifies the story. After all, we did not find a significant relation between maximizing and another marker of academic success, GPA. Furthermore, if one assumed maximizers' success in the job market to simply be about better credentials, one would expect proxies for high qualifications, such as university rank and GPA, to mediate the effects of maximizing on job-market performance. Yet even though our analysis controlled for these two indices, we found maximizing tendencies were still predictive of salary. Thus, whatever the relation between maximizing and high achievement, past achievement in and of itself seems inadequate to explain maximizers' negative affect. Why, then, do maximizers feel worse when they do better?

Perhaps the fact that maximizers start the job search process at T1 feeling worse than satisficers suggests that they are simply dispositionally less happy than satisficers, and therefore less satisfied with the outcome of any decision. However, even after accounting for initial negative affect at T1, we observed that option fixation and regret with choice set size mediated the effect of maximizing on outcome satisfaction at T2 and T3. Our findings support earlier research by Schwartz et al. (2002), which suggests that the contribution of maximizing tendencies to subjective evaluations is independent of dispositional happiness.

Instead, we suggest that maximizers may be less satisfied than satisficers and experience greater negative affect with the jobs they obtain because their pursuit of the elusive "best" induces them to consider a large number of possibilities, thereby increasing their potential for regret or anticipated regret, engendering unrealistically high expectations, and creating mounting opportunity costs. Such effects may be integral to identifying maximizing as a goal, and may detract from the satisfaction that maximizers ultimately derive from their decisions.

Although we treated maximizing tendencies as a global individual difference measure, it may well be that maximizing strategies to find the best are simply a set of learned behaviors or search strategies designed specifically for decision-making tasks, and not necessarily even all decision-making tasks. In fact, mediation analyses demonstrated that individual differences in maximizing tendencies were explained by differences in option fixation and reliance on external sources of information. Nonetheless, whether global or specific, maximizing tendencies seem to cast a long shadow on people's evaluations of their decision and search outcomes.

Of course, the findings from this investigation are limited in that salary is merely one measure of objective success in the job-search process. Our investigation did not allow us to assess whether maximizers' lesser job satisfaction stems from other measures of job-search success, such as working conditions, professional atmosphere, interaction with colleagues, organizational commitment, and opportunities for advancement. Additionally, our affective measures allowed us to assess decision makers' experiences with the process and their expected satisfaction with their impending employment, but did not assess job seekers' affective experience with their resulting employment.

Psychologists and economists alike have assumed the provision of choice to be beneficial, as it allows decision makers more opportunities for preference matching, and more generally enables utility maximization. However, the present investigation is part of a growing body of literature positing that decision makers' appraisals of their decision outcomes may have less to do with their ability to preference-match or increase the expected value of their decision outcomes than with their social values (Iyengar & Lepper, 1999), mispredicted expectations during the decision process (Frederick & Loewenstein, 1999; Kahneman, 1999; Loewenstein & Schkade, 1999; Wilson, 2002; Wilson & Gilbert, 2003), and the affect experienced during the decision process itself (Botti & Iyengar, 2004). Maximizers, then, epitomize the type of decision maker who may overestimate the affective benefits that result from pursuing the best objective outcome, and underestimate the affective costs of a process that involves evaluating as many options as possible and fixating on choices that may be nonexistent. Even when they get what they want, maximizers may not always want what they get. Individual decision makers, as well as policymakers, are thus confronted by a dilemma: If the subjective well-being of the decision maker and the objective value of the decision outcome are at odds, which should be prioritized? What should people do when "doing better" makes them feel worse?

ACKNOWLEDGMENTS

This research was supported by a National Science Foundation Young Investigator Career Award.

ENDNOTE

1. Detailed statistical information yielded by analyses of differences in subsamples' characteristics is also available upon request.

REFERENCES

Best national universities. (2001, September 17). *U.S. News & World Report*, p. 106.

Botti, S., & Iyengar, S. S. (2004). The psychological pleasure and pain of choosing: When people prefer choosing at the cost of subsequent outcome satisfaction. *Journal of Personality and Social Psychology, 87*, 312–326.

Frederick, S., & Loewenstein, G. (1999). Hedonic adaptation. In D. Kahneman, E. Diener, & N. Schwarz (Eds.), *Well-being: The foundations of hedonic psychology* (pp. 302–329). New York: Russell Sage.

Iyengar, S. S., & Jiang, W. (2004). *Choosing not to choose: The effect of more choices on retirement savings decisions.* Manuscript submitted for publication.

Iyengar, S. S., & Lepper, M. R. (1999). Rethinking the value of choice: A cultural perspective on intrinsic motivation. *Journal of Personality and Social Psychology, 76*, 349–366.

Iyengar, S. S., & Lepper, M. R. (2000). When choice is demotivating: Can one desire too much of a good thing? *Journal of Personality and Social Psychology, 79*, 995–1006.

Kahneman, D. (1999). Objective happiness. In D. Kahneman, E. Diener, & N. Schwarz (Eds.), *Well-being: The foundations of hedonic psychology* (pp. 3–25). New York: Russell Sage.

Killeen, P. R. (2005). An alternative to null-hypothesis significance tests. *Psychological Science, 16*, 345–353.

Kliger, M., & Schwartz, B. (2005). [Maximizing tendencies: Evidence from a national sample]. Unpublished raw data.

Loewenstein, G., & Schkade, D. (1999). Wouldn't it be nice? Predicting future feelings. In D. Kahneman, E. Diener, & N. Schwarz (Eds.), *Well-being: The foundations of hedonic psychology* (pp. 85–108). New York: Russell Sage.

Lyubomirsky, S., & Ross, L. (1997). Hedonic consequences of social comparison: A contrast of happy and unhappy people. *Journal of Personality and Social Psychology, 73*, 1141–1157.

Miller, G. A. (1956). The magic number seven plus or minus two: Some limits in our capacity for processing information. *Psychological Review, 63*, 81–97.

Schwartz, B. (2004a). *The paradox of choice: Why more is less.* New York: Ecco.

Schwartz, B. (2004b, April). The tyranny of choice. *Scientific American, 290*, 70–76.

Schwartz, B., Ward, A., Monterosso, J., Lyubomirsky, S., White, K., & Lehman, D. R. (2002). Maximizing versus satisficing: Happiness is a matter of choice. *Journal of Personality and Social Psychology, 83*, 1178–1197.

Simon, H. A. (1955). A behavioral model of rational choice. *Quarterly Journal of Economics, 59*, 99–113.

Simon, H. A. (1956). Rational choice and the structure of the environment. *Psychological Review, 63*, 129–138.

Simon, H. A. (1957). *Models of man, social and rational: Mathematical essays on rational human behavior.* New York: Wiley.

Wilson, T. D. (2002). *Strangers to ourselves: Discovering the adaptive unconscious.* Cambridge, MA: Harvard University Press.

Wilson, T. D., & Gilbert, D. T. (2003). Affective forecasting. In M. P. Zsana (Ed.), *Advances in experimental social psychology* (Vol. 35, pp. 345–411). San Diego, CA: Academic Press.

CRITICAL THINKING QUESTIONS

1. Think about changing one word in the title of this article so that it reads "Looking for the 'Best' *Relationship* Undermines Satisfaction." Do you think the concepts presented in this article could be applied to how individuals pursue relationships? If so, how? Be specific in your answer.

2. Does having too many options ultimately make people distressed and unhappy? Explain your reasoning using an example other than job or relationship satisfaction.

3. As the article states, "Our affective measures allowed us to assess decision makers' experiences with the process and their expected satisfaction with their impending employment, but did not assess job seekers' affective experience with their resulting employment." Do you think mazimizers would be equally dissatisfied with their actual employment, rather than just their anticipation of it? Why or why not?

4. Will the approach you took in applying to and then selecting a college to attend predict how you will go about getting your first job after graduation? Why or why not?

5. Recall the concept of cognitive dissonance discussed in Chapter Four, Articles 11 and 12. How might this concept be applied to mazimizers' satisfaction with their job choice? Explain your answer.

CHAPTER INTEGRATION QUESTIONS

1. The first article in this chapter dealt with employee turnover, the second with employee motivation, and the third with job satisfaction. What do these three articles have in common? Explain what you see as a common thread or threads running through all of the articles in this chapter.

2. What other factors besides those discussed in these articles may be important in understanding business psychology? For example, what topics of previous chapters may have particular relevance for the study of business psychology? Discuss why you think these topics/chapters may be relevant.

3. An old proverb tells us, "It is not whether you win or lose but how you play the game." Yet according to Vince Lombardi, a former professional football coach, "Winning isn't everything, it's the only thing." These quotes typically are associated with sports, but can they be applied to how people approach business, as well? How so? What are both the potential short-term and long-term implications for someone who follows either of these quotes in his or her approach to business? Explain.

Chapter Fourteen

FORENSIC PSYCHOLOGY

YOU PROBABLY HAVE had some contact with the legal system, in one form or another. Perhaps you (or someone you know) have been arrested and even tried for some offense. Maybe you have been asked to be a juror. More likely, you have watched televised trials or read about real or fictional trials in the media. Given your experience, does the legal system, as it presently operates, guarantee an objective, unbiased outcome?

Forensic psychology has emerged in recent years as a major discipline that tries to understand the entire judicial process and to make it as fair as possible. Originally an outgrowth of social psychology and other psychological disciplines, forensic psychology has become an area of study in its own right. Nonetheless, it remains strongly rooted in the principles and findings of social psychological research.

Social psychologists working in the field of forensic psychology have examined a number of factors that may influence the outcomes in legal settings. Many of the findings summarized in previous articles in this book can be applied to forensic settings, as well. For example, the findings pertaining to prejudice, discrimination, social influence, and attitude change, to name but a few, can easily be extended to the courtroom. Some of the biases that enter into the judicial process may be byproducts of how we think and process information (i.e., social cognition). Some of these biases may stem from how we naturally deal with the complex world around us, and as such, they may have been present from the first time that someone's guilt or innocence was put in question. However, there also may be some new biases entering the modern courtroom based on technological changes.

Article 40, "Can Psychology Prevent False Confessions?" examines why someone might do the unthinkable: namely, confess to a crime he or she did not commit. The article addresses some of the social psychological factors that may play a role in getting someone to admit guilt when he or she is actually innocent.

The classic study found in Article 41, "Beautiful but Dangerous: Effects of Offender Attractiveness and Nature of the Crime on Juridic Judgment," looks at the relationship between the attractiveness of the offender and the nature of the crime and how it may influence a jury's judgment. Often (but not always), having good looks is an asset when someone is on trial.

Article 42, "Looking Deathworthy: Perceived Stereotypicality of Black Defendants Predicts Capital-Sentencing Outcomes," is a contemporary exploration of variables that may influence the outcomes of a trial. Like the classic Article 41, which found that physical appearance may have a big impact on the perception of guilt or innocence, this article found that not only race but also how closely someone resembles the stereotype for that race affected decision making to sentence someone to death. The disturbing findings of this study are even more significant given that they were based on the analysis of actual capital-sentencing decisions.

ARTICLE 40

Since the advent of DNA testing, many individuals who have committed crimes have been convicted and sentenced based on genetic evidence. As any viewer of the myriad police shows on television will attest, the use of DNA evidence seems to be a cornerstone of modern forensic police work.

While the use of DNA testing has provided evidence to convict criminals who would not confess to their acts and for whom other evidence was lacking, the use of such testing also has produced another result. Namely, DNA testing has provided evidence that someone already convicted for a crime could not have committed it.

There are many reasons an innocent person may be convicted of a crime. The person's physical similarity to the actual offender, the existence of eyewitnesses who maintain he or she was the criminal, and the lack of competent legal representation are but a few of the reasons a person professing innocence may be convicted of a crime he or she did not commit. However, sometimes people are convicted of crimes they did not commit because they confess to committing them.

To many people, the last sentence seems implausible. Why in the world would an innocent person confess to a crime he or she did not commit? Common sense would lead most people to believe that if you voluntarily confess to something, you must be telling the truth. We expect people to lie to get out of being charged or convicted of a crime, not to get charged or convicted.

So why would someone confess to a crime of which he or she was innocent? Topics from many of the previous chapters pertain to this issue. Using just a few examples, *social influence* deals with how people respond by conforming to social pressure, *social cognition* addresses how people think and make sense of the world, and *attitudes* reflect how people sometimes use a process known as *cognitive dissonance* to justify their initial beliefs or statements. But other processes are at work, as well.

The following article by Zak Stambor explores some of the reasons people may confess to crimes they did not commit. It also discusses some of the ways the legal system might be improved to minimize the possibility of people making false confessions.

Can Psychology Prevent False Confessions?

■ Zak Stambor

In 1988, 22-year-old Chris Ochoa worked at a Pizza Hut in Austin, Texas. When he wasn't working he liked watching television and listening to rock bands like Aerosmith and Van Halen. And aside from a handful of parking and speeding tickets, the small, quiet, dark-eyed Ochoa had never had a problem with the law. He shared a two-bedroom apartment with his co-worker Richard Danziger and planned to attend community college and eventually transfer to the University of Texas.

But his ambitions were dashed when, on Oct. 24, Achim Josef Marino robbed another Austin-area Pizza Hut, took Nancy DePriest—the restaurant's 20-year-old manager—to the washroom, tied her up with her bra, raped and shot her.

When Ochoa and Danziger shared a pizza and beer at DePriest's Pizza Hut the following day, restaurant employees thought they might have been toasting to DePriest's death and called the police, who, three days later, picked up the two men and scuttled them to separate interrogation rooms.

"That's when the nightmare began," Ochoa says. For 12 hours, a parade of interrogators, who called themselves names like "The Bogeyman," presented Ochoa with a choice—confess and get a life sentence or refuse and be sent to the death chamber. When Ochoa asked for a lawyer, they told him he didn't have the right to one because he hadn't been charged with anything. Interrogators shoved photos of death row cells in his face and told him that this was where he would spend the remainder of his life.

"I was worried," he says. "I didn't know what they can and can't do."

After another grueling day of interrogation during which he thought to himself, "They're going to kill me. They're going to murder me for a crime I didn't commit," Ochoa confessed.

At the trial, Ochoa testified that he and Danziger—who refused to confess—robbed the Pizza Hut and raped and shot DePriest. Both men received life sentences, which they served until Marino confessed to the crime 12 years later.

Psychologists and other scientists who study false confessions say that Ochoa's experience is anything but unique. False confessions have accounted for more than 26 percent of the nation's first 130 convictions later overturned by DNA testing, according to the New York-based Innocence Project, which works to free the wrongly convicted. And those cases figure to be only the tip of the iceberg, says psychologist Saul Kassin, PhD, of Williams College.

A recent tide of psychological research suggests that false confessions often arise after innocent people waive their legal protections due to their ignorance of the system or their belief that the evidence will vindicate them. To stop the problem, psychologists are helping to educate interrogators about the power of social influence—especially when dealing with children, people with cognitive disabilities, or people like Ochoa who are psychologically coerced into confessing after failing to understand their rights.

WAIVING PROTECTIONS

It may seem baffling that any person would waive their Miranda rights and other legal protections, but many suspects—because of youth, intelligence level, lack of education or mental health status—lack the capacity to understand and apply the rights they are given, says Kassin.

And when innocent suspects give their alibis, their explanations are precisely the type of alibis that police are trained not to trust: They often state that they were alone or with friends and family members.

In a 2004 article published in *Law and Human Behavior* (Vol. 21, No. 2, pages 211–221), Kassin had participants pretend they were either guilty or innocent of a mock theft of $100. After being apprehended for investigation, 58 percent of suspects waived their rights. Moreover, innocent suspects signed a Miranda waiver twice as often as guilty suspects. The reason? They felt they had nothing to hide.

"Innocent people have the naïve and powerful belief that their innocence will set them free," says Kassin. "So they agree to come to the station and waive whatever safeguards are in place."

And when innocent people talk, police often figure that the chatter is an attempt to deceive them, says Kassin. To counter the deception, they move the suspected criminal into an interrogation room and offer a host of traps to garner a confession. They might suggest, for example, that a confession will be rewarded with lenient sentencing, or offer a host of mitigating factors that might have led to the crime, or even lie about the evidence. When people continue to refuse to confess after hours in the interrogation room, stress, fatigue and claustrophobia typically ensue, says Kassin.

"People figure they can give a confession as an escape hatch," he says. "They figure, 'It wasn't me, and the investigation will show that.' But they don't realize that the confession closes the investigation—it doesn't open it."

VULNERABLE POPULATIONS

Yet not all false confessions are a ploy to leave the interrogation room. Some confess because the interrogation causes them to doubt their own memory, and they begin to believe that they may have blacked out or repressed the crime. And as interrogators offer false evidence to fill in the gaps, many, including children and people with cognitive disabilities are put at risk.

In a 2003 study published in *Law and Human Behavior* (Vol. 27, No. 2, pages 141–155), psychologists Allison Redlich, PhD, and Gail Goodman, PhD, found that the younger a child is, the more likely they were to falsely confess in a lab environment. In the study, they sat 12- to 26-year-olds at a computer, and told them to type the letters that the researcher read to them and not to touch the "ALT" keys because it would crash the computer and all data would be lost. After researchers read 115 letters, the computer screen turned black and stopped working, and the researchers, acting distressed, asked "Did you hit the ALT key?"

About 69 percent of the participants falsely confessed to hitting the key and 39 percent of the participants came to believe they actually pressed the button but couldn't remember doing so. Although taking responsibility for crashing a computer is obviously different from confessing to a crime, Redlich suggests that the psychological processes are the same.

And because research suggests that at least 65 percent of children in the juvenile justice system have mental health disorders, it is essential that police officers alter their interrogation methods to be mindful of suspects' vulnerabilities, she says.

"We need interrogators to take what [developmental psychologists] have learned about children's development and apply it to child suspects," she says, noting that the consequences of children falsely confessing to crimes could ruin children's lives.

A SAFETY NET

In line with Redlich's suggestions, officials in the United Kingdom have recently instituted protections to prevent false confessions.

For instance, they train interrogators to no longer assume suspects are guilty and to not lie to suspects.

"When police can lie to suspects, they can decide on dubious grounds to try to trick a suspect into confession," says psychologist Gisli Gudjonsson, PhD,

of London's Institute of Psychiatry at King's College. "And often they persuade themselves that the person is guilty."

Along with other psychologists, Gudjonsson—who has developed measures that assess people's susceptibility toward compliancy and suggestibility—works as a consultant to police to help them determine the vulnerabilities of suspects with mental health disorders or issues. After interviewing and testing the suspect, Gudjonsson writes detailed reports that analyze the best interview strategies for the individual. The practice helps police obtain more reliable accounts, he says.

"There's a lot at stake if the wrong person is convicted," says Gudjonsson. "You cannot take a confession at face value. You have to corroborate it. Mistakes can cost people their lives." Even if the mistake is rectified, its effects can be long-lasting. For instance, since being released, Ochoa settled with Austin for $5.3 million and graduated from the University of Wisconsin School of Law. But success and financial security cannot make up for the 12 years he lost, he says. He's perpetually frustrated that people fail to grasp that his confession was not voluntary but grew out of circumstance.

"Exonerees aren't seen as victims," he says, suggesting that many fail to understand the system's ability to provoke duress.

To help prevent cases like Ochoa's, the British police now videotape all interviews and interrogations. The tapes provide an objective, accurate record of circumstances surrounding suspects' statements—which Kassin endorsed in a 2005 *American Psychologist* (Vol. 60, No. 3, pages 215–228) article that examined whether innocence puts innocent suspects at risk. In the United States, videotaping is only mandatory in Minnesota, Alaska, Illinois and Maine, despite data compiled by the Center on Wrongful Convictions at Northwestern University Law School showing that videotaping interrogations boosts police officers' effectiveness in catching criminals and keeping innocent people free.

Kassin's article suggests that videotaping could help judges and juries understand the context in which promises or threats were made and whether a confession's details grew out of interrogators' questions. And videotaping could also help deter police from conducting prolonged interrogations, like Ochoa's two-day interrogation, since research suggests that 73 percent of false confessions are given after more than six hours of interrogation.

"Psychologists need to help police develop a set of techniques to catch criminals and leave innocent suspects unharmed," he says. "We need to build a better mousetrap."

CRITICAL THINKING QUESTIONS:

1. The article states that only a handful of states require videotaping confessions. Do you think this should be required everywhere? Why or why not? Defend your position.

2. Working within the legal system, would better educating lawyers, judges, and juries about the psychology of false confessions help lessen the possibility of wrongful convictions? If so, how would you go about educating these individuals, especially jury members?

3. For what possible reasons might police use coercive techniques during interrogations that result in false confessions? In addition to better educating police about the psychology of false confessions, what other safeguards could be implemented to help reduce the likelihood of an innocent person being convicted of a crime he or she did not commit?

4. Based on the information in Chapters Two and Three (on social perception and social cognition, respectively), what other sources of bias may affect courtroom proceedings? Explain your answer.

ARTICLE 41_____

What factors may have an impact on determining the defendant's guilt or innocence? Jurors are asked to weigh the evidence presented during the trial. Hopefully, they will not permit irrelevant characteristics of the defendant—such as his or her physical appearance, race, or sex—to affect their judgment. But is it really possible to be totally objective in such situations? Or do irrelevant factors play a role in our beliefs about guilt or innocence?

The following article by Harold Sigall and Nancy Ostrove is a classic piece of research that investigated the impact of the defendant's physical attractiveness on the severity of sentences given to her. Earlier studies had indicated that physically attractive individuals often have great advantages over less attractive people in a variety of situations. This study not only examined the role of physical attractiveness in a trial-like setting but also how the nature of the crime and attractiveness interact to influence judgments about the defendant. The article also tests two different models that may explain why this particular effect occurs.

Beautiful but Dangerous

Effects of Offender Attractiveness and Nature of the Crime on Juridic Judgment

■ Harold Sigall and Nancy Ostrove

The physical attractiveness of a criminal defendant (attractive, unattractive, no information) and the nature of the crime (attractiveness-related, attractiveness-unrelated) were varied in a factorial design. After reading one of the case accounts, subjects sentenced the defendant to a term of imprisonment. An interaction was predicted: When the crime was unrelated to attractiveness (burglary), subjects would assign more lenient sentences to the attractive defendant than to the unattractive defendant; when the offense was attractiveness-related (swindle), the attractive defendant would receive harsher treatment. The results confirmed the predictions, thereby supporting a cognitive explanation for the relationship between the physical attractiveness of defendants and the nature of the judgments made against them.

Research investigating the interpersonal consequences of physical attractiveness has demonstrated clearly that good-looking people have tremendous advantages over their unattractive counterparts in many ways. For example, a recent study by Miller (1970) provided evidence for the existence of a physical attractiveness stereotype with a rather favorable content. Dion, Berscheid, and Walster (1972) reported similar findings: Compared to unattractive people, better-looking people were viewed as more likely to possess a variety of socially desirable attributes. In addition, Dion et al.'s subjects predicted rosier futures for the beautiful stimulus persons—attractive people were expected to have happier and more successful lives in store for them. Thus, at least in the eyes of others, good looks imply greater potential.

Since physical attractiveness hardly seems to provide a basis for an *equitable* distribution of rewards, one might hope that the powerful effects of this variable would occur primarily when it is the only source of information available. Unfair or irrational consequences of differences in beauty observed in some situations would cause less uneasiness if, in other situations given other important data, respondents would tend to discount such "superficial" information. Unfortunately, for the vast majority of us who have not been blessed with a stunning appearance, the evidence does not permit such consolation. Consider, for example, a recent study by Dion (1972) in which adult subjects were presented with accounts of transgressions supposedly committed by children of varying physical attractiveness. When the transgression was severe the act was viewed less negatively when committed by a good-looking child, than when the offender was unattractive. Moreover, when the child was unattractive the offense was more likely to be seen as reflecting some enduring dispositional quality: Subjects believed that unattractive children were more likely to be involved in future transgressions. Dion's findings, which indicate that unattractive individuals are penalized when there is no apparent logical relationship between the transgression and the way they look, underscore the importance of appearance because one could reasonably suppose that information describing a severe transgression would "overwhelm the field," and that the physical attractiveness variable would not have any effect.

Can beautiful people get away with murder? Although Dion (1972) found no differences in the punishment recommended for offenders as a function of attractiveness, Monahan (1941) has suggested that beautiful women are convicted less often of crimes they are accused of, and Efran (1974) has recently demonstrated that subjects are much more generous when assigning punishment to good-looking as opposed to unattractive transgressors.

The previous findings which indicate a tendency toward leniency for an attractive offender can be accounted for in a number of ways. For example, one might explain such results with the help of a reinforcement-affect model of attraction (e.g., Byrne & Clore, 1970). Essentially, the argument here would be that beauty, having positive reinforcement value, would lead to relatively more positive affective responses toward a person who has it. Thus we like an attractive person more, and since other investigators have shown that liking for a defendant increases

leniency (e.g., Landy & Aronson, 1969), we would expect good-looking (better liked) defendants to be punished less than unattractive defendants. Implicit in this reasoning is that the nature of the affective response, which influences whether kind or harsh treatment is recommended, is determined by the stimulus features associated with the target person. Therefore, when other things are equal, benefit accrues to the physically attractive. A more cognitive approach might attempt to explain the relationship between physical appearance and reactions to transgressions by assuming that the subject has a "rational" basis for his responses. It is reasonable to deal harshly with a criminal if we think he is likely to commit further violations, and as Dion's (1972) study suggests, unattractive individuals are viewed as more likely to transgress again. In addition, inasmuch as attractive individuals are viewed as possessing desirable qualities and as having relatively great potential, it makes sense to treat them leniently. Presumably they can be successful in socially acceptable ways, and rehabilitation may result in relatively high payoffs for society.

There is at least one implication that follows from the cognitive orientation which would not flow readily from the reinforcement model. Suppose that situations do exist in which, because of his high attractiveness, a defendant is viewed as more likely to transgress in the future. The cognitive approach suggests that in such instances greater punishment would be assigned to the attractive offender. We might add that in addition to being more dangerous, when the crime is attractiveness related, a beautiful criminal may be viewed as taking advantage of a God-given gift. Such misappropriation of a blessing may incur animosity, which might contribute to severe judgments in attractiveness-related situations.

In the present investigation, the attractiveness of a defendant was varied along with the nature of the crime committed. It was reasoned that most offenses do not encourage the notion that a criminal's attractiveness increases the likelihood of similar transgressions in the future. Since attractive offenders are viewed as less prone to recidivism and as having greater potential worth, it was expected that under such circumstances an attractive defendant would receive less punishment than an unattractive defendant involved in an identical offense. When, however, the crime committed may be viewed as attractiveness-related, as in a confidence game, despite being seen as possessing more potential, the attractive defendant may be regarded as relatively more dangerous, and the effects of beauty could be expected to be cancelled out or reversed. The major hypothesis, then, called for an interaction: An attractive defendant would receive more lenient treatment than an unattractive defendant when the offense was unrelated to attractiveness; when the crime was related to attractiveness, the attractive defendant would receive relatively harsh treatment.

METHOD

Subjects and Overview

Subjects were 60 male and 60 female undergraduates. After being presented with an account of a criminal case, each subject sentenced the defendant to a term of imprisonment. One-third of the subjects were led to believe that the defendant was physically attractive, another third that she was unattractive, and the remainder received no information concerning appearance. Cross-cutting the attractiveness variable, half of the subjects were presented with a written account of an attractiveness-unrelated crime, a burglary, and the rest with an attractiveness-related crime, a swindle. Subjects were randomly assigned to condition, with the restriction that an equal number of males and females appeared in each of the six cells formed by the manipulated variables.

Procedure

Upon arrival, each subject was shown to an individual room and given a booklet which contained the stimulus materials. The top sheet informed subjects that they would read a criminal case account, that they would receive biographical information about the defendant, and that after considering the materials they would be asked to answer some questions.

The case account began on the second page. Clipped to this page was a 5 × 8 inch card which contained routine demographic information and was identical in all conditions.[1] In the attractive conditions, a photograph of a rather attractive woman was

affixed to the upper right-hand corner of the card; while in the unattractive conditions, a relatively unattractive photograph was affixed. No photograph was presented in the control conditions.

Subjects then read either the account of a burglary or a swindle. The burglary account described how the defendant, Barbara Helm, had moved into a high-rise building, obtained a pass key under false pretenses, and then illegally entered the apartment of one of her neighbors. After stealing $2,200 in cash and merchandise she left town. She was apprehended when she attempted to sell some of the stolen property and subsequently was charged with breaking and entering and grand larceny. The swindle account described how Barbara Helm had ingratiated herself to a middle-aged bachelor and induced him to invest $2,200 in a nonexistent corporation. She was charged with obtaining money under false pretenses and grand larceny. In both cases, the setting for the offense and the victim were described identically. The information presented left little doubt concerning the defendant's guilt.

The main dependent measure was collected on the last page of the booklet. Subjects were asked to complete the following statement by circling a number between 1 and 15: "I sentence the defendant, Barbara Helm, to _____ years of imprisonment." Subjects were asked to sentence the defendant, rather than to judge guilt versus innocence in order to provide a more sensitive dependent measure.

After sentencing had been completed, the experimenter provided a second form, which asked subjects to recall who the defendant was and to rate the seriousness of the crime. In addition, the defendant was rated on a series of 9-point bipolar adjective scales, including physically unattractive (1) to physically attractive (9), which constituted the check on the attractiveness manipulation. A post-experimental interview followed, during which subjects were debriefed.

RESULTS AND DISCUSSION

The physical attractiveness manipulation was successful: The attractive defendant received a mean rating of 7.53, while the mean for the unattractive defendant was 3.20, $F(1, 108) = 184.29$, $p < .001$. These ratings were not affected by the nature of the crime, nor was there an interaction.

The criminal cases were designed so as to meet two requirements. First, the swindle was assumed to be attractiveness-related, while the burglary was intended to be attractiveness-unrelated. No direct check on this assumption was made. However, indirect evidence is available: Since all subjects filled out the same forms, we obtained physical attractiveness ratings from control condition subjects who were not presented with a photograph. These subjects attributed greater beauty to the defendant in the swindle condition ($X = 6.65$) than in the burglary condition ($X = 5.65$), $F(1, 108) = 4.93$, $p < .05$. This finding offers some support for our contention that the swindle was viewed as attractiveness-related. Second, it was important that the two crimes be viewed as roughly comparable in seriousness. This was necessary to preclude alternative explanations in terms of differential seriousness. Subjects rated the seriousness of the crime on a 9-point scale extending from not at all serious (1) to extremely serious (9). The resulting responses indicated that the second requirement was met: In the swindle condition the mean seriousness rating was 5.02; in the burglary condition it was 5.07 ($F < 1$).

Table 1 presents the mean punishment assigned to the defendant, by condition. Since a preliminary analysis demonstrated there were no differences in responses between males and females, subject sex was ignored as a variable. It can be seen that our hypothesis was supported: When the offense was attractiveness-unrelated (burglary), the unattractive defendant was more severely punished than the attractive defendant; however, when the offense was attractiveness-related (swindle), the attractive defendant was treated more harshly. The overall Attractiveness × Offense interac-

tion was statistically significant, $F(2, 108) = 4.55$, $p < .025$, end this interaction was significant, as well, when the control condition was excluded, $F(1, 108) = 7.02$, $p < .01$. Simple comparisons revealed that the unattractive burglar received significantly more punishment than the attractive burglar, $F(1, 108) = 6.60$, $p < .025$, while the difference in sentences assigned to the attractive and unattractive swindler was not statistically significant, $F(1, 108) = 1.39$. The attractive-swindle condition was compared with the unattractive-swindle and control-swindle conditions also, $F(1, 108) = 2.00$, *ns*. Thus, strictly speaking, we cannot say that for the swindle attractiveness was a great liability; there was a tendency in this direction but the conservative conclusion is that when the crime is attractiveness-related, the advantages otherwise held by good-looking defendants are lost.

Another feature of the data worth considering is that the sentences administered in the control condition are almost identical to those assigned in the unattractive condition. It appears that being unattractive did not produce discriminatory responses, per se. Rather, it seems that appearance had its effect through the attractive conditions: The beautiful burglar got off lightly, while the beautiful swindler paid somewhat, though not significantly, more. It can be recalled that in the unattractive conditions the stimulus person was seen as relatively unattractive and not merely average looking. Therefore, the absence of unattractive-control condition differences does not seem to be the result of a weak manipulation in the unattractive conditions.

Perhaps it is possible to derive a small bit of consolation from this outcome, if we speculate that only the very attractive receive special (favorable or unfavorable) treatment, and that others are treated similarly. That is a less frightening conclusion than one which would indicate that unattractiveness brings about active discrimination.

As indicated earlier, previous findings (Efran, 1974) that attractive offenders are treated leniently can be interpreted in a number of ways. The results of the present experiment support the cognitive explanation we offered. The notion that good-looking people usually tend to be treated generously because they are seen as less dangerous and more virtuous remains tenable. The argument that physical attractiveness is a positive trait and therefore has a unidirection-

TABLE 1 / Mean Sentence Assigned, in Years ($n = 20$ per cell)

Offense	Defendant Condition		
	Attractive	Unattractive	Control
Swindle	5.45	4.35	4.35
Burglary	2.80	5.20	5.10

ally favorable effect on judgments of those who have it, would have led to accurate predictions in the burglary conditions. However, this position could not account for the observed interaction. The cognitive view makes precisely that prediction.

Finally, we feel compelled to note that our laboratory situation is quite different from actual courtroom situations. Most important, perhaps, our subjects made decisions which had no consequences for the defendant, and they made those decisions by themselves, rather than arriving at judgments after discussions with others exposed to the same information. Since the courtroom is not an appropriate laboratory, it is unlikely that actual experimental tests in the real situation would ever be conducted. However, simulations constitute legitimate avenues for investigating person perception and interpersonal judgment, and there is no obvious reason to believe that these processes would not have the effects in trial proceedings that they do elsewhere.

Whether a discussion with other jurors would affect judgment is an empirical, and researchable, question. Perhaps if even 1 of 12 jurors notes that some irrelevant factor may be affecting the jury's judgment, the others would see the light. Especially now when the prospect of reducing the size of juries is being entertained, it would be important to find out whether extralegal considerations are more likely to have greater influence as the number of jurors decreases.

REFERENCES

Byrne, D., & Clore, G. L. A reinforcement model of evaluative responses. *Personality: An International Journal,* 1970, *1,* 103–128.

Dion, K. Physical attractiveness and evaluation of children's transgressions. *Journal of Personality and Social Psychology,* 1972, *24,* 207–213.

Dion, K., Berscheid, E., & Walster, E. What is beautiful is good. *Journal of Personality and Social Psychology,* 1972, *24,* 285–290.

Efran, M. G. The effect of physical appearance on the judgment of guilt, interpersonal attraction, and severity of recommended punishment in a simulated jury task. *Journal of Research in Personality,* 1974, *8,* 45–54.

Landy, D., & Aronson, E. The influence of the character of the criminal and victim on the decisions of simulated jurors. *Journal of Experimental Social Psychology,* 1969, *5,* 141–152.

Miller, A. G. Role of physical attractiveness in impression formation. *Psychonomic Science,* 1970, *19,* 241–243.

Monahan, F. *Women in crime.* New York: Washburn, 1941.

ENDNOTE

1. This information as well as copies of the case accounts referred to below, can be obtained from the first author.

This study was supported by a grant from the University of Maryland General Research Board.

CRITICAL THINKING QUESTIONS

1. This article used pictures only of females to show defendants of varying attractiveness. Would the same results be obtained if male defendants were used? In other words, do you think that attractiveness stereotypes operate in the same way for males as for females? Defend your answer.

2. As the authors of the article noted, the methodology of the study differed from real-life jury trials in several ways. For example, subjects made their decisions alone and were presented with a paper description of the person and deed, not a real-life person and crime. Design a study that would investigate the same variables studied in the article in a more natural environment.

3. Would the results of this study be generalizable to situations other than jury trials? Think of a situation in which the attractiveness of a person making a request or performing a certain action may result in his or her being treated differentially as a result of his or her attractiveness. Explain your answer.

4. What implications do these findings have for the U.S. legal system? How could the effects of irrelevant factors such as attractiveness somehow be minimized in the real-world courtroom? For example, would telling the jurors beforehand about the tendency to let attractiveness influence their judgments make any difference? Why or why not?

ADDITIONAL RELATED READINGS

Dabney, D. A., Dugan, L., Topcalli, V., & Hollinger, R. C. (2006). The impact of implicit stereotyping on offender profiling: Unexpected results from an observational study of shoplifting. *Criminal Justice and Behavior, 33*(5), 646–674.

Wuensch, K. L., & Moore, C. H. (2004). Effects of physical attractiveness on evaluations of a male employee's allegation of sexual harassment by his female employer. *Journal of Social Psychology, 144*(2), 207–217.

ARTICLE 42_____

In the legal systems of the United States, Canada, and many other countries, the conviction and sentencing of a defendant is supposed to be based on the admissible evidence presented in the courtroom. What is considered *admissible* usually is based on precedent and other rules concerning the appropriateness of certain types of evidence. However, there are certain factors pertaining to the defendant that, while not admissible as evidence, are impossible to conceal from the jury. For example, Article 41 demonstrated how the physical attractiveness of the defendant may play an important role in the likelihood of his or her being convicted and the severity of his or her recommended punishment.

Besides physical attractiveness, many other personal characteristics of the defendant are obvious to the jury yet should not necessarily affect the decision it makes. Race, ethnic background, and perceived intelligence are but a few of the defendant characteristics that cannot be concealed from the jury. While such factors presumably should not enter into the decision making of the jury, they certainly may.

The following article by Jennifer L. Eberhardt, Paul G. Davies, Valerie J. Purdie-Vaughns, and Sheri Lynn Johnson examines how race may impact trial sentencing. In particular, the article looks at whether how stereotypically black an individual appears will increase the likelihood of his or her receiving the death sentence, especially when the victim is white.

This article also is of interest in that it uses data from real court sentencing, rather than data from the more typical laboratory format. This article, along with the information already presented in Articles 40 and 41, further demonstrates that many potential sources of bias and error influence the workings of the criminal justice system.

Looking Deathworthy
Perceived Stereotypicality of Black Defendants
Predicts Capital-Sentencing Outcomes

■ Jennifer L. Eberhardt, Paul G. Davies, Valerie J. Purdie-Vaughns, and Sheri Lynn Johnson

ABSTRACT

Researchers previously have investigated the role of race in capital sentencing, and in particular, whether the race of the defendant or victim influences the likelihood of a death sentence. In the present study, we examined whether the likelihood of being sentenced to death is influenced by the degree to which a Black defendant is perceived to have a stereotypically Black appearance. Controlling for a wide array of factors, we found that in cases involving a White victim, the more stereotypically Black a defendant is perceived to be, the more likely that person is to be sentenced to death.

Race matters in capital punishment. Even when statistically controlling for a wide variety of nonracial factors that may influence sentencing, numerous researchers have found that murderers of White victims are more likely than murderers of Black victims to be sentenced to death (Baldus, Pulaski, &

Eberhardt, J. L., Davies, P. G., Purdie-Vaughns, V. J., & Johnson, S. L. (2006). Looking deathworthy: Perceived stereotypicality of black defendants predicts capital-sentencing outcomes. *Psychological Science, 17*(5), 383–386.

Woodworth, 1983; Baldus, Woodworth, & Pulaski, 1985, 1990, 1994; Baldus, Woodworth, Zuckerman, Weiner, & Broffitt, 1998; Bowers, Pierce, & McDevitt, 1984; Gross & Mauro, 1989; Radelet, 1981; U.S. General Accounting Office, GAO, 1990). The U.S. GAO (1990) has described this race-of-victim effect as "remarkably consistent across data sets, states, data collection methods, and analytic techniques" (p. 5).

In one of the most comprehensive studies to date, the race of the victim and the race of the defendant each were found to influence sentencing (Baldus et al., 1998). Not only did killing a White person rather than a Black person increase the likelihood of being sentenced to death, but also Black defendants were more likely than White defendants to be sentenced to death.

In the current research, we used the data set from this study by Baldus and his colleagues (1998) to investigate whether the probability of receiving the death penalty is significantly influenced by the degree to which the defendant is perceived to have a stereotypically Black appearance (e.g., broad nose, thick lips, dark skin). In particular, we considered the effect of a Black defendant's perceived stereotypicality for those cases in which race is most salient—when a Black defendant is charged with murdering a White victim. Although systematic studies of death sentencing have been conducted for decades, no prior studies have examined this potential influence of physical appearance on death-sentencing decisions.

A growing body of research demonstrates that people more readily apply racial stereotypes to Blacks who are thought to look more stereotypically Black, compared with Blacks who are thought to look less stereotypically Black (Blair, Judd, & Fallman, 2004; Blair, Judd, Sadler, & Jenkins, 2002; Eberhardt, Goff, Purdie, & Davies, 2004; Maddox, 2004; Maddox & Gray, 2002, 2004). People associate Black physical traits with criminality in particular. The more stereotypically Black a person's physical traits appear to be, the more criminal that person is perceived to be (Eberhardt et al., 2004). A recent study found that perceived stereotypicality correlated with the actual sentencing decisions of judges (Blair, Judd, & Chapleau, 2004). Even with differences in defendants' criminal histories statistically controlled, those defendants who possessed the most stereotypically Black facial features served up to 8 months longer in prison for felonies than defendants who possessed the least stereotypically Black features. The present study examined the extent to which perceived stereotypicality of Black defendants influenced jurors' death-sentencing decisions in cases with both White and Black victims. We argue that only in death-eligible cases involving White victims—cases in which race is most salient—will Black defendants' physical traits function as a significant determinant of deathworthiness.

PHASE 1: BLACK DEFENDANT, WHITE VICTIM

Method

We used an extensive database (compiled by Baldus et al., 1998) containing more than 600 death-eligible cases from Philadelphia, Pennsylvania, that advanced to penalty phase between 1979 and 1999. Forty-four of these cases involved Black male defendants who were convicted of murdering White victims. We obtained the photographs of these Black defendants and presented all 44 of them (in a slide-show format) to naive raters who did not know that the photographs depicted convicted murderers. Raters were asked to rate the stereotypicality of each Black defendant's appearance and were told they could use any number of features (e.g., lips, nose, hair texture, skin tone) to arrive at their judgments (Fig. 1).

Stanford undergraduates served as the raters. To control for potential order effects, we presented the photographs in a different random order in each of two sessions. Thirty-two raters (26 White, 4 Asian, and 2 of other ethnicities) participated in one session, and 19 raters (6 White, 11 Asian, and 2 of other ethnicities) participated in the second session. The raters were shown a black-and-white photograph of each defendant's face. The photographs were edited such that the backgrounds and image sizes were standardized, and only the face and a portion of the neck were visible. Raters were told that all the faces they would be viewing were of Black males. The defendants' faces were projected one at a time onto a screen at the front of the room for 4 s each as participants recorded stereotypicality ratings using a scale from 1 (*not at all*

FIGURE 1 / Examples of Variation in Stereotypi-cality of Black Faces. These images are the faces of people with no criminal history and are shown here for illustratiave purposes only. The face on the right would be considered more stereotypically Black than the face on the left.

stereotypical) to 11 (*extremely stereotypical*). In both sessions, raters were kept blind to the purpose of the study and the identity of the men in the photographs. The data were analyzed for effects of order and rater's race, but none emerged.

Results

We computed an analysis of covariance (ANCOVA) using stereotypicality (low-high median split) as the independent variable, the percentage of death sentences imposed as the dependent variable, and six nonracial factors known to influence sentencing (Baldus et al., 1998; Landy & Aronson, 1969; Stewart, 1980) as covariates: (a) aggravating circumstances, (b) mitigating circumstances, (c) severity of the murder (as determined by blind ratings of the cases once purged of racial information), (d) the defendant's socioeconomic status, (e) the victim's socioeconomic status, and (f) the defendant's attractiveness.[1] As per Pennsylvania statute (Judiciary and Judicial Procedure, 2005), aggravating circumstances included factors such as the victim's status as a police officer, prosecution witness, or drug-trafficking competitor; the defendant's prior convictions for voluntary manslaughter or violent felonies; and characteristics of the crime, such as torture, kidnapping, or payment for the murder. Mitigating circumstances included factors such as the defendant's

youth or advanced age, extreme mental or emotional disturbance, lack of prior criminal convictions, minor or coerced role in the crime, and impaired ability to appreciate the criminality of his conduct. The Baldus database of death-eligible defendants is arguably one of the most comprehensive to date; using it allowed us to control for the key variables known to influence sentencing outcomes.

The results confirmed that, above and beyond the effects of the covariates, defendants whose appearance was perceived as more stereotypically Black were more likely to receive a death sentence than defendants whose appearance was perceived as less stereotypically Black, $F(1, 36) = 4.11$, $p < .05$, $\eta_p^2 = .10$ (Fig. 2a). In fact, 24.4% of those Black defendants who fell in the lower half of the stereotypicality distribution received a death sentence, whereas 57.5% of those Black defendants who fell in the upper half received a death sentence.

PHASE II: BLACK DEFENDANT, BLACK VICTIM

Method

Using the same database and procedures described earlier, we examined whether this stereotypicality effect extended to cases in which the victims were Black. Of all cases that advanced to penalty phase, 308 involved Black male defendants who were convicted of murdering Black victims. The photographs for all of these defendants were obtained. The death-sentencing rate for these 308 defendants, however, was only 27% (as compared with 41% for the cases with White victims). Given both the low death-sentencing rate and the large number of cases involving Black defendants and Black victims, we selected 118 of these 308 cases randomly from the database with the stipulation that those defendants receiving the death sentence be over-sampled. This oversampling yielded a subset of cases in which the death-sentencing rate (46%) was not significantly different from that for the cases with White victims (41%; $F = 1$). Using this subset provided a conservative test of our hypothesis. We then presented this subset of Black defendants who murdered Black victims to 18 raters (12 White and 6 Asian), who rated the faces on stereotypicality.[2]

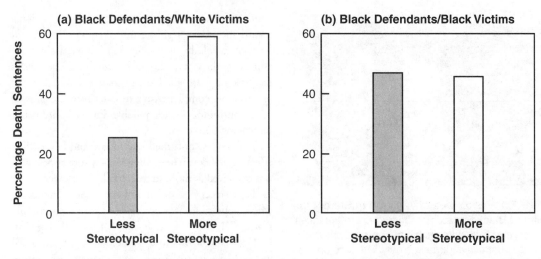

FIGURE 2 / Percentage of death sentences imposed in (a) cases involving White victims and (b) cases involving Black victims as a function of the perceived stereotypicality of Black defendants' appearance.

Results

Employing the same analyses as we did for the cases with White victims, we found that the perceived stereotypicality of Black defendants convicted of murdering Black victims did not predict death sentencing, $F(1, 110) < 1$ (Fig. 2b). Black defendants who fell in the upper and lower halves of the stereotypicality distribution were sentenced to death at almost identical rates (45% vs. 46.6%, respectively). Thus, defendants who were perceived to be more stereotypically Black were more likely to be sentenced to death only when their victims were White.

Although the two phases of this experiment were designed and conducted separately, readers may be interested in knowing whether combining the data from the two phases would produce a significant interactive effect of victims' race and defendants' stereotypicality on death-sentencing outcomes. Analysis confirmed that the interaction of victims' race (Black vs. White) and defendants' stereotypicality (low vs. high) was indeed significant, $F(1, 158) = 4.97$, $p < .05$, $\eta_p^2 = .03$.

DISCUSSION

Why might a defendant's perceived stereotypicality matter for Black murderers of White victims, but not for Black murderers of Black victims? One possibil-ity is that the interracial character of cases involving a Black defendant and a White victim renders race especially salient. Such crimes could be interpreted or treated as matters of intergroup conflict (Prentice & Miller, 1999). The salience of race may incline jurors to think about race as a relevant and useful heuristic for determining the blameworthiness of the defendant and the perniciousness of the crime. According to this racial-salience hypothesis, defendants' perceived stereotypicality should not influence death-sentencing outcomes in cases involving a Black defendant and a Black victim. In those cases, the interracial character of the crime may lead jurors to view the crime as a matter of interpersonal rather than intergroup conflict (Prentice & Miller, 1999).

These research findings augment and complicate the current body of evidence regarding the role of race in capital sentencing. Whereas previous studies examined intergroup differences in death-sentencing outcomes, our results suggest that racial discrimination may also operate through intragroup distinctions based on perceived racial stereotypicality.

Our findings suggest that in cases involving a Black defendant and a White victim—cases in which the likelihood of the death penalty is already high—jurors are influenced not simply by the knowledge that the defendant is Black, but also by the extent to which the defendant appears stereotypically Black. In fact, for those defendants who fell in the top half as opposed to the bottom half of the stereotypicality distribution, the chance of receiving a death sentence more than doubled. Previous laboratory research has already shown that people associate Black physical traits with criminality (Eberhardt et al., 2004). The present research demonstrates that in actual sentencing decisions, jurors may treat these traits as powerful cues to deathworthiness.

ACKNOWLEDGMENTS

The authors thank R. Richard Banks, Hazel Markus, Claude Steele, and Robert Zajonc for comments on a draft of this article and Hilary Bergsieker for preparation of the manuscript. This research was supported by a Stanford Center for Social Innovation Grant and by National Science Foundation Grant BCS-9986128 awarded to J. L. Eberhardt.

ENDNOTES

1. With the exception of defendant's attractiveness, all of the covariates employed here were included in the Baldus database and have been described in detail elsewhere (e.g., see Baldus et al., 1998). We added defendant's attractiveness, basing this variable on 42 naive participants' ratings of the defendants' faces using a scale from 1 (*not at all attractive*) to 11 (*extremely attractive*).

2. Faces of 15 of the Black defendants who murdered White victims were repeated in this session. Analysis of the ratings confirmed interrater reliability.

REFERENCES

Baldus, D.C., Pulaski, C.A., & Woodworth, G. (1983). Comparative review of death sentences: An empirical study of the Georgia experience. *Journal of Criminal Law and Criminology, 74,* 661–753.

Baldus, D.C., Woodworth, G., & Pulaski, C.A. (1985). Monitoring and evaluating contemporary death sentencing systems: Lessons from Georgia. *U. C. Davis Law Review, 18,* 1375–1407.

Baldus, D.C., Woodworth, G., & Pulaski, C.A. (1990). *Equal justice and the death penalty: A legal and empirical analysis.* Boston: Northeastern University Press.

Baldus, D.C., Woodworth, G., & Pulaski, C.A. (1994). Reflections on the "inevitability" of racial discrimination in capital sentencing and the "impossibility" of its prevention, detection, and correction. *Washington and Lee Law* Review, *51,* 359–419.

Baldus, D.C., Woodworth, G., Zuckerman, D., Weiner, N.A., & Broffitt, B. (1998). Racial discrimination and the death penalty in the post-Furman era: An empirical and legal overview, with recent findings from Philadelphia. *Cornell Law Review, 83,* 1638–1770.

Blair, I.V., Judd, C.M., & Chapleau, K.M. (2004). The influence of Afrocentric facial features in criminal sentencing. *Psychological Science, 15,* 674–679.

Blair, I.V., Judd, C.M., & Fallman, J.L. (2004). The automaticity of race and Afrocentric facial features in social judgments. *Journal of Personality and Social Psychology, 87,* 763–778.

Blair, I.V., Judd, C.M., Sadler, M.S., & Jenkins, C. (2002). The role of Afrocentric features in person perception: Judging by features and categories. *Journal of Personality and Social Psychology, 83,* 5–25.

Bowers, W.J., Pierce, G.L., & McDevitt, J.F. (1984). *Legal homicide: Death as punishment in America, 1864–1982.* Boston: Northeastern University Press.

Eberhardt, J.L., Goff, P.A., Purdie, V.J., & Davies, P.G. (2004). Seeing Black: Race, crime, and visual processing. *Journal of Personality and Social Psychology, 87,* 876–893.

Gross, S.R., & Mauro, R. (1989). *Death and discrimination: Racial disparities in capital sentencing.* Boston: Northeastern University Press.

Judiciary and Judicial Procedure, 42 Pa. Cons. Stat. § 9711 (2005).

Landy, D., & Aronson, E. (1969). The influence of the character of the criminal and his victim on the decisions of simulated jurors. *Journal of Experimental Social Psychology, 5,* 141–152.

Maddox, K.B. (2004). Perspectives on racial phenotypicality bias. *Personality and Social Psychology Review, 8,* 383–401.

Maddox, K.B., & Gray, S.A. (2002). Cognitive representations of Black Americans: Reexploring the role of skin tone. *Personality and Social Psychology Bulletin, 28,* 250–259.

Maddox, K.B., & Gray, S.A. (2004). Manipulating subcategory salience: Exploring the link between skin tone and social perception of Blacks. *European Journal of Social Psychology, 34,* 533–546.

Prentice, D.A., & Miller, D.T. (Eds.). (1999). *Cultural divides: Understanding and overcoming group conflict.* New York: Russell Sage Foundation.

Radelet, M.L. (1981). Racial characteristics and the imposition of the death penalty. *American Sociological Review, 46,* 918–927.

Stewart, J.E. (1980). Defendant's attractiveness as a factor in the outcome of criminal trials: An observational study. *Journal of Applied Social Psychology, 10,* 348–361.

U.S. General Accounting Office. (1990). *Death penalty sentencing: Research indicates pattern of racial disparities.* Washington, DC: Author.

CRITICAL THINKING QUESTIONS

1. The previous article (Article 41) found that attractive defendants generally were less likely to be convicted of crimes than less attractive individuals. In the present study, could it be that individuals who were less stereotypically black were perceived as being more attractive than their more stereotypically black counterparts and that that was the factor in determining sentencing? Agree or disagree, but defend your position.

2. In the Discussion section, the article offers the *racial-salience hypothesis* to explain why perceived racial stereotypicality only mattered when the victims were white. Do you agree or disagree with this hypothesis? Use information from other sources to substantiate your belief.

3. What other issues from social psychology might be used to explain the findings of this study? For example, what concepts from topics such as prejudice, social perception, social cognition, and attitudes may be of use in understanding these findings?

4. This article focused only on black defendants. Are there other groups in the United States that might be stigmatized similarly to black defendants? If so, which groups and in what ways? What about in other countries? Explain.

5. How can the information from articles such as this be used in a practical way to help reduce the sentencing biases (especially in death sentence cases) that exist in the current legal system? Be as specific as you can in your answer.

CHAPTER INTEGRATION QUESTIONS

1. By this time, you have undoubtedly read many of the previous chapters in this book. What other chapters and topics have particular relevance to the field of forensic psychology? Be specific in discussing how these chapters/topics may be of importance to forensic psychology.

2. What theme or themes are common to all three of the articles in this chapter? Explain.

3. "Justice is truth in action," according to Benjamin Disraeli, former British Prime Minister. What does this quotation mean to you? Based on the research presented in this chapter, how true is this quote? Explain your answer.

Chapter Fifteen

HEALTH PSYCHOLOGY

THIS FINAL CHAPTER addresses the contributions of social psychology to health issues. When we think of health, often the first thing that comes to mind is the medical or biological component of illness. But what about the behaviors that are linked to illness? Obviously, we can do many things to increase or decrease the likelihood of becoming ill. *Health psychology,* which has a long and strong connection with social psychology, is concerned with the psychosocial factors affecting the prevention, development, and treatment of physical illness.

Think of the various chapters and topics that you have read about in this book thus far. In one way or another, virtually every one of them has some implications for health psychology. For example, how we think about the social world around us (social cognition), our views of ourselves (social identity), how we form and change attitudes and the connection between attitudes and behaviors (attitudes), the impact of being subject to prejudice (prejudice), the role of supportive relationships (helping behavior), and the role of conformity in starting (or stopping) unhealthy behaviors (social influence) are all topics in social psychology that have direct implications for health.

Article 43 discusses the evidence that factors in American culture may be causing health problems. "America: A Toxic Lifestyle?" reports that as a whole, whether rich or poor, Americans tend to be less healthy than their foreign counterparts. Moreover, this fact might be attributed to two related cultural factors: an overemphasis on materialistic achievement and an underemphasis on interpersonal connectedness.

We all know that stress can cause illness, but can even positive events make us sick? Perhaps it is not just negative events but anything that makes us adapt and change that causes stress. From this view, getting married may be almost as stressful as getting fired from work. Article 44, "The Social Readjustment Rating Scale," is a classic article about pioneering work on how life changes in general may affect health.

Finally, Article 45 examines how the terrorist attacks of September 11, 2001, may have affected people. Unlike many studies on people's reactions to traumatic events, "Psychological Resilience after Disaster: New York City in the Aftermath of the September 11th Terrorist Attack," looked at the number of people who were exposed to that trauma yet did not exhibit negative reactions to it. The heartening message from this study is that people may be a lot more resilient to trauma than is commonly believed.

ARTICLE 43 _____

Over the years, numerous connections have been made between personality/lifestyle factors and health. Perhaps the best-known link is that between stress and health. But what is *stress?* To a large extent, it is subjective. What is a source of stress for one person may be a neutral or even positive experience for another. Effectively, then, *stress* may be defined as physical, mental, or emotional strain or tension. It has evolved as a shortened version of the word *distress*.

Many studies have linked the amount of stress people experience with negative health consequences. Sometimes, these negative consequences are the direct result of stress—for instance, developing cardiovascular disease as a result of having elevated blood pressure. In other cases, the health problems may stem from behaviors developed in response to stress, such as smoking out of nervousness and contracting lung cancer. Thus, an important factor in determining the impact of stress on health is one's ability to cope. Someone who has developed effective coping mechanisms in response to stress is less likely to develop stress-related health problems than someone with less effective coping mechanisms.

While the sources and manifestations of stress may be unique to each individual, certain factors seem to predispose most people to health risks. For example, anger and hostility have been linked to cardiovascular disease in numerous studies. Likewise, factors such as social isolation may not only predispose individuals to disease but also impair their recovery from illness.

A lot of health literature focuses on individual risk factors that may predispose someone to illness; however, it may be that the culture as a whole may be toxic in the sense that it promotes behaviors that ultimately compromise health. The following article by Tori Deangelis examines evidence that despite Americans' affluence, they may be less healthy than their foreign counterparts due largely to a set of cultural values that promotes material success over interpersonal connectedness.

America: A Toxic Lifestyle?

■ Tori Deangelis

It's no secret that the poor, uninsured, obese, heavy drinkers and smokers of the world tend to have the most health problems. However, cultural factors may be as important as these well-known health risks, according to a study that appeared last year in the *Journal of the American Medical Association* (Vol. 295, No. 17, pages 2037–2045). Simply living in America may be as risky as a diet of doughnuts and beer, researchers suggest.

In fact, study author epidemiologist Sir Michael Marmot, PhD, of University College London Medical School and his colleagues found that despite the fact that Americans spend 2.5 times more on health care, we are far sicker than the British in rates of diabetes, high blood pressure, heart disease, heart attack, stroke, lung disease and cancer. Unsurprisingly, the team also found that Americans are less healthy the farther down they are on the socioeconomic ladder. However, in absolute terms the richest, "healthiest" Americans are as sick as the poorest Brits, Marmot says.

"Why are rich people in [America] unhealthy too?" he asks. "That's the real puzzle."

Just as intriguingly, "the usual suspects" don't fully explain these differences—accounting for less than half of them, the team found. For instance, the British drink a little more alcohol than we do. And though Americans are more obese on average, the difference between American and British body mass indices doesn't account for all of the difference in chronic illness.

Marmot believes the psychic smog that's making Americans sick could be composed of two factors. One is that Americans' long work hours leave us more stressed and less healthy. The other is that Americans may feel friendless and isolated due to social stressors created by our country's widening income gap. In turn, that societal divisiveness may be bad for our health—not just poor people's health, but everyone's, he speculates.

NOMADS ON A TREADMILL

Currently Marmot can only guess why Americans are less healthy than physical measures suggest they should be. But psychologists have identified some intriguing possibilities.

In the realm of work stress, Marmot is right: We do work longer hours than people from other countries, observes cognitive psychologist Alan Hedge, PhD, a professor in Cornell University's department of design and environmental analysis.

International Labor Organization statistics show, for example, that we're more than twice as likely as Europeans to work 50 hours a week or more. Relatedly, downsizing and outsourcing have led to longer hours and more job insecurity for many Americans, and poorer Americans often work two jobs—a trend that is nearly unheard of in Britain, Hedge notes.

As a possible consequence of such factors, many Americans are obsessed with money, no matter how much or little they make, Hedge observes. "We're almost like a nomadic society on this treadmill, hoping that we'll either strike it rich with the lottery, or that if we work hard enough, somehow we'll become Google millionaires," he comments.

The way America deals with social building blocks such as health care, education and pensions compounds the problem, Hedge believes.

In England, for example, a university education costs about $3,000 a year, and everyone has access to adequate health insurance. British citizens must retire at age 65, with many companies encouraging earlier retirement, and they receive both a government and employer pension.

"And it's not linked to stock-market performance—your 401K doesn't evaporate because of the dirty dealings of an Enron!" he says.

By contrast, many Americans angst over how they can possibly make enough to cover insurance and other basics, while saving enough for retirement. In 2005, for instance, the average cost of a year at a private American college or university was $21,235, with some private institutions costing double that amount, statistics show.

ISOLATION NATION

Americans facing job insecurity and financial instability may lack sufficient social supports to help them through tough times, other observers say. While findings on our degree of isolation are mixed, a study in the June 2006 *American Sociological Review* (Vol. 71, No. 3, pages 353–375), by University of Arizona sociologist Miller McPherson, PhD, and colleagues, for instance, reports that Americans' network of confidantes dropped from about three to two people between 1985 and 2005. Meanwhile, a 2001 study by York University psychologist Ami Rokach, PhD, in *Social Behavior and Personality* (Vol. 29, No. 5, pages 477–489) found that North Americans scored higher than their Spanish counterparts on five factors related to the experience of loneliness, including feelings of social inadequacy and alienation, interpersonal isolation, and self-alienation.

Indeed, Americans with two jobs, for example, may not have the time to meet up with friends, says Hedge. Our tendency to pick up and move for new jobs, leaving friends and family behind, could also be a factor, undergirded by a culture that favors the individual over the group, adds psychologist, social observer and best-selling author Mary Pipher, PhD, whose most recent book is "Writing to Change the World" (Riverhead, 2006).

"We no longer live in a culture where we know most of the people we encounter," she says.

APA Task Force Report Decries Culture's Sexualization of Girls

—T. DeAngelis

One aspect of American culture that seems particularly toxic is the sexualization of young girls—whether it's marketing scantily clad dolls to 6-year-olds, thongs sized for grade-schoolers, or teens turning to heiress Paris Hilton and pop star Britney Spears as role models.

An APA task force has spent two years reviewing research on this phenomenon, and released a report on the topic in February.

Their findings? "We have ample evidence to conclude that sexualization has negative effects in a variety of domains, including cognitive functioning, physical and mental health, and healthy sexual development," says psychologist Eileen L. Lurbriggen, PhD, chair of the task force and associate professor of psychology at the University of California–Santa Cruz.

According to the task force, sexualization occurs when people value a woman or girl primarily for her sexual appeal or behavior; hold her to a narrow standard of beauty; equate her physical beauty with sexiness; view her as an object for sexual use; or inappropriately impose sexuality on her.

The six-member group pored over hundreds of studies to draw its conclusions, which it made in three areas:

■ **Prevalence.** The sexualization of women and young women in this country has, in fact, increased over time, says Zurbriggen. However, there is still little research in the area on young girls, though anecdotal evidence like the trend toward provocatively dressed dolls and sexy clothing marketed to young girls strongly suggests such a rise.

■ **Effects.** Sexualization has a range of negative consequences for young women, the task force finds. For instance, "studies show that when you begin to see yourself as a sex object, it leaves you with fewer cognitive resources to do things like math," Zurbriggen says. Sexualization also can lead to body shame, depression, eating disorders and low self-esteem, the report notes.

■ **Potential for progress.** There are a variety of steps parents, educators, policy makers and the media can rake to counteract this toxic trend, the report notes.

These include creating comprehensive sexuality-education programs for boys and girls that include a component on sexualization; adding media-literacy programs to school curricula; promoting healthy activities for girls, including athletics and art; and promoting religious or spiritual values that de-emphasize appearance and encourage qualities such as kindness, generosity and empathy.

The report also calls for more research on the topic, and for federal agencies to support the development of pro-girl programming aimed at counteracting the effects of sexualization.

The full task force report and an executive summary are available online at www.apa.org/pi/wpo/sexualization.html. Request hard copies by contacting the APA Women's Programs Office, at the APA address or at (202) 336–6050.

Indeed, the British and other Europeans place far more emphasis on social bonding than we do, Hedge says. Take the British pub: "The fact that you have a local place where neighbors go every night just to communicate—that seems to be completely different from the American approach where people vanish into their house at night and lock themselves in," he says. In fact, many studies show that compared with Americans, Europeans would rather forego more income for more leisure time, Marmot adds.

Is it possible such differences could affect a nation's health? Maybe, says Sheldon Cohen, PhD, professor of psychology at Carnegie Mellon University. In a 2005 study in *Health Psychology* (Vol. 24, No. 3, pages 297–306), for example, Cohen and colleagues found that first-year college students with smaller social networks and greater reported loneliness had a poorer immune response to flu vaccine than other students.

In related findings, people with the greatest number of social roles and domains of social connection are less likely to smoke and drink in the face of social pressure than those with less diverse networks, according to another forthcoming study by Cohen's team, also to appear in *Health Psychology.*

"We think the high-integration people may in fact be responding to social norms," Cohen says, "but to the larger norms of their network as a whole—to stay healthy and take care of yourself so you can take care of other people." By contrast, those low in social integration "may use smoking and drinking as a way of lubricating social interactions," he notes.

PASSING THE BUCKS?

Parents, both rich and poor, may be bequeathing this culture of stress to their children, adds Marin County, Calif., psychologist Madeline Levine, PhD, author of "The Price of Privilege: How Parental Pressure and Material Advantage Are Creating a Generation of Disconnected and Unhappy Kids" (HarperCollins, 2006).

Levine wrote her book after observing more and more well-off young people entering her office with depression, anxiety, loneliness and self-destructive behaviors, such as cutting, eating disorders and substance abuse. The epidemic, she thinks, results from messages from parents and teachers that tell children to excel and seek material success, even at the expense of healthy prosocial development—a phenomenon she calls "the culture of affluence." This trend isn't limited to wealthy families, she adds, but to any parents who tend to value material goods over relationships and competition over cooperation.

To begin to break up this consumeristic malaise that's poisoning Americans and their children, Levine teaches parents first to spend substantive, nonstressed time with their kids, and then to help them build relationships and become giving members of society—views she's sharing with sell-out crowds around the country.

"Research shows that a child's first community is their home," Levine says. "If they grow up believing they have a contribution to make, they'll have an easier time raising a family and being part of a community. I tell parents that if at the end of the day your kid doesn't have coping skills, it doesn't matter where he gets into school."

CRITICAL THINKING QUESTIONS

1. The article reports that most Americans would prefer to have more income over more leisure time. Based on your own observations of family and friends, do you agree with this proposition? Be specific in explaining why this may or may not be the case.

2. Do you think Americans are part of a so-called culture of affluence, one that values material success over interpersonal relationships? What evidence do you have to support or refute this concept? Be specific.

3. The box in the article also addresses the sexualization of girls in American culture. What examples can you cite to support this claim? What do you see as the possible negative outcomes of this trend? What, if anything, can be done about it?

4. The article maintains that, rich or poor, Americans' focus on wealth and work over interpersonal connectedness affects their health in negative ways. Is it possible to change cultural values such as these, or are they too entrenched to change? If they are possible to change, how might this be brought about? Be specific in your answers.

ARTICLE 44_____

Just about everyone these days accepts the idea that stress can cause illness. However, this concept was not always deemed to be true. In the past, it was commonly believed that illness was due to germs and organ pathology. There was not much focus on what was going on in a person's life that actually might be causing the illness.

A new view of the relationship between stress and illness was pioneered by the work of Hans Selye a half century ago. Selye defined *stress* as the body's physiological response to threatening events, whether physiological or psychological in nature. Thus, Selye was the first to clearly demonstrate that a purely psychological state, such as worrying too much about something, could produce a negative physiological state.

While Selye began to expand our understanding of how psychological states could produce physiological consequences, other researchers began to examine specifically what types of events might produce stress and consequently physical changes. The following classic article by Thomas H. Holmes and Richard H. Rahe represents the beginning of a line of research that tried to relate life events and health. Holmes and Rahe suggest that *stress* is the extent to which people have to readjust or change their lives in response to an outside event. Thus, a great deal of stress would be associated with a major life change, such as getting divorced, while considerably less stress would be associated with a lesser life change, such as getting a parking ticket. Furthermore, any life change, positive or negative, could produce such stress. Getting married, which involves many changes in a person's life, is a good example of how an event typically thought of as positive may nonetheless produce stress.

This article by Holmes and Rahe discusses the methodology that they used in developing their scale, which has been widely reproduced and used in many research studies. For example, several subsequent studies have found that the higher a person scores on this scale, the more likely his or her physical health will suffer.

Our understanding of the relationship between stress and health has become much more complex over the years. For example, the original Holmes and Rahe scale assumed that anyone experiencing a divorce would find that event to be extremely stressful. But isn't it possible that someone in a terribly abusive relationship might actually find that getting divorced lessens his or her stress? A critical factor may be our subjective interpretation of the events that we experience. That is, it may not be the event itself that causes stress but how we subjectively react to it. Certainly, a given event is not viewed the same by everyone who experiences it. While the Holmes and Rahe scale does not take this subjective reaction into account, it is nonetheless a good example of how the research on stress and health began.

The Social Readjustment Rating Scale[1]

■ Thomas H. Holmes and Richard H. Rahe

In previous studies [1] it has been established that a cluster of social events requiring change in ongoing life adjustment is significantly associated with the time of illness onset. Similarly, the relationship of what has been called 'life stress,' 'emotional stress,' 'object loss,' etc. and illness onset has been demonstrated by other investigations [2–13]. It has been adduced from these studies that this clustering of social or life events achieves etiologic significance as a necessary but not sufficient cause of illness and accounts in part for the time of onset of disease.

Methodologically, the interview or questionnaire technique used in these studies has yielded only the number and types of events making up the cluster. Some estimate of the magnitude of these events is now required to bring greater precision to this area of research and to provide a quantitative basis for new epidemiological studies of diseases. This report defines a method which achieves this requisite.

METHOD

A sample of convenience composed of 394 subjects completed the paper and pencil test (Table 1). (See Table 2 for characteristics of the sample.) The items were the 43 life events empirically derived from clinical experience. The following written instructions were given to each subject who completed the Social Rating Questionnaire (SRRQ).

(A) Social readjustment includes the amount and duration of change in one's accustomed pattern of life resulting from various life events. As defined, social readjustment measures the intensity and length of time necessary to accommodate to a life event, *regardless of the desirability of this event.*

(B) You are asked to rate a series of life events as to their relative degrees of necessary readjustment. In scoring, *use all of your experience* in arriving at your answer. This means personal experience where it applies as well as what you have learned to be the case for others. Some persons accommodate to change more readily than others; some persons adjust with particular ease or difficulty to only certain events. Therefore, strive to give your opinion of the average degree of readjustment necessary for each event rather than the extreme.

(C) The mechanics of rating are these: Event 1, Marriage, has been given an arbitrary value of 500. As you complete each of the remaining events think to yourself, "Is this event indicative of more or less readjustment than marriage?" "Would the readjustment take longer or shorter to accomplish?" If you decide the readjustment is more intense and protracted, then choose a *proportionately larger* number and place it in the blank directly opposite the event in the column marked "VALUES." If you decide the event represents less and shorter readjustment than marriage then indicate how much less by placing a *proportionately smaller* number in the opposite blank. (If an event requires intense readjustment over a short time span, it may approximate in value an event requiring less intense readjustment over a long period of time.) If the event is equal in social readjustment to marriage, record the number 500 opposite the event.

The order in which the items were presented is shown in Table 1.

RESULTS

The Social Readjustment Rating Scale (SRRS) is shown in Table 3. This table contains the magnitude of the life events which is derived when the mean score, divided by 10, of each item for the entire sample is calculated and arranged in rank order. That consensus is high concerning the relative order and magnitude of the means of items is demonstrated by the high coefficients of correlation (Pearson's *r*) between the dis-

This article was published in *Journal of Psychosomatic Research,* vol. 11, by T. H. Holmes and R. H. Rahe, "The Social Readjustment Rating Scale," pp. 213–218, Copyright Elsevier 1967.

TABLE 1 / Social Readjustment Rating Questionnaire

Events	Values
1. Marriage	500
2. Troubles with the boss	—
3. Detention in jail or other institution	—
4. Death of spouse	—
5. Major change in sleeping habits (a lot more or a lot less sleep, or change in part of day when asleep)	—
6. Death of a close family member	—
7. Major change in eating habits (a lot more or a lot less food intake, or very different meal hours or surroundings)	—
8. Foreclosure on a mortgage or loan	—
9. Revision of personal habits (dress, manners, associations, etc.)	—
10. Death of a close friend	—
11. Minor violations of the law (e.g. traffic tickets, jay walking, disturbing the peace, etc.)	—
12. Outstanding personal achievement	—
13. Pregnancy	—
14. Major change in the health or behavior of a family member	—
15. Sexual difficulties	—
16. In-law troubles	—
17. Major change in number of family get-togethers (e.g. a lot more or a lot less than usual)	—
18. Major change in financial state (e.g. a lot worse off or a lot better off than usual)	—
19. Gaining a new family member (e.g. through birth, adoption, oldster moving in, etc.)	—
20. Change in residence	—
21. Son or daughter leaving home (e.g. marriage, attending college, etc.)	—
22. Marital separation from mate	—
23. Major change in church activities (e.g. a lot more or a lot less than usual)	—
24. Marital reconciliation with mate	—
25. Being fired from work	—
26. Divorce	—
27. Changing to a different line of work	—
28. Major change in the number of arguments with spouse (e.g. either a lot more or a lot less than usual, regarding childrearing, personal habits, etc.)	—
29. Major change in responsibilities at work (e.g. promotion, demotion, lateral transfer)	—
30. Wife beginning or ceasing work outside the home	—
31. Major change in working hours or conditions	—
32. Major change in usual type and/or amount of recreation	—
33. Taking on a mortgage greater than $10,000 (e.g. purchasing a home, business, etc.)	—
34. Taking on a mortgage or loan less than $10,000 (e.g. purchasing a car, TV, freezer, etc.)	—
35. Major personal injury or illness	—
36. Major business readjustment (e.g. merger, reorganization, bankruptcy, etc.)	—
37. Major change in social activities (e.g. clubs, dancing, movies, visiting, etc.)	—
38. Major change in living conditions (e.g. building a new home, remodeling, deterioration of home or neighborhood)	—
39. Retirement from work	—
40. Vacation	—
41. Christmas	—
42. Changing to a new school	—
43. Beginning or ceasing formal schooling	—

TABLE 2 / Pearson's Coefficient of Correlation between Discrete Groups in the Sample

Group	No. in Group		Group	No. in Group	Coefficient of Correlation
Male	179	vs.	Female	215	0·965
Single	171	vs.	Married	223	0·960
Age < 30	206	vs.	Age 30–60	137	0·958
Age < 30	206	vs.	Age > 60	51	0·923
Age 30–60	137	vs.	Age > 60	51	0·965
1st Generation	19	vs.	2nd Generation	69	0·908
1st Generation	19	vs.	3rd Generation	306	0·929
2nd Generation	69	vs.	3rd Generation	306	0·975
< College	182	vs.	4 Years of College	212	0·967
Lower class	71	vs	Middle class	323	0·928
White	363	vs.	Negro	19	0·820
White	363	vs.	Oriental	12	0·940
Protestant	241	vs.	Catholic	42	0·913
Protestant	241	vs.	Jewish	19	0·971
Protestant	241	vs.	Other religion	45	0·948
Protestant	241	vs.	No religious preference	47	0·926

crete groups contained in the sample. Table 2 reveals that all the coefficients of correlation are above 0·90 with the exception of that between white and Negro which was 0·82. Kendall's coefficient of concordance (*W*) for the 394 individuals was 0·477, significant at $p = < 0.0005$.

DISCUSSION

Placed in historical perspective, this research evolved from the chrysalis of Psychobiology generated by Adolph Meyer [14]. His invention of the 'life chart,' a device for organizing the medical data as a dynamic biography, provided a unique method for demonstrating his schema of the relationship of biological, psychological, and sociological phenomena to the processes of health and disease in man. The importance of many of the life events used in this research was emphasized by Meyer: ". . . changes of habitat, of school entrance, graduations or changes or failures; the various jobs, the dates of possibly important births and deaths in the family, and other fundamentally important environmental influences" [14].

More recently, in Harold G. Wolff's laboratory,[2] the concepts of Pavlov, Freud, Cannon and Skin-

ner were incorporated in the Meyerian schema. The research resulting from this synthesis adduced powerful evidence that 'stressful' life events, by evoking psychophysiologic reactions, played an important causative role in the natural history of many diseases [15–19]. Again, many of the life events denoted 'stressful' were those enumerated by Meyers and in Table 1 of this report.

Beginning in this laboratory in 1949, the life chart device has been used systematically in over 5000 patients to study the quality and quantity of life events empirically observed to cluster at the time of disease onset. Inspection of Table 1 reveals that each item derived from this experience is unique. There are 2 categories of items: those indicative of the life style of the individual, and those indicative of occurrences involving the individual. Evolving mostly from ordinary, but some from extraordinary, social and interpersonal transactions, these events pertain to major areas of dynamic significance in the social structure of the American way of life. These include family constellation, marriage, occupation, economics, residence, group and peer relationships, education, religion, recreation and health.

TABLE 3 / Social Readjustment Rating Scale

Rank	Life Event	Mean Value
1	Death of spouse	100
2	Divorce	73
3	Marital separation	65
4	Jail term	63
5	Death of close family member	63
6	Personal injury or illness	53
7	Marriage	50
8	Fired at work	47
9	Marital reconciliation	45
10	Retirement	45
11	Change in health of family member	44
12	Pregnancy	40
13	Sex difficulties	39
14	Gain of new family member	39
15	Business readjustment	39
16	Change in financial state	38
17	Death of close friend	37
18	Change to different line of work	36
19	Change in number of arguments with spouse	35
20	Mortgage over $10,000	31
21	Foreclosure of mortgage or loan	30
22	Change in responsibilities at work	29
23	Son or daughter leaving home	29
24	Trouble with in-laws	29
25	Outstanding personal achievement	28
26	Wife begin or stop work	26
27	Begin or end school	26
28	Change in living conditions	25
29	Revision of personal habits	24
30	Trouble with boss	23
31	Change in work hours or conditions	20
32	Change in residence	20
33	Change in schools	20
34	Change in recreation	19
35	Change in church activities	19
36	Change in social activities	18
37	Mortgage or loan less than $10,000	17
38	Change in sleeping habits	16
39	Change in number of family get-togethers	15
40	Change in eating habits	15
41	Vacation	13
42	Christmas	12
43	Minor violations of the law	11

During the developmental phase of this research the interview technique was used to assess the meaning of the events for the individual. As expected, the

psychological significance and emotions varied widely with the patient. Also it will be noted that only some of the events are negative or 'stressful' in the conventional sense, i.e. are socially undesirable. Many are socially desirable and consonant with the American values of achievement, success, materialism, practicality, efficiency, future orientation, conformism and self-reliance.

There was identified, however, one theme common to all these life events. The occurrence of each usually evoked or was associated with some adaptive or coping behavior on the part of the involved individual. Thus, each item has been constructed to contain life events whose advent is either indicative of or requires a significant change in the ongoing life pattern of the individual. The emphasis is on change from the existing steady state and not on psychological meaning, emotion, or social desirability.

The method for assigning a magnitude to the items was developed for use in Psychophysics—the study of the psychological perception of the quality, quantity, magnitude, intensity of physical phenomena. This subjective assessment of the observer plotted against the physical dimension being perceived (length of objects, intensity of sound, brightness of light, number of objects, etc.) provides a reliable delineation of man's ability to quantify certain of his experiences [20]. In this research, the assumption was made that participants in the contemporary American way of life could utilize this innate psychological capacity for making quantitative judgments about psychosocial phenomena as well as psychophysical phenomena [21, 22]. The data generated by this investigation appear to justify the assumption. Although some of the discrete subgroups do assign a different order and magnitude to the items, it is the degree of similarity between the populations within the sample that is impressive. The high degree of consensus also suggests a universal agreement between groups and among individuals about the significance of the life events under study that transcends differences in age, sex, marital status, education, social class, generation American, religion and race.

The method used in this research, when applied to psychophysical phenomena, generates a ratio scale. A discussion of whether or not the magnitudes assigned to the items in Table 3 actually constitute a ratio scale is beyond the intent of this report [21, 22]. However, this issue will be dealt with in a subsequent report [23].

REFERENCES

1. Rahe R. H., Meyer M., Smith M., Kjaer G. and Holmes T. H. Social stress and illness onset. *J. Psychosom. Res. 8*, 35 (1964).

2. Graham D. T. and Stevenson I. Disease as response to life stress. In *The Psychological Basis of Medical Practice* (H. I. Lief, V. F. Lief, and N. R. Lief, Eds.) Harper & Row, New York (1963).

3. Greene W. A., Jr. Psychological factors and reticulo-endothelial disease—I. Preliminary observations on a group of males with lymphomas and leukemias. *Psychosom. Med. 16*, 220 (1954).

4. Greene W. A. Jr., Young L. E. and Swisher S. N. Psychological factors and reticulo-endothelial disease—II. Observations on a group of women with lymphomas and leukemias. *Psychosom. Med. 18*, 284 (1956).

5. Greene W. A., Jr. and Miller G. Psychological factors and reticulo-endothelial disease—IV. Observations on a group of children and adolescents with leukemia: an interpretation of disease development in terms of the mother-child unit. *Psychosom. Med. 20*, 124 (1958).

6. Weiss E., Dlin B., Rollin H. R., Fischer H. K. and Bepler C. R. Emotional factors in coronary occlusion. *A.M.A. Archs. Internal Med. 99*, 628 (1957).

7. Fischer H. K., Dlin B., Winters W., Hagner S. and Weiss E. Time patterns and emotional factors related to the onset of coronary occlusion. [Abstract] *Psychosom. Med. 24*, 516 (1962).

8. Kissen D. M. Specific psychological factors in pulmonary tuberculosis. *Hlth Bull. Edinburgh 14*, 44 (1956).

9. Kissen D. M. Some psychosocial aspects of pulmonary tuberculosis. *Int. J. Soc. Psychiat. 3*, 252 (1958).

10. Hawkins N. G., Davies R. and Holmes T. H. Evidence of psychosocial factors in the development of pulmonary tuberculosis. *Am. Rev. Tuberc. Pulmon. Dis. 75*, 5 (1957).

11. Smith M. Psychogenic factors in skin disease, Medical Thesis, University of Washington, Seattle (1962).

12. Rare R. H. and Holmes T. H. Social, psychologic and psychophysiologic aspects of inguinal hernia. *J. Psychosom. Res. 8*, 487 (1965).

13. Kjaer G. Some psychosomatic aspects of pregnancy with particular reference to nausea and vomiting, Medical Thesis, University of Washington, Seattle (1959).

14. Lief A. (Ed.) *The Commonsense Psychiatry of Dr. Adolf Meyer,* McGraw-Hill, New York (1948).

15. Wolff H. G., Wolf S. and Hare C. C. (Eds.) *Life Stress and Bodily Disease,* Res. Publs. Ass. Res. Nerv. Ment. Dis. Vol. 29. Williams & Wilkins, Baltimore (1950).

16. Holmes T. H., Goodell H., Wolf S. and Wolff H. G. *The Nose. An Experimental Study of Reactions Within the Nose in Human Subjects During Varying Life Experiences,* Charles C. Thomas, Springfield, Illinois (1950).

17. Wolf S. *The Stomach,* Oxford University Press, New York (1965).

18. Wolf S., Cardon P. V., Shepard E. M., and Wolff H. G. *Life Stress and Essential Hypertension,* Williams & Wilkins, Baltimore (1955).

19. Grace W. J., Wolf S. and Wolff H. G. *The Human Colon,* Paul B. Hoeber, New York (1951).

20. Stevens S. S. and Galanter E. H. Ratio scales and category scales for a dozen perceptual continua. *J. Exp. Psychol. 54*, 377 (1957).

21. Sellin T. and Wolfgang M. E. *The Measurement of Delinquency,* John Wiley, New York (1964).

22. Stevens S. S. A metric for the social consensus. *Science 151*, 530 (1966).

23. Masuda M. and Holmes T. H. This issue, p. 219.

ENDNOTES

1. This investigation was supported in part by Public Health Service Undergraduate Training in Psychiatry Grant No. 5-T2-MH-5939-13 and Undergraduate Training in Human Behavior Grant No. 5-T2-MH-7871-03 from the National Institute of Mental Health; O'Donnell Psychiatric Research Fund; and The Scottish Rite Committee for Research in Schizophrenia.

2. Harold G. Wolff, M.D. (1898–1962) was Anne Parrish Titzell, Professor of Medicine (Neurology), Cornell University Medical College and the New York Hospital.

CRITICAL THINKING QUESTIONS

1. Examine the methodology that Homes and Rahe used. For example, subjects were asked not only how stressful they found the events to be but also how stressful they thought other people typically found the events to be. Is this a problem? If so, why? If not, why

not? What other issues in how Holmes and Rahe collected their data might limit the conclusions that they have drawn? Be specific in your answers.

2. Examine the items on the Social Readjustment Rating Scale (Table 3). Are any "life events" missing from the scale that you think are important stressors? If so, what are they, and why are they important? Why do you think these items were not included in the original scale?

3. The introduction to the article mentioned how the subjective perception of events may be more critical in determining stress reactions than the objective events themselves. In other words, not everyone reacts to the same situation in the same manner. Select an item from the scale, and give a concrete example of how you have seen two people react to it in very different ways.

4. According to this scale, getting married is more stressful than getting fired and hence more likely to cause physical illness. Do you accept the premise that *positive* life events, such as getting married, are just as stressful as *negative* life events, such as getting fired? Why or why not? If positive life events cause stress and hence illness, why do people seek them out in the first place? Explain your reasoning.

ADDITIONAL RELATED READINGS

Lynch, D. J., McGrady, A., Alvarez, E., & Forman, J. (2005). Recent life changes and medical utilization in an academic family practice. *Journal of Nervous and Mental Disorders, 193*(9), 633–635.

Scully, J. A., Tosi, H., & Banning, K. (2000). Life events checklist: Revisiting the Social Readjustment Rating Scale after 30 years. *Educational and Psychological Measurement, 60*(6), 864–876.

ARTICLE 45 _____

Do you remember exactly where you were and what you were doing when you first heard of the terrorist attacks on September 11, 2001? For most people in the United States, and indeed the world, the destruction of the World Trade Center in New York City and the attack on the Pentagon in Arlington, Virginia, are events they will always remember. Whether we were 10 or 10,000 miles away from the horrific events of that day, few of us can say that we were not profoundly affected by them.

Given the impact of the events of 9-11, it only stands to reason that they represented a stressor in the lives of many people. Obviously, the more directly affected someone was by the attacks—such as knowing a person who was killed or injured—the more stressful the events were. But even people far removed from the events were profoundly affected. And so, the events of 9-11 were believed to be a major stressor and, as such, to have many negative effects on people's psychological well-being and physical health.

At least, that was what common sense and much media reporting reasoned. In the weeks, months, and years following the events of 9-11 (and other terrorist acts as well, such as the Madrid train bombings), commentators and experts alike took to the press and the airwaves to discuss how these events were going to affect us all. In particular, they claimed, children's sense of safety and security would be greatly diminished in the aftermath.

But do you think that all of the people who witnessed the events of 9-11 were affected in the same way? Current thinking on the impact of stress is that the subjective interpretation we make of the events is what causes stress, rather than the events per se. Thus, two people experiencing the same event could react quite differently to it, depending on their individual subjective interpretations of it.

The following article by George A. Bonanno, Sandro Galea, Angela Bucciarelli, and David Vlahov examines the resilience of the population exposed to the September 11 terrorist attack. Most studies on reaction to trauma have focused on the symptoms or problems people experience after being exposed to trauma. This study, in a sense, focuses on the opposite question: Namely, how many people were resilient to the traumatic event and did not experience any negative effects? The surprising (and optimistic) findings are that more people than we may think are capable of dealing with traumatic situations in positive ways.

Psychological Resilience after Disaster
New York City in the Aftermath of the September 11th Terrorist Attack

■ George A. Bonanno, Sandro Galea, Angela Bucciarelli, and David Vlahov

ABSTRACT

Research on adult reactions to potentially traumatic events has focused almost exclusively on post-traumatic stress disorder (PTSD). Although there has been relatively *little research on the absence of trauma symptoms, the available evidence suggests that resilience following such events may be more prevalent than previously believed.*

Bonanno, G. A., Galea, S., Bucciarelli, A., & Vlahov, D. (2006). Psychological resilience after disaster: New York City in the aftermath of the September 11th terrorist attack. *Psychological Science, 17*(3), 181–186. Copyright © 2006 by American Psychological Society. Reprinted with permission of Blackwell Publishers.

*This study examined the prevalence of resilience, defined as having either no PTSD symptoms or one symptom, among a large (*n = 2,752*) probability sample of New York area residents during the 6 months following the September 11th terrorist attack. Although many respondents met criteria for PTSD, particularly when exposure was high, resilience was observed in 65.1% of the sample. Resilience was less prevalent among more highly exposed individuals, but the frequency of resilience never fell below one third even among the exposure groups with the most dramatic elevations in PTSD.*

Bad things happen, and unfortunately they happen to most people. Epidemiological studies indicate that the majority of adults are exposed to at least one potentially traumatic event (PTE; e.g., physical or sexual assault or a life-threatening accident) in their lifetimes. However, not everyone reacts to PTEs in the same way, and although most people experience distress and confusion, typically only a small subset of exposed adults develop posttraumatic stress disorder (PTSD; Kessler, Sonnega, Bromet, Hughes, & Nelson, 1995). Given the health costs associated with severe trauma reactions, it is not surprising that a vast literature on PTSD and its treatment has arisen (McNally, 2003). However, one consequence of this focus is that relatively little is known about the adult capacity to maintain healthy, symptom-free functioning, or *resilience,* following PTEs.

For decades, developmental researchers have documented the prevalence of resilience among children growing up in caustic socioeconomic circumstances (Garmezy, 1991; Luthar, Doernberger, & Zigler, 1993; Masten, 2001; Rutter, 1987). Although fewer and farther between, studies of adults have also documented the pervasiveness of resilience following PTEs (Bonanno, 2004; Rachman, 1978) and highlighted the distinction between resilient individuals and those who show a more gradual recovery from trauma (Bonanno, 2004). Nonetheless, the empirical reality of this distinction is still poorly understood. Trauma investigators have often used the terms resilience and recovery somewhat interchangeably (McFarlane & Yehuda, 1996) or simply pooled these different types of outcome into a single, non-PTSD category (King, King, Foy, Keane, & Fairbank, 1999). And in the absence of an adequate database for the normal range

of trauma reactions, the near or complete absence of trauma symptoms had been commonly assumed to occur only in people with exceptional physical or emotional strength (Casella & Motta, 1990; McFarlane & Yehuda, 1996; Tucker et al., 2002). Even theorists sympathetic to the idea of adult resilience have tended to remain skeptical about its prevalence in the context of exposure to extreme stressor events (Litz, 2005; Roisman, 2005).

To date, the most explicit and systematic research on adult resilience has focused on one particular type of PTE: the death of a spouse. A growing number of prospective studies have shown, for example, that even in the early months following a spouse's death, many and sometimes the majority of bereaved individuals exhibit few or no overt symptoms of psychopathology and continue to function at or near their normal level across time (Bonanno, Moskowitz, Papa, & Folkman, 2005; Bonanno et al., 2002).

A comparable body of evidence on adult resilience in the aftermath of potentially more traumatic life events is not yet available. Proponents of the broader application of the resilience construct have tended to rely on estimates from previously published trauma studies (Bonanno, 2004; Rachman, 1978). Yet these estimates suffer from inherent methodological limitations. For example, many early studies cited as evidence for widespread resilience (Rachman, 1978) were based on retrospective and unsystematic assessments. Recent trauma studies (Bryant, Harvey, Guthrie, & Moulds, 2000), although more systematic, typically report only proportions of PTSD diagnosis and not data necessary to establish the presence of resilience. Several studies have explicitly examined adult resilience to PTEs using prospective or longitudinal designs (Bonanno, Rennicke, & Dekel, 2005; Saigh, 1988). However, these studies used small samples that limit generalizability and preclude examination of variations in exposure.

The potential implications of widespread adult resilience, coupled with the limitations of the existing evidence, suggest a need for more systematic research. Ideally, such research would involve a large, randomly selected sample representative of the broader population. The sample should vary in level of exposure to an isolated PTE of at least sufficient magnitude to produce PTSD reactions in a subset of individuals.

However, sufficient data should be available to permit examination of the full range of trauma reactions, from PTSD to the absence of trauma symptoms. Finally, it should be possible to examine how the range of trauma reactions varies in relation to demographics and levels of exposure.

We were able to meet these criteria in the current study by examining PTSD symptoms among a large probability sample of people living in or near New York City at the time of the September 11th terrorist attack (Galea, Ahern, et al., 2002; Galea, Resnick, et al., 2002; Galea et al., 2003). Few people would question the potentially traumatic nature of the September 11th attack. Although the probable prevalence of PTSD for the New York metropolitan area during the first 6 months after the attack was estimated at 6.0% (Galea et al., 2003), PTSD estimates were considerably higher among people most directly exposed during the attack. Nonetheless, a recent study using a relatively small high-exposure sample (N = 54) of people who had been in or near the World Trade Center (WTC) during the attack indicated that more than one third (35%) exhibited few or no PTSD symptoms (Bonanno, Rennicke, & Dekel, 2005).

In determining the cutoff for resilience in the current study, we considered that even ostensibly healthy individuals sometimes exhibit low levels of psychiatric symptoms (Bonanno, Moskowitz, et al., 2005; Judd, Akiskal, & Paulus, 1997). The PTSD diagnosis comprises 17 symptoms, which include nonspecific symptoms (e.g., difficulty sleeping) that may be present even in the absence of trauma exposure. When PTSD symptoms were assessed in the absence of trauma exposure, the normal range was found to be 2 or fewer symptoms (Bonanno, Moskowitz, et al., 2005). Studies of subthreshold depression have typically set a more conservative criterion for the absence of depression as 1 or 0 symptoms (Judd et al., 1997), and the same criterion has been used to determine resilience during bereavement (Zisook, Paulus, Shuchter, & Judd, 1997). Therefore, in the current study, we adopted this more conservative definition. Specifically, we defined *resilience* as 1 or 0 PTSD symptoms and *recovery* from trauma as 2 or more PTSD symptoms in the absence of the PTSD diagnosis. We then assessed the proportions of the sample exhibiting resilience, recovery, or a probable PTSD diagnosis across different demographic and exposure categories.

METHOD AND RESULTS

Participants were contacted by random digit dial approximately 6 months after September 11th. The sampling frame included all adults in New York City and contiguous geographic areas in New York State, New Jersey, and Lower Fairfield County in Connecticut. Participants were interviewed in English, Spanish, Mandarin, and Cantonese, using translated and back-translated questionnaires and a computer-assisted telephone interview system. The overall cooperation rate was 56%, and the overall response rate (the sum of the number of completed and partial interviews divided by the sum of all numbers that were either eligible as residential telephone numbers or of unknown eligibility) was 34%. Sampling weights were used to correct for potential selection biases related to the number of household telephones, the number of persons in the household, and oversampling (see Galea et al., 2003). The final sample (N = 2,752) adequately represented the broader New York population, as evidenced by comparison with the most recent census data (see Table 1). Of particular importance, the sample included a diverse spectrum of potential trauma experience both during the attack (e.g., being in the WTC at the time) and in its aftermath (e.g., losing possessions).

PTSD symptoms since September 11th were assessed using the National Women's Study PTSD module. This module showed good construct validity in previous research and was validated in a field trial (Kilpatrick et al., 1998), demonstrating that it has a sensitivity of 99% and specificity of 79% when compared against PTSD from the Structured Clinical Interview for DSM-III-R (Spitzer, Williams, Gibbon, & First, 1990). Both the 6-month cumulative PTSD estimates and raw PTSD symptom totals were found to be highly reliable with PTSD estimates obtained from similar samples 1 and 4 months after September 11th (Resnick, Galea, Kilpatrick, & Vlahov, 2004).

Despite our conservative definition for resilience, 65.1%[1] of the respondents *(n = 1,672)* had one or no PTSD symptoms during the first 6 months and thus provided striking evidence of an overall adjustment

TABLE 1 / Comparison of the Current Sample with 2000 Census Data for New York City

Category	Current Sample (%)	Census 2000 (%)
Gender		
Male	46.1	46.9
Female	53.9	53.1
Age		
18–24	13.7	11.7
25–34	24.1	20.4
35–44	20.5	21.9
45–54	18.9	17.7
55–64	12.2	11.8
65+	10.5	16.5
Race		
White	53.2	54.8
African American	16.7	16.5
Hispanic	20.6	18.5
Asian	5.4	7.7
Other	4.2	2.6

in the sample. Although there was variation in the prevalence of resilience across demographic categories (see Table 2), resilience remained high (over 50%) in all categories except Staten Island residents (48.0%) and unmarried couples (39.1%).

Although, as expected, there was meaningful variation in resilience, recovery, and PTSD proportions across the different exposure groups (see Table 3), we were particularly interested in resilience following different types of exposure, especially in categories that resulted in high rates of PTSD. The overall pattern of findings was consistent with the view that resilience is prevalent even among the most highly exposed individuals (Bonanno, 2004). Across the range of exposure conditions, the prevalence of resilience was more than 50% in most categories and never fell below one third even in exposure categories that generated the greatest proportion of probable PTSD. For example, more than half of the people who saw the attack in person or experienced the death of a friend or rela-

tive in the attack were resilient. Of particular interest were the two relatively small groups that had the highest proportions of probable PTSD: people who were physically injured ($n = 59$) or in the WTC ($n = 22$) during the attack. Although 26.1% of the respondents who were physically injured had probable PTSD, approximately one third (32.8%) in this category were resilient. The findings for respondents who were in the WTC at the time of the attack were even more compelling; 25.4% in this category had probable PTSD, yet more than half in this category (53.5%) were resilient.

The exposure categories were created so as to be relatively exclusive. However, the most widely represented category, people who saw the WTC attacks in person ($n = 798$), overlapped sufficiently with two other categories (people who lost a friend or relative in the attack and people who were involved in the rescue effort) to permit analyses of compound exposure.

Although in both of these latter groups the prevalence of resilience was above 50%, resilience was reduced among individuals with compound exposure, as in previous research (Bonanno, Rennicke, & Dekel, 2005). More than half (51.2%) of the respondents who were involved in the rescue effort ($n = 296$) were resilient. However, resilience was about 10 percentage points less prevalent (40.3%) for respondents who both were involved in the rescue effort and had seen the attack in person ($n = 119$). The effect of compound exposure was even more pronounced for people who had experienced the death of a friend or relative ($n = 392$); 53.9% in this category were resilient, whereas for respondents who both experienced the death of a friend or relative and saw the attack in person ($n = 142$), 33.4% were resilient.

DISCUSSION

On the, whole, these findings demonstrate widespread resilience in the New York City area during the 6 months after the September 11th attack. Even among the groups with the most pernicious levels of exposure and highest rate of PTSD, the proportion that was resilient never dropped below one third. Of particular interest, although the exposure categories that generated the highest estimates of probable PTSD tended to have lower levels of resilience than other categories,

TABLE 2 / Prevalence of Resilience across Demographic Categories

Category	n	Resilience (0 or 1 PTSD Symptom) n	Resilience (0 or 1 PTSD Symptom) %	Category	n	Resilience (0 or 1 PTSD Symptom) n	Resilience (0 or 1 PTSD Symptom) %
Gender***				**Marital status*****			
Male	1,273	858	71.3	Married	1,182	786	70.0
Female	1,479	814	59.8	Divorced	271	144	57.1
Age***				Separated	85	46	52.8
18–24	261	163	62.2	Widowed	182	117	65.2
25–34	667	360	57.7	Never married	927	525	62.5
35–44	598	368	68.4	Unmarried couple	93	47	39.1
45–54	521	294	62.2	**Living location*****			
55–64	333	214	69.4	Proximity to World Trade Center			
65+	341	256	79.5	Manhattan below 14th St.	669	342	54.5
Race***				Other	2,083	1,330	65.3
White	1,592	986	67.8	Borough			
African American	391	238	64.1	Bronx	85	51	58.6
Asian	166	126	82.3	Brooklyn	347	186	54.8
Hispanic	465	243	56.3	Queens	167	95	61.2
Other	91	47	53.2	Manhattan	907	485	58.7
Income*				Staten Island	64	30	48.0
< $20,000	400	214	58.3.	**State****			
$20,000–$29,999	242	145	63.1	Connecticut	53	36	73.3
$30,000–$39,999	270	143	59.2	New Jersey	66	451	69.5
$40,000–$49,999	195	124	64.3	New York	2,037	1,185	62.9
$50,000–$74,999	392	229	63.4	New York City**			
$75,000–$99,999	272	160	58.9	Yes	1,570	847	57.7
$100,000+	497	320	72.6	No	1,182	825	71.2
Education*							
No high school diploma	274	156	56.8				
High school or general equivalency diploma	600	376	65.2				
Some college	517	304	62.9				
College degree	875	521	65.8				
Graduate degree	469	301	72.3				

Note. The percentages shown reflect weighted proportions. Asterisks indicate a significant nonchance chi-square distribution within the category. PTSD = posttraumatic stress disorder.

$^*p_{rep} > .87.$ $^{**}p_{rep} > .95.$ $^{***}p_{rep} > .97.$

TABLE 3 / Prevalence of Resilience, Recovery from Trauma, and Probable PTSD across Exposure Categories

Exposure	*n*	Resilience (0 or 1 PTSD Symptom)			Recovery from Trauma (≥ 2 PTSD Symptoms)			Probable PTSD Related to the Attack		
		n	%	p_{rep}	*n*	%	p_{rep}	*n*	%	p_{rep}
Total sample	2,752	1,672	65.1	> .99	863	28.9	> .99	217	6.0	> .99
Saw attacks in person from outside WTC	798	396	55.6	> .99	289	31.9	> .87	113	12.5	> .99
In WTC	22	10	53.5	n.s.	5	21.1	n.s.	7	25.4	> .95
Friend or relative killed	392	192	53.9	> .99	151	34.9	> .87	49	11.2	> .95
Loss of possessions	105	41	42.6	> .95	35	36.0	n.s.	29	21.4	> .99
Physically injured	59	16	32.8	> .99	25	41.0	n.s.	18	26.1	> .99
Involved in rescue	296	141	51.2	> .99	110	37.0	> .87	45	11.8	> .95
Lost employment	147	54	39.1	> .99	64	43.4	> .95	29	17.5	> .99
Involved in rescue and saw attack	119	52	40.3	> .99	64	45.2	> .95	26	14.5	> .95
Friend or relative killed and saw attack	142	38	33.4	> .99	49	35.4	n.s.	32	31.3	> .99

Note. The percentages shown reflect weighted proportions. The p_{rep} values represent significant differences in chi-square tests comparing each group with all other groups combined. PTSD = posttraumatic stress disorder; WTC = World Trade Center.

the concordance between PTSD prevalence and resilience prevalence was far from perfect. For example, PTSD was almost twice as common in respondents who were in the WTC at the time of the attack compared with those who witnessed the attacks in person from outside the WTC. However, more than half the respondents in both groups were resilient. Similarly, although people who were physically injured had a relatively high PTSD prevalence (26.1%) and a relatively low resilience prevalence (32.8%), respondents who had lost possessions in the attack also had a high PTSD prevalence (21.4%) but were more resilient (42.6%).

The design of the current study made it possible to address the methodological limitations of previous studies. However, this design also generated its own limitations; most notably, although the measure of PTSD used had adequate reliability and validity, because these data were collected by telephone interview, more thorough clinical judgments about func-

tioning or the relative absence of PTSD symptoms were not possible. Another limitation, inherent in the use of a large probability sample, is that our operational definition of resilience was restricted. However, when we explored using either a more stringent or a more liberal definition of resilience, the results did not change meaningfully. For example, because some respondents may have been depressed even in the absence of PTSD symptoms, we tried further narrowing the definition of resilience to include the absence of depression. However, this added restriction did not appreciably lower the proportions of resilience across exposure categories. We also explored expanding the definition of resilience to include individuals with up to two PTSD symptoms. This more liberal definition did increase the proportion of resilience across the entire sample from 65.1% to 73.2%, and also increased resilience for some types of exposure (e.g., the prevalence of resilience for people with a friend or relative who was killed in the attack increased from

53.9% to 62.0%). However, increases were not uniform across exposure categories (e.g., the prevalence of resilience among people who were physically injured in the attack increased only slightly from 32.8% to 33.1%). Thus, the original cutoff of one or no symptoms produced a relatively stable, albeit conservative, pattern of findings and seems preferable for considering resilience in a general population sample.

These data, of course, do not solve the controversy about adult resilience to PTEs. They do, however, provide the most convincing data to date indicating that resilience is prevalent even following the most pernicious and potentially traumatic levels of exposure, and they are compatible with results of studies examining resilience using different types of outcome measures (Bonanno, Moskowitz, et al., 2005; Bonanno, Rennicke, & Dekel, 2005). It is our hope that future research will help untangle how both level and nature of exposure may influence the relation between resilience on the one hand and clinically relevant trauma reactions on the other. Additionally, if resilience is not limited to exceptionally healthy individuals, then as preliminary research has shown (Bonanno, Rennicke, & Dekel, 2005), there are probably many different ways to be resilient (Bonanno, 2004). A greater understanding of resilient functioning could shed light on new avenues for preparation and training in anticipation of expectable PTEs (e.g., war, terrorist attack) and could bolster arguments against the use of wholesale prophylactic psychological interventions in the aftermath of trauma (McNally, Bryant, & Ehlers, 2003). From a public-health standpoint, clear evidence for resilience would indicate a need to reconceptualize resource allocation and timing, as well as mental health practices and policies, following natural disasters or major terrorist attacks (van Ommeren, Saxena, & Saraceno, 2005; World Health Organization, 2003). Perhaps a silver lining of the terror of September 11th will be that the resilience observed in the New York area will inspire further research on these fundamental questions.

ACKNOWLEDGMENTS

This research was supported by Grants MH 66081, MH 66391, and DA 13146-S2 from the National Institutes of Health.

ENDNOTE

1. Percentages reported reflect weighted rather than actual proportions.

REFERENCES

Bonanno, G. A. (2004). Loss, trauma, and human resilience: Have we underestimated the human capacity to thrive after extremely aversive events? *American Psychologist, 59,* 20–28.

Bonanno, G. A., Moskowitz, J. T., Papa, A., & Folkman, S. (2005). Resilience to loss in bereaved spouses, bereaved parents, and bereaved gay men. *Journal of Personality and Social Psychology, 88,* 827–843.

Bonanno, G. A., Rennicke, C., & Dekel, S. (2005). Self-enhancement among high-exposure survivors of the September 11th terrorist attack: Resilience or social maladjustment? *Journal of Personality and Social Psychology, 88,* 984–998.

Bonanno, G. A., Wortman, C. B., Lehman, D. R., Tweed, R. G., Haring, M., Sonnega, J., Carr, D., & Neese, R. M. (2002). Resilience to loss and chronic grief: A prospective study from preloss to 18-months postloss. *Journal of Personality and Social Psychology, 83,* 1150–1164.

Bryant, B. A., Harvey, A. G., Guthrie, R. M., & Moulds, M. L. (2000). A prospective study of psychophysiological arousal, acute stress disorder, and posttraumatic stress disorder. *Journal of Abnormal Psychology, 109,* 341–344.

Casella, L., & Motta, R. W. (1990). Comparison of characteristics of Vietnam Veterans with and without posttraumatic stress disorder. *Psychological Reports, 67,* 595–605.

Galea, S., Ahern, J., Resnick, H., Kilpatrick, D., Bucuvalas, M., Gold, J., & Vlahov, D. (2002). Psychological sequelae of the September 11 terrorist attacks in New York City. *New England Journal of Medicine, 346,* 982–987.

Galea, S., Resnick, H., Ahern, J., Gold, J., Bucuvalas, M., Kilpatrick, D., Stuber, J., & Vlahov, D. (2002). Posttraumatic stress disorder in Manhattan, New York City, after the September 11th terrorist attacks. *Journal of Urban Health, 79,* 340–353.

Galea, S., Vlahov, D., Resnick, H., Ahern, J., Susser, E., Gold, J., Bucuvalas, M., & Kilpatrick, D. (2003). Trends of probable post-traumatic stress disorder in New York City after the September 11 terrorist attacks. *American Journal of Epidemiology, 158,* 514–524.

Garmezy, N. (1991). Resilience and vulnerability to adverse developmental outcomes associated with poverty. *American Behavioral Scientist, 34,* 416–430.

Judd, L. L., Akiskal, H. S., & Paulus, M. Y. (1997). The role and clinical significance of subsyndromal depressive symptoms (SSD) in unipolar major depressive disorder. *Journal of Affective Disorders, 45,* 5–17.

Kessler, R. C., Sonnega, A., Bromet, E., Hughes, M., & Nelson, C. B. (1995). Posttraumatic stress disorder in the National Comorbidity Survey. *Archives of General Psychiatry, 52,* 1048–1060.

Kilpatrick, D. G., Resnick, H. S., Freedy, J. R., Pelcovitz, D., Resick, P. A., Roth, S., & van der Kolk, B. (1998). The posttraumatic stress disorder field trial: Evaluation of the PTSD construct-criteria A through E. In E. Widiger, H. A. Pincus, M. B. First, R. Ross, & W. Davis (Eds.), *DSM-IV sourcebook* (Vol. 4, pp. 803–844). Washington, DC: American Psychiatric Association Press.

King, D. W., King, L. A., Foy, D., Keane, T. M., & Fairbank, J. A. (1999). Posttraumatic stress disorder in a national sample of male and female veterans: Risk factors, war-zone stressors, and resilience recovery variables. *Journal of Abnormal Psychology, 108,* 164–170.

Litz, B. T. (2005). Has resilience to severe trauma been underestimated? *American Psychologist, 60,* 262.

Luthar, S. S., Doernberger, C. H., & Zigler, E. (1993). Resilience is not a unidimensional construct: Insights from a prospective study of inner-city adolescents. *Development and Psychopathology, 5,* 703–717.

Masten, A. S. (2001). Ordinary magic: Resilience processes in development. *American Psychologist, 56,* 227–238.

McFarlane, A. C., & Yehuda, R. (1996). Resilience, vulnerability, and the course of posttraumatic reactions. In B. A. van der Kolk, A. C. McFarlane, & L. Weisaeth (Eds.), *Traumatic stress* (pp. 151–181). New York: Guilford.

McNally, R. J. (2003). Progress and controversy in the study of post-traumatic stress disorder. *Annual Review of Psychology, 54,* 229–252.

McNally, R. J., Bryant, R. A., & Ehlers, A. (2003). Does early psychological intervention promote recovery from posttraumatic stress? *Psychological Science in the Public Interest, 4*(2).

Rachman, S. J. (1978). *Fear and courage.* New York: Freeman.

Resnick, H., Galea, S., Kilpatrick, D., & Vlahov, D. (2004). Research on trauma and PTSD in the aftermath of 9/11. *PTSD Research Quarterly, 15,* 1–3.

Roisman, G. I. (2005). Conceptual clarifications in the study of resilience. *American Psychologist, 60,* 264–265.

Rutter, M. (1987). Psychosocial resilience and protective mechanisms. *American Journal of Orthopsychiatry, 57,* 316–331.

Saigh, P. A. (1988). Anxiety, depression, and assertion across alternating intervals of stress. *Journal of Abnormal Psychology, 97,* 338–341.

Spitzer, R. L., Williams, J. B., Gibbon, M., & First, M. B. (1990). *User's guide for the Structured Clinical Interview for DSM-III-R: SCID.* Washington, DC: American Psychiatric Association.

Tucker, P., Pfefferbaum, B., Doughty, D. B., Jones, D. E., Jordan, F. B., & Nixon, S. J. (2002). Body handlers after terrorism in Oklahoma City: Predictors of posttraumatic stress and other symptoms. *American Journal of Orthopsychiatry, 72,* 469–475.

van Ommeren, M., Saxena, S., & Saraceno, B. (2005). Mental and social health during and after acute emergencies: Emerging consensus? *Bulletin of the World Health Organization, 83,* 71–75.

World Health Organization. (2003). *Mental health in emergencies.* Geneva, Switzerland: World Health Organization, Department of Mental Health and Substance Dependence.

Zisook, S., Paulus, M., Shuchter, S. R., & Judd, L. L. (1997). The many faces of depression following spousal bereavement. *Journal of Affective Disorders, 45,* 85–94.

CRITICAL THINKING QUESTIONS

1. The article suggests that resilience to trauma is more prevalent than many would think. Although this study focused exclusively on people's reaction to the 9-11 terrorist attack, might similar findings be expected in other presumably traumatic events, such as Hurricane Katrina and the war in Iraq? What are some of the potential similarities and/or differences between the type of trauma exposure in the 9-11 attack and the types in other potentially traumatic events? Explain.

2. The article indicates that a lot more studies have been conducted on PTSD (posttraumatic stress disorder) than on resilience. In some ways, this parallels much of the research in psychology in general, in which there is a stronger tendency to study pathol-

ogy rather than the lack of pathology. Why do you think this may be the case? What, if any, potential problems might be associated with studying pathology as the main subject matter? Explain.

3. How might the media contribute to the common perception that people are more traumatized than they really are by certain events (e.g., hurricanes, floods, tornadoes, terrorist attacks, etc.)? In other words, how might the way an event is reported influence how widespread the trauma is perceived to be? Use examples to support your answer.

4. The article states, "A greater understanding of resilient functioning . . . could bolster arguments against the wholesale prophylactic psychological interventions in the aftermath of trauma." What does this statement mean? How could interventions be handled differently in response to traumatic events?

CHAPTER INTEGRATION QUESTIONS

1. "That which does not kill me, makes me stronger," wrote Friedrich Nietzsche, German philosopher. Discuss this quotation in the context of the three articles in this chapter.

2. The three articles in this chapter all dealt with stress in one form or another. Integrate the findings of the articles into one or more conclusions on how stress affects people. Explain your conclusions.

3. Again, all three articles in this chapter looked at stress. What social psychological factors other than stress might have an impact on health? Explain your answers.

Author Index

Subject Index